SECOND EDITION

# Programming the Mobile Web

*Maximiliano Firtman*

O'REILLY®

Beijing · Cambridge · Farnham · Köln · Sebastopol · Tokyo

**Programming the Mobile Web, Second Edition**

by Maximiliano Firtman

Printed in the United States of America.

Published by O'Reilly Media, Inc., 1005 Gravenstein Highway North, Sebastopol, CA 95472.

O'Reilly books may be purchased for educational, business, or sales promotional use. Online editions are also available for most titles (*http://my.safaribooksonline.com*). For more information, contact our corporate/institutional sales department: 800-998-9938 or *corporate@oreilly.com*.

| | | | |
|---|---|---|---|
| **Editors:** Simon St. Laurent and Meghan Blanchette | | **Indexer:** Lucie Haskins | |
| **Production Editor:** Melanie Yarbrough | | **Cover Designer:** Randy Comer | |
| **Copyeditor:** Rachel Head | | **Interior Designer:** David Futato | |
| **Proofreader:** Kiel Van Horn | | **Illustrator:** Rebecca Demarest | |

March 2013:     Second Edition

**Revision History for the Second Edition:**

2013-03-15:    First release

See *http://oreilly.com/catalog/errata.csp?isbn=9781449334970* for release details.

ISBN: 978-1-449-33497-0

[LSI]

*For my parents, Stella Maris and Edgardo, my brother, Sebastián, Inés and Antonio, and my lovely wife, Ani, who have supported me during all of my projects*

# Table of Contents

Preface. . . . . . . . . . . . . . . . . . . . . . . . . . . . . . . . . . . . . . . . . . . . . . . . . . . . . . . . . . . . . xvii

1. The Mobile Jungle. . . . . . . . . . . . . . . . . . . . . . . . . . . . . . . . . . . . . . . . . . . . . . . . 1
   The Mobile Ecosystem                                                        1
      What Is a Mobile Device?                                                 1
      Mobile Device Categories                                                 3
   Brands, Models, and Platforms                                              9
      Apple iOS                                                                9
      Android                                                                 13
      Windows                                                                 17
      Nokia                                                                   20
      BlackBerry                                                              24
      Samsung                                                                 26
      Sony Mobile                                                             27
      Motorola Mobililty                                                      27
      Amazon                                                                  28
      LG Mobile                                                               28
      HTC                                                                     29
      HP and Palm                                                             29
      Firefox OS                                                              30
      Ubuntu for Phones                                                       30
      Chinese Platforms                                                       31
      Other Platforms                                                         31
      Smart TV Platforms                                                      31
   Technical Information                                                      32

2. Understanding the Mobile Web. . . . . . . . . . . . . . . . . . . . . . . . . . . . . . . . . . 35
   Myths of the Mobile Web                                                    35
      It's Not the Mobile Web; It's Just the Web!                             35

You Don't Need to Do Anything Special About Your Desktop Website                36
One Website Should Work for All Devices (Desktop, Mobile, TV)                    36
Just Create an HTML File with a Width of 320 Pixels, and You Have a
    Mobile Website                                           37
Native Mobile Applications Will Kill the Mobile Web                              37
People Are Not Using Their Mobile Browsers                                       37
What Is the Mobile Web?                                                          38
  Differences                                                          38
Mobile Web Eras                                                                  39
  WAP 1                                                                39
  WAP 2.0                                                              41
The Mobile Browsing Experience                                                  43
  Navigation Methods                                                   43
  Zoom Experience                                                      45
  Reflow Layout Engines                                                46
  Direct Versus Cloud-Based Browsers                                   47
  Multipage Experience                                                 48
  Web Engines                                                          49
Fragmentation                                                                   50
  Display                                                              50
  Input Methods                                                        58
  Other Features                                                       60
Market Statistics                                                               60

3. Browsers and Web Platforms. . . . . . . . . . . . . . . . . . . . . . . . . . . . . . . . . . . . . . . . . . . . . .  63
Web Platforms That Are Not Browsers                                             64
  HTML5 Web Apps                                                       64
  Web Views                                                            67
  Pseudo-Browsers                                                      68
  Native Web Apps, Packaged Apps, and Hybrids                          69
  Ebooks                                                              72
Mobile Browsers                                                                 73
  Preinstalled Browsers                                               73
  User-Installable Browsers                                           82
  Browser Overview                                                     87

4. Tools for Mobile Web Development. . . . . . . . . . . . . . . . . . . . . . . . . . . . . . . . . . . . . . .  89
Working with Code                                                               89
  Adobe Dreamweaver                                                   89
  Adobe Edge Tools                                                     90
  Microsoft Visual Studio and WebMatrix                               91
  Eclipse                                                             91

    Native Web IDEs . . . . . . . . . . . . . . . . . . . . . . . . . . . . . . . . . . . . . . . . . . 91
  Testing . . . . . . . . . . . . . . . . . . . . . . . . . . . . . . . . . . . . . . . . . . . . . . . . . . . . 91
    Emulators and Simulators . . . . . . . . . . . . . . . . . . . . . . . . . . . . . . . . . . . 92
    Real Device Testing . . . . . . . . . . . . . . . . . . . . . . . . . . . . . . . . . . . . . . . . 114
    Remote Labs . . . . . . . . . . . . . . . . . . . . . . . . . . . . . . . . . . . . . . . . . . . . . . 116
  Production Environment . . . . . . . . . . . . . . . . . . . . . . . . . . . . . . . . . . . . . . 124
    Web Hosting . . . . . . . . . . . . . . . . . . . . . . . . . . . . . . . . . . . . . . . . . . . . . 125
    Domain . . . . . . . . . . . . . . . . . . . . . . . . . . . . . . . . . . . . . . . . . . . . . . . . . 125
    Error Management . . . . . . . . . . . . . . . . . . . . . . . . . . . . . . . . . . . . . . . . 125
    Statistics . . . . . . . . . . . . . . . . . . . . . . . . . . . . . . . . . . . . . . . . . . . . . . . . 126

**5. Architecture and Design.** . . . . . . . . . . . . . . . . . . . . . . . . . . . . . . . . . . . . . . . . **127**
  Mobile Strategy . . . . . . . . . . . . . . . . . . . . . . . . . . . . . . . . . . . . . . . . . . . . . 127
    When to Get Out of the Browser . . . . . . . . . . . . . . . . . . . . . . . . . . . . . 127
    Context . . . . . . . . . . . . . . . . . . . . . . . . . . . . . . . . . . . . . . . . . . . . . . . . . 130
    Server-Side Adaptation . . . . . . . . . . . . . . . . . . . . . . . . . . . . . . . . . . . . 131
    Progressive Enhancement . . . . . . . . . . . . . . . . . . . . . . . . . . . . . . . . . . 132
    Responsive Web Design . . . . . . . . . . . . . . . . . . . . . . . . . . . . . . . . . . . . 134
    RESS . . . . . . . . . . . . . . . . . . . . . . . . . . . . . . . . . . . . . . . . . . . . . . . . . . 139
  Navigation . . . . . . . . . . . . . . . . . . . . . . . . . . . . . . . . . . . . . . . . . . . . . . . . 140
  Design and User Experience . . . . . . . . . . . . . . . . . . . . . . . . . . . . . . . . . . 141
    Touch Design Patterns . . . . . . . . . . . . . . . . . . . . . . . . . . . . . . . . . . . . . 145
    Tablet Patterns . . . . . . . . . . . . . . . . . . . . . . . . . . . . . . . . . . . . . . . . . . 148
    Official UI Guidelines . . . . . . . . . . . . . . . . . . . . . . . . . . . . . . . . . . . . . 149
    What Not to Do . . . . . . . . . . . . . . . . . . . . . . . . . . . . . . . . . . . . . . . . . . 149

**6. Markups and Standards.** . . . . . . . . . . . . . . . . . . . . . . . . . . . . . . . . . . . . . . . . **153**
  First, the Very Old Ones . . . . . . . . . . . . . . . . . . . . . . . . . . . . . . . . . . . . . 153
    WML . . . . . . . . . . . . . . . . . . . . . . . . . . . . . . . . . . . . . . . . . . . . . . . . . . 154
  Current Standards . . . . . . . . . . . . . . . . . . . . . . . . . . . . . . . . . . . . . . . . . 158
    Politics of the Mobile Web . . . . . . . . . . . . . . . . . . . . . . . . . . . . . . . . . 159
    Delivering Markup . . . . . . . . . . . . . . . . . . . . . . . . . . . . . . . . . . . . . . . 160
  XHTML Mobile Profile and Basic . . . . . . . . . . . . . . . . . . . . . . . . . . . . . . 164
    Available Tags . . . . . . . . . . . . . . . . . . . . . . . . . . . . . . . . . . . . . . . . . . . 165
    Official Noncompatible Features . . . . . . . . . . . . . . . . . . . . . . . . . . . . . 166
    Creating Our First Compatible Template . . . . . . . . . . . . . . . . . . . . . . 167
    Markup Additions . . . . . . . . . . . . . . . . . . . . . . . . . . . . . . . . . . . . . . . . 169
  Mobile HTML5 . . . . . . . . . . . . . . . . . . . . . . . . . . . . . . . . . . . . . . . . . . . . 169
    Creating Our First HTML5 Template . . . . . . . . . . . . . . . . . . . . . . . . . . 170
    Syntax Rules . . . . . . . . . . . . . . . . . . . . . . . . . . . . . . . . . . . . . . . . . . . . 171
    New Elements . . . . . . . . . . . . . . . . . . . . . . . . . . . . . . . . . . . . . . . . . . . 172
  CSS for Mobile . . . . . . . . . . . . . . . . . . . . . . . . . . . . . . . . . . . . . . . . . . . . 172

WCSS Extensions                                                     172
CSS3                                                               176
HTML5 Compatibility Levels                                         177
Testing Your Browser                                              177

**7. Basics of Mobile HTML5.** . . . . . . . . . . . . . . . . . . . . . . . . . . . . . . . . . . . . . . . . **181**
The Document Head                                                 181
Title                                                            181
Website Icons                                                    183
Home Screen Icons                                                187
The Viewport                                                     200
Changing the Navigation Method                                   215
Removing Automatic Links                                         216
Metadata for Sharing                                             216
Hiding the URL Address Bar                                       218
Native App Integration                                           220
The Document Body                                                224
Main Structure                                                   225
HTML5 Mobile Boilerplate                                         227
The Content                                                      228
Block Elements                                                   228
Lists                                                           228
Tables                                                          229
Frames                                                          229
Links                                                           230
Accessibility                                                   232

**8. HTML5 Forms.** . . . . . . . . . . . . . . . . . . . . . . . . . . . . . . . . . . . . . . . . . . . . . . . . **235**
Form Design                                                      235
Form Elements                                                    238
Select Lists                                                    238
Radio Buttons and Checkboxes                                    241
Buttons                                                         242
Hidden Fields                                                   243
Text Input Fields                                               243
Range Slider Fields                                             254
Date Input Fields                                               255
File Selection Fields                                           257
Noninteractive Form Elements                                    264
Form Control Attributes                                          266
Placeholder                                                     266
autofocus                                                       267

autocomplete 267
readonly 268
Input Validation Attributes 268
Safari Extensions 268
Firefox Extensions 268
XHTML Mobile inputmode 269
Additional Form Attributes 270
Form Validation 270
HTML5 Validation 271
WAP CSS Validation 275

9. **Feature and Device Detection**..................................... 279
Possible Problems 279
Possible Solutions 280
Informational Websites 281
Can I Use 282
MobileHTML5.org 282
WebPlatform.org 284
Client-Side Detection 284
HTML Fallbacks 284
CSS Fallbacks 285
Vendor Prefixes 286
JavaScript Fallbacks 290
Modernizr 292
Polyfills 297
Platform Detection 298
Server-Side Detection 300
HTTP 300
Detecting the Context 307
Cloud-Based Browsers 309
Mobile Detection 311
Transcoders 312
Device Libraries 313

10. **Images and Media**................................................... 331
Images 331
Image Formats 331
Using the img Element 336
Responsive Images 337
Local Pictograms 340
Dealing with Multiple Screen Densities 342
Using Vector-Based Solutions 343

Providing One Single Image      344
Providing Image Alternatives      346
SVG      350
Canvas      357
Adobe Flash      365
Video      368
Containers and Codecs      368
Delivering Video      370
The HTML5 video Element      370
Streaming      376
Embedding with object      378
Video Compatibility      378
Audio      379
Invisible Audio Player      380
Web Audio API      380
Audio Compatibility      381

**11. CSS for Mobile Browsers.** . . . . . . . . . . . . . . . . . . . . . . . . . . . . . . . . . . . . . . . . **383**
Where to Insert the CSS      383
Media Queries      384
CSS3 Media Queries      385
Selectors      392
CSS Techniques      393
Reset CSS Files      393
Text Formatting      395
Common Patterns      404
Display Properties      404
Rounded Corners      408
Border Image      409
Pseudoclasses      413
Backgrounds      413
Scrollable Areas      414
Content      415
Opacity      416
Cursor Management      416
Selection Management      417
Touch Callout      420
Highlight Color      421
Appearance Override      421
CSS Sprites      422
Samples and Compatibility      422
CSS Sprites Alternatives      427

CSS3 Modules                                                       427
  Gradients                                              428
  Reflection                                             431
  Masks                                                  432
  Transforms                                             433
  Transitions                                            439
  Animations                                             442
  CSS Filter Effects                                     446
  CSS Regions and Exclusions                             447
  New CSS Values and Units                               448

**12. JavaScript Mobile** . . . . . . . . . . . . . . . . . . . . . . . . . . . . . . . . . . . . . . . . . . . . . . . **451**
Coding for Mobile Browsers                                        452
  HTML5 Script Extensions                                453
  Code Execution                                         453
  Cloud-Based Browsers                                   454
JavaScript Debugging and Profiling                                455
Battery Consumption                                               455
Background Execution                                              456
  Status Detection                                       457
  Background Tab Notification Trick                       460
  Background Execution Compatibility                      461
  Push Notifications                                      462
Supported Technologies                                            463
  The Document Object Model                               463
  The Selectors API                                       463
  JSON                                                    464
  Binary Data                                             464
  Web Workers                                             464
  HTML5 APIs                                              466
  Native Web App APIs                                     466
Standard JavaScript Behavior                                      467
  Standard Dialogs                                        467
  History and URL Management                              470
  Manipulating Windows                                    471
  Focus and Scroll Management                             472
  Timers                                                  473
  Changing the Title                                      476
  Cookie Management                                       476
  Event Handling                                          477
JavaScript Libraries                                              484
  Mobile Libraries                                        485

| | | |
|---|---|---:|
| | UI Frameworks | 487 |
| | Sencha Touch | 488 |
| | jQuery Mobile | 489 |
| | Enyo | 490 |
| | Montage | 491 |
| | iUI | 492 |
| | jQTouch | 493 |
| | JavaScript Mobile UI Patterns | 495 |
| **13.** | **Offline Apps, Storage, and Networks.** | **501** |
| | Offline Web Apps | 501 |
| | The Manifest File | 502 |
| | Accessing Online Resources | 503 |
| | Updating the Package | 504 |
| | Deleting the Package | 505 |
| | The JavaScript API | 506 |
| | Compatibility and Limits | 508 |
| | Client-Side Storage | 511 |
| | Web Storage | 511 |
| | The Web SQL Database API | 514 |
| | The IndexedDB API | 518 |
| | The FileSystem API | 520 |
| | User Intervention | 521 |
| | Debugging Storage | 521 |
| | Network Communication | 522 |
| | Ajax | 522 |
| | Server Sent Events | 525 |
| | WebSockets | 527 |
| **14.** | **Geolocation and Maps.** | **529** |
| | Location Techniques | 529 |
| | Accuracy | 529 |
| | Indoor Location | 529 |
| | Client Techniques | 530 |
| | Server Techniques | 532 |
| | Asking the User | 533 |
| | Detecting the Location | 534 |
| | The W3C Geolocation API | 534 |
| | Carrier Network Location APIs | 539 |
| | IP Geolocation | 540 |
| | Maps/Navigation App Integration | 541 |
| | Google Maps for Android | 541 |

|  | iOS Maps | 543 |
|  | Bing Maps | 545 |
|  | Showing a Map | 546 |
|  | Google Maps API v3 | 546 |
|  | Google Maps Static API | 549 |
|  | Nokia Here | 550 |

**15. Device Interaction.........................................................553**

|  | Mobile-Specific URIs | 553 |
|  | Making a Call | 554 |
|  | Sending Email | 556 |
|  | Sending an SMS | 557 |
|  | Other Communication Apps | 558 |
|  | Adding a Contact to the Phonebook | 559 |
|  | Integrating with Other Applications | 560 |
|  | JavaScript APIs | 564 |
|  | Touch | 564 |
|  | Gestures | 572 |
|  | Sensors | 579 |
|  | Network Information | 583 |
|  | File Management | 585 |
|  | Full Screen | 587 |
|  | Web Notifications | 588 |
|  | Camera | 590 |
|  | Battery | 593 |
|  | Vibration | 593 |
|  | Other APIs | 594 |

**16. Native and Installed Web Apps.........................................597**

|  | Web App Pros and Cons | 598 |
|  | Architecture of a Web App | 599 |
|  | Meta Configuration | 599 |
|  | Platform Access | 600 |
|  | Data Storage | 600 |
|  | Network Access | 600 |
|  | Logic | 600 |
|  | User Interface | 601 |
|  | Packaging | 601 |
|  | Distribution | 601 |
|  | Standards | 601 |
|  | Packaging and Configuration Standards | 601 |
|  | Official Platforms | 602 |

iOS Web Apps 602
Symbian Standalone Web Apps 612
Windows 8 Store Apps 613
Mozilla Open Web Apps 619
Chrome Apps 624
Samsung Web Apps 624
BlackBerry WebWorks Apps 624
Nokia S40 Web Apps 632
Nokia Symbian Web Apps 637
Apache Cordova/PhoneGap Apps 644
Template Creation 646
Cordova Web View 646
CordovaJS 647
Plug-ins 650
Distribution 650
iOS App Store 650
Android Stores 651
BlackBerry AppWorld 651
Microsoft Windows Store 651
Microsoft Windows Phone Store 651
Full-Screen App Patterns 652
Multiple Views 652
Layout 652
Input Method 652
One-View Widget 653
Dynamic Application Engine 653
Reload My Web App 653

17. Content Delivery................................................... 655
MIME Types 655
Static Definition 655
Dynamic Definition 657
File Delivery 658
Direct Linking 658
Delayed Linking 658
OMA Download 659
Application and Games Delivery 662
iOS Applications 663
Android Applications 665
Windows Applications 666

Java ME .................................................................. 667

18. **Debugging and Performance** .............................................. **671**
   Debugging                                                          671
      Server-Side Debugging                                           671
      Markup Debugging                                                676
      Client-Side Debugging                                           678
   Performance Optimization                                           686
      Measurement                                                     686
      Best Practices                                                  689

19. **Distribution and Social Web 2.0** ......................................... **695**
   Mobile SEO                                                         695
      Spiders and Discoverability                                     696
      Mobile Sitemaps                                                 696
   How Users Find You                                                 698
      SMS Invitation                                                  698
      Email Invitation                                                699
      Mobile Tiny URL                                                 699
      QR Codes                                                        699
      NFC Tags                                                        701
   User Fidelizing                                                    701
      Web Shortcuts                                                   702
      RSS                                                             702
      Open Search                                                     702
      Apple Passbook                                                  703
   Mobile Web Statistics                                              704
      Google Analytics for Mobile                                    704
      Yahoo! Web Analytics                                            705
      Mobilytics                                                      705
   Monetizing Your Website                                            705
      Mobile Advertisements                                           705
   Mobile Web Social Features                                         706
      Authentication and Sharing APIs                                 706
      Sharing Content                                                 707

A. **MIME Types for Mobile Content** ........................................... **709**

Index ..................................................................... **713**

# Preface

In your pocket is a device that has changed the lives of billions of people all over the world. The third personal screen (after the TV and the computer) is the most personal one, and bringing our services to it is one of the key business priorities of this decade.

Mobile development, however, is a more challenging activity than desktop development. Platforms are severely fragmented, and developers have to work with minimal resources. Fortunately, the mobile web makes it easier to deal with this fragmentation, allowing developers to create applications that run on many more platforms than native (or installable) applications. As we will see later, the mobile web and installable applications are not enemies. In fact, they work together very well.

All of that sounds great: billions of devices, web technologies, multiplatform solutions... where's the problem? More than half of your desktop web skills and the tips, hacks, and best practices you already know simply do not apply on the mobile web. The mobile web demands new usability patterns, new programming best practices, and new knowledge and abilities.

This is a second edition, prepared two years after the first one. At the time of the first edition there were almost no books, websites, or training courses focused on concrete mobile web programming. Today it's more common to find such information; however, it's not always good enough. We don't need vague information like "this may not work on some phones"; we need real, fresh, and working data. On which devices does a solution not work? Why? Is there another solution? That is why I've written this book: to help developers in programming mobile websites.

You may feel that you are advanced enough to go directly to the code, but I encourage you to start from the beginning of the book if you are new to the mobile world. This is another universe, and every universe has its own rules.

# Who This Book Is For

This book is for experienced web developers who want to learn what's different about designing for the mobile web. We will talk about HTML, CSS, JavaScript, Ajax, and server-side code as if you have experience with all those technologies. If you are a web designer with some basic programming skills, you will also find this book useful.

We will cover HTML5 features, but don't worry if you don't have any experience with this platform yet; we will cover it from the ground up, and your HTML 4 and XHTML 1.0 knowledge will be enough.

If you are an individual freelancer, if you work for a company in the areas of programming or web development, or if you work in a web design studio, this book is for you. Perhaps you need to create a mobile application or client for a current desktop service, you want to add new services to your portfolio, or you need to migrate an old mobile website to newer devices.

You may also be a web entrepreneur with—or looking for—a great idea for mobile devices, and you want to analyze what you can do with current mobile browsers. This book investigates compatibility device by device and discusses advanced features you can implement.

The book will also be useful if you are wondering how to identify devices and deliver proper and compatible content for ad campaigns, to sell content or to deliver free content to mobile users.

# Who This Book Is Not For

I don't really want to cut anyone out of the possibility of reading this book, but there are a lot of people who aren't likely to benefit from all of it. If you are a graphic designer, you will not find detailed tips and practices in this book, and you are likely to enjoy only the first four chapters.

If you are a web designer without programming skills, Chapter 1 through Chapter 7 are the ones you should read line by line; the rest will be useful to review so you know the capabilities you can request from a developer.

If you are a native mobile developer (iPhone, Android, Java mobile, Windows Phone), some web knowledge will be required in order to understand and follow all the samples in this book.

This is also not a book for learning basic HTML, CSS, or JavaScript. You will not find detailed samples or step-by-step instructions on how to implement every task. It is assumed that you are experienced enough to create code on your own, or at least know how to find out by searching the Web.

If you are a manager, a CTO, a project leader, or an entrepreneur without any web knowledge, you will find the first four chapters useful: they describe the current state of the art in this market and should help you decide how to organize your team.

## What You'll Learn

This book is an advanced reference for the mobile web today, and it is the most complete reference available at this time. This may seem an ambitious claim, but it is the truth. This book draws upon a mix of experience and very detailed research and testing not available in other books, websites, or research papers about the mobile web.

*Programming the Mobile Web* will teach you how to create effective and rich experiences for mobile web browsers, and also how to create native web applications that will be installed in a device's applications menu.

We will not talk only about the star devices, like the iPhone and Android devices; we will also cover mass-market platforms from Nokia, BlackBerry, Amazon, Microsoft, and other vendors.

## Other Options

The main challenge looking for books and online resources is finding solutions that contain information, not ones having plenty of "maybes," "perhapses," and "be carefuls."

If you need to learn web technologies, there are plenty of books and resources available. Take a look at *oreilly.com/css-html* and *oreilly.com/javascript* for some lists.

If you want a complement to this book in the areas of design, performance, and advanced programming, I recommend the following books:

- *Mobile Design and Development* by Brian Fling (O'Reilly)
- *Programming the iPhone User Experience* by Toby Boudreaux (O'Reilly)
- *JavaScript: The Good Parts* by Douglas Crockford (O'Reilly)
- *High Performance JavaScript* by Nicholas Zakas (O'Reilly)
- *High Performance Websites* by Steve Souders (O'Reilly)
- *Even Faster Web Sites* by Steve Souders (O'Reilly)
- *Website Optimization* by Andrew B. King (O'Reilly)
- *Mobile JavaScript Application Development* by Adrian Kosmaczewski (O'Reilly)
- *Mobile Usability* by Jakob Nielsen and Raluca Budiu (New Riders Press)

# If You Like (or Don't Like) This Book

If you like—or don't like—this book, by all means, please let people know. Amazon reviews are one popular way to share your happiness (or lack of happiness), and you can leave reviews on this book's website (*http://oreil.ly/program_mobile_web_2e*).

There's also a link to errata there, which readers can use to let us know about typos, errors, and other problems with the book. Reported errors will be visible on the page immediately, and we'll confirm them after checking them out. O'Reilly can also fix errata in future printings of the book and on Safari, making for a better reader experience pretty quickly.

We hope to keep this book updated for future mobile platforms, and will also incorporate suggestions and complaints into future editions.

# Conventions Used in This Book

The following font conventions are used in this book:

*Italic*
> Indicates pathnames, filenames, and program names; Internet addresses, such as domain names and URLs; and new items where they are defined.

`Constant width`
> Indicates command lines and options that should be typed verbatim; names and keywords in programs, including method names, variable names, and class names; and HTML/XHTML element tags.

**`Constant width bold`**
> Used for emphasis in program code lines.

*`Constant width italic`*
> Indicates text that should be replaced with user-supplied values.

 This icon signifies a tip, suggestion, or general note.

 This icon indicates a warning or caution.

# Using Code Examples

This book is here to help you get your job done. In general, if this book includes code examples, you may use the code in your programs and documentation. You do not need to contact us for permission unless you're reproducing a significant portion of the code. For example, writing a program that uses several chunks of code from this book does not require permission. Selling or distributing a CD-ROM of examples from O'Reilly books does require permission. Answering a question by citing this book and quoting example code does not require permission. Incorporating a significant amount of example code from this book into your product's documentation does require permission.

We appreciate, but do not require, attribution. An attribution usually includes the title, author, publisher, and ISBN. For example: "*Programming the Mobile Web,* Second Edition by Maximiliano Firtman (O'Reilly). Copyright 2013 Maximiliano Firtman, 978-1-449-33497-0."

If you feel your use of code examples falls outside fair use or the permission given above, feel free to contact us at *permissions@oreilly.com.*

# Safari® Books Online

**Safari**. Safari Books Online (*www.safaribooksonline.com*) is an on-demand digital library that delivers expert content in both book and video form from the world's leading authors in technology and business.

Technology professionals, software developers, web designers, and business and creative professionals use Safari Books Online as their primary resource for research, problem solving, learning, and certification training.

Safari Books Online offers a range of product mixes and pricing programs for organizations, government agencies, and individuals. Subscribers have access to thousands of books, training videos, and prepublication manuscripts in one fully searchable database from publishers like O'Reilly Media, Prentice Hall Professional, Addison-Wesley Professional, Microsoft Press, Sams, Que, Peachpit Press, Focal Press, Cisco Press, John Wiley & Sons, Syngress, Morgan Kaufmann, IBM Redbooks, Packt, Adobe Press, FT Press, Apress, Manning, New Riders, McGraw-Hill, Jones & Bartlett, Course Technology, and dozens more. For more information about Safari Books Online, please visit us online.

## How to Contact Us

Please address comments and questions concerning this book to the publisher:

O'Reilly Media, Inc.
1005 Gravenstein Highway North
Sebastopol, CA 95472
800-998-9938 (in the United States or Canada)
707-829-0515 (international or local)
707-829-0104 (fax)

We have a web page for this book, where we list errata, examples, and any additional information. You can access this page at *http://oreil.ly/program_mobile_web_2e*.

To comment or ask technical questions about this book, send email to *bookquestions@oreilly.com*.

For more information about our books, courses, conferences, and news, see our website at *http://www.oreilly.com*.

Find us on Facebook: *http://facebook.com/oreilly*

Follow us on Twitter: *http://twitter.com/oreillymedia*

Watch us on YouTube: *http://www.youtube.com/oreillymedia*

## Acknowledgments

I want to thank first all the members of my family, including my parents, Stella Maris and Edgardo, my brother, Sebastián, and my lovely wife, Ani, who have supported me during the writing of this book and all of my projects.

Second, thanks to the many people who have helped with comments, reviews, and criticisms on the first edition of this book and on the many training courses and conferences I've held since its publishing. Without them, I could not have learned as much as I have and gained experience in this minefield.

I want to thank my technical reviewers, who helped find some bugs and fill in some information gaps: Tomomi Imura, Carlos Solís, Dion Almaer, Luca Passani, and Edgar Parada.

A special thanks to Vivian Cromwell, Alejandro Villanueva, Nick Bortolotti, Fernando Freytes, John Koch, Robert Burdick, Adam Stanley, and Bryan Tafel for their support.

A special mention to Rachel Head, copyeditor of this book, who did a really great job making this book a perfect read even with my not-so-perfect English.

Finally, to Simon St. Laurent at O'Reilly Media, thanks for all your help and for trusting me when I presented this risky project in 2009, and for your help in continuing its evolution.

Creating a book about the mobile web was really a challenge; updating it after more than three years was hard, but it was worth it. Enjoy!

# CHAPTER 1

# The Mobile Jungle

Everyone wants to go mobile today. There are several reasons for this, such as more than 70% of the world's population having an active mobile device, and these being really the first personal devices (*really* personal), reading the user's context all the time, always and everywhere.

So what's the problem? Well, as I always say, "Mobile is a minefield." That is, everyone trying to enter into the mobile world feels as if they're in a minefield. Every step might be the right one, or might just be a waste of time.

Should we create native apps? Should we go with jQuery Mobile? Should we create a special version for tablets? Should we target feature phones?

We have lot of questions, and sometimes it's difficult to find answers. No step feels right enough. That's the "minefield sensation."

The mobile web appears to be a solution to some of the problems that the mobile space has. This book is about trying to get an idea of what we can do and how, and what the main problems we face are.

## The Mobile Ecosystem

If you are coming from the desktop web world, you are probably not aware of the complete mobile ecosystem. Maybe you have read a lot about mobile development, but I can assure you that it will be more complex than you think. Let's review the current state of affairs, so we can be sure we have all the knowledge we need to create the best solutions.

### What Is a Mobile Device?

It's really difficult to categorize every mobile device. Is it a smartphone? Is it a handheld? Is it a netbook? Is it a music player?

First, when is a device considered a mobile one?

For the purposes of this book, a mobile device has the following features:

- It's portable.
- It's personal.
- It's with you almost all the time.
- It's easy and fast to use.
- It has some kind of network connection.

Let's take a closer look at these features.

## Portable

A mobile device has to be portable, meaning that we can carry it without any special considerations. We can take it to the gym, to the university, to work; we can carry it with us everywhere, all the time.

## Personal

We've all heard it: "Don't touch my phone!" A mobile device is absolutely personal. My mobile is mine; it's not property of the family, nor is it property of my company. I choose the ringtone, the visual theme, the games and applications installed, and which calls I should accept. My wife has her own mobile device, and so do my kids. This personal feature will be very important in our projects. You can browse a desktop website from any computer—your familiar home PC, your computer at work, or even a desktop at a hotel or Internet café—and numerous people may have access to those machines. However, you will almost always browse a mobile website from the same device, and you are likely to be the only person who uses that device.

 Do a test: go now and ask some friends or colleagues to allow you to view your email or your Facebook account using their mobile devices. Pay attention to their faces. They don't want to! You will log them out from their accounts, you will use their phone lines, and you will touch their personal devices. It's like a privacy violation.

## Companion

Your mobile device can be with you anytime, anywhere. Even in the bathroom, you probably have your mobile phone with you. You may forget to take lots of things with you from your home in the morning, but you won't forget your wallet, your keys, and your mobile. The opportunity to be with the user all the time, everywhere, is really amazing.

### Easy to use

A notebook (or even a netbook) is portable; it can be with you at any time and it has a network connection, but if you want to use it, you need to sit down and perhaps find a table. Therefore, it's not a mobile device for the purposes of this book.

A mobile device needs to be easy and quick to use. I don't want to wait for the operating system to start; I don't want to sit down. If I'm walking downtown, I want to be able to find out when the next train will be departing without having to stop.

### Connected

A mobile device should be able to connect to the Internet when you need it to. This can be a little difficult sometimes, so we will differentiate between *fully connected devices* that can connect any time in a couple of seconds and *limited connected devices* that usually can connect to the network but sometimes cannot.

A classic iPod (non-touch) doesn't have a network connection, so it's out of our list, too, like the notebooks.

 Where do tablets, like the iPad, fit in? They are not so personal (will you have one tablet per member of the family?), and they may not be so portable. But they generally use mobile instead of desktop operating systems, as well as mobile browsers, so they are more mobile than notebooks or netbooks. I don't have the final answer, but they are considered mobile devices in this book.

## Mobile Device Categories

When thinking about mobile devices, we need to take the "phone" concept out of our minds. We are not talking about simply a phone for making calls—that's just one possible feature of a mobile device.

With this in mind, we can try to categorize the mobile devices on the market today.

### Mobile phones

OK, we still have basic mobile phones in some markets. These are phones with call and SMS support. They don't have web browsers or Internet connectivity, and they don't have any installation possibilities. These phones don't really interest us—we can't do anything for them—and in a couple of years, because of device recycling, such phones will probably not be on the market anymore.

The Nokia 1100 (see Figure 1-1) is currently the most widely distributed device in the world, with over 250 million sold since its launch in 2003. In terms of features, it offers nothing but a built-in flashlight. The problem for us, as developers, is that we can't create web content for it. Some companies may continue to make very low-end entry-level devices like this in the future, but hopefully Nokia and most other vendors will stop creating this kind of device soon. Even newer, cheaper mobile devices now have built-in browser support. This is because the mobile ecosystem (vendors, carriers, integrators, and developers) wants to offer services to users, and a browser is the entry point.

*Figure 1-1. 250 million devices worldwide sounds very attractive, but this device (Nokia 1100) is out of our scope because it doesn't have a web browser.*

For example, Nokia offers Nokia Mail, an email service for non-Internet users in emerging markets. Thanks to this service, many, many people who have never before had access to email have been able to gain that access, with a mobile device costing less than $40. This widespread solution meets a real need for many people in emerging markets, like some countries in Africa and Latin America.

### Feature phones

Feature phones, also known as low-end mobile devices, have a great advantage: they have web support. They typically have only a very basic browser, but this is the gross market. People who buy these kinds of devices don't tend to be heavy Internet users, although this may change quickly with the advent of social networks and Web 2.0 services. If your friends can post pictures from their mobile devices, you'll probably want to do the same, so you may upgrade your phone when you can.

Nokia, Motorola, Kyocera, LG, Samsung, and Sony Mobile have devices for this market. They do not have touch support, have limited memory, and include only a very basic camera and a basic music player. We can find phones in this category on sale from $40 all over the world.

Just to give you an idea of how big this market is, during 2011 70% of total phone sales worldwide were in the feature phone category (source: ZDNet (*http://zd.net/Y0vG4I*)). However, these users are usually phone and messaging users only, so they rarely consume web content.

## Social phones

Social phones are also known as mid-range and/or high-end mobile devices. The difference is that they are prepared for social users: apps such as Facebook, Twitter, and WhatsApp are always preinstalled and a minimum data plan is also usually included with the contract.

This is the mass-market option for a good mobile web experience. Mid-range devices maintain the balance between a good user experience and moderate cost. From $150, we can find a lot of devices in this market sector. In this category, devices typically offer a medium-sized screen, basic HTML browser support, sometimes 3G connection support, a decent camera, a music player, games, and application support.

One of the key features of mid-range devices is the operating system (OS). They don't have a well-known OS; they have a proprietary one without any portability across vendors. Native applications generally aren't available publicly, and some runtime, like Java ME, is the preferred way to develop installed applications.

The same vendors develop these devices as the low-end devices.

Originally the same category as smartphones, high-end devices are generally non-multitouch but have advanced features (like an accelerometer, a good camera, and Bluetooth) and good web support (but not the best in the market). They are better than mid-range devices but not on a par with smartphones. The enhanced user experience on smartphones is one of the key differences. The other difference is that high-end devices generally are not sold with flat Internet rates. The user can get a flat-rate plan, but he'll have to go out and find it himself.

 You will find different mobile categories defined in different sources. There isn't only one de facto categorization. The one used here is based on mobile web compatibility today.

## Smartphones

This is the most difficult category to define. Why aren't some social devices considered "smart" enough to be in this category? The definition of *smart* evolves every year. Even the simplest mobile device on the market today would have been considered very smart 10 years ago.

A device in this category can cost upwards of $400. You can probably get one at half that price from a carrier; the devices are often subsidized because when you buy them you sign up for a one- or two-year contract with a flat-rate data plan (hopefully). This is great for us as users, because we don't have to care too much about the cost of bytes transferred via the Web.

A smartphone, as defined today, has a multitasking operating system, a full desktop browser, Wireless LAN (WLAN, also known as WiFi) and 3G/4G connection support, a music player, and several of the following features:

- GPS (Global Positioning System) or A-GPS (Assisted Global Positioning System)
- Digital compass
- Video-capable camera
- Bluetooth
- Touch support
- 3D video acceleration
- Accelerometer
- Gyroscope
- Magnetometer

Currently, this category includes the Apple iPhone, every Android device (including the Samsung Galaxy series and the Sony Xperia series), the Nokia Lumia 920, and later BlackBerrys.

 The discussion about smartphones is always floating in the market. For example, BlackBerry believes that every device it has manufactured is a smartphone, even though they don't all have touch or WiFi connection support. On the other hand, Nokia's Asha series (in the social phone category) do have touch and WiFi support, so they may claim to be smartphones.

If you are still confused about the models, brands, and operating systems, don't worry, it will become clearer. Some confusion is normal, and I will help you to understand the mobile web ecosystem in the following pages.

### Tablets

A tablet is a flat device that usually doesn't fit in a pocket and that has a touch screen with a size ranging from 7 to 11 inches. Sometimes it uses a mobile operating system (such as iOS instead of Mac OS), and sometimes it uses a touch-optimized version of a desktop operating system (such as Windows for tablets instead of Windows Phone).

Tablets have the same functionalities as smartphones, including multitasking operating systems, installed applications, and full modern web browsers. Every tablet has WiFi support, and there are some with 3G or 4G connections.

Some devices are difficult to categorize—for example, the Samsung Galaxy Note is a 4G phone with a 5.3" pointer- and finger-based touchscreen that can also be included in the tablet category.

 There is an informal concept known as the *phablet*—a portmanteau of the words "phone" and "tablet"—describing phones with very large screens (5 to 7 inches), such as the Samsung Galaxy Note phone series.

### Nonphone mobile devices

This may sound a bit strange. Nonphone mobile pocket devices? Indeed, there are some mobile devices that have all the features we've mentioned and have a size similar to a phone, but without voice support using the normal carrier services.

For example, Apple's iPod touch is a device in this category. They aren't phones, but they can be personal, are portable and easy to use, can be kept with you most of the time, and have WiFi connections, so they fall into the category of limited connected devices. They can have great mobile browsers, so they will be in our list of devices to be considered for development.

We can also consider some of the new ebook readers. For example, I have an Amazon Kindle ebook reader, like the one shown in Figure 1-2, with data connection support (both WiFi and 3G). The Kindle has a great web browser, if you can get used to e-ink refresh delays. Ebook readers aren't phones, but they conform to all our other guidelines for mobile devices.

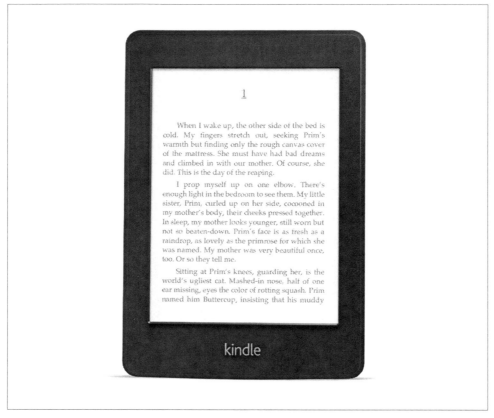

*Figure 1-2. The Amazon Kindle can be considered a mobile web device because of its network connection and web browser.*

At the time of this writing Google is working on a project called Google Glass, which is a connected pair of augmented reality glasses. We may be delivering services and widgets to our eyes in the near future with these new devices. We can develop solutions for them using a web service–based API.

### Netbooks

Netbooks have at minimum a nine-inch display, and they are more like desktops than mobile devices. Some have desktop operating systems and desktop browsers, while others have a reduced web-based operating system (such as the Chromebooks, which include Chrome OS).

If a device has a full operating system, you will need to install antivirus protection and a firewall on it, so it won't meet the easy usage criterion for a mobile device. Also remember that you can't use a netbook while walking, and that's one of the key features of mobile devices. Because of these limitations, netbooks are not considered mobile devices for the purposes of this book.

# Brands, Models, and Platforms

Now that we have established a set of categories in the mobile world, let's talk about the difficult part: the brands and models on the market. We are not going to talk about every model available, and we don't need to know about all of them. We only need to be aware of some information that will be useful for making decisions in the future.

Writing a book about brands and models is very difficult. The market changes a lot every year. In fact, during the months while I was writing this book, I had to update this information several times. So, I'll be general here and aim to give you not only an idea of what's out there now, but also of how to understand new devices that may appear on the market.

## Apple iOS

We are going to start with Apple, not because its devices are the best or because it has the greatest market share, but because Apple has caused a revolution in the market. It changed the way users see mobile devices and mobile web browsing, and it is the reason why many developers (web or not) have turned their attention to the mobile world.

Apple, a well-known desktop computer company, entered the mobile world with a revolutionary device: the *iPhone*. The iPod touch continued the iPhone revolution with a similar device without phone capabilities. Luckily for us, all of Apple's small mobile devices are quite similar. They have a multitouch screen, a 3.5" screen with medium or ultra-high resolution or a 4" screen with ultra-high resolution, WiFi connections, and Safari on iOS (formerly Mobile Safari) as the browser. The iPad series added a 9.7" screen size (medium and high resolution), with almost the same other features as the iPod touch and iPhone.

 As of June 2012, Apple had sold over 400 million iOS devices, including iPhones, iPod touches, and iPads.

Figure 1-3 shows a few examples of current Apple devices.

*Figure 1-3. We can find iPod touch and iPhone devices with a 3.5" or 4" screen; here you can see the iPhone 4S and iPhone 5.*

Apple's devices have a great feature: an operating system called *iOS* (formerly iPhone OS) that is based on Mac OS X (a Unix-based desktop OS). Usually, the last hardware versions of the iPhone can be upgraded to the latest operating system version. By default, the iPhone, iPad, and iPod touch are charged using a USB adapter; when you charge your device, iTunes (the Apple software for managing your device's content and music) will detect automatically if an OS update is available for your device, and you can install the update in minutes without any technical skill needed. Starting with iOS 5.0, the device can upgrade itself over the air (OTA), just using your wireless connection.

That is why today, for a mobile web developer, it's more important to know what OS version an Apple device has installed than which device it is. For those of us whose aim is to create great web experiences for the iPhone, it doesn't matter if the device is an iPhone (the original phone), an iPhone 4S (the S stands for speed, indicating a device with more power and speed), an iPhone 5, or an iPod touch (like the iPhone without the phone). Even within each device type, we have many generations. The same idea applies to the iPad.

 The Apple iPad is a 9.7" tablet running iOS. It includes the same functionality and browser as the iPhone, with minor differences because of the larger screen, which has a 768 × 1024 resolution in the first two generations and 1536 × 2048 in the third generation. Apple sold more than 84 million iPads in just the first two and a half years after this device's release.

So, the important thing is to know which OS version a device that accesses your website is running. It may be iOS 1.0, 2.2, 3.0, 3.2, 4.0, 5.0, 6.0, or newer (although versions 1.0 to 3.2 are rarely seen on devices in use today, so we can safely work with versions 4.0 and beyond). Up to version 4.0, iOS was called iPhone OS. Every version has upgrades in the browser—for example, the Gmail version for the iPhone is different if you have an iPhone running OS 2.2 or 6.0—and is backward compatible. Table 1-1 lists the iOS versions and the devices that support them.

*Table 1-1. List of iOS versions and devices supported per version*

| iOS version | Devices added | Highest version for | Released in |
|---|---|---|---|
| 1.0 to 1.1.5 | iPhone 1st gen.<br>iPod touch 1st gen. | | 2Q 2007 – 3Q 2008 |
| 2.0 to 2.2.1 | iPhone 3G<br>iPod touch 2nd gen. | | 3Q 2008 – 1Q 2009 |
| 3.0 to 3.1.3 | iPhone 3GS<br>iPod touch 3rd gen. | iPhone 1st gen.<br>iPod touch 1st gen. | 2Q 2009 |
| 3.2 to 3.2.2 | iPad 1st gen. (only) | | 2Q 2010 |
| 4.0 to 4.2.1 | iPhone 4<br>iPod touch 4th gen. | iPhone 3G<br>iPod touch 2nd gen. | 2Q 2010 – 4Q 2010 |
| 4.3 to 4.3.5 | iPad 2 | | 1Q 2011 – 3Q 2011 |
| 5.0 to 5.1.1 | iPhone 4S<br>iPad 3rd gen. | iPod touch 3rd gen.<br>iPad 1st gen. | 4Q 2011 – 2Q 2012 |
| 6.0 | iPhone 5<br>iPod touch 5th gen.<br>iPad mini 1st gen.<br>iPad 4th gen. | | 3Q 2012 – 4Q 2012 |

You can see some sample screens in Figure 1-4.

*Figure 1-4. This is the same Gmail account accessed from an iPhone running OS 2.0 and one running 6.0—the latter provides a more rich and contextual experience for the user.*

Today, we can develop applications for iOS devices on only two platforms: using mobile web techniques, and using the native *Cocoa Touch* framework built on Objective-C. There are other nonofficial platforms that can also compile iOS native applications, such as Adobe AIR, Corona, or Appcelerator Titanium.

 It's not widely known today that Apple, creator of the iPod and iPhone, was really one of the pioneers in the mobile device market. The Apple Newton was on the market from 1990 to 1998, and the ROKR E1, which Apple released in conjunction with Motorola in 2005, was the first phone connected with Apple's services (including iTunes). The phone was not a great success from Apple's perspective, and that was one of the reasons why the company decided to start the iPhone project.

Every iOS device has built-in access to the App Store, Apple's famous store for selling and distributing free native apps for the iPhone, iPod touch, and iPad.

 Later in this book, we are going to talk about how to detect the OS and use all the features available only in Safari on iOS. We will also talk about the App Store and how to distribute our mobile web applications via this store.

## Android

Android is a platform, not a manufacturer. Therefore, it may not seem to fit in this list. It does, though—if we are developing a website for an Android device, we don't need to bother too much about who the manufacturer is. This is because the Android platform is powerful enough to leave the brand and model in second place when we are talking about developer features.

Android is an open source, Linux-based operating system created and maintained by a group of software and hardware companies and operators called the *Open Handset Alliance*. Google mainly maintains it, so it is sometimes known as the "Google Mobile Operating System." As with any open source software, any manufacturer could theoretically remove all the Google-specific stuff from the operating system before installing it on its devices. However, as of this writing no vendor has done this, which is why every Android device is very "Google friendly."

 According to official Google data, as of July 2012 there were 400 million Android devices in use and 1 million new devices activating every day.

Android is a software stack including a Linux-core, multitasking operating system based on the concept of a virtual machine that executes bytecode, similar to .NET or JVM (Java Virtual Machine). Google chose Java as the main language to compile (not compatible with Java ME) with web users in mind. Android includes a bunch of Google services, such as Google Maps, Google Calendar, Gmail, and an email client, and provides connections to many free Google web services. It's not an obligation, but as of today every Android device is touch-based, and many of them have a QWERTY physical keyboard, GPS, a digital compass, and an accelerometer.

Android is the mobile platform with the most choices when talking about mobile browsers. From the default Android browser available before Android 4.1, to Firefox, Google Chrome, Opera Mobile, Opera Mini, UCWeb, and many others, there are multiple options available to download and install for free.

Today, HTC, Motorola, Samsung, LG, Acer, Asus, and Sony Mobile make Android devices. There are also some nonphone devices, such as tablets, that use Android. There are even some personal video-playing glasses that use Android, and Google TV, an interactive television platform, is based on this mobile operating system.

An Android device usually comes with the *Google Play Store* (previously known as Android Market), the official platform store for Android apps, music, books, and other multimedia content, preinstalled. Some Android-based vendors replace this or add their own stores, such as the *Amazon Appstore* or *Samsung Apps*.

 Android 3.0 was the first version supporting large screens and tablets. However, you can find lots of 7" tablets—such as the first generation of Samsung Galaxy Tabs—and some 10" tablets from low-budget manufacturers using Android 2.2 and Android 2.3 sold before 2012.

### Versions

As of the writing of this book, the Android OS comes in multiple versions. A device usually can update its OS only once or twice, because every manufacturer (and sometimes carriers) needs to create its own version of Android from Google's source code. That means that at any given time we can find on the market devices running at least three main versions of the OS that are stuck on that version and will not receive an update.

Knowing the OS version will be very useful to determine what browser features are available. Unfortunately, the documentation about the Android browser's features is not complete, although (as we will see in the next chapter) Google Chrome has appeared to solve some of these problems for the future.

Every Android version is known by its number and also by a codename that is always a dessert, beginning with successive letters of the alphabet. In Table 1-2 you will see a list of the Android versions that have been published or are scheduled to be published at the time of this writing. Google also maintains a website (*http://bit.ly/X3KDsh*) where you can see every version's market share over the last 14 days.

*Table 1-2. List of Android versions and code names*

| Android version | Codename | Released on | Optimized for |
|---|---|---|---|
| 1.0 & 1.1 | | 2008, 2009 | Smartphones (deprecated) |
| 1.5 | Cupcake | 1Q 2009 | Smartphones (deprecated) |
| 1.6 | Donut | 3Q 2009 | Smartphones (deprecated) |
| 2.0 & 2.1 | Eclair | 4Q 2009 | Smartphones |
| 2.2 | Froyo | 2Q 2010 | Smartphones |
| 2.3 | Gingerbread | 4Q 2010 | Smartphones |
| 3.0, 3.1 & 3.2 | Honeycomb | 2011 | Tablets |
| 4.0 | Ice Cream Sandwich (ICS) | 4Q 2011 | Smartphones & tablets |
| 4.1 & 4.2 | Jelly Bean (JB) | 2Q 2012 | Smartphones & tablets |
| Not confirmed | Key Lime Pie (KLP) | | Smartphones & tablets |

Figure 1-5 shows a few examples of Android devices.

*Figure 1-5. The Galaxy from Samsung and RZR from Motorola are the most famous Android device series; here you can see the Galaxy SIII and the RZR M.*

### Google's Nexus devices

In 2011, Google acquired Motorola Mobility, the well-known mobile device manufacturer. This means that Google is now itself a manufacturer of mobile devices—including the well-known tablet Motorola Xoom and the Motorola Droid series—and at the time of this writing Motorola is still working as a separate company under its own name. While Google has promised that Android will continue its current open source initiative and Motorola will not have special treatment, other competitors working closely with Android, such as Samsung and HTC, are looking for an alternate operating system in case the current status changes in the future.

 Rumor has it that Google plans to deliver a new phone under this new ecosystem at some point after this book is published, under the codename XPhone. To get updates on new devices and platforms after this book's publication, check out *www.mobilexweb.com*.

Despite its link with Motorola, Google has some devices that it identifies as key devices —examples of the best hardware for every Android version. Different vendors, such as HTC, Asus, and Samsung, manufacture these devices without any customization (pure Android), and they are usually very high-end devices, mostly acquired by developers. These Google key devices are under the Nexus series name; they include the Nexus One, Nexus S, Galaxy Nexus, and the multimedia home player Nexus Q. From 2012, Google offers different sizes for a Nexus experience, such as the smartphone Nexus 4 and the tablets Nexus 7 and Nexus 10.

### Fragmentation

One of the big problems of Android from a developer's perspective is its fragmentation. By fragmentation, I mean the diversity of manufacturers and devices on the market, from very low-end cheap hardware to very expensive high-end hardware, and from really small screens and resolutions to high-definition devices with large screens. Compared to iOS, where every device is basically the same with a few hardware improvements, the difference is huge.

The openness of Android makes it the perfect platform for customization. That is why you will find lots of Android devices with different user interfaces (UIs), and even with different mobile browsers. For example, Samsung adds its own UI layer to the basic Android interface on some devices, and there are also some tablets with a complete layer over the Android UI. Amazon has released tablets under the series name Kindle Fire that are Android devices with a different user interface; Barnes & Noble did a similar thing with Android and the Nook series.

# Windows

Microsoft has been trying to enter the mobile space as a big player for years. Windows Mobile was its main platform, until it decided to start from scratch: Windows Phone was the result, leading to Windows 8 on the desktop and tablets later. A new mobile operating system, developed from the ground up with a unique user interface (originally called Metro), it provides a different experience than the other main platforms. Both Windows Phone and the Windows tablet and desktop versions (from version 8) include an official Windows store for applications and content.

## Windows Phone

Microsoft launched its new operating system with companies such as HTC, LG, and Samsung, but it didn't get too much market share. A special agreement with Nokia changed this, providing much wider Windows Phone distribution worldwide starting in 2012. Most independent analysts conclude that in the following years iOS, Android, and Windows Phone are likely to be the main three platforms in the market.

The first version of the Windows Phone OS was 7.0 (following on from Windows Mobile 6.5). This was followed by the first big step: Windows Phone 7.5, also known as Mango, which supported multitasking and HTML5 in Internet Explorer 9. The operating system has the same restrictions as iOS when dealing with the balancing act of providing an easy-to-use platform and hiding some low-level stuff, such as the filesystem, app installation from unknown sources, or real multitasking. Windows Phone devices include Microsoft-related services and applications, such as Office, Internet Explorer, and Bing services. Applications on Windows Phone devices can only be installed through the official Windows store.

The second generation of this platform, known as Windows Phone 8, is not compatible with devices sold with 7.x, although these devices were upgraded to Windows Phone 7.8, which includes some of the new features of the second-generation platform (such as a new Home screen with tiles). Windows Phone 8 includes a new architecture and an optimized UI for better customization, including Kid's Corner, which provides a worry-free way for your kids to play with your phone. All Windows Phone 8 devices include the Windows Phone Store, formerly known as Windows Marketplace, for native app distribution. Figure 1-6 shows an example of a device running Windows Phone 8.

*Figure 1-6. Windows 8 and Windows Phone 8 include a new user interface, originally called Metro; here you can see the Nokia Lumia 820 with Windows Phone 8 installed.*

## Windows 8

Windows Phone is not intended for tablets because Windows 8—the big version—is prepared for bigger touch devices. Windows 8 includes the same user interface that appeared first in the phone version of Microsoft's mobile operating system.

 Microsoft originally named the Windows Phone and Windows 8 user interface *Metro*, but a trademark dispute forced it to drop this name. It is now called the "Windows 8–style UI" or "Windows Store UI."

Windows 8 is included with many tablets on the market, including Microsoft's own devices and those from different vendors, and every version supports Windows 8 Store apps—full-screen applications created with HTML5 or .NET. The operating system includes an official Windows Store for the first time, for app distribution.

This operating system is optimized for desktops, notebooks, and tablet devices. For tablets, it is available in two main versions: Windows 8 Pro and Windows 8 RT. The first version is the "classic" Intel chipset–based version, and it supports every Windows Vista or legacy Windows XP application in a "Desktop" mode.

Windows 8 RT is optimized for ARM-based devices and is more common on tablets than the more powerful (Pro) version of the operating system. This version has a limited desktop mode that works with Microsoft apps; it can't run any classic Windows application, just Windows Store certified apps.

Microsoft has also released its own tablets running Windows 8 under the series known as Microsoft Surface. Two main tablet categories are offered, with the first (cheaper) one shipping with Windows 8 RT and the second with Windows 8 Pro. One of the big advantages of the Surface over other tablets on the market today is the ability to use the cover as a keyboard—it's available as a touch surface or a physical keyboard version.

### Windows Mobile and Embedded Compact

One of the older mobile operating systems on the market is Windows Mobile (formerly Windows CE for PocketPC and Smartphones). For many years its market included the well-known PocketPCs, personal digital assistants (PDAs) without phone features. The "mobile revolution" pushed Microsoft to create a smartphone version of its mobile operating system, called Windows Mobile, which was available in two flavors: the Professional (formerly Pocket PC) and Smartphone editions.

Today Windows Mobile doesn't have too much market share, and it has been totally replaced by Windows Phone on the consumer side. However, it is still well received in some industries for specific-purposes devices.

Almost every mobile device with Windows Mobile that has launched since 2003 has .NET Compact Framework support. This means we can develop native applications for these devices using C# or Visual Basic with a reduced .NET Framework.

For industrial and corporate users, Windows Mobile continued as a separate mobile operating system with the Windows CE codebase, called *Windows Embedded Compact*. A 7.0 version of this operating system was released in March 2011, at almost the same time as Windows Phone 7. However, it's not intended for the mass market and is only for embedded systems. In early 2013, Microsoft released Windows Embedded 8 in several versions for vertical markets: Standard, Pro, Industry, Handheld, and Automotive. Table 1-3 lists the recent and current Windows versions.

*Table 1-3. List of Windows versions and code names for mobile web development*

| Name | Version and codename | Released on | Optimized for |
|---|---|---|---|
| Windows Phone 7 | 7.0 (Metro) | | Smartphones (deprecated) |
| Windows Embedded Compact | 7.0 | 1Q 2011 | Devices for the enterprise, industrial, and consumer electronics markets |
| Windows Phone 7.5 | 7.1 (Mango) | 3Q 2011 | Smartphones |
| Windows Phone 7.5 Refresh | 7.1.x (Tango) | 2Q 2012 | Smartphones |
| Windows Phone 7.8 | 7.x (Apollo) | 4Q 2012 | Smartphones |
| Windows Phone 8 | 8.0 (Apollo) | 4Q 2012 | Smartphones |
| Windows 8 | 8.0 | 4Q 2012 | Tablets and desktop |
| Windows Embedded 8 | 8.0 | 1Q 2013 – 2Q 2013 | Devices for the enterprise, industrial, consumer electronics, and automotive markets |

# Nokia

Nokia had the largest market share in mobile devices and smartphones worldwide for years (but not necessarily in specific markets, like the US). Nokia has devices in all the mobile categories, from very low-end devices to very high-end smartphones.

I've been one of the Nokia Developer Champions (a worldwide recognition program for top mobile developers) since 2006, and I know that Nokia really cares about the developer community. You can find the Nokia Developer website (*http://develop ers.nokia.com*).

The bad news for developers is that hundreds of different Nokia devices are available today. The good news is that they are very well organized by platform into different series, making it easier for us to develop, test, and port our web applications to most of them.

All Nokia devices, except the Windows-based ones, support the Nokia Store, formerly Ovi Store, for application distribution for all the supported platforms.

## Windows Phone

In late 2011, Nokia began using Windows Phone as the main smartphone platform in devices released under the marketing series name *Lumia*. These devices are replacing Symbian devices as Nokia's main high-end line and will coexist with them for a couple of years.

Nokia Lumia phones have Windows Phone 7.x, 8.0, or later and include Microsoft and Nokia software such as Internet Explorer, Bing, Nokia Maps, Nokia Drive, and the Windows Phone Store.

For most of our web development work we will follow Microsoft directives, tools, and documentation, as there is no specific work to do on Nokia Windows Phone devices in terms of mobile web development. The only exception may be the Nokia Xpress browser that Nokia offers to its users; we'll cover that later in this book.

## Tablets

At the time of this writing Nokia has confirmed that it will soon be creating tablets using Windows 8 RT as the operating system.

## Series 40

Nokia's Series 40 (S40) line consists of low-end and mid-range devices (both feature phones and social phones) using a proprietary Nokia OS focused on the mass market. The devices in this series first appeared in 2003, and today they are separated into different editions and even small update packages (called "feature packs") that help us to understand the abilities of each mobile device in this series. The "Lite" suffix on some editions and feature packs indicates low-end limited devices.

Between 2003 and 2007 lots of series were developed, from 1$^{st}$ Edition to 3$^{rd}$ Edition Feature Pack 3 (FP3), that today can be considered legacy platforms. There have been no new devices on the market in these subseries since the end of 2007.

In 2012 this series was renamed *Nokia Asha* for marketing purposes, and it now includes touch devices with 3G and WiFi connection support.

At the time of writing, Series 40 includes all the versions listed in Table 1-4.

*Table 1-4. List of Nokia S40 versions, release dates, and device types since 2007*

| Version name | Release dates | Device type | Features |
| --- | --- | --- | --- |
| 5$^{th}$ Edition and 5$^{th}$ Edition FP1 | 2Q 2007–4Q 2009 | Medium feature phones | Numeric keypad, 240×320 screen |
| 5$^{th}$ Edition Lite and 5$^{th}$ Edition FP1 Lite | 2Q 2007–4Q 2009 | Feature phones | Numeric keypad, 128×160 screen |
| 6$^{th}$ Edition and 6$^{th}$ Edition FP1 | 2Q 2009–3Q 2011 | Feature and social phones | Numeric keypad, QWERTY keyboard, and some small touchscreens; some with WiFi support |
| 6$^{th}$ Edition Lite | 2Q 2010–2Q 2012 | Feature phones | Numeric keypad, 128×160 screen |
| Developer Platform 1.x | 2Q 2010–1Q 2012 | Social phones | Numeric keypad or QWERTY keyboard, WiFi |
| Developer Platform 2.0 | From 2Q 2012 | Social phones | Full touch devices, WiFi |

Every edition has between 5 and 40 devices on the market today, and we can safely work with the fifth edition and beyond. The best part is that Nokia guarantees us that development for each device in one series (edition plus feature packs) is the same.

All the Series 40 devices have a mobile browser and *Java ME* (Micro Edition)—formerly known as J2ME (Java 2 Micro Edition)—support. From the third edition, they also support different versions of Adobe Flash Lite. Figure 1-7 shows a recent device, the Nokia Asha 306.

*Figure 1-7. The latest Series 40 devices in the social phone market, such as this Nokia Asha 306, include a full touchscreen, WiFi access, video streaming, and web browsing support.*

The platform now has an application store (Nokia Store) and a modern web browser. We can also create HTML5 native web apps for these devices, as we will see later in this book.

## Symbian

Series 60 (S60) began as the smartphone line from Nokia, using Symbian as the operating system. Today these devices are closer to the high-end category, but the limit is not clear. The Symbian company was formed by a group of manufacturers including Nokia, Ericsson, and Motorola. Later, Samsung and Sony Ericsson were added to the member list. For many years Nokia was the leading company using the Symbian platform, although there were also some Samsung, Sony Ericsson, and Motorola Symbian-based devices on the market.

This is history, though. In 2008, after the launching of Android as an open source operating system, Nokia made a decision: it bought 100% of Symbian, Ltd., from all the other manufacturers and created the Symbian Foundation to migrate the Symbian operating system to open source. At the end of 2010, Nokia decided to close the Foundation and now Symbian is 100% property of Nokia. A few months later, after a lot of criticism of how Symbian was evolving to compete with Android and iOS, Nokia did a 360-degree turn, making an arrangement with Microsoft to use Windows Phone as the main smartphone platform for Nokia's future devices.

In 2012, Nokia delivered both Symbian and Windows Phone devices, and in the following years Symbian may cease to exist. However, there are millions of Symbian devices on the market and in use today, so even if its market share is decreasing, we will have Symbian for a couple of years yet. If you are in the United States this may not seem like a big deal because Symbian was never a massive platform in the US, but you can see a very different perspective in Europe, Asia, and Latin America.

Symbian devices from Nokia were divided into different editions under the name S60, from the 1$^{st}$ to the 5$^{th}$ edition. After that, the S60 platform was renamed the Symbian platform and Nokia did not use the S60 name anymore. In the market today, we can find Symbian devices under the versions listed in Table 1-5.

*Table 1-5. List of Symbian smartphone platform versions available since 2008*

| Version name | Released on | Input type | Update ability |
|---|---|---|---|
| S60 3$^{rd}$ Edition FP2 | 1Q 2008 – 2Q 2011 | Numeric keypad and QWERTY keyboard, no touch devices | No updates |
| S60 5$^{th}$ Edition | 4Q 2008 – 3Q 2011 | Full touch devices, no keyboard | No updates |
| Symbian^3 | 2Q 2010 | Full touch devices with optional QWERTY keyboard | No updates |
| Symbian Anna | 2Q 2011 | Full touch devices with optional QWERTY keyboard | From Symbian^3 |
| Symbian Belle | 3Q 2011 | Full touch devices with optional QWERTY keyboard | From Symbian^3 and Anna |
| Symbian Belle FP1 | 1Q 2012 | Full touch devices with optional QWERTY keyboard | Only for some devices |
| Symbian Belle Refresh | 3Q 2012 | Full touch devices with optional QWERTY keyboard | Only for some devices |

 There isn't a fourth edition in Nokia's Series 40 or Series 60. Why is this? Nokia has a lot of market share in Asia, and in China 4 is considered bad luck (like the number 13 in the Western world) because it is pronounced "si," similar to "death" in Chinese.

All Symbian devices include a camera, a mobile browser, multitasking support, and a numeric or QWERTY keyboard. Fifth edition and later devices have touch support and the ability to upgrade to newer versions of the operating system. For example, the Nokia N8 originally came with Symbian^3 in 2010, and it has received free over-the-air upgrades to Symbian Anna in 2011 and to Symbian Belle in 2012.

Every Symbian device has a WebKit-based browser that allows it to browse almost any website on the Internet, including Flash-based sites like YouTube, thanks to Flash Lite.

### MeeGo

In 2005, Nokia introduced a new platform to replace Symbian, called Maemo. It's a Linux-based operating system designed for small netbooks or devices with full web-browsing support. In 2010, Nokia's Maemo merged with Intel's Moblin OS, creating the MeeGo OS. While Nokia originally intended MeeGo to be the replacement platform for smartphones, it subsequently moved to Windows Phone, so the MeeGo smartphones project was cancelled inside Nokia.

Before that, one MeeGo device was released to the market: the Nokia N9, sold in Europe and Latin America at the end of 2011, was the first and last device of its kind. To be honest, I have a Nokia N9, and the Linux-based operating system looks really great. Nokia has received some criticism about discarding this promising platform.

After Nokia discarded MeeGo, Intel began looking for a new partner to continue the project. Samsung was interested, and together they created a new project called Tizen as the evolution of some parts of MeeGo in conjunction with other projects from Samsung.

At the same time, a new company appeared in Finland, formed by ex-Nokia employees with the goal of continuing production of MeeGo devices. The company is called Jolla, and its version of the MeeGo operating system is called SailFish OS (*http://sail fishos.org*).

## BlackBerry

Research in Motion (RIM) was the Canadian manufacturer of the BlackBerry devices, mobile devices focused on being "always connected" with push technologies. The company was renamed "BlackBerry" in early 2013, dropping the RIM name for the future. Early adopters were primarily corporate users who needed to remain connected to intranets and corporate networks; then the devices appeared in new markets, becoming popular with teenagers and instant messaging fans. RIM used to call all its devices "smartphones," but others did not always consider them as falling into that category.

 In later chapters we will cover all the tools, SDKs, and emulators available from each manufacturer to make our lives as web developers easier.

For years RIM had few devices aimed at the mass market; most of them had QWERTY keyboards and were not designed for gaming. Many of these devices had proprietary input devices, like a scroll wheel or a touchpad, although some touch-enabled devices were launched in the last few years, giving users more multimedia and gaming support. Until 2012 all BlackBerry smartphones shipped with the BlackBerry OS, a proprietary operating system compatible with Java ME with extensions, and, of course, a mobile browser. We can categorize the devices by operating system version. The versions available on the market in 2012 were 4.7, 5.0, 6.0, 7.0, 7.1, and the new BB10 platform. Versions 4.7 and 5.0 should be considered legacy platforms; however, there are still some old devices in some markets working with these (more than three-year-old) versions.

All the BlackBerry devices support App World, the BlackBerry application store.

### The PlayBook tablet

In 2011, the company released its first tablet, the BlackBerry PlayBook (Figure 1-8), a 7" device with a new operating system, Tablet OS, derived from *QNX*, a Unix-based real-time operating system. This new operating system was prepared from the ground up to compete with iOS and Android and included many new and modern features, such as multitouch support, a modern web browser, multitasking support, and even Flash Player and AIR support.

*Figure 1-8. The BlackBerry PlayBook, including the Tablet OS, was the origin of the new BB10 platform, which has now also come to smartphones.*

In 2012, Tablet OS 2.0 appeared on the market, and every device is upgradable to the latest BB10 operating system. A 4G tablet version was also released in 2012. The distribution has never reached iPad or Android tablet levels, though, and the future of the platform is still uncertain.

### BlackBerry 10

Starting in 2013, BlackBerry is fully changing its smartphone platform in favor of the same PlayBook QNX-based operating system, adapted to the phone layout. This new platform is called BlackBerry 10 (*BB10*), and both the phones and the tablets from the company include it. BB10 is not compatible with BlackBerry OS versions earlier than version 7.1, and all the native applications must be developed using HTML5 or C++ using the Qt framework and a UI layer called Cascades. Adobe AIR (Flash) and Android Java applications are also compatible. (No, that's not a mistake—Tablet OS 2.0 on the PlayBook and BB10 on both tablets and phones support Android Java applications through an invisible virtual machine.)

The first BlackBerry 10 devices to hit the market are the full-touch Z10 and Q10, the latter of which is a square-screen device with a QWERTY keyboard. At the time of their launch in early 2013, the new BlackBerry 10 devices are among the most powerful HTML5 devices on the market.

## Samsung

Samsung has many devices on the market, most of which are divided into three different series: feature phones with a proprietary operating system, social devices with Bada, and smartphones with Android. From 2013, Samsung is also delivering devices with the new Linux-based Tizen operating system (partially based on MeeGo with Intel support).

Samsung's native devices are low-end and mid-range mobile devices with a proprietary OS including a browser and Java ME support, and typically a camera and a music player.

Bada is a mobile operating system managed completely by Android; it was released in 2010 and is optimized for mid-range devices to offer a touch interface without the need of high-end hardware. It includes a modern browser and native application installation support through the Samsung store, Samsung Apps.

In the smartphone category, Samsung is offering Android- and Windows Phone–based devices at the time of this writing, and will be offering Tizen-based devices from 2013.

 Samsung Tizen-based devices support first-class-citizen HTML5 apps and Android apps through an application compatibility layer.

Prior to 2010, the smartphones and high-end devices were divided into two categories by operating system—Symbian and Windows Mobile—with each having its own set of features. Subsequently, while delivering some Windows Phone devices (primarily the Omnia series), Samsung committed its smartphone and tablet platform to Android, and it has created different series, including the Galaxy series, with devices such as the Galaxy SIII or Galaxy Tab 10.1. Some of the Android-based devices from Samsung include a UI layer called TouchWiz, providing a different experience from other vendors' Android-based devices.

Android devices from Samsung support both the Google Play Store and the Samsung Apps store for application distribution.

## Sony Mobile

Ericsson built many mobile phones in the 1990s, and in 2001 it merged with Sony and created the Sony Ericsson company. Sony Ericsson produced a variety of low-end and mid-range devices and a couple of smartphones, including the *Xperia* series. In 2012, Sony became the sole owner of the company and "Ericsson" was removed from the name, converting the company into Sony Mobile.

Sony Mobile, like Samsung, has decided to offer devices with different operating systems. It offers low-end and mid-range devices using a proprietary operating system, as well as Windows Phone devices and Android devices. Before 2010, Sony Ericsson also delivered some Symbian and Windows Mobile devices to the market.

In the smartphone category, Android, Windows Phone, and Firefox OS devices are supported. The high-end series using Android is called Xperia, and it includes the Xperia Play, a PlayStation-certified phone optimized for gaming. Sony has also entered the tablet market with the Android-based devices Sony Tablet S and Sony Tablet P.

## Motorola Mobililty

For many years, Motorola has been a leading manufacturer of low-end and mid-range devices. Motorola's devices were the first mobile devices on the market, and the company pioneered the clamshell design with the classic Motorola StarTac. Motorola's mobile devices have traditionally used either a proprietary operating system (like the well-known Motorola v3), Symbian, Windows Mobile, or a Linux-based operating system the company created for its devices.

This situation created a very fragmented market for developers. Fortunately, today Motorola has changed its vision and has focused on a single solution for phones and tablets: Android. Motorola has also created some inexpensive mid-range devices with Android that might be considered social devices rather than smartphones, because the screen size, the hardware capabilities, and the performance are not high-end enough for them to be compared with other smartphones.

Google acquired Motorola in 2011, but at the time of this writing it continues operations under the Motorola name and as a separate company.

Motorola is the company behind some successful Android-based series, such as the Droid series (known as Milestone outside the US) and the Xoom tablet.

## Amazon

It may seem strange to see an online seller such as Amazon in this list. However, Amazon became a mobile device manufacturer with its Kindle ebook reader. The latest versions of the e-ink reader include a web browser, and while it is not one of the most-used browsers in the world, most users will use it as a backup browser.

Actually, Amazon appeared in the mobile market not with its ebook reader but with the Kindle Fire, the first tablet from the company. The first edition was a 7" tablet with a full touchscreen (not e-ink) using a customized version of Android and its own mobile browser. The Kindle Fire hit the market in November 2011 with a new price point for tablets: $199, less than half the cost of the iPad—or even other 7" Android-based tablets —at the time.

While it's difficult to know how many Kindle Fires are out there, Amazon reported millions of sales in the first weeks—more than the sales reported by other non-iPad tablets.

In September 2012, Amazon released the second generation of Kindle Fire tablets, known as the Kindle Fire HD, including WiFi connection support and a 4G-enabled 8.9" screen version.

 The bookseller Barnes & Noble has also released its own ereader and tablet, called Nook. The Nook Color and Nook Tablet are Android-based devices with their own UI and browser layer.

## LG Mobile

LG Mobile has many feature phones, social devices, and smartphones on the market today. Most are based on a proprietary OS with Java ME, Flash, and web support. However, LG also has devices with Android and Windows Phone on the market.

 LG Mobile has released one of the first auto-stereoscopic 3D devices on the market, the LG Optimus 3D: it's an Android device with a 3D screen that does not require the use of glasses. While there is an SDK that works with the Android SDK, there is no special 3D behavior that can be applied on web pages yet.

# HTC

HTC has become very popular in the mobile market since it created the first and second Android devices in the world and the first Google phone, the Nexus One. But HTC doesn't create only Android devices; it also produces a lot of Windows Phone devices. We can think of HTC devices as either Android devices or Windows devices; that's the only distinction that's needed.

# HP and Palm

My first mobile device was a Palm III, back in 1998. At that time, it was a great device. It was touch-enabled (used with a stylus), black and white, and very small. It was a revolution for me: I could install applications, read newspapers, and even program directly on the device with a Pascal for Palm interpreter. OK, the programming wasn't the best experience, but the concept was really powerful.

USRobotics bought Palm Computing, Inc., in 1995. At the time, it was the pioneer launching PDA devices. USRobotics later merged with 3Com, and as 3Com was dedicated to network cards and accessories, Palm Inc. was created as a subsidiary. Palm Inc. was very successful, and other manufacturers (including IBM) created other devices licensing its Palm OS. In 1998, a couple of Palm's directors left to create another company, HandSpring, which released the Treo devices to the market. Half PDA and half mobile phone, they can be considered the first smartphones on the market.

A few years later, Palm decided to divide the company into a hardware manufacturer, palmOne, and an operating system developer, PalmSource. This idea didn't work out: customers didn't accept the palmOne brand, so the company again acquired the Palm trademark and the operating system became the Garnet OS. In the meantime, Palm acquired HandSpring, so now we have Palm Treo devices.

In 2005, ACCESS (who also had other mobile technologies) acquired PalmSource and the operating system. Suddenly, the new-old Palm company made a difficult decision: it started to manufacture Treo devices with Windows Mobile, killing all hopes for the future of the Garnet OS (formerly Palm OS).

The Treo series was the only type of Palm device that survived in the mobile world, and BlackBerrys, the Nokia E Series, and other devices soon pushed Palm to the bottom of the market. In response, Palm created another operating system for mobile devices, aimed at being a web-oriented platform for iPhone-killer devices. *webOS* came to the market in 2009 with the first device, the Palm Pre. Other devices, such as the Palm Pixi, followed.

The company didn't do so well in the market, and in 2010, HP acquired Palm, promising evolution of webOS. In 2011, it even delivered new smartphones, such as the HP Pre 3, the HP Veer, and a new tablet, the HP TouchPad.

All this is history, to tell you that TouchPad tablet sales in 2011 proved disappointing; after that, HP decided to conclude its phone and tablet production and webOS became an obsolete mobile operating system. In 2012, HP decided to open source webOS; it became *Open webOS*, and at the time of this writing, there is no indication of who is going to use this operating system in the future. webOS is a powerful mobile operating system, so as an open source solution it seems reasonable to believe that some tablets, smartphones, or ebook readers will use this platform in the near future.

## Firefox OS

The Mozilla Foundation made a late entry into the mobile world. A Firefox mobile version for Android and MeeGo devices launched in 2011, but as of today it doesn't have too much market share. However, the Mozilla Foundation didn't give up, and in mid-2012 it created a new web-based operating system for smartphones, originally called Boot2Gecko but rebranded as Firefox OS.

This new platform is an open source Android-kernel-based platform utilizing the Gecko engine (the same engine that powers the Firefox browser), optimized for mid-range hardware delivering HTML5 and web experiences with lots of rich APIs. The first agreement that led this software project to a real implementation was with Telefónica.

Telefónica is the company behind many carriers in the world, including Movistar in Spain and dozens of countries in Latin America and O2 in the United Kingdom and Germany. Telefónica has committed to create and deliver devices using Firefox OS, called Open Web Devices (*http://www.openwebdevice.com*).

Following Telefónica, Deutsche Telekom, Etisalat, Smart, Sprint, Telecom Italia, and Telenor have announced their adherence to the Firefox OS project.

The idea is to offer inexpensive devices that are comparable with iOS, Android, and Windows Phone devices, with a rich user interface and an HTML5-based development platform. Sony, as well as other vendors, has announced Firefox OS devices.

## Ubuntu for Phones

Ubuntu for phones (*http://www.ubuntu.com/devices/phone*) is a mobile operating system presented at the beginning of 2013, with devices planned for release in 2014. It is based on the popular Ubuntu Linux distribution and was created by Canonical, the company behind Ubuntu support. The platform will support HTML5 and Qt native apps and includes a heavy gesture-based UI.

## Chinese Platforms

China has several of its own mobile platforms, typically based on Android. We can mention here *Baidu Yi*, an Android-powered operating system for the Chinese market, and *OPhone*, a Linux-based operating system based on the original Android (even before Google bought it) used by the operator China Mobile.

## Other Platforms

We've already covered almost 98% of the market. There are many other manufacturers, like Sanyo, Alcatel, Kyocera, and ZTE, but they don't have visible market share, and many of them produce devices based on platforms we've already discussed, like Windows Phone or Android. With the information I've shared with you in the preceding pages, I think you will be capable of understanding any new platform you can find on the market.

## Smart TV Platforms

I know what you're thinking: my TV is not too mobile! Well, you're right. We are not going to talk too much about TVs in this book, but it's important to give them a mention. Why? Because interactive TV systems are using web technologies, and most of them are imported from mobile operating systems. While TVs are not mobile, they usually have web browsers and engines similar to those of mobile devices. And mobile web developers usually are the first group of professionals to be called when a company needs a TV-based application.

At the time of this writing, interactive TV platforms are divided into native platforms and set-top box (STB) platforms. The first group includes companies that are delivering the interactive platform with the TV itself, while the latter are just set-top boxes that you can buy and attach to any HDMI-based TV.

As with smartphones and tablets, we can find low-end TVs and high-end TVs on the market, with radical differences in the engines behind them.

Interactive TV platforms typically include a web browser and native web or widget apps that can be attached to the TV home screen or even to a live channel to follow the video streaming. On the market today we can find Android-based, Opera-based, and custom-based TV platforms.

 Some console platforms, such as the PlayStation 3 or Wii, include a web browser, and they should be considered if you are creating a website for TV.

If you want more information about smart TV web platforms, you can look at the following websites for developers:

- Google TV (*http://developers.google.com/tv*)
- Samsung Smart TV (*http://www.samsungdforum.com*)
- Philips NetTV (*http://www.supportforum.philips.com*)
- LG NetCast (*http://netcastdev.lge.com*)
- Panasonic Viera Connect (*http://developer.vieraconnect.com*)
- Opera TV platform (*http://www.opera.com/business/tv/emulator*)

While Apple has the Apple TV platform based on iOS, at the time of this writing there is no web browser and no application installation process on this platform.

# Technical Information

After reading the previous section, you may be wondering where you can find information about all the individual devices on the market. What operating system does the Nokia Lumia 900 use? Does the BlackBerry PlayBook use the same browser as BlackBerry's smartphones? Which HTC devices use Android 4.0?

To get you closer to these answers, Table 1-6 lists the developer sites of all the major device manufacturers and platforms. Everyone has one, and almost all of them list the technical specifications of each of their devices. You can usually filter the devices by any characteristic, such as screen size, platform, operating system, or browser version. Sony Mobile's developer site is shown in Figure 1-9.

*Table 1-6. Mobile manufacturer and platform developer website URLs*

| Manufacturer/platform | Developer site URL |
| --- | --- |
| Apple iOS | developer.apple.com/ios |
| Android | developer.android.com |
| Nokia (S40, Symbian, MeeGo, Windows Phone) | developer.nokia.com |
| RIM/BlackBerry | developer.blackberry.com |
| Sony Mobile | developer.sonymobile.com |
| Microsoft Windows Phone | dev.windowsphone.com |
| Motorola Mobility | developer.motorola.com |
| Opera Mobile/Mini | dev.opera.com |
| LG | developer.lgmobile.com |
| Samsung | developer.samsung.com |
| Samsung Bada | developer.bada.com |
| Amazon Kindle | developer.amazon.com |

| Manufacturer/platform | Developer site URL |
| --- | --- |
| HTC | htcdev.com |
| HP webOS | developer.palm.com |
| Open webOS | openwebosproject.org |
| Barnes & Noble Nook | nookdeveloper.barnesandnoble.com |
| Tizen | developer.tizen.org |
| Firefox OS | developer.mozilla.org/apps |
| Ubuntu for Phones | developer.ubuntu.com/gomobile |

*Figure 1-9. The Sony Mobile Phone Gallery—almost every manufacturer website for developers allows you to filter the devices by features, such as the browser used.*

If you are new to the mobile development ecosystem, it's a good idea to register on all the developers' websites—and even the operators', if they have one. You will receive updates about tools, documentation, and news. You will also have access to download tools and emulators.

# CHAPTER 2

# Understanding the Mobile Web

Isn't the mobile web the same web as the desktop one? It does use the same basic architecture and many of the same technologies, though mobile device screens are smaller and bandwidth and processing resources are more constrained. There's a lot more to it than that, though, with twists and turns that can trip up even the most experienced desktop web developer.

## Myths of the Mobile Web

As the Web has moved onto mobile devices, developers have told themselves a lot of stories about what this means for their work. While some of those stories are true, others are misleading, confusing, or even dangerous.

### It's Not the Mobile Web; It's Just the Web!

I've heard this said many times in the last few years, and it's true. It's really the same Web. Think about your life. You don't have another email account just for your mobile. (OK, I know some guys that do, but I believe that's not typical!)

You read about the last NBA game on your favorite site, like ESPN; you don't have a desktop news source and a different mobile news source. You really don't want another social network for your mobile; you want to use the same Facebook or Twitter account as the one you use on your desktop PC. It was painful enough creating your friends list on your desktop, you've already ignored too many people...you don't want to have to do all that work again on your mobile.

For all of these purposes, the mobile web uses the same network protocols as the whole Internet: HTTP, HTTPS, POP3, Wireless LAN, and even TCP/IP. OK, you can say that GSM, CDMA, and UMTS are not protocols used in the desktop web environment, but they are communication protocols operating at lower layers. From our point of view, from a web application approach, we are using the same protocols.

So, yes…it's the same Web. However, when developing for the mobile web we are targeting very, very different devices. The most obvious difference is the screen size, and yes, that will be our first problem. But there are many other not-so-obvious differences. That's why the concept of the mobile web exists as a group of best practices, techniques, and frameworks specially designed for mobile devices. I'm pretty sure that in the near future all these techniques and best practices are going to become must-knows for every web developer, and perhaps the mobile web will disappear; it will just be the Web for different devices.

Don't get me wrong—this doesn't mean that, as developers, we need to create two, three, or dozens of versions duplicating our work. In this book, we are going to analyze all the techniques available for this new world. Our objective will be to make only one product, and we'll analyze the best way to do it.

## You Don't Need to Do Anything Special About Your Desktop Website

Almost every smartphone on the market today—for example, the iPhone and Android-based devices—can read and display full desktop websites. Yes, this is true. Users want the same experience on the mobile web as they have on their desktops. Yes, this is also true. Some statistics even indicate that users tend to choose desktop web versions over mobile versions when using smartphones.

However, is this because we really love zooming in and out, scrolling and crawling for the information we want? Or is it because the mobile versions are really awful and don't offer a great user experience? I've seen a lot of mobile sites consisting of nothing but a logo and a couple of text links. My smartphone wants more! In my opinion, for most cases, it is a much better idea to create a device-specific user interface. We are not trying to create fragmentation; we are trying to give the user the best experience her device can support.

## One Website Should Work for All Devices (Desktop, Mobile, TV)

As we will see, there are techniques that allow us to create only one file but still provide different experiences on a variety of devices, including desktops, mobiles, TVs, and game consoles. This vision is called "One Web," and there is also a technique called Responsive Web Design that aims to achieve it. This is, to an extent, possible today, but the vision won't fully be realized for years to come. Today, there are a lot of mobile devices with very low connection speeds and limited resources—nonsmartphones—that, in theory, can read and parse any file, but will not provide the best user experience and will have compatibility and performance problems if we deliver the same document as for desktops. Performance is so important for mobile devices that in most situations, if you consider all the pros and cons, the idea of providing the same document to every device seems like just a utopian ideal. Therefore, One Web remains a goal for the future. A little additional work is still required to provide the right user experience for each mobile device, but there are techniques that can be applied to reduce the work required and avoid code and data duplication.

 If you believe that the mobile web is about WML (Wireless Markup Language), a language deprecated several years ago, then you need to fast forward to the present. Today, it's almost an impossible mission to find a live phone supporting only WML as markup.

## Just Create an HTML File with a Width of 320 Pixels, and You Have a Mobile Website

This is the other fast-food way to think about the mobile web. Today, there are more than 3,000 mobile devices on the market, with almost 30 different browsers (actually, more than 300 different browsers if we separate them by version number). Creating one HTML file as your mobile website will be a very unsuccessful project. In addition, doing so contributes to the belief that mobile web browsing is painful.

## Native Mobile Applications Will Kill the Mobile Web

Every solution has advantages and disadvantages. The mobile web has much to offer native applications, as this book will demonstrate later. The mobile web (and the new concept of the native web app or hybrid application) offers us a great multidevice application platform, including local applications that don't require an always-connected web with URLs and browsers.

## People Are Not Using Their Mobile Browsers

How many Internet connections are there in the world?

> 2,267,233,742 (33% of the world's population) at the beginning of 2012 (*http://www.internetworldstats.com*).

How many people have mobile devices?

> 5,981,000,000 (86% of the population) at the end of 2011 (U.N. Telecommunications Agency (*http://www.itu.int*))

Opera Mini is a mobile browser for all ranges of devices. It is free, and as of January 2012 it had 159 million active users. This tells us that 159 million users wanted to have a better mobile web experience, so they went out and got Opera Mini. Do all the nearly 6 billion worldwide mobile device users know about Opera Mini? Perhaps not, so it's difficult to know how many would be interested in trying this different mobile web experience. However, 159 million unique users for a browser that the user had to install actively is a big number for me. When Opera Mini appeared in Apple's App Store, from which users can download and install applications for the iPhone, iPod, and iPad, 1 million users downloaded the browser on the first day. That's quite impressive.

The percentage of total web browsing from mobile devices is increasing month by month. Mobile browsing may become as popular as desktop browsing in the coming months and years. According to StatCounter (*http://gs.statcounter.com*), in mid-2012, 10% of total web browsing was done from mobile web devices—5 times more than at the same time one year before and 10 times more than two years before.

# What Is the Mobile Web?

The mobile web, from a user's perspective, is basically just web content accessed from a mobile device. We can even discuss whether the mobile web exists as a concept from a user's perspective.

From a developer's perspective, however, the mobile web definitely does exist, and it's a group of best practices, design patterns, and even new code that we need to learn. And that's why this book exists.

## Differences

If you are an experienced web developer or web designer, you may feel confident about creating mobile web experiences. It seems like the same thing in a smaller package, right? Wrong. The mobile web is really different, and even if you're a senior, experienced web professional you still have lot to learn.

Some of the main differences from the desktop web include:

- Slower networks with higher latency
- Slower hardware and less available memory
- Different browsing experience
- Different user contexts
- Different browser behavior (for example, do you know that usually only the current tab on a mobile browser is active and running effectively?)
- Too many mobile web browsers, with different versions on the market at the same time
- Some browsers are too limited, some browsers are too innovative
- Several browsers without identity (it's just…the browser), documentation, or developer tools

- Differences in testing and debugging (in the mobile web this is a challenge, and it's different from in classic web development)

# Mobile Web Eras

Don't panic; this isn't a history class. However, it is useful to be aware of the history of the mobile web. This is recent history: the first mobile web platform was developed less than 15 years ago. Analyzing this history can help us to understand the technologies behind the mobile web, and compatibility issues.

## WAP 1

The mobile Internet appeared at the end of the last millennium. I remember all the advertising on the streets and in TV commercials. A wide range of operators started to offer mobile web browsing, with one or two devices with Wireless Application Protocol (WAP) browsers.

---

### What Is WAP?

The Wireless Application Protocol is a standard for application-layer network communication in the mobile world. With the exception of the i-mode protocol used in Japan and briefly in other countries, WAP is the primary protocol used by operators worldwide.

The WAP standard describes a protocol suite that allows the transportation of information between a device and the Internet (via a WAP gateway), and a list of standard recommendations for the content to be transmitted. It was created by the WAP Forum (converted in 2002 to the Open Mobile Alliance, or OMA).

For many years the term "WAP" was used incorrectly, to refer to a document type ("a WAP file") or a website as a whole ("I've developed a WAP").

WAP has two main versions: 1.1, released in 1998, and 2.0, released in 2002 (this is the actual standard). Many users are not even aware of the existence of the newer version, and today it has been replaced by classic HTTP web browsing.

---

I can remember traveling by train in my home city in 2000, using the first device with a WAP browser (my Nokia 7110, famous because of its similarity to Neo's phone in the film *The Matrix*). My operator had an excellent promotion: free browsing for two months. I was browsing a website with an ICQ client, and nobody in my buddy list could believe that I was chatting from my mobile phone. The free browsing promotion wasn't very popular, because at the time few people understood what the mobile Internet was. When I received a $300 bill for "voice calls," I realized that I was probably the only one using that promotion (of course, I didn't pay the bill, because it was supposed to be free!).

 Some WAP 1.x browsers were so simple that they didn't even have a "back" feature—the developer was responsible for providing a link back to the previous page.

At that time, mobile devices connected to the Internet using a voice call as a modem communication. So, every minute you were connected was charged as a voice call minute. The devices with browsers had black and white screens without image support (or very basic support) and could display only three or four lines of text on the screen. This early version of the mobile Internet was a failure. It was expensive and did not offer any useful services. The overall user experience was very poor.

A few years later, 2.5G technologies such as the General Packet Radio Service (GPRS) appeared on the market. These technologies allowed us to browse the Internet (even WAP 1 sites) and be charged according to the number of kilobytes transferred, no matter how many minutes we were connected to the Internet.

This first mobile web was defined by the WAP 1.0 standard (which, in practice, never existed on the market, having quickly been replaced by WAP 1.1). That standard suggested Wireless Markup Language (WML)—an XML version designed for mobile devices that was not compatible with the HTML standards—as the document type for the web content. The devices communicated with the operators' WAP gateways using WAP protocols, and the gateways translated the communications to HTTP and passed them on to the destination web servers. WAP 1.x is not recommended today, as it has been replaced by new technologies.

 The HTML 3.2 subset in the Japanese i-mode service was one of the first languages that shifted the mobile web away from the old Handheld Device Markup Language (HDML) and WML and pushed it toward HTML and, eventually, XHTML.

Mobile browsers in this era were called "WAP browsers," and websites using this standard were called "WAP sites"—"WAP" was used instead of "web." This created a perceived distinction between the two (WAP appeared to be different from the Web).

At this time, the de facto standard for publishing WAP sites on the Internet was the use of the *wap* subdomain. So, for example, we could access Yahoo!'s WAP site using the URL *http://wap.yahoo.com*. Even today, it is not uncommon to find this domain pattern in use for mobile websites.

Most low-end and mid-range devices on the market today still support WAP content, but the browsers on newer smartphones (like the iPhone, and Android and Windows Phone devices) don't support WML content anymore.

## WAP 2.0

The last OMA standard, WAP 2.0, was released in 2002. The first WAP 2.0 devices appeared in 2002, and almost every device on the market today is WAP 2.0 compatible (with some exceptions in the last few years). This standard is nearer to the web standards than the previous version and allows HTTP communication between the device and the server. The WAP gateway acts only as a proxy in the operator network.

WAP 2.0 deprecated WML and created XHTML MP (Mobile Profile), along with other companion standards that we will analyze in detail in Chapter 6. Surprisingly, after this new standard was released the word "WAP" dropped out of usage and "mobile web" started to be used. So, if we talk about a "WAP site" today, it will be understood that we are referring to a WAP 1.1 website.

Many sites continued to use the *wap* subdomain for mobile websites, while others started using the other de facto standard for publishing mobile websites, the *m* subdomain ("m" for mobile). For example, today we can access the Google Mobile website using *http://m.google.com*, or the popular Facebook social networking site using *http://m.facebook.com*.

---

### WAP Push

WAP Push is a standard available since WAP 1.2 that allows content to be pushed to a mobile device at any time. A WAP Push is generally an SMS (Short Message Service) message to a special port with a URL to content or a website. When a device receives a WAP Push, it asks the user if he wants to go to that URL. Content portals use this method to push games, ringtones, and other premium content when you ask for that content using SMS. There are also some silent pushes from the operator that the user doesn't receive any feedback about.

WAP Link is a similar solution, but it sends an SMS to the user's inbox. The message contains a URL. Modern devices autodetect URLs inside the text messages and convert them into links that the user can click on.

Modern smartphone platforms support Push messages using an operating system layer that is out of the scope of carriers, working through TCP protocols.

---

### The dotMobi era

dotMobi (*.mobi*) is a top-level domain (TLD) approved by the Internet Corporation for Assigned Names and Numbers (ICANN) in 2005 and made available to the public at the end of 2006. It was approved to be used as the main domain for the mobile Internet and it had the support of many software companies, Internet companies, manufacturers, and operators. The idea was that if you had the domain *yourcompany.com*, you should use *yourcompany.mobi* for your mobile website. The concept was original and some big companies have gotten on board (for example, Nokia uses *nokia.mobi*), but it's not as well supported as everyone wanted. For example, there is no browser with a shortcut to *.mobi* when you are typing in a URL address (there are shortcuts for *.com*, *.net*, and *.org*).

The TLD is managed by mTLD, an organization with many services and web portals centered around the mobile web. Any *.mobi* site should be WAP 2.0 compatible, but there is no technical obligation for this. You can buy a dotMobi domain from any registrar and host it anywhere, without any limitation.

The main criticism of dotMobi is that it created two Internets, a desktop web (*.com*, *.net*, and so on) and a mobile web (*.mobi*), rather than promoting a single Web that can be browsed from different devices.

### The iPhone era

In 2007, the iPhone appeared, and it was a big hit in the market because it was the first device with a browser encouraging users to browse the "desktop/full web" instead of the mobile web. While often this is not a good idea, as we are going to see later, Safari on the iPhone completely changed the mobile web space. Almost every mobile browser today has some behavior and UI elements inspired by the iPhone browser.

Safari supported HTML5 stuff even before it had that name; they were called "Apple extensions" and led developers to create iPhone-specific websites.

The iPhone gave us another way to use the Web: applications. Lots of users use the Web through apps, such as Twitter, Facebook, or Gmail. This is not true of all users, but installed apps have become important in the mobile world if we want to be discovered and used frequently.

### The mobile HTML5 era

When all the major browser vendors entered the HTML5 world, a new era started. While it is still well received to have an *m.** subdomain, mobile HTML5 is starting to promote the idea of not having a different URL for the mobile and desktop web. The same URL can have different views, served client-side or server-side with different techniques that we are going to see later in this book.

The recommended way to implement mobile websites is using the same URL for every device. However, using a mobile subdomain is still valid.

With mobile HTML5, new abilities appeared, such as the creation of installed apps and native web apps.

 Back in 2005, installed apps for using web services used to be called On Device Portals (ODP), and around 2007 native web apps used to be called *widgets*. These names are legacy now and you won't find too many usages in the mobile web space today.

# The Mobile Browsing Experience

The mobile browsing experience varies among different devices, and even among different browsers running on the same device. The user interfaces work very differently.

## Navigation Methods

A mobile website can be navigated using different techniques. Every mobile browser uses one or many of these modes of navigation. The modes are:

- Focus navigation
- Cursor navigation
- Touch navigation
- Multitouch navigation

*Focus navigation*, illustrated in Figure 2-1, is the most frequent mechanism used for browsing websites on low-end and mid-range devices. (Smartphones that have hardware cursor keys, a touchpad, or a scroll wheel sometimes use focus navigation as an alternative to touch.) With this mode, a border or a background color is used to show the user where the focus is. In general it is used in nontouch devices: the user uses the cursor keypad to navigate between links and scroll the website. Pressing the down arrow key makes the browser change the focus to the next focusable object (for example, a link, a text field, or a button), or scroll a couple of lines in the content if there is no other focusable object nearby.

*Figure 2-1. Focus navigation on a low-end device*

*Cursor navigation*, illustrated in Figure 2-2, emulates a mouse cursor over the screen that can be moved using the arrow keys. A mouse click is emulated with the Fire or Enter key. For a better experience, many browsers jump the cursor to a nearby focusable object to reduce the distance the user has to move the pointer to use a link or a button.

*Figure 2-2. Cursor navigation on nontouch devices shows a typical mouse pointer that allows mouseover events and mouse effects in a website*

*Touch navigation* may seem obvious, but we need to be aware of one thing: the user may navigate using a finger or a stylus. The differences in design can be huge; precision is much lower if fingers are used. Touch devices allow the user to use detectable gestures to easily perform some actions. We will cover gesture detection in later chapters.

Some devices are also *multitouch,* allowing the users to select many objects at the same time and incrementing the number of gestures that can be detected.

## Zoom Experience

Analyzing how browsers manage zoom options reveals two different types of browser. The first type offers *basic zoom* capabilities: the web page is always rendered at 1:1 scale to the original design, and the user can only change the font size. If the design doesn't fit on the screen, the scroll bar comes in to solve the problem.

The second type offers *smart zoom* capabilities: the web page can be viewed at any zoom scale the user wants, and the zooming action affects the font size, the images, and the web page as a whole. Based on a user gesture or menu option, we can switch from a full-page view to a paragraph view, as shown in Figure 2-3.

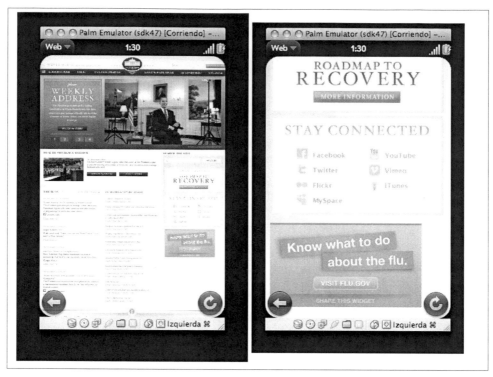

*Figure 2-3. The webOS browser, like many others, offers smart zooming: the entire web-site layout is rendered first, and when the user double-taps on part of the page, the smart zoom focuses in on that area*

Some browsers use smart zooming like on a desktop: if a paragraph extends beyond the page width, when you zoom in you need to scroll horizontally (Safari on iOS is one example). Some others reflow the text when zoomed in to fit the page width (the Android browser does this), and still others (such as Opera Mini) reflow the page even when zoomed out.

## Reflow Layout Engines

Some mobile browsers aim to offer a better experience to mobile users browsing web-sites that were not designed for mobile devices by reflowing the pages to a one-column design. The smart zoom option has started to replace this technique, but there are still some browsers that use a reflow algorithm. For example, Figure 2-4 shows the result of using Opera Mini's "Single Column View" on a web page.

*Figure 2-4. The same website browsed with Opera Mini in normal mode and in "Single Column View," with a reflow engine that autodetects navigation bars, content zones, and footers and shows us a one-column view of the site*

## Direct Versus Cloud-Based Browsers

Another difference we will find is between *direct* browsers, which get content directly from the website server, and *cloud* browsers (also known as proxied browsers), which go through a proxy server on the cloud. The proxy server usually does many of the following actions on the fly:

- Reduces the content, eliminating features that are not mobile-compatible
- Compresses the content (images included)
- Pre-renders the content, so it can be displayed in the browser faster
- Converts the content, so we can see Flash video on devices with no Flash support
- Encrypts the content
- Caches the content for quick access to frequently visited sites

Cloud-based browsers, such as Opera Mini and the Nokia Xpress browser, consume less bandwidth, increasing performance and reducing total navigation time at the same time. From a developer's perspective, the main difference is that the device is not directly accessing our web server; it's the proxy server on the cloud that is requesting all the files from our server, rendering those files on the cloud, and delivering a compressed, proprietary result to the browser.

## Multipage Experience

There are very different approaches to multipage browsing (such as opening more than one web page at the same time). This can be initiated by the user, or by the developer opening a pop-up window or a link in a new window. Different browsers take different approaches and may support any of the following:

- Only one page
- Multiple windows (shown in Figure 2-5)
- Window stacks
- Tab navigation

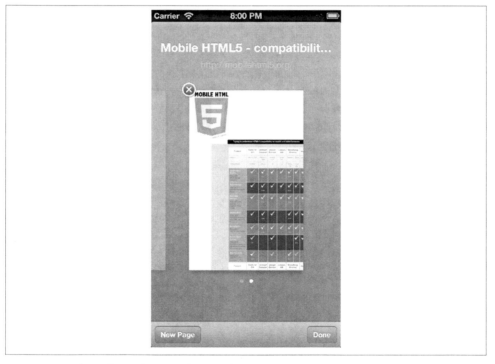

*Figure 2-5. The iPhone browser has multiwindow support, allowing the user to maintain up to eight different websites open at the same time.*

The iPhone, Android, and Windows Phone browsers all support multiple windows.

# Web Engines

The rendering engine is the heart of the browser. It's the native code that parses, understands, and renders the page after reading the HTML and CSS or executing JavaScript code. While some rendering engines come with a default JavaScript execution engine, some browsers upgrade it to a different one.

### Rendering engines

With regard to mobile devices, the king of rendering engines is WebKit.

WebKit is an open source layout engine for web browsers. Apple created it based on the open source KHTML engine (used in the Linux Konkeror browser) to be used in its Safari web browser for Mac OS X, and later for Windows and iOS. As an open source project, there are many ports of the rendering engine, and today we can find many applications using it—for example, Google Chrome and Adobe AIR.

The great thing about WebKit is that almost everyone in the mobile world is using it. This means that even on very different mobile devices we can expect very similar web rendering with simple markup and styles, which is good news for developers. However, it isn't perfect—as we'll see in later chapters, many differences do exist between WebKit implementations, as well as in HTML5 compatibility.

 WebKit2 is a new project created from the ground up supporting a new internal architecture that splits the web content process from the application UI process. At the time of this writing the only mobile browser supporting this new version is the Nokia Browser for MeeGo.

Firefox on Android, Firefox OS, Windows 8, and MeeGo use Gecko, another open source rendering engine created by the Mozilla Foundation; Opera used a proprietary engine called Presto until 2013; and Microsoft uses its own engine called Trident on Internet Explorer. Other browsers for older devices or feature phones use their own engines.

As of January 2013, according to StatCounter (*http://gs.statcount er.com*), WebKit has 44% of the desktop web browsing market and 66% of the mobile web browsing market. In the mobile world, Opera and the Presto engine have the next biggest share, with 17%, and the UC browser has 10%.

### JavaScript engines

JavaScript is a scripting language used by interpreters, not compilers. However, starting in 2010, some new JavaScript engines appeared in the market, increasing execution speeds by two or three times. The main difference in these new engines is a precompilation process that accelerates JavaScript code execution time, known as the JIT (Just in Time) compiler.

The first of the new engines was Carakan, created by Opera for its desktop browser; this was followed by V8, an open-source JavaScript engine developed by Google that is currently used in Google Chrome and other projects. Other modern JavaScript engines include JägerMonkey (Mozilla Foundation), IonMonkey (Mozilla Foundation, since 2013), SquirrelFish Extreme (WebKit, marketed as Nitro for Safari), and Chakra (Internet Explorer).

 While WebKit is important in the mobile web world, we need to develop, test, and profile on all the other engines too. The market changes so fast that we need to be multiplatform to be future-proof. Embrace WebKit while ensuring compatibility with standards and the whole browser ecosystem.

# Fragmentation

If you are a newcomer to the mobile world, we need to discuss some things affecting web browsing before we do any coding. I know you want to start coding right now, but believe me, your project will be more successful if you know a bit about the environment.

*Fragmentation* in this context refers to how the market is "fragmented" in pieces supporting different interfaces, hardware, operating systems, and abilities offered to developers.

# Display

I know what you're thinking: "You're going to talk to me about the small screen problems." Yes, I was going to start with that. A mobile device has a very small screen compared with a desktop. While in desktop development we talk about 19-, 21-, and

25-inch screen sizes (diagonally), in mobile development we talk about 1.5, 2.5, or 4 inches. It's really a big difference. Similarly, while in desktop development we talk about 1024×768-pixel resolution, in mobile development we talk about a quarter or half of that (or in some cases, double that).

## Resolution

Resolution is the primary concern in mobile design. How many pixels (width and height) are available on a given device? This was the only portability problem for many years in the area of mobile development.

 *Portability* refers to the ability of a mobile application to be used on multiple devices with different hardware, software, and platforms.

There are no mobile device standards regarding screen resolution. One phone-sized device may have a resolution of 128×128 pixels, and another 720×1280. The third-generation iPad has a 2048×1536 screen. But if we talk about devices sold from 2009, we can separate most of them into these groups:

- Feature phones: 128×160 or 128×128 pixels
- Social phones (group #1, nontouch): 176×220, 176×208, 240×320, or 320×240 pixels
- Social phones (group #2, touch): 240×320, 320×240, or 240×400 pixels
- Touch-enabled smartphones (group #1, low resolution): 240×480, 320×480, or 360×480 pixels
- Touch-enabled smartphones (group #2, higher resolution): 480×800, 480×854, 540×960, 640×960, 640×1136, 720×1280, or 768×1280 pixels
- Tablets: 1024×768, 1024×600, 1280×800, 1920×1200, or 2048×1536 pixels

 Touch-only devices typically have a higher resolution than devices with a keyboard because no space needs to be reserved for the keypad.

Most screen sizes have recognizable names that you will find in technical documentation and inside emulator settings. Table 2-1 shows the most important names you need to understand and their relation to DPI (dots per inch) for typical smartphones on the today.

*Table 2-1. List of screen resolutions available on the market for smartphones and tablets, in portrait mode*

| Short name | Name | Resolution (w×h in portrait mode) | Aspect ratio | Sample devices | Average screen size | PPI |
|---|---|---|---|---|---|---|
| QQVGA | Quarter Quarter VGA | 120×160, 128×160 | 4:3 | Nokia C1-01, LG LX150 | 1.5″ – 1.8″ | 111 – 133 |
| QVGA | Quarter VGA | 240×320 | 4:3 | Nokia Asha 300, Sony W910 | 2.4″ | 166 |
| WQVGA | Wide Quarter VGA | 240×400 | 5:3 | Samsung Wave 2 | 3″ | 155 |
| FWQVGA | Full Wide Quarter VGA | 240×432 | ~16:9 | Samsung F490 | 3.2″ | 155 |
| LQVGA | Landscape Quarter VGA | 320×240 | 4:3 landscape | BlackBerry 8320 (Curve), Sony Aspen | 2.5″ | 160 |
| HVGA | Half VGA | 320×480 | 5:3 | Apple iPhone 3GS, BlackBerry 9550 (Storm 2) | 3.2″ – 3.5″ | 165 – 180 |
| nHD | Ninth of High Definition | 360×640 | 16:9 | Nokia 808 PureView, Nokia N8 | 3.0″ – 3.5″ | 210 – 250 |
| WVGA | Wide VGA | 480×800 | 5:3 | Samsung Galaxy SII, Nokia Lumia 900 | 3.7″ – 4.3″ | 220 – 252 |
| FWVGA | Full Wide VGA | 480×854 | 16:9 | Nokia N9, Motorola Droid X, Sony Xperia Play | 3.9″ – 4.3″ | 228 – 251 |
| VGA | Video Graphic Adaptor | 640×480 | 4:3 landscape | Nokia E6 | 2.5″ | 320 |
| DVGA | Double-Size VGA | 640×960 | 3:2 | Apple iPhone 4S | 3.5″ | 330 |
| WDVGA | Wide DVGA | 640×1136 | 16:9 | Apple iPhone 5 | 4″ | 330 |
| QHD | Quarter High Definition | 540×960 | 16:9 | Motorola Droid RAZR, HTC Sensation | 4.3″ | 256 |
| WSVGA | Wide Super VGA | 600×1024 | ~5:3 | BlackBerry PlayBook, Samsung Galaxy Tab 7″ | 7″ | 170 |
| HD (also known as FWXGA/ WXGA) | High Definition | 720×1280 | 16:9 | Galaxy Nexus, Sony Xperia S, Samsung Galaxy SIII | 4.3″ – 4.8″ | 320 – 342 |
| Sq.HD | Square HD | 720×720 | 1:1 | BlackBerry Q10 | ~3.5″ | ~300 |
| XGA | Extended Graphic Adaptor | 768×1024 | 4:3 | iPad 2, iPad mini, HP TouchPad | 7.0″ – 9.7″ | 163 – 132 |
| WXGA #1 | Wide XGA | 768×1280 | 15:9 | Samsung Galaxy Tab 10.1, Motorola Xoom, Nexus 7, BlackBerry Z10 | 4.2″ – 10″ | 356 – 151 |

| Short name | Name | Resolution (w×h in portrait mode) | Aspect ratio | Sample devices | Average screen size | PPI |
|---|---|---|---|---|---|---|
| WXGA #2 | Wide XGA | 768×1366 | 16:9 | Microsoft Surface | 10.6" | 148 |
| WXGA #3 | Wide XGA | 800×1280 | 16:10 | Nexus 4 | 4.8" | 320 |
| Full HD | Full HD 1080p | 1080×1920 | 16:9 | Sony Xperia Z | 5" | 443 |
| WUXGA | Widescreen Ultra XGA | 1200×1920 | 16:10 | Kindle Fire HD 8.9" | 8.9" | 254 |
| QXGA | Quad XGA | 1536×2048 | 4:3 | iPad 3rd gen. | 9.7" | 256 |
| WQXGA | Wide Quad XGA | 1600×2560 | 16:10 | Nexus 10 | 10" | 300 |

There are also still a lot of devices with custom resolutions. Web technologies will simplify this problem for us, as we'll see later in this book.

## 3D Stereoscopic Screens

In 2011, 3D screens started to appear on the market. Examples of these devices are the LG Optimus 3D and the HTC Evo 3D.

They use stereoscopic screens (sometimes known as autostereoscopic screens) and they don't require the use of glasses for the immersive 3D experience. Instead, there is a parallax barrier over the LCD screen, allowing us to receive different information in each eye and to create 3D images in our heads.

Usually these platforms provide an SDK for native developers to create 3D immersive experiences, but unfortunately for mobile web developers, at this time there is no 3D support for web browsing or inside a web browser. There are some extensions to known formats, such as 3D MPEG-4 video formats and the JPS image format (a JPEG file with the image for both eyes in the same file), but true 3D web development is not yet possible at the time of this writing.

### Physical dimensions

The resolution isn't the only thing we can talk about with regard to a mobile device's screen. One feature as important as the resolution is the physical dimensions of the screen (in inches or centimeters, diagonally or measured as width × height), or the relation between this measure and the resolution, which is known as the *PPI* (pixels per inch) or *DPI* (dots per inch). This is very important, because while our first thought may be that a screen with a resolution of 128×160 is "smaller" than a screen with a resolution of 240×320, that may be a false conclusion. Consider the iPad 2 and the third-generation iPad: they have resolutions of 1024×768 and 2048×1536, respectively, in the same 9.7" screen. Also, you can find on the market 10" tablets with only as many pixels as a high-resolution 4.5" smartphone.

We can categorize screen sizes as follows:

- Small phone screens: from 1.5" to 3"
- Normal/medium phone screens: from 3" to 4"
- Large phone screens: from 4" to 5"
- Small tablet screens: from 5" to 8"
- Large tablet screens: from 8" to 11"

Every screen size type can have different density options:

- Low density: 100 to 130 PPI
- Medium density: 130 to 180 PPI
- High density: 180 to 270 PPI
- Ultra-high density: more than 270 PPI

That's why, on the market, we can find medium phone screens with medium density, high density, and ultra-high density with resolutions of 320×480, 480×854, and 640×960, all having the same physical screen size (meaning more or fewer pixels in the same area).

 Android offers an online statistics site (*http://developer.android.com/ about/dashboards/index.html*) that gives information on the market share of devices with different screen sizes and densities. At the time of this writing, 50% of Android devices are normal phone size with high-density screens, 25% are normal phone size with ultra-high-density screens, 4.6% are large tablet screens with medium-density screens, and the rest is shared between all the other combinations.

One of the phones I owned back in 2006, thanks to a gift from Nokia, was an N90. The device was like a brick, but the great (or not so great, as it turned out) feature was its resolution at the time: 352×416. The problem was that the screen size was very similar to those of other devices on the market at the time that used resolutions like 176×208. Therefore, I couldn't use any game or application on the device, or browse the Web; I needed a magnifier to see the normal font size. Every programmer thought that more available pixels meant a bigger screen, so why bother increasing the font? "Let's use the extra space to fit more elements," everyone thought. Wrong.

---

# Retina Display

In June 2010 Apple presented the iPhone 4, the first device with a "Retina display"—that is, a display with 326 dots per inch (DPI). The human retina can discern up to a limit of 300 DPI at a certain distance, so this device, with 960×640 pixels in landscape mode, has more pixels per inch than we can really perceive distinctly at that distance.

The third-generation iPad (known as the "new iPad") has double the previous iPad 2's resolution—264 PPI—and the same is true of some new MacBook devices with Retina displays.

The Retina display is a trademark from Apple that today means "double the resolution (or four times the available pixels)" and has no direct relationship with a certain PPI value—as we've seen, it can be 326 DPI on the iPhone and 264 DPI on an iPad.

In response, in January 2013, Sony announced the Xperia Z, the first device with 443 DPI, naming it a device with a "Reality Display."

---

The iPhone 4S has a display size of 4.5" × 2.31" (11.52 cm × 58.6 cm) – 326 PPI (or 0.07 mm dot pitch), in comparison with other devices with a similar screen size, which have between 180 and 220 PPI.

You can find a PPI and DPI calculator (*http://pxcalc.com*) online.

### Pixel density ratio

To solve the problem of having different-resolution devices in the same device category, some mobile browsers support a feature called *device pixel ratio*. This is a multiplier that, when available, is automatically applied to our web content.

Be careful to not confuse *device pixel ratio* with *pixel aspect ratio*, which describes how the width of one pixel relates to its height.

When this feature is available inside a browser, instead of working with physical dimensions we are working with something known variously as *device-independent pixels*, *density-independent pixels*, *CSS pixels*, or *virtual pixels*. That means that if we define something to be 100 pixels wide and 20 pixels high, we are not talking about real device pixels. Instead, our measures will be multiplied by the current device pixel ratio, so it may be 150×30 pixels on a 1.5 pixel ratio device or 200×40 pixels on a 2 pixel ratio device.

The objective of the pixel ratio idea is to simplify our lives as designers and developers: we can design for one virtual, average device and the result will look fine on every screen size. Remember, more pixels doesn't necessarily mean more space to insert content.

Thanks to pixel ratio, we can design one website for the iPhone 3GS and iPhone 5, the iPad 2 and fourth-generation iPad, or every Android smartphone, without worrying about differences in resolution. However, there are some exceptions; for example, the iPad mini exposes the same pixel ratio as the iPad 2, while they have different screen sizes (7.9" versus. 9.7" diagonally). Therefore, everything on the iPad mini looks the same as on the iPad 2, but 19% smaller.

Table 2-2 lists the device pixel ratio values that are most common on mobile devices currently on the market (as of the beginning of 2013).

*Table 2-2. Most common device pixel ratio values, and sample devices using these ratios*

| Device pixel ratio value | Resolution | Platform using this value | Sample devices |
|---|---|---|---|
| 0.75 | Low | Android | Samsung Galaxy Mini, Motorola Charm, Sony Xperia Mini |
| 1 | Medium | iOS, Android, BlackBerry, Symbian | iPhone 3GS, iPad 2, iPad mini 1st gen., Nokia 500, LG Optimus One, HTC Explorer, BB Torch 9810 |
| 1.3 to 1.4 | Medium | Symbian, Android tablets | Nokia N8 (1.3), Nexus 7 (1.325...) |
| 1.5 | High | Android, Symbian, MeeGo | Samsung Galaxy SII, LG Optimus, Nexus One, Sony Xperia Play, Nokia E6, Nokia N9 |
| 2 | Ultra high | iOS, Android | iPhone 4S, iPhone 5, iPad 3rd & 4th gen., Galaxy Nexus, Galaxy SIII |
| 2.1 to 2.5 | Ultra high | Android, BlackBerry | Galaxy Nexus, Galaxy SIII, BlackBerry Z10 |
| 3 | Ultra high | Android | Sony Xperia Z |

Some ultra-high-resolution devices (or browsers inside those devices) report a value of exactly 2, even when the correct pixel ratio value should be greater than 2. Other devices report inexact numbers, such as 2.2437500953674316 on the BlackBerry Z10; therefore, you should always ask about range and not exact values.

## Aspect ratio

A device's *aspect ratio* is the ratio between its longer and shorter dimensions. There are vertical (or portrait) devices whose displays are taller than they are wide, there are horizontal (or landscape) devices whose displays are wider than they are tall, and there are also some square screens. To complicate our lives as designers even more, today there are also many devices with rotation capabilities. Such a device can be either 320×240 or 240×320, depending on the orientation. Our websites need to be aware of this and offer a good experience in both orientations.

 BlackBerry recently announced a new device (known as the Q10) with a square screen of 720×720 pixels, creating the first modern smartphone with a 1:1 aspect ratio screen. Ten years ago it was common to find square resolutions at a much smaller size, such as 128×128.

The most recognizable aspect ratios are:

- Standard 4:3, used in classic TV and old CRT computer monitors
- Standard 3:2, used in classic 35 mm film
- Wide-screen 16:9, used in standard high-definition TV
- Wide-screen 15:9, used in LCD desktop computer monitors
- European wide-screen 5:3, used in Super 16 mm film

The other important part of aspect ratio in terms of mobile phones is the phone factor. You will encounter all of the following:

- Phones and tablets with portrait (wider than high) and landscape (higher than wide) modes
- Phones with screens wider than they are high, such as most BlackBerry smartphones before BB10
- Phones with screens higher than they are wide with no rotation mechanism, such as most feature phones

While your first thought may be that most mobile devices should be wide-screen because they are "modern," you should check that—for example, every iPad on the market right now is using the standard 4:3 aspect ratio, and the iPhone 4S uses 3:2.

Wide-screen PC monitors used to be 16:10, but since 2008 the HD TV standard has popularized the 16:9 aspect ratio. However, in the tablet world we can find both 16:10 and 16:9 wide-screen tablets, as well as 15:9 and 4:3 devices.

## Input Methods

Today, there are many different input methods for mobile devices that change how a mobile web app should be developed. A given device may support only one input method, or many of them. Possibilities include:

- Numeric keypad
- Alphanumeric keypad (ABC or QWERTY)
- Virtual keypad on screen
- Touch
- Multitouch
- External keypad (wireless or not)
- Handwriting recognition
- Voice recognition

And of course any possible combination of these, like a touch device with an optional onscreen keyboard and also a full QWERTY physical keyboard (see Figure 2-6).

If you are thinking that QWERTY sounds like a *Star Trek* Klingon's word, go now to your keyboard and look at the first line of letters below the numbers. That's the reason for the name; it's a keyboard layout organized for the smoothest typing in the English language, created in 1874. This layout is preserved in many onscreen keyboards (see Figure 2-7).

*Figure 2-6. The Motorola Droid has a full slider QWERTY keyboard and, when that is closed, an onscreen touch keyboard.*

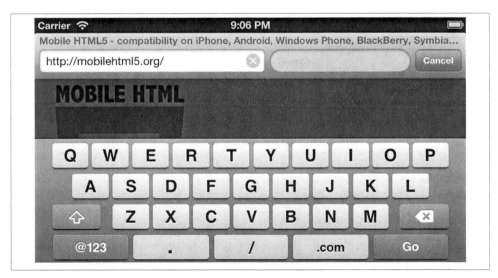

*Figure 2-7. The iPhone and iPod touch, like many other touch devices, use an onscreen virtual keyboard when the user needs to type something on a website.*

## Other Features

We could talk for hours about mobile device features, but we'll focus on the ones that are most useful for us as mobile web programmers. Key features include:

*Geolocation*
> Many devices can detect the user's geographical location using one or many technologies, like GPS (Global Positioning System), A-GPS (Assisted GPS), WPS (WiFi Positioning System), or cell-based location tracking.

*Phone calls*
> Yes, mobile devices also make phone calls!

*Accelerometer*
> An accelerometer is a sensor that measures proper acceleration in three axes— $x$, $y$, and $z$—and can be used for games and orientation purposes.

*Gyroscope*
> A gyroscope is a sensor that measures orientation based on the principles of angular momentum. It can be used in conjunction with the accelerometer.

*Magnetometer*
> A magnetometer is a sensor that measures the direction of magnetic fields and can be used as a digital compass.

*Application installation*
> Many devices allow the user to download and install applications over the air (OTA). This means that we can serve applications to a device from our websites.

# Market Statistics

At this point, you may be tempted to close this book and leave the mobile web jungle via a shortcut. However, believe me, the path through the jungle is clearer than you probably think right now.

Let's analyze some market share information. This will help us to make some decisions about how our work will be done.

Sometimes it's difficult to decide what to target. Should we develop for all devices, or only for iOS and Android devices? How can we decide how many versions to create?

The mobile world is very different from the desktop world. If we are developing for desktops, we can assume that the market share of the available browsers will be similar worldwide. In the mobile world, this is not the case. Because of commercial agreements and cultural differences, we find very diverse market shares in different regions of the world (US & Canada, Latin America, Europe, Asia, Oceania). For example, for a long time Nokia had a huge market share in Europe and Asia, but not in the United States.

It's important to define who our targets are. Worldwide users? US users? What about gender and age? Depending on the target demographic, we can define our porting strategy.

 Always keep in mind that a multiplatform solution will be preferred. Excluding users because they don't have the platform you like is not a good idea—bear that in mind when you decide about which platforms to target.

Overall mobile device sales statistics aren't the only ones we need to analyze. The market shares are very different if we look only at people using their mobile devices to browse the Web. A device with a very low total worldwide market share, such as the iPhone, can prove to have a big market share if we only analyze devices with high web consumption.

Some websites providing information on mobile web market share are:

- StatCounter Global Stats (*http://gs.statcounter.com*)
- NetMarketShare (*http://www.netmarketshare.com*)
- Akamai Internet Observatory (*http://www.akamai.io*)
- Wikimedia stats (*http://stats.wikimedia.org/wikimedia/squids/SquidReport Clients.htm*)
- Chitika Insights (*http://insights.chitika.com*)
- 51Degrees.mobi's Interactive Mobile Analytics (*http://51degrees.mobi/Products/ MobileAnalytics.aspx*)

To demonstrate how different the mobile web market can be from country to country, Table 2-3 shows information on the same period (late December 2012/early January 2013) provided by StatCounter Global Stats. Different providers may list different numbers for their market share. You should compare every source of information, understand how it's being measured, and use the information just to give you an idea of the tendencies.

*Table 2-3. Comparison chart of mobile web market share by browser (source: gs.stat-counter.com, January 2013)*

| Top | Global market | US | Germany | Argentina | India |
|-----|---------------|------|---------|-----------|-------|
| #1 | Android – 28% | Safari on iOS – 50% | Android – 50% | Android – 53% | Opera – 29% |
| #2 | Safari on iOS – 23% | Android – 39% | iOS – 35% | Opera – 17% | UC Browser – 26% |
| #3 | Opera – 17% | UC Browser – 3% | Opera – 5% | Nokia – 11% | Nokia – 17% |
| #4 | UC Browser – 10% | BlackBerry – 2% | Internet Explorer – 2% | Safari iOS – 5% | NetFront – 11% |
| #5 | Nokia – 9% | Nokia – 1% | Chrome for Android – 2% | BlackBerry – 3% | Android – 7% |

| Top | Global market | US | Germany | Argentina | India |
|---|---|---|---|---|---|
| #6 | NetFront – 4% | Internet Explorer – 1% | Firefox – 1% | Internet Explorer – 2% | Dolfin – 2% |
| #7 | BlackBerry – 3% | | | Chrome Android – 2% | Samsung – 2% |
| #8 | Dolfin – 1% | | | Firefox – 1% | Jasmine – 1% |

 You can find a list of updated mobile browser and device market share statistics in the statistics section of this book's blog (*http://www.mobilexweb.com/go/stats*).

# CHAPTER 3

# Browsers and Web Platforms

Understanding the big picture about platforms, operating systems, brands, and models is important for getting started in the mobile market, but the most important information for us will be which mobile browser or platform is used. Browsers will guide the rest of this book and most of our work as mobile web developers.

Many web developers curse desktop browsers and compatibility issues between them. Maybe you are one of them. But compared with the mobile world, in the desktop world the browser war is really simple: we have Google Chrome, Internet Explorer, Firefox, Safari, and Opera. That's about it. In the mobile world, there are more than 5,000 devices on the market. The good news (compared with this number) is that there are fewer than 25 mobile browsers in common usage—every smartphone OS has its own mobile browser, but the proprietary operating systems for the low-end and mid-range devices mostly use similar browsers. Still, the situation is far more complex than in the desktop world!

All mobile devices come with one preinstalled mobile browser, and very few of them can be upgraded or uninstalled. There are some exceptions: the browsers included with iOS, Windows Phone, Symbian, and Android (up to 4.0) are upgraded when you update the operating system firmware.

To complicate the situation, almost every device on the market allows users to add an alternative web browser, and some carriers, like Vodafone in Europe, include a copy of an alternative web browser customized for that operator, such as Opera Mini or Mobile, along with the factory-installed browser.

To add more complexity to the ecosystem, now we can also install browsers that are not complete browsers but rather different UIs for the same default browser (what we might call "pseudo-browsers"), and we can also execute mobile web code in native apps.

# Web Platforms That Are Not Browsers

I can guess what you're thinking: "Platforms that aren't browsers? I thought this book was all about creating content for mobile web browsers!" Well, that's true, but it's also true that we will deal with other platform types when creating mobile HTML5 content, whether we want to or not. That is, in some situations our content will be executed not in a browser, but inside some other native app or platform that can take web development to a different level.

While the market doesn't have concrete names for all of these things yet, in this book we are going to talk about the following:

- Browser-based websites or web apps
- HTML5 apps
- Web views
- Native web apps
- Ebooks

While browser-based websites or web apps is the easiest category to understand, with mobile web technologies including HTML5 we can deliver experiences that can get users out of the browser.

## HTML5 Web Apps

Some platforms allow us to create application-like experiences by using the browser as the installation platform, and providing from then on a full-screen experience based on the browser. While the name "HTML5 apps" can also be used for any web apps that can run on a browser—and even hybrids, which we'll cover shortly—in this case we are talking about browser platforms that are offering something special to a web developer to upgrade the user experience to a new level, in terms of the user interface and/or device access.

Usually this category involves installation through the browser itself or a store accessed via the browser. We don't need to compile or sign anything, and usually it involves a way to define the package of files to use and the metadata.

 There may be some confusion between these HTML5 web apps and hybrid or native apps. In the latter case we are creating HTML5 apps but wrapping them inside a native app, including compilation, signing, and native store distribution. HTML5 web apps are hosted-based (must be hosted on a web server) and distributed through the browser, and there is no way to call native code outside of the HTML5 APIs available.

### iOS web apps

On iOS devices we can upgrade a mobile website to a full-screen HTML5 app with a series of meta tags and techniques that we'll cover later in this book. With this technique (Apple calls it a web app), the user can install an icon in the Home screen, sharing the space with the native apps. When opened, instead of being just a shortcut to our website, the user will have a full-screen experience and no browser UI will be provided.

Mixing this technique with HTML5 APIs, we can create an offline experience like that the user gets with any installed application. Testing your app in this new environment is a must, as some behaviors are different from in the browser, and this can frustrate you if you are not aware of them (for example, the page being reloaded every time the user opens the app). Figure 3-1 shows an example of an iOS web app.

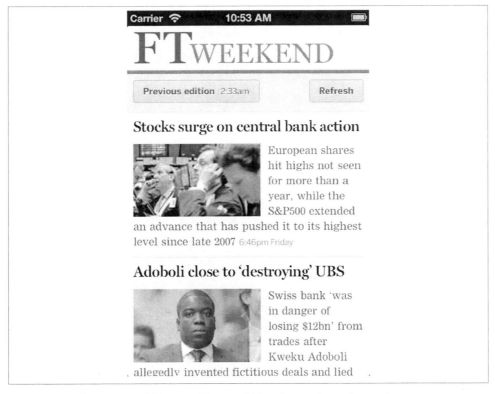

*Figure 3-1. The Financial Times offers an iOS web app through app.ft.com—as you can see, once it's installed, there is no Safari UI (including the address bar and toolbar buttons).*

### Chrome apps

Google Chrome started with the idea of HTML5 apps on the desktop and notebook side, even delivering a store for app distribution, the Chrome Web Store. Today the Chrome app platform is available on Windows, Mac, Linux, and Chrome OS, and in mid-2012 Google announced that Android would be supported soon. Chrome apps are also known as *packaged apps*.

Once an app is installed in the system, it can be launched from Chrome or a system icon, and using HTML5 and Chrome APIs it can leverage a full-screen and offline experience.

At the time of this writing, Chrome apps for Android are not available, so we don't know if they will be hosted-based (as on the other platforms) or packaged as native web apps (as covered later).

### Firefox open web apps

Firefox supports on all of its platforms—desktops, tablets, and smartphones—the ability to create apps and distribute them through the Mozilla Marketplace. Every application is based on HTML5, with an app manifest defining all the information needed to install the application and run it out of the scope of the browser.

We can expect these apps to work on Firefox OS, Firefox for Android, and desktop Firefox.

### Symbian standalone web apps

Following iOS web apps syntax, the latest version of the Symbian browser supports the installation of Home screen icons that open full-screen web apps without the browser UI.

### S40 web apps

Nokia provides a web app platform for its mid-range device series, called Series 40. This platform allows us to create cloud-based apps with web technologies that can be distributed (and sold) through the Nokia Store. Once installed, an S40 web app can be launched from the applications menu via an icon and from inside the Nokia Browser.

### Samsung web API

In early 2013 Samsung released an SDK to create web apps for smartphones and smart TVs using web technologies and a JavaScript API. At the time of this writing it's compatible with devices such as the Galaxy SIII and Galaxy Note II, and it can also communicate with a Samsung smart TV. The platform supports mobile web apps, TV web apps, and convergence web apps, which interwork between a Samsung smartphone and a TV.

# Web Views

A native application is compiled and signed using official SDKs and nonweb programming languages, such as C, Objective-C, Java, or C#. Almost every native mobile platform includes a control or component that allows web content to be embedded inside a native application. This component is generically known as a *web view*, while having specific class names on every platform (such as *UIWebView* on iOS).

While sometimes the rendering engine in a web view is exactly the same as the one used in the browser, in some situations the behavior (in terms of markup, APIs, and performance) can be quite different. In later chapters, we'll see how to manage the special behaviors we need to be careful of.

 Even if you are not creating a native application with a web view inside, your website may be rendered in a web view: some social media–related native apps for iOS, Android, and other mobile operating systems use this mechanism to show web content to users instead of opening the default web browser.

Examples of web views in action include most social networking applications for smartphones and tablets. When you find a post or tweet with a link to the Web, these applications open a web view for you to see this web page inside the social app, not in the browser. Usually there is a way to open the link in the web browser, but the default initial behavior is to open the URL inside a web view. In Figure 3-2 we can see this in action in the Twitter application for iPod.

 From a developer's point of view a web view acts like the native default browser, but with some limitations and differences that can change expected behaviors. For example, on iOS, Safari (the native web browser) supports a JIT JavaScript engine for high-performance execution, while the web view for iOS doesn't support it for security reasons. Some HTML5 APIs can have limitations, too, as we'll see later in this book.

*Figure 3-2. When a user clicks on a post including a link in a social networking app, the web page is loaded in a web view, not in the browser.*

## Pseudo-Browsers

I'm pretty sure you've never heard about *pseudo-browsers*. It's really a new category that I'd like to create. A pseudo-browser is a native application marketed as a web browser that, instead of providing its own rendering and execution engines, uses the native web view.

From a user's point of view, it's a browser. From a developer's point of view, it's just the web view with a particular UI. Therefore, we have the same rendering engine as in the preinstalled browser, but with a different UI. These pseudo-browsers are mostly available for iOS and Android, and they offer the same service as the native browser but with different services on top of them.

This can lead to some philosophical questions about what a browser is. From a developer's perspective, it's important to understand that pseudo-browsers are not adding fragmentation—they're not new engines, but simply the web view from the operating system.

Google Chrome for iOS (Figure 3-3) is a key example of a pseudo-browser. Because of an App Store licensing limitation, Google cannot deliver its own rendering and execution engine with a native app. Therefore, Google decided to deliver a Chrome experience application with the default iOS web view engine. This means Chrome for iOS does not have the same HTML5 compatibility or features as Chrome for Android or desktop Chrome, but it does have the same features as the iOS web view.

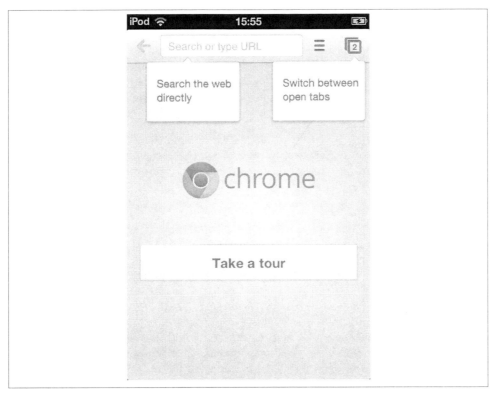

*Figure 3-3. Chrome for iOS is an example of a pseudo-browser: the rendering and execution engines are provided by the iOS web view, not by the Chrome team, so only updates to iOS will enable more developer features for this "browser."*

## Native Web Apps, Packaged Apps, and Hybrids

Also known as a *hybrid* application, a *native web* application is a compiled native application that usually uses a full-screen web view as the whole application container. In one approach, the whole application is developed using web technologies (HTML, CSS, JavaScript), but it is packaged and compiled as a native application so we can distribute it in native application stores. Another approach is to use some native layers and some web layers at the same time, such as native UI components with only some parts in a web view, with JavaScript logic.

Some web view platforms, as we'll see later in this book, allow us to communicate between JavaScript and native code, either one way or bidirectionally, opening the possibility to extend the browser's limits with native code (such as C, Java, Objective-C, or C#).

 Apache Cordova is an open source native web application framework for multiple platforms that is well known in the market because of one of its implementations: PhoneGap from Adobe. We need to remember that these multiplatform frameworks are based on the web view components from each platform, so we will be dealing with different engines.

We can also use web views ourselves if we have native know-how, such as Objective-C on iOS or Java on Android. We just need to add the web view and connect the component to some local or generated HTML code.

If we don't have any native know-how or just want to make it work fast and across multiple platforms, we can use a framework that will help us with the process. Some frameworks add a layer of JavaScript and native code, offering new APIs for web developers to use. We will cover native web frameworks later in this book.

## Facebook and the HTML5 Problem

For a while, the native Facebook apps for iOS and Android were hybrid apps using HTML5 for the main browsing experience. After a couple of months of using this technique and encountering some performance issues, Facebook decided to migrate some of the web view–based screens (such as the main timeline) to full native code, increasing the performance by a factor of two.

Mark Zuckerberg, CEO of the company, said in September 2012: "When I'm introspective about the last few years I think the biggest mistake that we made, as a company, is betting too much on HTML5 as opposed to native…because it just wasn't there. And it's not that HTML5 is bad. I'm actually, on long-term, really excited about it. One of the things that's interesting is we actually have more people on a daily basis using mobile web Facebook than we have using our iOS or Android apps combined. So mobile web is a big thing for us."

That said, Facebook has more mobile browser–based users than native users, and on the browser it's always HTML5. Facebook also has other HTML5-based apps, such as for Firefox OS and other platforms, and even the updated native apps are still using HTML5 in some situations.

Three months after Facebook made its changes, the Sencha (*http://sencha.com*) team—believing that the Facebook team was wrong and that HTML5 was ready—created an HTML5-redesigned Facebook app called *Fastbook* to prove the point. You can try it yourself by accessing *fb.html5isready.com* from your mobile phone. The Fastbook web app has reached the same levels of performance and UI responsiveness as the native app, using optimization techniques.

If you want to know more about Facebook's difficulties with HTML5, check out *mobilexweb.com/go/html5fb*.

Some platforms don't need any real compilation or signing process, but just need to be packaged in a ZIP or other format with a configuration file inside. The operating system will create the web view for us and load the main HTML defined in the configuration file. The main difference from HTML5 web apps, discussed earlier in this chapter, is that in a packaged app we don't use a web server to host the files.

Let's briefly review some of the most important native web frameworks on the market.

### Platform-specific solutions

The following operating systems offer a way to compile and sign a package that can be distributed as a native app while being developed with HTML5:

*BlackBerry WebWorks*
Available for BlackBerry 5.x, 6.x, 7.x, and 10 (including the PlayBook).

*Windows 8 HTML5 apps (previously known as Metro apps)*
Available for Windows 8 (only the desktop and tablet versions, no support yet on Windows Phone up to version 8).

*Tizen apps*
Available from Tizen 1.0 devices.

*Symbian WRT*
Available from Series 60 3rd edition. This is a legacy platform; while it's still working, Nokia has not added any new features to the platform since 2011.

*QtWebKit*
Available for Symbian and MeeGo devices from Nokia; allows developers to compile an HTML5 application as a native Qt-based package with a WebKit engine integrated inside.

*Ubuntu for mobile apps*
HTML5 apps with native integration.

### Apache Cordova and Adobe PhoneGap

PhoneGap was the pioneer in offering a multiplatform solution for native web development. After a couple of years working as a small open source project, Adobe acquired Nitobi (the company behind PhoneGap), donated the project to the Apache Foundation, where it was renamed Apache Cordova, and continued evolving the project with the power of Adobe.

 Adobe has a free and commercial service called PhoneGap Build that is a cloud-based Cordova compiler, so we don't need to deal with the native SDK on our computers. You can find more information on this service at *build.phonegap.com*.

We'll look at Apache Cordova in more detail later in this book, but for now it's important to say that we can compile native web apps and distribute them via official stores using this open source framework.

### Sencha Touch

While Sencha Touch is a UI framework, from version 2.0 it includes a native packager for iOS and Android available to Windows and Mac developers. The packager is included in the developer tools of the UI framework that can be downloaded from *sencha.com/products/touch*.

### Appcelerator Titanium

This framework allows the creation of iOS, BlackBerry (7.x/10), and Android native web apps, providing a bridge that enables developers to use native UI components from JavaScript. That means that your JavaScript will be converted to native code when your app is compiled, so your app can feel more "native" than if it were using web views directly (because in most situations there is no HTML involved). You can download the free Appcelerator Titanium Studio IDE (*http://appcelerator.com*).

## Ebooks

The latest ebook readers support some kind of HTML5 and web content based on different formats such as EPUB 3 or Kindle Format 8. These formats are based on HTML5, meaning that we can create interactive ebook experiences with HTML, CSS, and JavaScript.

While ebook creation is outside the scope of this book, most of the code and techniques that we are going to see can be applied easily to ebooks and digital magazines.

---

# Mobile Browsers

When browsing the Web on our mobile devices, we can use the preinstalled browser available by default on every device or we can install new browsers through the application stores. Let's review the most important browsers in both categories.

## Preinstalled Browsers

Practically every mobile device on the market today has a preinstalled browser. One of the big features of these browsers is that the average user typically doesn't install a new web browser; therefore, on each device the preinstalled browser is the most-used one. One main disadvantage of preinstalled browsers is that usually there is no way to update the browser independently from the operating system. If your device doesn't get operating system updates, usually you will not get browser updates.

### Safari on iOS

Safari is a WebKit-based browser bundled with iOS that offers a great browsing experience and smart zoom options. It is updated with every operating system change to include new features that allow us, as developers, to create better user experiences.

Safari on iOS (formerly known as Mobile Safari) was the first mobile browser to support a range of new features, including those that allow us to create animations, transitions, 3D effects, and Flash-like experiences using HTML, JavaScript, and CSS (but without Flash—what we currently know as HTML5). We will cover these topics in Chapters 7, 11, and 12.

 For many years, Safari on iOS was the best mobile browser in terms of HTML5 API compatibility, performance, and distribution. As of September 2012, it had more than 90% of the web browsing market share on tablets.

This browser is designed for touch and multitouch navigation. It can support focus navigation if the user is attaching an external keyboard, and it was also the first browser to support accessibility features such as a screen reader for people with visual disabilities.

Most of the HTML5 APIs were first implemented in Safari on iOS, and even most of the nonstandard code that we will see later in this book was invented in Safari and then cloned in other mobile browsers.

While the iPad/iPad Mini and iPhone/iPod touch versions are pretty similar, the tablet version additionally supports tab navigation.

Safari on iOS was the first mobile browser to support *chromeless* Home screen applications, which fall somewhere between browser-based apps and native web apps.

The official documentation for Safari on iOS can be found at *www.mobilexweb.com/go/safaridocs*. Safari on iOS doesn't follow the same versioning as desktop Safari (for Mac or Windows); usually it is named with the iOS version number, so we are talking about Safari on iOS 5.x or 6.0. This browser can't be updated using the App Store; it's only updated when the operating system is.

The latest versions of the mobile and desktop versions of Safari are starting to match up, so it's possible that in the near future Safari will be exactly the same on desktops, notebooks, tablets, and smaller devices.

### Android browser

Up to and including Android 4.0 (Ice Cream Sandwich), the Android OS came with its own browser, based on WebKit. It is called the Android browser, sometimes referred to as Android WebKit. While many developers believe that it is similar to Google Chrome or even Safari on iOS, the truth is that the Android browser has always lagged behind other mobile browsers in terms of performance, HTML5 compatibility, and even bugs found.

The browser has changed a lot between different versions of the operating system, to the extent that versions 2.2 and 4.0 can be considered two distinct browsers. Even in the same version of the operating system, we can find customized versions of the browser on devices from different vendors, such as Samsung, Sony, or Barnes & Noble (with its Nook tablet).

Google realized that the Android browser was not good enough for its platform, so it started a completely separate project, Google Chrome for Android, to replace this browser.

The Android browser is considered a legacy browser after Android 4.1 (from late 2012) and has been replaced by Google Chrome. However, the web view still executes the Android browser engine.

Google Chrome for Android is now the default browser preinstalled on most new devices coming to the market with Android 4.1. However, devices that were upgraded to 4.1 from 4.0 still have the Android browser.

## Google Chrome

In 2012, Chrome appeared in the mobile world as a downloadable browser for Android 4.0, and since Android 4.1 (Jelly Bean) it has begun to replace the default browser. It shares most of its code with the desktop version of Google Chrome and is one of the most modern HTML5 browsers on the market.

Unfortunately, only Android 4.0 or newer devices can install Chrome. However, one of the key features is that the browser is upgradable through the Google Play Store without the need to wait for an operating system upgrade. That means that Chrome users will have new HTML5 features available sooner than users of other platforms.

Google has released a new operating system called *Chrome OS* that is totally based on HTML5. Currently you can find this operating system on netbooks, known as *Chromebooks*, and on desktop computers, known as *Chromeboxes*. This version is not yet available for mobile devices—phones or tablets—so it's outside the scope of this book.

Chrome for Android will follow as quickly as possible updates on the desktop and Chrome OS side. The desktop version has Beta and Canary channels, where we can follow future versions of the browser closely. On Android, only the Beta channel is available. From version 26, it supports a cloud-based network compression feature.

In mid-2012, Google also released *Google Chrome for iOS*, a pseudo-browser for iPhone, iPod, and iPad users that delivers the Chrome experience—UI, omnibox URL search box, tab and info synchronization—but uses the default web view engine on iOS devices. That means that Chrome for iOS is not really Chrome. If you don't believe me, it's enough to say that Chrome for iOS does not even identify itself to servers as Chrome—it uses the same user agent name as Safari, adding a string called *CriOS* (presumably for "Chrome for iOS") so developers looking for the Chrome string inside that name will not be confused and decide to deliver Chrome-only code.

Chrome for iOS, like other pseudo-browsers, uses the iOS web view's rendering and execution engines. The same Chrome for iOS version may have different compatibility on different devices, depending on the current iOS version.

While the rendering and execution engines are from iOS and not from Chrome, this pseudo-browser adds a network layer that is different from that of Safari or the default web view, and will prefetch content and accelerate the downloading of resources.

### Amazon Silk

Tablets from Amazon—the Kindle Fire family—include a new browser created by Amazon based on the Android browser, called Amazon Silk. The main difference of Silk is that it has an "accelerated mode" that proxies the rendering in the Amazon cloud servers. That means that when you are browsing in accelerated mode, part of your HTML, CSS, or JavaScript can be parsed in some Amazon servers, and a compressed result is delivered to the browser. From a user's perspective there is no real difference in the UI experience while browsing the Web.

Silk had a major upgrade in 2012 with the release of the second generation of Kindle Fire devices, including better support for HTML5 and modern techniques.

### Internet Explorer

Microsoft's browser can be considered to have been one of the first mobile browsers on the market. The first version was released in 1996, for Windows CE 1.0: it was first known as Pocket Internet Explorer (PIE), then Internet Explorer Mobile, and is now just called Internet Explorer. While maintaining the same name, the truth is that the browser has changed from the ground up many times. Up to version 6.0, it had its own rendering engine (based on IE4), but today these can be considered legacy versions. With Windows Mobile 6.5, the browser was upgraded to an IE6-based rendering engine.

The new operating system from Microsoft, launched in 2010 as Windows Phone 7, came with a new version of Internet Explorer Mobile that was based on the IE7 engine, with some IE8 features mixed in (some have called it an IE 7.5 engine). It offers similar behavior to Internet Explorer 7, and multitouch support.

 Older Windows Mobile devices supported an IE4 or IE6 engine.

The free upgrade to Windows Phone 7.5 came with the first HTML5-compatible browser from Microsoft: Internet Explorer 9, using the same codebase as IE9 for desktops with some special mobile additions. This was the start of a new way of Microsoft seeing the mobile web browser. Now, every desktop version is followed by a mobile version using the same rendering engine.

Windows 8 and Windows Phone 8 come with Internet Explorer 10 (IE10), which represents a big step forward in terms of mobile HTML5 API support.

## Nokia Browser

Nokia Browser is a generic name for different real products available for different platforms inside the Nokia world.

**Nokia Browser for Series 40.** Every Nokia Series 40 device comes with a built-in web browser created by Nokia. Up to S40 5th Edition, it was a simple browser without smart zoom capabilities, designed with feature phones in mind. It was basically a focus navigation browser, based on Nokia's own rendering engine.

Beginning in the 6th Edition, the browser was updated to WebKit (similar to Nokia's Symbian browser), creating a new browsing experience for low-end and mid-range devices. The main problem with this browser was that the low-end and mid-range devices are not created with high-quality hardware, which can lead to some performance problems.

In 2010, Nokia acquired a browser company called Novarra that offers cloud-based web support. Nokia has since created a new Java-based browser called the Nokia Xpress browser (formerly Ovi Browser) that offers a new experience for feature phones and social devices. This browser was originally available as a free download from the Nokia Store and is now being preinstalled in newer Series 40 devices, such as the Asha series devices.

Nokia has also released Nokia Xpress for Lumia, a cloud-based browser for Windows Phone, based on the same Xpress browser.

The new browser renders websites on the server and delivers a compressed, already rendered version to the phone, giving users a fast browsing experience. This browser works with touch- and focus-based devices, and it adds the ability to create installed web apps for Nokia Store distribution with HTML5 support—all rendered from the Nokia servers.

**Nokia Browser for Symbian.** In 2005, Nokia created the first open source WebKit-based mobile browser for Symbian devices (known for many years as the S60 OSS browser). Depending on the device, it supports focus, cursor, and multitouch navigation. Many devices support more than one navigation type; for instance, the Nokia E7 supports touch (finger and stylus) navigation, and cursor navigation when the keyboard is opened.

From Symbian Anna, the browser has support for HTML5; however, it tends to lag behind other browsers even for the same operating system, such as Opera Mobile for Symbian.

**Nokia Browser for MeeGo.** Nokia has also created the first WebKit2 browser in the mobile market: the Nokia Browser for MeeGo. It has great HTML5 support, but unfortunately there aren't many devices on the market today supporting this operating system.

### webOS browser

The HP operating system comes with a WebKit-based browser that supports the latest web technologies. It supports touch navigation and a card concept that allows the user to open many websites at the same time and flip between them using a finger.

> Older Palm devices using Garnet OS (Palm OS) 3.1 and later shipped with a browser known as Blazer. Future devices will include the Open webOS operating system and an updated, open source browser named Isis (*http://isis-project.org*).

### BlackBerry browser

Every BlackBerry device comes with a mobile web browser with focus navigation and, more recently, touch navigation support. Many versions of the browser are available, depending on the device. There are devices with trackball and cursor navigation, older devices with focus navigation, and newer smartphones with touch support.

The first generation of the BlackBerry browser was included with Device Software version 4.5 and earlier. The second generation, available from versions 4.6 to 5.0, had a redesigned rendering engine but was still far behind other mobile browsers in terms of performance and compatibility.

BlackBerry devices running OS 6.0, 7.0, and 7.1 have a WebKit-based browser that was completely redesigned for the tablet PlayBook and the new BlackBerry 10 platform.

> The browser on the BlackBerry 10 platform was totally created using web technologies—that means the whole browser was engineered using JavaScript, CSS, and web views.

### UC Browser

The UC Browser (formerly known as UCWEB) is the #1 browser in the Chinese market (and #2 in the Indian market) and is now available in English for other markets as a downloadable browser. It is a cloud-based browser supporting full HTML and Java-Script, multiple windows, and many advanced features.

It works on some 3,000 different mobile device models, including Android, Symbian, BlackBerry, Windows Phone, Java-based devices, and the iPhone.

According to StatCounter (*http://gs.statcounter.com*), in December 2012 the UC Browser had 10% usage share of the global mobile browser market and 43% usage share of the Chinese market, with some 300 million active users (85% from China).

You can download the browser from www.uc.cn/English.

### Samsung Dolfin & Jasmine

The WebKit-based browser installed with the Bada OS is called *Dolfin*. This browser has included HTML5 support from Bada 2.0 and is installed on social devices.

Don't confuse Samsung's Dolfin browser with Dolphin, another option available for Android and iOS as a user-installable browser.

On low-end devices featuring a proprietary operating system, Samsung also has another browser called *Jasmine*.

### LG Phantom

This is the browser included on some social devices from LG, based on WebKit. It doesn't have much market share, and there is not much information available for developers.

### NetFront

NetFront is a mobile browser created by the Japanese company ACCESS, targeting low-end and mid-range devices including phones, digital TVs, printers, and game consoles. It is licensed by the manufacturer, and that's why we can find devices of many different brands using the same browser engine. NetFront is installed on thousands of Sony Ericsson, LG, Samsung, and ZTE devices, as well as on Amazon Kindle ebook readers. It is also included with the PlayStation 3, PSP, and Nintendo 3DS.

The browser has many different versions, and it uses its own rendering engine. From NetFront 3.5, it supports cursor navigation and a feature called Smart-Fit that reorganizes websites to fit into a single column without horizontal scrolling. NetFront 4.2, released in late 2011, includes some basic HTML5 support, enhanced JavaScript performance, and an optional Flash Lite Player.

While it's probable that most web developers and designers have never heard of NetFront as a browser, as of July 2012 it had 3% usage share of the global mobile browsing market, according to StatCounter (*http://gs.statcounter.com*).

ACCESS has also released two WebKit-based spin-off browsers: NetFront Life Browser for smartphones and tablets and NetFront Browser NX for other devices, such as set-top boxes. The first is available as a free download for Android devices via the Google Play Store and the Amazon Appstore for Android. As a "different" feature, the NetFront Life Browser offers a "Tilt" browsing mode that allows you to view a web page diagonally, giving you the widest possible view of the page (see Figure 3-4).

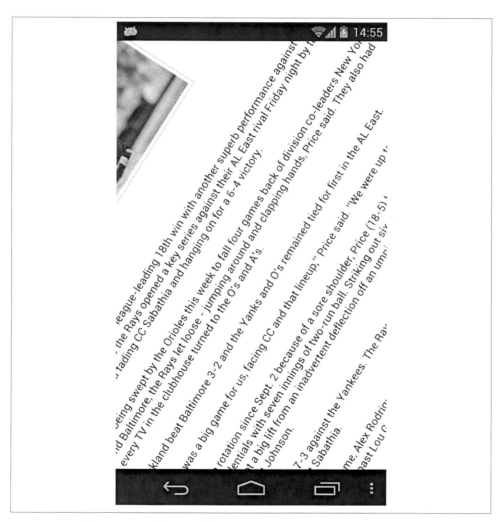

*Figure 3-4. It's not a problem in the image: the NetFront Life Browser allows you to browse the Web in "Tilt mode," where you can read text diagonally, getting the widest view for a paragraph.*

## Myriad browser

The Openwave browser was, for many years, one of the preferred mobile browsers to be preinstalled on low-end devices. In conjunction with NetFront, it was used for the majority of low-end and mid-range browsing. Openwave was acquired by Myriad in 2008, and since that time it has been known as the Myriad browser. Like NetFront, it has been used by many vendors, including Motorola, LG, Sharp, and Kyocera.

## Obigo browser

The Obigo mobile browser from Obigo/Teleca claimed 14% browser market share in 2007 (before the smartphone revolution). It was found in Samsung, LG, Motorola, and Sony Ericsson devices and in many CDMA devices from some operators, like Verizon. Obigo also offers a widget solution implemented by LG Mobile.

In this era, it's still being used in some LG and BREW devices, and the latest versions are WebKit-based.

## Legacy mobile browsers

There are also a few legacy mobile browsers that are worth mentioning.

**MicroB for Maemo.** Maemo, the platform that merged with Intel's Moblin OS in 2010 to form MeeGo, shipped on one Nokia device: the N900. This device included a Gecko-based browser known as MicroB. Maemo and MicroB were subsequently replaced by MeeGo and the Nokia Browser.

**Sony Mobile (formerly Sony Ericsson) browsers.** If we analyze Sony Mobile's non-smartphone devices—that is, those not based on an operating system like Android or Windows Phone—we can find three primary browsers in use, depending on the device's release date:

- Sony Ericsson WAP browser before 2004
- Sony Ericsson web browser from 2004 to 2006
- NetFront browser (version 3.3, 3.4, or 3.5) from 2006

Other browsers, such as Opera and even Openwave, were also preinstalled on some devices.

**Motorola Mobile Internet Browser (MIB).** Motorola devices based on the Motorola proprietary OS (excluding the company's Linux, Windows Mobile, Android, and Symbian devices) came with a simple proprietary browser that allows focus navigation and page scrolling. The last version was 2.2. As an indication of its limits, it can render only documents up to 10 KB.

Some other older devices came with the Openwave, Obigo, or Opera browser preinstalled. The same device model shipped at different dates and in different markets did not necessarily come with the same browser.

---

### Japanese Mobile Web

In the mobile web world, the Japanese market is quite an exception. The three main carriers in Japan (DoCoMo, Softbank, and Au) each had their own mobile web standards for years regarding markup, Emoji, geolocation, and so on, that browsers preinstalled on their devices were required to support. They didn't actually make their own browsers.

ACCESS's i-mode browser was the most common on DoCoMo devices, while Openwave was more common on Softbank and Au devices. Today, popular platforms such as iOS, Android, and other major brands are on the market, using their own browsers and operating systems.

---

## User-Installable Browsers

The market complicates the situation further: we also need to think about *user-installable browsers*. These are free and commercial web browsers that you can install after you buy a device. Sometimes (mostly on feature phones and social devices) they are included on the device by the vendor or the operator in a particular country or region.

 On iOS there is no way to replace the default browser—Apple's policies don't allow anything but the default rendering or execution engine, and the OS does not support the ability to change the default browser. Even if we install apps using the web view, such as Chrome for iOS, the operating system will always open Safari when we click on links in any app.

We need to remember that for iOS and Android there are plenty of pseudo-browsers (native apps marketed as browsers but using the default web view). Besides that, on Android we can find several browsers with their own rendering engines that can replace the default browser (see Figure 3-5).

*Figure 3-5. There are a lot of browsers that can be installed on Android devices; these can be used on a per-usage basis or as the default browser.*

### Opera Mobile

I was an addict of Opera for the desktop for many, many years. Opera has lost the desktop browser war, but it took its experience in browser creation and entered the mobile world in 2000.

Opera Mobile is a full browser supporting tab and cursor navigation that comes factory-preinstalled on some devices and is sometimes preinstalled by the carrier using an OEM license, replacing the default device browser.

Opera Mobile is also available for download by users of Android, MeeGo, and Symbian devices. Usually, users can download the latest version and a beta of the next version, known as the Opera Mobile Labs build.

### Opera Mini

My Opera addiction continues: Opera Mini remains one of the best Java ME applications ever produced for feature phones. It is a free browser that works on almost any device, including feature phones from Nokia, LG, Samsung, and Sony, and smartphones such as Android and iOS devices (iPhone, iPod, iPad). It supports "the full web" as a proxied browser. This means that if you browse using Opera Mini, you won't be accessing web-sites directly. Instead, the application will contact an Opera Mini server that will compress and pre-render the websites. This allows very quick full web navigation for every device, whether low-end or smartphone.

From version 4, it supports video playback, Ajax, offline reading, and smart zooming, even in low-end devices (see Figure 3-6). From version 5, it also supports tabbed browsing, a password manager, and touch navigation in devices with touch support. Versions 6 and 7 include new rendering engines, more CSS3 support, and performance improvements. Opera offers a beta version of future versions of the browser known as Opera Mini Next.

 In early 2013, Opera Mobile and Opera Mini were merged into one browser on Android, known as "Opera for Android". It has the option to enable optionally cloud-based compression using Mini servers. Version 14 of this browser is the first edition using a Chromium (WebKit) engine instead of the previous Presto engine.

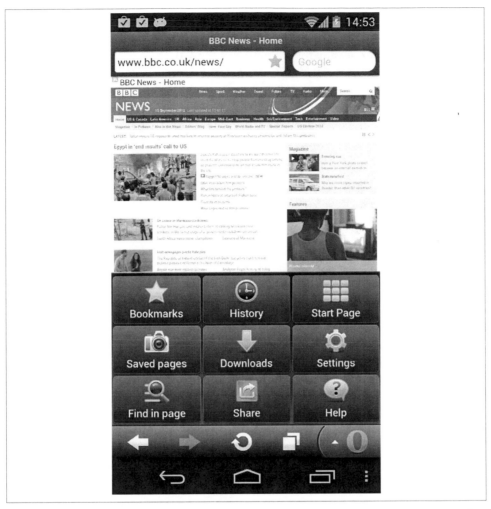

*Figure 3-6. Opera Mini is an excellent option for low-end and mid-range devices, offering a proxied browser with smart zooming for almost any mobile phone with Java ME support. The same browser is available for smartphones.*

You can download Opera Mini for free by browsing to *m.opera.com* from your mobile device. Opera Mini had 194 million users in October 2012, compared to 21 million Opera Mobile users. For Android and iOS devices, you can find Opera Mini in the Google Play Store and the App Store.

### Firefox

The Mozilla Foundation arrived a bit late to the mobile browser world. Mozilla offers a downloadable Firefox version for Android and MeeGo (the Nokia N9) and a working version for the Windows 8 Metro UI (optimized for tablets), and it has been updated in sync with the desktop version.

You can download the mobile version of Firefox from stores and from *m.firefox.com*. It uses the same Gecko engine as the Firefox desktop browser and it works on smartphones and tablets.

As we saw in Chapter 1, in 2013, Mozilla has worked on its own operating system, Firefox OS: the browser is preinstalled in the OS as the whole base of the platform.

 Three versions of Firefox for Android are available: the latest version, a beta of the next version (both available from Google Play Store), and Aurora, an alpha version of a future release that can be downloaded only from www.mozilla.org/firefox/channel/#aurora.

### Dolphin

Dolphin (not to be confused with Samsung's Dolfin) started as a pseudo-browser for Android, adding features to the default engine in the Android web view; this was soon followed by a similar iOS version. The latest versions of this application for Android replace the web view with their own WebKit-based engine, which has one of the top scores in terms of HTML5 compatibility and performance. You can download Dolphin from Apple's App Store, the Google Play Store, or the Dolphin website (*http://dolphin-browser.com*).

### Baidu Browser

Baidu, the most-used search engine in China, has released a browser for Android- and Windows Phone–based devices that can be downloaded from *shouji.baidu.com/browser*. The Baidu Browser uses a WebKit-based engine called *T5*.

### SkyFire

SkyFire is a pseudo-browser available for iOS and Android with the particularity of delivering Flash and video content from its own servers, which transcode nonmobile content to be compatible with these platforms. SkyFire is available for download from the App Store and the Google Play Store.

As of December 2010, SkyFire was rebranded as a proxied browser for Android and iOS. Before that, it was a Gecko-based browser for Symbian, BlackBerry, and Windows Mobile. SkyFire was acquired by Opera in 2013.

## Browser Overview

That list of browsers is a lot to digest. Table 3-1 compares key features of the most commonly used browsers on the market.

*Table 3-1. Features of mobile browsers available on the market as of 2012*

| Browser | Current platforms | Engine | Proxied | Navigation |
|---|---|---|---|---|
| Safari | iOS | WebKit | No | Multitouch |
| Android browser | Android up to 4.1 | WebKit | No | Multitouch and focus |
| Chrome | Android > 4.0 (iOS as a pseudo-browser) | WebKit | No | Multitouch and focus |
| Nokia Browser | S40 6th Edition | WebKit | No | Cursor, touch, and focus |
| | S40 new platform (Nokia Xpress browser) | Gecko | Yes | Focus, touch, and multitouch |
| | Symbian | WebKit | No | Cursor, multitouch, and focus |
| | MeeGo | WebKit2 | No | Multitouch |
| webOS browser | webOS, Open webOS | WebKit | No | Multitouch and focus |
| BlackBerry browser | BlackBerry OS 5.x | Custom | In some situations | Cursor and multitouch |
| | BlackBerry OS 6.0, 7.0 | WebKit | No | Cursor and multitouch |
| | Tablet OS / BB10 | WebKit | No | Multitouch and cursor |
| Internet Explorer | Windows Phone, Windows | Trident | No | Multitouch |
| Firefox | Android, MeeGo, Firefox OS | Gecko | No | Multitouch |
| NetFront | Low-end devices | Custom | No | Focus or touch[a] |
| Opera Mobile | Android, Symbian | Presto/Webkit | Yes/No[b] | Focus |
| Opera Mini | Android, iOS, Symbian, Java, BlackBerry | Presto/Webkit[c] | Yes | Cursor or touch[d] |
| Bada Browser | Bada | WebKit | No | Touch |
| UC Browser | Android, iOS, Java, BlackBerry | Custom | Yes | Multiple |

[a] Depending on the device.

[b] Depending on the usage of the optional compression option.

[c] Presto was used before 2013. From version 14, Opera is based on Chromium/WebKit.

[d] Depending on the device.

# CHAPTER 4

# Tools for Mobile Web Development

Unlike desktop web development, where you're likely to create and test your work on the same device, mobile development generally requires setting up and managing several development environments.

## Working with Code

For coding our markup, JavaScript, and CSS, we can use almost any web tool available on the market, including Adobe Dreamweaver, Microsoft Visual Studio, Eclipse, Aptana Studio, and of course any good text editor, such as Sublime Text, Textmate, WebStorm, or Notepad++. In mobile web development, it is often easier and cleaner to work directly with the code rather than using a visual tool or IDE.

## Adobe Dreamweaver

Since the CS5.5 version, Dreamweaver has worked better with mobile markup and allows us to validate against mobile web standards. In this editor, when we create a new document we can choose HTML5 as the document type, as shown in Figure 4-1.

Version CS6 includes several enhancements that support mobile web design and development, such as:

- HTML5 support and code hinting
- Multiple screen preview
- jQuery Mobile integration
- PhoneGap Build integration for native web app compilation from the IDE

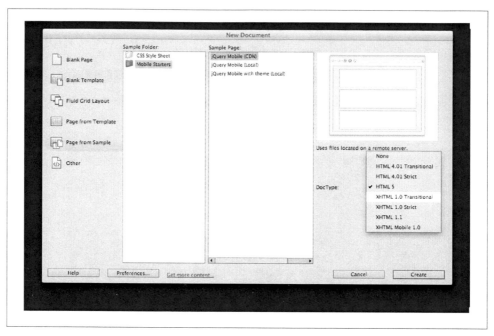

*Figure 4-1. Dreamweaver allows us to define new files as HTML5 or XHTML Mobile Profile documents, as well as giving us the ability to start with a jQuery Mobile template.*

## Adobe Edge Tools

Adobe offers a group of tools under the name of Edge that help designers and developers to create HTML5 applications. They include:

*Edge Code*
> A complete HTML5 editor based on web technologies. This tool is based on the open source editor Brackets and it includes several interesting ideas on how to code HTML, CSS, and JavaScript quickly and easily.

*Edge Reflow*
> A tool that helps designers to create responsive web design solutions.

*Edge Inspect*
> A tool for mobile HTML5 testing. We'll cover this tool later in this chapter.

*Edge Animate*
> A tool to design HTML5 animations visually.

You can download these tools from Adobe's website (*http://html.adobe.com*).

## Microsoft Visual Studio and WebMatrix

Microsoft IDEs have supported HTML5 syntax and IntelliSense since version 2010 SP1. You can also use WebMatrix (*http://web.ms/WebMatrix*) for mobile web development; it's available for free.

WebMatrix has supported mobile websites since version 2, including:

- Mobile-friendly templates
- Connection with the Windows Phone emulator and iOS simulation through partners, such as Electrium Plumb
- Code completion for HTML5 and the jQuery Mobile UI framework

# Eclipse

If you would like to use Eclipse as your development environment, there are several plug-ins you can use to create mobile HTML5 apps. I suggest Aptana from Titanium, a free Eclipse-based IDE for HTML5 and mobile development. You can download a free version from Aptana's website (*http://aptana.com*).

## Native Web IDEs

If you are going to target native web or hybrid apps, some platforms offer tools and IDEs you can use to develop, test, and build your final packages. The most important products include:

*Nokia Web Tools (http://mobilexweb.com/go/nokiawebtools)*
> For testing and compilation of S40 web apps. A legacy 1.2 version that will help with the legacy WRT Symbian format is still available.

*Tizen IDE (https://developer.tizen.org/sdk)*
> For the creation of Tizen apps based on HTML5.

*Intel XDK (http://dev.appmobi.com/?q=node/153)*
> A nonofficial for creating tool for creating Apache Cordova HTML5 native apps.

*Titanium Studio (http://www.appcelerator.com/platform/titanium-studio/)*
> An Eclipse plug-in to create Appcelerator Titanium JavaScript mobile apps.

# Testing

Testing with a desktop browser is not good enough. Mobile browsers are really different, and we need to test our mobile apps using tools that are as accurate as possible.

Emulators are very useful and provide a simple, fast, and fairly accurate testing solution. If it doesn't work in the emulator, it probably will not work on the real device, and if it works in the emulator, it probably will work on the real device (yes, again "probably"!).

There are some problems with this testing approach, though. For one thing, there are hundreds of differences between real devices, and hundreds of bugs. Furthermore, there are several platforms without emulation. That is why real device testing is mandatory.

But how can we get access to multiple real devices? Here are a few suggestions:

- Acquire as many friends as you can (with different devices, if possible).
- Buy or rent devices. Some vendors offer promotions for buying or renting devices for developers and their partners.
- Use a testing house company. This is an expensive solution and is not recommended for mobile web developers; we need to be as close as possible to the devices.
- Create a beta tester program, for receiving feedback.
- Access a community mobile lab in your city, see www.opendevicelab.com (*http:// opendevicelab.com*) for more information.
- Use a remote device lab.

In Chapter 18, we will review tools and services that will help us to test and measure performance on mobile websites.

Let's first review emulators and simulators before talking about the other solutions we can use.

 Mob4Hire (*http://www.mob4hire.com*) is a mobile social network aimed at joining testers with mobile devices around the world and developers who want to test applications or websites using a payment service. You can find a similar solution from UserTesting (*http://www.user testing.com/mobile*) (at a cost of $39 per tester).

## Emulators and Simulators

The most useful tools for our work will be emulators and simulators. Generally speaking, an *emulator* is a piece of software that translates compiled code from an original architecture to the platform where it is running. It allows us to run an operating system and its native applications on another operating system. In the mobile development world, an emulator is a desktop application that emulates mobile device hardware and a mobile operating system, allowing us to test and debug our applications and see how they are working. The browser, and even the operating system, is not aware that it is running on an emulator, so we can execute the same code that we would execute on the real device.

We should also add to our mobile development environments classic tools for project and configuration management, like bug tracking, version control, and project management tools.

Emulators are created by manufacturers and offered to developers for free, either stand-alone or bundled with the Software Development Kit (SDK) for native development.

There are also operating system emulators that don't represent any real device hardware, but rather the operating system as a whole. These exist for Windows Phone and Android.

On the other hand, a *simulator* is a less complex application that simulates some of the behavior of a device, but does not emulate hardware and does not work over the real operating system. These tools are simpler and less useful than emulators. A simulator may be created by the device manufacturer or by some other company offering a simulation environment for developers. As the simulator does not simulate all the device features, we can also find tools that will be helpful not for mobile web development but rather for other technologies, like Java ME. In mobile browsing, there are simulators with pixel-level simulation, and others that neither create a skin over a typical desktop browser (such as Firefox, Chrome, or Safari) with real typography nor simulate these browsers' rendering engines.

For mobile web development, we will find emulators from Nokia, BlackBerry, Android, webOS, and Windows Phone, and simulators from Apple for iOS (though only for Mac OS X). A multiple mobile browser simulator is available from Adobe, called Device Central, but we will not find any help from Sony Mobile, LG, Motorola, or Samsung with their proprietary OSs (used on their low-end and mid-range devices).

Emulators and simulators don't replace real device testing, but they are useful for UI testing, JavaScript debugging, and testing different scenarios. These tools are useless to test performance, touch interaction, and some hardware scenarios, such as the accelerometer and lighting conditions.

Some browser-based emulators, like the Opera Mini emulator, are also available. An up-to-date list of emulator download URLs can be found at *emulato.rs*.

As the emulators have the same operating system and applications as the real devices, you'll need to wait for the OS to load before opening a web page.

### Android emulator

The Android emulator is available in conjunction with the SDK to create native Java applications for Android. You can download it for free from the Android Developer page (*http://developer.android.com*); the base SDK and the different Android OS versions are available separately. The Android emulator is available for Windows, Mac OS X, and Linux. Once you've downloaded it, create a folder for the contents on your hard drive and unzip the package. On Windows, there is an installer version that will do the work for you.

In the folder where you extracted the package, there is an `android` terminal command on Mac OS X/Linux and an *SDK Setup.exe* application for Windows that opens the *Android SDK Manager* shown in Figure 4-2, where you can download and configure Android platforms (known as packages or targets) after installing the base SDK.

You can download as many packages as you want, one per operating system version; you can even download vendor-specific emulators, such as for the Motorola Xoom 2, LG Optimus 3D, or Galaxy Tab. Try to download the latest releases of every Android version, such as Android 2.3.3, Android 4.0, and Android 4.1.

---

## Android on Intel Computers

Most of the Android version SDKs execute slowly on Intel computers, as they are emulating a whole different hardware. Fortunately, now we have an Intel-based porting of Android that will work much faster on our development computers. You can download it from the Android SDK Manager, searching for the package named "Intel Atom x86 Image."

You can also find a different project at www.android-x86.org that was ported to Android to work as a whole operating system on Intel machines (remember, Android is Linux-based). Therefore, you can run this Android x86 operating system as a virtual machine, like VMWare or VirtualBox.

---

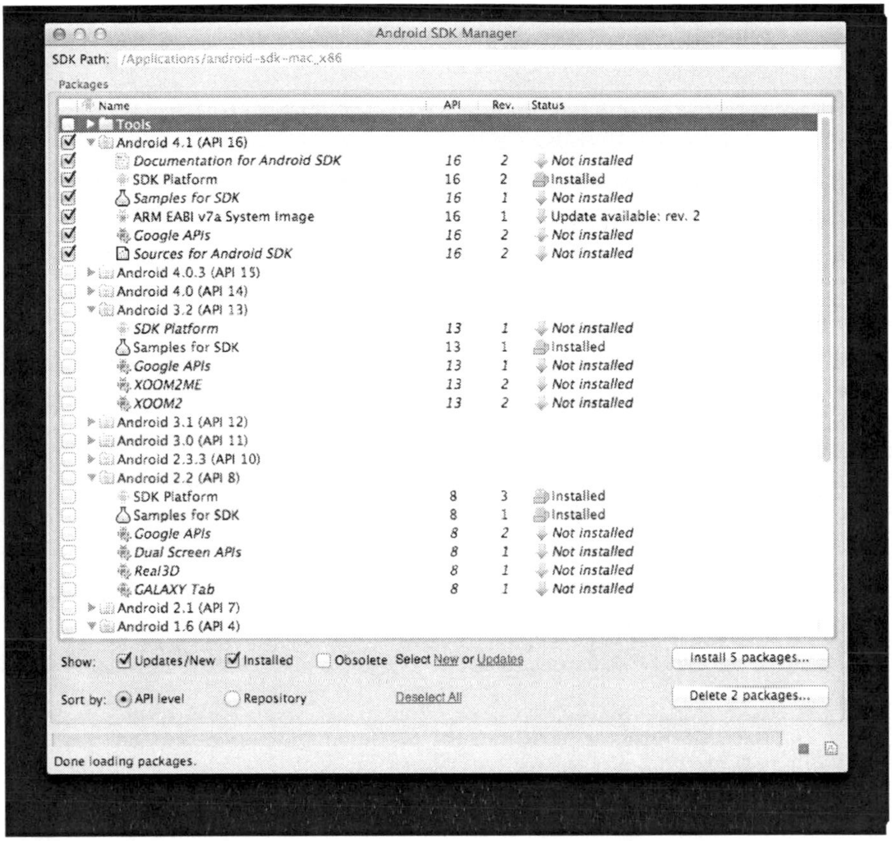

*Figure 4-2. After downloading the Android SDK, open the SDK Manager and download the platforms you want—the Google APIs are needed for native development using Google's services.*

Opening the Android emulator can be a little tricky the first time. You can open it from an IDE such as Eclipse, but first you need to install the Android plug-in and create a native empty application. Alternatively, you can open the emulator from a console window (Terminal or the command prompt, depending on the operating system) or from the AVD (Android virtual device) Manager. The AVD Manager can be opened from the SDK Manager, using the Tools→Manage AVDs menu option.

Once you've installed a platform, you need to create a new virtual device using the AVD Manager. Creating a new device involves selecting the target (of the installed packages), defining a name, and specifying the size of the SD card, the screen size, and other optional hardware features, as you can see in Figure 4-3. To understand the screen size names, refer back to Table 2-1.

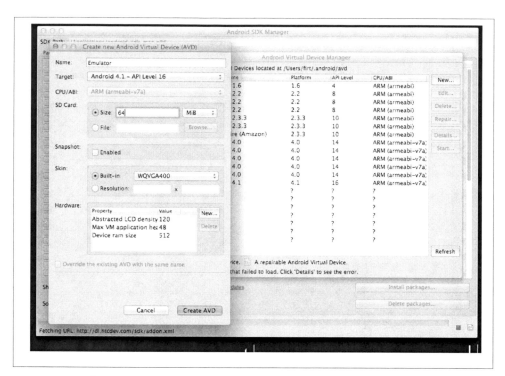

*Figure 4-3. After installing the SDK and the platform, you must create virtual devices for each platform and screen combination you need.*

 If you add external sites in the Android SDK Manager, you can install third-party Android emulators. For example, you can install Kindle Fire emulators by adding *kindle-sdk.s3.amazonaws.com/addon.xml*.

One you've created the device, you can select it and click Start to reach a result like the one shown in Figure 4-4.

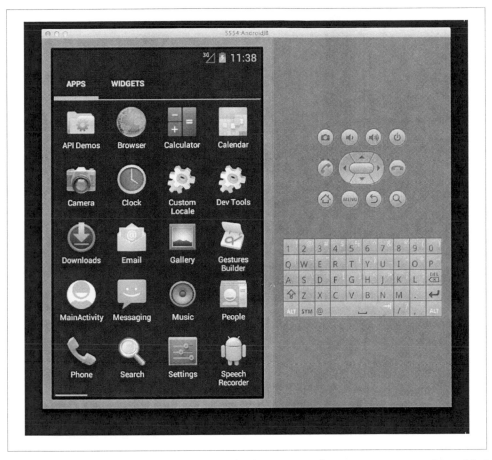

*Figure 4-4. At this point, you can open the browser as if you were on a touch-enabled Android device and use the mouse over the emulator's screen to emulate the user's gestures.*

When you start the Android virtual device (AVD), you will be prompted with an opening configuration window, as seen in Figure 4-5. In this Launch Options window you can scale the emulator if it's bigger than your own computer screen—a possible situation when opening tablet emulators—using the "Scale display to real size" option. If you want to delete all the settings and applications installed on that emulator, you can use the option "Wipe user data."

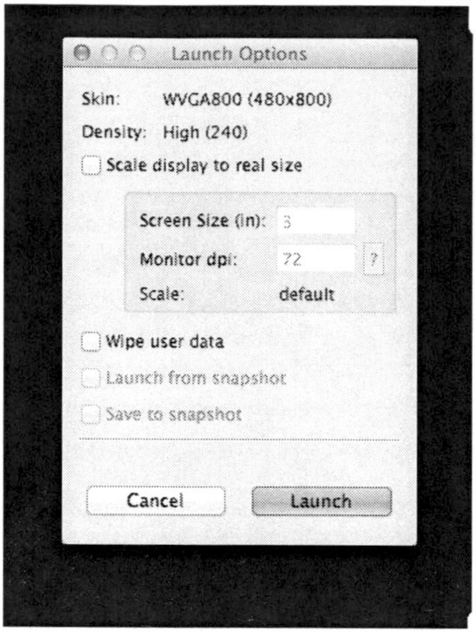

Figure 4-5. When opening an AVD we need to select some configuration attributes, such as display scaling.

When using the Android emulator, you can use the shortcuts Ctrl-F11 and Ctrl-F12 to change the emulator's orientation.

With the emulator opened, you can open a mobile website by finding the browser using your mouse (remember that almost all Android devices are touch-capable) and typing the URL in its location bar. The emulator doesn't support opening local files directly using the *file://* protocol, so you'll need to set up a local web server (for example, Apache) or upload your files to a web server on the Internet.

If you want to load a local web server in the Android emulator, you can't use *localhost* or 127.0.0.1 because the browser will point the request to Android itself. There is a special IP address available to point to the host computer: 10.0.2.2.

Up to version 4.0, the Android emulator comes with only the Android browser. You can install other browsers if you find the installation packages at the Google Play Store. Inside the emulator, you can download other browsers from the URL www.mobilex-web.com/go/android-browsers.

The Android Emulator doesn't officially include the Google Play Store. Therefore, there is no way to download or buy native apps there. If you want to install other apps—such as an alternative browser—you need to look for the installation package (*.apk* file) on a different source.

## iOS Simulator

Available for only Mac OS, the iOS Simulator (shown in Figure 4-6) offers a free simulation environment for the iPhone and iPad, including the mobile browser Safari. It is not an emulator, so it does not really provide a hardware emulation experience and is not a true performance indicator. However, it is perfectly suitable for seeing how your website is rendering and how your code is working. It's especially convenient for loading local or remote files by typing in the URL field using your desktop keyboard.

*Figure 4-6. The iOS Simulator allows us to rotate the screen as in the real device.*

Some websites, such as www.TestiPhone.com and www.iPhoneTester.com, try to simulate the iPhone browser, but the experience isn't the real thing; they are just iframes with the skin of the iPhone.

The iOS Simulator is included with the SDK for native development, available for free at the Mac App Store (search for Xcode) or at from Apple's website (*http://developer.apple.com/ios*). The SDK may take a while to download, because it's about 1.5 GB.

You will always download the latest version of the operating system and can then add previous versions (such as 6.0), in which case you can switch between versions using the Hardware→Version menu option.

To download a previous version of the operating system to the simulator, you need to open the Xcode app, open Preferences, and select Downloads, as seen in Figure 4-7.

*Figure 4-7. Opening Preferences in Xcode allows us to download previous iOS versions that will be available later on the simulator.*

 When simulating high-resolution devices, we can change the scale of the simulator using the Window→Scale menu or using the hot keys with ⌘-1, with ⌘-2, and with ⌘-3.

Within the Simulator, you can also select what device you want to simulate using the Hardware→Device menu option. Options include:

*iPhone*
Emulates low-resolution iPhone and iPod Touch devices, such as the iPhone 3GS

*iPhone Retina 3.5-inch*
Emulates high-resolution 3.5"-screen iPhone and iPod touch devices, such as the iPhone 4S

*iPhone Retina 4-inch*
Emulates 4"-screen iPhone and iPod touch devices, such as the iPhone 5

*iPad*
Emulates low-resolution iPads, such as the iPad 2 and iPad Mini first generation

*iPad Retina*
Emulates high-resolution iPads, such as the third and fourth generation iPads

 At the time of this writing, there is no way to emulate the real iPhone browser on Windows or Linux machines. There are some free and commercial tools that will help you simulate some behaviors on Windows, however, such as the Electric Mobile Simulator (*http://electric plum.com*), the MobiOne emulator (*http://www.genuitec.com/mobile*), and BrowseEmAll (*http://browseemall.com*).

Once the emulator is open, you can open the Safari application and type a URL in the address bar. To open a local file, use the *file:///* protocol in the address field (for example, *file:///Users/myUser/Desktop/test.html* to open an HTML file on the desktop of the *myUser* user). You can also drag and drop an HTML file from the desktop to the Simulator while it's opened to browse it.

Pasting a URL from the clipboard can be a little tricky. When you paste text using the keyboard or the Edit menu, the text will be pasted into the iPhone's internal clipboard. You then need to paste it again using the iPhone's gesture, tapping once over the text input and selecting Paste from the contextual menu (as shown in Figure 4-8), or use the Edit→Paste Text menu option.

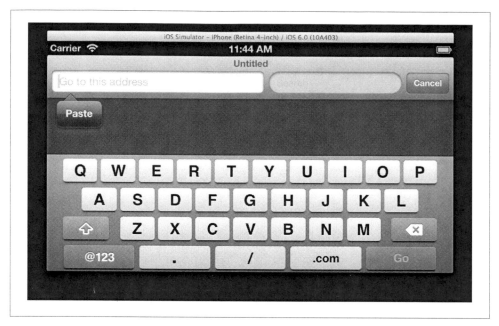

*Figure 4-8. You can use your desktop keyboard or Edit→Paste to paste text to the iPhone's clipboard, and then tap once on the text input and press Paste on the screen to paste it where you want it to go.*

 There is no App Store available in the iOS Simulator, meaning that you can't download alternative browsers or pseudo-browsers such as Opera Mini or Google Chrome for iOS.

## Nokia emulators

Nokia has always had the better emulators, since the beginning of mobile web development. Instead of one emulator per device, you'll find one emulator for each version of each platform. You can download emulators for Series 40 devices (feature phones and social devices) and for Symbian smartphones at the Nokia forum (*http://www.forum.nokia.com*).

 Nokia also has a tool called the Nokia Mobile Browser Simulator, developed in 2003 to test mobile websites for old WAP 1.0 devices and the first WAP 2.0 ones. Today, this tool is still available but deprecated; we don't need it.

Unfortunately, Nokia emulators, like that shown in Figure 4-9, are available only for the Windows operating system.

*Figure 4-9. A touch-based browser running in a Nokia S40 emulator—if you use File→Open, you must type http:// first.*

If you need to emulate a Nokia device, first find the correct platform version for that device at Nokia's website (*http://developer.nokia.com/devices*) and then download the emulator for that platform. Nokia guarantees (and it works almost all the time) that every device based on the same platform version has the same browser and rendering engine and even the same hardware features.

The Nokia emulators will add shortcut icons to your Start menu, so it will be easy to find them. Once you've launched the emulator, you can open the browser and type in the URL or use the shortcut File→Open, which allows you to type or paste a URL or browse for a file in your local filesystem. The emulator will open the browser automatically.

Some of the latest S40 emulators have predictive text input active by default, and this will deactivate the usage of your desktop QWERTY keyboard to type. Before using them, you'll need to disable predictive input.

Nokia S40 emulators support the use of *localhost* or 127.0.0.1 to connect with your desktop host computer.

## Running Mac OS or Linux?

If you are taking mobile web programming for multiple devices seriously, it will be very useful to have at least one development desktop with Windows, even if it is on a virtual PC. Some emulators work only in Windows environments. Hopefully this will change with time; emulators for Mac OS X and Linux are already available for some platforms.

### BlackBerry simulators

Research in Motion (RIM), vendor of the popular BlackBerry devices, has two different tools available for web developers: emulators and a simulator for web apps known as Ripple.

RIM has done a great job with emulators, with only one problem: it is very difficult to decide which one to download and use. Dozens of different installers are available at BlackBerry's developer site (*http://www.blackberry.com/developers*); you can download the proxy server and the emulators. The BlackBerry Smartphone Simulators (for BlackBerry OS versions up to 7.1) are compatible only with the Windows operating system, but the emulators for BB10 and PlayBook are also available for the Mac and Linux platforms.

**Ripple.** Ripple (Figure 4-10) is a free tool available as a Google Chrome for desktop plug-in that helps us test HTML5 web content and WebWorks native web applications in a simulation environment. It's available for free (*http://mobilexweb.com/go/ripple*) and it's compatible with Mac and Windows. There is also a standalone version that may be deprecated in the future, based on Chromium.

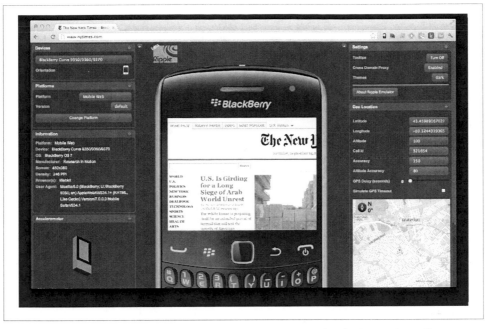

*Figure 4-10. Ripple is a free plug-in for Google Chrome for desktops that allows us to simulate some mobile devices, such as BlackBerrys, and native web platforms, such as Apache Cordova/PhoneGap or WebWorks.*

You can simulate different scenarios, from BlackBerry 7 to PlayBook and the newest BlackBerry 10 platform, and it includes mobile web support and WebWorks support (adding support for native web API testing). While Ripple is good for a first testing, remember that it is really the Chrome engine, not the real web engine running on BlackBerry devices. Also, Ripple requires an HTTP connection (local or external), so you cannot just open files from the local filesystem.

**BlackBerry smartphones.** The first requirement for older emulators is to download the BlackBerry Email and MDS Services Simulator Package. This proxy allows any simulator to access the network and emulates email services and an enterprise server. Before opening a browser, you need to start this service on your computer.

The BlackBerry Smartphone Simulators (*http://na.blackberry.com/eng/developers/ resources/simulators.jsp*) are available. The first step is to select the smartphone you want to emulate (for example, the BlackBerry Tour 9630) and choose either the carrier you want (or Generic), or the OS version. One example of a BlackBerry simulator is shown in Figure 4-11.

*Figure 4-11. Some BlackBerry simulators are pointer-based, so you need to use the onscreen keys or the arrow keys on your desktop keyboard; others are touch-based, so you can use your mouse on the screen.*

Once you've installed your emulator, you can launch it, open the browser, and type the URL you want to access (if it's an older version, remember to open the BlackBerry MDS Services Simulator before launching the emulator!). These emulators don't support local files or accessing them through *localhost*; you can use the local IP address of your desktop if you're on a network or the public IP address if you are connected directly to the Internet.

**PlayBook and BB10.** The BlackBerry PlayBook tablet and BlackBerry 10 emulators are available for different operating systems. Before installing them, you need to have installed VMWare Player (*http://www.vmware.com/products/player*) on Windows or VMWare Fusion on Mac (*http://www.vmware.com/products/fusion*).

Both the PlayBook and BB10 emulators are virtual machines, and you can use the whole operating system, including the BlackBerry browser to test your web applications. If you want to open local files, you need to set up a server and verify on your VMWare which IP address is your host machine.

### webOS emulator

Palm has been in the emulator market for more than 10 years and has always had great support for these tools. We have already talked about the history of Palm and Palm OS; in this book we will cover only webOS, the operating system available since Palm Pre. You can download the Palm SDK (*http://developer.palm.com*), which includes the Palm emulator. It is available for Windows, Mac OS X, and Linux. To use it, you must have VirtualBox (*http://www.virtualbox.org*), a free virtualization tool, installed on your machine. If everything goes OK, you can open the webOS emulator from the Start menu, the command line/Terminal, or your applications list.

 For the future, all the webOS emulation tools will be available as an open source project from Open WebOS Project (*http://openwebospro ject.org*).

### Windows emulators

If you want to test your applications on Windows Phone, you can download the free Windows Phone SDK or buy a license of Visual Studio. The Windows Phone emulator (Figure 4-12) comes with the SDK (*http://mobilexweb.com/go/wpsdk*) and includes the current version of Internet Explorer to test web content.

*Figure 4-12. The Windows Phone 7.x emulator needs a Windows 7 desktop environ-
ment and the Windows Phone 8 emulator needs a Windows 8 desktop environment.*

 The Windows Phone emulator is compatible with only Windows Vista
SP2, Windows 7, or Windows 8 and requires a graphic driver with
WDDM 1.1 support. You can check your hardware specifications to
verify whether your graphic driver is compatible. If not, you will see the
emulator, but you will see only a white page when trying to load Internet
Explorer.

If you want to emulate Windows 8 for tablets, you have two options:

- Use your own Windows 8 for desktop environment.
- Use the Windows Simulator included with Visual Studio for Windows 8 (even with Express, a free version of the IDE). It includes Internet Explorer 10.

The Windows Simulator works only on Windows 8 desktop machines; it emulates a tablet touch environment, where you can emulate touch gestures, geolocation, and different screen sizes and orientations.

 If you are looking for the legacy Windows Mobile emulation, you can find a guide from the first edition of this book (*http://mobilexweb.com/ go/winmobemu*).

### Opera Mobile Emulator

In 2010 Opera released the first emulator for its Opera Mobile browser, available for Mac OS X, Linux, and Windows. The emulator runs the exact same code as the mobile version, so it is accurate. With this emulator you can also debug your mobile web applications using Dragonfly, a debugging service for Opera that we will cover in Chapter 18.

As you can see in Figure 4-13, this emulator comes with different real mobile device profiles, and you can create your own combinations of screen resolution, pixel density, and type (touch, keypad, or tablet).

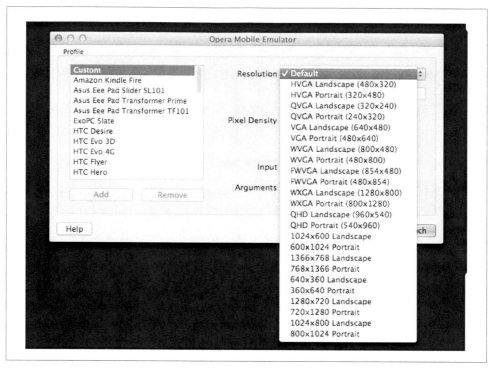

*Figure 4-13. With the Opera Mobile Emulator, we can select a device profile or create our own profile by defining each property's values.*

You can download the emulator for free at *www.opera.com/developer/tools*.

**Opera Mini Simulator.** You can enjoy a full Opera Mini simulation (*http://www.opera.com/mini/demo*) in a Java applet (see Figure 4-14). This URL is for the latest version of the software (at the time of this writing, 7.0).

 Remember that Opera Mini and other user-installable browsers are available as normal native or Java ME applications, so you can use any emulator to download them. The Nokia, Android, and BlackBerry emulators are great for this purpose.

*Figure 4-14. The Opera Mini Simulator is an online free service running the same Java browser as the one on real devices.*

### Other official emulation platforms

Other platforms have their own emulators, but they are often not so simple to use or are not optimized for web development:

- The Tizen emulator (*http://developer.tizen.org*) is part of the SDK.
- The Firefox OS emulator (*https://addons.mozilla.org/es/firefox/addon/firefox-os-simulator/*) is available as a Firefox plug-in
- The Bada emulator (*http://developer.bada.com/devtools*), part of the native SDK, is not prepared for web testing.
- The MeeGo emulator (*http://developer.meego.com/meego-sdk*) is prepared for net-books and smartphones.

### Adobe Device Central

This tool was included with Adobe Dreamweaver, Adobe Flash Professional, and some of the suites up to CS5.5, and it had an updated list of devices, including their screen sizes and Flash Lite capabilities. However, for browser emulation it is just a miniature

WebKit browser on the desktop. It doesn't provide real (or even almost-similar) simulation in terms of typography, browser bars, and markup rendering. From CS6, Adobe has abandoned the project.

### Keynote MITE

The Mobile Interactive Testing Environment (MITE) is a piece of software from Keynote for testing, validating, and monitoring mobile websites using thousands of simulated devices. You can download it from *mite.keynote.com*.

### Comparison

Table 4-1 shows how the different platform emulators and simulators allow us to access files and the clipboard on our host machines.

*Table 4-1. Comparison of available emulators and simulators*

| Platform | Able to open local files | Accesses host's local server via | Devices | OS compatibility |
|---|---|---|---|---|
| Android | No | 10.0.2.2 | Smartphones and tablets | Windows, Mac, and Linux |
| iOS | Yes | *localhost* | Smartphones and tablets | Mac |
| Nokia S40 | Yes | *localhost* | Phones | Windows |
| Windows Phone | Yes | *localhost* | Smartphones | Windows |
| BlackBerry | No | Network IP address | Smartphones | Windows |
| BlackBerry PlayBook/BB10 | No | VMWare IP address | Smartphones and tablets | Windows, Mac, and Linux |
| webOS | No | Virtual box IP address | Smartphones and tablets | Windows, Mac, and Linux |
| Opera Mobile | Yes | *localhost* | Smartphones and tablets | Windows and Mac |

 For emulators without URL pasting abilities, you can generate a free mobile-optimized short URL for easy typing on a mobile device or in an emulator at Mobile Tiny URL (*http://www.mobiletinyurl.com*).

### Remote emulation services

The cloud has come to us to solve some problems: now, we don't need to have everything installed on our own computers. In this case of mobile web development, there are some cloud-based solutions that we can use for mobile testing.

**BrowserStack.** BrowserStack (*http://browserstack.com*) is a cloud-based service optimized for cross-browser testing. While it's been useful for desktop web testing for a while, it recently added mobile web browsers. Instead of having emulators installed on our own development machines, we can use this web-based solution and use a remote emulator or simulator.

 With BrowserStack we can use the official iOS Simulator on Windows and Linux machines. You can request a trial account at BrowserStack's website (*http://browserstack.com*).

BrowserStack includes emulation of Safari on iOS, the Android browser, and Opera through different device profiles, such as the iPhone 3GS, iPhone 4S, iPad, Samsung Galaxy SII, HTC Evo 3D, and Motorola Xoom (see Figure 4-15).

*Figure 4-15. With BrowserStack we can emulate Android and iOS devices remotely— even the iOS Simulator on Windows computers.*

Using a Java-based tunnel, we can test local files on our development machines, or on a private server that is not accessible through the public Internet.

**Browshot.** Browshot allows us to take screenshots of our mobile websites with iOS, Android, and BlackBerry devices. While we can't interact with the emulations, sometimes a screenshot is enough. You can request an account at Browshot's website (*http://browshot.com*).

## Real Device Testing

There is nothing like real devices when testing mobile websites. You will find differences not only in performance but also in behavior, like when you use your fingers to navigate and not a precise mouse pointer. And while creating your own testing lab is ideal, it's also expensive and needs to be updated frequently. At the time of this writing, I currently have around 45 devices for testing.

If you have a limited budget, you should try to buy one key device per platform, and if you are targeting tablets you should get one—don't rely on smartphones for tablet testing as the browsers don't act the same way.

 While you can potentially copy your web files to the memory of your phone and open them locally, it's not a good idea; using an HTTP server—local or remote—is the way to do it.

When you have a real device, the first question is how to easily test your web development. The answer is through a web server. If your device supports WiFi (almost every social device, smartphone, and tablet supports WLAN at the time of this writing), you can run a web server on your computer—such as Apache—and access it from your device using your local IP address. Remember that your computer must be connected to the same network and you should have a firewall or a router allowing internal port connections.

On Windows hosts you can get your IP address by opening a command line/terminal (from the Start menu, type `cmd`) and using the `ipconfig` command. On Mac hosts you can get your IP address from System Preferences→Network.

 Typing IP addresses on mobile devices can be a little complicated. You can create a shorter version of your URL and even generate a QR code for camera scanning using the free service Mobile Tiny URL (*http://mobiletinyurl.com*).

If you want to test your mobile website on cellular network or you have no possibility to run a local web server on your development environment, you can always use a normal shared web service to host your files.

## Adobe Edge Inspect

When you have real iOS and Android devices, you can use the tool Adobe Edge Inspect —formerly known as Adobe Shadow—to help with your testing and debugging. Adobe Edge Inspect is a solution involving different applications that work together and help you carry out multidevice testing with almost no effort. All the information and download links are available at Adobe Edge Inspect's website (*http://adobe.com/go/edgeins pect*).

The tool is available as part of the Adobe Creative Cloud services. If you have a free account, you can connect with one device at a time. If you have a premium account, you can connect multiple devices simultaneously.

To make it work, you need to download the following parts:

- Google Chrome for Windows or Mac and the Edge Inspect extension, available at the Chrome Web Store
- The Edge Inspect server for Windows or Mac, connected to your Adobe Creative Cloud account
- The Edge Inspect client, available for iOS via the App Store, for Android via the Google Play Store, and for the Kindle Fire via the Amazon Appstore

When you have everything installed, you can open the Edge Inspect app (the server) and Chrome on your desktop computer. Then, on your mobile devices, open the Edge Inspect mobile app (the client), which will automatically try to find the server on your local network.

 It's important to understand that both the desktop computer (the server) and the mobile device (the client) must be connected to the same local network in order for Edge Inspect to work.

If your device can't connect to your computer, you can add it manually. Once connected, Chrome for desktop and all your connected devices will be synchronized, as seen in Figure 4-16. That means that browsing to a website in Chrome on your Windows or Mac machine will automatically fire a browsing to the same URL on every device connected to Edge Inspect.

*Figure 4-16. Adobe Edge Inspect allows us to keep our desktop browsing experience in sync with a real Android or iOS device, take screenshots, and do basic HTML and CSS debugging.*

Edge Inspect supports some advanced features, such as:

- Mobile screenshots
- Debugging your HTML and CSS dynamically through a Weinre session (covered in Chapter 18)
- HTTP authentication
- Clearing the cache on your devices

 Adobe Edge Inspect does not use the browser on your iOS and Android devices, but rather the default web view engine. That means that you can't use Edge Inspect to test on a different browser on your mobile device, such as Chrome or Firefox. While mostly similar, some behaviors on the web view differ from the browser (for example, the iOS web view does not support the Nitro JavaScript engine).

# Remote Labs

"Any sufficiently advanced technology is indistinguishable from magic," said sci-fi writer Arthur C. Clarke in 1961. When I demonstrate some of these remote labs in my classes, I see a lot of astonished faces.

A remote lab is a web service that allows us to use a real device remotely without being physically in the same place. It is a simple but very powerful solution that gives us access to thousands of real devices, connected to real networks all over the world, with a single click. You can think of it as a remote desktop for mobile phones.

There are three kinds of remote lab solutions for mobile devices:

- Software-based solutions, using a resident application on the device that captures the screen, sends it to the server, and emulates keyboard input or touches on the screen

- Hardware-based solutions, using some technology (magic, I believe) to connect the server to the hardware components of the device (screen, touch screen, keypad, lights, audio, and so on)

- Mixed solutions, having some hardware connection, some software additions, and maybe a video camera for screen recording

 As these are real devices, only one user can make use of them at any given time. As such, the devices are a limited resource.

In terms of services provided, we have two kinds of solutions:

- Free usage, where we can use the remote device freely. That is, we can install apps, browse the Web, and use the whole operating system.

- Closed usage, where we can just run a series of tests available on our website or app and receive a report. We can't interact with the device.

Let's take a look at some of the remote lab solutions currently on the market.

### Nokia Remote Device Access

Nokia offers a free (yes, free!) remote lab solution for Symbian, MeeGo, and S40 devices called Remote Device Access (RDA), shown in Figures 4-17 and 4-18. To use the service, go to www.mobilexweb.com/go/rda (you'll need to have already created a free Nokia account). You will need Java Runtime 5.0 or newer, because RDA is a WebStart Java application.

*Figure 4-17. Remote Device Access is a free and simple way to test on real Symbian, S40, MeeGo, and Windows Phone devices.*

At present, usage is limited to eight hours per day. The main features are:

- Complete usage of the device
- 3G and WiFi connection support
- Application installation
- Device rebooting
- Changing screen orientation
- Browser and app support
- Reservation of devices for future usage
- Usage of devices with SIM cards connected in Europe
- Saving screenshot images
- Incoming calls and SMS available

*Figure 4-18. The devices are connected to real 3G networks (you can even call them), so you can accurately test speeds and transfers.*

At the time of this writing, there are more than 200 devices available. There is no audio or accelerometer support, and depending on your network bandwidth you can select the video quality you want.

 AppThwack (*https://appthwack.com*) is a commercial service that uses the virtual test lab idea to work with real Android and iOS devices. It has an option for mobile web testing (available only on Android at the time of this writing): give it a URL, and it will generate dozens of screenshots of that website in different browsers—the Android browser, Opera Mobile, Opera Mini, Firefox, Chrome, and Dolphin—on different real devices.

### Samsung Remote Test Lab

Samsung also offers a free remote lab web service, similar to Nokia's RDA, called Remote Test Lab (RTL). RTL, shown in Figure 4-19, includes Android smartphones, Android tablets, and Bada phones at the time of this writing. The devices don't have SIM cards, though, so you can test only WiFi connections (not 3G).

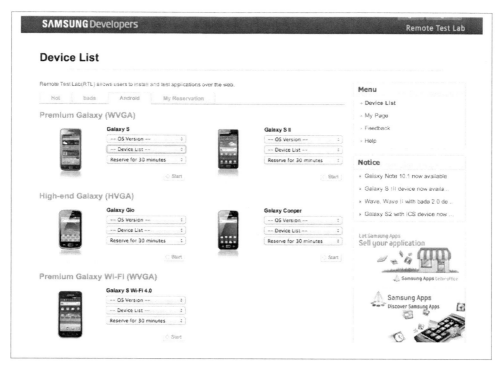

*Figure 4-19. Samsung's Remote Test Lab is a free service where you can use real Android and Bada devices remotely.*

You can access this remote lab from www.mobilexweb.com/go/labdev.

### Keynote DeviceAnywhere

Keynote DeviceAnywhere is the leader and pioneer in remote lab solutions for mobile testing. It offers a hardware solution that allows any device (low-end, mid-range, or smartphone, from any vendor) to plug into the architecture.

The company offers a product called *Test Center Developer*, with different price models depending on the package. DeviceAnywhere Test Center offers more than 2,000 devices (iOS, Android, Nokia, Motorola, Sony Ericsson, Samsung, BlackBerry, LG, Sanyo, Sharp, HTC, and more) connected to more than 30 live networks all over the world.

You can apply for a free trial at the DeviceAnywhere website (*http://www.keynotedevi ceanywhere.com*). The IDE (DeviceAnywhere Studio) is a Java application, so it should work on any OS. Easy-to-install packages are available for Windows and Mac OS X. The company offers a special free plan prepared for mobile web testing of only the 10 most popular devices. The free service doesn't require the IDE; it uses a web environment for the testing.

The solution includes:

- Access to the registered packages and devices from DA Studio
- Access to all hardware features (lock/unlock, close and open, change orientation, power off and on)
- Ability to place calls, send and receive SMS messages, access the carrier's portal, and buy premium content (as the devices are on live networks)
- Pixel-based perfect image rendering, so you can save screenshots and videos of your testing for offline review (audio is also supported as an optional feature)
- Ability to manage multiple devices at the same time
- Virtual onscreen keyboard, and shortcuts to use your own desktop keyboard for testing
- Team management for testing a device and sharing the screen with other users
- DOM Inspector and HTTP headers viewer using an included proxy

Many manufacturers and carriers have selected DeviceAnywhere as the official testing solution for their Virtual Developer Labs (VDLs). Some of the Virtual Lab solutions include:

- Nokia VDL (Series 40 and Symbian)
- Sony Ericsson VDL
- Palm VDL (Palm OS, Windows Mobile, and webOS)
- Motorola VDL (Motorola OS, Windows Mobile, and Android)
- BlackBerry VDL

To use the full DeviceAnywhere service, you'll need to subscribe to one or more packages. At the time of this writing, a yearly contract is needed, and on top of the monthly subscription fee (starting at $100) you will either pay on a per-hour basis or subscribe to a prepaid plan. On a per-hour basis, the maximum price is $16/hr. There are also other promotions available on the website, and different manufacturers' VDLs can have different pricing models.

The time spent on the system is calculated beginning from when you open a device and finishing when you release it, in six minute minimum time slots.

For web development testing purposes, Keynote offers a free option that allows you to test websites on real browsers in an unlimited quantity of 10-minute sessions, on the most popular devices. It's a good service to start working with the system, and if you decide you need more devices or more time, you can upgrade your account to a professional or corporate plan.

 If you apply for a free trial, you will get three hours of free usage and you will have to enter valid credit card details. It is safe to add this information, and it is a requirement because this is a live network where you can buy premium content.

**Usage for mobile web testing.** As DeviceAnywhere uses real devices from different manufacturers, you will need to learn to use every operating system interface to access the web browsers. You will generally find an icon in the Home screen or applications menu labeled "Browser," "Internet," or even the name of the carrier's online service (for example, "MediaNET," the AT&T Wireless service).

When in the mobile browser, you will need to type your URL using the phone's features: a numeric keyboard, a QWERTY keyboard, or an onscreen touch keyboard. DeviceAnywhere also offers a feature where you can type or paste any URL and then press a button to automatically generate all the keypresses required on the hardware to type the URL.

In numeric keypad devices, the URL typing process can be slow, so it's better if you first minimize the URL using a shortener service, like www.mobiletinyurl.com.

For mobile web debugging purposes, DeviceAnywhere includes an excellent proxy-based browsing solution that brings into the IDE an HTTP sniffer and a DOM Inspector so you can see what markup is actually rendered on the device.

 Remember that these are real devices on real networks. If you want to test an application or installable widget, you will need to first upload it to a web server (DA offers a solution) and then access the URL from the browser, typing it or sending it by SMS to the device.

**Testing automation.** DeviceAnywhere offers many advanced features. One of them is testing automation, a premium service that allows you to create testing scripts and schedule them to be tested on several devices automatically. You can then access the results via a web report.

### Perfecto Mobile

Perfecto Mobile (*http://www.perfectomobile.com*) is a company offering a software/hardware hybrid solution for mobile testing, shown in Figure 4-20. Perfecto Mobile uses a video camera for screen recording on some devices. A good point for Perfecto Mobile is that the whole environment is built on top of the Adobe Flash Player, so you don't need to install anything, and it works from any desktop browser. You can try the system by registering for a free trial; it will be activated in minutes.

*Figure 4-20. With Perfecto Mobile you can manage real phones (here, a Kindle Fire and an iPhone 4S) with a Flash-compatible desktop browser.*

With this service, you have access to the whole list of devices and carriers from the same pricing policy. The devices are on real networks in Canada, Israel, the US, the UK, and France.

 If you are using nontouch devices, for website scrolling it is better to have a key pressed down for a long time. You can emulate this using the Control key on your desktop keyboard.

**Pricing structure.** Perfecto Mobile has a simple pricing model. You can access the full cloud of devices with a prepaid monthly plan starting at $17/hr with a minimum 10 hours, or buy a flexible per-project solution at $250 per 10 hours. There is also a flat-rate plan where you can use the full cloud for as many hours as you need.

Sometimes Perfecto Mobile runs special promotions per platform, such as BlackBerry-only or Android-only devices at very low prices.

 In both DeviceAnywhere and Perfecto Mobile, you can use two or more devices at the same time. However, your per-minute charges will be counted separately, so you will be charged for two or more minutes at a time.

**Main features.**  The main features of Perfecto Mobile for mobile web testing are:

- When you take screenshots it uses the real screen image, not the camera image.
- You can record videos and share or embed them easily.
- You can send an SMS or invoke a call to the device from the UI.
- You can transfer files to the device (if file transfer is supported).
- There is an OTA mechanism where you can upload your app or widget and the device will receive an SMS link to download it within a 15-minute time slot.
- You can easily share a URL, so customers and coworkers can see what you are doing with the device via live streaming. The only requirement for the other parties is that they use a browser with Adobe Flash Player support.
- You can request Automation, a macro-like recording feature that supports advanced actions and wait conditions using screen recognition and OCR (for example, "go to this URL, wait for the word 'Hello' to appear on the screen, then take a snapshot").
- In Automation, there is a ScriptOnce technology that includes multiplatform templates for common actions.
- You can test how your mobile website is rendering on multiple devices at the same time without your intervention. This feature, called Website Validation, is available on premium plans.

# Production Environment

The mobile production environment, surprisingly, doesn't differ too much from a classic web environment. Although many web hosting companies used to offer a "premium WAP hosting" option (obviously, more expensive than the nonmobile options), there is no need for any such distinction.

## Web Hosting

To get started, you will need a web server with your favorite platform installed. It should support either static or dynamic files on all platforms you plan to work with (PHP, ASP.NET, Java, Ruby, Python, and so on). Cloud hosting (via a service like Amazon EC2, Google App Engine, Aptana Cloud, or Microsoft Azure) will work well, too.

You will need to have permissions to manage MIME types on the server. We will talk about this in Chapter 17, but for now, just remember that it will allow you to make compatible mobile websites more easily.

 There is no special need to use HTTPS (secure connections) for mobile devices. If you want to, just remember that the most widely accepted certificates are from Thawte and VeriSign.

## Domain

Which domain alternative should you use? I have no answer for this; you will have to decide for yourself. You can create a subdomain of your desktop website (if you have one), like *m.mydomain.com*, or you can use the main entry point (*mydomain.com* or *www.mydomain.com*. My only recommendation is that, whatever decision you make, you should try to have the other options available and set up a 301 HTTP Redirect to the domain you've chosen. I've tried myself many times to guess a mobile URL using *m.<anysite>.com* or *<anysite>.mobi*, and you should support that user behavior.

 No matter which mobile domain you will be using, remember to create a 301 HTTP Redirect to the chosen one from all the possibilities (*m.yourdomain*, *wap.yourdomain*, *mobile.yourdomain*, and, if possible, *yourdomain.mobi*). You don't want to lose visitors because they couldn't guess your mobile address.

## Error Management

You'll need to ensure that your error pages will be mobile compatible. You should be able to configure the default error pages for most common HTTP error codes, like 404 (Page Not Found) and 500 (Internal Server Error), on your server. These files must be mobile compatible; we don't want to waste traffic for the user on a server error or deliver pages that aren't compatible with low-end devices. If you're not sure how to configure the default error pages, ask your server provider.

If you are providing both the desktop and mobile versions of your website from the same domain, you should create dynamic code to detect whether or not the device accessing your site is a mobile device. In the case of a 500 error, deliver a very simple HTML page for both desktop and mobile users; you won't know whether the problem was in your dynamic platform. You can use responsive web design techniques on the error pages.

## Statistics

Statistics about mobile website usage are typically the same as those for desktop usage, but a mobile-friendly tool will be very helpful in understanding mobile-specific features. You can log requests on the server for later processing with a log analysis tool, or you can use a third-party tool for help in your statistics management. We will cover mobile-friendly statistical tools in Chapter 19.

# CHAPTER 5

# Architecture and Design

While this is not a book about design, understanding some architectural and usability concepts is critical to creating useful mobile services. Many common desktop web design patterns and usability concepts do not apply in a mobile environment.

 If you want to inspire yourself, check out Mobile Awesomeness (*http://www.mobileawesomeness.com*) to see some of the best mobile websites available.

## Mobile Strategy

When creating mobile web applications, we need to remember that we can create browser-based apps, full-screen web apps, or native web apps. All the types have some architectural rules in common, but there are also some practices that are useful only for a particular type.

My first piece of advice is, "Be responsible." Don't discriminate against your users just because they don't have the mobile browser or device that you prefer. I've seen plenty of websites (even from big companies) showing messages like "You can only browse this site with iOS" or providing a good experience only for WebKit-based browsers. If you browse such websites with modern non-WebKit browsers, such as IE10, Firefox, or Opera, you get an awful outdated version, that may even be not touch optimized when browsing with touch devices.

### When to Get Out of the Browser

We know that with mobile web we can create that with the mobile web we can create full-screen web apps and native apps. Determining when to get out of the browser depends on your particular case.

With full-screen web apps you gain more space, as well as an icon in the device's Home screen or applications menu. That can help the user remember your web app in the future; he won't need to type in the URL again.

You get the same visibility advantage with a native app, but you also have the ability to run native code (and extend what the browser can give you in terms of API support), and you win some discoverability, as the user will find your app when searching or browsing inside the application store.

It's up to your project what solution is the best. Usually you will offer at least a browser-based website, and possibly more advanced features through a full-screen or native web app. Never force the user to follow your idea; if you have a website and the user wants to use the browser to access your service, let her do that. Don't remind the user on every entry that she can install the app; do it a couple of times and hide the invitation after that.

Just to give you some examples, the *Financial Times* (*http://app.ft.com*) provides a website for every platform, a full-screen optional experience for some devices, and a native web application for other devices, as you can see in Figure 5-1.

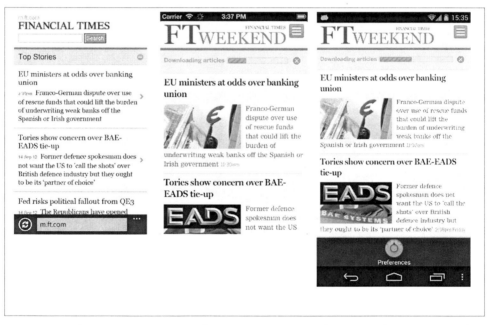

*Figure 5-1. The Financial Times offers a mobile website for some (first image), a full-screen web app for iOS, and a native web application through the stores for Android and other platforms.*

Similarly, Wikipedia (Figure 5-2) has a mobile website for all platforms and a native web app—created with Apache Cordova—available for iOS through the App Store, BlackBerry through App World, and Android through the Google Play Store. This app received more than 6 million downloads in the first few months after its release.

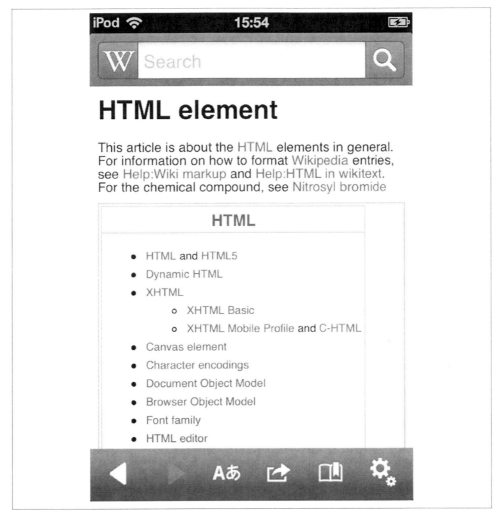

*Figure 5-2. Wikipedia has an open source native web application using Apache Cordova as the web view wrapper, available for iOS, Android, BlackBerry PlayBook, and other platforms.*

If you are providing a full-screen web app or a native app, every platform will have a way to invite the user to install it while browsing your website. On some platforms you can even send parameters from the website to the native app so the user can continue the experience on the native side using the same context as the website (for example, continuing to read the same article).

## Context

Remember that a mobile user has a different context than a desktop user. You should think about and define your users' possible contexts:

- Where is the user?
- Why is the user accessing your mobile website?
- What is the user looking for?
- What can you offer from a mobile perspective to help solve the user's problem?
- Where will the user be when accessing your website? Walking on the street, using public transportation, at the office, traveling as a tourist, sitting on the couch watching TV?

The context will tell you many things about your navigation, use cases, and the usability needs for your mobile site.

---

### A Bad Example of Navigation

I have imprinted in my mind a bad example for navigation in a mobile website. In my city, years ago (but still online today), there was a free mobile web service to get public bus schedules. This is a great service for mobile web users; you are on the move, you need to take the bus, but you're not sure when it will arrive. Should you go for a coffee first?

When you first enter the site, you see a welcome page with a Begin link. After that, you have to choose from a list which bus line you want to query. Then you see a list of final stops for that line, to select your orientation. The first problem is whether you know the name of the final stop in the direction you want to travel. After selecting your orientation, you have to choose the stop or station where you want to get on the bus. There is a list of around 50 addresses, ordered alphabetically. If you don't know the street name for the stop you want, you will need to make an average of 25 clicks to find the right one.

Once you've found your stop, you need to select whether you want a normal bus or a bus with accessibility support. Finally, the service informs you when the next two buses will be arriving. You have to navigate through six pages and choose from a 50-item list to get the result.

---

In my city, on weekdays during the day buses run very frequently (approximately every five to eight minutes), so what will be the most common context for the service? Probably night and weekend services. The first time I really needed the service was at 1 a.m., coming back from an event. I completed the six-step query only to receive a "There is no information" message. The service did not work at night!

What could be done to improve navigation? Avoid the welcome screen, the accessibility support selection page, and maybe also the direction selection (we can usually guess it from the stop, and even if the stop has service in two directions, information for both can be shown). The stop selection could be improved with features such as a search box, a list filtered by neighborhood, a list of nearby points of interest (museums, cinemas), a location query, a history of stops used before (perhaps using cookies), and so on.

# Server-Side Adaptation

A different approach is to create *n* different versions of your site and redirect the user to the appropriate one depending on the device detected. The main problem with this approach is that you need to maintain *n* different versions of the same documents.

If this will be your strategy, expect to need a minimum of four versions for a successful mobile website, with an optional fifth. If you create fewer versions, some users will probably have a bad experience with your site.

Using a server-side adaptation mechanism, you can reduce the number of required versions to two: one for low-end and mid-range devices and one for high-end devices and smartphones. In the high-end and smartphone world it will be better to use an adaptation strategy for the many features that are not compatible with all devices. Broadly, here are the features you will need to consider for each device category:

*Low-end devices*
> Basic XHTML markup, maximum screen width of 176 pixels, basic CSS support (text color, background color, font size), no JavaScript

*Mid-range devices*
> Basic XHTML markup, average screen width of 320 pixels, medium CSS support (box model, images), basic JavaScript support (validation, redirection, dialog windows)

*High-end devices*
> XHTML or HTML 4 markup, average screen width of 240 pixels, advanced CSS support (similar to desktops), Ajax and DOM support, optional touch support, optional orientation change support (for an average screen width of 320 pixels)

*Smartphones*
> HTML5, large screen size and high resolution, touch support, support for CSS3 (animations, effects) and Ajax, local storage, geolocation

*Web app for smartphones*
> Same as smartphones, plus offline support, full-screen and icon installation, native integration, and device APIs

 I've seen a lot of browser grouping techniques to determine which versions or features we can use in each browser group. The reality is that browsers are so different that there is no way to group them that guarantees all members will have the exact same features. In the next chapters, we will analyze compatibility browser by browser and feature by feature. I suggest you create your own groups based on your code features and the website versions you will design.

## Progressive Enhancement

*Progressive enhancement* is a simple but very powerful technique used in web design that defines layers of compatibility that allow any user to access the basic content, services, and functionality of a website and provide an enhanced experience for browsers with better support of standards.

The term was coined by Steven Champeon (*http://www.hesketh.com*) in 2003, and while this approach wasn't defined specifically for the mobile web, it really is perfect for mobile web design. The concept subverts the typical web design strategy, known as "graceful degradation," where designers develop for the latest technologies and browsers and their designs automatically work with the lesser functions available on older browsers. This technique is not useful for mobile browsers because, as we will see, there are serious compatibility and performance issues in the mobile world. If we develop a website for the latest device (for example, the iPhone), it may not automatically work on other, less advanced or older devices.

Progressive enhancement has the following core principles:

- Basic content is accessible to all browsers.
- Basic functionality is accessible to all browsers.
- Semantic markup contains all content.
- Enhanced layout is provided by externally linked CSS.
- Enhanced behavior is provided by unobtrusive, externally linked JavaScript.
- End user browser preferences are respected.

We will add some other ingredients to this recipe when talking about mobile devices. The objective is to have only one set of code that is compatible with all devices. And, as we are going to discuss later, we must provide the right user experience on every device. We shouldn't create lowest common denominator websites just so that they will be compatible with all devices, and we shouldn't create overly complex mobile websites that will only work on high-end smartphones.

In the mobile web, a progressive enhancement approach will also include some server-side detection and adaptation that will be mandatory for some specific mobile markup (sending an SMS, for example).

 *Regressive enhancement* is the inverse concept: start by supporting high-end platforms and then add polyfills—libraries that fill gaps—to support older or less-capable platforms. In the mobile ecosystem regressive enhancement is not usually a good idea, because adding more overhead to less-capable platforms impacts directly on already bad performance.

From my point of view, a mobile web design approach should have the following layers, using a progressive enhancement strategy:

1. Create valid and semantic markup containing only the content—no CSS, no frames or iframes, no JavaScript, and no Ajax. All the content and services on the website (with the exception of some nonstandard features, like geolocation) should work with this simple version.

2. Insert in the document any special tags or classes required for device-specific functionality, such as call-to links or a file upload form control.

3. Optionally, from the server, decide which MIME type you will be using (this will be covered in Chapter 17) and recognize the device.

4. Optionally, from the server, replace the special tags inserted in step 2 with real markup depending on the device's capabilities.

5. Add one CSS layer for basic devices, one for high-end devices, and one for some specific smartphones (Android and iPhone devices, for example). You can insert all the markup at the same time using CSS media queries (to be covered in Chapter 11), or use a server-side mechanism to decide which CSS file to apply.

6. Add an unobtrusive basic JavaScript layer for form validation and other basic features.

7. Add an unobtrusive Ajax layer for content updating, capturing the `onclick` event of every link.

8. Add an unobtrusive JavaScript layer and a CSS layer for advanced features (animations, effects, geolocation, offline storage, and so on).

9. Optionally add full-screen installation support using a new layer.

10. Optionally add native web support using a new layer.

We will cover most of these technologies in the next few chapters. The most important part to understand right now is that using this strategy, all devices receive similar markup (with minor changes if we use a server-side adaptation engine); using CSS and Java-Script, we add layers of behavior and design adapted to each device.

## Responsive Web Design

The term *Responsive Web Design*, or RWD, was coined by Ethan Marcotte in 2010 in his article "A List Apart" (*http://www.alistapart.com/articles/responsive-web-design*), which was followed by his own short book *Responsive Web Design* (published by A Book Apart). It follows the progressive enhancement idea, as the same document will provide the best experience on every device using the same URL.

It's a simple and powerful idea to provide one HTML document that will automatically adapt (respond) on the client side to different scenarios, usually meaning available screen size or current orientation (landscape versus portrait). RWD is implemented using CSS3 media queries (covered in Chapter 11), which allow the same HTML to automatically change the layout and design in different conditions, so it can be used to separate between:

- Feature phones
- Smartphones
- Tablets
- Desktop browsers
- Smart TVs

A different CSS stylesheet (or a portion of one) will be executed in every scenario, so the layout and full design can be different on each type of device. In Figures 5-3 and 5-4, we can see two examples of the same website serving Responsive Web Design solutions.

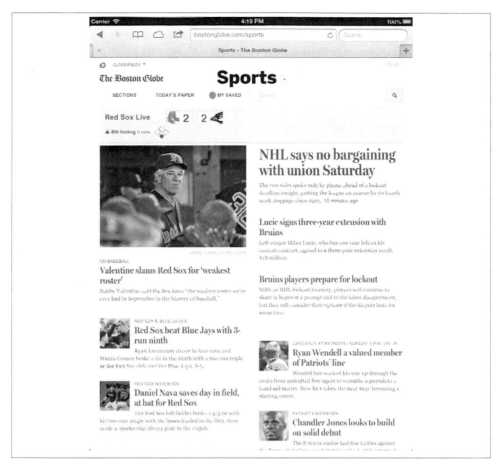

*Figure 5-3. The Boston Globe uses Responsive Web Design to deliver the best design for each device and orientation—on a portrait iPad, it has a two-column design and a collapsed menu.*

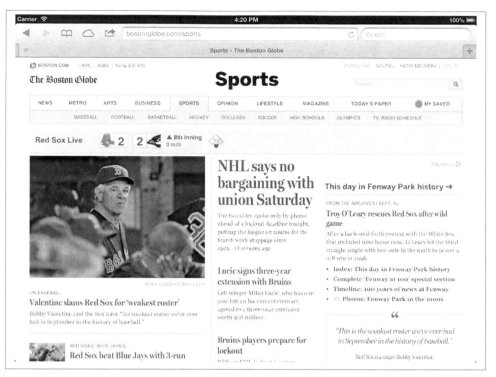

*Figure 5-4. When you change the orientation of an iPad to landscape, the Boston Globe website automatically changes to a three-column design with a visible top menu.*

While Responsive Web Design can be extremely useful, we need to be careful with this approach in some situations. Not every website is an ideal candidate for a full RWD experience at this time, sharing the same HTML document for desktops, tablets, smartphones, feature phones, and smart TVs. Performance is the key issue—when providing the same document across device types, we can fail in creating a high-performance experience.

While in a desktop browser we can resize a window, that is not possible on mobile devices—or even on smart TVs—so the magic of RWD is only useful for different orientations (portrait or landscape) or some special behaviors, such as the full-screen versus in-browser experience.

In RWD, the HTML file served is exactly the same, while the CSS may vary based on the device specifics (for example, screen width, screen height, pixel density, or orientation). Unfortunately, there is no way yet to recognize touch versus nontouch devices or other mobile-specific features using CSS3 standards.

I have to be honest with you: I like and promote the use of RWD techniques in mobile or tablet web versions as part of the progressive enhancement idea. However, using RWD to serve the same HTML document for all devices, including desktops, may not be a good idea for most websites. Problems include:

- The desktop HTML may include old browser hacks that are not necessary in mobile browsers.

- Unless images are inserted with a responsive technique—to be covered later in this book—the images served may be larger than the visible pixels on the screen.

- Desktop websites may contain large JavaScript frameworks, such as jQuery and its plug-ins, that, as we will see later, may not be a good idea on mobile websites.

- Ads and other third-party content usually are not responsive to the current context or device, so we may find problems if we use these solutions.

- In a content-based website, such as a newspaper, usually the desktop website will contain more text on the home page and inner pages, so we will be delivering content (consuming bandwidth and creating delays) just to hide that content from the CSS side.

- Mobile websites and mobile apps can only respond to orientation changes and, on some platforms, full-screen versus in-browser experiences. Mobile users will not receive changes in window dimensions; therefore, we determine the user experience and the design on the server side or at the load event instead of having RWD mechanisms waiting for a scenario change.

- Mobile apps sometimes take advantage of nondesktop features that can't be discriminated using CSS and RWD, such as geolocation, the accelerometer, and call-to-action links.

Therefore, unless you have a simple website in terms of content provided and external framework used, you should think of having at least two versions: desktop/classic and mobile. You can still use RWD inside the desktop version and inside the mobile version to make adaptations to different contexts. This may change in the following years if mobile networks and browsers become more powerful, but today performance is a key problem in mobile web browsing and mobile web apps.

If you want to browse hundreds of Responsive Web Design examples on the Web, you can check out *mediaqueri.es*. You can start accessing websites using a desktop browser and resize the window until you see that layout changes are being applied.

### Responsive layouts

RWD is usually accompanied by a fluid grid layout allowing a site to adapt easily to different screen sizes. On the desktop side, sometimes it's common to have one or more fixed-width layouts (such as for 800px wide, 1024px wide, or 1280px wide).

 Later we will cover best practices and free frameworks that will help us in creating Responsive Web Design websites and apps.

As you can see in Figure 5-5, Starbucks Coffee's US website has a fixed-width layout for large screen sizes, moving to a fluid-width layout for medium and small screens.

### Responsive images

While we can change dimensions dynamically using CSS3, a problem appears with regard to images and how to make them react to different screen sizes. *Responsive images*, also known as *flexible images* or *fluid images*, make use of a group of techniques that may involve CSS resizing (using the same original file), supplying different image sizes on the server side, or cropping the images using CSS to adapt to different screen sizes and orientations.

We will cover responsive image techniques in Chapter 10.

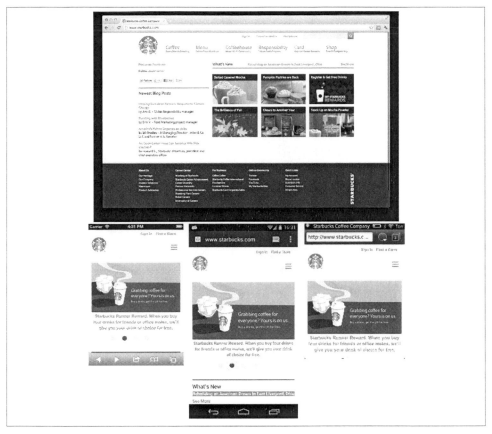

*Figure 5-5. Starbucks Coffee's US website uses a responsive layout, having a fixed width for large screens (white bars on both sides) and a fluid-width layout for smaller screens.*

# RESS

*Responsive Web Design + Server Side Components* (RESS) incorporates the best of two worlds: RWD and server-side adaptation. With this technique, we can decide on the best version and/or compatible experience on the server side, and then RWD on the client side will make the final adjustments, such as having a fluid layout and reacting to different orientations.

While the concept has been around for a while—it was even published in the fist edition of this book as a possible implementation of progressive enhancement—the RESS name was first suggested by Luke Wroblewski (*http://www.lukew.com*) in 2011 and involves the idea of having one version of the HTML on the server and changing some portions on the server side before delivering it to the client.

RESS solves some of the problems of Responsive Web Design, such as ensuring high-performance HTML for mobile devices and serving mobile-specific code, responsive images, and compatible ads.

For example, we can have a template that will change the header and the footer for feature phones, smartphones, tablets, and desktops, while the main section of the HTML remains the same. The same URL will deliver the current device version, which RWD will then adapt as the context changes.

---

## Mobile First

"Mobile First" refers to the idea of creating a new web-based project first on mobile devices and then adapting it to bigger screens. Luke Wroblewski, author of the book *Mobile First* (A Book Apart), created this idea, too. Some big companies, including Google, Adobe, and Facebook, are already applying this practice in their own products.

Mobile devices' ubiquity, their ability to force us to focus on the product because of the small screen, the explosion in mobile web browsing figures, and the ability to read the user's context on a mobile device (such as through geolocation) are some of the reasons that Luke uses to promote Mobile First.

The idea behind this approach is that if you start with a large desktop website and then try to "mobilize" it (or worse, minimize it), you will end up with a not-so-optimized desktop website and probably a terrible mobile app.

If you start with your mobile website first, however, you will be forced to think about the best user interface, and the use cases; you will focus on the main business areas, and your mobile website will be better as a result. From that version you can then start on your larger-screen versions, which will end up being more optimized and usable.

---

# Navigation

When creating your mobile web concept, before you do any coding you should define what will be in the navigation tree for the user. To do that, you need to understand what services and information will be available for the mobile user. Always remember the *80/20 law*: 80% of your desktop site will not be useful to mobile users. Therefore, you need to research the 20% you should be focusing on.

You can decide that you won't have a mobile website and just want to allow access to your desktop site to full HTML smartphones. If you're sure you will have mobile users I don't recommend you leave the desktop website as-is, but if you do decide not to create a separate mobile site, you will see later in this book how to optimize your desktop website for better visualization in smartphones.

Here are some tips you will need to follow:

- Define the use cases (for example, find a product price, find a store near you, call us, or perform a search).
- Order the use cases by the most frequent for a mobile user. Use your best guess, statistical information, and usability tests to keep this order updated.
- If you have a desktop website, try to maintain visual consistency with it.
- Do your best to make every use case successful in no more than three clicks or at a page depth of no more than three.
- Define no more than five main sections below the home page. If you need more, you should separate your service into more mobile pages.
- Always offer a link to the desktop website, sometimes called the "classic version."
- Determine whether locating the user is useful for your services.
- Reduce the form pages for user text input to the minimum. While mobile users are used to typing a lot—just look at SMS and the adoption of messaging apps!—typing in a long form usually results in a bad experience, as there is not much available space.
- Avoid startup or welcome screens in browser-based apps.
- Do your best to predict users' input based on the context and their browsing history, to reduce the number of page selections and clicks required.
- In full-screen web apps or native web apps, always provide navigation mechanisms such as back buttons. Remember that in those cases there will be no browser toolbar or UI.

# Design and User Experience

Designing a mobile website or mobile app can be a challenge at the beginning. Unless you are working on a website for only one device, forget about creating an exact pixel-by-pixel web design. Your mobile website will look different on every device it's viewed on; you need to accept this and, keeping it in mind, develop a strategy to create the best web design you can.

The best advice I can give you about mobile web design is: Keep It Simple! However, that doesn't mean Keep It Ugly.

A mobile website ideally consists of vertically scrollable documents. The typical two- or three-column design is not suitable for mobile web pages, unless you are targeting tablets or devices with a landscape orientation mode. Every mobile web document has a few identified zones:

- Header
- Main navigation
- Content modules
- Second-level navigation
- Footer

These sections will be created one after the other in a vertical scope. Only for devices with a landscape orientation and smartphones is it suitable to create an alternative organization, where you can move the main navigation section to a right-side column.

 On high-end smartphones, your main navigation can become a top or bottom tab bar, and the content modules can shrink with an accordion or master-detail design.

When you are creating a mobile version of an existing desktop website, you need to understand that you are *mobilizing* the website, not *minimizing* it. Minimizing (or miniaturizing) a desktop website simply involves displaying the same content on a smaller screen. Mobilizing is more than that; it requires understanding the context and offering your services and content in a manner that is useful and allows for quick access by the user.

 If you are designing a mobile app or a website using Ajax, you should always insert in the UI a background operation icon to alert the user when a background connection is in progress. An offline button could be useful if the user is not on WiFi or is in roaming mode and doesn't want to get updates for a while.

Some best practices include:

- Avoid horizontal scrolling (unless you know what you are doing).
- Use Responsive Web Design to provide the best possible design in different scenarios, such as orientation changes.
- Maintain visual consistency with your desktop site, if you have one.
- Reduce the amount of text.
- Use fonts that will be legible on every screen; don't rely on the resolution.
- Use background colors to separate sections.
- Keep the main navigation to four or five links.
- Maintain the total link count at no more than 15 per page.
- For low-end and mid-range devices, don't insert more than one link per line.
- Use all the available width (not columns) for links, list elements, text inputs, and all possible focusable elements. Use HTML by-default focusable elements for clickable areas (for example, avoid using divs; use an anchor with a div).
- Provide a "Go to Top" link in the footer.
- Provide a Back button in the footer (some browsers don't have a Back button visible all the time).

 If your navigation requires going back frequently, you should check whether the browser maintains the scroll position after going back. If not, you should probably create back links with anchors to scroll to directly where the user was.

- Provide the most-used features at the top.
- Group large lists by categories, each with no more than 15 items (for example, country selection by selecting the continent first).
- Use standard dialog windows.
- Use standard drop-down menus, such as HTML selects. Don't customize them or create them using JavaScript.
- Minimize the amount of user text input required if you have multiple fields.
- Save the user's history and settings for future predictive usage.
- Split large text articles into pages for feature phones (with page size depending on the richness of the browser).

- Try your color palette in different environments. Users may be in a place with poor lighting, on public transport, at the beach in bright sunlight, or in an office with fluorescent lighting.

- Provide different styling for touch devices.

- Think about fluid (liquid) designs for best adaptation.

- Use lists rather than tables.

- Embrace accessibility support. For example, use HTML5 ARIA or be careful when disabling zooming.

- Don't discriminate against your users; provide the best possible experience to every mobile device.

- For touch and cursor-based devices, use full-width links so that a link will activate if the user clicks on any pixel in the line containing it. Make sure there is only one link in each line.

- Use high-quality color images and fancier features for smartphones (we will discuss optimizing later).

- For cursor navigation, create medium-sized clickable zones for the cursor, moving by 5 or 10 pixels every time. Do not make the user travel a lot using the cursor; design all the clickable buttons near each other.

- Provide images that are sized on the server side for the current device's screen size and pixel density.

- Don't rely on fixed-position elements or on scrollable small areas (such as using `overflow: scroll`). Test them and provide alternatives if they are not compatible on some browsers.

- If you are providing a shortcut, a native app, or an offline version of your mobile website, create an alert at the top of the design alerting the user to download it. Don't show that alert after the first few views, or after the user has entered the download area. We will cover these techniques later.

 Keep the text on your site to a minimum. Read every paragraph five times, and you will always find some word you can remove or a shorter way to say the same thing.

For low-end and mid-range devices, it is preferable to use a table design instead of floating `div`s, like in the first years of the desktop web. But keep in mind that using more than one item, link, or idea per line isn't a good practice on those devices.

### I Didn't Want to Buy It!

Many years ago, I was browsing my operator's deck portal checking the games and content available for my device. I remember accessing the details of one game and seeing a screen that offered to let me buy it and have the charge added to my phone bill. I didn't want to buy the game.

The page asked me for permission to make the charge and offered two links, YES and NO. Both links were in the same line, one after the other. The focus was in the YES link (of course). What did I do? Instinctively, I pressed the right key to shift focus to the NO link.

What happened? The right key was a "go-to-link" action for my browser! I could only change the link focus using the up and down keys (like a tab), no matter where the links were located. So, because of a usability problem, I had to pay for content I didn't want.

That is why we need to test our websites on a wide range of real devices, and why I advise you to use only one link per line when targeting low-end and mid-range devices.

If you want to get deeper into mobile web design, you can read *Mobile Design and Development*, by Brian Fling (*http://www.flingmedia.com*) (O'Reilly). You can also find some useful native mobile user interface books on the market.

To get deeper information on usability research based on user testing, read *Mobile Usability*, by Raluca Budiu and Jakob Nielsen.

*Mobile Web Best Practices* (*http://mobilewebbestpractices.com*) is also a good source of links and information on mobile web design patterns.

Some low-end and mid-range devices have buggy CSS implementations, like the 100% width bug that generates a minimal (and annoying) horizontal scrolling action when this style is used on an element. You should test your design and change your strategy when problems like this crop up.

## Touch Design Patterns

Touch devices have unique features in terms of design and usability. With the same amount of effort, the user can access every pixel on the screen; this encourages a different way of thinking about a design. Another difference is that the user will use her finger for touch selection (unless it is a stylus-based device). A finger is big compared to a mouse pointer, and the hit zone should reflect this.

The Touch Gesture Reference Guide is a great resource put together by Luke Wroblewski (*http://www.lukew.com*) that contains an overview of core gestures for most touch commands, tips on how to utilize gestures, visual representations of each one to use in documentation, and an outline of popular software platforms supporting them. You can download it from *www.mobilexweb.com/go/touchguide*.

Here are some useful design tips for touch devices:

- When the user touches the screen, parts of it will be obscured. Think about what will be hidden, and if it is important. Consider both right- and left-handed users.

- Provide a reasonable amount of space (20 pixels or more) between clickable elements.

- For frequently used buttons and links, provide a big clickable area (minimum 40 pixels width and height).

- For less frequently used buttons, you can use a smaller area (minimum 25 pixels).

- Provide quick feedback when a touch is accepted.

- Think about how scrolling will work.

- When using form input fields, try to insert the label above and hints below, not to the right or left of the input field. Generally, touch devices with virtual keyboards zoom in on the field when the user moves the focus to it, so the user will not see what is at the right or left of the input field while typing.

- Use finger gestures on compatible devices.

- Use infinite lists instead of pagination. An infinite list, like that shown in Figure 5-6, has a "More" final item that the user can click to dynamically add more elements to the list (via Ajax or other techniques). For performance purposes, you should reduce the number of pages shown at the same time. When adding new pages, the best way to approach this is to eliminate the first page from the DOM and create a "Previous" first item when the count reaches *n* pages (for example, 5). Doing this ensures that you will not have more than *n* pages shown at the same time.

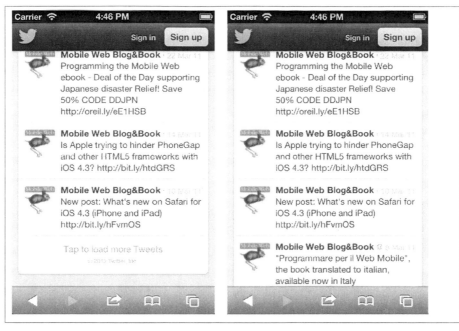

*Figure 5-6. An infinite list offers an option to load more items in the same list using Ajax.*

- Use an auto-clear textbox feature for the most common text inputs. This is just an X icon at the right of the text input box that the user can click to automatically clear the input.

- Use the long-press design pattern (also known as "touch and hold") for contextual actions. This means that if the user presses a zone for two seconds or more, you can show a pop-up menu with contextual options.

- Prefer bottom-fixed to top-fixed tab navigation. The bottom of the screen (or the right, in landscape mode) is nearer the finger while browsing than the top zone.

- Analyze native touch applications for usability ideas.

- Hide the URL bar so you can have more space available for your app.

- Don't create touch gestures on the borders of your page (top, bottom, left, or right), as some mobile browsers will capture those gestures for their own actions.

- When using touch gestures, make them obvious (following operating system patterns), such as swipe right or left for picture gallery navigation; if they're not obvious, provide alternative buttons and/or an example tutorial at the first load.

# Tablet Patterns

Designing tablet a website leads us to a big question: should we base it on the desktop version or on the mobile version? The answer may differ, depending on factors such as tablet size (7" or 10") and how your content is structured.

 If you want to browse a large selection of mobile design patterns, you can check out Mobile Patterns (*http://www.mobile-patterns.com*) and Pttrns (*http://pttrns.com*).

If you are not providing a specific layout for tablets, starting from the desktop version is frequently the preferred way, as the screen size allows the display of more content. However, remember that tablets may be using cellular networks or not-so-fast WLAN networks, such as a public WiFi connection.

Providing smartphone-optimized experiences for landscape tablets doesn't seem that good an idea, as too much space is being wasted (as you can see in Figure 5-7).

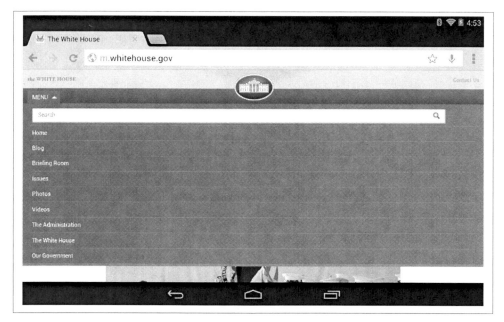

*Figure 5-7. When creating tablet experiences, starting from the smartphone version usually leads to waste of space.*

If you are starting from a desktop website, two suggestions are important:

- Replace all the Flash content with alternative versions, as most tablets either don't support Flash or may remove its support in the near future.
- Provide more padding and bigger areas for clickable elements—Google's home page for desktops and tablets, shown in Figure 5-8, provides an example.

## Official UI Guidelines

Official user interface guidelines from the manufacturers, links to which you can find at www.mobilexweb.com/go/uiguides, are another source of inspiration for mobile web design. Here, you will find guidelines, samples, tips, and descriptions of common mistakes. Many of the guidelines focus on native application development, but we can apply most parts of them to mobile web design, too.

 If you apply the long-press (touch and hold) design pattern, you should be aware that browsers have their own long-press actions for clickable elements, like links, images, or text, for copying and pasting. In WebKit-based browsers, you can disable text selection on text items using the `webkit-user-select:none` style and then create your own menu.

The most important guides are:

- iOS Human Interface Guidelines
- UI Guidelines for BlackBerry Smartphones
- Android User Interface Guidelines
- Nokia Design & User Experience Guidelines
- Windows Touch UI Guidelines

## What Not to Do

The website WTF Mobile Web (*http://wtfmobileweb.com*) collects dozens of examples of what not to do on mobile websites. There is a quote on this site that I would like to mention here:

> Respect your users' time and context. Don't penalize people for how they choose to access your sites, products and services. Work towards universal access to content.

While there's a long list of websites with big usability problems on this site, I've made a quick selection in Figure 5-9 whose problems you should be able to spot pretty easily.

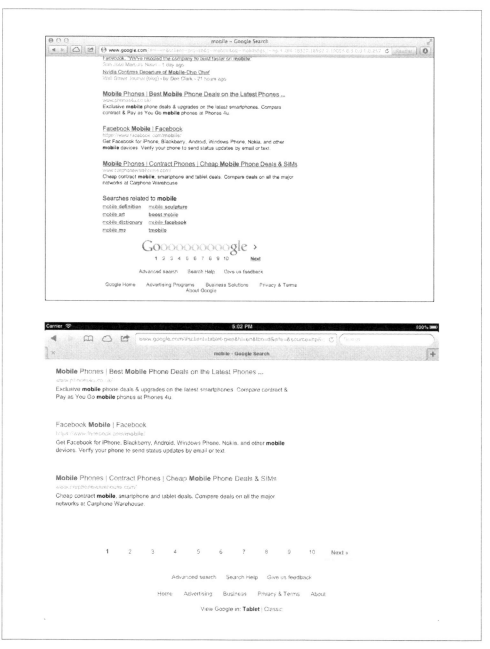

*Figure 5-8. The Google home page offers the desktop version for tablets, but with some small enhancements, such as larger clickable areas.*

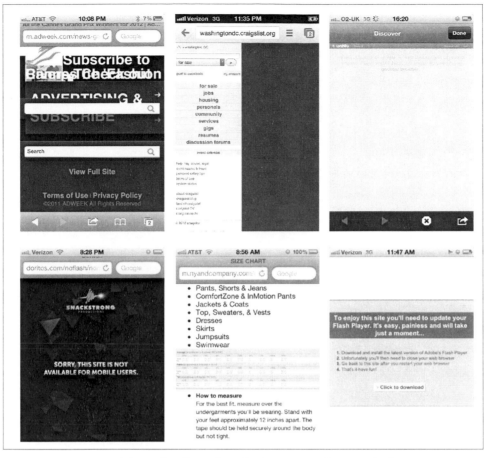

*Figure 5-9. WTF Mobile Web offers a list of what you need to avoid when creating mobile websites.*

 If you don't know yet what WTF means, well…you can search for its definition on the Web.

The list of problems can be summarized as follows:

- Too-small text whose size cannot be increased.
- "Unsupported browser" messages (remember, it's the Web!). These are worst when they suggest that the user download IE or some other desktop browser.
- Big fixed elements that create unusable experiences.
- "Install Flash Player" messages.

- "Mobile version available soon" messages, without even a link or a way to open the desktop version.
- Full-Flash websites that show only an error icon on the screen.
- Too-narrow small links for a touch device.
- Very large paragraph elements that can't fit on the screen, so the user needs to scroll right and left to read them.
- Forcing the user to install a native app instead of providing a website (even if a website exists).
- Providing a 320px-wide fixed view on a large tablet.
- Providing full-screen installation invitation dialogs when the user is not in the browser (such as when the user is in a web view or inside a pseudo-browser).

# CHAPTER 6

# Markups and Standards

Finally, we have arrived at the best part: coding! If you are reading this chapter but have skipped the previous ones, I encourage you to read them. Mobile web development is not just about coding; it is important to understand the full ecosystem, including what types of devices and browsers are available, and to be aware of mobile design and usability issues. That said, let's take a look at the available markup languages and the relevant standards.

## First, the Very Old Ones

Although you're unlikely to use them in mobile web projects today, some familiarity with at least the basic concepts of the old markup languages can be useful. One day you may need to migrate an old mobile website, or work with older devices, and I wouldn't be satisfied if I didn't talk a little about them.

One of the first mobile web markup languages to be developed was *HDML* (Handheld Device Markup Language). Similar to HTML, it was developed by a company called Unwired Planet (the company that became Openwave and was later taken over by the Myriad Group). This markup language was never released as a standard, but it helped in the creation of WML (Wireless Markup Language).

## Why Not HTML from the Beginning?

The first specialized language for the mobile web, HDML, appeared in 1996. Why not use the well-known HTML from the beginning? There were a few main issues. For one thing, mobile devices were so limited in terms of network access and CPU and memory resources that it was necessary to create very small rendering solutions. A mobile browser couldn't process nonstrict markup and decide what to do if the developer forgot to close a tag, for example. The other issue was the need to create mobile-specific functionality in the markup, like keyboard shortcuts.

Over time, mobile devices evolved into what we know today; now some mobile devices are even more mature than desktop ones, and mobile devices began using HTML5 before desktops, well before the standard (still in draft format) was finished.

## WML

WML was incorporated into the WAP 1.1 standard and was the first standard of the mobile web. It was standardized not by the World Wide Web Consortium (W3C), but rather by the WAP Forum (known today as the Open Mobile Alliance), an organization made up of many players from the mobile industry working on standards in this market.

We have already agreed that WML is absolutely deprecated today. Any nonsmartphone will still understand WML, but I want you to consider it a historic language, like Latin, instead of a current standard. Depending on your target, you may still want to create a basic WML version like that in Figure 6-1, but it is not the place to start.

*Figure 6-1. A typical WML document used to contain just text, links, and maybe some small image; it was always focus-based and optionally could execute WMLScript code, but that was very rarely used.*

In fact, some modern browsers (Safari on iOS, Android browser, IE) do not read this format anymore, as shown in Figure 6-2. It was the markup for WAP 1.1, and the first (and almost the last) version was created in 1998! Just think about what mobile phones were like that year. Still, if you search for "filetype:wml" in Google, you'll find nearly a billion results using this format. And Google did not index the majority of the WAP 1.1 mobile web!

*Figure 6-2. Both Safari on iOS and the Android browser show the WML source code instead of rendering it.*

A couple of years ago, I asked some big mobile portals about their WML usage. The Weather Channel (*http://m.weather.com*) was the first to give me a good answer (from Cathy Rohrl, Product Manager – Mobile Web):

> To have a WML-compliant site is not that big of an issue. It was easy to build and it's just out there. But the importance of having WML today is supporting the concept of access to EVERYONE, everywhere. You start tempting people with older handsets, and they'll want more. Another year and we may completely mothball the site, but even then I don't think we'll take it down. It will just become a site that is not actively maintained.

Internal nonaudited private reports of US traffic on The Weather Channel's mobile site indicate that 5% of traffic in 2008 was WML-only, decreasing to 2% in 2009 and even less in early 2010.

A WML file is an XML file, normally using the *.wml* extension. It is similar to HTML in some ways and very different in others. Let's take a look at a typical WML file:

```
<?xml version="1.0"?>
<!DOCTYPE wml PUBLIC "-//WAPFORUM//DTD WML 1.1//EN"
    "http://www.wapforum.org/DTD/wml_1.1.xml" >
<wml>
    <card id="home" title="Welcome to Old Mobile">
        <p mode="wrap">This is a <b>typical</b> paragraph in WML</p>
        <p mode="wrap">It can include images,
            <a href="http://wap.yahoo.com">External Links</a> and
            <a href="#two">Internal Links</a>.
        </p>
    </card>
    <card id="two" title="Second screen">
        <p>This is like a second page in the same document</p>
    </card>
</wml>
```

We can recognize many tags found in HTML here, like p, b, and a, and they have the same functionality. Other tags the two standards have in common include img, br, and input.

 Today it is common to use the self-closed tag <br /> in XHTML files instead of the classic <br> without a closing tag. WML, as one of the first XML-based markup languages, was the pioneer in using the self-closed tag.

However, you'll also notice some differences. First, a WML file starts with a root wml tag after the DOCTYPE declaration. A WML document is also called a *deck*. Every deck can contain many cards. A *card*, identified by a tag with the same name, is one visible page in a browser; it is like the contents of a body tag in HTML. So yes, a WML file can contain many pages in the same document. This was a great feature for speeding up the performance of the mobile web in the early 2000s.

The Document Type Declaration (known as the DOCTYPE) is an instruction in an XML document (or an SGML document, such as HTML) that allows the browser to match that document with a Document Type Definition (DTD) so it can tell how to understand the document.

WML was conceived for mobile devices. Consequently, we will find tags and attributes supporting mobile device functionality (such as voice calls, keyboard support, adding contacts to the phone book, and accessing the SIM card) in the standard. The best part is that we can use the well-known anchor tag to create an absolute link, a link to a relative document, or a link to another card in the same document using the *#card_name* URL.

 The multiple cards design pattern in WML is very useful. We will use it in our modern mobile websites using JavaScript, the Document Object Model (DOM), and even Ajax. You'll need to wait a few pages for that, though!

There is a lot to say about WML; in fact, I have a book on WML on my bookshelf that's more than 600 pages long. But to be honest, WAP 1.1 pages today are so simple that this quick introduction should be enough for you to understand WML.

 WML is not compatible with CSS, and its minimal design support includes the use of the tags big, small, b, and i using a "best effort" mechanism. Many old WML browsers had only one font and no bold or italic support.

If you are still curious about WML, you can use Adobe Dreamweaver to create WML files with code hinting support. When you select File→New, you will find WML in the "Other" section. Of course, you can also use any text editor and a WML-compatible emulator. The best WML emulators today are the Nokia Series 40 emulators (only for Windows), as they show real rendering and work well on modern desktops running Windows.

## WML Was Not Alone

WML does not generally support GIF, JPEG, or PNG images (although some browsers did accept GIF and JPEG images, starting with color screens). Images in WML files were typically in *WBMP* (Wireless Bitmap) format. WML also supports scripting using a language called *WMLScript*, loosely based on ECMAScript. They aren't worth discussing; just know that they existed and talk to your grandchildren about them. A WBMP file is just a 1-bit-per-pixel bitmap file, in black and white.

Other common scenarios involved compiled WML and WMLScript files. These files were compiled by the developer or by a proxy or WAP gateway between the user and the web server. A free tool for compiling WMLScript files is the old Nokia Mobile Internet Toolkit, still available for download.

At the same time that WML appeared on the market, in 1998, compact HTML (cHTML) also appeared, mainly in the Japanese market. cHTML is a subset of HTML with additions for mobile features, like support for access key shortcuts, pictorial characters (emoticons, or Emoji), and Japanese characters. It was submitted as a standard to the W3C but its adoption was mainly in Japan, with some implementations in the Netherlands, Italy, France, Australia, and the United States. Early versions of cHTML lacked support for JPEG, tables, backgrounds, frames, and stylesheets.

# Current Standards

In terms of the mobile web today, our real work will be directly related to the following standards and pseudo-standards:

- HTML5 and other sub-standards
- XHTML Mobile Profile 1.0, 1.1, and 1.2
- XHTML Basic 1.0 and 1.1
- HTML 4.01
- De facto standard mobile HTML extensions
- WAP CSS
- CSS Mobile Profile (CSS MP)
- CSS 2.1
- CSS 3.0 and other sub-standards, such as CSS3 transitions and CSS3 columns

This may seem overwhelming, but don't panic: it isn't really that complicated. We can distinguish two main types of standards: HTML-based and CSS-based.

## Politics of the Mobile Web

Why are there so many standards? The first answer is politics. Politics? Yes. Many actors are involved in the mobile web, and everyone wants to be part of the decision-making process. Were mobile web standards "mobile enough" to be managed by mobile standards organizations, like the Open Mobile Alliance (OMA)? Were they "web enough" to be managed by web standards organizations, like the W3C? Do the manufacturers have enough power to decide on their own markup?

Those kinds of questions are responsible for the nightmares that can occur with markup. Here's another look at the preceding list, grouped by owners:

*W3C mobile web & web standards:*
- XHTML Basic 1.0 and 1.1
- CSS Mobile Profile (MP)
- HTML5 and subsequent standards
- CSS3 and subsequent standards

*Web Hypertext Application Technology Working Group (WHATWG) web standards:*
- HTML Living Standard

*OMA mobile web standards:*
- XHTML Mobile Profile (MP) 1.0, 1.1, and 1.2
- Wireless CSS (WCSS) or WAP CSS

*Manufacturers' extensions to the standards:*
- De facto standard HTML extensions
- CSS custom extensions

### Managing multiple standards

The first bit of good news is that, with the exception of some new features in HTML5 and CSS3, all the standards are similar and compatible with each other. The second piece of good news is that HTML-based browsers—including every mobile browser on the market today—have a "good effort" mechanism to manage nonrecognized tags and attributes. This is at the heart of HTML's evolution.

 On today's mobile web, we will use HTML5 and CSS3 for smartphones and tablets and XHTML MP with WAP CSS for feature phones and some other devices.

I remember my first desktop HTML project in 1996, and the projects after that. The list of compatible tags was different for each browser on the market (at that time, Mosaic, Netscape Navigator, the AOL Browser, and, a bit later, Internet Explorer). However, it wasn't a big problem. If the browser did not understand a tag or an attribute, it just ignored it. The same is true of most mobile browsers. This will be very helpful in enabling us to manage all standards at the same time (with some exceptions: basically, older devices).

As the mobile device manufacturers were nearer to OMA than the W3C, they officially implemented the WAP 2.0 standard using XHTML MP and WAP CSS. However, almost all browsers also understand XHTML Basic and CSS MP, and most mid-range and high-end devices understand full desktop web standards (HTML and CSS).

 Don't rely only on the standards. Even two devices supporting the same standard may render different results for many tags, attributes, and styles. We will analyze every usage, and I'll recommend the best solution.

## Delivering Markup

Before we talk about the individual standards and the differences between them, we will analyze how to deliver each standard to a mobile device. First, as in the desktop web, all static document markups use the *.html* extension, and the style ones use the *.css* extension. Of course, we can deliver HTML5, XHTML MP, or XHTML Basic using a dynamic template, a *.php* or *.aspx* file, or servlet Java.

So, how does the device know which standard we coded a website in? By reading the MIME type and the DOCTYPE. The MIME type is a string sent by the server telling the browser the format of the document, and the DOCTYPE is the first line in the HTML file. If you omit the DOCTYPE the file should still work in many browsers, but don't do this! The other thing to notice is that in HTML 3.2, 4.0, and optionally HTML5 the opening tag should be:

```
<html>
```

while for all the other XHTML subtypes it should be:

```
<html xmlns="http://www.w3.org/1999/xhtml">
```

All CSS standards use the same MIME type as in the desktop web (text/css), and there is no format indicator inside the CSS. That is why for the style file, we will not need to define which standard we are using. The selectors and attributes used will determine compatibility. Figure 6-3 illustrates how MIME types and DOCTYPEs travel through the network, one in the header and the other inside the document.

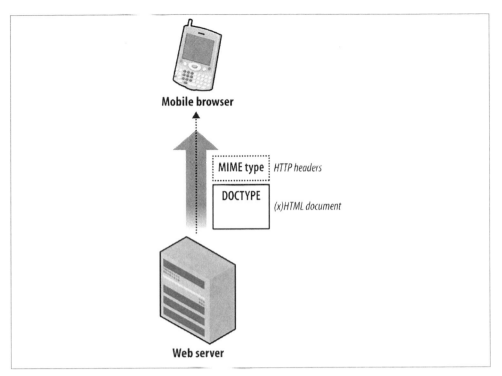

**Mobile browser**

MIME type : *HTTP headers*

DOCTYPE

*(x)HTML document*

**Web server**

*Figure 6-3. The MIME type travels with the server's response headers and the DOC-TYPE is defined inside the HTML document.*

The preferred MIME types and DOCTYPEs are listed in Table 6-1.

*Table 6-1. MIME types and DOCTYPEs for today's standards*

| Standard | Preferred MIME type | DOCTYPE |
|---|---|---|
| XHTML MP 1.0 (first version) | application/xhtml+xml | `<!DOCTYPE html PUBLIC "-//WAPFORUM//DTD XHTML Mobile 1.0//EN" "http://www.wapforum.org/DTD/xhtml-mobile10.dtd">` |
| XHTML Basic 1.1 | application/xhtml+xml | `<!DOCTYPE html PUBLIC "-//W3C//DTD XHTML Basic 1.1//EN" "http://www.w3.org/TR/xhtml-basic/xhtml-basic11.dtd">` |
| XHTML MP 1.2 (last version) | application/ vnd.wap.xhtml+xml | `<!DOCTYPE html PUBLIC "-//WAPFORUM//DTD XHTML Mobile 1.2//EN" "http://www.openmobilealliance.org/tech/DTD/xhtml-mobile12.dtd">` |

| Standard | Preferred MIME type | DOCTYPE |
|---|---|---|
| XHTML 1.0 | application/xhtml+xml | `<!DOCTYPE html PUBLIC "-//W3C//DTD XHTML 1.0 Transitional//EN" "http://www.w3.org/TR/xhtml1/DTD/xhtml1-transitional.dtd">` |
| HTML 4.0 | text/html | `<!DOCTYPE HTML PUBLIC "-//W3C//DTD HTML 4.01 Transitional//EN" "http://www.w3.org/TR/html4/loose.dtd">` |
| HTML5 | text/html | `<!DOCTYPE html>` |

Safari on iOS will render a file differently if the markup is using the HTML5 or the XHTML Mobile Profile DOCTYPE, as shown in Figure 6-4. The biggest difference will be the viewport used. This will be covered in Chapter 7, but for now, it's good to know that a file in XHTML MP markup will not start zoomed out, like a normal HTML file.

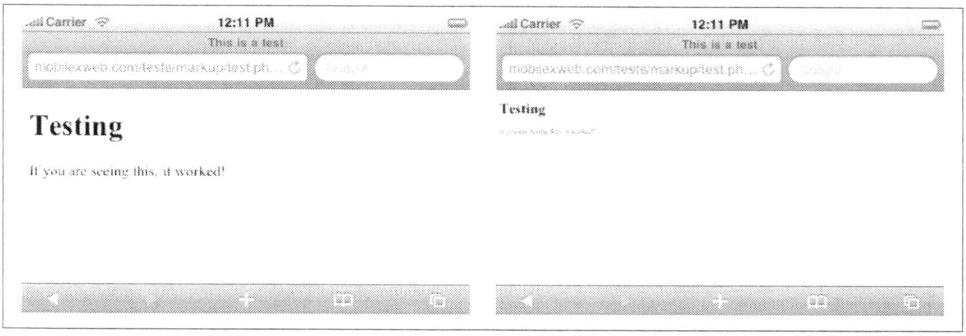

*Figure 6-4. The same document, with the same MIME type, rendered in Safari on iOS: the version on the left is using the XHTML Mobile Profile DOCTYPE and the version on the right a nonmobile XHTML one.*

If we are delivering XHTML (any version) we should also include the `meta` tag to tell the browser the content type of the file, using the right MIME type or `text/html` (even if we are using XHTML or XHTML MP, as the W3C recommends), and define the charset used (UTF-8 in almost all situations):

```
<meta http-equiv="Content-Type" content="text/html; charset=UTF-8" />
```

In HTML5, this `meta` tag becomes:

```
<meta charset="UTF-8">
```

This is optional, but it may be useful if we don't define the charset used in the HTTP header and we don't use the XML header. Using the header alternative is the preferred and most compatible way to do it.

If we use basic markup compatible with all standards, some old and basic devices will not understand the text/html MIME type, and some smartphones will not understand the XHTML MP MIME type. In a later chapter we will learn how to change this attribute dynamically, even when we deliver the same code.

XHTML MP can be delivered using the OMA MIME type (application/vnd.wap.xhtml+xml), the XHTML type (application/xhtml+xml), or even the HTML type (text/html), with the same result. The OMA recommends using the first one, but using the XHTML type will work well in almost all situations. Some older and low-end devices render the page differently depending on the MIME type used.

---

## This Book's Testing Suite

All the testing documents used in this book are available for free at www.mobilex-web.com/tests; you can test every feature tested here yourself with any mobile browser. For less typing, you can use the Mobile Tiny URL, typing *t.ad.ag* in your browser's address bar (you will need to type *8123124* on almost every numeric keypad). This is a valid URL on the Internet, and it uses only the first characters associated with each numeric key to reduce keypresses. You can create your own URLs for easy mobile typing by accessing www.mobiletinyurl.com from your desktop browser.

Every suite was tested on the latest versions of some of the platforms available at the time of this writing, on all the major versions available on the market, and on older versions of the same platforms. As mobile browsers are evolving quickly, new versions could have different results. You can follow my blog (*http://www.mobilexweb.com*) or my Twitter account (*http://www.twitter.com/mobilexweb*) for updates.

---

### Charset encoding

For the best compatibility for Latin languages, we should deliver any XHTML with UTF-8 defined in the XML header or in the Content-Type HTTP header. If we are delivering just HTML or content in other languages, we can use other encodings.

### Conclusion about MIME types and DOCTYPEs

What is the advantage of using the mobile headers? On some devices (those using Safari on iOS, for example) the behavior may differ if you use or don't use the mobile headers, and for some devices using them is the semantically correct solution. This will be our flag saying, "Hey, this is a mobile website, and it is not intended to be used from a desktop." This metadata is very helpful for search engine robots to determine which pages are mobile-ready.

In the mobile HTML5 era, on smartphones and tablets, the way to determine if a page is mobile-ready is through other meta tags that we will see later in this book, such as the viewport meta tag.

# XHTML Mobile Profile and Basic

XHTML MP is based on the W3C's XHTML Basic, and they are almost the same. The W3C has an online mobile validator (*http://validator.w3.org/mobile*); it accepts XHTML Basic and MP as valid markup.

XHTML Mobile Profile is a subset of XHTML. It is XML-based, so we need to follow the strict rules. If you have never worked with XHTML 1.0 or 1.1, let's analyze the differences compared with working with HTML5:

- The file must have a root element (`html` tag).
- Every tag name and tag attribute must be in lowercase.
- Every attribute must have a value, and it must be enclosed in quotes. For example, `<option selected>` is invalid; you must use `<option selected="selected">`.
- Every tag must be closed. This may seem obvious, but it is not; tags like `<img>`, `<input>`, and `<br>` don't need to be closed in HTML, but they do need to be closed in XHTML. The general rule is to use self-closed tags, like `<br />`.
- The tags need to be closed in reverse order. If you open a paragraph and then a link, you must close the link before closing the paragraph.
- XHTML entities must be well formed. A mandatory space should be ` ` and an ampersand character should be `&amp;`.
- The DOCTYPE declaration is mandatory, and the XML opening tag is optional. In fact, for mobile browsers we should not insert the XML opening tag.

 This is not a book about XHTML, HTML5, CSS, or even JavaScript. I assume you have some basic experience with these markup and programming languages; if not, you will find a lot of resources on the Web and excellent books from O'Reilly Media to help you get started.

## Available Tags

We have finally arrived at the level of code. XHTML MP, as a subset of XHTML derived from HTML, will look familiar to most web developers.

---

### The Space Before the Final Closing Slash

You may be familiar with the use of `<br />` in recent years, whether in XHTML or in HTML. Do you know why the space is included before the closing slash? In an XML file, we can use `<br/>` without a space, and it's valid. The space is for backward compatibility with non-XHTML browsers that don't expect a final slash in the tag. Using the space ensures that most older browsers will understand the tag as a line break.

---

The tags available in both XHTML Mobile Profile 1.2 and XHTML Basic 1.1 (the two standards are almost at the same level) are listed in Table 6-2. Some features, like scripting support, were added in XHTML MP 1.1 and others, like object support, in the last standard (1.2).

*Table 6-2. HTML tags available in XHTML MP 1.2 and Basic 1.1*

| Tag types | Tags available |
| --- | --- |
| Structure | body, head, html, title |
| Text | abbr, acronym, address, blockquote, br, cite, code, dfn, div, em, h1, h2, h3, h4, h5, h6, kbd, p, pre, q, samp, span, strong, var |
| Links | a |
| Presentation | b, big, hr, i, small |
| Stylesheet | style |
| Lists | dl, dt, dd, ol, ul, li |
| Forms | form, input, label, select, option, textarea, fieldset, optgroup |
| Basic tables | caption, table, td, th, tr |
| Other | img, object, param, meta, link, base, script, noscript |

If we compare previous versions of XHTML MP and Basic, the differences are bigger. The last XHTML Basic standard (1.1) added almost every addition in XHTML MP 1.2, and now the two are almost equivalent.

 XHTML Mobile Profile 1.2 is the last standard from the OMA. The first draft was presented in 2004 and the approved version was released in 2008. Remember that it takes some time for browser developers to comply with new standards, and more time for manufacturers to get devices using the new standards to the market.

We can still use a tag that is not supported in our declared DOCTYPE. It will not validate against the DTD, but most mobile browsers that don't support it will simply ignore the tag without any error visible to the user.

## Official Noncompatible Features

Every mobile browser on the market today should understand and render the tags listed in Table 6-2. However, in XHTML MP (and Basic), there are also several tags, techniques, and technologies that are officially not supported. We will still test them in every browser, though, because as we've seen there are many full HTML browsers on the market, and others that will understand some noncompatible features. All of the following are officially unsupported:

- Nested tables (tables inside other tables)
- Full table tags: `thead`, `tbody`, `rowspan`, and `colspan` attributes
- Full form tags: `<input type="image">`, `<input type="file">`
- Editing tags: `ins`, `del`
- Image maps
- Frames
- Iframes
- Deprecated formatting tags: `font`, `dir`, `menu`, `strike`, `u`, and `center`

We will check all browsers for compatibility with those features, as well as the following:

- Adobe Flash
- The `XMLHttpRequest` object (Ajax)
- SVG
- The `canvas` HTML5 tags
- Other embedded objects: Windows Media, QuickTime, Java applets
- Multimedia HTML5 tags: `audio` and `video`
- Opening links in new tabs or windows

We will also verify which URL schemas are available for each browser.

# Creating Our First Compatible Template

Let's create a very simple markup template that will be compatible with all devices. I really recommend that you use the source code view if you are using a visual web tool, like Adobe Dreamweaver or Microsoft Expression Web. You should feel comfortable with nonintrusive, semantic HTML code for mobile web development.

Our template will look like this:

```
<!DOCTYPE html PUBLIC "-//WAPFORUM//DTD XHTML Mobile 1.2//EN"
    "http://www.openmobilealliance.org/tech/DTD/xhtml-mobile12.dtd">
<html xmlns="http://www.w3.org/1999/xhtml">
<head>
    <title>First Template</title>
</head>

<body>
    <h1>First Template</h1>
    <h2>Programming the Mobile Web</h2>
    <p>Welcome to the first template of this book</p>
    <p>It <strong>should work</strong> in every mobile browser
       on the market</p>
    <ol>
        <li><a href="http://m.yahoo.com" accesskey="1">Yahoo!</a></li>
        <li><a href="http://m.google.com" accesskey="2">Google</a></li>
        <li><a href="http://m.bing.com" accesskey="3">Bing</a></li>
    </ol>
    <p><img src="images/copyright.gif" width="150" height="50"
            alt="(C) mobilexweb.com" /></p>
</body>
</html>
```

Here are some comments on this code; the results are shown in Figure 6-5:

- We are using the XHTML MP DOCTYPE.

- We are using standard header tags for titles; that is, h1 ... h6, not p or div tags.

- We are using the paragraph tag (p) to enclose text.

- We are using an ordered list to show a link menu. The option numbers match the accesskey attributes of the anchor (a) tags.

- We provide a width, height, and alternate text for all images.

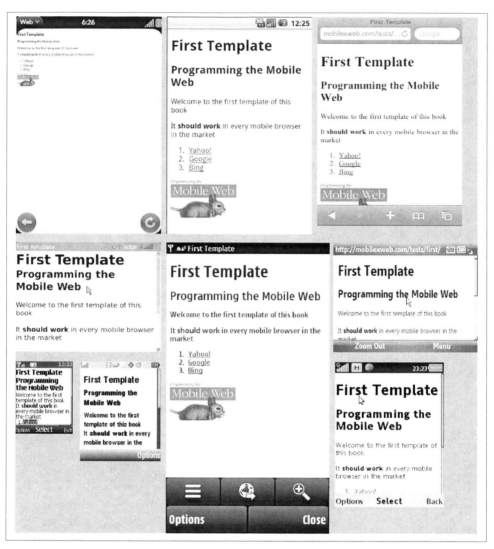

*Figure 6-5. The same template without CSS in the webOS, Android, iOS, BlackBerry 5.x, Symbian, Windows Mobile, Nokia S40 (low-end device), Motorola, and NetFront browsers.*

As these images prove, this code works on every platform. I know what you're thinking: "Hey, this is an awful experience for the iPhone." If you're tempted to throw away this book right now, wait! Give me a chance. Using this exact code, we will create a great iPhone (or other smartphone) experience in the following pages. Well, OK, there may be some little changes to the code, but not so many. Our goal will be to keep our document template as simple as this one, even for very complex HTML5 web apps.

## Markup Additions

WML, as a mobile-specific language, has many mobile-prepared tags and attributes. This is not true of XHTML MP or Basic, and that's why many developers were against WAP 2.0 in the early 2000s. Some vendors, such as Nokia, even tried to create their own markup supersets over XHTML with mobile-specific features.

The only mobile-specific addition is present in XHTML Basic 1.1, but even with the XHTML MP DOCTYPE it will work if the browser understands that markup. The addition is the attribute `inputmode`, available for the `input` and `textarea` tags; it allows us to specify input mode tokens indicating the expected type of the input characters (`latin`, `thai`, `arabic`) and modifier tokens for the text input (such as `predictOff` to deactivate predictive input). XHTML MP adds similar support with WAP CSS, which we will cover later.

WML had a `format` attribute for the `input` tag that was similar to `in putmode`. Some browsers, such as Openwave, still understand this attribute in an XHTML file.

# Mobile HTML5

Let's be clear: there is nothing officially called "Mobile HTML5" in terms of standards. We are talking about the same HTML5 as we can use on other platforms. However, there are some specific behaviors, hacks, and even tags that we will want to use when creating HTML5 documents for the mobile web.

While many developers still do not have a clear idea of exactly what HTML5 is, the W3C has created its own description, and it has reached a point where it will not add any more features to it; the W3C has also begun working on the next version, called HTML 5.1 (*http://www.w3.org/TR/html51*), which is in a very early draft state at the time of this writing. While versioning HTML5 is still a subject of much discussion in the community, the truth is that today we don't need to define a version number; we can just use features when they are compatible with the current browser.

The history of HTML5 deserves more space than I can dedicate here. To keep it brief, originally the W3C was against it and was promoting XHTML 2.0. Some W3C participants disagreed, and they split off and created a new organization called WHATWG (*http://whatwg.org*), whose purpose was discussing and creating the next generation of markup languages for the Web.

Originally called Web Applications 1.0 before HTML5, the new standard began as a couple of tags and JavaScript APIs that modern browsers should implement. Apple was one of the first companies to apply these ideas (in Safari for iPhone), trying to fill the gap created by the lack of Flash support. At that time, the term HTML5 was not yet in use.

 The W3C created the HTML5 logo to promote all technologies around the Web. You can find out more about the HTML5 logo from the W3C (*http://w3.org/html/logo*).

After a couple of years, the W3C finally gave up on XHTML 2.0 and created a new project called HTML5 based on the WHATWG discussion. It then started the normal discussion—and, let me say, necessary large steps—to arrive at a standard language. The standard is still in draft and in discussion today, but HTML5 has become a buzzword with a broad meaning. That is why WHATWG decided to change its own name for the new standard to "HTML Living Standard," indicating something that is evolving every day and doesn't have snapshots or versions. That living standard idea is more representative of what HTML5 really is today, from a community perspective: a standard in constant evolution. From the W3C's perspective, however, HTML5 is a spec that will have a limit (to be finished in 2014), and then we will be talking about other versions, such as HTML 5.1, for adding more features.

## Creating Our First HTML5 Template

HTML5 does not follow XML rules, so it's less strict in terms of syntax. The minimum HTML5 template looks like this:

```
<!DOCTYPE html>
<title>My title</title>
```

If you are wondering where the html, body, and head are, they are all optional tags in HTML5. Even if you open them, you don't need to close them, so the following code is also valid HTML5:

```
<!DOCTYPE html>
<title>My title</title>
<html>
<head>
<body>
```

Usually, a mobile HTML5 template also includes some important meta tags; we'll cover these in the next chapter.

Many of the new features in HTML5 have a fallback mechanism, meaning that, with the same code, we can provide alternative solutions with noncompatible browsers. In some cases, we can use JavaScript libraries that will also provide the same solution, known as *polyfills*. However, in the mobile web space we need to be careful about adding large Java-Script frameworks.

## Syntax Rules

Being a non-XML language, HTML5 has its own rules. The most important rules for understanding the rest of the code in this book are:

- The html, body, and head tags are optional.

- There are elements that must always be closed, such as ul, script, select, or div.

- There are elements that you can close, self-close, or not close at all, such as p, li, option, input, head, body, img, br, or link. For example, <br></br>, <br />, and <br> are equivalent.

- Element and attribute names are not case-sensitive.

- Boolean attributes exist. In those cases, you don't need to provide a value. The mere presence of the attribute (as in <input required>) indicates a true value. If you really need to define a value, then the same name as the attribute means true while anything else means false; for example, <input required="required"> means true.

- Attribute values require quotation marks (double or single) only when the value includes spaces or other special characters. Therefore, in most situations you don't need quotation marks, such as <input type=text>.

 Even though HTML5 doesn't follow XML rules, you can still stick to those rules, and it will be fine. In multiplatform mobile web development where you can support older browsers, you should stay with XML syntax so you can then reuse templates with HTML code with XHTML MP documents.

You can find a lot of resources to learn HTML5, including excellent books from O'Reilly Media and other publishers, so I won't take too much time explaining all the differences here; we'll just look at what's necessary to create our multiplatform mobile web solutions.

## New Elements

We are going to talk about the usage of new elements (elements not present in XHTML 1.0) in the following chapters. In the meantime, here's a quick list of new elements that we have in HTML5:

- Semantic block elements: `header`, `footer`, `article`, `section`, `nav`, `aside`
- Semantic inline elements: `time`, `output`, `progress`, `mark`
- Text elements: `wbr`, `ruby`
- Multimedia elements: `video`, `audio`, `canvas`

 As we'll see in Chapter 10, we can inline SVG static or animated content using an `svg` element, and it will work on mobile smartphones.

# CSS for Mobile

Web (and mobile) browsers have a great feature that makes our lives much easier in the CSS world. If we use any selector or attribute that the browser doesn't understand, the browser will just ignore it. This will be very helpful in the following pages. Usage of CSS 2.1, CSS 3.0, CSS Mobile Profile, and WAP CSS is the same; we specify CSS selectors and attributes for those selectors. The standards only tell us which selectors and attributes are supported, and we will find browsers that do not properly render standard ones and do properly render noncompatible tags.

If you are interested in having W3C-valid markup, remember that XHTML Basic 1.0 doesn't support CSS, and 1.1 added support, but only for a `style` or `link` tag with external styles. The W3C standard doesn't support the inner styles defined in the `style` attribute.

WCSS, or WAP CSS (the OMA standard that comes with XHTML MP), is a CSS 2.0 subset, like CSS MP (the W3C standard that comes with XHTML Basic). That's why we will focus here on CSS 2.0 features (and beyond). We'll begin by talking generally about "mobile CSS," and later we will see how the different mobile browsers handle each of those features.

## WCSS Extensions

The Open Mobile Alliance standard added to CSS2 some new attributes that we can use in mobile browsers. As this is how CSS defines extensions, every new attribute has a dash (-) as a prefix. We will see later that some mobile browsers also understand some nonstandard extensions, like WebKit-based browsers. But again, don't worry; we will look at compatibility attribute by attribute so you understand how to manage incompatibilities the best you can.

## Access keys

The first attribute is -wap-accesskey; it is the counterpart of the XHTML accesskey attribute. It can be used with any interactive element (generally, the a, textarea, label, input, and button tags). The possible values are the digits 0 through 9 and the special values * and #. For some browsers on devices with numerical keypads, this attribute can be used to create shortcuts to access those elements. Some browsers do nothing with it, some browsers set the focus on that element when the user presses the key, and other browsers directly fire the action associated with it (go to a link, submit a form).

 We should use only the standard keys 0–9, *, and # as access keys. We cannot assign functions to soft keys or any other special keys in HTML. WML allows us to assign links to soft keys, but this functionality has no effect in modern browsers.

We can assign the same key to only one element in the same page. That's why the -wap-accesskey attribute is useful only with ID selectors or with inline styles. You shouldn't use this attribute with element or class selectors.

The next three samples all have the same result:

```
<a href="http://mobilexweb.com" accesskey="0">Our website</a>
<input type="submit" value="Send" accesskey="9" />

<a href="http://mobilexweb.com" style="-wap-accesskey: 0">Our website
    </a>
<input type="submit"" value="Send" style="-wap-accesskey: 9" />

<style type="text/css">
#linkWeb {
    -wap-accesskey: 0;
}
#btnSubmit {
    -wap-accesskey: 9;
}
</style>

<a href="http://mobilexweb.com" id="linkWeb">Our website</a>
<input type="submit"" value="Send" id="btnSubmit" />
```

Access keys work with only a few browsers today. This is because many of them use the keypad for accelerators (shortcuts for browser functions like scrolling, going back, or reloading). That is why we can use them only if they are not the preferred or only way to access functionality on the website.

### Marquees

If you've been doing web development for a long time, like me, you probably hate the nonstandard marquee element that many people used to insert in web pages. WAP CSS revived this technique to create small animations without images that do not require Flash. A marquee is generally a text that scrolls from one side of the screen to the other, wrapping around continuously. In some mobile browsers it can contain any HTML code, including images and even tables. However, don't scroll too much heavy markup, for the sake of your visitors and the performance of your website.

To create floating, scrolling text, use any paragraph element, like p or div, define the display attribute as -wap-marquee, and assign values to some of the CSS attributes listed in Table 6-3.

*Table 6-3. Marquee WAP CSS attributes*

| Attribute | Possible values | Description |
|---|---|---|
| -wap-marquee-dir | ltr or rtl | Direction of the scrolling. Can be left to right (ltr) or right to left (rtl). |
| -wap-marquee-loop | Any number or infinite | Animation count. The infinite value creates a never-ending animation. |
| -wap-marquee-speed | slow, normal, or fast | Speed of the animation, without fine control. |
| -wap-marquee-style | scroll, slide, or alternate | Possible styles for the animation. |

The following sample shows how to use a marquee to present an offer to the user:

```
<!DOCTYPE html PUBLIC "-//WAPFORUM//DTD XHTML Mobile 1.0//EN"
    "http://www.wapforum.org/DTD/xhtml-mobile10.dtd">
<html xmlns="http://www.w3.org/1999/xhtml">
<head>
<meta http-equiv="Content-Type" content="text/html; charset=UTF-8" />
<title>Mobile Web Test</title>
<style type="text/css">
.offer {
    display: -wap-marquee;
    -wap-marquee-dir: rtl;
    -wap-marquee-speed: medium;
    -wap-marquee-loop: infinite;
    -wap-marquee-style: scroll;
}
```

```
.offer strong {
    color: red;
}
</style>
</head>

<body>
<div class="offer"><strong>Fly to the Moon</strong> Special offers this
month starting at US$145.00. Apply now and see us from the sky.</div>
<h1>TravelWithUs.com</h1>
(...)
</body>
</html>
```

The result is shown in Figure 6-6.

*Figure 6-6. A Nokia Asha showing a marquee animation in progress using standard WAP CSS.*

Now let's take a look at how browsers react to this tag. We may be tempted to use this display type to show a large amount of text in a small space, but if the mobile browser doesn't understand the marquee display, all that text will appear on the page, pushing down the important content! That is why we should consider alternative solutions for noncompatible browsers, like hiding the content. For example:

```
.offer {
    display: none;
    display: -wap-marquee;
    -wap-marquee-dir: rtl;
    -wap-marquee-speed: medium;
    -wap-marquee-loop: infinite;
    -wap-marquee-style: scroll;
}
```

In the preceding code, we first assign display: none to remove the text from the display. Then we assign display: -wap-marquee. If the browser understands the WAP CSS marquee styles, it will replace the none value. If not, it will just ignore the second setting and the none will win. We can also apply this style to a marquee HTML element, so it can work in all possible marquee-compatible browsers. The problem is that the code will not validate against standards (if we are interested in that).

Try to avoid using marquees for important information. You may want to use them to reduce the space taken up by information that is not directly relevant, or to have some kind of animation free of plug-ins. Avoid the usage of links, images, or any other nontext markup inside a marquee, and create an alternative CSS stylesheet for noncompatible devices.

### CSS form extensions

Another great enhancement in WAP CSS is the ability to define useful information for form input. We will talk about this in depth later, but for now let's see what extensions are included in the standard. They are listed in Table 6-4.

*Table 6-4. WAP CSS form extension attributes*

| Attribute | Possible values | Description |
|-----------|-----------------|-------------|
| -wap-input-format | Complex pattern (see Chapter 11) | Defines the pattern of the text. Can be applied to text fields, password fields, and textareas. |
| -wap-input-required | true or false | If true, requires the user to provide some content before exiting the field. Can be applied to text fields, password fields, and textareas. This attribute has precedence over the format attribute in the input tag, if both are defined. |

# CSS3

CSS version 3.0 is now split into different subgroups of standards. Therefore, we have basic CSS3 support and a group of other sub-standards in the W3C, such as:

- CSS Background and Borders
- CSS 2D & 3D Transforms
- CSS Transitions
- CSS Animations
- CSS Columns
- CSS Flexible Box Layout
- CSS Fonts
- CSS Device Adaptation
- CSS Regions

# HTML5 Compatibility Levels

HTML5 in mobile devices is usually thought of as a mix of W3C standards, drafts, and de facto practices, including HTML, CSS, and JavaScript APIs. The W3C maintains the *Mobile Web Initiative* (*http://w3.org/mobile*), where you can find some useful links, discussions, and best practices.

 In the following chapters, we will analyze all the HTML5 JavaScript APIs that we can use on mobile web platforms, including resources to understand current compatibility.

W3C discussion groups have reached some conclusions, including the following resources:

- Mobile Web Best Practices 1.0 (*http://www.w3.org/TR/mobile-bp/*), from July 2008
- Mobile Web Applications Best Practices 1.0 (*http://www.w3.org/TR/mwabp/*), from December 2010
- Standards for Web Applications on Mobile (*http://www.w3.org/Mobile/mobile-web-app-state/*), current state and roadmap, updated frequently

## Testing Your Browser

One of the biggest problems with HTML5 is that every browser has different compatibility in terms of the standards supported. While there is no standard to define how "HTML5 compatible" a browser is, there are some initiatives in the community to solve this problem.

### HTML5 Test

The most-used resource today to measure HTML5 support is *html5test.com*. This website will execute a test suite on your browser and give you a score based on the APIs/features supported, plus a bonus score for any optional features supported (such as video codecs). In my opinion, this website is primarily useful for comparing different versions of the same browser, as in Figure 6-7; if you compare two different browsers the temptation is to interpret a higher score as indicating better compatibility, but the problem is that this algorithm does not consider which APIs are most useful to you—maybe Browser A has a better score than Browser B, but only Browser B supports the API you are looking for.

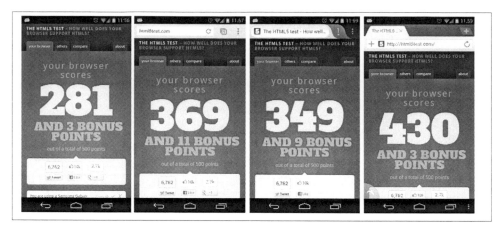

*Figure 6-7. Different Android browsers on the same device will have different scores on the HTML5 test.*

 HTML5 Test does not test all the mobile-specific APIs. Therefore, the score on your mobile phone will not take into consideration some of these standards.

### Ringmark

Ringmark (*http://rng.io*) is an open source mobile browser testing suite that will give you not an exact score, but a compatibility level (a ring) regarding your current support. The test has three different rings covering several standards and features that a browser may support. If one feature on one ring fails, the suite will not execute the next ring's tests.

 Later in this book, we will analyze all the APIs and features that Ringmark tests.

Ringmark will identify a browser as being Ring 0, Ring 1, or Ring 2 compatible. Therefore, if you are creating an app or a game, you can say that it is compatible only with Ring 1 browsers, for example, so you will know which APIs and features will work properly.

 If you want to test your own mobile browser, just point it to *rng.io*.

At the time of this writing, no mainstream mobile browser has reached the Ring 1 mark. The first Ring 1 compatible browser was Dolphin for Android, released in August 2012, as seen in Figure 6-8. The prize for the first Ring 1 compatible default installed browser was claimed by BlackBerry with the new BlackBerry 10 platform at the beginning of 2013.

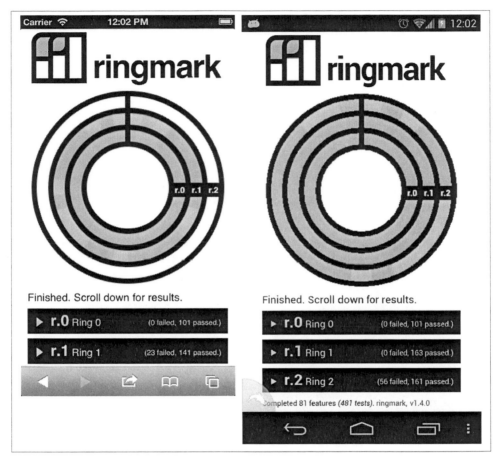

*Figure 6-8. Ringmark is a mobile browser HTML5 testing suite; here we can see that Safari on iOS 6 reaches Ring 0, and Dolphin for Android reaches Ring 1.*

 It's OK to be a little confused after reading about all the incompatibilities. This is just an introduction to general and mobile-specific standards—just theoretical information. Actual concrete practice will make it much clearer!

# CHAPTER 7

# Basics of Mobile HTML5

The standards are sometimes utopias, while the real world is something different. Many devices officially support standards, but in practice some feature is missing; many other devices add support for more technologies besides what is covered by the standards.

They are decent resources, though, and they contain much good advice for multiplatform mobile web development. We will take that a bit further here, testing every feature in the standards (and some nonstandard ones) to draw real conclusions about their usage.

We will go through a typical document, from the heading to the body structure, looking at the most common design patterns for document structure, including forms, frames, tables, links, and images. We will test every possible solution for each topic on every mobile platform so we can get some useful information about what we can and cannot use.

## The Document Head

The head part of a mobile web document will be very similar to that in a desktop web document, with the addition of some new meta tags useful only in mobile browsers.

### Title

First we'll define a title, as for any other web page. The space available for the title in a mobile browser is small compared with a desktop browser (Table 7-1 gives the average lengths of the titles displayed on the different phone-factor platforms). The page title is used as the heading at the top of the screen on some devices; other devices also use the title as the default text for bookmarks and the history list.

*Table 7-1. Average characters used in titles on smartphone platforms*

| Browser/platform | Average number of chars used in titles |
|---|---|
| Safari on iOS | 40 chars in portrait and 60 in landscape (75 on 4.5" devices). Hidden after the user scrolls the page. Hidden in full-screen web apps. |
| Android browser | After 2.0, titles are not displayed on the screen. |
| Chrome for Android | Titles are not displayed on the screen. You can see the first 15 chars on the window list, or tabs on tablets. |
| Internet Explorer | No usage. |
| Symbian/S60 | 35 chars in portrait, 20 in landscape. |
| Nokia Series 40 | 20 chars in third edition.<br>No usage in fifth and sixth editions. |
| Firefox | 15 chars in portrait and 50 in landscape, replacing the URL when the page loads. |
| BlackBerry | 15–30 chars, depending on screen width. |
| webOS | No usage up to webOS 1.3. In webOS 1.4, the title appears only if the user scrolls down from the top. |
| NetFront | No usage. |
| UC browser | 10 chars in portrait and 30 in landscape, replacing the URL when the page loads. |
| Opera Mobile | Depends on the screen, between 20 and 60 chars. |
| Opera Mini | Depends on the screen, between 20 and 60 chars. |

Every mobile title needs to be:

*Meaningful*

Avoid duplicate titles for every page of your mobile site using only your company name. However, on your home or entry page, don't use "Home Page," use your company or product name and keep it very short. This may be the most bookmarked page.

*Short*

Keep the title between four and eight words long. If mentioning the name of your company, do that last (for example, "Big Mac - Meals in McDonald's"). Use small words first; some old devices truncate the title after 10 or 12 characters.

*Concise*

Don't waste words. For example, avoid using "Mobile" in the title; the user knows that she is using a mobile device.

When creating full-screen experiences or native web apps, usually the title seems useless. However, there are two reasons why you should always add a title element: 1) some APIs, such as dialogs and permission-based APIs, will use it as a dialog window title; and 2) the title element is mandatory if we want to validate against HTML5.

## Website Icons

In the early 2000s, everyone rushed to insert *favicon.ico* files in their websites' root files to see how the icons would be added to Internet Explorer's address bar. Today, in the desktop web those icons are more useful for tab iconography. But what about in mobile browsers?

In HTML, the standard way to add an icon file is to use the following `link` tag:

```
<link rel="icon" href="favicon.png">
```

Originally, the icons were in Windows ICO format (similar to BMP), but these files are difficult to export from well-known graphic editors and are not optimized in size. Today, you can use PNG for mobile compatibility. Originally the icon size had to be 16×16 pixels, but now they can be any square size and the browser will resize them. Usually, the preferred size for this icon is 32×32 pixels.

 X-Icon Editor (*http://www.xiconeditor.com*) is an online HTML5-based icon creator tool specially created for the Internet Explorer ICO format. When you download the editor, you can upload your PNG icon and it will be exported to ICO format. It is recommended that you start with a 64×64-pixel icon.

Internet Explorer 9 for Windows Phone 7.5 ignores the icon, but IE10 uses it for tablets and other devices running Windows 8. It ignores the `rel="icon"` definition and accepts `rel="shortcut icon"` instead; also, the icon must be in ICO format. Therefore, we should also include the definition:

```
<link rel="shortcut icon" href="favicon.ico">
```

 If you are creating XHTML documents—for example, using XHTML Mobile Profile—remember that you need to close every element (as in `<link ... />`). In HTML5 self-closing is not necessary.

Browser support for icons varies. As you can see in Figure 7-1, some tablet browsers, such as Safari on the iPad, do not use the tab icon, while other browsers, such as Google Chrome IE10 for Windows 8, do.

*Figure 7-1. Some tablet browsers use the icon for the tab, while others—such as Safari on the iPad—ignore it completely.*

SVG is an excellent icon format because it is resolution-independent. However, while some desktop browsers support this format, it is not yet supported on mobile devices. PNG is the recommended solution for most browsers, other than Internet Explorer (IE supports the ICO format only, and it may include different-resolution icons in the same file).

In Figure 7-2 we can see different mobile browsers using the website icon.

*Figure 7-2. The website icon is rendered on some mobile browsers and ignored on others.*

Some browsers support bookmarking, and others also support adding icons to the Home screen. Let's talk first about bookmarking. Some platforms don't associate any image with the bookmark, some platforms take a screenshot of your website (as seen in Figure 7-3) and use that as the icon, and some others use the website icon.

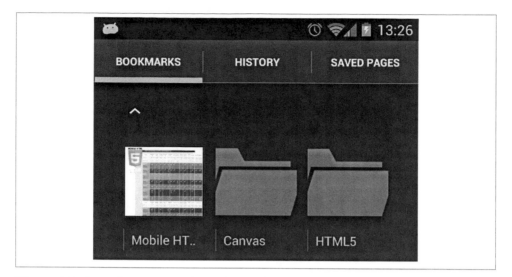

*Figure 7-3. Some browsers, such as the Android browser on Android 4.1, will take a screenshot of the current page and add that to bookmarks instead of using the website icon.*

In Table 7-2 we can see current browser compatibility with website icons.

*Table 7-2. Icon display compatibility table*

| Browser/platform | Usage on toolbar | Usage on tab/ window list | Preferred format and size (px) |
|---|---|---|---|
| Safari on iOS | No | No | |
| Android browser | In the URL bar | No | PNG or ICO 32×32 |
| Chrome for Android | No | Yes | PNG or ICO 32×32 |
| Nokia Browser for Symbian | No | No | |
| Nokia Browser for S40 | No | No | |
| BlackBerry < 7.1 | In the title area (some devices) | No | PNG or ICO 16×16 |
| BlackBerry PlayBook and BB10 | Yes | Yes | PNG or ICO 16×16 |
| NetFront | No | No | |
| Internet Explorer | No in IE9, yes in IE10 for Windows 8 | No | ICO multiresolution 64×64 and 32×32 |
| Opera Mobile | Some versions | No | PNG or ICO 32×32 |
| Opera Mini | Some versions | No | PNG or ICO 32×32 |
| Firefox for Android | Yes | Yes | PNG or ICO 32×32 |
| webOS browser | No | No | |

# Home Screen Icons

Some platforms support a way to create shortcut icons for the device's Home screen or applications menu. For this purpose, they usually ignore the website icon because of its low resolution.

## Apple Touch Icons

Safari on iOS was the first platform to support Home screen icons, and for that purpose Apple created another type of icon, known as a *Web Clip*. Safari on iOS requires a square PNG file (with no transparency preferred) using a `link` element with a `rel` value of `apple-touch-icon` or `apple-touch-icon-precomposed`, so it can coexist with the previous icon declarations:

```
<link rel="apple-touch-icon" href="iphone_icon.png">
```

If we use the `apple-touch-icon` version the icon will automatically be given rounded borders, a shadow, and a reflective shine, like the one shown in the middle of Figure 7-4. If you don't want your icon to have the reflective shine effect, instead use the following meta tag alternative:

```
<link rel="apple-touch-icon-precomposed" href="iphone_icon.png">
```

*Figure 7-4. The original iOS icon file, the final appearance once the website has been added to the Home screen using the nonprecomposed version, and the icon using the precomposed link version.*

Up to iOS 3.1 (known as iPhone OS at that time), 57×57 pixels was the only available size for the Web Clip. Starting with iOS 3.2, 72×72 appeared as the icon size for the original iPad. Before iOS 4, server-side techniques were necessary to deliver iPhone or iPad icons using the same `link` element.

 The `rel` HTML attribute accepts multiple value declarations using spaces. However, Safari on iOS will ignore the whole `link` element if we try to provide more than one `rel` value at the same time, such as `rel="icon apple-touch-icon"`.

For iOS 4.0 and newer, Safari supports a `sizes` attribute that we can apply to different link definitions. The value defines the possible icon sizes that we can use on different iOS devices with different pixel densities. For example, devices with higher DPIs (such as the iPhone 5) need an icon size of 114×114 pixels, while high-resolution iPad devices (such as a third-generation iPad) require a size of 144×144 pixels.

If we don't provide different sizes, the device will resize the icon with quality loss.

You should always provide an icon with 90-degree corners for iOS. Safari will add rounded corners to your icon by default. If you provide an icon with an alpha transparent background, Safari will use a black background by default.

If we want to provide Home screen icons for every iOS version, the code for `apple-touch-icon` will look like this:

```
<-- iPad icons -->
<link rel="apple-touch-icon" href="icons/72.png" sizes="72x72">
<link rel="apple-touch-icon" href="icons/144.png" sizes="144x144">

<!-- iPhone and iPod touch icons -->
<link rel="apple-touch-icon" href="icons/57.png" sizes="57x57">
<link rel="apple-touch-icon" href="icons/114.png" sizes="114x114">
```

While you can provide only one big icon without a `sizes` definition and Safari will resize it, remember you are delivering a big file for older devices, which may cause performance issues. Also, the icon might not look good on lower-resolution devices.

If more than one icon appears to be valid for the current context, Safari will take the last one. Therefore, up to iOS 3.2 (which does not support the `sizes` attribute), the last declaration will be taken.

If we don't provide one version of the iOS sizes, Safari will use the next-lower version. For example, if we provide only 57-, 72-, and 114-pixel versions, the third-generation iPad (expecting 144 pixels) will use the 114-pixel version.

## When Is the Web Clip Icon Retrieved?

The appropriate icon for the current device is not retrieved when the page loads. Instead, on iOS 6 and beyond, the icon is retrieved when the user presses the Share icon before selecting "Add to Home Screen," as seen in Figure 7-5. Prior to iOS 6, the icon is retrieved from the server when the user selects "Add to Home Screen." The Share icon, which looks like a box with an arrow jumping out of it, is located in the bottom bar on iPhone and iPod devices and the top bar on the iPad (see Figure 7-6).

With that in mind, there is a possibility that the page will have loaded entirely, but when the user tries to add it to the Home screen, the network will not be available anymore. In that case, the icon will be replaced by a screenshot. If you want to force the icon, you can pre-cache it using typical image caching techniques or using a data URI.

In Chapter 10, we will get further into the data URI protocol; for now you just need to know that it means that the icon will be embedded inside the HTML page and will not be retrieved by a different network request. The advantage is that the user will have the icon immediately and will not get the strange effect of seeing a screenshot of the website being replaced by the icon after a while. The main disadvantage is that the icon is always inside the HTML and there is no cache opportunity.

*Figure 7-5. This is the process on iOS 6 for adding a page to the Home screen—once installed, it looks like any other native app on the operating system.*

*Figure 7-6. On the iPad the add to Home screen process is similar to the iPhone, but the Share icon inside Safari is in the top bar as opposed to the bottom bar on the iPhone and iPod touch.*

If you don't define the `apple-touch-icon` or `apple-touch-icon-precomposed` link element, Safari will look for the existence of the file anyway on the server when the user tries to add the page to the Home screen. From iOS 4.0, the search algorithm will look for the files in the following order:

- */apple-touch-icon-<size>x<size>-precomposed.png*
- */apple-touch-icon-<size>x<size>.png*
- */apple-touch-icon-precomposed.png*
- */apple-touch-icon.png*

Therefore, if an iPhone 5 is accessing your website and you don't provide an Apple-specific Home screen icon, the browser will try */apple-touch-icon-114x114-precomposed.png* first, and then continue with the other three options. If there is no file available on the server, Safari will take a screenshot of your website and use that as the icon.

If you don't provide a Home screen icon though a link element, Safari will make four requests to your server anyway that will generate 404 error codes.

**Icon titles.** The title that appears below the icon, as seen in the last sequence in Figure 7-5, is automatically taken from the `title` element of your HTML document. The text will be cropped if it has more than 13 characters; therefore, if you have a long title, you need to be careful and make sure the first 13 characters are the title you want on the Home screen. If necessary, you can pad it with spaces to control the display.

In iOS 6 and beyond, a new meta tag appears to solve this problem, allowing you to provide an alternative title for the Home screen. We will cover iOS web app meta tags later in this book, but for now, here's how to provide alternative text for the Home screen icon using the `apple-mobile-web-app-title` meta tag:

```
<meta name="apple-mobile-web-app-title" content="My App Name">
```

### Other platforms using Apple's link

Some versions of the Android, BlackBerry, and Nokia browsers use the `apple-touch-icon` link element (yes, even using the Apple name).

**Nokia Browser for Symbian.** Since version 8.3.1 of the Symbian browser, Nokia has supported the `apple-touch-icon` link element and also a `nokia-touch-icon` link element with the same syntax. Using the `nokia`-prefixed one, we can differentiate Symbian icons from other platform icons. Symbian icons should be 54×54 pixels.

We can add support for Symbian icons as follows:

```
<!-- Nokia Symbian -->
<link rel="nokia-touch-icon" href="icons/54.png">
```

**Nokia Browser for MeeGo.** The browser available on the Nokia N9 also supports the `apple-touch-icon` link element and expects an icon size of 80×80 pixels, reading the `sizes` attribute when the user adds the page to the Home screen (as seen in Figure 7-7). There is no support for this icon in the Symbian or S40 edition of the browser.

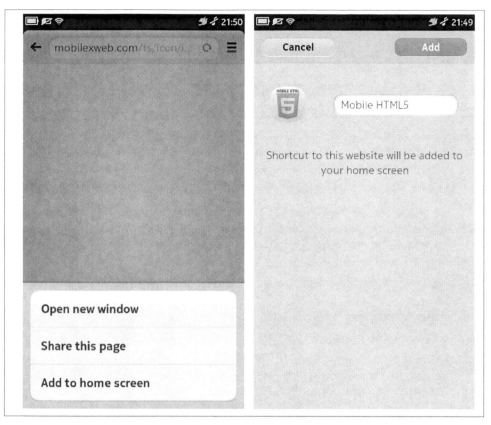

*Figure 7-7. The Nokia Browser for MeeGo (available on the Nokia N9) supports 80×80-pixel icons using the same apple-touch-icon declaration, but be aware that your icon will be inside some Nokia-specific rounded corners.*

We can add support for icons in the Nokia Browser for Meego using:

```
<!-- Nokia MeeGo -->
<link rel="apple-touch-icon" href="icons/80.png" sizes="80x80">
```

**BlackBerry browser.** The BlackBerry browser for devices running OS versions 7.0 and 7.1 also supports the apple-touch-icon link element when adding a website to the Home screen, but it does not support the sizes attribute. The BlackBerry browser supports two different icon sizes, depending on the current device's resolution: 68×68 and 92×92 pixels. However, because it ignores the sizes attribute, in the end it will just take the last definition of a series and resize it if necessary, as seen in Figure 7-8.

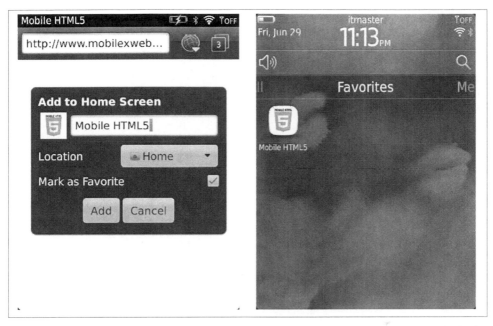

*Figure 7-8. The BlackBerry browser on OS 7.x supports the apple-touch-icon link element but ignores the sizes attribute; it will take the last declaration and resize the icon to 68×68 or 92×92 pixels.*

The browser on BlackBerry 10 devices also allows us to define the icon for the Home Screen menu using the Apple's syntax. The recommended icon size is 150×150 pixels.

Here's how to define the icon for BlackBerry devices:

```
<!-- iOS and Nokia icons -->
...
<!-- BlackBerry icon, last declaration -->
<link rel="apple-touch-icon" href="icons/bb.png" sizes="others">
```

**Android browser.**   From version 1.5 to version 2.1,the Android browser supports the icon link and the apple-touch-icon-precomposed link; from version 2.2 it also supports the apple-touch-icon link. Android ignores the sizes attribute, like the BlackBerry browser. Therefore, if we want to provide an icon for iOS devices and a different icon for Android in the same HTML, we can use the following trick:

```
<!-- Android icon precomposed so it takes precedence -->
<link rel="apple-touch-icon-precomposed" href="icons/android.png"
    sizes="1x1">
```

Android devices ignore the sizes attribute, but if the browser finds different icon declarations, it will take the last one. iOS devices after 4.0 will ignore the sizes="1x1" link because it has an invalid value.

When you have different declarations, the precomposed declaration has priority. If you don't have any precomposed declarations, Android will use the first link available and not the last, unlike the BlackBerry browser.

Providing only a website icon with rel="icon" or providing a small Home screen icon makes the Android browser use a small icon inside a standard bookmark icon, as seen in Figure 7-9.

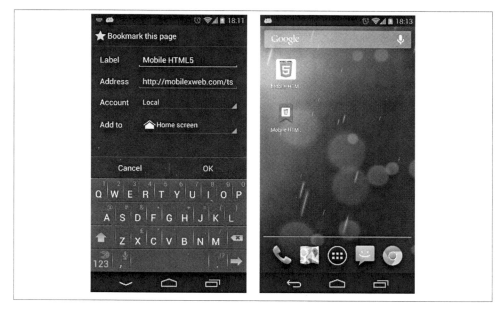

*Figure 7-9. The process to add an icon to the Home screen on the Android browser may vary per Android version and manufacturer.*

The Android icon sizes for the Home screen (Launcher) are:

- Low-density screens: 36×36 pixels
- Medium-density screens: 48×48 pixels
- High-density screens: 72×72 pixels
- Ultra-high-density screens: 96×96 pixels

There is no way to define four different icons in HTML right now. Therefore, the best solution is usually to deliver a 96×96 icon, which will be automatically resized as necessary; we can also use a server-side technique to provide the right one, but this probably involves more work than it's worth. From version 3.0, the Android browser adds rounded corners to the icon.

Google Chrome for Android doesn't have a way to add icons to the Home screen at the time of this writing. Firefox for Android supports adding a bookmark to the Home screen, but it has no support for apple-touch-icon. Instead, it uses the rel="icon" link for the Home screen icon, if it has enough resolution. Opera for Android always uses a default icon when adding a website to the Home screen.

In Android the applications menu has icon support, as well as the home screen. There is no way to add an icon in the applications menu using this technique, though. You need to create a native application to insert an icon into the applications menu.

Android 2.3 and later do not have an option for "Add to Home screen." However, on 2.3, if the user adds the page to his Bookmarks, there is an "Add shortcut to Home" contextual option. On 3.x and 4.x the user can add a Bookmark and select the Home screen as the destination.

 As device manufacturers may customize the Android browser, there are some versions on some devices that will never take your icon and will always insert a default bookmark icon on the Home screen.

### Windows Start tiles

The Metro user interface available in Windows Phone and Windows 8 includes a way for Internet Explorer to "pin" a website to the Start screen—a sort of Home screen. The icons are called *tiles*, and the way to define what is shown there differs according to the Windows and IE versions.

 Opera for desktops has a way to define an icon through the link element—even with apple-touch-icon—for the Speed dial access (a sort of Opera Home screen). With meta tags and/or HTTP headers, we can even customize how the icon and mini view render, and we can update it frequently. Unfortunately, this feature is not enabled at the time of this writing for Opera Mobile.

In Windows Phone 7.x, there is no official way to define the tile. When the user pins a website, the browser will automatically take a screenshot of a portion of the rendered HTML. The trick to define your own icon is to create a separate page that includes the icon you want. Google, for example, will suggest that the user add it to the Home screen, then take the user to a second page containing the desired icon, as seen in Figure 7-10; IE then takes the screenshot and creates the final icon.

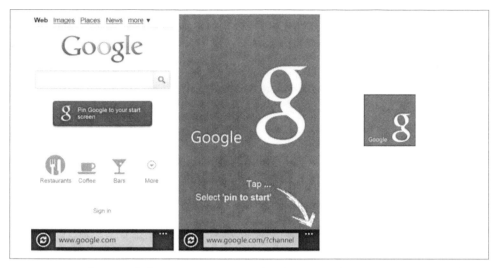

*Figure 7-10. The Google home page creates a hack to provide its customized tile for the Start screen on Windows Phone 7.x.*

In Internet Explorer 10, from Windows 8, we can define our own tile icon and the background image to be used in the Start screen when the user pins the site, as we can see in Figure 7-11. To do so we use the `msapplication-TileImage` and `msapplication-TileColor` meta tags:

```
<meta name="msapplication-TileImage" content="tile.png">
<meta name="msapplication-TileColor" content="#ef0303">
```

*Figure 7-11. Internet Explorer 10 allows us to "pin" websites to the Start screen and define our own tile icon and preferences.*

The tile image should be a 144×144-pixel PNG file, preferably with a transparent background; the tile color accepts as a value a CSS color that should be the main color of your logo or visual presence. We can use hexadecimal RGB values (such as #333333), named values (such as red), or CSS functions, such as rgb. If you don't provide a color, IE will use the most prominent color of your website icon or your tile image.

 To fit in with Metro styles, you can just use a small white or black icon over a plain color instead of a big colorful image.

The image and color you specify are also used in history searches and other places inside Internet Explorer.

 The IE10 tile size of 144×144 is the same as the high-resolution iPad's icon size. However, be careful using the same icon for both platforms, as the idea behind how they are rendered on the screen is really different.

Internet Explorer 10 will use the title of the current page for the tile's title. If we want to define a different one, we can use the `title` meta tag.

**Live badge notifications.** Windows 8 includes the ability to update the badge number for a tile in the Start screen, so it becomes a *live tile*. Internet Explorer will poll for updates for pinned sites if we provide the right details.

The first action is to create a badge XML file, using a predefined template. This is a really simple XML file that defines the current badge value (number) to show inside the tile. Of course, we can make a dynamic XML file.

The XML looks like this:

```
<?xml version="1.0" encoding="utf-8" ?>
<badge value="5" />
```

Then we define the live badge notification settings, using an `msapplication-badge` meta tag. We provide the polling frequency and the badge XML URL:

```
<meta name="msapplication-badge"
      content="frequency=1440;polling-uri=http://mysite.com/badge.xml">
```

The possible values for `frequency` are:

- 30 for 30 minute polling
- 60 for 1 hour polling
- 360 for 6 hours polling
- 720 for 12 hours polling
- 1440 for 1 day polling (default value)

### Summary of Home screen icon compatibility

Table 7-3 explores browser compatibility for Home screen icons in HTML documents, including sizes and implementation method. If you want to support all of these browsers in the same HTML, you can use the following snippet, in this specific order:

```
<!-- iPad high-resolution -->
<link rel="apple-touch-icon" href="icon_144.png" sizes="144x144">
<!-- iPhone/iPod high-resolution -->
<link rel="apple-touch-icon" href="icon_114.png" sizes="114x114">
<!-- Nokia N9 -->
<link rel="apple-touch-icon" href="icon_80.png" sizes="80x80">
<!-- iPad low-resolution -->
<link rel="apple-touch-icon" href="icon_72.png" sizes="72x72">
<!-- iPhone/iPod low-resolution -->
<link rel="apple-touch-icon" href="icon_57.png" sizes="57x57">
<!-- Nokia Symbian -->
<link rel="nokia-touch-icon" href="icons_54.png">
```

```
<!-- BlackBerry 7.x -->
<link rel="apple-touch-icon" href="icon_92.png" sizes="1x1">
<!-- Android Browser (and also iOS 3.2 and older) -->
<link rel="apple-touch-icon-precomposed" href="icon_96.png"
      sizes="1x1">

<!-- Internet Explorer 10 icon -->
<meta name="msapplication-TileImage" content="tile_144.png">
<meta name="msapplication-TileColor" content="#ef0303">
```

*Table 7-3. Home screen icon display compatibility table*

| Browser/platform | Supported link rel types | Supports sizes attribute | Icon sizes to provide |
| --- | --- | --- | --- |
| Safari on iOS | apple-touch-icon and apple-touch-icon-precomposed | Yes | 57×57 for iPhone and iPod touch low resolution, 72×72 for iPad low resolution, 114×114 for iPhone and iPod touch high resolution, 144×144 for iPad high resolution |
| Android browser 1.5 to 2.1 | apple-touch-icon-precomposed | No | 72×72 (will be resized on some devices) |
| Android browser 2.1, 3.x, and 4.x | apple-touch-icon and apple-touch-icon-precomposed | No | 96×96 (will be resized on some devices) |
| Nokia Browser for Symbian | apple-touch-icon, nokia-touch-icon, and touch-icon | No | 54×54 |
| Nokia Browser for MeeGo | apple-touch-icon and apple-touch-icon-precomposed | Yes | 80×80 |
| BlackBerry 7.x and 10 | apple-touch-icon and apple-touch-icon-precomposed | No | 92×92 (will be resized on some devices) 150×150 for BlackBerry 10 |
| Firefox for Android | icon | No | 96×96 (will be resized on some devices) |
| Internet Explorer 10 | No link, uses meta tag | No | 144×144 (background color can be defined) |

 The HTML5 specification supports the sizes attribute for the `<link rel="icon">` element with a different syntax from the Apple solution, but at the time of this writing no mobile web browser is using this feature.

### Native and installed web app icons

In Chapter 16, we will see how to deal with icons for native and installed web apps through package metadata.

## The Viewport

We talked about the MIME type and DOCTYPE in the last chapter. As you saw, these are very helpful in telling browsers that documents are prepared for mobile delivery. However, this is not enough for mobile browsers that can read any desktop website. Those browsers treat the pages differently if they are for desktop users or are optimized for mobile devices. The differences are in the initial zoom scale and some possible changes in the layout.

If you are creating a mobile-optimized version of your website, you need to tell the browsers to be aware of this. The most common approach to say to the browser, "Hey, I'm a mobile website" is to use a `viewport` declaration.

### The problem

The `viewport` is the area in which the page fits. The W3C defines it as "a window or other viewing area on the screen through which users consult a document." In classic web development, the viewport was usually exactly the current browser window.

 Some mobile browsers, such as Safari on iPhone and iPod, define a default value of 980 pixels for the viewport width. You should redefine this if you want to take control of how many pixels you are going to use on the screen.

The W3C defines the `canvas` as "the space where the formatting structure is rendered." The canvas is conceptually infinite, so we can define a width of 10,000 pixels, and it usually works. Different algorithms can define the canvas's limits, depending on the browser, how we are defining an element's dimensions, and its content (such as an image greater than the current viewport's size).

If the canvas is larger than the viewport, browsers usually add scroll bars and implement panning behaviors on mobile devices.

In classic browsers, if you shrink the window, the viewport shrinks. In mobile browsers, starting with Safari for iPhone in 2007, that's not what happens. In mobile browsers, there is no "window" concept. Therefore, as the iPhone 5 has a screen width of 640 pixels and the iPhone 3GS has a screen width of 320 pixels, it seems logical to assume that the viewport—the area available for your content—is 640 pixels wide on the iPhone 5 and 320 pixels wide on the 3GS. That's not true.

In Figure 7-12, the Apple website is using the default viewport. Therefore, on the iPhone 3GS and iPhone 5 the website is being rendered as if it were a 980 pixel-wide window on a desktop, shrunk to fit the smaller screen sizes.

*Figure 7-12. Apple.com has no mobile website or viewport declaration, so Safari defines a desktop-like viewport, using a width of 980 pixels, even though the iPhone 3GS (left) has a screen width of 320 pixels and the iPhone 5 (right) has a width of 640 pixels.*

The viewport's default size may vary per browser, but it has no direct relationship with the screen's width, as on desktops.

Safari on iOS (for all devices, including the iPad) has a default value of 980 pixels wide for the viewport. That means that if we render an image that is 980 pixels wide, it will be scaled down to fit the available width on every iPhone and iPod touch on the market. It also means that if we define a body's child element as 100% width it will be rendered as 980 pixels wide in the canvas, if there are no margins and no padding.

You may be wondering why a default value of 980 is used, when the real widths are 320 or 640 pixels. The answer is that Safari on the iPhone/iPod believes that your website is optimized for desktops by default, and usually all desktop websites work properly in a 980-pixel-wide browser window. Of course, there are not 980 real pixels on the iPhone in portrait mode; therefore, Safari scales the page to fit the current real width.

In mobile browsers, the viewport concept has been divided in two:

- The *initial viewport* or *device viewport* is the "real" viewport that the current screen has, without any rules applied. This is like the classic concept of the viewport available on most desktop browsers (for example, 320 pixels wide on the iPhone 3GS).

- The *actual viewport* or *layout viewport* is the current viewport, imaginary at some point, that was applied by the browser because of its default behavior or the developer's definition—for example, 980 pixels wide on the iPhone and iPod, if we don't override the defaults. This is the important viewport from a CSS and HTML perspective.

From a designer and developer's perspective, it's like having a 980 pixel-wide browser window that someone has applied the *Honey, I Shrunk the Kids* machine to. Therefore, to get a horizontal scroll bar we need to define an element with a width greater than 980 pixels (in this particular case), ensuring that the canvas will be larger than the actual viewport.

 Before Safari on iOS, all mobile browsers defined the actual viewport as the initial viewport. Therefore, as the screens on mobile devices are usually smaller than desktop windows, websites that were not mobile-optimized had horizontal scrolling (the canvas was larger than the viewport).

When the actual viewport is a different size than the initial viewport, a formula is applied to the dimensions to determine how the canvas is rendered. First, the viewport relationship needs to be calculated—that is, the initial viewport size divided by the current viewport size.

For example, if the width of the initial viewport is 320 and the width of the current viewport is 980, the calculation for the initial zoom factor equals 0.3265. That is the ratio of the zoom that is being applied to the canvas when it is rendered on the first load.

 To simplify the problem, some mobile browsers change the current viewport size if the canvas doesn't fit inside, overriding defaults or developer declarations. Therefore, if you change the canvas dimensions—for example, increasing the size of an image—the current viewport size will be increased and the zoom factor will be recalculated, resulting in an automatic zoom-out behavior. Usually, the default limit for a zoom-out operation is the bigger of the current canvas size and the current viewport size.

If you're confused, just give me a couple more minutes. When the user zooms in or out using the pinch gesture or any other zoom gesture (such as double tap), the zoom ratio is changed from the original calculation, and then scroll bars may appear. On mobile browsers scroll bars are applied not in the actual viewport, but to the initial viewport. To understand how this works, Figure 7-13 shows a diagram of what is happening in the case of a canvas larger than the actual viewport that is being applied on a different initial value. An example might be a 1,500-pixel image being drawn on a 980-pixel actual viewport that is shown on a 320-pixel initial viewport.

> *Initial viewport* and *current viewport* are names defined by the W3C CSS Device Adaptation group, while *device viewport* and *layout viewport* are names defined by the community on the Web for the same concepts.

### Viewport declaration

While some browsers have a default current viewport size and others calculate it from the current canvas size, we have a method to define our own specific current viewport size though a meta tag. This method was invented by Apple on the original iPhone, and after that it was cloned by almost every modern smartphone and tablet browser out there.

For the near future, the W3C is trying to standardize it through the CSS Device Adaptation standard (*http://dev.w3.org/csswg/css-device-adapt*). The W3C is trying to move the declaration to CSS instead of using a meta tag, as we will see later.

The meta declaration follows the following syntax:

```
<meta name="viewport" content="{declaration}">
```

The {*declaration*} should be replaced with one or more *attribute*: *value* declarations, comma-separated.

> You can think about the viewport width definition as defining a logical window size that will be used on all compatible devices, regardless of real screen size: it is a way to normalize your design to one "virtual screen."

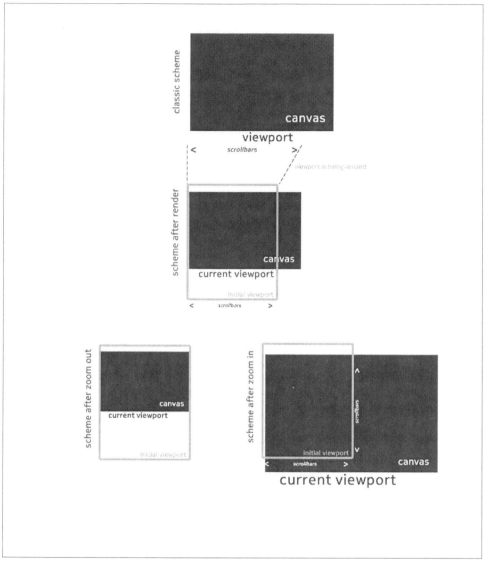

*Figure 7-13. Some browsers will increase the current viewport size if the canvas is larger than the defined value, to simplify the operation.*

You can specify the current viewport's width or height, and it can be larger or smaller than the total visible area of the screen (the initial viewport). This is where the initial scale and zoom features of the mobile browser come into play. If you are creating a mobile-friendly website, it shouldn't need to be zoomed in or out, so you can say to the browser that you want to start with a scale of 1:1 (current viewport = initial viewport = visible area).

The content of the tag can be a comma-separated list of one or more of the attributes listed in Table 7-4.

*Table 7-4. Viewport metadata attributes*

| Attribute | Possible values | Description |
|---|---|---|
| `width` | Integer value (in CSS pixels) or the constant `device-width` | Defines the viewport width |
| `height` | Integer alue (in CSS pixels) or the constant `device-height` | Defines the viewport height |
| `initial-scale` | Floating value (0.1 to *n*); 1.0 is no zoom | Defines the initial zoom scale of the viewport |
| `user-scalable` | no or yes | Defines whether we will allow the user to zoom in and out in the viewport |
| `minimum-scale` | Floating value (0.1 to *n*); 1.0 is no scale | Defines the minimum zoom scale of the viewport |
| `maximum-scale` | Floating value (0.1 to *n*); 1.0 is no scale | Defines the maximum zoom scale of the viewport |
| `target-densitydpi` | Integer value (70 to 400) in DPI, or one of the constants `device-dpi`, `high-dpi`, `medium-dpi`, or `low-dpi` | Defines how to manage different resolutions regarding the viewport's width |

You can define a viewport with a fixed size (in case you are showing a desktop-friendly website), or with a size relative to the visible area. The most common approach for our mobile template is to define the `width` as `device-width`:

```
<meta name="viewport" content="width=device-width">
```

If you don't want the user to be able to zoom in and out, you can define both the `maximum-scale` and the `minimum-scale` as `1.0`, or just set `user-scalable=no`:

```
<meta name="viewport"
      content="width=device-width,minimum-scale=1.0, maximum-scale=1.0">
<meta name="viewport" content="width=device-width,user-scalable=no">
```

Even if you believe that your design is good enough and perfectly readable for a mobile screen, some users will still want to zoom in to get a closer look at your content, so disabling zooming may make some users angry. Also be aware that some mobile browsers will always provide the zoom ability, even if you force `user-scalable=no`.

 Safari on iOS will use a default viewport of 320px on iPhone/iPod and between 480px and 640px on iPad when your website has an XHTML MP DOCTYPE, or if it's hosted on a *.mobi* domain, instead of the default 980px.

Some browsers allow us to change the viewport dynamically using JavaScript, or even start without one and inject the meta tag after the page has loaded. Other browsers will just ignore any updates to the viewport meta tag after the page has loaded. Figure 7-14 shows the same image viewed in viewports of different sizes and at different `device-width` scales.

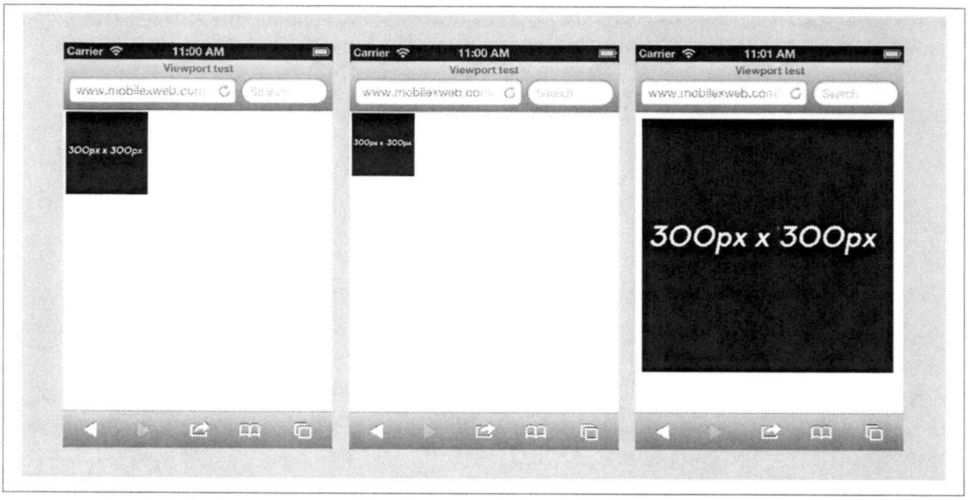

*Figure 7-14. The same 300×300-pixel image viewed in the default Safari viewport, in a 1,500-pixel viewport, at a device-width scale of 1.0, and at a device-width scale of 2.0.*

### What is device width?

Just when you think you're getting to grips with all of this, I have a bad news: `device-width` is not exactly the device's screen width. I've told you that usually providing a viewport with `width=device-width` for a mobile version leads to the best results. However, consider the following device examples:

- Apple iPhone 3GS, Safari on iOS, screen width = 320 pixels
- Nokia N8, Nokia Browser for Symbian, screen width = 360 pixels
- Nokia Lumia 900, Internet Explorer 9, screen width = 480 pixels
- Samsung Galaxy SII, Android browser, screen width = 480 pixels
- Apple iPhone 5, Safari on iOS, screen width = 640 pixels
- Samsung Galaxy SIII, Android browser, screen width = 720 pixels

Our first thought may be that `<meta name="viewport" content="width=device-width">` will give us a current viewport equal to the initial viewport or the screen width. Well, here comes the other tricky part of the viewport—the good news is that it exists to simplify our lives.

Most of the devices listed here report `width=320` when we define `width=device-width`, although some Android devices with wider screens (such as the Galaxy SIII) report `width=360` so you can fit more content. That means we can design to one and only one virtual device with a width of 320 pixels, and every browser will adapt the design to the initial viewport. Basically, we don't need to worry about the different screen sizes.

As many websites are optimized for a viewport width of 320 resolution-independent pixels, the Android browser on 4.x devices with wider screens (such as 4.5–5" screens) overrides the `320` value with `360` so you have more space on the screen to fit more content, instead of just resizing it. Google Chrome on the same devices uses `320` if you specify the exact value and `360` if you set `width=device-width`.

 Viewporter (*https://github.com/zynga/viewporter*) is a JavaScript mini-framework created by the game developer company Zynga to simplify setting up the viewport and help immersive apps get the most out of it.

To summarize, the most-implemented width values (in resolution-independent pixels) when using `width=device-width` at the time of this writing are:

320
> iPhone/iPod, Android browser/Google Chrome (medium-sized screen), Windows Phone (all screen sizes), BlackBerry (all screen sizes), Firefox/Opera for Android (all screen sizes), and other phone platforms

360
> Android browser and Google Chrome 4.x or greater on a wider screen (4.5–5"), Symbian devices

400
> Android browser on large-screen devices (more than 5", also known as *phablets*, such as the Samsung Galaxy Note)

600
> 7" tablets, such as the Kindle Fire and BlackBerry PlayBook

768
> iPad, iPad mini, and other tablets

600-1024
> Browsers on Android-based tablets (based on device's width in resolution independent pixels)

Usually on mobile phones device-width is 320, as this is the average screen width on devices with a medium-density screen. Scales are measured on medium-resolution devices; a scale of 1:1 on a high-resolution device such as the iPhone 5 is defined in CSS pixels, and it will give you 320 pixels as the current viewport width instead of the real 640 device pixels.

### Give me back the pixels

In some specific situations—such as for immersive apps or games—you may want to have a current viewport equal to the initial viewport, so that you have available every pixel that is there on the screen. That is, on the Galaxy SII, your viewport will have 480 pixels, and on the Galaxy SIII 720 pixels, instead of both being resized to 320. Of course, in this situation it's up to you to manage differences, and you need to be careful about minimum font sizes and other visible stuff.

The Android browser added an extension to the viewport meta tag to provide this feature: the target-densitydpi attribute. At the time of this writing, the Android browser, BlackBerry browser 7.0+, Chrome for Android, Opera for Android, and Nokia Browser for Symbian support this extension.

It basically defines the DPI values that we want to use for the width and height viewport definitions. We can use a specific DPI value (such as target-densitydpi=320), or some Android constants, such as low-dpi, medium-dpi (the default), or high-dpi. If we want every pixel for us, we need to use width=device-width and target-densitydpi=device-dpi:

```
<meta name="viewport"
      content="width=device-width,target-densitydpi=device-dpi">
```

Safari on iOS will just ignore the target-densitydpi declaration. If you want to have every iOS pixel for you, you need to manually define double the width for the viewport for high-resolution devices, such as width=640. However, this isn't a good idea in most situations.

### Landscape behavior

What happens when the user switches to the landscape orientation? The initial viewport gets wider and shorter, but your current viewport usually maintains the default width value, or the value you defined in the viewport meta tag. Therefore, if you provide a specific value, such as width=320, when the user switches to landscape the result will be the viewport stretching your content, as you can see in Figure 7-15.

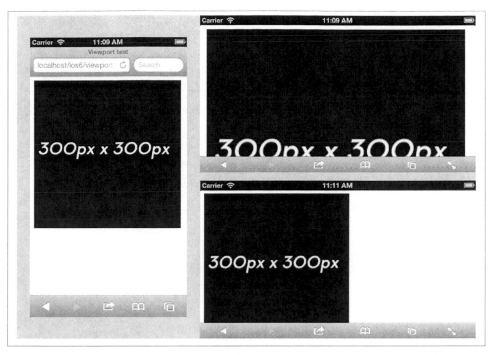

*Figure 7-15. By default, Safari on iOS will maintain your current viewport when going to landscape (top right), but with some hacks you can force it to give you a new current viewport with all the available space (bottom right).*

The problem with the lack of standards comes when you define `width=device-width`. There are two approaches:

- Take the portrait's `device-width` as the landscape's width value.
- Take the portrait's `height` value as the landscape's width value.

Safari on iOS and the Nokia Browser for MeeGo always use the `device-width` in portrait mode as the width value, so basically when you go landscape you are not getting more width for your content; your canvas is just resized. Other browsers understand that now the `device-width` should be the previous available height in portrait mode, which means you will have a wider current viewport by default.

 Be careful when trying to get all the possible width in landscape mode, because some devices on the market are wider than others in this orientation. Just take the example of the iPhone 4 and iPhone 5: you will get 480 CSS pixels (960 device pixels) and 568 CSS pixels (1,136 device pixels), respectively.

While Apple appears to see this as the proper result—your website will render exactly as in portrait mode, but bigger—some developers refer to this as the *iPhone Safari Viewport Scaling Bug*. One solution is to use maximum-scale=1.0 on the viewport. That forces Safari on iOS not to use a scale greater than 1, so you will always get 1:1 scale. The problem is that you are also limiting the user's rights to scale the content.

The solution for Safari involves some JavaScript that changes the viewport meta tag dynamically based on the context.

 Some versions of Safari also have a bug on the orientation change event where the viewport is being scaled or moved from the original position. The JavaScript hacks, such as the solution presented by Scott Jehl on his GitHub (*https://github.com/scottjehl/iOS-Orientationchange-Fix*), usually fix this strange behavior.

For example, Shi Chaun devised a solution, available on his blog BigHub (*http://www.blog.highub.com*), and later improved on at *www.gist.github.com/901295*—that involves these steps:

- Change the viewport's width when the screen orientation changes.
- Define maximum-scale=1.0, capture the pinch gesture (when the user zooms), and dynamically reset the viewport's minimum-scale and maximum-scale to the defaults when that occurs.

This solution involves defining the viewport as follows:

```
<meta name="viewport" content="width=device-width,initial-scale=1.0">
```

And using the following JavaScript code:

```
(function(doc) {

    var addEvent = 'addEventListener',
        type = 'gesturestart',
        qsa = 'querySelectorAll',
        scales = [1, 1],
        meta = qsa in doc ? doc[qsa]('meta[name=viewport]') : [];

    function fix() {
        meta.content = 'width=device-width,minimum-scale=' +
                    scales[0] + ',maximum-scale=' + scales[1];
        doc.removeEventListener(type, fix, true);
    }

    if ((meta = meta[meta.length - 1]) && addEvent in doc) {
        fix();
        scales = [.25, 1.6];
        doc[addEvent](type, fix, true);
```

```
    }
}(document));
```

 Be careful when testing viewport changes on simulators or real devices because some of them cache current viewport settings in memory and if you just refresh, you will not see the changes reflected. You need to close the window and start again, or type the URL again.

### Viewports in CSS

While Apple went for the meta tag and every mobile browser today supports it, the W3C, based on an Opera proposal, is going to a CSS-based solution for the future viewport definition. At the time of this writing, only Opera Mobile and Internet Explorer 10 support the CSS viewport standard, defined as a draft at www.dev.w3.org/csswg/css-device-adapt.

The definition includes the @viewport declaration that today may be prefixed by vendors, as in @-ms-viewport on IE10 or @-o-viewport for Opera browsers. For example:

```
@viewport {
    width: 320px;
}
@-ms-viewport {
    width: 320px;
}
@-o-viewport {
    width: 320px;
}
```

The attributes compatible with the viewport CSS declaration are listed in Table 7-5.

*Table 7-5. Viewport CSS declaration attributes*

| Attribute | Possible values | Related meta attribute | Description |
| --- | --- | --- | --- |
| max-width, min-width | Any CSS measure, auto, or the device-width constant. Usually a constant with px unit. | None | Defines the viewport maximum or minimum width |
| width | Any CSS measure, auto, or the device-width constant. Usually a constant with px unit. | width | A shortcut for both max-width and min-width at the same time |
| max-height, min-height | Any CSS measure, auto, or the device-height constant. Usually a constant with px unit. | None | Defines the viewport maximum or minimum height |
| height | Any CSS measure, auto, or the device-height constant. Usually a constant with px unit. | height | A shortcut for both max-height and min-height at the same time |

| Attribute | Possible values | Related meta attribute | Description |
|---|---|---|---|
| zoom | Floating value (0.1 to *n*) or percentage; 1.0 is no zoom. | initial-scale | Defines the initial zoom scale of the viewport |
| user-zoom | fixed or zoom. | user-scalable | Defines whether we will allow the user to zoom in and out in the viewport (zoom) or not (fixed) |
| min-zoom | Floating value (0.1 to *n*) or percentage; 1.0 is no scale. | minimum-scale | Defines the minimum zoom scale of the viewport |
| max-zoom | Floating value (0.1 to *n*) or percentage; 1.0 is no scale. | maximum-scale | Defines the maximum zoom scale of the viewport |
| orienta tion | One of the constants auto, portrait, or landscape. | None | Forces browser orientation lock to portrait or landscape; auto means accepting default browser values |

One of the biggest advantages of defining the viewport inside CSS is that it allows us to use CSS media queries, which we will cover in Chapter 11. That means we can say things such as, "If the current device's width is less than 480 pixels, then define a current viewport of 320 pixels; if not, fix it at 800 pixels." In other words, it's easy to implement threshold values and make fixed viewport declarations. The same idea can be applied to other conditionals, such as the current orientation.

For example, Internet Explorer 10 for Windows 8 supports viewport definitions for different orientations with the following syntax:

```
@media screen and (orientation: landscape) {
  @-ms-viewport {
    width: 1024px;
    height: 768px;
  }
  /* CSS for landscape layout goes here */
}

@media screen and (orientation: portrait) {
  @-ms-viewport {
    width: 768px;
    height: 1024px;
  }
  /* CSS for portrait layout goes here */
}
```

Internet Explorer in Windows Phone 8 has some unexpected behavior when working with viewports. If the meta tag is used with width=device-width, the viewport is always defined as 320 pixels. On the other hand if the CSS viewport declaration is used with width: device-width, the current real device width is used, such as 480 on medium-resolution devices and 768 on high-resolution devices. Using the CSS version will create different size experiences on different devices.

**Viewport compatibility.** Table 7-6 shows what happens if you try the viewport meta tag in different browsers, to see which ones detect it and do something with it. Remember that we can still add it in noncompatible browsers because the meta tag accepts any content.

*Table 7-6. Viewport usage compatibility table*

| Browser/platform | Default width | Meta version | CSS version | Can disable zoom | target-density-dpi support | device-width on landscape |
|---|---|---|---|---|---|---|
| Safari on iOS | 980px | Yes | No | Yes | No | PW |
| Android browser 2.x | 800px or CW | Yes | No | Yes | Yes, 2.2+ | PH |
| Android browser 3.x and 4.x | 980px | Yes | No | Yes | Yes | PH |
| Chrome for Android | 980px | Yes | No | No | Yes | PH |
| Nokia Browser for Symbian | IV or CW | Yes, 5th+ | No | Yes | Yes, ^3+ | PH |
| Nokia Browser for MeeGo | 980px | Yes | No | Yes | Yes | PW |
| Nokia Browser for S40 | IV | Yes, 2011+ | No | No | No | N/A |
| BlackBerry browser for smartphones | IV or CW | Yes, 4.6+ | No | Yes | Yes, 7.0+ | PH |
| BlackBerry browser for PlayBook and BB10 | IV or CW | Yes | No | Yes | Yes | PH |
| Internet Explorer | 1024px | Yes, 7+ | Yes, 10+ (-ms- prefix) | Yes | No | PH |
| Opera Mobile (Presto) | 980px or CW | Yes | Yes, 11+ (-o- prefix) | Yes | Yes | PH |
| Opera Mini | 980px or CW | Yes from 6 | Yes from 6 | Yes | Yes | PW |
| Firefox | 980px | Yes | No | Yes | No | PH |
| webOS browser | 980px or CW | Yes | No | No | No | PW |

[a] IV: initial viewport's width; CW: canvas width if wider than the default value.

[b] PH: portrait's height; PW: portrait's width.

While on smartphones usually `device-width` is `320` or `360`, on tablets the `device-width` value may change per device. The iPad (even third generation) will give you `768`, Chrome for Android and the Android browser use the initial viewport's width (changes per device), and the BlackBerry browser for PlayBook will give you `600`.

**Viewports for older devices.** Devices shipped before 2009 didn't work with the viewport meta tag. However, some platforms offered an alternative meta tag that defines a similar concept: "Don't try to zoom out or reflow my content because it's already mobile-optimized."

BlackBerry and some other platforms use this meta tag for defining mobile-friendly documents:

```
<meta name="HandheldFriendly" content="True" />
```

This meta tag is still detected on modern browsers because of backward compatibility, but should use the viewport for today's devices. If we define both, the viewport will take precedence.

Internet Explorer Mobile (formerly Pocket IE) introduced this meta tag in Windows Mobile 5—like the `HandheldFriendly` tag, it still works today, but the viewport meta tag takes precedence if both are defined:

```
<meta name="MobileOptimized" content="width" >
```

 Mobile Internet Explorer allows us to activate the ClearType technology to smooth fonts for easier reading using the tag `<meta http-equiv="cleartype" content="on">`.

A not-so-standard variation is to use the `alternate` link meta tag. This is intended to be used in desktop documents, defining an alternative URL for the same content intended for viewing on different media (`handheld`, in this case):

```
<link rel="alternate" media="handheld" href="http://m.mysite.com" >
```

Some mobile sites (like the Google mobile home page) also include the same `link` tag in the mobile page with an empty `href` attribute, like a flag saying that this is alternative content for mobile devices and should not be considered as duplicated content:

```
<link rel="alternate" media="handheld" href="" >
```

I don't have real evidence yet that this works in any mobile browsers or for search engine optimization (SEO) purposes, but it won't do any harm.

Defining mobile meta tags can be useful for transcoders, helping them determine whether to show the mobile version as we've created it rather than transcoding the content as a full website. We will talk about transcoders in Chapter 9.

## Changing the Navigation Method

The Symbian browser (on third edition and later devices) has two possible methods of browsing on devices with keyboards: the standard/normal way (cursor-based) and a hidden focus-based mechanism. A meta tag available for these devices allows us to change the default navigation method to a simple focus mechanism:

```
<meta name="navigation" content="tabbed">
```

This should be used only if you have a vertical tabular design (for example, a list of links using the whole width of the page). Using this tag will disallow the mouse events and hover effects over the page. If your design supports only vertical navigation, focus-based navigation will be faster for the user than the standard cursor navigation.

BlackBerry browser for smartphones (version 7.0+) and all versions of the PlayBook and BB10 platforms support two meta tags: `cursor-event-mode` and `touch-event-mode`. The first one defines how to handle trackpad events. The default value is `processed` and means the browser will take care of some UI behaviors, such as click to zoom or click and hold to display a context menu. If we want to override that behavior and have total control of the trackpad events from JavaScript, we should use the `native` value, as follows:

```
<meta name="cursor-event-mode" content="native">
```

We can create a similar effect on touch devices for the default touch gestures using the `touch-event-mode` meta tag. By default, the value `processed` is applied, meaning that the browser handles some touch gestures (such as pinch-to-zoom, conversion from touch events to mouse events). We can override all the defaults using the `native` value:

```
<meta name="touch-event-mode" content="native">
```

or use the value `pure-with-mouse-conversion`, allowing us to detect some touch events while others are passed directly to the browser. We'll talk about touch events later, in Chapter 15.

Later in this book we will cover other meta tags that we can use for specific purposes on some platforms, but that are not useful for all kinds of websites.

## Removing Automatic Links

Safari on iOS and the BlackBerry browser include an automatic behavior that can lead to confusion and problems: every number in the body content that looks like a phone number (the same pattern) will be converted to a call action link. We'll cover how to create this kind of link in a later chapter, but for now you just need to be aware that this automatic link behavior can lead to some weird false positives.

To remove the automatic behavior, Safari on iOS looks for the following meta tag:

```
<meta name="format-detection" content="telephone=no">
```

The BlackBerry browser uses a different meta tag to disable the automatic link function:

```
<meta name="x-rim-auto-match" content="none" forua="true">
```

If we don't provide this meta tag, the BlackBerry browser will also autodetect email addresses and convert them to links.

## Metadata for Sharing

Sharing on social networks is a popular feature with users. Modern mobile browsers, such as Safari on iOS 6 (see Figure 7-16), the BB10 browser, and Internet Explorer 10, include a simple way to share the currently open website on Twitter or Facebook. However, to enable our mobile websites to be shared properly, we need to include some metadata.

Sharing a mobile web page raises the question, "What happens when a follower or friend tries to access this URL on a desktop browser?" We have different options for handling this, depending on the architecture of the mobile solution.

If you are providing a different URL for mobile devices, you can:

- Deliver the same experience to desktop users (the default, not recommended).
- Redirect the user to a desktop version of the same URL. For this, you need to have a mapping mechanism from mobile to desktop web and vice versa.

If you are using the architecture of one URL for all devices, either because you are using Responsive Web Design or a server-side detection and delivery mechanism, you don't need to do anything about the URL.

Some browsers leave the hard work of reading our websites and getting useful content (such as the title and a description) up to the social networks, while others do the dirty work themselves. In both cases, the information that we should provide is the same, as (fortunately) most elements are part of the Open Graph standard (*http://ogp.me*).

*Figure 7-16. Some mobile browsers allow the user to share the current page easily on different social networks—we should prepare our content so it's optimized for that operation.*

The most useful meta elements you can define on your website for sharing are:

title
> The page title. While the `title` element is usually fine, sometimes we want to change the title when a page is being shared. For this purpose, some platforms use a `title` meta tag, if it's defined. IE10 uses this tag to prepare the preview content.

description
> A short description of the current document. IE10 uses this tag to prepare the preview content.

og:title
> Same as `title`, but from the Open Graph standard. This is used when the social network is gathering information from our document.

`og:description`

Same as `description`, but from the Open Graph standard. This is used when the social network is gathering information from our document.

`og:image`

The URL of the image that will be shown with the title and description on the social network

You can find more information on the Open Graph protocol website (*http://ogp.me*).

The following is an example of the sharing metadata we can use:

```
<meta name="title" content="Programming the Mobile Web, 2nd edition">
<meta name="description" content="A book with all the information you
    can find on mobile web development using HTML5">
<meta name="og:title" content="Programming the Mobile Web, 2nd
    edition">
<meta name="og:description" content="A book with all the information
    you can find on mobile web development using HTML5">
<meta name="og:image" content="http://mobilexweb.com/images/cover.png">
```

 The classic desktop web meta options, like `refresh` and `cache-control`, work well on mobile browsers. Usage of the `refresh` meta tag for autoupdating documents is not good practice for mobile devices, though: it is difficult to scroll on some mobile browsers, and an unsolicited page refresh can be unpleasant for the user. You can do an Ajax autoupdate if it is really necessary to keep the document updated.

Almost every mobile browser supports caching, either in meta tags or using HTTP headers. For example:

```
<meta http-equiv="expires"
      content="Mon, 5 Mar 2015 01:01:01 GMT">
```

## Hiding the URL Address Bar

Some browsers hide the URL bar when the document is loaded, so there is more space for content. Some other browsers do this when the user starts to scroll the page; the user can get the URL back again by scrolling to the top or opening the contextual menu. And there are yet other browsers, such as Chrome for Android and almost every tablet browser, that do not support any option to hide the URL bar.

To hide the URL bar in browsers without any automatic URL-bar-hiding behavior, such as Safari on iOS or the Android browser, we just need to scroll the window to 0 pixels (iOS) or 1 pixel (Android) on the *y*-axis, as in the following example:

```
If (window.addEventListener) {  // Make sure addEventListener exists
    window.addEventListener("load", function() {
        setTimeout(function() { window.scrollTo(0, 1)}, 0);
```

```
        });
    }
```

The main disadvantage of the previous code is that if the user is trying to load the page with a hash (an internal page anchor), we will still be sending her to the (0,0) coordinate of the window.

Scott Jehl (*http://scottjehl.com*) has released a full snippet, open source, that works properly in both the Android browser and Safari on iOS (and other browsers as well) that we can use to hide the address bar without encountering this problem. The fix is available at *gist.github.com/1183357*, and the latest version at the time of this writing looks like the following:

```
/*
 * Normalized hide address bar for iOS & Android
 * (c) Scott Jehl, scottjehl.com
 * MIT License
 */
(function( win ){
    var doc = win.document;

    // If there's a hash, or addEventListener is undefined, stop here
    if( !location.hash && win.addEventListener ){

        //scroll to 1
        window.scrollTo( 0, 1 );
        var scrollTop = 1,
            getScrollTop = function(){
                return win.pageYOffset || doc.compatMode === "CSS1Compat"
                && doc.documentElement.scrollTop || doc.body.scrollTop || 0;
            },

            //reset to 0 on bodyready, if needed
            bodycheck = setInterval(function(){
                if( doc.body ){
                    clearInterval( bodycheck );
                    scrollTop = getScrollTop();
                    win.scrollTo( 0, scrollTop === 1 ? 0 : 1 );
                }
            }, 15 );

        win.addEventListener( "load", function(){
            setTimeout(function(){
                //at load, if user hasn't scrolled more than 20 or so...
                if( getScrollTop() < 20 ){
                    //reset to hide addr bar at onload
                    win.scrollTo( 0, scrollTop === 1 ? 0 : 1 );
                }
            }, 0);
        } );
    }
})( this );
```

# Native App Integration

Some platforms allow us to integrate a website with a related native application. There-fore, if a user arrives at our website from a search engine or other source and we have a native application that can offer more services to the user, the browser will invite the user to install the app (if it's not already installed) or to open the app directly from the browser.

At the time of this writing, only iOS since 6.0 and Windows 8 allow this kind of native and web app integration, but more platforms will be getting on board soon. For updates on this feature, see www.mobilehtml5.org.

## iOS Smart App Banners

Since iOS version 6.0, Apple allows us to link a website with a native app through a service called *Smart App Banners*. When the user accesses a website with a Smart App Banner definition, Safari will check if the user has the associated app installed or not. If so, it will invite the user to open the app from the website using an OPEN button. If it's not installed, it will check the current device and App Store country to see whether the user can install the app. If so, the user will be invited to install the app directly from the website using a VIEW button.

The banner shown in Figure 7-17 takes up 156 pixels (312 on high-resolution devices) at the top of the screen until the user clicks on the screen below the banner or on the close button, at which point your website gets the full height. It acts like a DOM object at the top of your HTML, but it's not really on the DOM. On the iPad, especially in the landscape orientation, it seems a little space-wasting.

If the app is not installed, the banner will show a "loading" animation for a few seconds while the system verifies whether it will work on the user's current device and whether it's available via the App Store in the user's country. If the app is not available in the user's country or will not work on the current device, the banner hides automatically (for example, if it's an iPad-only app and the user is browsing with an iPhone, or if the app is available only on the German App Store and the user's account is in the US).

*Figure 7-17. The Smart App Banner appears when you don't have the app installed.*

To define a Smart App Banner in an HTML document, we use a meta tag called `apple-itunes-app` with a few declarations, including:

`app-id` *(mandatory)*
   The ID of the native app.

`app-argument` *(optional)*
   Arguments that the native app will receive from the website; should be formatted as a URL.

`affiliate-data` *(optional)*
   If you participate in the iTunes Affiliate Program to earn a commission on sales, you can add the relevant information here. The format is `siteId=9999&partnerId=ID`.

To make it work, the app you want to link to needs to be already approved on the Apple App Store. Then, you can go the iTunes Link Maker (*http://itunes.apple.com/linkmaker*) to retrieve the application ID you need to use in the meta tag. The ID is a nine-digit numeric value; to find it, search for your app by name on the Link Maker and extract the number from the URL, as seen in Figure 7-18.

*Figure 7-18. On the iTunes Link Maker website we can find the application ID to be used in the Smart App Banner meta tag.*

 Your native app in the App Store can also be created using HTML5, such as an Apache Cordova or Adobe PhoneGap application.

For example, to create a Smart App Banner for the app available for the iOS version of this book, we would use the following code:

```
<meta name="apple-itunes-app" content="app-id=393555188">
```

If you want to send arguments to the app, you can do this using a URL specified in the `app-argument` declaration. The URL can be the URL that the user came to the app from, where you can extract useful information, or any data in URL format that you can parse from the native side. The idea is that the user can continue working in the native app or seeing the same information that he was seeing on the website, without having to start from scratch. The value of this argument can be generated dynamically on the server or client side.

 From Objective-C, you can implement the method `application:open URL:sourceApplication:annotation:`. The second parameter of that method will be the URL passed from the website.

## Windows Store app connections

If you have a Windows Store app (on Windows 8), you can connect your website to it with some meta tags. Internet Explorer will show a menu like the one in Figure 7-19, allowing the user to quickly get the app from the store if it's not already installed. If the app is installed, the menu option changes to "Switch to *<name>* app."

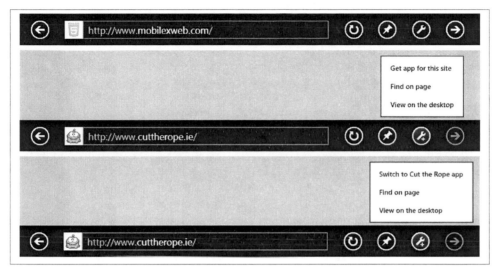

*Figure 7-19. When a Windows Store app connection is defined, the tools icon changes to a + symbol and it offers an invitation to install or switch to the app.*

There are five meta tags that we can define in our website for this connection:

msApplication-ID *(mandatory)*
    The identifier defined in the application manifest.

msApplication-PackageFamilyName *(mandatory)*
    The package family created by Microsoft Visual Studio to identify the app.

  Instead of using Visual Studio to get the package family name, you can browse the web version of the Windows Store, locate your desired app, and look at the source code. You will find the information in a packageFamilyName JavaScript variable.

msApplication-Arguments *(optional)*
    A string that will be passed to your app. If we don't provide this meta information, Internet Explorer will pass the current URL automatically.

**msApplication-MinVersion** *(optional)*

Enforces a minimum version of your app. Therefore, if the user has an older version of the app, when she tries to switch to it she will first be sent to the store to update it.

**msApplication-OptOut** *(optional)*

Allows your HTML document to not use the connection in some situations. Possible values are `install` to prevent the installation invitation if the app is not installed, `switch` to prevent the switch invitation if the app is installed, and `both`.

 A Windows Store app can be created using HTML5, C++, C#, or Visual Basic, and it must be approved by Microsoft. To submit an app to the Windows Store, you must have a developer account.

Cut the Rope (*http://cuttherope.ie*) is an addictive game available on many mobile platforms, such as iOS and Android; an HTML5 version, sponsored by Internet Explorer 10, is available online. The game is also available as a Windows Store app. To offer the functionality seen in Figure 7-19, the following meta tags are used:

```
<meta name="msApplication-ID" content="App" />
<meta name="msApplication-PackageFamilyName"
      content="ZeptoLabUKLimited.CutTheRope_sq9zxnwrk84pj" />
```

# The Document Body

The body is the most important section of the document, as it defines the content that the user will see.

Key best practices include:

- Avoid formatting tags such as `big`, `format`, and `center`.
- Use semantically correct, clean XHTML or HTML5; we will define styles later with CSS.
- Don't create a large document. Larger documents cause problems on old browsers (and caching problems even on some modern ones).
- If you have a lot of text to show, for feature phones, separate the content into many pages.
- Don't use tables for layout.

# Main Structure

A typical mobile document will be divided into four main sections:

1. Header
2. Main navigation
3. Content
4. Footer

The header should be as simple as possible, using an h1 title or a logo or company banner. The main navigation should consist of no more than five main links, ordered by likelihood of use in a mobile context (most to least probable). The content is obvious; the footer should include very brief copyright information, a home link, a back link, and optionally other related links (such as "go to top").

This is a simplification, I know, but most mobile pages should fit this structure. If your structure is more complex, give some careful thought to whether that complexity is necessary.

---

## The Hell of Transcoders

Some carriers have decided to install and execute in their networks a *transcoder* that proxies every mobile web request—even those made with nonproxied browsers—to create a "better experience" for the user. This is a very bad practice from a developer's perspective, for the following reasons:

- It compresses the content, the document, the CSS, the JavaScript, and the images without our consent.
- It changes our layout and design.
- It can even change our markup language.
- It removes all the original HTTP headers from the browser, blinding us from knowing which devices are accessing our websites.

Luca Passani, a well-known mobile web developer, created a manifesto in 2008 addressing content reformatting problems, available at *wurfl.sourceforge.net/manifesto*. The W3C is also taking part in this issue; it has issued a document on the Content Transformation Landscape (*http://www.w3.org/TR/ct-landscape*).

---

The basic document structure should look like this. Separating every section with a div tag is not necessary for the document definition, but it is useful later for CSS styling. The main navigation can be an unordered list (ul) instead of a div:

```
<body>
    <header>
        <h1>Mobile Web</h1>
    </header>
    <nav>
        <ul>
            <li><a href="Tests">Tests</a></li>
            <li><a href="Blog">Blog</a></li>
            <li><a href="Contact">Contact</a></li>
        </ul>
    <nav>
    <div id="content">
    </div>
    <footer>
    </footer>
</body>
```

The main content div should have as children only the tags h2–h6, p, ul, and, if necessary, other semantic elements such as section or article. I know, this doesn't seem so exciting. However, using CSS and maybe JavaScript libraries prepared for smartphones, we can take this simple markup and create great experiences for high-end devices. Using a simple document structure will be one of our best practices in the mobile world, to avoid duplication.

---

## Navigation Link Menus

XHTML MP 1.2 recommends the usage of linked resources for navigation purposes. A navigation link menu is a series of link tags, generally defined in the head element, that refers to the main index file (the home page) and optionally the next and previous pages in a series of related documents. These links can be useful for indexing and search engine optimization purposes. While almost no browser today actually uses this information, it's useful for SEO purposes (IE10 has a similar behavior called jump lists). Here is an example of a navigation link menu for a photo gallery showing photo #2:

```
<link rel="start" href="index.html" />
<link rel="next" href="photo3.html" />
<link rel="prev" href="photo1.html" />
```

---

### Go to top

Some mobile browsers, like Safari on iOS, allow the user to tap with a finger in the top section of the screen to scroll the page to the top. Other browsers have keyboard shortcuts for that. And many others don't have any such mechanism, or if they do, it's so obscure that most users probably don't know what it is. So, it is a good mobile web practice to insert an anchor at the top of the page (in the header) and a link to that anchor at the bottom:

---

```
<body>
    <header>
        <a name="top"></a>
        <h1>Mobile Web</h1>
    </header>
        ...
    <footer>
        <ul>
            <li><a href="#top">Go to Top</a></li>
            <li><a href="/">Go Home</a></li>
        </ul>
    </footer>
</body>
```

# HTML5 Mobile Boilerplate

Wikipedia (accessed September 2012) defines boilerplate as follows:

> [B]oilerplate is the term used to describe sections of code that have to be included in many places with little or no alteration. It is more often used when referring to languages which are considered verbose, i.e. the programmer must write a lot of code for minimal functionality. The need for boilerplate can be reduced through high-level mechanisms.

When creating a new website, it is helpful to have a template (boilerplate) with all the well-known hacks, solutions, and best practices already implemented to use as a starting point, rather than having to start from scratch. HTML5 boilerplate (*http://html5boiler plate.com/mobile*) is starting to emerge: a mobile-specific version is maintained by the community as an open source project.

The latest version at the time of this writing includes many of the techniques that we have covered in this chapter, and you can of course add your own code to it. The template includes:

- Meta tags, such as viewport and icon references
- *normalize.css*, an alternative to CSS reset (a way to normalize defaults on different browsers)
- Some JavaScript libraries, such as Zepto.js and Modernizr (two libraries we will cover later in this book)
- A JavaScript helper class useful for some JavaScript-based hacks, such as the iOS viewport bug fix
- High-performance and mobile-specific configuration files for Apache

# The Content

If we focus our content semantically, we will not have big problems adapting our design to different mobile scenarios. By "semantically," I mean using the well-known paragraph, structure, and list HTML5 elements. Be sure to understand and make proper use of every HTML element, such as header, footer, article, abbr, and address.

## Block Elements

If we define a viewport allowing user scaling, most browsers support a way to zoom into a block element (such as a paragraph), using a double-tap gesture, for example. To make this work properly we should not use paragraphs that are forced to be wider than the screen (because we have defined the width and the font-size as fixed); this will force the browser to zoom out and the paragraph will be unreadable.

## Lists

Using standard lists will help us a lot in defining our designs later with CSS and for semantic search engine optimization. For the mobile web, we should use the following list types:

*Ordered lists (ol tag)*
    For navigation link menus

*Unordered lists (ul tag)*
    To present lists of similar objects

*Definition lists (dl tag)*
    To show key/value details

The last one is perhaps the lesser-known list tag in web development. For example, if we are showing a product detail page, in many browsers it's better to use a definition list rather than a table for attributes:

```
<h2>iPhone 5</h2>
<dl>
    <dt>Price</dt>
    <dd>300 EUR</dd>
    <dt>Memory</dt>
    <dd>32Gb</dd>
    <dt>Network</dt>
    <dd>LTE, 3G, WiFi, Bluetooth</dd>
</dl>
```

The dt tag is used for the key (definition term) and the dd tag for the value (definition description). This is very useful, semantically correct, and clearer than using a table. Later, with CSS, we can rearrange the elements.

# Tables

Repeat after me: "I will not use tables for document layout." Write it with a red marker on your bedroom ceiling, if it will help you remember. Using tables for document layout is bad in desktop web development. It is hell for the mobile web.

Mobile browsing is more a one-column experience, unless we are working with tablets. If you do want or need to use a table, you should limit it to at most five columns of tabular data (preferably with short column headings and data values).

We can define the table title (`caption`), the header (`thead`), the body (`tbody`), the footer (`tfoot`), and the columns (`colgroup`, `col`), and finally the rows (`tr`), the header cells (`th`), and the data cells (`td`). Cells can be merged using the `rowspan` and `colspan` attributes, and the design should be defined in CSS.

 On some older devices and basic browsers for feature phones, sometimes the only way to add different elements in a row is to design with tables, as floating elements are not available.

# Frames

Frames are one of the "better if you avoid it" features in the mobile world. I remember, back in 1997 (the Microsoft FrontPage era), being happy with the frames technique, creating fixed menu bars and dealing with links between frames. It was a happy time, until search crawlers came into action and frames became the worst thing you could ever do in a website. OK, background music can be even worse, but it is true that today the usage of frames is suitable only for intranet sites and noncrawled applications. Similar functionality can now be provided with the much more versatile Ajax.

The HTML frames mechanism allows the developer to split a document into *n* subdocuments, vertically and/or horizontally. Every frame is a different document (that's the problem for search engine spiders), and every frame manages its own scrolling (this is the problem for the mobile world).

We already know that in the mobile world, even though the viewport can be large, the screen is small. Splitting this small screen into smaller windows as frames can be difficult. The biggest problem is scrolling. As mobile browsers don't show visible scroll bars, the user has no clear indication where a frame or iframe exists to scroll inside. Some mobile browsers will not even allow the user to scroll inside a frame or iframe.

So, my final advice is: don't use frames when developing for the mobile web.

The inline frame (or *iframe*) is a modern way to do frames (although it was introduced by Internet Explorer in 1997). The `iframe` tag produces better results than frames. Today, iframes are often used by ad servers to serve advertisements from a third-party server. If you can, it's still best to avoid them; if you can't, offer content that doesn't need to be scrolled inside the iframe.

---

## i-mode XHTML

Japanese devices from NTT DoCoMo used to have their own version of XHTML with extensions for XHTML and CSS, based on the old cHTML. Serving i-mode XHTML files requires using a new DOCTYPE and defining the charset UTF-8 or Shift-JIS for Japanese characters. For example, for the latest version, the first two lines of the file might look like this:

```
<?xml version="1.0" encoding="Shift_JIS"?>
<!DOCTYPE html PUBLIC "-//i-mode group (ja)//DTD XHTML i-XHTML(Locale/
Ver.=ja/2.3) 1.0//EN" "i-xhtml_4ja_10.dtd">
```

The latest version of i-mode XHTML at the time of this writing is 2.3; there is also a non-XML version, called i-mode HTML, which is currently at version 7.2. i-mode Browser 2.0 is the browser delivered by devices manufactured after May 2009; it includes the latest versions of both i-mode HTML and i-mode XHTML.

There is an excellent portal of information (*http://bit.ly/ZpVJUJ*) in English for versions 1.0 and 2.0 of the i-mode Browser.

The good news is that the latest versions of i-mode HTML and i-mode XHTML support almost every tag used in XHTML MP. The list of supported attributes differs, though, and a lot of new attributes and values are available as i-mode extensions. For example, an `li` element can have a `type` attribute with `circle` as the value, and a numeric text input can be defined with `type="text"` and `istyle="3"`.

---

## Links

Hyperlinks are the heart of the Web, and this holds for the mobile web, too. You might think there isn't much to say about links, but that's not the case.

Every link in a mobile website should have the well-known `href` attribute, set to the URL of the desired resource, and the most important links on the page can have an `accesskey` attribute assigned for easy access via keyboard shortcuts, on devices that support access keys. The `target` attribute should be avoided for feature or social phones because those browsers don't have tab or multipage support.

---

Some devices support the usage of `tabindex` for focusable elements (links, form controls) to change the element order for browsers with focus-based navigation. However, changing the natural order of tabbing is discouraged, unless you have a difficult design and you want to improve the user experience.

If you are making a link to the desktop version of your website (a must-have, as discussed earlier), use `rel="alternate"` to specify that the link is to the same page in an alternative format.

In devices that support focus-based navigation (most low-end devices, and even some touch devices with a touchpad or scroll wheel, like the Nexus One and some BlackBerrys), it is important to define whole clickable zones. For example, if you want to make a title and description both clickable, use one link tag for both elements instead of two separate links to the same page. A single focus border will appear around the whole area you want to be clickable.

### New windows

Some browsers accept the `target="_blank"` attribute, but depending on the browser the behavior is different. Some browsers simply open the URL in the same window, others create a new tab or window (allowing the user to browse between them), and still others open the new URL as a modal pop-up, in which case the user cannot go back to the first page until he closes the new one.

On tablet-based browsers, usually we have a tab navigation user interface, as we are used to in desktop browsers.

In Chapter 15, we are going to analyze how we can integrate with device services through different URIs using links.

### Navigation lists

A navigation list is any list of links that are related in some manner and listed one after the other. The recommended way to create such a list is with `ol` or `ul` tags. With the ordered list, the number of the key to press to access each option is printed for us for free, but we still need to add the `accesskey` attributes to the `a` tags by hand:

```
<ol>
    <li><a href="option1.html" accesskey="1"></li>
    <li><a href="option2.html" accesskey="2"></li>
</ol>
```

Remember to use the nav container that is available in HTML5 to clearly mark navigational areas on the screen.

## Accessibility

The accessibility of a mobile website should be as important as the graphic design, the performance, or the user experience. Some mobile operating systems, such as iOS, support accessibility features such as screen voice readers, gesture helpers, or contrast color utilities.

If your mobile website or app is *accessible* it means that anyone can use it, with any device. Here's some good advice for mobile web solutions:

- Leave zooming capabilities in place at all times.
- Provide your content using progressive enhancement, so it will work properly without any CSS enhancement or JavaScript layer.
- Verify that the website can be browsed with focus-based navigation.
- Use semantic HTML, not just divs and spans.
- Use HTML5 WAI-ARIA attributes.
- Provide alternate content when necessary, such as alt attributes for images or alternate information for video or canvas elements.
- Browse your website with accessibility tools enabled.

 If you want to know more about mobile web accessibility, you can check out the W3C Mobile Accessibility website (*http://www.w3.org/WAI/mobile/*).

### WAI-ARIA

Accessible Rich Internet Applications (*http://www.w3.org/TR/wai-aria*) (WAI-ARIA) is a W3C standard for accessibility that is compatible with some HTML5 mobile browsers. The main goal is to make accessible, rich pages that are not just plain documents but services and applications.

A compatible browser will understand a role attribute that can be applied to any HTML element, such as a div or section. The role definition allows the browser to understand your rich content, indicating whether the element is a navigation area, a slider, or some other rich element. The available roles are listed at www.w3.org/TR/wai-aria/roles.

For example, we can explicitly define that aul is a toolbar with role="toolbar":

```
<ul role="toolbar">
</ul>
```

A screen reader, for example, will then understand that our `ul` is a toolbar and will react appropriately, such as by inviting the user to select one of the `li`s. WAI-ARIA also adds new `aria-*` attributes to define more specific metadata information, such as `aria-pressed`, which indicates if a push button is pressed or not.

 Screen readers provide spoken feedback on what is touched and selected for blind and low-vision users. Semantic content and WAI-ARIA will help the reader to understand what the content really is. You can try it on your own smartphones and tablets on some operating systems.

If you want to know more about accessibility, check out the *Accessibility HandBook* by Katie Cunningham (O'Reilly).

### Accessibility testing

If you want to test how accessible your mobile website is, you can:

- Browse your website from a focus-only device, such as a feature phone or a non-touch Kindle ereader.
- Enable VoiceOver on iOS, a screen reader available from Settings→General→Accessibility→VoiceOver.
- Enable TalkBack on Android, a screen reader available from Settings→System→Accessibility→Services in conjunction with the "Enhance web accessibility" option in 4.1.
- Search the application stores for accessible browsers and use them to view your own content.

# CHAPTER 8

# HTML5 Forms

Forms are a key issue on mobile devices. While some people claim that typing on mobile devices is painful, we can see how much typing happens today on mobile devices: from SMSs to WhatsApp, Twitter, and Facebook. Even if typing on these devices is not as comfortable as on desktops, users are doing a lot of it, and it's our job to make it as good an experience as possible.

To maximize compatibility and accessibility, the input controls should be inside the classic `form` tag, with `method="GET"` or `"POST"` and `action="serverScriptURL"`. If we want to use Ajax or any other sort of rich behavior, that's fine, but we must be sure to always have a basic HTML form as a fallback.

## Form Design

Avoid using tables for form layout. The best solution is to use definition lists, labels, and input controls. Using CSS you can enhance the form and even with different layouts for different devices and orientations. If you start your design with a fixed-layout from the HTML, such as using tables, you will not have the ability to modify it from CSS.

 The older BlackBerry browser for smartphones—not BB10—allowed offline form submission. If the device was offline when the user completed the form, it was placed in a queue and was automatically submitted when the device went back online.

A typical key/value form should look like the following code:

```
<form action="formAction" method="post">
  <dl>
    <dt><label for="name">Name</label></dt>
    <dd><input type="text" name="name"></dd>
```

```
  </dl>
</form>
```

The usage of the `label` tag is very important for mobile input controls, and especially for touch devices. For example, if you insert a checkbox without a `label` tag, the user will need to tap (click) over the tiny checkbox to select it, which can be fiddly. Using a label allows the user to tap anywhere in the text assigned to the checkbox to select it.

 As discussed in Chapter 5, mobile forms should have a vertical design, so it is better to put the label above each input field instead of to the right or left. This is because touch devices zoom in on the field when it's in focus and do not show what is to the right or left of the control. Tables don't help in this design.

So, a form with a checkbox should look something like the following:

```
<form action="formAction" method="post">
  <input type="checkbox" name="accept" id="accept" value="yes">
  <label for="accept">I accept terms and conditions</label>
</form>
```

 Some mobile browsers have a lower limit for the URL length than desktop ones. That is why we should avoid long forms using the `GET` method.

We can also assign access keys to the form controls (using the `accesskey` attribute in the `input` tags) and show which keys are assigned in the labels, with a CSS class. This method is very useful in devices with QWERTY keyboards, where you can assign a letter to each field instead of numeric values:

```
<form action="formAction" method="post">
  <input type="checkbox" name="accept" id="accept" value="yes"
        accesskey="a">
  <label for="accept">I <span class="accesskey">A</span>ccept terms
    and conditions</label>
</form>
```

A typical form should include one or more `fieldset` tags, each with a `legend` inside. The `fieldset` is just a container for form controls, and the `legend` is a child tag that defines the title or legend for its parent:

```
<fieldset>
  <legend>Personal Information</legend>
  <!-- controls here -->
</fieldset>
```

Some mobile browsers will add navigation between all interactive form elements, such as Previous or Next buttons (Figure 8-1) on virtual keyboards that will jump between elements in the current order, or `tabindex` declarations, as if it were tabbed navigation on a desktop. Therefore, it's important to define a coherent order for the elements.

*Figure 8-1. Some browsers allow tabular navigation between form controls using Previous and Next buttons*

To reduce submissions you should add JavaScript form validation, and to secure your app you must add a validation process on the server side.

# Form Elements

An HTML5 mobile form can contain the following form elements:

- Single-line text boxes for different types of input
- Password boxes
- Multiline text boxes
- Date and time selectors
- Select lists for single selection
- Select lists for multiple selection
- Checkboxes
- Radio buttons
- File selectors
- Range selectors
- Noninteractive elements, such as hidden input fields and keygen elements

As we are going to see later, not every platform supports every form type, so we need to be careful about which ones we use.

## Select Lists

The select tag should be one of the most-used tags in a mobile form. Selection from a list is the first option for reducing typing. In a mobile browser, when you click on a select element, typically you will see a pop-up window (modal or not) showing all the options. As shown in Figures 8-2 and 8-3, how select lists are rendered varies across devices.

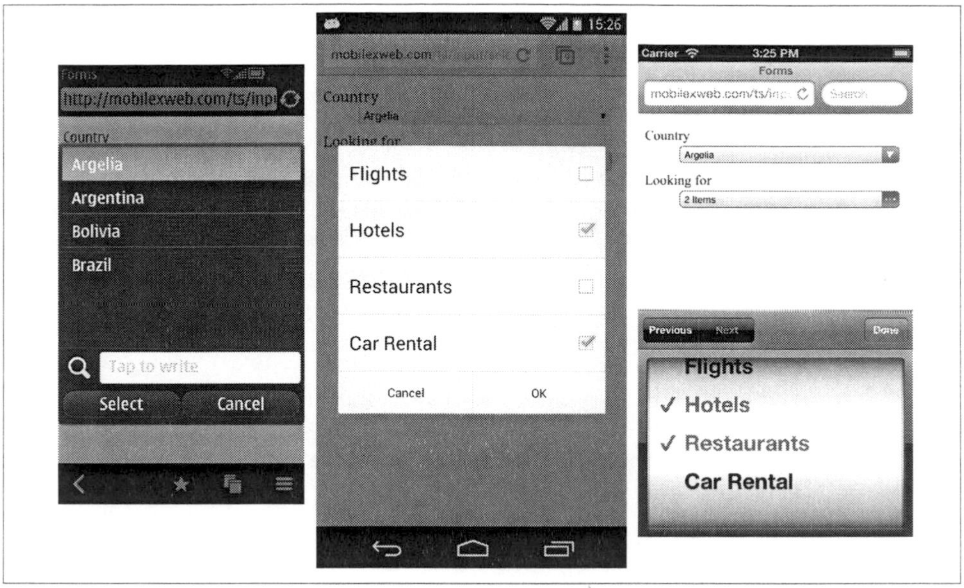

Figure 8-2. Most mobile browsers show nice native dialogs when selecting elements using standard form controls.

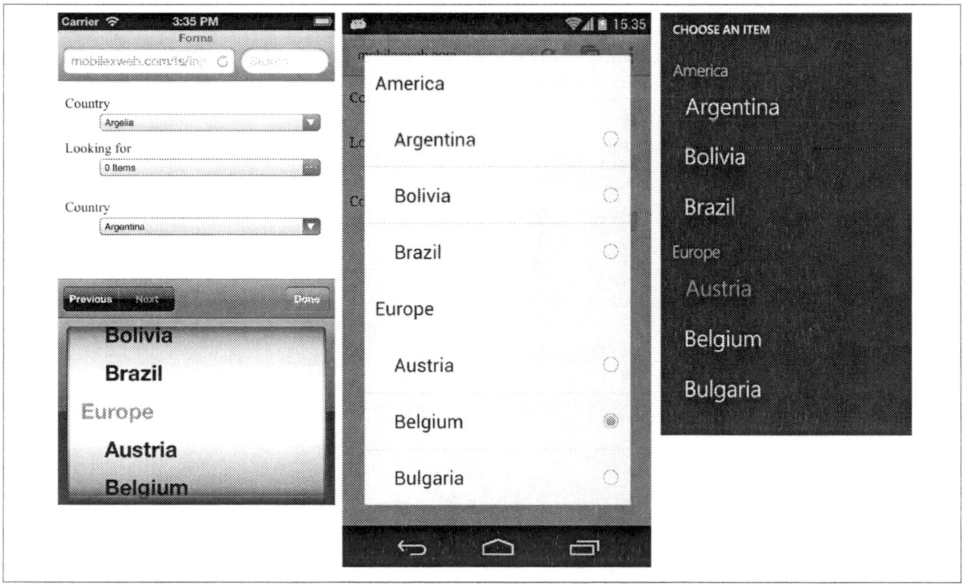

Figure 8-3. Symbian select lists offer a search box for all the options, Android shows a modal pop-up, and Safari uses a wheel selector.

You can use the `size` property of the `select` tag to define a list with a predefined height, but the result is not usually good enough on mobile browsers .

You can specify that the list accepts multiple selection using the Boolean attribute `multiple`. The multiple-selection feature is more useful in mobile forms than desktop forms. In a desktop form, the user generally uses Shift or Control to select multiple options. In a mobile form, we generally present a pop-up window with checkboxes for the user to make his selections and a confirm action to go back to the main page, as seen in Figure 8-2.

 With HTML5, Boolean attributes such as `multiple` don't need to have a value definition. If you want to force a value or if you are validating against an XHTML DOCTYPE, the value must be the same name as the attribute name, such as `multiple="multiple"`.

The code for the `select` lists shown in Figure 8-3 looks like the following:

```
<form action="formAction" method="post">
   <dl>
      <dt><label for="country">Country</label></dt>
      <dd>
         <select name="country">
            <option>Argelia</option>
            <option>Argentina</option>
            <option>Bolivia</option>
            <option>Brazil</option>
         </select>
      </dd>
      <dt><label for="filter">Looking for</label></dt>
      <dd>
         <select name="filter" multiple>
            <option>Flights</option>
            <option>Hotels</option>
            <option>Restaurants</option>
            <option>Car Rental</option>
         </select>
      </dd>
   </dl>
</form>
```

Safari for iOS uses a spinning wheel for selections in HTML, but the native similar control also supports a multicolumn spinning wheel to select multiple fields at the same time. This functionality is not provided in HTML and can only be used natively in Objective-C. However, there is a JavaScript library that emulates the multicolumn control available at *www.mobilexweb.com/go/wheel*.

### Option groups

Option groups are an underused feature of `select` lists, even in desktop web development. Defining an `optgroup` allows you to provide a label for a set of children, so you can group the available options by category. Here's an example:

```
<dl>
    <dt><label for="country">Country</label></dt>
    <dd>
        <select name="country">
            <optgroup label="America">
                <option value="ar">Argentina</option>
                <option value="bo">Bolivia</option>
                <option value="br">Brazil</option>
            </optgroup>
            <optgroup label="Europe">
                <option value="at">Austria</option>
                <option value="be">Belgium</option>
                <option value="bg">Bulgaria</option>
            </optgroup>
        </select>
    </dd>
</dl>
```

The result is shown in Figure 8-4. Again, different devices may render option groups differently!

## Radio Buttons and Checkboxes

The usage of radio buttons and checkboxes is the same on mobile devices as on desktops. The only recommendation I can give you is to avoid using these controls if there are more than four options, using in that case a `select` with single or multiple selection, as appropriate. A group of more than four radio buttons is likely to increase the page height and may require scrolling, which can impact the usability of the form.

Using a label attached to a radio button or a checkbox is a must, as the little icon (the box or circle) is too small for a touch experience.

*Figure 8-4. Option groups can be rendered strangely on older devices, but on devices shipped after 2011 they usually work well.*

## Buttons

HTML has five types of buttons:

*Image map buttons*
```
<input type="image">
```

*Submit buttons*
```
<input type="submit">
```

*Clear buttons*
```
<input type="reset">
```

*Custom buttons*
```
<input type="button">
```

*Submit buttons with HTML support*
```
<button></button>
```

The image map button allows us to use an image as a button and receive on the server the coordinates of the point inside the image where the user clicked. Of course, this functionality is possible only on mobile devices supporting touch- or cursor-based navigation. This type of button should be avoided if possible (this is the recommendation of the W3C) and replaced with a classic submit button. We can later add an image or icon using CSS.

The submit button is the most widely compatible, and for the lowest common denominator devices it should work fine. I've always hated (yes, hated!) the clear button. How many times have you clicked a clear button thinking it was the submit button? This button should be avoided when developing for mobile devices: why potentially add more scrolling and take up more space for a function that few people use? If you want to include this functionality in your form, please be sure to use a different style for the clear button (smaller, darker) than the style you use for the submit button.

The custom buttons should be avoided if you want full mobile compatibility because they work only with JavaScript. For compatible devices, you can still use submit buttons and capture the submit action with JavaScript.

## Hidden Fields

Hidden fields (`<input type="hidden">`) are fully compatible with mobile browsers. They are useful for passing information from one page to another because any hidden field will be sent to the server as if the user has entered it on the form. Thanks to modern server-side techniques, hidden fields are not as important today as they once were.

## Text Input Fields

Text input on mobile devices is a key area for improving usability.

QWERTY devices are the only ones that don't require a new window to insert the text: when the text input has focus, the user can start typing. In all other device types, when the field has focus the user can either click (or tap) in it or start typing to open a modal pop-up window with all of the OS's typical text typing features (such as predictive text, onscreen keyboard, character recognition, dictionary, and symbol list). Some devices show a full-screen text input window (hiding the entire web interface), and others show a smaller window inside the browser window. In the first case, a descriptive label is required so the user knows what to type.

We can divide the possible text inputs into:

- Single-line inputs
- Multiline inputs
- Rich inputs
- Pop-up inputs

Before iOS 3.0, an undocumented feature allowed us to force a numeric keyboard using the name property of the text input. If the name of the input contained the string "zip" or "phone," the keyboard would change to numeric. However, using this feature was not good practice because it's inconvenient in non-US countries where the zip code can contain letters (the United Kingdom and Argentina, for example).

For the single-line inputs, HTML5 uses the standard input element with different type values. The type will determine which keyboard to show on the screen on touch devices. For nontouch devices, every type will react in the exact same way. The possible input types we have are:

- Any-character textbox: `<input type="text">` or just `<input>`
- Numeric textbox: `<input type="number">`
- Phone number textbox: `<input type="tel">`
- Email textbox: `<input type="email">`
- URL textbox: `<input type="url">`
- Any-character secure box: `<input type="password">`
- Search textbox: `<input type="search">`
- Date textboxes: to be covered later in this chapter

As we can see in Figure 8-5, Safari on iOS, the Android browser, and the BlackBerry browser for PlayBook and BB10 will show different virtual keyboards for each input type. For example, there is an email-optimized keyboard that includes the @ character, and a URL-optimized keyboard with a ".com" button and no space bar. In some other browsers, every nonsecure input type will be treated as a `type="text"`.

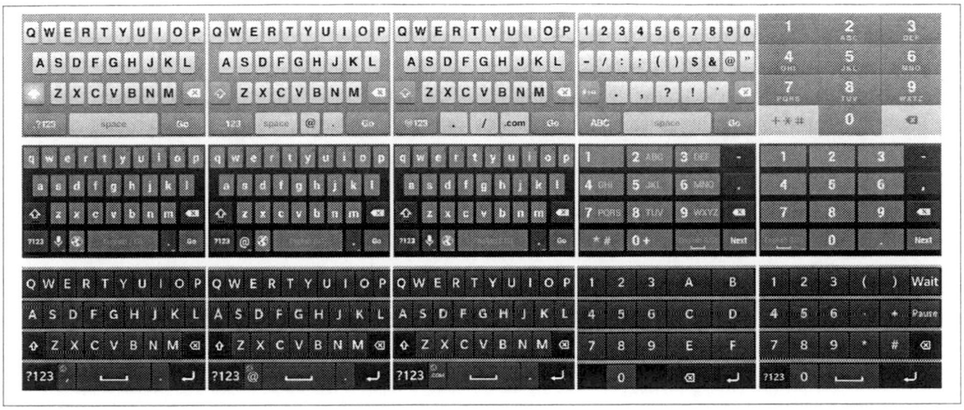

Figure 8-5. *Different virtual keyboards displayed on iOS, Android, and BlackBerry 10 devices—in order: text, email, url, number, and tel.*

> Even when you are using a numeric input type, JavaScript always treats the value as a string, and on some devices the user can switch to an alphanumeric keyboard and enter nonnumeric characters. Therefore, input constraints must not be used as a validation mechanism, just a feature that will improve usability on some devices.

The search box is just a text box with a different semantic meaning; it lets external search engines know that your site search engine is there. In some browsers, such as Safari on iOS, the search input type is shown with a different UI and the virtual keyboard will use "Search" instead of "Go" on the submit button, as you can see in Figure 8-6.

Some browsers also support the new `autosave` attribute, which works only with `type="search"` input types. By defining that attribute with a unique ID, we allow the browser to save a user's searches for future suggestions. We can define how many entries we want to save using the `results` numeric attribute, as in:

```
<input type="search" autosave="mysearch" results="5">
```

*Figure 8-6. When using `type=search`, some virtual keyboards will replace the default "Go" button with a search button.*

## Password or No Password

The usage of the password text input (`<input type="password">`) on mobile devices is a subject of much debate. The password text input (with the classic stars or circles displayed instead of the typed characters) was originally created because of the possibility of a password or other sensitive data being stolen by someone standing behind the user with a view of the screen.

In the mobile ecosystem, the situation is different. With the limited screen size and font size, it is very difficult for another person to see what the user is typing on his mobile phone. Furthermore, typing on non-QWERTY devices is difficult, and if we show a star instead of the real character typed the user may be unsure that he's entered the text correctly (even if, as is done on some devices, the character is displayed for a second before it's changed to a star).

Jakob Nielsen (*http://useit.com*), guru of web usability, agrees. In a 2009 Alertbox column, Nielsen wrote: "Usability suffers when users type in passwords and the only feedback they get is a row of bullets. Typically, masking passwords doesn't even increase security, but it does cost you business due to login failures."

A good solution to this problem is to add a checkbox to make it visible (changing `type="password"` to `type="text"`), or leave it as `type="text"` and provide a checkbox to make it hidden. Another solution, used by many websites (such as Facebook), is to offer a `type="password"` field on the first login page. If the login details provided are incorrect, it automatically changes to `type="text"` so you can see what you are typing, as you can see in Figure 8-7.

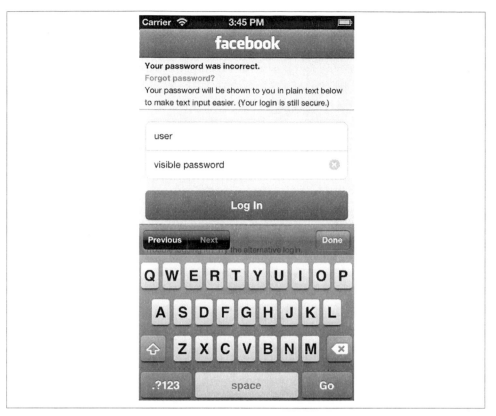

Figure 8-7. Facebook makes the password visible after a login error to improve usability.

 For some older devices, such as BlackBerry 5.0 devices, we can also define that we want a numeric input box using the XHTML MP `input mode="digits"` attribute or using the WAP CSS `-wap-input-format` style.

### Data lists for suggestions

HTML5 also adds a new `datalist` tag that is useful for autocomplete features. The data list is useful when an input type is open to any value, but we want to show the user some suggested values. As of this writing, the BlackBerry browser and IE10 for Windows 8 (not Windows Phone) support it.

We can define a data list with an ID and a set of child `option` elements:

```
<datalist id="dataCountries">
    <option value="France">
```

```
    <option value="Portugal">
    <option value="Spain">
</datalist>
```

Then, we can use that list for suggestions in a text input, matching the list attribute with the data list's id:

```
<input type="text" id="txtCountry" list="dataCountries">
```

The data list will not have any UI if it is not associated with one or more form elements. When the user focuses on an associated text input and starts typing, the browser will suggest matching options from the data list.

### Multiline text controls

When more space is required (like in a mail message body), we can use a textarea, and depending on the device the experience should be the same as with a normal text input. The biggest problem with multiline input controls is what happens when the content is larger than the available space. The scrolling mechanism inside a textarea element is a usability problem. To solve it, we can create an autogrowing text control.

This UI pattern was created by the Google Mobile team and is currently used in Gmail. The problem is that if we have a large amount of text in a textarea, scrolling inside it is very painful in some browsers (Safari on iOS is one of them). The solution is to grow the textarea to fit the contents, so the user can use the normal page scrolling instead of the textarea's.

 HTML5 supports several new attributes for textareas: maxlength to constrain the length of the content, wrap="hard" to add a newline character at the end of each line when sending the data to the server, placeholder to show placeholder text in the text area, and the new attributes that can be applied to every control, such as autofocus or required.

We can capture the onkeyup event and grow the textarea if necessary. We also need to capture onchange because pasting in iOS doesn't generate an onkeyup event.

The complete solution is available at *www.mobilexweb.com/go/autogrowing*. The code, borrowed from the Google Code Blog with a few changes, is:

```
<script>
// Value of the line-height CSS property for the textarea.
var TEXTAREA_LINE_HEIGHT = 13;

function grow(event) {
    var textarea = event.target;
    var newHeight = textarea.scrollHeight;
    var currentHeight = textarea.clientHeight;
    if (newHeight > currentHeight) {
```

```
                textarea.style.height = newHeight + 5 * TEXTAREA_LINE_HEIGHT +
                    'px';
        }
    }
    </script>
    <textarea onkeyup="grow(event);" onchange="grow(event);" >
```

Figure 8-8 shows the result.

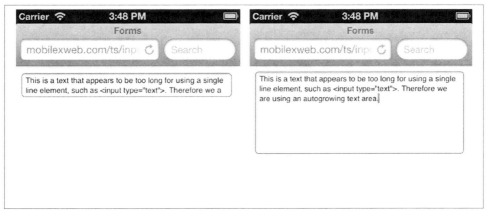

*Figure 8-8. The autogrowing multiline textarea in action—the height of the control changes dynamically as the content grows.*

### Rich text controls

Rich text input controls are not very common in the mobile world, and they were really difficult to implement for many years because of the browser internals. Usually, desktop-based rich text input controls used iframes and were not compatible with mobile browsers.

On touch smartphones, the onscreen keyboard usually takes up too much space on the screen to have a toolbar around. However, on some larger devices, such as the iPhone 5, we can fix a toolbar over the keyboard zone and still have some space to type. On tablets we have enough space to provide a rich input control, and some solutions are appearing to provide this feature.

 The BlackBerry 10 browser supports an extension HTML attribute, `data-blackberry-end-selection-on-touch="on"`, that disables the default behavior when the user selects text on the screen: after a selection is done, instead of opening the clipboard menu on tapping, it will just deselect the text.

**contenteditable.**  HTML5 officially includes something that has been around on the Web unofficially for many years: the `contenteditable` attribute. This attribute accepts `true` or `false` as its possible values; most browsers will also parse it as a Boolean attribute, where its mere presence means true.

When we use `contenteditable="true"` on any HTML element, the whole element and its content becomes an editable control. As weird as it sounds, you can make a whole body element editable!

Safari on iOS from version 5 was the first mobile browser supporting `contenteditable`; when you tap on the editable element the keyboard and cursor will appear on the screen. In Figure 8-9, we can see this feature in action on the Windows Phone.

*Figure 8-9. Here we can see* `contenteditable` *in action on Windows Phone with Internet Explorer—the whole section becomes a rich editor.*

`contenteditable` compatibility as of the time of this writing is shown in Table 8-1.

*Table 8-1. contenteditable compatibility*

| Browser/platform | Supports contenteditable |
| --- | --- |
| Safari on iOS | No until iOS 4.3<br>Yes from iOS 5.0 (contextual menu from 6.0) |
| Android browser | No until Android 3.2<br>Yes from Android 4.0 |
| Chrome for Android | Yes |
| Internet Explorer | Yes |
| Nokia Browser for Symbian | No |
| Nokia Xpress browser for S40 | No |
| Firefox | Yes |
| BlackBerry browser | No on smartphones up to 7.1<br>Yes on PlayBook from 2.0<br>Yes on BB10 |
| webOS | Yes from 3.0 (tablet only) |
| NetFront | No |
| UC browser | No |
| Opera Mobile | No until 12.0<br>Yes from 12.1 |
| Opera Mini | No |

From iOS 6, Safari offers a new feature for content-editable elements: when the user selects text, a menu will appear offering the user the ability to apply bold, italic, or underline styling to that text, as we can see in Figure 8-10. This feature adds the proper HTML elements to the content itself.

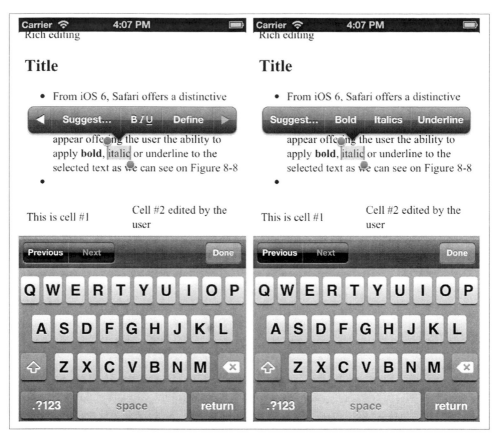

*Figure 8-10. On iOS 6 and beyond, Safari shows a contextual menu on selections allowing you to apply bold, italic, and underline styles to them.*

From iOS 6, Safari will always add a submenu for applying bold, italics, or underline styles to selected text. If you don't want this feature, be sure to remove those tags from the element after the user has ended the editing action.

If you want the user to be able to apply rich formatting—such as color, font size, bold/ italics, or any other HTML styling—you can provide a toolbar near the editable content that will wrap the current selection in a new DOM element. When the user is typing new text or modifying current elements, she is changing the DOM directly, as if she were writing the `innerHTML` property of your content-editable element.

On compatible devices, it's a good idea to offer a fixed toolbar so it will not disappear when the user scrolls the content area.

I know what you're thinking: "How can we detect changes in the editable element?" The onchange event is not useful here because elements like a div or a section don't have that event, unlike form controls. There are four possible solutions:

- Read the innerHTML property of the desired element when the user submits the info, or frequently with a timer.
- Capture key events on the element, so we detect every keypress (or a specific keypress, such as the Return key).
- Use a *DOM mutation observer*, a modern technique available in some mobile browsers that will monitor any changes to the DOM, including the ones defined by the user on a contenteditable element.
- Use *DOM mutation event listeners*, such as DOMNodeInserted, DOMNodeRemoved, and DOMCharacterDataModified.

To provide our own rich toolbar options, we can use the document.execCommand method available in browsers that support contenteditable.

The execution command mechanism receives three arguments: the command's name, whether the default UI for the command should be shown, and some optional extra value information for the command. Commands include features such as apply bold, change colors, clipboard actions, and undo. Not every action is supported on each mobile browser, so we should test them before use.

 All of these features were included in Internet Explorer for desktop, and now they are being discussed by the W3C as the HTML Editing API. We can find more information and a complete list of available actions at W3C's website (*http://www.w3.org/community/editing*).

**WYSIHTML5.** WYSIHTML5 is an open source rich text editor created fully in HTML5 that is compatible with mobile browsers. You can download it and see a live demo (*http://xing.github.com/wysihtml5*).

This framework will downgrade to a normal and basic textarea when the feature is not compatible with the current browser. The library supports a good way to define your own toolbar using just HTML5 elements, as in:

```
<a data-wysihtml5-command="italic">apply italic</a>
<a data-wysihtml5-command="foreColor" data-wysihtml5-command-value="red">
 apply red</a>
```

Every action can be applied to the current selection or, if there is no selection, the next values that the user types.

### Pop-up controls

If we just need one quick text input, we can use the standard JavaScript `prompt` dialog instead of an HTML element. As you can see in Figure 8-11, the dialog has a nice native UI on different mobile browsers. Unfortunately, there is no way to customize the dialog's title or the virtual keyboard type.

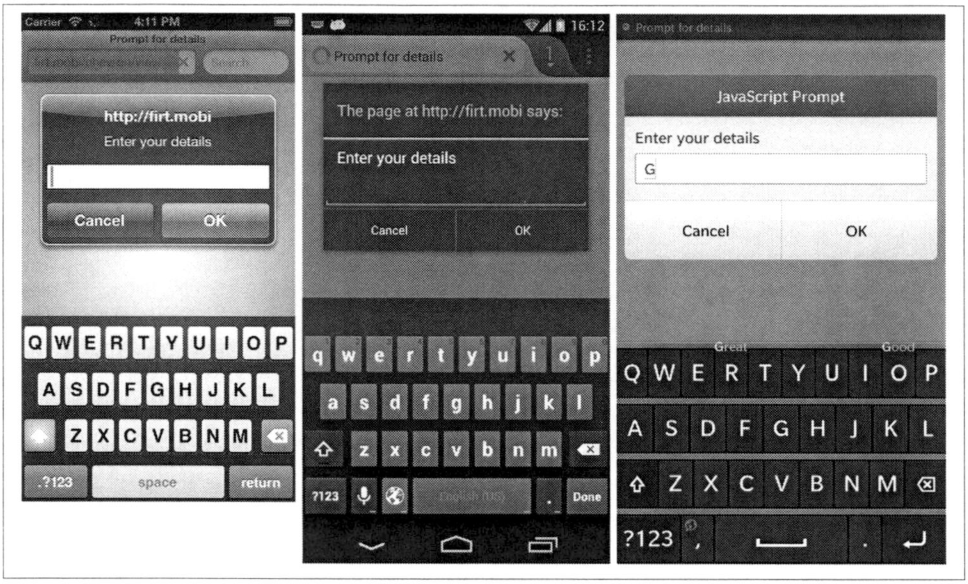

*Figure 8-11. Using the standard dialog prompt, we can replace single-element forms.*

You use it as follows:

```
var input = window.prompt("Enter your details", "");
```

> When we are creating native web experiences, the default JavaScript dialog is not good enough as it shows *file://* or the name of the HTML file as the dialog title. However, many native web platforms allow us to use a nonstandard native dialog instead.

## Range Slider Fields

HTML5 includes the `<input type="range">` that will render on compatible devices as a range slider on the screen. The input needs at least the maximum (`max`) attribute defined so it knows the limit; you can also define a minimum (`min`) attribute different than the default zero value, and the `step` attribute, which will define the jump that the slider will make. For example:

```
<input type="range" min="0" max="100" step="10">
```

The range input type has some usability problems on mobile browsers:

- The draggable selector is too small on most mobile browsers, as you can see in Figure 8-12, and it's difficult to move it.
- The user does not see the current value in all browsers, which can make the control useless.

 Internet Explorer 10 is one of the browsers that show the current value of the range input type while the user is dragging the control.

Because of these usability problems, the UI framework jQuery Mobile enhances the range input control with a much nicer user interface, including a bigger scrollable element and a numeric input that is synchronized with the slider automatically, as shown in Figure 8-12.

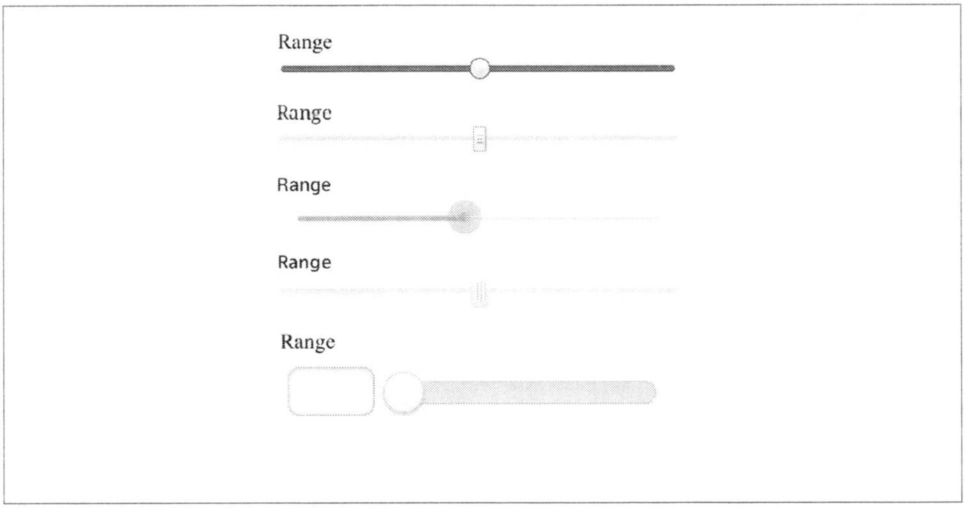

Range
Range
Range
Range
Range

*Figure 8-12. The standard `type=range` slider element in Safari on iOS, the Android browser, Google Chrome for Android, and the BlackBerry browser, and the jQuery Mobile enhanced control.*

## Date Input Fields

HTML5 defines new input types for date and time selectors. Unfortunately, not every mobile browser supports this feature at this time, but the good news is that if the browser is not compatible, the input field will fall back to a normal text input field.

The following type values are available:

- Date selector: `<input type="date">`
- Time selector: `<input type="time">`
- Date and time selector: `<input type="datetime">`
- Local date and time selector: `<input type="datetime-local">`
- Month selector: `<input type="month">`
- Week selector: `<input type="week">`

 The date and datetime selectors will give you a string value in the value property. However, the browser guarantees that if you instantiate a new Date object with that string it will create a proper and valid date object.

Figure 8-13 shows how Safari on iOS and Chrome for Android render the different input types, usually as a pop-up control. The datetime selector will include the time zone when getting the value, but the datetime-local selector will not. The week selector is not compatible with most mobile browsers, so it will fall back to a text input control.

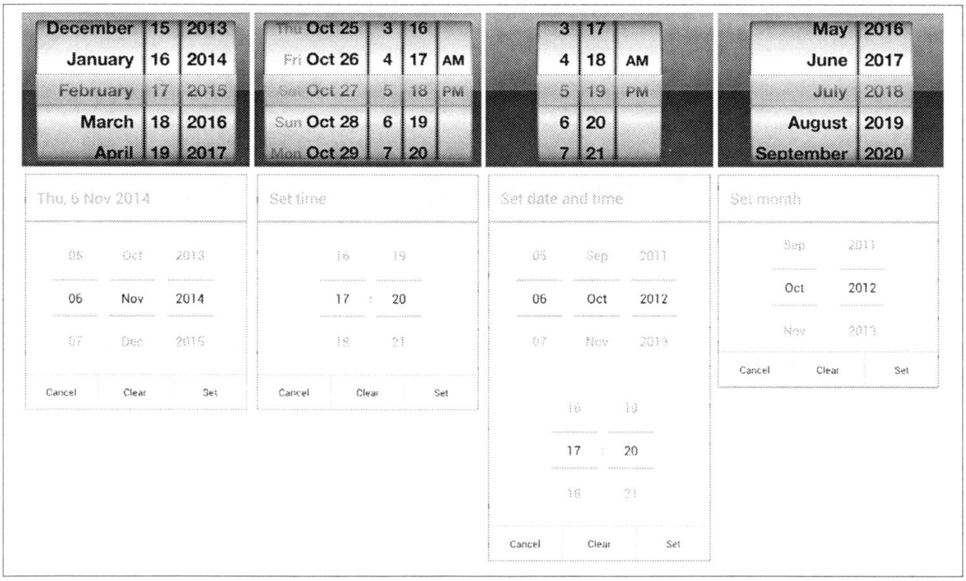

*Figure 8-13. The date selectors in action (in order: date, datetime, time, and month— the datetime-local selector is the same as datetime, and the week selector is not compatible). Chrome for Android has removed support for datetime from version 26.*

HTML5 defines a color picker control `<input type="color">`. However, at the time of this writing, only Opera for Android and BlackBerry 10 support it; all other browsers will fall back to a text input control.

## File Selection Fields

The file selection control is the control typically used to browse for a local file to send to the server. When the user selects this control a modal pop-up window appears, allowing him to select a file from the public internal memory folders or from the additional memory card. A simple upload form might look like this:

```
<label for="photo">Upload a photo</label>
<input type="file" name="photo">
```

HTML5 adds two attributes to the `<input type="file">` element: the `multiple` Boolean attribute for multiple file selection and the `accept` attribute that allows us to filter the kind of files we want. We can choose to accept:

- Images only: `image/*`
- Videos only: `video/*`
- Audio only: `audio/*`
- Any specific format (MIME type)
- A comma-separated list of MIME types

Let's take a look at some samples:

```
<label for="manyfiles">Upload multiple files </label>
<input type="file" name="manyfiles" multiple>

<label for="video">Upload only a video</label>
<input type="file" name="video" accept="video/*">
```

Some mobile browsers, such as the Android browser up to 2.1 and Safari on iOS up to 5.1 inclusive, are not compatible with any kind of file upload. Therefore, if you use a file upload selector it will be rendered on the screen as disabled, as shown in Figure 8-14.

Single upload:

Single upload:
Choose File  no file selected

Single upload:
Choose File   1 photo

*Figure 8-14. The file upload input type will not work on older devices, but here it's being rendered properly on newer ones.*

Figure 8-15 shows a QR code that you can use in your own mobile browser to test for yourself how this new attribute works on your device.

*Figure 8-15. If you want to test the file upload or any other code in this book by yourself, just point your mobile browser to http://t.ad.ag or scan this QR code.*

Some browsers, such as Safari on iOS from version 6, Firefox for mobile, and Chrome for Android, will invite the user to use the camera when `accept="image/*"` is defined.

### Actions with files

When the user selects one or more files, we can:

- Send the file to the server using `POST` and `enctype="multipart/formdata"` in the `form` element.
- Use the File API (to be covered in Chapter 15) to do something with the file locally using JavaScript. We can manage it as a binary file or, if it's an image, as a data URI element.
- Use `XMLHttpRequest` 2 (Ajax) to upload the file to the server and use progress events to show a progress bar while the file is being uploaded.

### The HTML Media Capture extension

The W3C has released an HTML extension called *HTML Media Capture* (*http://www.w3.org/TR/html-media-capture*), which allows us to make use of the device's camera and microphone from an `<input type="file">` including the new `capture` Boolean attribute.

 An old spec defined `capture` as a string attribute instead of a Boolean, supporting `camera`, `camcorder`, `microphone`, or `filesystem` as values. Version 2.x of the Android browser, Google Chrome up to version 18, and other browsers still support the old spec; if you use the Boolean version, they will just ignore it.

The `accept` attribute defines how to capture the media. Therefore, if we accept only images (`image/*`) or audio (`audio/*`) and we define a `capture` attribute, if the HTML Media Capture extension is available the user will get the camera or recorder app instead of a file picker when she clicks on the Browse icon (Figure 8-16).

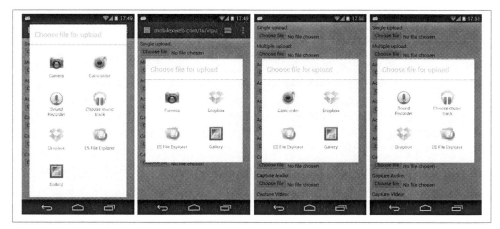

*Figure 8-16. With HTML Media Capture support, when the user clicks on "Browse" or "Choose File" the camera app or the sound recorder app will be opened directly as a picker for a temporary file.*

Using the File API, we can get the file from the user and do some actions on the client side, such as resizing the image or performing face or QR code recognition.

With the new spec, the code should look like the following:

```
<label for="photo">Take a Picture now </label>
<input type="file" name="photo" accept="image/*" capture>
```

```
<label for="video">Record a video now</label>
<input type="file" name="video" accept="video/*" capture>

<label for="mic">Record audio now</label>
<input type="file" name="mic" accept="audio/*" capture>
```

For browsers still supporting the old spec, such as Android browser 2.x, the code must look like the following:

```
<label for="photo">Take a Picture now </label>
<input type="file" name="photo" accept="image/*" capture="camera">

<label for="video">Record a video now</label>
<input type="file" name="video" accept="video/*" capture="camcorder">

<label for="mic">Record audio now</label>
<input type="file" name="mic" accept="audio/*" capture="audio">
```

Usually, on mobile browsers HTML Media Capture will work only on nonmultiple file controls, as most camera applications do not have a specific UI to take a group of pictures and send all those pictures back to the browser at once. Therefore, if you want to use HTML Media Capture for multiple files you will have to either add several controls or add a new control dynamically with JavaScript after every selection.

### Mobile browser compatibility

Safari on iOS was not compatible with file upload at all until iOS 6, nor was Android until 2.2; the webOS browser does not support file upload either. Therefore, there is no way to upload a file to a website on those devices. Remember that the original iPad and iPod touch (first generation) are not compatible with iOS 6; if you have users with these devices, they will see just a disabled element (as shown in Figure 8-14).

Safari on iOS from version 6 supports the multiple attribute and the accept attribute, but only with a value of image/* or video/*. Any other combination will just give the user a way to upload images or videos—there is no way to upload audio or other kinds of files, such as a PDF.

While Safari on iOS 6 does not support HTML Media Capture, if you use `accept="image/*"` or `accept="video/*"` without the `multiple` attribute, the user will be prompted to pick a file or open the camera application at that time to take a picture or record a video (see Figure 8-17).

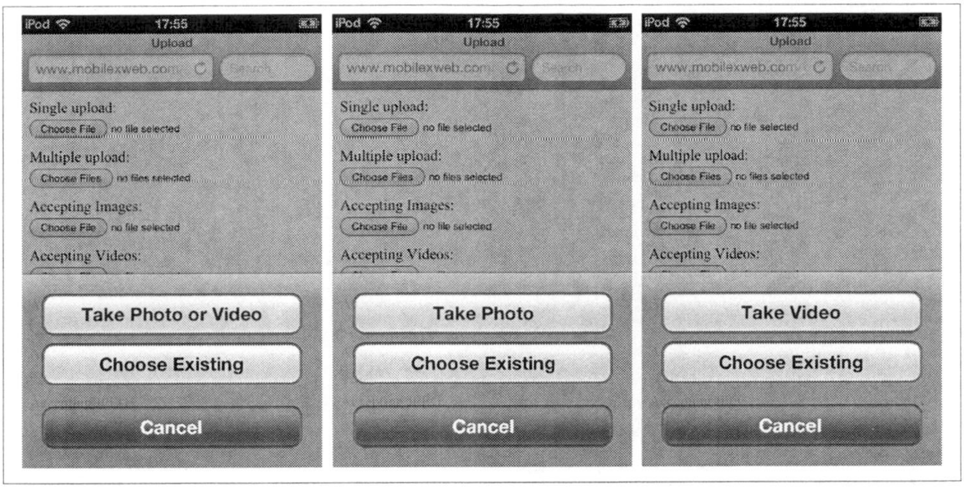

*Figure 8-17. Safari on iOS from version 6 will show different dialogs depending on the accept attribute's current value—if you add multiple, the gallery is shown by default and you can't use the camera app directly.*

On Android devices, usually every browser (Chrome, the Android browser, Firefox, Opera) will ask for an *Intent* to pick a file based on the current `accept` value. Intents are a way on Android to integrate all the installed apps in an agnostic way—for example, if an app subscribes as an image picker, it will appear as an option when the user taps on a file upload control accepting only images, as you can see in Figure 8-18.

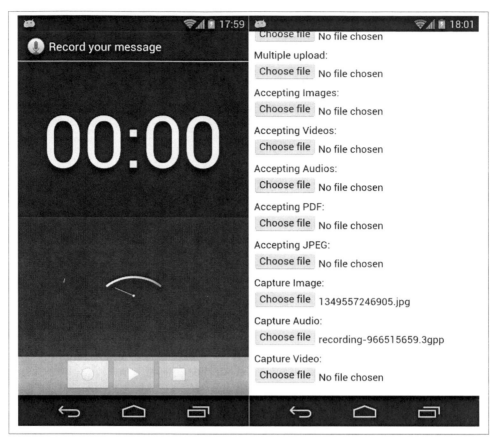

*Figure 8-18. The Android browser and Google Chrome for Android show an Intent selector where you can choose which installed native app to use to pick the file, based on the accept attribute's current value.*

As you'll see in Table 8-2, some browsers on Android devices support HTML Media Capture; if the capture attribute is included, the proper app (camera or voice recorder) will be opened automatically when the control is activated without any dialog being shown.

Browsers such as Nokia's Xpress browser for S40 and Opera Mini running on social phones will open a filesystem browser that will look into the internal or external memory to select a file and upload it every time they encounter a file upload control.

We can classify mobile browsers in terms of file upload compatibility as having:

*No compatibility at all*
    Your field will be disabled.

*Basic compatibility*
> Users can upload a single file, but there is no filtering ability and no HTML Media Capture support. Some browsers will offer users the ability to capture the file on the screen at that moment using the camera app.

*Filter compatibility*
> Users can upload only a single file, but you can use the `accept` attribute to filter files (usually at least images and videos).

*HTML5 compatibility*
> Users can upload one or more files, and the `accept` attribute works fully.

*HTML Media Capture compatibility*
> All possible options are available. When using `capture`, usually `multiple` can't be used at the same time.

Table 8-2 summarizes browser compatibility at the time of this writing.

*Table 8-2. File upload compatibility table*

| Browser/platform | Basic support | File picker/capture | accept attribute | multiple attribute | capture attribute |
|---|---|---|---|---|---|
| Safari on iOS | No <= 5.1 Yes, 6.0+ | Picker and camera capture | Yes, only images and videos | Yes | No |
| Android browser | No <= 2.1 Yes, 2.2+ | Picker, camera, and voice capture | Yes, only images, videos, and audio | No | No <= 2.3 Yes, 3.0+ |
| Chrome for Android | Yes | Picker, camera, and voice capture | Yes | No | Yes |
| Internet Explorer | No <= IE9 Yes, IE10+ | Picker and camera capture | Yes | Yes | No |
| Nokia Browser for Symbian | Yes | Picker | Partial (shows warning) | No | No |
| Nokia Xpress browser for S40 | Yes | Picker | No | No | No |
| Firefox | Yes | Picker, camera, and voice capture | No | No | No |
| BlackBerry browser | Yes, 4.2+ | Picker | No | No | Yes on BB10 |
| UC browser | Yes | Picker and camera capture | No | No | No |
| Opera Mobile | Yes | Only picker | No | No | No |
| Opera Mini | Yes | Only picker | No | No | No |

## Noninteractive Form Elements

In addition to supporting labels and hidden fields (`<input type="hidden">`), HTML5 defines some new noninteractive elements that are related to forms or value definitions. The new elements are `output`, `progress`, and `meter`. While not every browser renders these new elements properly at this time, we always have a fallback mechanism.

The `output` element is intended for the result of a calculation on a form. It receives a `for` attribute whose value is a space-separated list of controls involved in the calculation and a `form` attribute if we are using it outside of a `form` element.

 You can make any interactive form control read-only by applying the new HTML5 Boolean attribute `readonly`.

For example, if we were working on a currency calculator project we might have a form like the following:

```
<form id="currencyCalculator">
    <label for="value">Value in US Dollars</label>
    <input type="number" id="value">

    <label for="currency">
    <select id="currency">
        <option value="EUR">Euro</option>
        <option value="GBP">British pound</option>
        <option value="JPY">Yen</option>
    </select>

    <input type="button" value="Convert">
</form>

<output for="value currency" form="currencyCalculator"></output>
```

We could use JavaScript, Ajax, or a server postback to fill the output value.

The `progress` element provides a way to render a progress bar on the screen:

```
<progress>Loading...</progress>
```

When the browser is not compatible, it will just show the element's contents (here, "Loading..."). An indeterminate progress element (with no `value` attribute) is used when we don't know how much time (or what percentage) is left to complete the operation. Usually, a browser will render it as a progress animation—for example, Internet Explorer 10 shows a points floating animation typical of the Windows Phone and Windows 8 user interface.

If you are creating Windows 8 Store apps with HTML5—not browser-based apps—Microsoft allows a progress bar to be rendered as an animated ring using the nonstandard style `-ms-progress-appearance: ring`.

If we know the current value and the maximum value, we can create a determinate progress bar using the `value` and `max` attributes, which can be changed dynamically using JavaScript:

```
<progress max="100" value="60">60%</progress>
```

 If you don't provide a maximum value for a progress bar, a floating-point value between 0 and 1 is expected.

If we want to show a fractional value that is not expected to change as a progress indicator, we can use the `meter` element. For example, to show the available space on some account:

```
<meter max="1000000" value="450000">
```

`meter` is not yet well implemented in mobile browsers, but it supports more semantic attributes to indicate how good the current value is—we can specify `optimum`, `low`, and `high` values that may be used in the future by compatible browsers to show different areas on the meter in different colors.

Figure 8-19 shows the `progress` and `meter` elements rendered in two browsers that support these new elements.

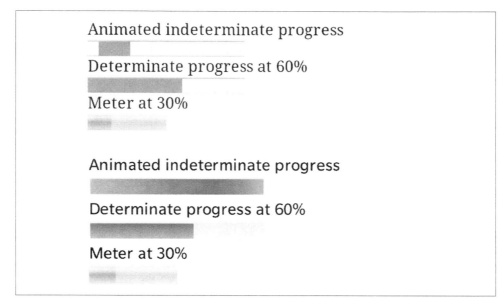

*Figure 8-19. The progress and meter elements rendered in Google Chrome for Android and the BlackBerry 10 browser.*

 HTML5 also includes the keygen element, which generates a public/private key pair and sends the public key to the server in the form. Mobile usage at the time of this writing is quite rare and compatibility is not yet good enough for me to recommend its use.

# Form Control Attributes

HTML5 includes new attributes that can be applied to almost every form element, including input, textarea, and select. Some of the attributes are semantic flags, and some others provide new behavior.

## Placeholder

A placeholder is a hint that is shown inside a text box until the user inserts text in that field. When the user starts typing, the placeholder is hidden, as shown in Figure 8-20. This feature is very useful in mobile designs because of the lack of space to add more information or hints about what the field should contain.

URL

e.g. http://mobilexweb.com

*Figure 8-20. The placeholder is the gray descriptive text inside the text box that is automatically deleted when the user begins typing a value in the box.*

The `placeholder` attribute is available in HTML5, and for noncompatible browsers we can create a little script to give this functionality, even using the standard `placehold er` attribute as the source:

```
<input type="text" name="zip" placeholder="Your ZIP Code">
```

We can customize the appearance of the placeholder using some nonstandard CSS hacks, such as `::-webkit-input-placeholder` for WebKit-based browsers, `:-ms-input-placeholder` for Internet Explorer 10, and `:moz-placeholder` for Firefox:

```
input::-webkit-input-placeholder, input:-ms-input-placeholder,
    input:moz-placeholder {
    color: #AFEFAF;
}
```

## autofocus

Adding the `autofocus` Boolean attribute to a control tells the browser to focus on that element once the page is loaded, so we don't need to rely on JavaScript hacks to support that feature. For example, if we are working on a search engine, we can focus on the main search field using:

```
<input type="search" autofocus>
```

 A JavaScript library can add support for `placeholder` and `autofocus` even on devices with no support for those attributes. You can download this library from GitHub (*http://gist.github.com/330318*).

## autocomplete

The `autocomplete` attribute accepts an `on` or `off` value, and it can be applied to the `form` element as a whole or to individual `input` elements. This allows us to enable or disable the autocompletion or autosuggestion features that the browser may use in forms.

## readonly

If for some reason we don't want the user to interact with a form element, we can disable it with `disabled` or make it `readonly`. Both attributes are Boolean:

```
<select disabled></select>
<input readonly type="tel">
```

## Input Validation Attributes

As we'll see later in this chapter, HTML5 includes a validation feature that can be used by JavaScript or CSS. In this category, we can find the following new attributes:

`required`
> A Boolean attribute that can be applied to any input type

`min`
> Specifies the minimum valid value; can be applied to numeric (`number` or `range`) or date input types

`max`
> Specifies the maximum valid value; can be applied to numeric (`number` or `range`) or date input types

`pattern`
> Specifies a regular expression against which the input value should be validated

`step`
> Used for numeric (`number` or `range`) input types; specifies the legal number intervals

## Safari Extensions

Safari on iOS includes `autocorrect="{on|off}"` and `autocapitalize="{on|off}"` attributes, to activate/deactivate automatic spelling correction (preferred for non-dictionary input fields) and automatic capitalization for the input.

 For BlackBerry 5.0 devices, we can also define that we don't want prediction on our input fields using the XHTML MP `inputmode="predictOff"`.

## Firefox Extensions

Firefox for mobile devices includes mobile devices includes the `mozactionhit` attribute that is used to define the label of the label/return key on virtual keyboards. The possible options are `go`, `done`, `next`, `search`, and `send`, and the value will be mapped to the appropriate string in the current language.

For validation purposes, Firefox shows an error bubble when a field doesn't comply with its constraints (for example, the email address does not have valid syntax). To replace the default error message, Firefox supports a nonstandard attribute, x-moz-errormessage:

```
<input type="text" name="name" required x-moz-errormessage=
        "You must enter your name">
```

## XHTML Mobile inputmode

Some non-HTML5 devices, such as BlackBerry smartphones running OS 5.0, also accept the XHTML Basic/Mobile Profile inputmode attribute with a comma-separated list of tokens. The tokens can be script tokens (language charsets) or modifier tokens.

 The inputmode attribute is also defined by WHATWG in the HTML specification, but not by the W3C.

The available script tokens are:

- arabic
- bopomofo
- cyrillic
- georgian
- greek
- han
- hangul
- hebrew
- hiragana
- kanji
- katakana
- latin
- simplifiedhanzi
- thai
- traditionalhanzi
- user

The possible modifiers are:

- `lowerCase`
- `upperCase`
- `titleCase`
- `startUpper`
- `digits`
- `symbols`
- `predictOn`
- `predictOff`

## Additional Form Attributes

Before HTML5, every form control needed to be inside the `form` element to work without JavaScript. From HTML5, there are new attributes that we can apply to form elements that define to which form a control should be applied. We need to be careful on mobile browsers, though, as compatibility is not very good yet and there is no simple way to create a fallback.

In this category, we can find attributes such as `form` (to specify the IDs of one or more forms that an `input` element belongs to), `formnovalidate` (for elements that should not be validated on form submission), and button-specific attributes such as `formaction`, `formenctype`, `formmethod`, and `formtarget`.

# Form Validation

To reduce the number of client-side scripts and server-side trips required for validation and to improve the usability of our forms, we should provide as many input validation properties as we can.

The first typical option is to define the maximum size accepted for the text input using the `maxlength` property, expressed as a number of characters. Many platforms automatically add a character counter while the user is typing. A second popular option is to define the right input type for `input` elements, such as `number` or `date`. That will definitely improve usability and validation.

To add more layers of validation without our own custom algorithms, HTML5 and WAP CSS (from XHTML MP) offer us some solutions.

# HTML5 Validation

As we saw earlier, HTML5 adds some validation attributes, such as `required`, `pat tern`, `min`, and `max`. The question is, what happens if a required input field is left without content, or if a numeric input field has a value greater than the `max` definition? What happens if the user doesn't type a valid email address in an `<input type="email">` field?

 Even though not all browsers support the HTML5 validation attributes, it's a good idea to use them as flags for our JavaScript validation algorithms instead of hardcoding the validation rules into our scripts.

The behavior changes per mobile browser, but here are some of the things that may happen:

- A validation bubble appears if the control doesn't validate against the rules.
- The form can't be submitted until the whole form validates against the rules.
- The JavaScript API is used to validate the input.
- We can use the new CSS validation pseudoclasses to show the validation process dynamically.

On desktops, most browsers add a validation bubble or halt the submission if validation rules are not met. However, most mobile browsers ignore that and leave it up to our CSS or JavaScript code to enforce the validation rules.

At the time of this writing only Firefox halts submission and shows an error bubble by default, as we can see in Figure 8-21.

*Figure 8-21. Firefox shows an error bubble when the element is not valid—we can define the error text using the nonstandard x-moz-errormessage attribute.*

If you want to disable validation in some situations, you can use <form novalidate> or apply the formnovalidate attribute to one specific button, as in <input type="submit" formnovalidate>.

### CSS validation pseudoclasses

CSS3 added new validation pseudoclasses that can be applied dynamically to form elements. The available pseudoclasses are:

`:required` *and* `:optional`
   Applied automatically for elements with or without the `required` Boolean attribute

`:read-only` *and* `:read-write`
   Applied automatically for elements with or without the `readonly` Boolean attribute

`:valid` *and* `:invalid`
   Applied automatically for all the rules, such as `type`, `min`, `max`, `pattern`, and `required`

`:in-range` *and* `:out-of-range`
   Applied automatically when the `min` and `max` attributes are defined

> If you don't use `required` on an attribute but do use another rule such as `pattern`, `type`, or `max`, an input without content will always be validated as valid. If the user enters at least one character, the other rules will define the validity of the input.

With these new pseudoclasses, we can change borders or backgrounds for inputs when they become valid or invalid:

```
input:valid {
    border: 1px solid green;
}
input:invalid {
    border: 1px solid red;
}
```

We can also mix these new features with other pseudoclasses such as `:focus`, so we can define a different style for invalid input types only when they are in focus:

```
input:focus:invalid {
    border: 1px solid red;
}
```

> WebKit-based browsers that show a bubble error message on submit allow customization through pseudoelements. You can customize styles using `::-webkit-validation-bubble`, `::-webkit-validation-bubble-message`, `::-webkit-validation-bubble-arrow`, and `::-webkit-validation-bubble-arrow-clipper`.

## Constraints validation API

HTML5 comes with a new API for form constraints validation. On compatible devices, the form element has a checkValidity() method that runs the constraints validation evaluation process and returns a Boolean value indicating the result, and a setCustom Validity(*message*) method that allows us to force a false validation result because of a custom validation process. We can use this method inside a change or input event listener.

Every form element, such as an input element, also has the following properties:

willValidate
  A Boolean value that defines the current state of the constraints evaluation. A false value means there is a problem.

validity
  A ValidityState object defining Boolean attributes for every possible constraint problem, such as validity.typeMismatch, validity.valueMissing, validi ty.customError, validity.patternMismatch, validity.rangeOverflow, or val idity.rangeUnderflow.

validationMessage
  A message describing failures.

 The onchange DOM event fires after the form element has lost focus. The new oninput DOM event available in some browsers will be fired any time the element is changed because of the user's intervention, such as pressing a key.

If we want to halt form submission if there is a problem in the validation process, we can use the following code:

```
<form onsubmit="return this.checkValidity()">
```

If we want to know whether an element such as <input type="number" max="110" id="age"> has any problem with validation, we can use:

```
var ageInput = document.getElementById("age");
var isNotNumeric = ageInput.validity.typeMismatch;
var isOverflow = ageInput.validity.rangeOverflow;
```

When working with numeric input fields, we need to remember that the value property always returns a string version of the value. We can force a number using parseInt or parseFloat; modern browsers also support the new valueAsNumber attribute on input elements.

---

The constraints validation API doesn't remove the need for server-side validation scripts to avoid security issues.

## WAP CSS Validation

As mentioned earlier, WAP CSS added the property -wap-input-format, which allows us to define the type and number of characters that the user can input (known as the *input mask*). Specifying an input mask will reduce the user's error possibilities; it can yield error messages like the one shown in Figure 8-22. There is also the -wap-input-required attribute, which prevents the user from moving the focus away from a field until she has entered some text in it.

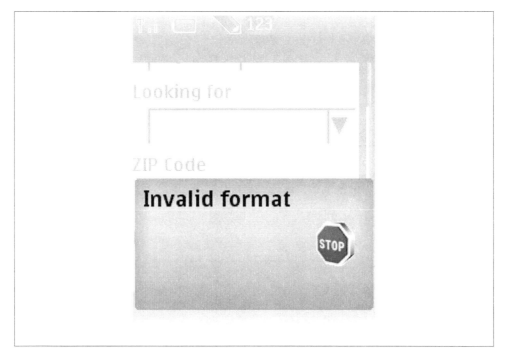

*Figure 8-22. Browsers compatible with WAP CSS input constraints show some kind of error message when the user enters text in an invalid format and then tries to move the focus away from that field.*

The content of the -wap-input-format attribute is a string mask using the special characters in Table 8-3.

*Table 8-3. WAP CSS input format patterns*

| Pattern | Usage |
|---|---|
| a | Any character, letter, number, or symbol. |
| A | Any uppercase alphanumeric character. |
| n | Any numeric character or symbol. |
| N | Any numeric character. |
| x | Any lowercase alphanumeric character or symbol. |
| X | Any uppercase alphanumeric character or symbol. |
| m | Any character, lowercase by default, but with uppercase possible. |
| M | Any character, uppercase by default, but with lowercase possible. |
| {n}{pattern} | A fixed number of repeats (n) of the pattern defined. For example, 4N means four numeric-only characters. |
| *{pattern} | Any number of repeats of the pattern defined. For example, *A means any number of uppercase alphanumeric characters. It can be used only once per pattern. |
| {pattern}{pattern} | Pattern combination. For example, A*a means one uppercase character and then any number of any other character. |

We can also escape other characters to create complex patterns, but this is not recommended because the pattern matching engines are not the same on all platforms and strange behavior can result.

 Internet Explorer Mobile before Windows Phone also accepted the nonstandard attribute `emptyok`, defining whether a value was required (`false`) or not (`true`).

The next sample shows the standard way to define a required US zip code text input, an optional phone number text input, and a required password numeric field using XHTML MP and WAP CSS:

```
<dl>
   <dt><label for="zip">ZIP Code</label></dt>
   <dl><input type="text" name="zip" style="-wap-input-format: '5N';
              -wap-input-required: true" /></dl>
   <dt><label for="phone">Phone Number</label></dt>
   <dl><input type="text" name="phone" maxlength="15"
              style="-wap-input-format: '*n';" /></dl>
   <dt><label for="password">Password</label></dt>
   <dl><input type="password" maxlength="8" name="password"
              style="-wap-input-format: '8N';
              -wap-input-required: true'" /></dl>
</dl>
```

Many older XHTML mobile browsers understand the inputformat or format attribute, imported from WML. The syntax is the same as for the WAP CSS attribute. If we want to add the same feature for older Openwave-based devices, for example, we can use the inputformat attribute. Internet Explorer uses the format attribute with the same pattern inside:

```
<input type="text" name="zip" inputformat="5N" format="5N"
       maxchars="5" />
```

# CHAPTER 9

# Feature and Device Detection

Before moving on with more HTML5, CSS, and JavaScript code that we can use on mobile devices, we need to pause and talk about feature and device detection. As we saw in the last chapter, not every browser supports exactly the same features, and even different versions of the same browser may have differences in terms of what we can use.

This book was likely finished a few months (or maybe even years) before you picked it up. I can assure you that what some browsers support today may differ from what they supported at the time I was writing it.

This is not just a book authoring issue. It's also a development issue, because we can't constantly update every website and web app we create to suit every new browser version or platform on the market.

Therefore, we need a way to design and develop our code that makes it as future-proof as possible. To that end, we are going to look at some techniques that will be useful for feature detection, device detection, and fallback mechanisms.

In combination with all these techniques, we can use the progressive enhancement technique (covered in Chapter 5) and some graceful degradation hacks to ensure that our code works as well as possible on as many platforms as possible.

## Possible Problems

To find the right solutions, first we need to recognize all the possible problems we may need to deal with. We can summarize the possible problems with regard to features as follows:

- An HTML feature we want to use is not available, such as the `progress` element.
- A CSS feature we want to use is not available, such as CSS animations.

- A JavaScript API we want to use is not available or only partially available, such as Geolocation.
- We need to deal with different contexts: different input modes, screen resolutions, pixel densities, and screen sizes.
- A feature may not work properly even when it is officially implemented.
- Some APIs (such as video-playing codecs) are technology-agnostic, so we need to know current compatibility.
- We need to deliver content that is platform-specific, such as an Android native application, an ebook, or a Passbook coupon for iOS.
- We want to use a feature that is prefixed—that is, for which every browser has a different prefix, usually on CSS or JavaScript API.

## Possible Solutions

Different types of solutions are available to solve problems we detect. For example, we can:

- Use internal HTML, CSS, or JavaScript mechanisms to provide a fallback, so if A is not available, B will automatically be executed.
- Use a *polyfill*, so if A is not available, some code is being executed on top of the browser that emulates A compatibility.
- Use a client-side feature detection framework, so if A is not available the framework will warn us somehow so we can use another solution.
- Use a client-side device detection mechanism, so if we already know that browser X doesn't support A, we can use another solution.
- Use a server-side feature library, so if A is not available, we change the code from the server or redirect the user to another page.
- Use a server-side device detection mechanism, so if we already know that browser X doesn't support A, we can change the code from the server or redirect the user to another page.

Which solution is the best one? Well, unfortunately there is no unique answer. Let's analyze it.

Device detection mechanisms should be avoided as much as possible, because as we know from Chapter 1 to Chapter 3 there are too many platforms and too many versions out there, and creating an infinite if-else-if algorithm (if it's iOS 6 then A, if it's iOS 5 then B, if it's Android then C...) is not a good idea for our mental health. However, in some specific situations, there is no other way to solve a problem than asking for the specific platform.

Device detection always creates new problems for the future. For example, until 2012 most websites were not delivering `<input type="file">` for iOS because it was not supported until iOS 6. So every developer must go now and change the condition if they realize that now iOS 6 supports them.

Generally, you should always try to rely on internal HTML, CSS, and JavaScript mechanisms to provide fallbacks, as we'll cover in the next few pages. However, you can't solve every problem this way, so using feature detection is the next recommended pattern. Client-side frameworks use automatic tests to mark a feature as compatible, but occasionally that may lead to false positives, or you may encounter features that cannot be detected automatically. Server-side feature libraries are manually tested server-side databases, so their reliability in some situations can be higher than that of automatic tests.

### About polyfills

While a polyfill may seem like a good idea for classic web development in some situations, when developing for the mobile web I recommend avoiding them as much as possible. A polyfill is usually a JavaScript framework that fills a gap for some feature that the browser doesn't recognize natively: it offers compatibility by emulating the same behavior. (Of course, a polyfill for every feature is not always possible.)

HTML5 Please (*http://html5please.com*) is a community-updated website where you can find information on every HTML5 feature and advice on whether you can use it with confidence or should use it with a fallback, use a polyfill, or avoid usage.

The problem on mobile browsers is performance. Like every JavaScript framework, a polyfill will take time and battery power to "fill the gap," and if a browser does not support a feature it may be because it's an old platform—and old platforms mean less memory and slower performance. Therefore, doing something that harms performance may be a very bad idea. That's not always the case, but you should at least test what the possible performance impact may be before deciding to use a polyfill.

# Informational Websites

If we want to know the current state of one API on different platforms, we can use some informational websites that will help us to understand compatibility. In Chapter 6, we covered browser testing tools such as HTML5 Test (*http://html5test.com*) and Ringmark (*http://rng.io*) that will assess current compatibility dynamically. There are also informational websites that provide compatibility tables to help us better understand current compatibility on all the browsers after manual or automatic tests.

## Can I Use

The most well-known website that provides compatibility information for web browsers is Can I Use… (*http://caniuse.com*). It has a good amount of information on features and sub-features of CSS, HTML5, SVG, JavaScript APIs, and others. Every feature is compared across many desktop and some mobile platforms. On the mobile side, compatibility information is currently limited to Safari on iOS, Opera Mini, the Android browser, and the BlackBerry browser. One of the important features is that we can see every feature's compatibility in the latest version, previous versions, and expected future versions of every browser platform. The site also includes links to related articles for almost every feature that is listed.

 If you want to run the tests that define the information on the Can I Use website, you can point your browser to Can I Use… test page (*http://tests.caniuse.com*).

Global usage share statistics from StatCounter Global Stats (*http://gw.statcounter.com*) are also provided for each feature, so we have an idea of the market share of compatible browsers. Unfortunately, at the time of this writing that data is not separated between mobile and desktop platforms, so the statistics are difficult to interpret from a mobile-only point of view.

 If you want to see an overview graph of the Can I Use data, you can point your browser to the HTML5 and CSS3 Readiness website (*http://html5readiness.com*).

In Figure 9-1, we can see compatibility for the WebGL JavaScript API at the time of this writing.

## MobileHTML5.org

Because I couldn't find any good and reliable resource on the Web specifically about HTML5 compatibility on mobile devices, I decided to create the website Mobile HTML5 (*http://mobilehtml5.org*), with the goal of covering as many mobile platforms as possible with real manual testing examples. Thanks to the fact that I own 45 mobile devices, I have the ability to manually test every feature on every platform; the results are displayed on the site in a quick-reference table to help viewers understand where we are in terms of compatibility (see Figure 9-2).

WebGL - 3D Canvas graphics - Other

*Usage stats: Global
Support: 28.19%
Partial support: 24.77%
Total: 52.96%

*Method of generating dynamic 3D graphics using JavaScript, accelerated through hardware*

| Show all versions | IE | Firefox | Chrome | Safari | Opera | iOS Safari | Opera Mini | Android Browser | Blackberry Browser |
|---|---|---|---|---|---|---|---|---|---|
| | | | | | | | | 2.1 | |
| | | | | | | 3.2 | | 2.2 | |
| | | | | | | 4.0-4.1 | | 2.3 | |
| | 7.0 | | | | | 4.2-4.3 | | 3.0 | |
| | 8.0 | 14.0 | 21.0 | 5.1 | | 5.0-5.1 | | 4.0 | |
| Current | 9.0 | 15.0 | 22.0 | 6.0 | 12.0 | 6.0 | 5.0-7.0 | 4.1 | 7.0 |
| Near future | 10.0 | 16.0 | 23.0 | | 12.1 | | | | 10.0 |
| Farther future | | 17.0 | | | 12.5 | | | | |

Parent feature: Canvas (basic support)

Notes    Known issues (0)    Resources (6)    Feedback                    Edit on GitHub

Support listed as "partial" refers to the fact that not all users with these browsers have WebGL access. This is due to the additional requirement for users to have up to date video drivers. This problem was solved in Chrome as of version 18. Note that WebGL is part of the Khronos Group, not the W3C.

*Figure 9-1. With Can I Use, we can check the current and future compatibility of dozens of features and abilities.*

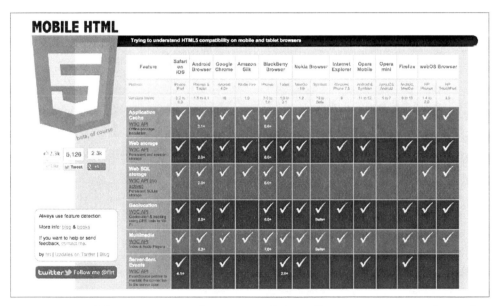

*Figure 9-2. Mobile HTML5 provides a compatibility table containing up-to-date information on every mobile platform with at least some basic HTML5 support.*

Most browser vendors are also helping me to maintain the website and ensure that the information published is correct and up-to-date.

The website's focus is on HTML5 JavaScript APIs and some big CSS features, such as animations.

## WebPlatform.org

Working with a selection of big vendors such as Google, Opera, Nokia, Adobe, Apple, Microsoft, and Mozilla, the W3C started a project in late 2012 to document the Web and provide a central place where developers can find useful articles and compatibility information on HTML, JavaScript, and CSS topics.

It's a community project, so anyone can participate and contribute to it; as it grows, it will become a great resource to find articles, API documentation, and compatibility information.

To access it, just browse to Web Platform's website (*http://webplatform.org*).

# Client-Side Detection

On the client side (in the browser), we can detect features, provide fallbacks, and issue queries about the current platform using a mix of technologies. Let's review them.

HTML, from its origins, has included a beautiful fallback mechanism that has helped the Web to grow without big incompatibilities. Basically, every browser will make the following assumptions without firing an error or stopping the rendering:

- If an element is unknown, the browser will ignore the open element, such as `<progress>` with all its attributes, and its closing element, such as `</progress>`; however, it will render its child content, such as other HTML elements or plain text.
- If an element is known but one or more of its attributes are unknown, the element will be rendered properly and the unknown attributes will just be ignored.
- If a CSS selector or CSS at-rule is unknown, the whole declaration will be ignored.
- If a CSS selector is valid but a style is unknown, only that definition will be ignored.
- If a CSS selector and a style are valid, but the value for the style is unknown, only that definition will be ignored.
- If the same CSS style on the same element is declared more than once, the last valid declaration will be used.

## HTML Fallbacks

Providing fallbacks for new HTML elements is really easy. Hopefully, browsers will provide the fallback mechanism by default. Let's continue with the `progress` example:

```
<progress max="100" value="8">
    <img src='loading.gif'>
    Progress 8%
</progress>
```

Browsers supporting the `progress` element will completely ignore all the child elements: that is, the `img` element and the `Progress 8%` text. Browsers that don't support the `progress` element will just ignore it, and they will parse the `img` and the text properly.

When it comes to attributes, it's even easier: we just use any attribute we want, and noncompatible browsers will ignore it or take a default action. Therefore, `<input required>` will render properly on all browsers (with some ignoring the `required`), and `<input type="date">` will fall back to a `type="text"` input field on browsers that do not support date input controls.

## CSS Fallbacks

Let's focus on CSS style declarations. If a browser doesn't understand a style it will just ignore it, without affecting any other declarations. For example:

```
#logo {
    background-image: url('logo.png');
    background-size: 50%;
}
```

The `background-size` style is new in CSS3; noncompatible browsers will just ignore it and use only the `background-image` style.

When we want to use a style value that may not be compatible with all browsers, we should use a multiple declaration, with the first value being the most widely compatible and the last one the most specific. Let's take a look at a sample:

```
#logo {
    background-image: url("logo.png"); // most compatible version first
    background-image: image-set(url("logo2x.png") 2x,
      url("logo.png") 1x));
}
```

In this example we want to use the new `image-set()` function that can be used to define different images for different resolutions. The problem is that it is not widely supported today, and if we use it on its own, noncompatible browsers will just ignore the whole declaration, meaning there will be no image for the logo.

The solution involves using two declarations for the same style. The first one should be the most compatible solution, which can be used by every browser. Browsers compatible with `image-set()` will also understand the last declaration, which will replace the first one. Noncompatible browsers will ignore the last declaration, considering it invalid, and the first one will win.

### CSS conditionals

A recent W3C draft standard, CSS3 conditionals (*http://www.w3.org/TR/css3-conditional*) allows us to define @supports rules for conditional processing—that is, we can define new styles and provide alternatives for browsers that do not yet support them:

```
@supports (box-shadow: 2px silver) {
    #element {
        box-shadow: 2px silver;
    }
}
/* Provides alternative when it is not supported */
@supports not (box-shadow: 2px) {
    #element {
        border: 2px solid red;
    }
}
```

Unfortunately, at the time of this writing, there is no mobile browser supporting this ability.

 Don't confuse CSS conditionals with CSS media queries. Conditionals query on browser CSS support, and media queries query on device or browser abilities.

## Vendor Prefixes

According to the CSS standard, when a browser is implementing a feature that is experimental, proprietary, or not yet mature enough for general usage, or if the discussion of how to implement it is not yet finished, the implementation must use a prefix so developers know that the final standard may change.

That was a good idea when browsers and the Web were evolving slowly, over the course of a few years. However, today's browsers (and mobile devices) can change a lot in just a few months, and because of their nature, they are hungry for more and more features. Therefore, today we use more prefixed features than we really want to, and the prefix system seems somewhat obsolete and nonsensical.

 The problem with prefixes is that we need to clone our code to define every possible prefix available today, such as -webkit- for WebKit-based browsers, -moz- for Firefox, -o- for Opera (Presto), or -ms- for Internet Explorer. Also, some values are not compatible between browsers, so we need to use different ones for each prefix.

There is a big discussion in the community about what to do with prefixes and the rules because we developers have seen that they make our website code longer, and harder to read and maintain. I will keep that discussion out of this book, and focus just on describing the problem and some possible solutions.

When a feature is mature in terms of the standard discussion, browsers can stop requiring the prefixes and use the standard style directly. Let's look at an example. To make rounded corners, the CSS3 style is `border-radius`. Today it's safe to use the standard, nonprefixed style. However, older browsers, such as Safari on iOS 4, needed a `-webkit-border-radius` definition to make it work. Similarly, older Firefox versions required `-moz-border-radius`. So, back in 2010, we needed to add every possible prefixed version in order to ensure compatibility, but today we can safely use the standard definition because all browsers with significant market share support it.

 When a feature is evolving to a standard, nonprefixed style, future versions of the browser will support both versions (prefixed and non-prefixed) until the prefixed version is removed.

Vendor prefixes have created a new problem on the Web for mobile devices. As Safari on iOS and Android—the top browsers when the mobile HTML5 era started—are WebKit-based, many developers just used the `-webkit-` prefix. Therefore, no Mozilla, Opera, Microsoft, or standard definitions were declared on millions of mobile websites, leading to a discrimination problem.

This problem led to some browsers, such as Opera and Firefox, announcing that from 2012 they would use the `-webkit-` prefix definition if the developer defined no `-o-` or `-moz-` prefixes, respectively. As Bruce Lawson (*https://twitter.com/brucel*), Opera Evangelist, said in .net magazine (*http://bit.ly/10RpF0Q*):

> Opera, along with Microsoft and Mozilla, announced at a CSS Working Group meeting that we would support some WebKit prefixes. This is because too many authors of mobile sites only use the WebKit-prefixed version, and not even the standard, unprefixed one, when it is available. This leads to a reduced user experience on Opera, Mobile Firefox and Mobile IE, which don't receive the same shiny effects, such as transitions, gradients and the like, even if the browser supports those effects.

 Remember that Opera for Android, from version 14, has changed its engine from Presto to WebKit. Therefore, `-webkit-` prefixes are the native ones now on this platform.

A similar statement was made by Mozilla's web standard lead in an interview published on the A List Apart website (*http://bit.ly/15Oo4Yz*). As yet, Microsoft has announced no plans to support `-webkit-` prefixes.

Even if Firefox may understand -webkit- prefixes on some attributes, we should use and test every possible prefix to maximize compatibility and ensure that everything works as expected when using experimental features.

As developers, the solution we can implement is to use the CSS fallback mechanism. We have two kinds of prefix usages in CSS: styles and values.

For prefixed styles, we can just define all the possible prefixes, and every browser will just take the right one and ignore the others as unknown values. For example:

```
article {
    -webkit-column-count: 2;    /* Webkit-based browsers */
    -moz-column-count: 2;       /* Firefox */
    column-count: 2;            /* W3C standard; IE and Opera use it
                                   today, and Firefox and WebKit will
                                   use it in the future  */
}
```

For prefixed values or functions, we just re-declare the same style with different values, as we saw before. For instance:

```
#logo {
    background-image: url("logo.png"); // most compatible version first
    background-image: -webkit-image-set(url("logo2x.png") 2x,
                                        url("logo.png") 1x));
    background-image: image-set(url("logo2x.png") 2x,
                                url("logo.png") 1x));
}
```

### CSS preprocessors

To manage all the possible prefixes, we can use a CSS preprocessor or dynamic language. Examples of dynamic languages are LESS and SASS (Syntactically Awesome Stylesheets). Both can be defined as CSS-based stylesheet languages with utilities and extensions not available in the standard CSS. Although browsers today do not support LESS or SASS styles directly, we can use a preprocessor tool that will "compile" our LESS or SASS styles to a final, standard CSS.

Remember that when we use dynamic stylesheet languages such as SASS or LESS we always need to precompile them to CSS before deploying our code for mobile platforms.

**SASS.** SASS (*http://sass-lang.com*) is defined as a CSS metalanguage that will be interpreted or compiled to standard CSS. It has two different syntaxes: the original syntax, based on the language Haml (using only indentation), and a modern syntax known as SCSS that is more similar to CSS (using braces).

SASS supports *mixins*, a way to define functions that can be applied on our stylesheets to simplify repetitive tasks, such as adding prefixes. For example, we can define the following mixin using SCSS syntax:

```
@mixin column($count) {
    -webkit-column-count: $count;
    -moz-column-count: $count;
    column-count: $count;
}
```

Then, when we want to use the mixin, we just use:

```
article {
    @include column(2);
}
```

The compiler (*http://sass-lang.com/try.html*) is available for Ruby.

 Compass (*http://compass-style.org*) is a SASS plug-in that will help you create more compatible CSS3 websites. It includes prefixes for some properties.

**LESS.** LESS (*http://lesscss.org*) was based on SASS, with a cleaner syntax and some more abilities. It is available for free and is distributed as a client-side processor (not recommended for mobile browsers) and a server-side processor based on Node.js and Rhino. LESS prefixer (*http://lessprefixer.com*) will give you a collection of LESS mixins that you can use to prefixize all your stylesheets.

To illustrate how LESS works, we can define a LESS stylesheet (with the LESS prefixer included) as:

```
article {
    .column-count(2); //  This is a LESS mixin that will be executed
}
```

When we compile LESS to CSS, if we define a `column-count` mixin function, we will receive complete, standard CSS with prefixes:

```
article {
    -webkit-column-count: 2;
    -moz-column-count: 2;
    column-count: 2;
}
```

Both LESS and SASS are more complex, interesting, and useful than the examples shown here suggest. If you like the idea and want to find out more, just go to their websites or buy some books on the topic.

### -prefix-free

The JavaScript framework *-prefix-free (http://leaverou.github.com/prefixfree)* is an open source solution to the prefix problem. It identifies the current browser and automatically adds all the necessary prefixes for you, on the fly.

There are plug-ins available for -prefix-free that allow you to detect changes in stylesheets on the fly and to use the jQuery css function without prefixes.

The main advantage of using this technique instead of a server-side or static solution is that you are not sending a big CSS file over the network to be parsed by the browsers. And the big disadvantage is that you are relying on JavaScript for your styles to be applied, which causes a small performance penalty while the page is being loaded.

To use this framework, just download the JavaScript file, include it in your HTML, and write your CSS without prefixes. That's it!

### Static tools for prefixes

There are some tools that you can use before deploying your website. That is, you can code with no prefixes or using the prefix you want, and then pass your stylesheets through these tools, which will give you the final code you should use with all the prefixed versions.

The best of these tools are:

- Prefixr (*http://prefixr.com*)
- prefixMyCSS (*http://prefixmycss.com*)
- CSSPrefixer (*http://cssprefixer.appspot.com*)

# JavaScript Fallbacks

With JavaScript APIs everything looks simpler, as we can use simple conditionals to verify whether an API, attribute, or feature is available.

JavaScript APIs are usually implemented as:

- Constructor functions, such as new WebSocket()

- Functions on standard elements, such as `window.openDatabase()`
- Properties or styles on standard elements, such as `DOMElement.style.transform`
- Event names, such as `touchstart`

### Are you there?

For constructor functions, object functions, and properties, we can just check if they are there—are not `undefined`—before trying to use them. We can also use the "false" value of an undefined declaration in JavaScript, so the following examples are equally valid:

```
if (navigator.geolocation!=undefined) {
    // Geolocation is available
} else {
    // Fallback
}

if (window.openDatabase) {
    // SQL API is available
} else {
    // Fallback
}

// We can check on property existence
var isGeolocationAvailable = 'geolocation' in navigator;

// Or we can use the double exclamation mark trick to receive
// a Boolean value
var isSQLAvailable = !!window.openDatabase;
```

Using the double exclamation mark (the not not operator), we can force any value to convert to a Boolean value: if the property exists it will return `true` and if not it will return `false`.

When working with event names, we can bind to them without worrying about incompatibilities. If the event is not available it will never be triggered, but no error will be raised.

 If you are testing against a global function or variable, such as `openDatabase`, always use explicit object syntax (`window.openDatabase`) or your conditional will create an error.

### Vendor prefixes

Vendor prefixes are also available in JavaScript. While it's not as common as in CSS3, some properties, event names, and CSS style declarations are prefixed. While CSS uses dash, prefix name, dash, such as `-moz-`, JavaScript can't use dashes inside property names. Therefore, in JavaScript prefixes are just webkit, Moz, ms, or O, without dashes and following camel case. The Mozilla and Opera with Presto engine prefixes use uppercase for the first letter, WebKit browsers usually accept either, and Microsoft uses lowercase.

Therefore, for an imaginary prefixed property hologram, the prefixed versions should be webkitHologram, MozHologram, OHologram, and msHologram.

 CSS prefixed styles are bound to prefixed JavaScript attributes on the style property with the same rules; therefore, -webkit-mask is bound to element.style.webkitMask.

Using the idea of undefined properties having a false Boolean value, we can simplify the problem if every vendor-specific version of the API or property uses the same syntax with the following pattern:

```
var hologram = window.hologram || window.webkitHologram ||
               window.MozHologram || window.OHologram ||
               window.msHologram || false;
if (!hologram) {
   // API is not supported
}
```

The engine will take the first nonundefined attribute, or it will just select the last false as the value. If you are providing a polyfill, you should replace the false with it.

 When unifying prefixed properties or functions under one name, be sure that all implementations are using the same syntax. You don't need to use any possible prefix, as some APIs are available only on some platforms.

## Modernizr

Modernizr (*http://modernizr.com*) is a free and open source JavaScript library that will detect whether certain HTML5 and CSS3 features are available in the user's browser and expose the results as Boolean JavaScript flags and CSS classes.

When you download the framework you can select one by one all the features that you want to detect, so you get a customized build (Figure 9-3).

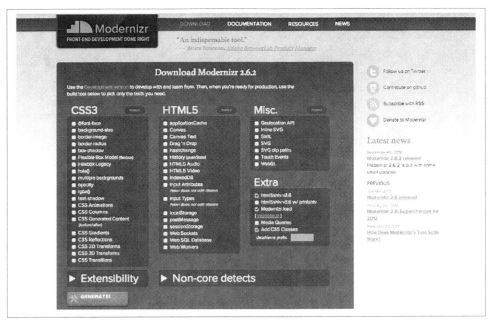

*Figure 9-3. Modernizr allows us to select which features of HTML5 and CSS3 we want to detect to create our own customized build.*

On the desktop side, Modernizr adds support for semantic HTML5 elements, such as `section` in IE6.

When you include the framework, after the page loads you will receive a `Modernizr` global object with Boolean flags for every feature checked. For example, if you want to know if CSS columns are available you can use the Boolean attribute `Modernizr.csscol umns`.

Besides the JavaScript flags, the framework adds classes to the body element for each selected feature. If the feature is available, the JavaScript property name is added as a class name. If the feature is not available, a `no-<name>` class is added. For example, for CSS columns, the class name added would be either `csscolumns` or `no-csscolumns`.

Besides all the Modernizr CSS classes, the framework adds the `no-js` class to the body when JavaScript is not enabled in the current context.

As all the website content is inside the body element, we can make use of cascade selectors in the same stylesheet to define different styles, as in:

```
// This style will be applied to columns-compatible browsers
.csscolumns article {
    column-count: 2;
    padding: 10px;
}

// This style will be applied to non-columns-compatible browsers
.no-csscolumns article {
    padding: 5px 50px;
}
```

 Modernizr does not remove the need to prefix features. However, there is an optional feature that you can add to your build that will give you a tool that will prefix an attribute for you, as in:

```
var propertyName = Modernizr.prefixed('column-count');
```

It can also look for a prefixed object in a container, as in:

```
var raf = Modernizr.prefixed('requestAnimationFrame', window);
```

### Conditional loading

Modernizr adds (as an optional feature) a conditional resource loader that will help you load JavaScript files based on current compatibility. The basic syntax is:

```
Modernizr.load({
    test: Modernizr.feature,
    yep : 'feature-yes.js',
    nope: 'feature-no.js'
});
```

With this tool you can load different JavaScript files based on feature compatibility (replace *feature* with any of the properties that Modernizr supports). The feature can be any Boolean attribute, so we can mix more than one feature, as in `test: Modern izr.geolocation && Modernizr.touch`. The yep and nope attributes accept one string or an array of strings to load multiple files.

Besides yep and nope, we can also define scripts with both that will always be loaded, and a complete callback that will be executed after all scripts have been loaded and parsed.

### All the properties

The properties that we can query with Modernizr up to version 2.6 are listed in the following subsections. Remember that you can customize your build to contain only the tests you want to use, and more properties can be added as plug-ins. Later in this book, I'll mention some of these properties that can be detected using Modernizr.

Some properties have a subset of properties that we can query on, such as different form input types or video codecs. These properties are not added to the body element as CSS classes; they only appear in the list of JavaScript attributes, such as `Modernizr.inputtypes.date`.

We can use the following feature names to check for compatibility, as properties in JavaScript and as class names that are applied as-is if compatible or with a `no-` prefix if not.

 Modernizr uses JavaScript tests to define compatibility. Some false positives are known to occur, and there may be others that have not been identified as yet.

### HTML5 main features

- `applicationcache`
- `canvas`
- `canvastext`
- `hashchange`
- `history`
- `input` (subtypes available)
- `inputtypes` (subtypes available)
- `audio` (subtypes available)
- `video` (subtypes available)
- `indexeddb`
- `localstorage`
- `postmessage`
- `sessionstorage`
- `websockets`
- `websqldatabase`
- `webworkers`

### CSS main mobile features

- `backgroundsize`
- `borderimage`

- borderradius
- boxshadow
- mediaqueries
- multiplebgs
- opacity
- overflowscrolling
- textshadow
- cssanimations
- csscolumns
- generatedcontent
- cssgradients
- cssreflections
- csstransforms
- csstransforms3d
- csstransitions

## Other features

- geolocation
- inlinesvg
- smil
- svg
- svgclippaths
- touch
- webgl
- devicemotion
- deviceorientation
- fileinput
- getusermedia
- notification

If you want to see a complete list of the features that Modernizr can test and the compatibility results on your own device, just visit the Modernizr Test Suite (*http://modernizr.github.com/Modernizr/test*) or haz.io.

To help you understand how it works, if we go back to the last chapter and try to get an idea of form feature compatibility, Modernizr will give us flags on:

- `autofocus` attribute support: `input.autofocus`
- `placeholder` attribute support: `input.placeholder`
- `required` attribute support: `input.required`
- The date/time picker: `inputtypes.datetime`
- The date picker: `inputtypes.date`
- The range slider: `inputtypes.range`
- The HTML5 form validation API: `formvalidationapi`

Some features are available as extensions. To use an extension you just need to download a JavaScript file from Modernizr's GitHub (*http://bit.ly/YbkxBt*).

## Polyfills

A polyfill is a JavaScript framework that will replace a feature that is not currently available on a browser with an alternative that will emulate the same syntax as the standard. Therefore, with a polyfill loaded we can use the same standard code even on a browser that doesn't support it.

The Modernizr team maintains a good, updated list of polyfills (*http://mobilexweb.com/go/polyfills*) available for every feature.

Polyfills are not always a good idea on mobile browsers, as we discussed earlier, because of the performance overhead they add to (usually older and less-capable) mobile platforms.

# Platform Detection

JavaScript has a native `navigator` object that represents the client browser on which the code is running. We'll take a look at server-side detection shortly, but for now, we can use this technique to detect what device our code is running on and make a decision about what to show based upon that.

The `navigator` object has many properties, but the most useful are `appName` (the browser's name), `appVersion` (the browser's version), `userAgent` (a long string identifying the browser), `plugin` (an array of supported plug-ins for the `object` tag), `platform` (the operating system), and `userLanguage`.

Generally, we will use the string function `indexOf` to verify whether some of these attributes have the values we are looking for. We can also use `match` and a regular expression. For example:

```
// Detects if it is an Android device
var isAndroid = navigator.platform.indexOf("android")>=0;

// Detects if it is an iOS device
var isIOS = navigator.userAgent.match(/iPhone|iPad|iPod/);
```

The big problem here is that there is no standard. Most browsers will just give you a `Netscape` value for the name, for compatibility with browsers from the '90s. Table 9-1 gives you an overview of what you get in the `navigator` object for each browser. In this table, assume that *<UA>* will be replaced with each device's user agent ID.

*Table 9-1. JavaScript navigator object properties compatibility table*

| Browser/Platform | appName | appVersion | Strings to identify in the User Agent | Platform |
|---|---|---|---|---|
| Safari on iPhone and iPod touch | `Netscape` | `5.0 (<UA>)` | `iPhone`, `iPhone OS` | `iPhone` or `iPod` |
| Safari on iPad | `Netscape` | `5.0 (<UA>)` | `iPad` | `iPad` |
| Android Browser | `Netscape` | `5.0 (<UA>)` | `Android` and `Mobile` | `null` or `Linux armv7l` |
| Chrome for Android | `Netscape` | `5.0 (<UA>)` | `Chrome` and `Mobile` | `Linux armv7l` |
| Firefox | `Netscape` | `5.0 (An droid/)` | `Firefox` and `Mobile` | `Linux armv7l` |
| Nokia Browser for Symbian | `Netscape` | `5.0 (<UA>)` | `Symbian` and `NokiaB rowser` | `S60` or `Symbian` |
| Nokia Browser for S40 before 6th Edition | `Nokia` | Empty string | `Series40` | Undefined |
| Nokia Browser for S40 from 6th Edition | `Netscape` | `2.0` | `Series40` | `Nokia_Ser ies_40` |

| Browser/Platform | appName | appVersion | Strings to identify in the User Agent | Platform |
|---|---|---|---|---|
| Nokia Xpress browser | `Netscape` | `5.0 (X11)` | `OviBrowser` or `NokiaBrowser` | `Linux x86_64` |
| webOS | `Netscape` | `5.0 (<UA>)` | `wOSBrowser` | `webOS` |
| BlackBerry browser for smartphones <= 7.1 | `Netscape` | `<Platform ver sion>` or `5.0 (<UA>)` | `RIM` | `BlackBerry` |
| BlackBerry browser for PlayBook | `Netscape` | `5.0(<UA>)` | `Tablet OS` | `BlackBerry` |
| BlackBerry 10 browser | `Netscape` | `5.0(<UA>)` | `BB10` | `BlackBerry` |
| Internet Explorer on Windows Mobile | `Microsoft IE Mobile` | Empty string | `Windows CE` | `WinCE` |
| Internet Explorer on Windows Phone | `Microsoft In ternet Explor er` | `5.0 (<UA>)` | `Windows Phone OS` | `Win32` |
| Internet Explorer on Windows 8 | `Microsoft In ternet Explor er` | `5.0 (<UA>)` | `Windows NT 6.2` | `Win32` |
| Opera Mobile (Presto engine) | `Opera` | `<engine ver sion>` | `Opera Mobi` | `Symbian, An droid, or Win dows` |
| Opera Mini | `Opera` | `<engine ver sion>` | `Opera Mini` | `Pike <version info>` |
| Amazon Silk | `Netscape` | `5.0(<UA>)` | `Silk` | `armv7l` |
| UC browser | `Netscape` | `UC/<version> (<UA>)` | `UCBrowser` | Empty string |

## Detect Mobile Browsers

If you want to detect whether your code is running on a mobile browser or not, the simple way is to look for some keywords in the User Agent, such as `mobile` or well-known mobile OS's names. There is a free open source framework that can help you with this—available as JavaScript code and many server-side scripts—from Modern-izr (*http://bit.ly/Wf44wB*).

 A big question is whether a tablet should be considered a mobile device. Tablet browsers don't usually use the word "mobile" inside the User Agent string, which is a clue that you can provide a more desktop-like version.

# Server-Side Detection

Before we get into detection of mobile devices and services on the server, we need to go back a bit and consider an old friend: the HyperText Transfer Protocol, also known as HTTP. Knowing a bit about its internals will help us determine what we can do in terms of mobile web development.

 There are no special server requirements for mobile websites; you can just use the same Apache, Internet Information Server (IIS), or other server you are currently using for desktop websites.

## HTTP

HTTP is a protocol originally defined in 1991 for document transportation over TCP/IP networks. It has two main versions: 1.0 and 1.1 (the last and current version of the protocol, defined in 1996). This same protocol is the one that we need to use from the server side in mobile web development.

Actually, that last sentence isn't strictly true if we consider WAP 1.1, where the device communicates with the WAP gateway and the WAP gateway is the one connecting to our server via HTTP. A similar approach is used in proxied browsers, like Opera Mini and the Nokia Xpress browser (see Figure 9-4). However, from the server's point of view the requests coming in will always be HTTP requests.

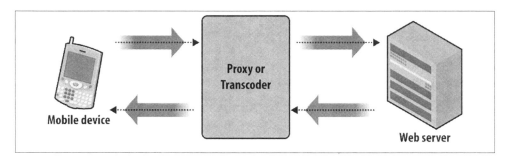

*Figure 9-4. When the user is accessing our website via a cloud-based browser or a transcoder, we will not receive the request directly from the user's mobile device.*

### The request

An HTTP request involves a client (the browser) sending a request to a server using its IP address (previously converted from a domain name). That request has a header and an optional body. The body is generally sent when we are doing a POST request. The most common request type is a GET, requesting a document or a file from the server.

The server responds with a response status code (hopefully not the famous 404), a header, and an optional (but generally sent) body. The body is the requested file.

Why are we taking this two-minute networking class? Because it illustrates many of the techniques we will use in server-side detection.

---

# SPDY and HTTP 2.0

Because HTTP 1.1 was created in 1996 and the Web has evolved enormously over the past few years, Google has developed an open network protocol to replace HTTP, with the particular objectives of reducing page loading latency and improving performance and security. SPDY (pronounced "speedy") multiplexes and prioritizes all the resources loading through only one connection, maximizing performance without the need of hacks or tricks.

SPDY is based on HTTP, so any HTTP server can work with SPDY if we add a translation layer in between. While SPDY is a trademark of Google, the IETF—the organization behind network standards—is starting work on the proposal of HTTP 2.0, and SPDY will be the starting point.

Google has released an Apache module (*http://code.google.com/p/mod-spdy*) to add support for this protocol. However, at the time of this writing, only big sites such as Google and Twitter are using SPDY on the server side.

As performance is a key issue in mobile browsing, mobile platforms have been among the earliest adopters, with some offering SPDY support from late 2011. The Android browser (from version 3.0), Google Chrome for Android, Amazon Silk, Opera Mobile from 12.1, and Firefox from version 15 support SPDY.

---

### The request header

The request header has many fields that are defined by the browser and sent to the server (if no proxy, gateway, or transcoder is in the middle). Some of the ones that we will find useful are listed in Table 9-2.

*Table 9-2. Most common HTTP request header fields*

| Header field | Description |
| --- | --- |
| User-Agent | The name of the browser or platform that originated the request |
| Accept | A comma-separated values (CSV) list of MIME types accepted by the browser |
| Accept-Charset | A CSV list of charsets accepted by the browser (e.g., ISO-8859-1, UTF-8) |
| Accept-Language | A CSV list of preferred languages in the browser |
| Accept-Charset | A CSV list of compression methods available for the response (e.g., gzip, deflate) |

Every mobile browser supports HTTP authentication, showing a modal window for username and password entry so the user can log in to a website.

The following is the header of a real request from a mobile device to a server:

```
GET / HTTP/1.1
Host: mobilexweb.com
Accept: application/vnd.wap.wmlscriptc, text/vnd.wap.wml,
application/vnd.wap.xhtml+xml, application/xhtml+xml, text/html,
multipart/mixed, */*
Accept-Charset: ISO-8859-1, US-ASCII, UTF-8; Q=0.8, ISO-10646-UCS-2;
Q=0.6
Accept-Language: en
DRM-Version: 2.0
Cookie2: $Version="1"
Accept-Encoding: gzip, deflate
User-Agent: Nokia5300/2.0 (03.50) Profile/MIDP-2.0
Configuration/CLDC-1.1
x-wap-profile: "http://nds1.nds.nokia.com/uaprof/N5300r100.xml"
```

 Many mobile browsers send */* as the list of accepted MIME types to avoid the server prefiltering the content that it can deliver using the Accept header. Other mobile browsers have known bugs in the MIME type lists that they provide.

### The user agent

The user-agent string identifies the browser. It has had a complex history, with the result that today there are browsers that identify themselves as six different browsers at the same time in the same string. This somewhat complicates browser detection. There is an excellent history of the user-agent string, presented in a very funny way, at We-bAIM (*http://bit.ly/Yd6Sqo*).

In brief, in the beginning of the web era, developers often looked for a particular string in the User-Agent header to determine what content to deliver, many browsers—starting with Microsoft Internet Explorer—started using a hack that today has resulted in user agent hell. The hack was for Internet Explorer to identify itself as Mozilla (the way that the Netscape browser, IE's main competitor, was identified). After this initial identification, it clarified that it was not actually Mozilla, but rather a compatible browser (IE). Microsoft also added other information to the user-agent string, like the operating system and details on the plug-ins and languages supported. The end result was a very complex user agent syntax with no standards.

In the mobile world, the situation is even worse. Some browsers use the IE hack and identify themselves as Mozilla (with some clarification), others identify themselves with the correct browser name, and still others send the device brand and model number in the User-Agent header. The same device may even provide a different user-agent string, depending on the OS version or the firmware used. This makes device detection using this string a bit complex.

 If you don't want your site to be transcoded, you can use Cache-Control: no-transform both in the HTML document and in the HTTP headers. Some transcoders use this information to decide whether or not to transcode a document, but there is no guarantee that this will work.

The following is a list of some mobile user-agent strings provided by a Nokia N95, a Nokia 3510, a Samsung Galaxy SIII, a BlackBerry, an iPhone 5, a Windows Phone 8 device, a Nexus 7, and a Japanese phone from the carrier Au:

- Mozilla/5.0 (SymbianOS/9.2; U; Series60/3.1 NokiaN95/20.0.015 Profile/MIDP-2.0 Configuration/CLDC-1.1) AppleWebKit/413 (KHTML, like Gecko) Safari/413
- Nokia3510i/1.0 (05.30) Profile/MIDP-1.0 Configuration/CLDC-1.0
- Mozilla/5.0 (Linux; U; Android 4.0.4; en-gb; GT-I9300 Build/IMM76D) AppleWebKit/534.30 (KHTML, like Gecko) Version/4.0 Mobile Safari/534.30
- BlackBerry8100/4.2.0 Profile/MIDP-2.0 Configuration/CLDC-1.1 Vendor ID/125
- Mozilla/5.0 (iPhone; CPU iPhone OS 6_0 like Mac OS X) AppleWebKit/536.26 (KHTML, like Gecko) Version/6.0 Mobile/10A405 Safari/8536.25
- Mozilla/5.0 (compatible; MSIE 10.0; Windows Phone 8.0; Trident/6.0; IEMobile/10.0; ARM; Touch; NOKIA; Lumia 920)
- Mozilla/5.0 (Linux; Android 4.1.1; Nexus 7 Build/JRO03D) AppleWebKit/535.19 (KHTML, like Gecko) Chrome/18.0.1025.166 Safari/535.19
- UP.Browser/3.04-TS14 UP.Link/3.4.4

As you can see, there is no standard for this string. So, the initial approach is to search for some term—for example, "iPhone" or "Android"—to try to determine which device or platform a request has originated from. Don't worry if this sounds nightmarish, though; in a few pages we will talk about a better solution.

### What we can identify

Identification is useful for context definition. We need to remember that the user is a mobile user, and for these users the context is very important. We want to get all the information we can about that context, so we can provide the most useful experience possible.

The mobile browser doesn't send information about:

- The International Mobile Equipment Identity (IMEI) or serial number to identify the device uniquely
- The type of network used (WiFi, 3G, GPRS, EDGE, CDMA)
- The carrier (operator) providing service to the device
- The country of the user
- If the user is roaming
- The phone number of the user
- The device's brand and model number (at least, not directly)

Some of this information (carrier, brand, and model number) can be inferred, but the other identification data will not be available. That is why we cannot identify users automatically without a login, as in desktop web applications.

 If you are working closely with the carrier for your mobile website, you may be able to have yourself added to the WAP gateway's URL whitelist. You will then be able to receive a customer ID or phone number in a new, nonstandard header.

Here's what we can glean from the device headers:

- The carrier and country, from the IP address of the request (if it is using a wireless network, such as 3G or 4G)
- The country (and maybe city or even exact location), from the IP address of the request (if it is using a WiFi network)
- The brand and model number, inferred from the User-Agent header
- The language in which the operating system is defined
- What markups and document types are accepted, if the header is not defined as */*

---

## The iOS Detection Problem

The user-agent string on iOS devices includes the operating system version (such as 5.1 or 6.0) and the device type (such as iPod, iPhone, or iPad), but it doesn't include any reference to the current device hardware or generation. Therefore, there is no way of using HTTP headers to determine if the user is browsing with an iPhone 3GS, an iPhone 4, or an iPhone 5. Likewise, you can't tell if the user has a first- or third-generation iPad.

Apple has done this intentionally to avoid developers trying to create different experiences per generation of device. Up to iPhone 5 it was not a big problem, as all the devices in a given category (all the iPhones, all the iPads) were quite similar in terms of how websites intended for viewing on those devices should be. On the iPhone 5 and fifth-generation iPod touch, the larger screen may require some attention, but if you design your website with good practices, you should not have any problem. Anyway, on the server side there is no way to tell if the user is on a larger screen device.

The problem continues with the iPad mini, as it exposes the same user agent as other iPads with the same iOS versions—there is no way to detect if the user is on a 7.9" or 9.7" iPad.

The inability to differentiate between hardware generations is also a problem for statistics, as we don't know how many visitors to our websites are on newer devices.

The only trick we can apply is to use a JavaScript solution that will look into the pixel ratio and screen dimension values to make assumptions about the type of device, and store that information in a cookie for later visits (or use Ajax to send that information to the server). This client-side trick can't be applied to the iPad mini, though, as every CSS and JavaScript property on this device exposes the same values as on the iPad 2.

### The User Agent Profile

The *UAProf* (User Agent Profile) is a voluntary standard defined by the Open Mobile Alliance (formerly WAP Forum). It takes the form of an XML file defining the abilities of the device, including its screen size, download features, and markup support.

The XML is defined by the manufacturer or the carrier, and a link to the XML is defined in a header (typically `x-wap-profile`). If you look back at the sample headers we saw earlier in this chapter, you'll see it:

```
x-wap-profile: "http://nds1.nds.nokia.com/uaprof/N5300r100.xml"
```

This URL will have been defined when the browser was created, which may have been several years before. If the URL is still working, we should get XML like the following extract:

```
<prf:ImageCapable>Yes</prf:ImageCapable>
<prf:Keyboard>Qwerty</prf:Keyboard>
<prf:Model>BlackBerry 8100</prf:Model>
<prf:NumberOfSoftKeys>0</prf:NumberOfSoftKeys>
<prf:PointingResolution>Character</prf:PointingResolution>
<prf:PixelAspectRatio>1x1</prf:PixelAspectRatio>
<prf:ScreenSize>240x260</prf:ScreenSize>
<prf:ScreenSizeChar>26x18</prf:ScreenSizeChar>
```

UAProf files have many problems. First, we need to download the XML for each request, process it, and either extract the properties we want or make a local copy on our server. Second, the community has found lots of bugs and problems in this official information. Some devices (the iPhone, for example) don't define a UAProf file, and they don't all define the same properties. Also, UAProf does not have the right granularity of information; for example, you can read that Flash is supported, but no information is there about which version.

So, another problem added to our list.

Some mobile browsers, mostly on smartphones and tablets, support a feature called something like "Request desktop site." When the user enables this feature, the browser changes its user agent to a desktop browser user agent. The result is that on the server side there is no way to tell that the user is on a mobile device, so you will most likely deliver a desktop experience.

### User agent tricks

As we already know, there are different versions of Firefox available for Android, Mee-Go, and Firefox OS. However, while the user-agent strings for Firefox reveal which platform the user is on, they do not identify the brand and model of device the user is using to browse the Web.

Opera Mobile had a similar problem, but starting with version 12.1 it includes a Device-Stock-UA header whose value is that of the user agent of the default browser on the current device, so we can detect which device it is regardless of which Opera version the user has. The User-Agent header doesn't include any reference to the device hardware.

On Windows 8 we can identify if the user is on a touch device by looking for the Touch token inside the user-agent string. We can also tell that it's a Windows 8 tablet if the ARM string is there; if not, it may be an Intel-based tablet, a notebook, or a desktop, and we can use Touch to figure out if it's a touch device. Microsoft does not indicate the brand and model of the device anywhere in the user-agent string.

Web views, such as native web apps, usually browse the Web with the default web browser user agent. However, on some platforms, developers can customize those user agents. For example, Chrome for iOS adds a CriOS token to the default Safari on iOS user agent.

For browsers that are available on different device types, such as tablets and smartphones, usually the way to differentiate them is to look for the Mobile token for smartphones and the Tablet token for tablets. This rule applies to Firefox, the BlackBerry browser, and Opera. For the Android browser and Chrome, you know the user is on a tablet if the Android token is there and the Mobile token is not. For iPads, you just look for the iPad substring.

## Detecting the Context

We've already seen how the network protocol works, and what information is provided and not provided in a mobile browser request. Now let's get some data and information from the context.

## How to read a header

The specifics depend on the language, but all server-side platforms offer a way to read the request's header. Some languages use the parameter name as the header name (for example, `Accept-Charset`), and others use a longer version with the syntax `HTTP_X`, where *X* is the header name in all uppercase and with the dashes (-) replaced by underscores (for example, `HTTP_ACCEPT_CHARSET`).

 Some Nokia devices expose a custom HTTP header that defines the connection type. The header is `x-nokia-musicshop-bearer` and the possible values are `WLAN` or `GPRS/3G`. We can try to read this header and, if it exists, get more information about the context.

In Java Servlets or JSP, we read a header using:

```
request.getHeader("header_key")
```

And in PHP:

```
$_SERVER["header_key_large"]
```

In ASP.NET with C# or Visual Basic, we have a `Headers` collection and public members for most of the common headers:

```
// This is the C# version
Request.Headers["header_key"]

' This is the VB version
Request.Headers("header_key")
```

 Older BlackBerry devices expose a custom HTTP `via` header that can be used to see which browser is being used. For example, if the value contains an `MDS` string, the user may be connected via the BlackBerry Browser through the corporate server; if it contains `BISB` the user is using the Internet Browser connecting through the carrier; and if the value is not defined, the user may be using the WiFi Hotspot Browser.

## How to read the IP address

The IP address from which the request originated can be read with the following code:

```
// In Java
String address = req.getRemoteAddr();

// In PHP
$address = $_SERVER["REMOTE_ADDR"];
```

```
// In C#
String address = Request.UserHostAddress;
```

What can we do with the IP address? The next chapter will talk about geolocation. However, if we want to define the user's carrier and country right now, we need to get an updated list of the IP ranges assigned to each carrier. The carriers distribute this information to their partners, and it can also be found in forums and communities or through commercial services.

 Massive's Operator Identification Platform is a community-based database service that allows us to determine visitors' countries and network operators, if detected, using a simple HTTP service request. You can request an account from massive (*http://www.werwar.com*).

# Cloud-Based Browsers

As mentioned earlier, there are some cloud-based browsers on the market (Opera Mini is the most widely installed), and we need to take care of differences in the headers in such browsers. Even on a well-known device, such as a BlackBerry or an iPhone, if Opera Mini is in use the requests we receive on our servers will come from the Opera Mini proxy and not from the device itself. So, the client IP address will be Opera's server address, and the user-agent string will be the proxy's one.

 Remember that cloud-based browsers are not just something for feature phones or older devices. Modern platforms can also browse the Web using these browsers, such as Opera Mini on iPhone/iPad or Android devices, Chrome on Android, the Nokia Xpress browser on Windows Phone devices, or Silk on an Amazon Kindle Fire.

## Opera Mini

On any device, the Opera Mini user-agent string looks like this:

```
User-Agent: Opera/9.80 (J2ME/MIDP; Opera Mini/6.1.25378/25.692; U; en)
Presto/2.5.25 Version/10.54
```

The substring between the open parenthesis and the first semicolon is the device's platform.

Possible options are:

- Android
- BlackBerry
- BREW

- J2ME/MIDP
- iPhone
- iPad
- MTK
- Series 60
- Windows Mobile

Fortunately, Opera Mini offers the original IP address and the original user-agent string, along with other information, in new headers (listed in Table 9-3) that we can read using the techniques we have already seen.

 Other cloud-based browsers are not as developer-friendly as Opera Mini and remove all the original headers, so we are blind in terms of detecting the device and its origin.

*Table 9-3. Opera Mini additional optional HTTP headers*

| Header | Description |
|--------|-------------|
| X-OperaMini-Phone-UA | Provides the user-agent string identifying the device that downloaded the Opera Mini client (or the current device's user-agent string if not available). |
| X-OperaMini-Phone | Provides the device's brand and model, separated by a hash (*<brand>#<model>*). |
| X-Forwarded-For | Provides a CSV list of all the proxy servers in the chain that have forwarded the request from the device to Opera Mini's proxy. Opera recommends using the last IP address listed for geolocation purposes. |
| X-OperaMini-Features | Provides a CSV list of phone features, from the following list:<br>• basic (Java MIDP 1.0 device, low resources, almost nonexistent today)<br>• advanced (Java MIDP 2.0 device, high resources)<br>• camera (camera detected, so we can provide a file upload input for pictures)<br>• file_system (filesystem support detected, so the user can download and upload files)<br>• download (the device supports download files)<br>• touch (the device has a touch screen)<br>• viewport (the viewport meta tag is compatible with the device)<br>• secure (connection between phone and proxy is encrypted) |

## Xpress browser

The Xpress browser is the cloud-based browser available for Nokia Series 40 and Windows Phone devices. Sometimes the browser will use the NokiaBrowser or OviBrowser identification, as it was also known as the Nokia Browser or Ovi Browser on older devices. Novarra is also used a lot inside headers, because this browser was developed as a result of Nokia's acquisition of Novarra, Inc. (a company that used to create transcoders and proxies for mobile web).

The specific HTTP headers the Xpress browser supports are listed in Table 9-4.

*Table 9-4. Nokia Xpress browser additional HTTP headers*

| Header | Description |
|---|---|
| X-Mobile-Gateway | Specifies the proxy server version: for example, Novarra-Vision/8.1. |
| X-Forwarded-For | Provides a CSV list of all the proxy servers in the chain that have forwarded the request from the device to the cloud's proxy. The last IP address (or the only value, if there's only one) is the user's IP address. |
| X-Nokia-Device-Type | Undocumented feature; in tests it's always zero (0). |
| X-WAP-Profile | Provides the URL to the current device's User Agent Profile (forwarded from the original request from the device; not available on all devices). |

### Amazon Silk

The Kindle Fire browser does not add any additional headers when the acceleration mode is enabled and the Amazon Cloud is between your server and the user. However, the Silk user agent will have the string Silk-Accelerated=true at the end if the acceleration mode is enabled, indicating that it's using the cloud-based acceleration proxy. If not, it's acting like a direct browser.

> If you are using a server-side detection to provide different layouts, you can try them with a User Agent Switcher plug-in for desktop browsers or use the online tool Hydra Multi-Device Proxy (*http://hydra.mobi forge.com*).

## Mobile Detection

If you only want to know whether the user is browsing from a desktop or a mobile device (perhaps for doing a redirection), the quickest way to find out is to check for some different well-known strings (iPhone, iPod, Nokia) inside the User-Agent header. Based on their presence or absence, you can make an educated guess about whether or not the user is on a mobile device.

> There is an excellent collection of mobile-specific User-Agent headers at mobiForge (*http://bit.ly/YtOvwx*).

Andy Moore has developed a very simple but powerful PHP script for detecting mobile user agents and browsers. The latest version (free for nonprofit purposes) can be downloaded from Detect Mobile Browsers (*http://detectmobilebrowsers.mobi*). You can also define what to do in specific situations, such as whether or not to consider iPads mobile devices.

A simple but effective script that will look into dozens of substrings inside the user agent is available from Detect Mobile Browsers (*http://detectmobilebrowsers.com*). You will find scripts for PHP, ASP.NET, ColdFusion, JSP, Node.js, Perl, Python, and Rails. You can also download configuration files for Apache or IIS.

 Some older devices used to support multipart document delivery. A multipart document includes XHTML and resources (images, CSS) in the same HTTP response, enhancing the download performance. To determine whether a device supports multipart documents, check for the `multipart/mixed` or `application/vnd.wap.multipart` MIME type in the `Accept` header. SPDY and HTTP 2.0 came to use the same idea on modern websites.

## Transcoders

With WAP 1.1, operator gateways were required to precompile WML and make it lighter and more easily parsable by devices with limited memory/CPU resources. Gateways were also relied upon to manage cookies on behalf of the devices (which did not have enough memory) and for integration with the operator's backend (for example, the gateway was able to inject the users' phone numbers into HTTP headers, so that authorized content providers could recognize them and bill them for services).

With WAP 2, precompilation was no longer needed, but other aspects of gateways were, and still are today, to some extent. In a lot of different contexts, the presence of a WAP gateway is beneficial to developers and content providers.

Around 2002, some companies started selling tools to "mobilize" web content. That is, users could type a URL into a field, and the transcoder/content reformatter would chop it up into pages that could be viewed by mobile devices.

Around 2006, some kind of genetic mutation happened: transcoder vendors realized that transcoders could be deployed in proxy mode and the whole Web could be transcoded behind the backs of the users and content providers, regardless of the presence of a mobile-optimized experience for any given site. This dangerous move posed a serious threat to the mobile ecosystem.

Hopefully, in the HTML5 era transcoders will not be used as they were before. If you want to know more about transcoders, check out *www.mobilexweb.com/go/transcoders*.

The W3C has released a couple of guidelines (*http://www.w3.org/TR/ct-guidelines*) for transcoders to follow. The community of mobile developers on the WMLProgramming list have also created their own guidelines, known as the Manifesto for Responsible Reformatting (*http://wurfl.sourceforge.net/manifesto*).

The official HTTP way to define that we don't want our content to be transformed is to add the following header in our HTTP responses: `Cache-Control: no-transform`.

# Device Libraries

As we've discussed, just looking at the HTTP headers and the UAProf will not give us enough useful information about the mobile devices that are accessing our websites. This is where device libraries come to our assistance. Device libraries are offline databases (or cloud-based services) that take a user-agent string (or all of the request headers) and return to us dozens of properties about the detected device, from screen size, to HTML5 compatibility, to Ajax support and video codec compatibility.

Device libraries are also known as Device Description Repositories (DDRs).

The most well-known libraries available today are WURFL, DeviceAtlas, and DetectRight, but we'll also look at a few other projects, including 51Degrees.mobi and OpenDDR.

### WURFL

The Wireless Universal Resource File (known as WURFL) is an open source device capabilities repository maintained by ScientiaMobile (*http://www.scientiamobile.com*) under a dual AGPL v.3 and Commercial license. It also includes APIs for the major server-side platforms and a cloud-based service.

The WURFL Framework consists essentially of two components: an API and the repository in XML format. The API is dually licensed (AGPL/Commercial), while the repository is distributed with a license that only allows usage with the APIs released by ScientiaMobile. The AGPL license allows free usage of the software only as long as one is willing to open source the entire application, irrespective of the fact that the application may be hosted on a web server. ScientiaMobile has also launched a WURFL Cloud Service, which includes a free-of-charge offering for hobbyists and small projects.

Before 2011, WURFL was a free and open source project. According to Luca Passani, CTO of ScientiaMobile and creator of the project, WURFL had reached the point where further improvements were not possible without the injection of development resources and this was the driver of the new commercial open source approach.

If you have been using WURFL for a while, you should check the new license conditions. There is a version of the cloud-based service you can still use free of charge.

The WURFL APIs can be downloaded from the WURFL website (*http://wurfl.source forge.net*). Repository updates are made available to commercial licensees on a weekly basis and community (AGPL) users are offered quarterly snapshots.

The AGPL v.3 license allows free usage if you are ready to open source your code. If not, you should acquire a commercial license from ScientiaMobile.

The sources of information include official technical information published by manufacturers, UAProf files, and data collected by the community and the company after testing on real devices. Today, the WURFL database contains thousands of devices (15,000 profiles, 8,000 of which have a unique brand and model), with information on subversions, operating systems, firmware and hardware variations, and hundreds of attributes that we can query for each one.

WURFL is available as three possible implementations:

- Standalone for web languages (Java, PHP, .NET)
- Standalone for C++ (high performance and integration with network-level software)
- Cloud (Java, PHP, .Net, Perl, Ruby, Python, and Node.js)

With the standalone license (also known as WURFL OnSite), you will be able to install the repository and the API on your own server; you'll need to update the repository frequently on your own but you can use it for free under AGPL v.3. If your site is commercial and you don't intend to comply with the AGPL terms, you can acquire a commercial license.

With the standalone commercial license you will receive:

- Weekly repository updates

- The Java, PHP, Database (previously known as Tera-WURFL), or .NET API

 The WURFL InFuze product series includes a C++ API as well as three enterprise-level products based on it: the WURFL Modules for Varnish Cache, Apache Web Server, and NGINX Web Server. These products enable features such as the ability to enrich the HTTP headers or the ENV environment variables with WURFL capabilities, effectively relieving organizations from the need to deploy device detection libraries as part of their applications.

With the Cloud Service, you don't need to install anything on your server with the exception of a light client; you will have a continually updated repository available to you at different monthly rates, and even a free service. The main disadvantage of the Cloud Service is that every time a new user makes a request, your script needs to contact the ScientiaMobile servers and wait for the response before getting the WURFL data and releasing the response to the user.

The Cloud Client comes with enough intelligence to save unnecessary round-trips for devices that have already been detected. Exactly which caching strategies are adopted also depends on the actual WURFL Cloud plan you select. The options are:

*Free*
    Allows you two capabilities of your choice, 5,000 detections per month, and one domain/IP address

*Basic ($10/month)*
    Allows you five capabilities of your choice, 50,000 detections per month, and one domain/IP address

*Standard ($40/month)*
    Allows you 10 capabilities of your choice, 2 million detections per month, three IP addresses, and two domains

*Premium ($500/month)*
    Allows you unlimited capabilities, 10 million detections per month, 25 IP addresses, and three domains

With any plan you will get access to the full list of capabilities that you can detect, and a WURFL Cloud Client available in PHP, Java, Ruby, Python, Node.js, and .NET.

**Architecture.** WURFL groups the devices into a hierarchy of devices and capabilities. Some devices are equivalent to other devices from the same series, possibly with some new features, so there is a fallback mechanism in WURFL allowing a device to extend the features of another one. The same applies for different models in the same brand or even different brands with the same operating system.

Also, there is a feature called "actual device root" that manages multiple sub-versions (different firmware) of the same device, so the information is not duplicated in two records; the sub-version will be based on the main record with any added or different abilities noted.

The WURFL database has a root fallback device called "generic device" that is matched when the device, the brand, and the series can't be determined.

 The WURFL repository also includes detection for desktop browsers and smart TV platforms.

**Capabilities.** Every ability, property, or attribute is called a *capability* in the WURFL world. Capabilities are organized into groups. Each capability for each device has an optional string value (taken from the device itself, or from the fallback mechanism). That value can be converted to a Boolean, a number, a string, or an empty string. You can find an updated list of capabilities at ScientiaMobile (*http://www.scientiamobile.com/wurflCapability*).

The most useful groups at the time of this writing are shown in Table 9-5.

*Table 9-5. Most useful WURFL capability groups*

| Group name | Capabilities related to |
|---|---|
| product_info | Device information, such as the brand, model, operating system, and browser |
| xhtml_ui | XHTML rendering, including tel URI scheme support, accesskey support, iframe support, and file upload support |
| ajax | Ajax and DOM support, including support for getElementById, innerHTML, and CSS manipulation |
| markup | Markup compatibility |
| cache | Cache support |
| display | The screen and display (physical dimensions, resolution, line rows, and so on) |
| image_format | Image formats, including support for animated GIFs and SVG |
| wta | WTAI, including voice call support |
| security | Encryption, including HTTPS support |
| bearer | Networks, including WiFi and VPN support |
| storage | Limits (such as max URL length) |
| object_download | Formats and object downloading support for each typical format |
| streaming | Audio and video streaming per format and codec |

| Group name | Capabilities related to |
|---|---|
| wap_push | WAP Push attribute support |
| j2me | Java ME configuration and profile versions and API compatibility |
| mms | MMS support |
| sms | SMS support |
| sound_format | Support for audio codecs and formats |
| flash_lite | Flash support on the browser, for standalone applications, and for wallpaper or screensavers |
| css | CSS properties |
| transcoding | Whether the client is detected as a transcoder |
| rss | RSS support |
| pdf | PDF viewing support |
| playback | Formats that can be played by the device |
| smarttv | Smart TV support |

As you can see, the information that the XML provides is really complete. If you want to browse all the capabilities, you can do so at ScientiaMobile (*http://dbapi.scientiamo bile.com/explore*).

Table 9-6 shows the most important capabilities we can query, based on the compatibility problems outlined in the preceding chapters. Remember that there are dozens of other properties that you can query; take a look at the library so you'll have an idea of all the possibilities.

*Table 9-6. Most useful WURFL capabilities*

| Capability name | Type | Indicates |
|---|---|---|
| brand_name | String | The device's brand name (such as Apple, Nokia, or HTC) |
| model_name | String | The device's model name (such as iPhone, N97, Nexus One) |
| marketing_name | String | The device's marketing name, including the brand, model, and possibly another part of the name (Pearl, touch) |
| ux_full_desktop | Boolean | Whether the device is optimized for a full desktop experience (true) or not |
| is_wireless_device | Boolean | Whether the device is a mobile device (true) or not |
| is_tablet | Boolean | Whether the device is a tablet device (true) or not |
| is_smarttv | Boolean | Whether the device is a Smart TV (true) or not |
| pointing_method | String | Which pointing method is accepted (joystick, stylus, touchscreen, clickwheel, or the empty string) |
| device_os | String | The name of the operating system |
| device_os_version | String | The version of the OS |
| mobile_browser | String | The name of the browser |
| mobile_browser_version | String | The version of the browser |

| Capability name | Type | Indicates |
|---|---|---|
| resolution_width | Integer | The screen width in pixels |
| resolution_height | Integer | The screen height in pixels |
| max_image_width | Integer | The display's usable width in pixels |
| max_image_height | Integer | The display's usable height in pixels |
| xhtml_support_level | Integer | The level of XHTML compatibility, from −1 to 4: <ul><li>−1: No support</li><li>0: Basic support (poor or no CSS support, basic form support, basic or no table support)</li><li>1 and 2: Advanced basic support (basic CSS and table support)</li><li>3: Medium support, including excellent CSS support</li><li>4: Advanced support, including Ajax support</li></ul> |
| preferred_markup | String | The markup best supported by the device (even if it supports a newer one) |
| xhtml_format_as_css_property | Boolean | Whether -wap-input-format is available |
| xhtml_make_phone_call_string | String | The prefix preferred for making phone calls in a URL |
| xhtml_send_sms_string | String | Whether and how the device supports triggering the SMS client from a link (can be sms:, smsto:, or the empty string, meaning not supported) |
| xhtml_file_upload | String | Whether the device allows file uploading (returns not_supported, supported, or supported_user_intervention) |
| xhtml_supports_iframe | String | Whether the device supports iframes (returns none, partial, or full) |
| ajax_supports_javascript | Boolean | Whether the device supports JavaScript with basic operations (dialogs, form values, timers, and document.location) |
| ajax_support_event_listener | Boolean | Whether the browser allows event registration through event listeners |
| html_wi_oma_xhtmlmp_1_0 | Boolean | Whether the browser supports XHTML MP 1.0 |
| html_web_4_0 | Boolean | Whether the browser supports HTML4 |
| gif_animated | Boolean | Whether animated GIFs are supported |
| svgt_1_1 | Boolean | Whether SVG 1.1 is supported |
| svgt_1_1_plus | Boolean | Whether SVG 1.1+ is supported |
| flash_lite_version | String | Which version of Flash is supported |
| fl_browser | Boolean | Whether the browser supports Flash content |
| is_transcoder | Boolean | Whether a transcoder was detected as a proxy from the real device |
| transcoder_ua_header | String | Which header we can find the original device's user-agent string in, if a transcoder was detected |
| viewport_supported | Boolean | Whether the viewport meta tag is supported |
| image_inlining | Boolean | Whether the data URI scheme is supported to inline images |
| css_spriting | Boolean | Whether CSS sprites are supported |

**WURFL Standalone API (OnSite).** These APIs allow us to use WURFL in a couple of lines, with many advantages:

- Automatic device detection using the header information
- Two-step user agent analysis (optimized and clever user-agent searching inside the XML)
- Detection of transcoders and proxies, and matching of the correct user agent and device information
- Merging of the static XML provided by WURFL with patches (the web patch or your own), providing a simple and unique way to query capabilities
- In-memory caching of the XML parsing for the best performance on every request

When you have your license activated, you can download snapshots weekly and update them manually on your server, or you can create a direct download link that will be unique for you and will let you download the latest WURFL snapshot (the device and capability database) and automatically apply it on your own server. Just go to My Account and look for the direct download section.

**PHP API installation.** We are going to use PHP to illustrate the use of the WURFL Standalone API. To begin, you should download the PHP API from ScientiaMobile (*http://www.scientiamobile.com/downloads*) and extract the contents of the ZIP file. The package contains documentation, examples, resources, unit tests, and a *WURFL* folder where the API resides.

The PHP WURFL API allows us to save persistence information (device profiles) and cached request information using memcache instead of using the filesystem. The filesystem was chosen as the default because it maximized users' ability to get the WURFL API to work out of the box, but it's not the preferred option in the long term.

To make it work, follow these steps:

1. Copy the *WURFL* folder into your web server root folder.
2. Copy the *examples/resources* folder into your web server root folder (you can change the name).

3. Optionally, download the latest *wurfl-<version>.zip* file from WURFL (*http://wurfl.sourceforge.net*) and copy it to the new *resources* folder.

4. Verify that PHP scripts have write permissions on the *resources/storage* folder.

5. Edit the *resources/wurfl-config.xml* file and check that the `<main-file>` tag matches the name of the ZIP file containing the main XML repository. It can also be a decompressed XML file.

6. Edit the *resources/wurfl-config.xml* file, go to the persistence and cache nodes, and check that the `<params>` tags match the names of the *cache* and *persistent* folders inside *resources/storage*, as in `<params>dir=storage/cache</params>`. The path needs to be relative to the *config* XML folder.

Once WURFL is installed, we can create our first PHP script that uses the repository. Using version 1.4 of the API, the code will be:

```php
<?php
$wurflDir = dirname(__FILE__) . '/WURFL';
$resourcesDir = dirname(__FILE__) . '/resources';
$wurflConfigFile = $resourcesDir.'/wurfl-config.xml';

require_once $wurflDir.'/Application.php';

// Create WURFL Configuration from an XML config file
$wurflConfig = new WURFL_Configuration_XmlConfig($wurflConfigFile);

// Create a WURFL Manager Factory from the WURFL Configuration
$wurflManagerFactory = new WURFL_WURFLManagerFactory($wurflConfig);

// Create a WURFL Manager
$wurflManager = $wurflManagerFactory->create();

// Get device object with all capabilities
$device=$wurflManager->getDeviceForHttpRequest($_SERVER);
?>
```

The first time you run this file on your web server (local or remote), you will need to wait a minute or two while it creates the persistent data to enable quick detection in future requests. If you receive a blank page, great! If you get an error, you need to check all the steps again.

 If you're working on a local server and are going to upload your website to another server using FTP or some other protocol, it will be better not to upload the cache folder because it will contain thousands of files. It is better to leave the server to re-create them locally.

**Using the PHP API.** The PHP API is an object-oriented API. Once you have the WURFL Manager object, you can use it.

If your server is too heavily loaded, you may get a timeout error when processing WURFL the first time. If this happens, ask your server provider how to increase the maximum script time limit or change the *PHP.ini* file.

A typical usage is getting a device object using the manager's methods:

- `getDeviceForHttpRequest($_SERVER)`
- `getDeviceForUserAgent($user_agent)`
- `getDevice($deviceId)`

If you want to access the capabilities of the current device accessing your website, the first option is the best one. If you want to get properties for other devices, you can use the `user_agent` method or the `deviceId` method. Every device in WURFL has an ID that you can store in your databases for statistical or logging purposes. You can then look for its capabilities later, after the mobile request.

 You can browse the WURFL device database using the free online tool ScientiaMobile Tera-WURFL Explorer (*http://dbapi.scientiamo bile.com/explore*).

You can also get all the possible groups and capabilities using `getListOfGroups()` and `getCapabilitiesNameForGroup(groupId)`, both methods of the manager.

Once you have the device object, you can get all the properties with the `getAllCapa bilities()` method or query for one particular feature with `getCapability($capabi lityName)`.

If you are using the desktop web patch, you can determine whether the client is a desktop or a mobile device:

```
if ($device->getCapability('is_wireless_device')==false) {
    // It is not a mobile device
    header('Location: http://yourdomain.com');
}
```

To detect if it is an Apple device, use:

```
if ($device->getCapability('brand_name')=='Apple') {
    // It is an iPhone, iPod or iPad, redirect to a prepared version
    header('Location: http://yourdomain.com/ios);
}
```

With the capability, you can then decide whether or not to provide some feature. For example:

```
if ($device->getCapability('xhtml_file_upload')=='supported') {
    echo '<input type="file">';
}
```

A great option if you are offering content is to explicitly display to the user his phone model in the marketing information:

```
echo 'Download compatible content for your ' .
    $device->getCapability('brand_name') . ' ' .
    $device->getCapability('model_name')  ;
```

 If you want to test whether your WURFL code is working on your desktop browser, you can use Firefox and the free plug-in User Agent Switcher that allows Firefox to change its user-agent string to that of any other device of your liking. We will cover this plug-in in Chapter 18.

**The WURFL Cloud API.** If you go with the Cloud API, you first need to get a key from a free or paid plan from ScientiaMobile (*http://www.scientiamobile.com/cloud*). When you are done, you will get a dashboard page where you can see the status of your account (detections for the month, capabilities you can detect, and so on).

The first step is to create a key and save it. The key is a string that looks like `995405:LU7z6FfYuaaabQVWvPZT8gk5G2qDMSps`.

After that, use the Cloud Capabilities Selector to choose all the capabilities you want to enable (Figure 9-5), and download the appropriate version of the WURFL Cloud Client software for your development environment. We will use PHP for demonstration purposes.

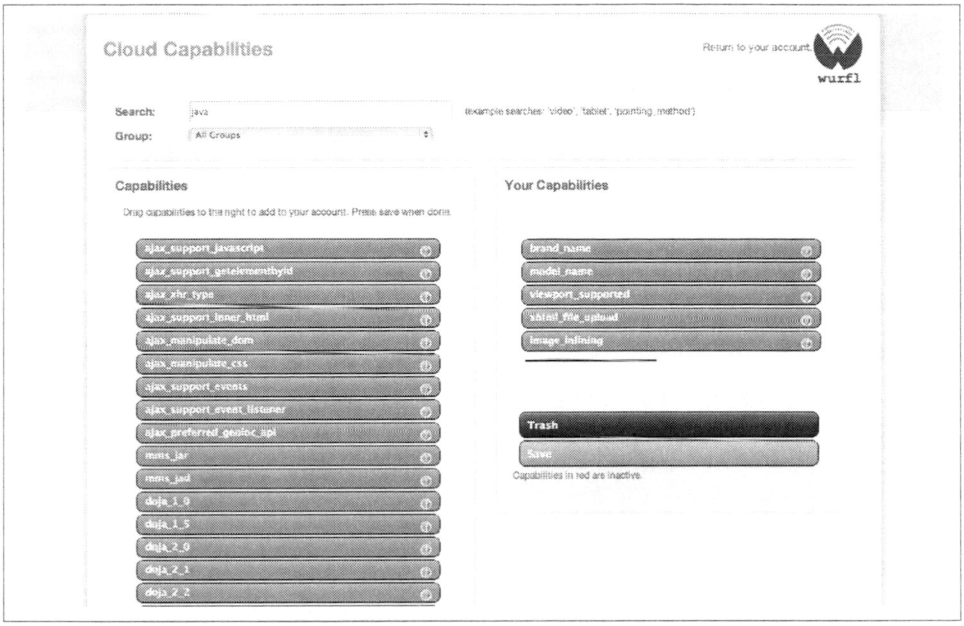

*Figure 9-5. Using ScientiaMobile's WURFL Cloud Service, we can select which capabilities we want to detect, based on our license level—the free service allows us to select up to two capabilities.*

When you download the PHP library, you can unzip it in your root folder and then use the following code snippet. Be careful to define where you copied the API as `wurfl-cloud` in this example. You should copy all the folders, except the examples:

```php
<?php
// Include the WURFL Cloud Client
// You'll need to edit this path
require_once 'wurfl-cloud/Client/Client.php';

// Create a configuration object
$config = new WurflCloud_Client_Config();

// Set your WURFL Cloud API key
$config->api_key = 'xxxxxx:xxxxxxxxxxxxxxxxxxxxxxxxxxxxxxxxx';

// Create the WURFL Cloud Client
$client = new WurflCloud_Client_Client($config);

// Detect your device
$client->detectDevice();

// Use the capabilities
if ($client->getDeviceCapability('is_tablet')) {
    echo "This is a tablet";
```

```
    }
?>
```

Remember that when using the WURFL Cloud Service you don't need
to download or update any WURFL repository on your server. When
you install the Cloud Client, you will always be accessing the latest
database.

## DeviceAtlas

In February 2008 (many years after WURFL was created), the dotMobi company, which
owns the *.mobi* top-level domain, launched its own device database that is similar in
many ways to WURFL.

DeviceAtlas (*http://deviceatlas.com*) is a commercial product that has partnerships with
many data providers.

The main features are:

- Monthly, weekly, daily, or constant updates to the database, depending on your
  license
- A data explorer to browse the database from the Web
- JSON data format support
- APIs for PHP, Java, .NET, Python, and Ruby
- Apache server module (with the enterprise license)
- Cloud-based service available

At the time of this writing, the service is available as an Enterprise plan for standalone
installation with no public prices and as a cloud-based service with two plans available:

*Standard ($40/month)*
> 1 million detections per month, single applications, weekly updates, standard set
> of capabilities

*Premium ($399/month)*
> 5 million detections per month, 50 applications, daily updates, premium set of ca-
> pabilities

At the time of this writing, DeviceAtlas has no free option (standalone
or cloud-based), unlike WURFL. You can, however, request a free evaluation license for testing purposes.

The Enterprise API is available for Java, PHP, .NET, Python, and Ruby. You'll need to download the JSON repository yourself, at whatever frequency your license allows. The cloud-based API is available for Java, PHP, .NET, and Python.

**Properties.** The data available in DeviceAtlas is segmented into categories. In the cloud-based services, some properties are available only with the premium plan.

The most important properties in each category are:

*Device name*
> vendor, model

*Hardware*
> displayHeight, displayWidth, mobileDevice, touchScreen, displayPpi, isER eader, isTablet, isMobilePhone, isGamesConsole, isTV, isMediaPlayer

*Environment*
> developerPlatform, developerPlatformVersion, osAndroid, osLinux, osOsx, os Proprietary, osRim, osSymbian, osWindowsPhone, osVersion

*Web browser*
> markup.xhtmlMp10, memoryLimitMarkup, uriSchemeSms, uriSchemeSmsTo, uri SchemeSmsTel, vCardDownload, usableDisplayWidth, usableDisplayHeight, flashCapable

*JavaScript*
> js.supportsBasicJavaScript, js.xhr, js.json

*Network protocols*
> EDGE, GPRS, HDSPA, UMTS

*HTML5*
> html.audio, html.canvas, html.svg, html.video, js.applicationcache, js.ge olocation, js.touchevents

*AudioPlayer*
> aac, amr, mp3

*Streaming*
> stream.3gp.aac.lc, stream.3gp.h263, stream.3gp.h264.level1, stream.mp4 .aac.lc

*VideoPlayer*
> 3gp.h263, 3gp.h264.level1, mp4.aac.lc, wmv

You can browse all the data available with your license at DeviceAtlas (*http://deviceat las.com/explorer*).

Remember that if you have a developer account (the free evaluation license) your database file will not be updated if you download it again, and if you have a basic license with monthly downloads a new file will not be available until 30 days from when you downloaded the previous version.

**Cloud API.** For demonstration purposes, we are going to use the PHP Cloud API from DeviceAtlas.

Inside the PHP Cloud API you will find just a *DeviceAtlasCloud/Client.php* file that you need to add to your project.

Then, your PHP will look like this:

```php
<?php
include './DeviceAtlasCloud/Client.php';

// Get the data - this automatically uses the browser/device User-Agent
// If TRUE, then a test device will be used to query DeviceAtlas Cloud
$test_mode = true;

$da_data = DeviceAtlasCloudClient::getDeviceData($test_mode);

if (isset($data_data['properties']['isTablet'])) {
    echo "This is a tablet";
}

?>
```

If you want a cache implementation, you'll need to do it yourself.

 Microsoft used to have an open source mobile browser database (*http:// mdbf.codeplex.com*) for ASP.NET. This project was abandoned; now you can use the *.browser* file to detect a device library such as WURFL, or see other ideas at ASP.NET (*http://www.asp.net/mobile*). ASP.NET MVC is recommended instead of Web Forms to create mobile websites.

## DetectRight

DetectRight is a detection engine, device database, analytics engine, and API/SDK with both service-based and dedicated server options. It offers a standalone API, a cloud service, and a local cloud service for enterprise applications.

Free nonprofit, community, and developer licenses are available, as well as commercial enterprise licenses. DetectRight features include SOAP and REST access, unique custom identification, country-level geolocation, and profiles in WURFL, DeviceAtlas, UAProf,

DetectRight, and Java ME Polish–compatible formats. Its database includes over 20,000 devices at the time of this writing.

 If you want easy and quick mobile detection, at Detect Mobile Browsers (*http://www.detectmobilebrowsers.mobi*) you will find a little piece of PHP code that allows you to determine whether the user is using a mobile browser, without any repository, database, or service call.

If you register at DetectRight (*http://www.detectright.com*), you will receive via email a key that enables you to access a variety of PHP, Java, and SOAP samples and APIs.

 Remember that when using cloud-based solutions, your mobile website's performance will depend on the reliability of the third-party server to which you are connecting.

You can download the PHP or Java API for easy usage on those platforms.

In PHP, once you've downloaded the API, you can use the service as shown in the following sample:

```
include_once("detectRight.php");

DetectRight::$druser = '<detectright.com username>';
DetectRight::$drpassword = '<detectright.com password>';
// possible values: DR, WURFL, W3C, UAProfile, J2MEPolish
DetectRight::$defaultSchema = 'DR';

$profile=DR_Customer::deduceCustomer($_SERVER);
$value = $profile['<property>'];
```

The API can also be used to download lists of manufacturers and devices, and to request individual profiles by manufacturer/model name.

## Movila DetectFree

Movila Detection (*http://www.moviladetection.com*) is a server-side Java solution to detect in 500 microseconds which device is using an embedded repository. It also works as a tool for URL rewrites. However, Movila's most-used feature is the free service called DetectFree.

DetectFree is a free light version of the service available for PHP and JavaScript (and for any other platform that sends HTTP requests) that allows you to detect whether the connecting device is a mobile device. You can find samples and documentation at DetectFree's website (*http://www.moviladetection.com/detectfree*). Just to illustrate how easy it is to use, the following sample is a JavaScript detection mechanism:

```
<script src="http://detectfree.moviladetection.com/detectfree.js"
        type="text/javascript"></script>

<script type="text/javascript">
if (is_mobile) {
   alert("This is a mobile device");
}
</script>
```

### 51Degrees.mobi

51Degrees.mobi (*http://51degrees.mobi*) offers free and premium tools for mobile device detection, providing open source APIs for PHP, Java, C, and .NET. The device database itself is delivered as an XML file, with two options:

*Lite data file*
> A free version offering basic user interface optimization properties, optimized to just separate mobile from nonmobile traffic.

*Premium data file*
> The full commercial database of phones, tablets, ebook readers, games consoles, and more, with a big list of properties available. The price starts at $360 for an annual subscription.

51Degrees.mobi's data used to rely on the WURFL database, but a different scheme and vocabulary were developed after ScientiaMobile restricted the WURFL license.

### OpenDDR

OpenDDR (*http://www.openddr.org*) is a recent project whose stated goal is to offer a community-based and open source device database. At the time of this writing, APIs are available only for Java and .NET, but the device format used is based on the W3C DDR format, which is as an open format that can be used from any language.

The APIs and the database are free to use. The device library started with the last WURFL repository version that was completely free, before ScientiaMobile changed the license; some of the OpenDDR vocabulary is also based on WURFL.

New versions of the database are being distributed monthly, and anyone can contribute to it. Compared to other libraries, the most important criticism is the lack of some capabilities; other drawbacks include its dependence on WURFL, a not-so-easy-to-use API, and the contributors' anonymity, which may have an impact on support and maintenance.

Apache DeviceMap (*http://incubator.apache.org/devicemap*) is an incubating project whose aim is to create a data repository for mobile device information. At the time of this writing, no product has been released, but OpenDDR has announced its forthcoming incorporation into DeviceMap; in the future we may see both projects merging.

# CHAPTER 10

# Images and Media

It's often said that a picture is worth a thousand words. This is true in the mobile web, too. However, we need to find a balance with regard to the number of images and media elements in a document. Every image or resource adds to the network traffic, number of requests, and load time, unless we use best practices and techniques to optimize performance.

Let's take a look at what options we have for images and other media elements, such as video and audio playing.

## Images

When we talk about images, your first thought is probably the img element. While this is one of the most-used solutions for images on the Web, it's not the only one available in mobile HTML5. With HTML5 we can render images with Scalable Vector Graphics (SVG), the canvas element, and Cascading Style Sheets (CSS).

 With CSS3 we can replace images for a lot of use cases, such as gradients, rounded corners, shadows, and other effects. If you can do it with CSS, do it and don't use images.

## Image Formats

There's good news here. Almost every mobile browser understands standard static web image formats: GIF, JPEG, and PNG. On tablets and modern smartphones, all of these formats will work without any major issues. That said, there are some differences with regard to indexing and alpha transparency on devices shipped before 2011.

Some mobile browsers also support SVG as a replacement for a bitmap image, as in the `img` element or `background-image` in CSS.

---

## Image Size and Memory Consumption

When you load an image in a web application, the original file size matters only in the data transfer. Once the file is on the browser, it is decoded in memory and it is always treated as a bitmap. Therefore, the size in memory can be calculated as width × height × bits per pixel. We should be careful, therefore, about loading big image files even if they are small in terms of bytes. Just to give an example, a full-screen image on a third-generation iPad will typically use around 12 MB of RAM.

Using more RAM will impact website performance when loading, scrolling, and returning from a frozen state (for example, when changing tabs).

---

A new format that is compatible with some mobile browsers is *WebP* (read it as "wep-py"). WebP is an open format created by Google, based on the VP8 video codec; it is intended to replace the JPEG and PNG formats as it has a better compression algorithm for both lossy and lossless images. For example, an image of the same image quality will have a file size in WebP that is, on average, 25%–45% smaller than in JPEG. WebP is also smaller for lossless images (on average, a WebP image is 26% smaller than the same image in PNG format). Therefore, it's a good candidate for the mobile web, as it is likely to enhance performance (less traffic, less time).

 To find out more about the WebP format and conversion tools, you can check out the Google Developers WebP page (*https://develop ers.google.com/speed/webp*).

The problem with WebP files is compatibility: at the time of this writing, only the Android browser, Opera (both Mobile and Mini), and the UC browser have complete support. Google Chrome for Android supports it, but there's a bug in version 18 that changes the color palette, making it useless.

### Animation formats

For animation, the standard in mobile web development is the *animated GIF*. As Flash support isn't included in many browsers (as you'll see later in this chapter), and even when it is included it can be slow, banners and animations will be most widely compatible using this classic format, until SVG or other solutions become more widely supported.

Animated GIFs were having problems before 2011, such as on Android 2.0, but today support is good enough to use them without any problem.

*APNG* (Animated PNG) is an unofficial standard for using PNGs for animations. The draft specification can be found at the Mozilla wiki (*https://wiki.mozilla.org/APNG_Spec ification*). At the time of this writing, only Opera Mobile and Firefox since version 14 support APNG on mobile websites. The polyfill *APNG-canvas* should make APNG work with Safari on iOS, the Android browser, and Chrome. Browsers that don't support APNG will just render the first frame of the animation. Modernizr has an extension attribute, apng, that will give us current compatibility information.

> APNG-canvas is a polyfill that is compatible with mobile browsers that use the Canvas API to run the animation. You can download it and check out a demo at Davidmz's GitHub (*https://github.com/davidmz/ apng-canvas*).

The advantage of APNG over animated GIFs is the ability to use alpha channels and 32-bit images. A quick way to create APNG files is using APNG Edit, a free Firefox for desktop plug-in available from Mozilla's Add-Ons (*http://bit.ly/16xxyZE*).

> An SVG element can also be animated, and it can be packaged as an *.svg* file or as a full URL that we can load as an iframe with all the contents inside.

Later in this book we will also cover CSS3 transitions and CSS3 animations.

> Older devices had support for XHTML+SMIL animation format (*http://www.w3.org/TR/XHTMLplusSMIL*). It is an obsolete standard today.

## 3D formats

As some mobile devices—such as the Evo 3D and LG Optimus 3D—have 3D screens, as we saw in Chapter 1, we can use some 3D image formats. However, having a 3D screen doesn't mean that those devices browse the Web in 3D. Therefore, usually we'll only use these formats to deliver content that the user can open, if desired, in a 3D image viewer.

The most often used format is the JPS (JPEG Stereoscopic) format, which is basically just two JPEG images side by side (one for each eye). If you use the JPEG extension, viewers will just see two images, one beside the other. Special 3D software will understand it better if the JPS extension is used; this tells it to load the image in the right way.

Always compress your images as much as possible to reduce bandwidth consumption and improve performance. Cloud-based browsers will compress your images automatically, sometimes with quality loss. In these browsers it's the user who decides on the image quality, not the developer.

### Inline images

A *data URL (http://www.ietf.org/rfc/rfc2397)* or data URI is a mechanism for defining a URL with embedded content (such as an inline image), defined in 1998. For example, we can define an img tag with the image itself inside it, without using an external file. This can be done using a base64 encoding of the image file—basically, storing the binary file as a set of visible ASCII characters in a string. This is great for small images, icons, backgrounds, separators, and anything else that doesn't merit a new request to the server. Where is the catch? No catch! All modern mobile browsers are compatible with this feature.

 The size of an image (or any other binary file) will increase by about 30% when it's converted to a base64 string for a data URI, but its size will be reduced again if we are serving the document using GZIP from the server. Therefore, at the end it will be the same size or even smaller, and it won't require a new request (with all the overhead that involves).

The best part about data URIs is that they can be used in a CSS file, with caching and multipage support, or they can be stored in any string-based storage. We will cover that later in this book.

To convert an image file to a base64 string representation, we can use any online converter or command-line utility. There are free and online alternatives at Web Utils (*http://bit.ly/13XAqza*) and Base64 (*http://www.base64encode.org*).

---

## PHP Base64 Conversion

Many web server platforms offer base64 conversion. For example, PHP offers a base64_encode() function for this purpose. To generate the code based on a real file on your server, use something similar to base64_encode(file_get_contents($path)). You'll need to add error support and insert the result in an img tag.

---

The syntax is *data:[MIME-Type][;base64],data*. The *data* can contain spaces and newlines for readability purposes, but some browsers won't render it properly. It's better to maintain it in one line.

For example, the O'Reilly logo (original PNG file 75 pixels wide) attached as a data URI image looks like this:

```
<img width="100" height="17" alt="O'Reilly" src="data:image/png;base64,
iVBORw0KGgoAAAANSUhEUgAAAEYAAAARBAMAAACSi8f4AAAAA3NCSVQICAjb4U/gAAAAGF
BMVEX//////8AAACpqanMzMxmZmaHhoQ/Pz9kt3AEAAAACHRSTlMA/////////9XKVDIA
AAAJcEhZcwAACxIAAAsSAdLdfvwAAAcdEVYdFNvZnR3YXJlAEFkb2JlIEZpcmV3b3Jrcy
BDUzQGstOgAAAAFnRFWHRDcmVhdGlvbiBUaW1lADEyLzExLzA5ueqApgAAAQNJREFUKJGV
kUFTwyAQhfMXXiH1LA3hDMTeSVDPidW7WnMvkxn/vo+MsamX6s7wgOy3O29JgetR/I2Rdy
8B8HICAyhj8PLIrOdsuYlDF8i8KWWC/BRKaVCUTaJmkhcDuNOHLVCaJg6VfJY6JivqGJHE
jn00q3tpsGcfd0KuuGdx2+fsmSl3m2r2k2gGg30i434xSMlmht0YbR+EflAU71dMW89zzW
cy2W61eF6YssK5j3vlII81Lj0vzOKHaXCuSz8334ybgC2bkdlUK6ZeMVvTdMM0M0IL3fmQ
skbD08LA8YHDzGDw9Nyn7Hziuv1hsH/PltCQi9770MmsXFaGf/z3q/EFatlL/IFsBmgAAA
AASUVORK5CYII=" />
```

I know what you're thinking: "This is awful, didn't you tell me to create clean HTML?" Maybe you're right. However, we can automate the encoding, or use it in many other ways, such as adding it in CSS or loading multiple images at the same time using Ajax techniques and a JSON file.

You should deliver data URI images only to known compatible browsers. In Modernizr, you can check the `datauri` attribute, and in WURFL the capability is `image_inlining`.

In CSS this image could be a `background-image`, like:

```
#logo {
    width: 70px; height: 17px;
    background-image: url('data:image/png;base64,
iVBORw0KGgoAAAANSUhEUgAAAEYAAAARBAMAAACSi8f4AAAAA3NCSVQICAjb4U/gAAAAGF
BMVEX//////8AAACpqanMzMxmZmaHhoQ/Pz9kt3AEAAAACHRSTlMA/////////9XKVDIA
AAAJcEhZcwAACxIAAAsSAdLdfvwAAAcdEVYdFNvZnR3YXJlAEFkb2JlIEZpcmV3b3Jrcy
BDUzQGstOgAAAAFnRFWHRDcmVhdGlvbiBUaW1lADEyLzExLzA5ueqApgAAAQNJREFUKJGV
kUFTwyAQhfMXXiH1LA3hDMTeSVDPidW7WnMvkxn/vo+MsamX6s7wgOy3O29JgetR/I2Rdy
8B8HICAyhj8PLIrOdsuYlDF8i8KWWC/BRKaVCUTaJmkhcDuNOHLVCaJg6VfJY6JivqGJHE
jn00q3tpsGcfd0KuuGdx2+fsmSl3m2r2k2gGg30i434xSMlmht0YbR+EflAU71dMW89zzW
cy2W61eF6YssK5j3vlII81Lj0vzOKHaXCuSz8334ybgC2bkdlUK6ZeMVvTdMM0M0IL3fmQ
skbD08LA8YHDzGDw9Nyn7Hziuv1hsH/PltCQi9770MmsXFaGf/z3q/EFatlL/IFsBmgAAA
AASUVORK5CYII=') top left no-repeat;
}
```

The best part about using data URI images in CSS is that we can use them in more than one document without downloading the image content again (by caching the same CSS), and we still have cleanXHTML.

With HTML5 features, you can save in a database or in a JSON object a list of base64 image files that will be cached for the user on the device for future usage in URLs. See Chapter 13 for more information.

### Format compatibility

Table 10-1 explores image features and the browsers that support them. Remember that static GIF, PNG, and JPEG formats are supported on all platforms.

*Table 10-1. Image format compatibility table*

| Browser/platform | WebP | Animated GIF | APNG | APNG with polyfill | SVG as an image format | Data URI |
|---|---|---|---|---|---|---|
| Safari on iOS | No | Yes | No | Yes | Yes | Yes |
| Android browser | No up to 3.2 Yes from 4.0 | No up to 2.1 Yes from 2.2 | No | Yes | No up to 2.3 Yes from 3.0 | Yes |
| Chrome for Android | Yes (buggy on 18) | Yes | No | Yes | Yes | Yes |
| Nokia Browser for Symbian | No | Yes | No | No | No | Yes |
| Nokia Xpress browser | No | No | No | No | No | Yes |
| BlackBerry browser | No | Yes | No | Yes | Yes | Yes |
| Internet Explorer | No | Yes | No | No up to 9 Yes from 10 | No up to 7.x Yes from 9 | Yes |
| Firefox Mobile | No | Yes | Yes | Yes | Yes | Yes |
| Opera Mobile | Yes | Yes | Yes | Yes | Yes | Yes |
| Opera Mini | Yes | No | No | No | Yes | Yes |
| Amazon Silk | No | Yes | No | Yes | No | Yes |
| UC browser | Yes | Yes | No | No | No | Yes |

## Using the img Element

The `img` element should be used only for semantic images, or images that deserve to be images. That means, don't use the `img` tag for:

- Buttons
- Icons for links or menus
- Backgrounds
- Visual separators
- Titles

That doesn't mean that you shouldn't use images for any of those purposes—just don't use the `img` tag. That tag is semantically correct for images that the user understands as images in their own right, not for visual aids. Most users don't consider an arrow icon to be an image; it's just a button, or a link. We will follow the same rule.

The mandatory attributes for an `img` tag are `src`, `width`, `height`, and `alt`. It is very important to define the width and height of every image in a mobile document. This will reduce the initial rendering time, because the mobile browser won't need to wait for the image to load to know how much space it will take up and how to draw the rest of the content.

The alternative text (`alt` attribute) is also mandatory, because the user can disable images or they can be very slow to load, and the document must work without them. The `alt` text should provide enough information for the user to understand what is missing.

 Image maps should be avoided on the mobile web. Focus-navigation devices don't have image map support, and while cursor-navigation devices may support them, usability is a problem for the users. They can even be problematic on touch-navigation devices, because of the finger size. Only use image maps when targeting compatible devices, and if those devices support touch navigation, use large areas for every link.

Out of all of these complications and possibilities, some guidelines emerge:

- Use images in HTML only for logos, photos, and maps.
- Compress the images with normal web image methods.
- Define the width, height, and alternative text for every image.
- Use data URIs for small images whenever possible.
- Leave icons, buttons, backgrounds, and visual alert images for CSS.
- Open your mind to the usage of Emoji and pictograms with known compatible devices.
- Avoid the usage of image maps.
- Analyze the use of `canvas` or SVG for compatible devices and for some graphic types. These technologies will be covered later in this chapter.

## Responsive Images

When developing for the mobile web, we need to adapt to different contexts, and when using Responsive Web Design we need a way to have adaptive images, or images that are available in different sizes for different contexts. The ability of a web app to adapt images involves a technique called *responsive images*.

 Matt Wilcox wrote a good article on problems with responsive images and possible solutions, titled "Responsive images: what's the problem and how do we fix it?" (*http://bit.ly/XyWte9*)

When using Responsive Web Design techniques and background images, we can make it work with `background-size` and `background-position` to change the image's clip based on the current available screen size or orientation. In Figure 10-1, we can see how Food Sense (*http://foodsense.is*) applies this idea—same background image, different size and clip.

*Figure 10-1. The Food Sense website changes the size and position of the background image to create different masks of the same image and support different layouts and orientations in the same HTML file.*

A different solution that can be applied in different scenarios is to have a really big image on the server that will be automatically resized to suit the current context—mixed with some JavaScript or cookies, this can help us deliver the right image for every context. We can use a client-side framework that will leave a cookie so the server can determine the current necessary image dimensions, or we can use any server-side library, like WURFL to determine the correct image sizes (as we saw in Chapter 9). One already created solution (involving server-side code) is available from Adaptive Images (*http://adaptive-images.com*).

## Sencha.io Src

Sencha (*http://sencha.com*), the company behind the Sencha Touch framework and many other solutions for web developers, offers a free service for creating responsive images in one second: the *Src* service. The documentation is available in Sencha docs (*http://docs.sencha.io/current/index.html#!/guide/src*); it's really easy to use and we don't need to install anything.

Let's say we have a logo that we want to be 100% the width of the device's screen, such as:

```
<img src="http://mobilehtml5.org/img/logo.png" width="100%">
```

 Sencha.io Src always needs an absolute URL for the source definition, as it doesn't know where to get the file if we use a relative URL.

The problem with this approach is, what size should we use for the file? If we deliver a small file it will be resized and lead to poor visual results; if we deliver a large file we are wasting bandwidth and valuable loading time. Instead of having different sizes or providing a server-side algorithm to resize the file, we can just add `http://src.sencha.io/` as a prefix for the image URL:

```
<img src="http://src.sencha.io/http://mobilehtml5.org/img/logo.png"
width="100%">
```

That's all? Yes. The image request will be done to the free Src service, which will take the image from our server and resize it automatically to the current device's screen width. Therefore, the image file that is transferred from the server to the browser will be the most suitable one.

The service offers us different options to customize how it delivers the file. For example, if we don't want to use 100% of the device's screen as a limit, we can add a different percentage using x*<percentage>*/, as in:

```
<img src="http://src.sencha.io/x35/http://mobilehtml5.org/img/logo.png"
width="35%">
```

We can also make some other complex calculations, such as a percentage of the screen minus a fixed margin value, as in 35% – 20px:

```
<img width="35%"
src="http://src.sencha.io/x35-20/http://mobilehtml5.org/img/logo.png">
```

And we can force the image to take landscape values:

```
<img src="http://src.sencha.io/landscape/http://mobilehtml5.org/img/logo.png"
                               width="100%">
```

Another great feature is the data URI conversion (discussed earlier in this chapter), which we can call using `data`:

```
http://src.sencha.io/data/http://mobilehtml5.org/img/logo.png
```

We can use a JSONP technique to get a callback when the data URI is available, creating a callback function such as `dataReady` and defining its name inside the script we are injecting:

```
<script src="http://src.sencha.io/data.dataReady/http://
mobilehtml5.org/img/logo.png">
</script>
<script>
function dataReady(dataURI) {
    // Do something with the data URI representation of the image
}
</script>
```

The API offers lots of other features that we can check on the Sencha website. As an experimental service, Sencha offers a JavaScript file that we can also add that will detect orientation changes and resize the image accordingly.

 Firefox for mobile devices supports the `image-rendering` CSS attribute, which accepts different values (such as `optimizeSpeed`) that change how a bitmap image is scaled when zooming in or on high-resolution devices. More information about this property can be found at the Mozilla Developer Network (*http://mzl.la/Ydew4b*).

## Local Pictograms

The Japanese carriers have created a de facto standard for using small icons in HTML without really using images and requests. The images (called *Emoji*, a Japanese word combining picture and letter) are based on a list of dozens of icons available to use, with the real rendering done by the browser. For example, say you would like to insert a heart icon. Every compatible browser will display a heart icon, but you might not know the exact image that the browser will use. Today, NTT i-mode services include *Basic Pictograms* (176) compatible with all devices and *Expansion Pictograms* (76) added in HTML 4.0. Other Japanese carriers (Au and Softbank) have their own pictograms (and their own usage mechanisms), so if you need to cover all Japanese carriers there are a lot of conversion tables between codes.

To display these pictograms, you can just embed the binary code into your HTML (saved as a Shift-JIS file, not UTF-8) or define them as Unicode standard characters using &#x9999, where *9999* should be replaced with the pictogram number. The list of possible pictograms can be found at *www.mobilexweb.com/go/pictograms*.

This is a very underused feature in the occidental world. Even Safari on iOS supports these icons, although I have not seen too many websites using them. iOS has supported an Emoji keyboard since version 2.2 (though only for devices sold in Japan), and the browser allows Emoji pictograms for users worldwide.

The list of iPhone Emoji is available at Wikipedia (*http://en.wikipedia.org/wiki/Emoji*) and is best browsed with an iOS device. The list is long—there are more than 450 Emoji —and the icons have great designs. Moreover, remember, they are images that don't use network resources! For example, for the iPhone we can show a message with a smiley at the end, as shown in Figure 10-2, with the following code:

```
<p>Thanks for your message! &#xe415;</p>
```

*Figure 10-2. Safari on iOS shows the Emoji icon, but other older browsers show only a rectangle indicating a noncompatible character.*

There is also a polyfill available that will use high-resolution PNG files using the same iOS Emoji codes. You can see the full list and download the polyfill at *code.kwint.in/ emoji/*.

 Remember, iPhone Emoji work all over the world, not just in the Japanese market. You can detect compatibility dynamically using the Modernizr extension property `emoji` or the WURFL capability `emoji`.

### ISO pictograms

In the last few years, Unicode 6.0 (*http://www.unicode.org/charts*) has standardized some emoticons and other characters from Apple and Android proposals under the name *ISO pictograms*. At the time of this writing, Android (since 4.1), Safari on iOS 6.0, and Windows Phone (since 7.5) support ISO pictograms, either totally or partially. ISO pictograms use the same syntax as Emoji characters on iOS, using HTML-encoded Unicode characters.

A list of emoticons and other symbols that we can use today (and their compatibility with modern browsers) can be found at MobiForge (*http://bit.ly/WfjeSu*).

For example, to show a star symbol we can just use:

```
<p>A star symbol: &#127775;
```

### OMA pictograms

The Open Mobile Alliance (OMA) standardized pictograms in XHTML MP using an `object` tag like this:

```
<object data="pict:///core/arrow/right" />
```

The standard supports alternative content. That is, if the pictogram is not available, you can add a child to the object with an alternative. The alternative can be another pictogram or a classic image:

```
<object data="pict:///time/season/summer">
   <object data="pict://weather/sunny">
      <img src="images/sun.png" width="32" height="32" alt="Sunny" />
   </object>
</object>
```

The pictogram sets are not standardized between browsers, and that's why today they are not widely used in mobile websites.

 A good resource for Emoji and pictograms is the Google site for Emoji symbols (*http://bit.ly/XyXP8G*).

# Dealing with Multiple Screen Densities

As discussed earlier in this book, in the mobile world we have to deal with screens with different pixel densities, or DPI (dots per inch), and DPI always has a direct relationship with images. If you remember from Chapter 2, we have devices with low, medium, high, and ultra-high density. If we don't take this into account, we may get undesirable results.

Recall also that when we use HTML or CSS px dimension values, they are expressed in CSS pixels, or resolution-independent pixels. And we already know from Chapter 7 that our dimensions will be calculated based on the current viewport and zoom level.

Therefore, when we say:

```
<img src="logo.png" width="200" height="80">
```

we are not saying "always render this logo at 200×80 pixels."

The same is true when we use:

```
#logo {
    width: 200px; height: 80px;
    background-image: url(logo.png);
}
```

We are saying lot of things at the same time here, such as (with a viewport using device-width and no scaling):

- On a medium-density screen (such as the iPhone 3GS), render the image at 200×80 pixels.
- On some other medium-density screens (such as the Nexus 7 tablet, with a pixel ratio of 1.325), render the image at 265×106 pixels.
- On a high-density screen (such as the Samsung Galaxy SII, with a pixel ratio of 1.5), render the image at 300×120 pixels.
- On an ultra-high-density screen (such as the iPhone 5, with a pixel ratio of 2), render the image at 400×160 pixels.

## Using Vector-Based Solutions

The first option that does not cause image-definition problems or require delivering different files is to use a vector-based solution. The possible implementations are:

- Use SVG for any nonbitmap content, such as logos or icons. SVG is scalable, so every device will get the right resolution by default. Always provide an alternative for noncompatible browsers, such as version 2.x of the Android browser.
- Use CSS effects. Everything that is rendered by CSS will have the right resolution by default. That includes gradients, shadows, rounded corners, reflections, and other effects. We will cover these in Chapter 11.
- Use custom fonts. Instead of using fonts in images, you can use custom fonts. Fonts are scalable by default and they will have the right resolution for the current device. You can even create your own fonts and use them for iconography or other vector-based assets in your app. We will cover how to use your own fonts in Chapter 11.

IcoMoon (*http://icomoon.io*) is a free online service that creates an icon gallery as a custom font. It includes lots of icons that are ready to use, and you can upload your own scalable icons to the gallery.

---

### Custom Fonts Versus SVG

When creating a vector-based icon gallery, SVG and custom fonts are two possible solutions. In most situations creating custom fonts will result in much smaller files, but there are also some disadvantages, such as the icons being monochrome only.

SVG, on the other hand, can support multiple colors, more complex paths, and gradients; it can also be manipulated from the DOM API in JavaScript, and SVG files are based on XML, so they are easier to edit than custom font files.

---

## Providing One Single Image

A simple approach is to provide a single file (say, 200×80 pixels, 400×160 pixels, or something in between) that will be rendered at different sizes on different devices. The problems with that solution are:

- If we provide an image smaller than the current density (for example, a 100×100 image on a device with a pixel ratio of 2 that is expecting a 200×200 image), the browser will resize the image, and that means we will lose quality. Even if the result is not so bad and there are no visual glitches or problems, the user may realize that the image does not have "good resolution" and is not as sharp as it could be.

- If we provide an image larger than the current density, the browser will again resize the image. Usually resizing down doesn't cause problems in terms of visual quality. The problem is that we are delivering a big file (from 2 to 4 times bigger than necessary), meaning more bandwidth, a longer download time, and more memory consumption. And usually devices with lower density are older or cheaper, meaning they have less power and less memory.

### Using img elements

If we decide to provide an `img` image with a resolution higher than the medium standard one, it's important to explicitly define the width, height, or both. If not, we may have a problem. Let's say we use:

```
<img src="logo.png">
```

and we expect the logo to be 200 CSS pixels wide. If we provide a 400-pixel-wide image (ultra-high density), the browser will use 400px as the width value, so it will render at double the size. Even worse, on ultra-high-density screens it will be rendered as 800 device pixels wide (400 multiplied by the pixel ratio of 2).

 When providing an `img` image with a resolution higher than medium, you must explicitly define the dimensions, in CSS pixels.

## Using background images

The problem is worse with CSS background images. Going back to our example:

```
#logo {
    width: 200px; height: 80px;
    background-image: url(logo.png);
}
```

In this case we are defining a 200-CSS-pixels-wide box with the logo image. If we define the image as double the size for ultra-high-density devices, we will get the wrong effect, as seen on the left in Figure 10-3. The background image size will be multiplied by the pixel ratio automatically. To solve the problem, we can use the new CSS3 `background-size` property. That property allows us to define the size in CSS pixels or as a percentage of the background inside the box.

If we want to use percentages in `background-size`, for high-resolution images we should always use 100% to match the box's size. We can also use specific values (width first, then height) so we get the desired result, as seen in the image on the right in Figure 10-3:

```
#logo {
    width: 200px; height: 80px;
    background-image: url(logo.png);
    background-size: 200px 80px;
}
```

*Figure 10-3. Left: high-resolution image with the background-size equal to the image's size. Right: same image with a background-size equal to the CSS element's size.*

# Providing Image Alternatives

As the Web evolves and changes, new features, techniques, and solutions appear in the browsers. That means if we already have variants of the same image for different resolutions, we can use some new techniques to deliver them. These techniques include:

- JavaScript and the `devicePixelRatio` property
- CSS media queries
- Image sets

As we saw in Table 2-2, there are different devices out there with different pixel density ratios. Providing a different image for every possible pixel ratio seems an impossible mission, as new devices are constantly appearing on the market.

 As we may need images with more density in the future, it's a good idea to always store vector-based versions of all our logos, icons, and so on, and high-resolution versions of all our bitmap images (around 300–400 DPI).

The best solution is to define ranges. For example:

- Version 1, from 0.75 to 1.25: your original CSS pixel size
- Version 2, from 1.25 to 1.75: your size multiplied by 1.5
- Version 3, from 1.76 to infinite: your size multiplied by 2

Some resizing will still occur, but the results should not be so problematic. To name your files, you can have different folders, such as *images/*, *images-1.5x/*, *images-2x*, or use the same filename with a suffix, such as *logo.png*, *logo-2x.png*, *logo.2x.png*.

 In native iOS development, the convention is to use the `@2x` suffix for high-resolution images. In HTML5, we should avoid using the at sign (`@`) inside filenames to avoid URL problems.

## Using devicePixelRatio

Some browsers expose the current device pixel ratio as a JavaScript variable of the `window` context, called `devicePixelRatio`. You should always provide a default value of 1 if the attribute is not defined (the assumption being that it is an older device with a medium-density screen):

```
var pixelRatio = window.devicePixelRatio || 1;
if (pixelRatio <= 1.25) {
```

```
    // Group #1, low and medium resolution
} else if ((pixelRatio > 1.25) and (pixelRatio <= 1.75)) {
    // Group #2, medium and high resolution
} else {
    // Group #3, ultra-high resolution, usually 2, 2.25
}
```

Because iOS devices often have a pixel density ratio of 2, it's a common technique to search for this exact ratio. That is not a good practice, as there are devices with higher density than iOS devices that deserve high-resolution images, but they receive the low-resolution versions just because their pixel density ratios are greater than 2. Always use greater than or less than when specifying resolutions inside conditionals.

When you detect every group, you can then define the corresponding image URL using the src attribute or CSS styles. The main problem with this technique is that the browser will not start downloading and rendering any image until your JavaScript code is executed.

Another solution, used by Apple on its home page, is to always load the low-resolution version first: the JavaScript code will replace it as soon as possible. The main problem with this approach is that in many cases the browser ends up downloading two versions of the image(s), wasting time and traffic.

### Using media queries

We will cover media queries in depth in Chapter 11. For now, suffice it to say that it is a CSS3 feature allowing us to define different styles for different conditions. Most browsers with different densities support an extension to the media queries standard allowing us to query about the pixel ratio in the CSS itself.

The browsers call the pixel ratio extension device-pixel-ratio, and it's prefixed. To make a "greater than" condition, we can use min-device-pixel-ratio instead. To further complicate our lives, the WebKit prefix version is -webkit-min-device-pixel-ratio and the Mozilla version is min--moz-device-pixel ratio (with a double -).

Because the CSS standard already had a similar property for the pixel ratio (resolution) but using dpi as the unit, the W3C group decided in mid-2012 to define a new unit so it wouldn't need to formalize the nonstandard device-pixel-ratio. The new unit is dppx (dots per pixel), and it's equal to the pixel ratio value. Therefore, for future compatibility we can start adding the standard resolution version.

Opera with Presto engine supports the prefixed pixel ratio extension but accepts fractions (the relation between resolutions) instead of float values: so, 1.5 becomes 3/2 and 2 becomes 2/1.

To give an example, we can make the following groups using CSS:

```
/* Definitions for all resolutions; dimensions will stay the same in
   CSS pixels */
#logo {
  width: 200px; height: 80px;
  background-size: 200px 80px;
}

/* We define the default value out of any media query */
#logo {
  background-image: url(logo.png);
}

/* We use different declarations for all the possible prefixes */
  @media screen and (min--moz-device-pixel-ratio: 1.5),
      only screen and (-o-min-device-pixel-ratio: 3/2),
      only screen and (-webkit-min-device-pixel-ratio: 1.5),
      only screen and (min-device-pixel-ratio: 1.5),
      only screen and (min-resolution: 1.5dppx) {

  /* This definition will replace the default value when the pixel
     ratio is at least 1.5 */
  #logo {
    background-image: url(logo_1.5x.png);
  }
}

/* We use different declarations for all the possible prefixes */
@media screen and (min--moz-device-pixel-ratio: 2),
      only screen and (-o-min-device-pixel-ratio: 2/1),
      only screen and (-webkit-min-device-pixel-ratio: 2),
      only screen and (min-device-pixel-ratio: 2) ,
      only screen and (min-resolution: 2dppx) {

  /* This definition will replace the default value when the pixel
     ratio is at least 2 */
  #logo {
    background-image: url(logo_2x.png);
  }
}
```

Before the device-pixel-ratio extension to the media queries standard was created, the spec included the resolution conditional, which accepts DPI values. We can convert from pixel ratio to DPI easily; the problem is that not every browser supports the resolution conditional, as we might expect. Therefore, some devices will honor 96dpi, no matter what the real resolution is. The new unit dppx will solve this problem in the near future.

You may be thinking about changing the background-size for every density definition—for example, using background-size: 50% on devices with a pixel ratio of 2 because the image size is double that of the original. However, you need to remember that when you give background-size a percentage value, that value applies to the image container—that is, the HTML element. And in our case, the HTML element is always the same size in CSS pixels, no matter what resolution the device has. Therefore, the background-size should not change from its original value.

 Instead of specifying dimensions in the background-size property, we can use the constant cover that will just fit the image into its container.

## Using image sets

Safari on iOS 6 has added a new nonstandard feature to support multiresolution images: the image-set() CSS function. As an experimental feature, it's prefixed, so the final name is -webkit-image-set(). At the time of this writing, only Safari on iOS 6 supports it.

image-set() is a CSS image function, meaning that we can use it any time we can use an image in CSS, such as in background-image. It accepts a set of comma-separated declarations, each consisting of an image and a resolution.

 Image sets have been added to the CSS4 standard discussion as a Resolution Negotiation feature (*http://bit.ly/Ydf6Pe*).

As with any other CSS property, we can make a fallback by defining a standard value first. This should become clearer with an example:

```
#logo {
    width: 200px; height: 80px;
    background-size: 200px 80px;
    background-image: url('logo.png'); // Standard fallback
    background-image: -webkit-image-set(url('logo.png') 1x,
    url('logo-2x.png') 2x);
}
```

In this case, in one declaration we are defining two images, one for a pixel ratio of 1 and the other for a pixel ratio of 2. Remember that iOS supports only devices with pixel ratios of 1 and 2 at the time of this writing. If other browsers, such as Chrome for Android, begin supporting this feature in the future, it's probable that they may use other values, such as 1.5x.

The main advantage of image sets over CSS media queries is the simplicity of the syntax and the fact that we don't need to search all over our stylesheets to find all the possible values for the same image on devices with different resolutions.

### The picture element

The main problem with using CSS media queries or image sets is that we are always talking about CSS background images. From an HTML perspective, there is no way to do the same thing without adding JavaScript code. In recognition of this, the W3C has started a new discussion group—the Responsive Images Community Group (*http:// bit.ly/ZPtuAL*)—that is focused on creating one new element for the future of HTML5: the picture element.

The picture element draws upon a mix of media query and image set techniques, but from an HTML point of view, to replace the img element. At the time of this writing no browsers support this new element, but some probably will soon.

 Scott Jehl (*http://scottjehl.com*) has created an open source polyfill for the picture element that validates against HTML5, using divs with a very similar syntax to the W3C's proposed picture element. It's available at Scott Jehl's GitHub (*https://github.com/scottjehl/picturefill*).

The picture element can have different source elements, providing different images by defining different media attributes and one src or srcset definition (following the image set syntax). Let's look at a sample:

```
<picture width="500" height="500">
    <source media="(min-width: 50em)" src="large.jpg"
            alt="Single image by media query">
    <source media="(min-width: 20em)"
            srcset="medium.jpg 1x, medium_2x.jpg 2x"
            alt="Multiple image set">
    <img src="small.jpg"
         alt="Fallback image if picture is not supported">
</picture>
```

Any browser that is compatible with the picture element will ignore the img element, which will be used only by noncompatible browsers.

# SVG

Standard Vector Graphics is an open XML specification describing 2D vector graphics. An SVG document can be static (declared in an XML file or tag) or dynamically generated from a JavaScript script using the DOM API. As a vector-rendering engine, a great feature is the adaptation to different screen sizes and resolutions without loss of quality.

SVG is a W3C standard for desktop platforms, with two subsets prepared for mobile platforms: *SVG Basic* and *SVG Tiny*. Thanks to this standards fight (as with XHTML mobile versions), we can use either SVG Basic or SVG Tiny with the same code and results.

The latest version available is SVG Tiny 1.2, but the most compatible version of SVG Tiny for mobile browsers is 1.1 (*SVGT 1.1*), which offers some support for animation. This version has been adopted by the OMA and the 3rd Generation Partnership Project (3GPP). Opacity and gradients are not part of the mobile standard, but some devices still render them. This addition is known in the market as *SVGT 1.1+*.

Modernizr will give you two important flags for compatibility checks, svg and inlinesvg. WURFL, on the other hand, has the capabilities svgt_1_1 and svgt_1_1_plus to detect SVGT and SVGT 1.1+ support.

One compatibility issue between SVGT devices is text support. Some devices allow us to use system fonts to declare text in the SVG, but others do not, forcing us to convert text to curves in a graphic design tool.

One of the biggest problems of using SVG today is the lack of support in Android browser 2.x, which still has a big portion of the Android market share.

Smartphones and tablets support the last non-Tiny SVG standard without any issue.

SVG can be used in different ways:

- As an external file using `img`
- As an external file using `object`
- As a CSS background
- As a CSS effect
- As a font
- As inline SVG

*The New York Times* uses a GIF logo on its desktop website (*http://nytimes.com*). However, when the desktop website is being browsed by a smartphone or tablet, the logo is replaced with an SVG version (Figure 10-4) so it is sharp at any zoom level and different resolutions, such as on the original iPad and iPad third generation.

*Figure 10-4. Because* The New York Times *uses an SVG logo, there is no loss of quality when the user zooms in or when the site is browsed by a high-density device.*

### Tools for SVG

Most vector graphic design software supports SVG as an export format. Adobe Illustrator, for example, can export to SVGT 1.1, SVGT 1.1+, and SVGT 1.2. Corel Draw is another useful tool for SVG conversion. Sometimes the markup generated by Illustrator has more tags than you need, so you may want to open it with another tool and export it again. The most useful tool for mobile SVG currently on the market is Ikivo Animator. It is intended for mobile devices and can create animations using SVGT 1.1. You can download a trial version from Ikivo (*http://www.ikivo.com/animator*).

 Google Maps uses SVG on the Street View HTML5 version. When you view a street view panorama on Google Maps (*http://maps.google.com*) on a mobile device, the panorama is a bitmap and the direction arrows and street names are a transparent SVG image laid over the top. It's a vector image, so it's easy to rotate and change properties as you browse in the panorama.

In the open source world, Inkscape (*http://inkscape.org*) offers SVG support, and for Windows only we can use SVGmaker Tiny (*http://svgmaker.com*), a printer driver that converts any printed document into SVGT.

In the online world, we can find free SVG editors (*http://code.google.com/p/svg-edit*).

 Google Swiffy (*https://www.google.com/doubleclick/studio/swiffy/*) is an online tool that converts Flash movies (ActionScript 2 and experimental ActionScript 3) to SVG and JavaScript.

The recommendations for SVG document generation are:

- Keep the quantity and size of the objects used to the minimum.
- Avoid big gradient areas; they decrease performance.
- Reduce path points to the minimum.
- If the object is too complex, a raster PNG may be better.
- Use GZIP if compatible.
- Combine paths when possible.
- Maintain one copy of each object online.
- Export text as curves.
- For simple shapes, don't use a graphic design tool.

### SVG for beginners

SVG is beyond the scope of this book, but here is a very quick lesson on SVG Tiny.

An SVG document is an XML document with a root svg tag defining an original viewport size (width and height), but remember that it is a vector image, so you can resize it. Inside the image, we can draw the following kinds of shapes:

- Rectangles (rect)
- Circles (circle)
- Ellipses (ellipse)
- Lines (line)
- Polylines (polyline)
- Polygons (polygon)
- Paths (path)

The following is an SVG Tiny 1.1+ compatible document (it uses a `LinearGradient`, which is not included in the SVGT 1.1 standard):

```
<?xml version="1.0" encoding="utf-8"?>
<!DOCTYPE svg PUBLIC "-//W3C//DTD SVG 1.1 Tiny//EN"
    "http://www.w3.org/Graphics/SVG/1.1/DTD/svg11-tiny.dtd">

<svg version="1.1" baseProfile="tiny"
    xmlns="http://www.w3.org/2000/svg"
    xmlns:xlink="http://www.w3.org/1999/xlink"
    x="0px" y="0px" width="200px" height="200px">

<linearGradient id="grad1" gradientUnits="userSpaceOnUse"
            x1="54" y1="61" x2="147" y2="61">
   <stop offset="0" style="stop-color:#FFFFFF"/>
   <stop offset="1" style="stop-color:#000000"/>
</linearGradient>

<rect x="0" y="0" fill="url(#grad1)" stroke="#000000"
        width="193" height="84"/>

<ellipse fill="#FF0000" stroke="#000000" cx="30" cy="100"
        rx="25" ry="25"/>

</svg>
```

This document creates a 200×200-pixel SVG image containing a rectangle (`rect` tag) and a circle (`ellipse` tag with equal radius `rx` and `ry` centered at `cx`, `cy`). The circle is filled with a plain red color and the rectangle is filled with a linear gradient defined with an `id` of `grad1`. This gradient is not compatible with SVGT 1.1 (without the +).

 Google Drive (*http://drive.google.com*) has an online free vector graphic designer for diagrams and graphs. It has the option to export to SVG.

This document has a size of 670 bytes (0.6 KB) as an SVG file. A 24-bit PNG with the same image has a size of 5.77 KB, and an 8-bit PNG with quality loss has a size of 1.31 KB. Clearly, SVG is better from a size (and network traffic) perspective. The bad thing is that the browser has to render the image on the mobile device (although this is not the case for cloud-based browsers, such as Opera Mini, where the SVG is pre-rendered on a server).

### Embedding the SVG in XHTML

To insert an SVG document inside an XHTML document, we can use the `object` tag, defining the `data` attribute with the URL of the SVG, the type as `image/svg+xml`, and the `width` and `height`. As an SVG is a vector-based image, we can use percentages for the size attributes to adapt the content to the viewport size. If SVG is not available, we can use the fallback feature to create an alternative image in another format as a child of the object tag:

```
<object data="logo.svg" type="image/svg+xml" width="100" height="30">
    <img src="logo.jpg" width="100" height="30" alt="Logo not SVG" />
</object>
```

### Embedding the SVG using img

Some HTML5 browsers (as seen in Table 10-1) also use the classic img tag for SVG files:

```
<img src="logo.svg" width="100" height="30">
```

 Filter Effects (*http://mobilexweb.com/go/w3cfilter*) is a W3C draft that allows us to use simple effects or SVG effects on DOM elements. At the time of this writing there is no mobile browser supporting SVG effects, but it's possible that we will see this kind of compatibility in the future.

### Inline SVG

HTML5 offers the ability to embed an SVG document using an svg element. Inside the svg element we must follow XML rules. With this approach we don't need to load an external file, as we do when using object or img. The following HTML5 document is valid and includes the previous SVG drawing:

```
<!DOCTYPE html>
<title>SVG demo</title>

<h1>SVG demo</h1>

<svg xmlns="http://www.w3.org/2000/svg" id="svg1" version="1.1"
     viewBox="0 0 100 100"
     preserveAspectRatio="xMidYMid slice" width="300" height="300">

    <linearGradient id="grad1" gradientUnits="userSpaceOnUse"
                    x1="54" y1="61" x2="147" y2="61">
      <stop offset="0" style="stop-color:#FFFFFF"/>
      <stop offset="1" style="stop-color:#000000"/>
    </linearGradient>

    <rect x="0" y="0" fill="url(#grad1)" stroke="#000000"
          width="193" height="84"/>

    <ellipse fill="#FF0000" stroke="#000000" cx="30" cy="100"
             rx="25" ry="25"/>
</svg>
```

Figure 10-5 shows the result.

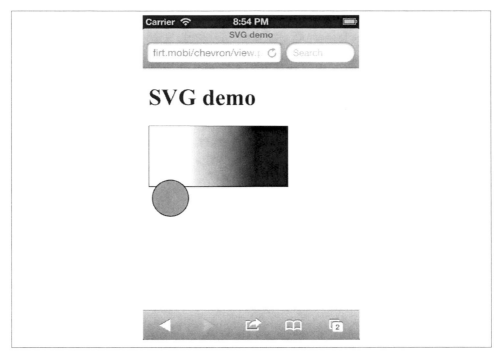

*Figure 10-5. With inline SVG we can embed a vector graphic inside any HTML5 document on compatible browsers.*

With SVG we can use the DOM API to manage elements, such as creating new SVG elements, or changing elements or attributes. For example, this JavaScript code will add a circle over the svg element with the ID svg1:

```
var newCircle = document.createElementNS('http://www.w3.org/2000/svg',
  'circle');
newCircle.setAttribute('r',20);
newCircle.setAttribute('id','leftEye');
newCircle.setAttribute('cx',50);
newCircle.setAttribute('cy',40);
newCircle.setAttribute('fill','red');
newCircle.setAttribute('stroke','white');
document.getElementById('svg1').appendChild(newCircle);
```

### Raphaël

While SVG is getting more important in the HTML5 world for vector-based graphics, lots of other frameworks are available. One of the most important is *Raphaël* (*http://raphaeljs.com*).

Raphaël can create really cool graphics, animations, and effects with just a few lines of code. Once you add the Raphael.js library to your HTML project, you can start using the API, as in this example:

```
// Creates 320 × 200 canvas at 10, 50
var paper = Raphael(10, 50, 320, 200);

// Creates circle at x = 50, y = 40, with radius 10
var circle = paper.circle(50, 40, 10);

// Sets the fill attribute of the circle to red (#f00)
circle.attr("fill", "#f00");

// Sets the stroke attribute of the circle to white
circle.attr("stroke", "#fff");
```

 In Chapter 11, we will talk about using custom fonts, and we will see how to use SVG as a font format.

# Canvas

The possibility of a drawing API was the dream of every web designer in the '90s, but it has only recently become available in browsers. canvas is an HTML5 element that defines a rectangular area where we can draw using a JavaScript API. The drawings are not vector-based, and we cannot browse through them using the DOM or any other mechanism. canvas is not a competitor for SVG; it's just another way to generate dynamic graphics in a browser window.

 canvas was originally defined by Apple in WebKit, and today it is the oldest and the most widely adopted HTML5 feature in the web developers' world. You will find a lot of resources on the Web on the usage of this element.

For our purposes, the only useful attributes are an id and the dimensions width and height. As child elements, we can insert any HTML code that will be used as a fallback:

```
<canvas width="300" height="300" id="canvas">
  Here goes text, images, or other tags for noncompatible browsers
</canvas>
```

## The context

Once we have defined a canvas we get what is called a *2D context*: a JavaScript object that we can use for drawing bitmaps over that canvas.

We can get the context pointer using the following code, with the code checking for API support first:

```
var canvas = document.getElementById('canvas');
if (canvas.getContext) {
    // canvas is supported
    var context = canvas.getContext('2d');
}
```

### Lines and strokes

Once we have the context, we can define the line type using the color properties fill Style and strokeStyle and the integer property lineWidth. Then we can start drawing.

### Drawing methods

The available drawing methods of the 2D context are listed in Table 10-2.

*Table 10-2. Useful drawing methods in the HTML5 canvas context*

| Method | Description |
| --- | --- |
| fillRect(x, y, width, height) | Draws a filled rectangle with the current styles. |
| strokeRect(x, y, width, height) | Draws a stroked rectangle with a transparent fill. |
| clearRect(x, y, width, height) | Clears the area and makes it transparent. |
| beginPath() | Begins a path drawing. |
| closePath() | Closes the shape by creating a line from the first path line to the ending path line. |
| moveTo(x, y) | Moves the pen to the coordinates for the next line in the path. |
| lineTo(x, y) | Draws a line from the current pen coordinates to the ones provided. |
| arc(x, y, radius, startAngle, endAngle, anticlockwise) | Draws an arc with its center at x, y and with the defined radius. The anticlockwise parameter is a Boolean value. Angles are defined in radians. |
| quadraticCurveTo(controlx, controly, x, y) | Draws a quadratic Bezier curve. |
| bezierCurveTo(control1x, control1y, control2x, control2y, x, y) | Draws a cubic Bezier curve. |
| stroke() | Draws the path defined since the last beginPath(). |
| fill() | Closes the path defined since the last beginPath() and fills it. |
| drawImage(x, y) | Draws an image (Image JavaScript object) on the canvas. Other optional parameters also exist. |
| createImageData(width, height) | Creates an ImageData object with a data attribute that is an array of pixels to be manipulated as integers. |
| getImageData(x, y, w, h) | Gets an ImageData object from the current drawing to be manipulated. |
| putImageData(image_data, x, y) | Puts an ImageData object into the drawing. |

| Method | Description |
|---|---|
| strokeText(*string*, *x*, *y*) | Draws a stroked string. |
| fillText(*string*, *x*, *y*) | Fills a string. |

canvas as a whole is outside the scope of this book. If you want to dig deeper into this API, you can read the book *HTML5 Canvas* by Steve Fulton and Jeff Fulton (O'Reilly).

An excellent example of drawing curves on a canvas is provided by Mozilla's documentation, which shows how to draw a dialog box with the following code:

```
context.beginPath();
context.moveTo(75,25);
context.quadraticCurveTo(25,25,25,62.5);
context.quadraticCurveTo(25,100,50,100);
context.quadraticCurveTo(50,120,30,125);
context.quadraticCurveTo(60,120,65,100);
context.quadraticCurveTo(125,100,125,62.5);
context.quadraticCurveTo(125,25,75,25);
context.stroke();
```

 Angles in the Canvas API are defined in radians, not degrees. To make the conversion we can use the formula (Math.PI/180)*degrees.

### Advanced features

Some other advanced features for canvases include a Text API (to draw text), text shadowing, gradients, image scaling, transparency, fonts, line styles, patterns, and other drawing methods.

 In WURFL, the property that we can query server-side is canvas_sup port; in Modernizr, we have canvas and canvastext for the Canvas Text API.

With canvas we can do lots of cool stuff in mobile web apps, including creating games (using a game loop), drawing apps, charts, and more. There are hundreds of frameworks and libraries out there that we can use as a high-level API instead of talking directly to the Canvas API.

### Canvas as native code

Ejecta (*https://github.com/phoboslab/Ejecta*) is an open source iOS Canvas implementation allowing us to create high-performance native Canvas apps and games without a web view and without the HTML rendering engine being in memory. It's possible that in the next few years we will see this kind of solution available across platforms, allowing the creation of high-performance HTML5 games that will rely not on an HTML/CSS rendering engine but only on a JavaScript execution engine and a native Canvas implementation on each platform.

 At the time of this writing, Canvas 2.0 (*http://www.w3.org/TR/2dcontext2/*)—also known as HTML Canvas 2D Context, Level 2—is being discussed as a draft specification. As yet, there is no browser implementation.

### Canvas as a background

WebKit has released an extension to the Canvas API that allows us to define a drawing context as a CSS background instead of a `canvas` element. To do that we need to first define the background in CSS as `-webkit-canvas(`*id*`)` and use a `document.getCSSCanvasContext` function to retrieve the context. That function will receive the context type (`2d`), the `id` defined in CSS, and the desired width and height.

For example:

```
<!DOCTYPE html>
<title>Canvas Background</title>
<style>
#element {
    width: 200px; height: 100px;
    background: -webkit-canvas(myCanvas);
}
</style>

<div id="element"></div>

<script>
var context = document.getCSSCanvasContext("2d", "myCanvas", 200, 100);
// All my drawings here
</script>
```

At the time of this writing, this ability is only available on modern WebKit-based mobile browsers, such as the Android browser, Safari on iOS, BlackBerry 7/10, and Chrome for Android.

 On Firefox, we can achieve a similar effect using `background: -moz-element(#canvasId)` and a hidden `canvas` element on the screen connected though the `id`.

### Exporting canvas drawings

Another extension of the `canvas` element is the ability to export the canvas drawing as a bitmap image in data URI format. With this API, we can then use Ajax to send the drawing to the server, or use a storage API to store it locally. Remember that the basic Canvas API already has a way to export the drawing as an array of pixels. This API will export the bitmap as a real, valid PNG file, unless we define a different MIME type as a parameter. When we define JPEG as the result format, we can use a second argument (from `0.0` to `1.0`) indicating the JPEG compression value.

The method used is `toDataURL`, and it can be applied to the `canvas` element itself:

```
var bitmapDataPNG = canvas.toDataURL();
var bitmapDataGIF = canvas.toDataURL("image/gif");
var bitmapDataJPG = canvas.toDataURL("image/jpeg", 0.8);
```

 Exporting the canvas is particularly useful when the drawing is created by the user, or when we want to provide a local way to manipulate an image and export a new version, such as applying a bitmap effect, resizing an original image, or some other manipulations.

Some modern browsers also support a way to get the image as a Blob object using `toBlob()` or as a File API object using `getAsFile()` (this function is prefixed, as in `mozGetAsFile()`). You should check the context object for the presence of these functions before trying to use them.

 Adobe Flash Professional (*http://adobe.ly/Z6aJHX*) from version CS6 supports the CreateJS toolkit extension that helps Flash animators to export assets, animations, and drawings to the Canvas 2D drawing API using the open source CreateJS framework.

### Canvas and pixel density

As we already know, we need to deal with screens having different pixel densities, and when we create a 300×200-pixel canvas, it's measured in CSS pixels. On most mobile platforms, canvases are considered as bitmap images, so by default we will get a resized image that will not use the full definition of the device. For example, Safari on iPhone 5 will render your drawing as a 300×200 bitmap and then resize it to 600×400, with the consequent quality loss. Safari on the Mac with a Retina display acts differently, though: the canvas will use all the possible definition available.

To manage these differences, WebKit has added a new property to the canvas context, called `webkitBackingStorePixelRatio`. This means that you will get a device pixel ratio of 2 on both a Mac with a Retina display and an iPhone 5, but on iOS you will get a backing store pixel ratio of 1.

If we want to force a high-definition canvas, one solution is to double the canvas size in HTML and also the viewport width (for example, to 640 pixels on the iPhone or iPod).

 Pay attention to the performance, as when you double the canvas size, your rendering will take more processing time.

Another solution to force a high-definition canvas is to force a double-size canvas. Canvases have a virtual dimension that usually is 1:1 with CSS pixels. We can change that using the scale() function of the context. That is, if we say:

```
context.scale(2, 2);
```

our canvas will be double the size. The problem is that the drawing will also be double the size in our container. To solve this problem, we need a trick. The solution is to define the canvas dimensions in HTML (as double the desired size) and also in CSS (as the desired size):

```
<canvas width="600" height="600" style="width: 300px; height: 300px">
```

With that solution we will finally have a 300×300 CSS pixels canvas that is being rendered as a 600×600 real pixels image on high-resolution devices.

 Be careful to apply the high-resolution techniques only for devices with a high-density screen and when you know that the canvas is not being doubled in size automatically (as with the backing store pixel ratio value).

## WebGL

WebGL (*http://www.khronos.org/registry/webgl/specs/1.0*) brings 3D to the mobile web through a canvas element. The API is not a W3C standard; it was created by the Khronos Group. The API is based on OpenGL ES 2.0, and to be honest, it's not too webby. That means that the API doesn't look like a JavaScript API, but more like a C++ API with JavaScript syntax.

You need development knowledge to work with WebGL because it's not as simple as working with the 2D standard Canvas API. We use the same canvas element and we just change the context we look for:

```
var context = canvas.getContext("webgl") ||
              canvas.getContext("experimental-webgl");
```

Some browsers will use webgl and others experimental-webgl as the context name. With the context we can access the graphics or video card directly from JavaScript.

Even when a mobile browser supports WebGL, it doesn't mean that the performance will be good enough for some kinds of 3D content. Because of performance and some security issues, some browsers ask the user for permission before starting WebGL sessions, or allow the user to disable it from the preferences.

WebGL compatibility on mobile browsers is quite rare today, being limited to the BlackBerry browser for PlayBook and BB10, Firefox, and Opera for Android from version 12. At the time of this writing there is no support in Chrome, the Android browser, Internet Explorer, or Safari on iOS. The only exception is some Sony Xperia devices on Android 2.3 that have added WebGL support on top of the default browser.

 Safari on iOS from version 4.2 includes all the necessary properties and objects of WebGL in the engine, but it's completely disabled for developers. iAds, the advertisement system from Apple for native iOS apps, can make use of WebGL for 3D content under Apple's approval.

If you have a compatible browser, you can check out the open source TunnelTilt (*http://blackberry.github.com/WebGL-Samples/tunneltilt*) game created by BlackBerry. The source code is available at BlackBerry's GitHub (*https://github.com/blackberry/WebGL-Samples*).

Because the WebGL API accesses the video card as a low-level API, some security issues have been found that allow a website to potentially take information from other windows that the user may have open. That is why the BlackBerry browser for PlayBook shows a security warning before enabling WebGL, as seen in Figure 10-6.

For more information on WebGL, check out the book *WebGL: Up and Running* by Tony Parisi (O'Reilly).

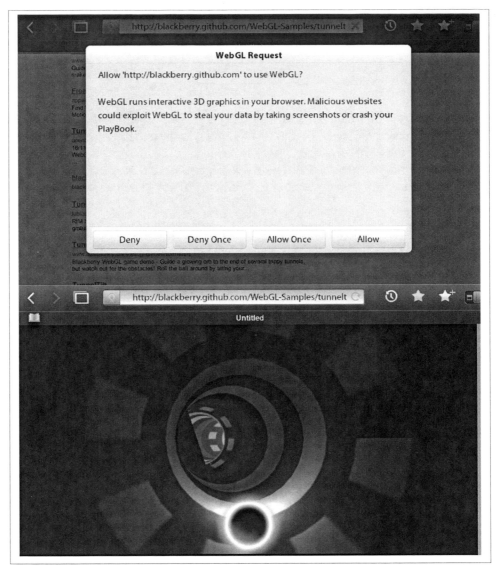

*Figure 10-6. The BlackBerry browser for PlayBook shows a security warning before starting a WebGL 3D session (in this case, the TiltTunnel game).*

### Canvas compatibility

Table 10-3 lists browser support for basic canvas functionality. For updated compatibility information, please visit Mobile HTML5 (*http://mobilehtml5.org*).

*Table 10-3. HTML5 canvas compatibility table*

| Browser/platform | 2D canvas | High-resolution canvas | Canvas as background | Export to data URI | WebGL |
|---|---|---|---|---|---|
| Safari on iOS | Yes | No | Yes | Yes | No |
| Android browser | Yes | No | Yes | Yes from 4.0 | No |
| Chrome for Android | Yes | No | Yes | Yes | No |
| Nokia Browser for Symbian | Yes from Anna | N/A | No | No | No |
| Nokia Xpress browser | No (only exported as data URI) | No | No | Yes | No |
| BlackBerry browser for smartphones until 7.x | Yes from 6.0 | N/A | Yes | Yes | No |
| BlackBerry for PlayBook | Yes | N/A | Yes | Yes | Yes from 2.0 |
| BlackBerry for BB10 | Yes | No | Yes | Yes | Yes |
| Internet Explorer | Yes from 9 | No | No | No | No |
| Firefox Mobile | Yes | No | No | Yes | Yes |
| Opera Mobile | Yes | No | No | Yes | Yes from 12.0 |
| Opera Mini | Yes, rendered on the server | No | No | Yes | No |
| Amazon Silk | Yes | No | Yes | No | No |
| UC browser | Yes | No | Yes | No | No |

# Adobe Flash

The Flash Player has long been the de facto standard in desktop browsers: Flash Player 8 penetration was at more than 99.5% at its peak in September 2009. However, the world has changed, and mobile devices are part of the change. While Adobe has tried to bring the same experience to the mobile browser, it has found many stones in the road.

Adobe had two mobile lines: Flash Lite and the major Flash Player for mobile devices. The first one was intended for low-end and mid-range devices (and high-end devices shipped before 2010), and the major player was available for Android and BlackBerry for PlayBook starting in 2010. However, after a couple of months it became clear that the experience and performance on Android were not good enough, and finally Adobe gave up and started to support HTML5 as the way to go.

 Flash Player for Android was available from Android 2.2 to Android 4.0. With Jelly Bean (4.1), Adobe has removed support, and it will not invest in enhancements to the already deployed versions of the player.

At the time of this writing only the BlackBerry PlayBook tablet and the BlackBerry 10 platform have the full Adobe Flash Player; all modern Symbian devices support Flash Lite 4 (similar to Flash Player 8 in terms of compatibility). Internet Explorer 10 on Windows 8 supports Flash in Desktop mode (not available on ARM tablets); in Windows 8 mode it is disabled by default.

The future of Flash on mobile devices is about creating native apps for iOS, Android, and BlackBerry 10 using Adobe AIR, not about mobile websites. Use HTML5 for the browser and multiplatform native web apps.

If your website really needs to use Flash content for Internet Explorer 10, you can add a header:

```
X-UA-Compatible: requiresActiveX=true
```

or a meta tag:

```
<meta http-equiv="X-UA-Compatible" content="requiresActiveX=true" />
```

indicating that it is required. Either of these will invite the Internet Explorer to open the website in Desktop mode in Windows 8, so your Flash content will run properly.

Mozilla Shumway (*http://mozilla.github.com/shumway/*) is an open source Flash Player completely written in JavaScript. It can run SWF files with ActionScript 3 on HTML5 browsers. The project is based on an older one known as Gordon.

Also, as long as your website does not make use of certain APIs (such as 3D or hardware access), you can request that Microsoft add you to a whitelist so Flash Player will be activated in IE10 Windows 8 mode on your website. More information is available at Breaking the Mobile Web (*http://mobilexweb.com/go/win8flash*).

## Apple Versus Adobe

Apple versus Adobe, Adobe versus Apple…this is one of the great fights in the mobile web world today. When the iPhone SDK arrived in 2008, Adobe wanted to create a Flash Player for it. Apple appeared to agree. A year later, Adobe accused Apple of not providing any help, and months later Apple announced that the iPhone would not have Flash support. The justification was the high battery consumption of Flash content in the browser, and the fact that it was not necessary because iPhone extensions to CSS and JavaScript allow any developer to create Flashy content without Flash.

One of the off-the-record causes, though, was that if Apple enabled Flash content in the iPhone, it would lose political control over the content, games, and applications available for the device.

In early 2010, Adobe announced that starting with Adobe Flash CS5, the tool would export SWF to native iPhone applications that could then be distributed in the App Store. However, Apple counterattacked by changing the terms of the App Store and saying that those applications would not be allowed. A year after that, Apple removed the "anti-Flash" restriction and Flash applications started to be accepted again at the App Store.

The issue of Flash compatibility is an important one because of the undesirable results when we attempt to show Flash content on noncompatible devices (as illustrated in Figure 10-7).

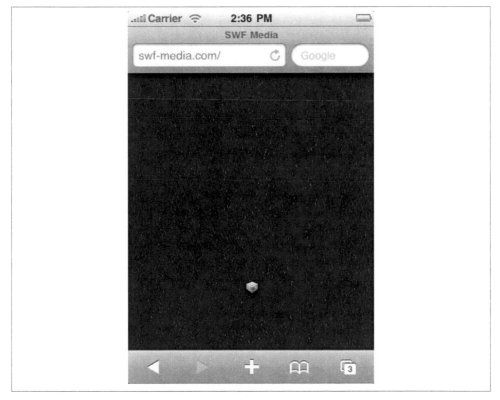

*Figure 10-7. As we can see, showing Flash content on noncompatible devices is a big mistake.*

Microsoft Silverlight had a short life in the desktop world as a browser plug-in. In the mobile world it was only a flash in the pan, with beta versions for Windows Mobile and Symbian released in 2010 that never even graduated to final releases.

# Video

Serving video content to mobile devices is very important for many portals and content providers.

We can provide multimedia content in three formats:

- Downloadable content
- On-demand streaming content
- Live streaming content

Before we look at any code, let's talk about the codec hell.

## Containers and Codecs

Video and audio files come with two technologies: a container format and one or more codecs inside. The container is what you usually see more frequently: the file extension, such as *.mov* or *.mpeg*. The codec is the algorithm that encodes and decodes the media; these are usually divided into video and audio codecs.

MPEG-4 containers are the most common. For these containers, AAC is the typical audio option, and the most compatible video codecs are H.263 and H.264; of the two, H.264 is preferred because of its compression algorithm (you get a smaller file for the same quality). The combination of MPEG-4/H.264/AAC is the most compatible solution for today's smartphones, social devices, and tablets. However, even when we say "H.264" there are several different configurations that the video can use, and not every one is compatible with every device, so testing is really important.

 It's important to understand the difference between containers and co- decs. When you talk about "an MP4 video," you are not saying anything about the audio and video codecs involved, which may be incompatible with some browsers.

There are also devices with support for other containers, such as Flash Video (FLV), Audio Video Interleave (AVI), Real Video (RV), QuickTime Movie (MOV), and Windows Media Video (WMV) containers, but compatibility varies and using them is not a good idea in terms of multiplatform accessibility.

H.264, also known as AVC, is one of the most used codecs and is commonly distributed inside MPEG-4 files. Its power is defined by its ability to provide high quality with smaller sizes. The problem is that its use also involves some royalties, which caused some desktop browsers to remove support for this codec. This isn't an issue on mobile devices because the video playing is usually managed by the operating system, so H.264 is well supported on most platforms.

Because of the proprietary nature of MPEG-4 and its associated codecs, the community has been working on some open and free alternatives over the last few years. The mobile community also created a container specifically designed for mobile devices a few years ago: the 3GP container.

The MPEG-4/H.264 alternatives include:

- The *Ogg* container, which usually comes with a Theora free video codec and a Vorbis audio codec (sometimes known as Ogg/Theora/Vorbis). On desktop, it's compatible with Firefox, Opera, and Google Chrome but on mobile it's right now only on Firefox.

- The *WebM* container, open and free project created by Google for HTML5 era. This container uses a VP8 video codec and Vorbis for audio. On desktop, Firefox, Opera, and Google Chrome support it, and on mobile only Android Browser from 2.3 and Google Chrome for Android.

- The *3GP* and *3GP2* containers, created by the 3GPP organization. These are based on MPEG-4 and optimized for mobile devices; they are still well distributed on mobile devices, but MPEG-4 is a much more modern solution and is referred today.

 Handbrake (*http://handbrake.fr*) is a free and open source video transcoder for Mac OS, Linux, and Windows that will help us with video conversions for mobile devices.

### Reference movies for iOS

Safari on iOS also supports "reference movies," created with QuickTime Pro or a similar tool. A reference movie provides a list of movie URLs with different bit rates (for example, for WiFi, 3G, or EDGE), so QuickTime can select the correct one for the device.

 You can find an Objective-C Mac tool (*http://www.mobilexweb.com/go/refmovie*) provided by Apple to generate iOS reference movie files from the command line.

## Delivering Video

We can deliver files using HTTP or a multimedia-streaming server, such as Adobe Flash Media Server. Unfortunately, most mobile browsers only support HTTP as the transport layer.

 Multimedia files are generally large. If we deliver noncompatible files, the user will be paying for useless traffic and will not be happy with us.

Check your server configuration, because using HTTP 1.1 we can support partial downloads and the ability to seek to any part of the file. For the best HTTP streaming technique, we need the server to support partial downloads. If your server doesn't support that, there is a great PHP script (*http://www.mobilexweb.com/go/phppartial*) available.

### Linking to video files

Usually, if MIME types are well defined on the server side, the user clicking on a link to a video file will start a video download automatically. On modern devices, instead of downloading the file, the browser will open the default video player application, which (if both client and server are compatible) will start playing your file using HTTP streaming. Only older feature phones will not play the video until the complete file has been downloaded.

 WURFL and Modernizr provide capabilities to help you understand video container and codec compatibility on both the server and the client side.

## The HTML5 video Element

HTML5 includes a new `video` element that can be used to embed and/or play videos in full-screen mode. We must specify a `width`, a `height`, and one or more video files to play. We can define one source video file using the `src` attribute, as in:

```
<video width="300" height="200" src="video.mp4"></video>
```

Because of the codec hell discussed earlier, the `video` element accepts a multiple-video definition using child `source` elements. That is, we can define different videos using different containers and codecs, and the browser will take the first one that is compatible with the current environment:

```
<video width="300" height="200">
    <source src="video.mp4" type="video/mp4">
    <source src="video.ogg" type="video/ogg">
```

```
    <source src="video.webm" type="video/webm">
</video>
```

The `type` attribute can contain just the MIME type for the container (such as `video/mp4`), or it can also include codec version declarations, such as:

```
<source src='video.mp4' type='video/mp4; codecs="avc1.58A01E,
    mp4a.40.2"'>
```

The `video` element typically acts as a video player in a rectangular area on the HTML page. However, on most smartphones it simply acts as a placeholder on the page; when we start playing the video, it always moves to a full-screen mode managed by the media player app, such as QuickTime on iOS. We can see this in action in Figure 10-8.

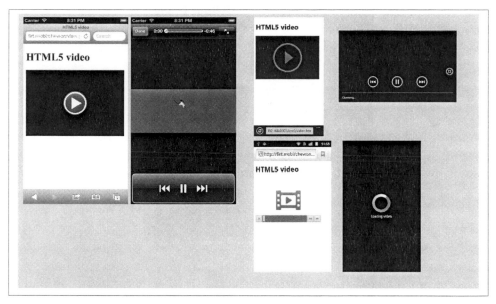

*Figure 10-8. A video element is shown as a placeholder that will open a full-screen player on some mobile browsers (in this case, Safari on iOS 6, Internet Explorer 9, and Android browser 2.3)—in some cases, the playing is in landscape mode.*

 Safari on iOS will only show the Play icon over the placeholder after loading the video metadata, so it knows that the video can effectively be played. If the video can't be played or doesn't exist, an error icon is shown instead.

On tablets, the `video` element acts similar to on a desktop: the video is rendered inside the HTML page and not in fullscreen mode, as on smartphones. Figure 10-9 illustrates.

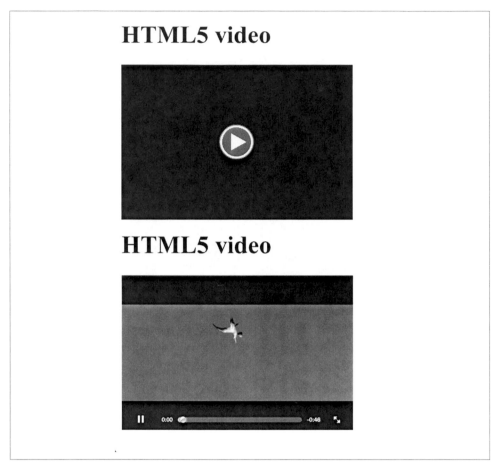

*Figure 10-9. On tablets, the video is usually embedded in the HTML page with a manual option to change to full-screen.*

By default most browsers will add a black background to the video area when the video is not playing. We can change that using the `poster` attribute, which defines an image to be displayed before the video starts playing:

```
<video width="300" height="200" src="video.mp4" poster="video_poster.png">
    </video>
```

You don't need to add a Play button image inside the poster picture, as most browsers will add a custom icon by default (as we can see in Figure 10-10).

*Figure 10-10. When we define a poster image, we should not add a Play icon; most browsers add one automatically.*

The HTML5 video element supports one or more track child elements that will define Closed Captions or subtitles for the video. However, at the time of this writing no mobile browser supports this.

For devices that will show the video embedded in the page, we have to use the Boolean controls attribute that, if present, forces the browser to show playing controls (such as Play, Pause, Stop, volume sliders, or track elements). On smartphones we will always have these controls, and there is no way to remove them. On some tablets, we have the option to use default controls or provide our own (see Table 10-4, later in this section).

For example, on the iPad, if we want a video player to have controls we must define the controls attribute:

```
<video width="300" height="200" src="video.mp4" controls></video>
```

On most mobile browsers there is no way to play more than one video at the same time.

### Advanced declarations

The video element supports more attributes that we can define. However, support on mobile browsers is quite rare, as the browser or the media player application will take control of the player, and not our HTML code. These attributes are:

autoplay
> A Boolean attribute that, if present, will start the video playing automatically. On mobile browsers it's usually disabled as the playing action will be triggered only by a user action.

loop
> A Boolean attribute that, if present, will start playing the video from the beginning again when it reaches the end.

muted
> A Boolean attribute that, if present, will start the video in silent mode.

preload
> Defines how to buffer or preload the video. It accepts the values none, metadata, or auto.

 On desktop browsers we can apply any CSS attribute to the video player, such as transformations, shadows, or transitions, and we can also use a video player as a canvas context image. However, because of the nature of video playing on mobile browsers (only full-screen or as a plug-in), these browsers do not support these features.

### Providing fallbacks

Anything inside the video element, apart from the source elements, will be ignored by HTML5-compatible browsers but used by noncompatible browsers, so we can, for example, add a message, a link to the video, or an alternative embedded system, such as object, embed, or Flash:

```
<video width="300" height="200" src="video.mp4">
    <!-- Fallback HTML code -->
    Embedding video is not compatible with your browser.
    <a href="video.mp4">Download the video</a>
</video>
```

Flash Lite (from version 3.0) supports only Flash Video format (FLV), while the major Flash Player supports FLV and MPEG-4. We can use the Flash Player as a fallback if HTML5 video is not available.

### Video player API

HTML5 browsers include a video player API that we can use to manage video playing from JavaScript. This API usually involves events that we can bind to so we can detect video download errors, codec errors, and video playing time events (such as `onplay` and `onpause`). With this API we can also use JavaScript to provide our own video playing controls, as any video DOM element has `play()` and `pause()` methods and properties such as `volume` and `currentTime`. Safari on iOS will ignore any `volume` definition, as the user can change it using the hardware keys:

```
var player = document.getElementById("player");
player.volume = 0.5;
player.play();
```

The problem with mobile browsers is again the full-screen playing experience. With that problem, our website is frozen while the video is playing, so we have no option to customize the experience unless the user's device is a tablet.

There are a few open source video player solutions available on the market, such as HTML5 VideoJS (*http://videojs.com*) and jPlayer (*http://jplayer.org*).

On most mobile browsers, such as Safari on iOS, we can only execute the `play()` method after a user action, such as a `click` event. Other solutions, such as using `load` events of timers, will be ignored.

### Streaming to Apple TV

If the user has an iOS device (iPod, iPad, or iPhone) and also an Apple TV, the set-top box from Apple, we can allow the user to stream a video from her device to the TV automatically. The wireless streaming is called *AirPlay*. To define how our `video` element should work with AirPlay, Apple offers a nonstandard `x-webkit-airplay` attribute supporting the values `allow` or `deny`.

If we have video playing rights for iPads and iPhones but not for TVs, we can deny AirPlay explicitly. The user will not be happy, but crazy license terms are around us all the time!

To allow streaming to Apple TVs, we should use x-webkit-airplay="allow":

```
<video src="video.mp4" width="300" height="200" controls
    x-webkit-airplay="allow">
</video>
```

When an Apple TV is available on the same network as the iOS device, the user will see the AirPlay TV icon, as shown in Figure 10-11. From iOS 5, AirPlay is enabled by default; before that version AirPlay is disabled by default.

*Figure 10-11. When using x-webkit-airplay="allow", we can allow the user to stream the video file to an Apple TV on the same network (the last icon on the right).*

## Streaming

Streaming audio or video is a difficult solution if we want to be compatible with all devices, because different platforms support different streaming technologies.

Some devices, including Symbian, Windows, and BlackBerry devices, support the Real Time Streaming Protocol (RTSP). When a link with this protocol is used (such as in rtsp://server/content), the default media player—Real Player or Windows Media— is opened. The content can be a file to be streamed (a prerecorded audio or video file) or a live event (such as radio or TV show, sports event).

Modern smartphones, such as Android and iOS devices, don't support these streaming standards, which were created for the desktop world and direct connections. Consequently, different streaming solutions have appeared on the market over the last year to use HTTP as a streaming transport protocol. These standards are:

- Apple HTTP Live Streaming (HLS)
- Adobe HTTP Dynamic Streaming
- Microsoft Smooth Streaming
- Dynamic Adaptive Streaming over HTTP (DASH)

Today, the Apple solution seems to be the most compatible with at least some mobile browsers.

## HTTP Live Streaming

Apple has created a new way to deliver live streaming using HTTP, called HTTP Live Streaming, which it has presented to the IETF as a proposed Internet standard. It is supported from iOS 3.0, and on Android since 3.0, and allows the transmission of live video (such as a live event) using the same HTTP method we know. In fact, this is the only streaming solution that works on iOS, webOS, and Android devices using the video element.

Implementing HTTP Live Streaming requires some changes on the web server end. The simplified explanation of the protocol is that on the server, the live stream is buffered in little packages that are sent to the client. It's like transmitting a live radio show by sending a series of 10-second MP3s.

 The well-known Akamai application acceleration service provider offers live streaming services for mobile devices from the Akamai iPhone Showcase (*http://iphone.akamai.com*). Influxis (*http://www.influxis.com*) also offers mobile streaming services as a shared hosting solution, for the iPhone/iPad and BlackBerry and Android devices. Cloud-based solutions such as Vimeo also support video streaming on mobile devices.

HTTP Live Streaming supports the H.264 codec for video and AAC or MP3 for live audio streaming, as well as a bandwidth switcher for different qualities. However, the best feature is that it passes any firewall or proxy because it is HTTP-based.

The implementation involves an extended M3U file (*.m3u8*) including links to different streaming segments, supporting different bandwidths. For example:

```
#EXTM3U
#EXT-X-STREAM-INF:PROGRAM-ID=1, BANDWIDTH=688301
http://qthttp.apple.com.edgesuite.net/1010qwoeiuryfg/0640_vod.m3u8
#EXT-X-STREAM-INF:PROGRAM-ID=1, BANDWIDTH=165135
http://qthttp.apple.com.edgesuite.net/1010qwoeiuryfg/0150_vod.m3u8
#EXT-X-STREAM-INF:PROGRAM-ID=1, BANDWIDTH=262346
http://qthttp.apple.com.edgesuite.net/1010qwoeiuryfg/0240_vod.m3u8
```

The video element will point to that file:

```
<video width="300" height="200" controls src="live.m3u8"></video>
```

Apple offers a prerelease toolkit for this solution called HTTP Live Streaming Tools, supported by the latest versions of the Flash Media Server, Microsoft IIS Media Services, and many others. You need to be part of the Apple Developer Connection to download it. The open source IceCast Server (*http://www.icecast.org*) also supports iPhone streaming, from version 2.3.2.

For Android, iPhone, and Flash Lite 3 or Flash Player 10 devices, we can safely upload video content to YouTube and embed it in our websites or link to it. The devices will render this content properly using the HTML5 iframe video player or a native YouTube application, if available.

## Embedding with object

Before HTML5 appeared on the market, the way to embed a video without any Flash support was to use the object tag:

```
<object data="video.mp4" type="video/mp4" width="300" height="300" />
```

The previous example worked on Symbian devices for many years.

The HTML fallback mechanism allows us to use the video element as the first option, with a fallback to a Flash Player, a fallback to the object element, and finally a fallback to a link to the video file.

An alternative solution was the embed tag, preferred for iOS 1 and 2.x (but completely replaced by the video tag on newer iOS devices):

```
<embed src="poster.jpg" href="video.m4v" type="video/x-m4v" />
```

## Video Compatibility

Table 10-4 shows video compatibility for the main mobile platforms.

*Table 10-4. HTML5 video compatibility table*

| Browser/platform | Preferred delivery | Playing UI | JS API | HLS |
|---|---|---|---|---|
| Safari on iPhone/iPod | video element | Full-screen | Only for play | Yes |
| Safari on iPad | video element | Embedded | Yes | Yes |
| Android browser | video element from 2.2 | Full-screen up to 2.3 Embedded from 3.0 | Yes | Yes from 3.0 |
| Chrome for Android | video element | Embedded | Yes | Yes |
| Nokia Browser for Symbian | video element from Anna object element before Anna | Full-screen | No | No |
| Nokia Xpress browser | File link (no video element) | N/A | No | No |
| BlackBerry browser | video element from 6.0 File link on 5.x | Embedded | Yes | No |
| Internet Explorer | video element from 9.0 | Full-screen on Windows Phone Embedded on tablets | Yes | No |

| Browser/platform | Preferred delivery | Playing UI | JS API | HLS |
|---|---|---|---|---|
| Firefox Mobile | `video` element | Embedded | Yes | No |
| Opera Mobile | `video` element | Embedded | Yes | N/A |
| Opera Mini | File link (no `video` element) | N/A | No | No |
| Amazon Silk | `video` element | Full-screen | Only for play | No |
| UC browser | `video` element | Full-screen | Only for play | No |

# Audio

Audio is another media element that we can use in our mobile websites. HTML5 includes a new `audio` element that is almost the same as the `video` element in terms of attributes and compatibility.

While some mobile browsers support WAV and Vorbis audio files, they all work well with the MP3 audio format. Therefore, we can usually use only one source definition with the MP3 audio file, such as:

```
<audio width="300" height="50" controls src="audio.mp3">
    Audio playing not available.
    <a href="audio.mp3">Download the file</a>
</audio>
```

 Before iOS 4, all `audio` elements played as a full-screen blank page following the video player action. From version 4, audio playing is embedded in the HTML page.

If you want the user to have audio controls on the page, as in Figure 10-12, you should always define the `controls` attribute. If not, you may consider creating an invisible `audio` element, as described in the next section.

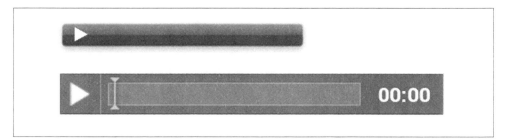

*Figure 10-12. The Safari on iOS and Chrome UIs for the audio element—when using audio we need to use the controls attribute if we want something to render on the screen.*

## Invisible Audio Player

When it comes to audio, we don't need any visual element on the HTML page in most situations—we just want to play a song or a sound effect for a game. To avoid the onscreen controls, we can create a full audio player from JavaScript without using HTML code. The JavaScript API is the same as for the video element. To load an audio file and play it, we can use the following code:

```
var player = document.createElement("audio");
player.src = "audio.mp3";
player.load();   // You can call play() directly or load it first
player.addEventListener("load", function() {
    player.play();
}, true);
```

> SoundJS (*http://www.createjs.com/#!/SoundJS*)—part of the CreateJS family—is a cross-platform audio JavaScript API.

The big problem for games is that usually in mobile browsers you can only play one audio file at a time (as we'll see later, in Table 10-5). To solve that problem, the Web Audio API appeared to enable low-level audio control.

## Web Audio API

The Web Audio API made its debut in the mobile web space with Safari on iOS 6. It's a pretty new API created by Google and at the time of this writing is in early draft with the W3C.

As a low-level API, we can use it to play binary audio files, create our own sounds dynamically, or apply audio effects in our web apps. To use this API completely, you need some advanced technical knowledge of audio management.

The API is available through an AudioContext global constructor or a prefixed version, as shown here:

```
var context = false;
if (window.AudioContext || window.webkitAudioContext) {
    context = window.AudioContext ? new AudioContext() :
        new webkitAudioContext();
} else {
    // API not available;
}
```

For simple audio playing purposes, the following code will bring an audio file by binary Ajax request and play it:

```
var request = new XMLHttpRequest();
var audioBuffer;
request.open("GET", "myaudio.mp3", true);
request.responseType = "arraybuffer";  // Defines binary file
request.onload = function() {
    context.decodeAudioData(request.response, function(buffer) {
        var audioSource = context.createBufferSource();
        audioSource.buffer = buffer;
        // We connect the audio with speakers
        audioSource.connect(context.destination);
        audioSource.noteOn(0);  // Play without delay
    });
};
request.send();
```

We can also create much more complex effects with the Web Audio API, such as mixing two audio files, cross-fading them, applying audio filters, and much more.

## Audio Compatibility

Table 10-5 shows audio compatibility for the main mobile web platforms.

*Table 10-5. HTML5 audio compatibility table*

| Browser/platform | Preferred delivery | Playing UI | Invisible audio support | Web Audio API |
|---|---|---|---|---|
| Safari on iOS | audio element | Embedded from 4.0 Full-screen before 4.0 | Yes | Yes from 6.0 |
| Android browser | audio element | Embedded | Yes | No |
| Chrome for Android | audio element | Embedded | Yes | No (until 18) |
| Nokia Browser for Symbian | audio element from Anna object before Anna | Embedded | No | No |
| Nokia Xpress browser | File link (no audio element) | N/A | No | No |
| BlackBerry browser | audio element | Embedded | Yes | No |
| Internet Explorer | audio element | Embedded | Yes | No |
| Firefox Mobile | audio element | Embedded | No | No |
| Opera Mobile | audio element | Embedded | Yes | No |
| Opera Mini | File link (no audio element) | N/A | No | No |
| Amazon Silk | audio element | Embedded | No | No |
| UC browser | audio element | Embedded | No | No |

# CHAPTER 11

# CSS for Mobile Browsers

In earlier chapters we discussed the many standards in the mobile CSS world and noted the CSS extensions available in WAP CSS. Whether we decide to use CSS 2.1, CSS3, CSS Mobile Profile, WAP CSS, or nonstandard extensions, it will be just the same; we'll use CSS at-rules, CSS selectors, and attributes for those selectors. The standards only tell us which ones are supported. What's more, we will find some browsers that do not render standard styles but do render nonstandard ones.

This chapter is not intended as an introduction to basic CSS; instead, we will focus on features that are specific to or important on mobile devices.

## Where to Insert the CSS

The first question to answer is: where should we tell the browser what styles to apply? We have many options:

- `<style>` tags inside the XHTML or HTML markup
- External stylesheets (*.css* files)
- `style` attributes inside the tags

The third option might seem like the most efficient approach, but it is not the best one. That said, there are times when it is useful. For the CSS WAP extensions for form controls described in Chapter 6, for instance, it is easiest to insert inline styles to avoid defining IDs and ID selectors for each control:

```
<input type="text" name="name" style="-wap-input-format: A*a">
```

 On BlackBerry devices running Device Software 4.5 or earlier, stylesheets can be disabled from the browser or from a corporate policy.

If the website you are creating is a one-page document, it will be faster to include the CSS in the <style> HTML tag to avoid a request and a rendering delay. The other ideal situation for this technique is if your home page is very different from the other pages in your site. Otherwise, odds are good that external stylesheets will help you manage your site more efficiently.

# Media Queries

Is one CSS stylesheet adequate for all devices? Maybe. The first factor to consider is whether we are working on a desktop HTML site or a mobile-specific one.

If we decide to use only one HTML site for both desktop and mobile devices, our only option for changing the design and layout is the CSS file, unless we don't want any mobile design adaptation. This situation is a good fit for the media attribute.

The CSS standard allows us to define more than one stylesheet for the same document, or one stylesheet with different definitions on different types of media. The media attribute was part of the CSS 2.1 standard, and the most-used values for media attributes are screen (for desktops), print (to be applied when the user prints the document), and handheld (for… yes, mobile devices). There are also other values, like tv and braille, but no browsers currently support these.

Great! We've found the solution. We can just define two stylesheets, one for screen and one for handheld, and all our problems will be solved. The two stylesheets can define different properties for the same elements, and we can even use display: none to prevent some elements from being shown on mobile devices:

```
<link rel="stylesheet" type="text/css" media="screen"
    href="desktop.css" />
<link rel="stylesheet" type="text/css" media="handheld"
    href="mobile.css" />
```

However, this "ideal" situation becomes hell when we test it. Many modern mobile browsers rely on screen stylesheets because they can render any desktop website (that is, they feel they have power enough to render any website, not just mobile-specific ones). And other browsers use screen when they think a site is a desktop website and use handheld when they think it is a mobile website, depending on the DOCTYPE, a meta tag, or the user's view preferences.

 We can't rely on the media="handheld" attribute for mobile-specific style definitions.

# CSS3 Media Queries

CSS3 comes to our help with *media queries*. These complex media definitions include conditions about different properties, such as screen size or current orientation.

For example, we can say: "Apply this stylesheet for devices with a maximum screen width of 480 pixels." This will apply to an iPhone, because in landscape mode it has a screen width of 480px and it doesn't support print, handheld, or any other media type. Here's how to write this as a conditional media query:

```
<link rel="stylesheet" media="screen and (max-device-width: 480px)"
    href="mobile.css">
```

We can also define CSS media queries inside the same stylesheet file. For example, the following code will change the background color displayed on a mobile device:

```
@media screen and (max-device-width: 480px) {
    body {
        background-color: red;
    }
}
```

 If you want to test media queries dynamically in your browser, check out the Media Queries Test (*http://mediaqueriestest.com*) or browse to *m.ad.ag* on your mobile device.

The standard is defined as a media type and at least one expression. The types are the same ones available in CSS2, including screen, print, handheld, and all. However, most modern browsers accept expressions without any type definition, in which case they apply all and—for example, (width: 480px) is equal to all and (width: 480px).

 Defining a media type and using parentheses for expressions are required by the standard. However, most browsers will evaluate the expression without them.

Media queries accept expressions and some operators. Parentheses are required around expressions. The possible types of conditional expressions are:

*Boolean attributes*
    Such as color or monochrome.

*Attribute value equal to*

The syntax is `<attribute>`: `<value>` and it is always evaluated as "equal to," such as `width: 500px` or `density: 326dpi`. The values can accept CSS units and constants.

*Attribute greater than or equal to*

The syntax is `min-<attribute>`: `<value>`, such as `min-width: 500px` (meaning "if the width is equal to or greater than 500 CSS pixels").

*Attribute less than or equal to*

The syntax is `max-<attribute>`: `<value>`, such as `max-width: 1024px` (meaning "if the width is no greater than 1,024 CSS pixels").

The possible operators between expressions are:

*NOT operator*

Using the `not` keyword before a conditional. `not` has a low precedence, meaning that it will always be applied to the whole expression unless we segment it using parentheses.

*ONLY operator*

Using the `only` keyword before a conditional. This means exclusivity. For example, `only screen` evaluates as true only on devices that don't support any other type, such as `print`. Usually it's a way to separate mobile devices from desktops, as desktop browsers support the `print` scheme.

*AND operator*

Using the `and` keyword between two conditions, such as `only screen and width: 320px`. We can use parentheses in conditions to avoid possible logical problems.

*OR operator*

There is no `or` keyword available; however, using a comma, we can emulate an OR operation, such as for orientation: `all and (orientation: landscape)`, `all and (min-width: 700px)`.

## Media features

In Chapter 10, we covered the pixel ratio extension to media queries (such as `-webkit-device-pixel-ratio`) and the discussion around compatibility to support different screens with different pixel densities. The following are the standard CSS media query features that we can use on mobile devices:

`aspect-ratio`

Defines the aspect ratio of the display area. The value must be two integers separated by a slash (horizontal/vertical), such as `aspect-ratio: 3/4`. This defines the relation between `width` and `height`, and it changes as the dimensions change. In mobile browsers, changing the device's orientation usually changes `aspect-ratio`.

`device-aspect-ratio`

> Defines the aspect ratio of the device. The value must be two integers separated by a slash (horizontal/vertical), such as `aspect-ratio: 4/3`. This defines the relation between `device-width` and `device-height`. On mobile devices it is the aspect ratio in portrait orientation.

`device-width` *and* `device-height`

> Define the width or height of the device in the default orientation (portrait on mobile devices). The value is expressed in CSS pixels.

 We can use `in` (inches) or `cm` (centimeters) in many media queries; however, these properties are not attached to real physical dimensions, but rather to a specific pixel relationship. Therefore, they are usually useless for making queries on physical dimensions.

`width` *and* `height`

> Define the width or height of the current viewport. The value is expressed in CSS pixels. If we don't provide a viewport definition, the available width will be the default one (from 800 to 1,024px; see Chapter 6 for more information).

`orientation`

> Defines the current device orientation, such as `landscape` or `portrait`. This is reevaluated automatically when the user changes the orientation.

`resolution`

> Defines the current resolution (pixel density) of the device's screen. It accepts values in dots per inch (`dpi`) and dots per cm (`dpcm`). As we discussed in Chapter 10, this feature will accept dots per CSS pixel (`dppx`) in the near future. We should not rely on this property for every device, as some of them don't support it, and others just report a generic `96dpi` resolution and not the real resolution. For today's devices, using the prefixed `device-pixel-ratio` is the solution.

*Browser extensions*

> Mozilla accepts the `-moz-touch-enabled` Boolean attribute, which will be evaluated only on touch devices, and the `-moz-device-pixel-ratio` extension. WebKit-based browsers support `-webkit-device-pixel-ratio` and Opera (Presto engine) supports `-o-device-pixel-ratio`.

 Firefox from version 16 and Opera from version 12 support `resolution` queries with dppx, such as `min-resolution: 1.5dppx` for high-resolution devices, to avoid the usage of the nonstandard and prefixed `device-pixel-ratio`.

### all versus only screen

It's common in modern media queries to use the `only screen` type before any query instead of using `all`. The first big difference is that when we use `all`, our styles will also be applied when the page is printed. Besides that, the usage of `only screen` is preferred because starting the media definition with the `only` keyword hides the whole stylesheet from noncompatible browsers.

> If a browser is not compatible with CSS3 media queries, it will understand CSS2 media queries, where only one word was used. So, if the first word of the `media` value is something that was valid in CSS2, such as `screen` or `all`, it will evaluate as true in these browsers, no matter what query follows it.

### Useful queries

To define different styles for portrait and landscape, we can use the following declaration:

```
@media only screen and (orientation: portrait) {
    // Portrait declarations
}

@media only screen and (orientation: landscape) {
    // Landscape declarations
}
```

> The `orientation: portrait` and `orientation: landscape` declarations have been supported in Safari since iOS 3.2. It's a good idea to include both declarations in one stylesheet and not in separate files, so the browser won't need to make a new download when changing orientations.

If we are targeting only iPhone and iPod devices, to separate between original-size devices and larger devices (such as the iPhone 5) we can query on `device-aspect-ratio`:

```
@media only screen and (device-aspect-ratio: 2/3) {
    // Original-size devices, such as iPhone 4S
}

@media only screen and (device-aspect-ratio: 40/71) {
    // Larger devices, such as iPhone 5
}
```

For iPhone and iPod devices in landscape mode, we can detect if the user has the full-screen option enabled (from version 6.0) using the following media query (with the viewport width equal to device-width and no JavaScript fix for the viewport scaling bug running):

```
@media only screen and (orientation: landscape) and (height: 214px),
       only screen and (orientation: landscape) and (height: 181px) {
   // Full-screen mode with the default viewport
   // If you are changing viewport width, height values may change
}
```

For the aspect-ratio and device-aspect-ratio, we can apply any equivalent fraction, including the full width and height, such as 2/3, 4/6, or 320/480.

 Remember that width and height are based on the current viewport; if we leave the default viewport, mobile devices will have the same dimensions as desktop windows. We can use device-width and device-height to rely on the device's dimensions regardless of the current viewport definition.

The Responsive Web Design approach is based on defining breakpoints on the current window width using a device-width viewport definition. The best solution is to start from the default values, then the smallest form, and add larger breakpoints one by one. For example:

```
// All default styles
@media only screen and (max-width: 480px) {
    // Smartphone-specific stylesheet
}
@media only screen and (min-width: 481px) {
    // Larger devices, tablets, and desktops
}
@media only screen and (min-width: 769px) {
    // Usually desktops
}
```

Another solution is to define all the groups as exclusive so they will not share any code, such as:

```
// All default styles
@media only screen and (max-width: 480px) {
    // Smartphone-specific stylesheet
}
@media only screen and (min-device-width: 481px) and
  (max-device-width: 768px){
    // Only tablets
}
@media only screen and (min-width: 769px) {
    // Usually desktops
}
```

Unfortunately, there is no media query to differentiate iPad 2 devices from iPad minis; they both have the same screen size in pixels and the same pixel ratio. While they have different screen densities, we don't have a way to query that.

### CSS4 media queries

At the time of this writing, a working draft for CSS4 (*http://dev.w3.org/csswg/mediaqu eries4*) is under discussion. It includes new attributes, such as:

script
> A Boolean feature that means that JavaScript is available and enabled.

pointer
> An enumeration that defines the presence and accuracy of a pointing device. The possible values are none, coarse for a pointing device with limited accuracy, and fine for an accurate pointing mechanism.

hover
> A Boolean feature that means that hover events can be rendered on the device (such as mouseover or the :hover pseudoclass).

### Internet Explorer 10 snap state

Windows 8 for desktops and tablets supports a Windows Store App mode for full-screen apps (previously known as Metro apps). These apps can work full-screen landscape, full-screen portrait, or "snapped." The snap state, available on screens with a width of at least 1,366 pixels, allows us to have more than one app on the screen at the same time. The snapped app will have a width of 320 pixels.

Internet Explorer (the Windows Store version) can be also snapped. By default, IE10 will freeze the default viewport when the window is narrower than 1,024px. That means that if your IE window has a width of 320, 500, or 1,000px, the default viewport will remain at 1,024px, so your content will be scaled down. The same goes for IE10 in the snapped state with our website inside (as we can see in Figure 11-1).

To provide a different layout in IE10 when in snapped mode, you need to use media queries and use the Microsoft viewport extension that we discussed in Chapter 6. With this approach we can define that in windows narrower than 400 pixels we don't want a, scaled-down viewport and we instead want a 320px viewport, as a mobile view:

```
@media screen and (max-width: 400px) {
  @-ms-viewport {
    width: 320px;
  }
  /* CSS for a 320px viewport in snapped mode goes here */
}
```

Some e-ink book readers come with a web browser, such as the Amazon Kindle. They are the only monochrome web browsers out there today that can access our websites. Unfortunately, the Kindle browser evaluates itself as a `color` screen and not a `monochrome` one.

*Figure 11-1. The Windows Store version of Internet Explorer in Windows 8 snap mode will narrow the viewport unless we override it using the viewport CSS extension.*

If your website follows Responsive Web Design, you can use:

```
@-ms-viewport {
    width: device-width;
}
```

When we're defining the viewport to use in snap mode, the `device-width` constant is not really the device's width but the available width in snap mode, usually 320px.

When we're creating HTML5 Windows 8 apps—*not* websites for IE—Microsoft accepts two extensions to media query attributes: `-ms-view-state` and `-ms-high-contrast`. The first one accepts as values `fullscreen-portrait` and `fullscreen-landscape` when your app is the only app in the foreground, `snapped` when it's in snap mode, and `fil led` when it is sharing the screen with another app in snap mode. The second attribute defines the current contrast mode on the system, as in `white-on-black` or `black-on-white`.

# Selectors

The classic CSS 2.1 selectors are compatible with every device, and for the few that don't recognize them entirely, it may not be worth the effort to create alternatives. The mobile CSS–compatible selectors we can trust for every device are:

*Universal*
> \* (compatible but not recommended)

*Element*
> `tagName`

*Class*
> `.className`

*Unique ID*
> `#elementId`

*Descendant*
> `selectorselector`

*Child*
> `selector > selector`

*Multiple*
> `selector, selector`

*Pseudoclasses (*`link`*,* `visited`*,* `active`*,* `focus`*)*
> `selector:pseudoclass`

As we discussed previously, most mobile browsers today support CSS3. A compressed list of other selectors to use for these mobile browsers is:

*Selector with attribute*
> `selector[attribute]`

*Selector with attribute condition*
> `selector[attribute<operator>value]`

 `operator` can be one of the following: equals (=), contains as one value (~=), begins with (^=), ends with ($=), contains as a string (\*=), or begins with and followed by hyphen (|=).

*Negation*
> `selector:not(selector)`

*Immediately preceded by*
> `selector + selector`

---

*Preceded by*
```
selector ~ selector
```

*Pseudoclasses (*`after`, `before`, `root`, `nth-child(n)`, `first-child`, `last-child`, `empty`,
*and others)*
```
selector:pseudoclass
```

 Some CSS3 selectors don't work for mobile devices. How complex should a mobile website be, though? If it has that much complexity, perhaps we should consider simplifying.

If a browser has only partial support for some attribute or selector, that means the behavior is not complete. For example, the browser may not accept all the possible values, or it may render a selector properly in the original document but not apply the style if we change the DOM dynamically. This stylesheet fragment illustrates a noncritical use of CSS3 selectors:

```
input {
    background-color: yellow;
    border: 1px solid gray;
}
/* The next style will only work in CSS3-compatible browsers */
input[type=button] {
    background-color: silver;
}
```

# CSS Techniques

In this section we are going to talk about some well-known CSS techniques (reset CSS files, text formatting, and the box model) and see how the different browsers react to these features.

## Reset CSS Files

It is very common in desktop web design to create a CSS hack to reset all the default margins and padding for common HTML elements. We can use this technique when developing for the mobile web, with some considerations: we should only reset the elements we are going to use, we should avoid the usage of the global selector (*) for performance purposes, and if we are using an external reset-CSS file we should consider merging it with our local CSS file.

Modern versions of reset files are available as part of the open source project Normalize.css (*http://necolas.github.com/normalize.css*), and are included in HTML5 Boilerplate (*http://html5boilerplate.com*).

Some browsers always create a margin around the whole document that cannot be deleted. And in the browsers that do allow you to delete the margin, remember that a zero margin may not be a good design decision.

Nokia also offers two markup and CSS templates for mobile web design for free through its developer site (*http://bit.ly/WpMswX*). Every template has a reset-CSS file. The following code is extracted from the mid-range device template, and we can adapt it to our needs:

```
html, body, div, span, object, blockquote, pre,
abbr, acronym, address, big, cite, code,
del, dfn, em, font, img, ins, kbd, q, s, samp,
small, strike, strong, sub, sup, tt, var,
b, u, i, center, dl, dt, dd, fieldset, form, label, legend,
caption, tr, th, td {
    margin: 0;
    padding: 0;
    border: 0;
    font-size: 100%;
    font-weight: normal;
    vertical-align: baseline;
    background: transparent;
}

p {
    border: 0;
    font-size: 100%;
    font-weight: normal;
    vertical-align: baseline;
    background: transparent;
}
a {
    margin: 0;
    padding: 0;
    font-weight: normal;
}

h1, h2, h3, h4, h5, h6 {
    margin: 0;
    padding: 0;
    border: 0;
    vertical-align: baseline;
    background: transparent;
}

body {
    line-height: inherit;
}

body table {
    margin: 0;
    padding: 0;
```

```
        font-size: 100%;
        font-weight: normal;
        vertical-align: baseline;
        background: transparent;
}

/* remember to highlight insertions somehow! */
ins {
        text-decoration: none;
}
del {
        text-decoration: line-through;
}

/* tables still need 'cellspacing="0"' in the markup */
body table {
        border-collapse: collapse;
        border-spacing: 0;
}
```

> The Nokia Mobile Web Templates (*http://bit.ly/WpMswX*) are a set of templates (including XHTML and CSS files) for low-, mid-, and high-end devices that generate similar experiences across different devices, including hacks that solve some bugs, like the 100% width bug. They have been optimized for the Series 40 browser, Symbian browser, Maemo browser, and Opera Mini.

# Text Formatting

Text is the most common content type in a mobile website, and styling it in a way that maximizes compatibility can be a little tricky. Bold (`font-weight: bold`) and italics (`font-style: italic`) are reliably compatible, but support for other text-formatting features varies.

## Font family

This will be our first problem in styling text for mobile browsers. There are no standards in terms of fonts for mobile operating systems, and most platforms have only one system font (generally sans serif).

> NTT DoCoMo markup (for the Japanese market) still uses the old font tag for defining font properties like face, color, and size. Newer devices also support CSS. Other WebKit-based mobile browsers also support the font tag, but its use is not recommended. Use CSS instead.

We can provide specific font names (like Arial, Verdana, or Times New Roman) or generic font types (like serif, sans-serif, monospace, cursive, or fantasy).

For the best compatibility, you should use the default font and apply other attributes (color, size, etc.), unless you are on a known platform such as iOS or are defining your own custom fonts. If you want to define a font name, you should consider providing a list of alternatives. If the first font isn't available, the browser will try the second, then the third, and so on; if none of the listed fonts is available, it will use the default one.

Most browsers rely on the operating system for the available fonts, and apart from iOS—remember Steve Jobs's fanaticism about typography—almost every other mobile operating system has just one or a couple of fonts available.

 When an operating system (like Android 2.x) has only a couple of proprietary font styles, even fonts that are safe on desktops, such as Arial or Times New Roman, will be rendered as the default one. Usually, these proprietary fonts are optimized for mobile screen reading.

Up to version 3.0, Android used a font called *Droid Sans*; a new font called *Roboto* replaced it in Android 4.0. Both are free fonts available from Google. For its devices, Nokia uses a *Nokia Sans* variation, and Microsoft uses *Segoe* for Windows Phone. BlackBerry 10 uses *Slate Pro* as the default font family, but it includes many others, such as Arial, Comic Sans, Browalia New, Georgia, Impact, Times New Roman, Trebuchet MS, and Verdana. For all these devices, leaving the default font or using font-family: sans-serif is enough.

iOS has included several fonts from the beginning, and the list grows with every version. The website (*http://www.iosfonts.com*) has a complete list of the available fonts with a nice preview, and you can filter the list by operating system version, as we can see in Figure 11-2. Some of the fonts available on iOS are AmericanTypeWriter, Arial, Courier New, Georgia, Helvetica, Times New Roman, Trebuchet MS, Verdana, Zapfino, Marker, AppleSDGothicNeo, Avenir, Chalkboard, Futura, GillSans, HelveticaNeue, Optima, and Palatino. We can safely use these fonts on iOS, and provide alternatives for other devices.

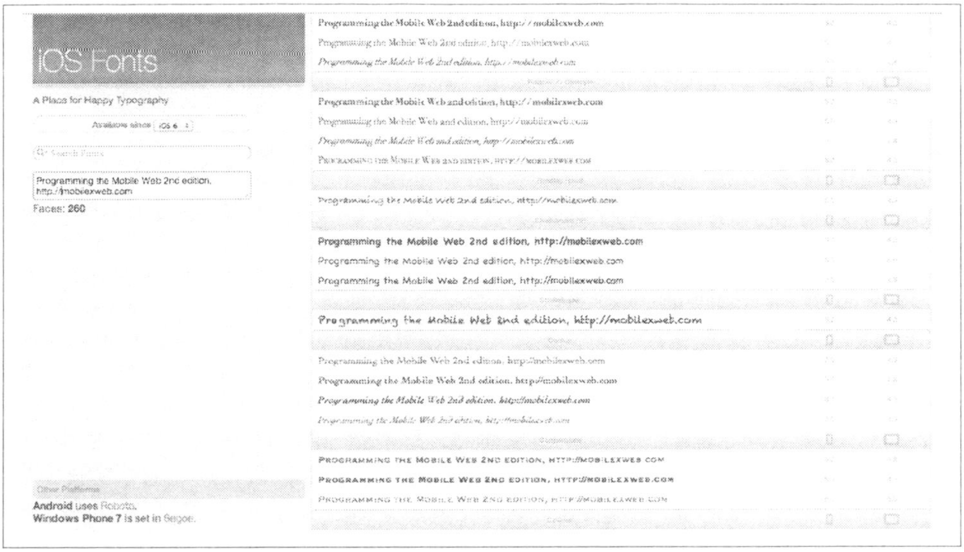

*Figure 11-2. Some operating systems support different font faces—iOS is the leader in this area, offering more than 60 system fonts.*

### CSS3 font-face

Before CSS3, some obscure techniques—including frameworks such as *sIFR* on Flash-enabled devices and *Cufón* for SVG-enabled devices—were used. CSS3 includes @font-face (*http://www.w3.org/TR/css3-fonts*), a custom font declaration that we can use on most modern smartphone and tablet platforms.

> If you're delivering a custom font, you need authorization to distribute it. The font may be copyrighted, and you should make sure you have the right to distribute it as a custom font for your website. Google Web Fonts and Adobe Edge Web Fonts are all license-free. Adobe TypeKit allows you to use licensed fonts if you pay the royalties.

Delivering your own fonts means that the browser needs to download the font family file and store it temporarily in memory while your page is being rendered. That means you're adding a download overhead that will impact directly on your website's performance.

To create a font face definition, we use a new at-rule that will define a src attribute pointing to a source file for the font. For example:

```
@font-face {
  font-family: OReilly;
  src: url(http://myfonts.com/OReilly.ttf);
}
```

Then, any time we define `font-family: OReilly` in a CSS style, it will use that file. Font files define only one variant, so when we need a bold, italic, bold+italic, or any other weight variation, we need to define a different `@font-face` rule with the same `font-family` name, such as:

```
@font-face {
  font-family: OReilly;
  font-weight: bold;
  src: url(http://myfonts.com/OReillyBold.ttf);
}
```

The main problem with `font-face` is that the standard is format-agnostic. That means that we need to deal with format inconsistencies between platforms. Fortunately, we can define more than one format using comma syntax in the `src` style.

Google Web Fonts (*http://www.google.com/webfonts*) and Adobe Edge Web Fonts (*http://html.adobe.com/edge/webfonts*) are two projects that we can use for free (see Figure 11-3); they each provide hundreds of fonts. With these solutions, we just need to add one CSS `link` declaration or a `script` declaration. On the server side, their websites will deliver the right file format for the browser. We can use their servers as a content delivery network, getting the cache advantage, or download the files and host them ourselves.

*Figure 11-3. With Google Web Fonts and Adobe Edge Web Fonts, we can use customized fonts in all modern tablet and smartphone browsers.*

For example, to add the ABeeZee font from Google Web Fonts, we just need to add:

```
<link href='http://fonts.googleapis.com/css?family=ABeeZee'
      rel='stylesheet'>
```

Remember that fonts are vector-based, so they will deliver great quality at every resolution. If you are not using dynamic content and are just using a custom font for your logo, you can compress your font file to just the characters you are going to use.

You can even create your own scalable icon gallery as a font file; Ico-Moon (*http://icomoon.io*) can help you with the task.

### Font size

Which elements need a defined font size? For most cases, we should only define font sizes for headers and for element selectors (h1, h2, p, div).

We can use any measure for the font size, and almost every browser will understand it. However, it may not be rendered any differently. Only smartphone browsers with smart zoom support allow any font size to be rendered (like 13.5px in Safari on iOS).

For most of the mobile browsers, the best font size technique is to use relative constants (xx-small, x-small, smaller, small, medium, large, larger, x-large, xx-large) or relative units, such as em.

Operating systems have different font support. Some of them have only three possible sizes for text, and if we use the typical pixel definitions, two different sizes (for example, 12px and 14px) may be rendered identically. If we use relative constants (e.g., large), we have more probability of that text being rendered in a larger font. Another compatible way of specifying font sizes is to use em values. Using em values is perfect for supporting different screen sizes and DPIs because this unit is relative and scalable to the standard font in the device.

The default (medium) font size is generally the perfect size in the operating system for normal paragraph text, and for normal text we should leave it that way.

### Text shadows

Another CSS3 feature is text-shadow. It allows us to define the color, *x*-offset, *y*-offset, and blur radius of a shadow to be applied to a text selector. For example, we can produce a shadowed headline with code like this:

```
h1 {
    text-shadow: 0.1em 0.1em #AAA
}
```

We can also define multiple shadow effects, using a comma to separate them.

If you're thinking about using this feature, remember that in the mobile world, the clearer the text is, the better for usability. Use text shadows with extreme care.

### Text overflow

CSS3 adds a very useful feature for mobile web designs: text overflow. This property, available in some mobile browsers, allows us to specify that an ellipsis should appear at the end of a piece of text if it doesn't fit in its container in a single line, depending on the font and space available. This is great for reducing the amount of space taken up by links, and for previews or summaries that will be shown completely in a details page after the user clicks on them.

For example, we can show a title, and a truncated description with `text-overflow` set to `ellipsis`. When the user clicks on the title, via JavaScript we remove the `text-overflow` property, and the whole text of the description is shown. This maximizes the amount of content we can display on a page. This feature also works well on devices that support both landscape and portrait orientations: with text overflow we can assure the usage of only one line in both modes.

To use this feature, the paragraph (or other element containing the text) must have `overflow: hidden` set to avoid the continuing of the overflow text on the next line, `white-space: nowrap` to avoid wrapping, and some value for `text-overflow`.

The possible standard values for `text-overflow` are `clip` and `ellipsis`. The `ellipsis` value causes an ellipsis to appear after the last character that fits in the box (as shown in Figure 11-4, below). `clip` is the default value, which truncates the text without showing the ellipsis.

 If you don't want to show the full text but you want to display more than just one line, there's no standard way to show the ellipsis at the end of the last line. Opera (and its mobile versions) supports the `text-overflow: -o-ellipsis-lastline` extension to solve that problem. On other browsers, however, we must rely on some large JavaScript frameworks, such as Three Dots (*http://www.jquerycode.com/theming/threedots*).

The BlackBerry 10 browser supports an extension (`text-overflow: -blackberry-fade`) that fades the text with an opacity gradient from left to right, as seen in Figure 11-4. Thanks to the fallback behavior of CSS3, we can first define `ellipsis` for all devices and then provide the `-blackberry-fade` declaration for BB10; all other browsers will ignore this.

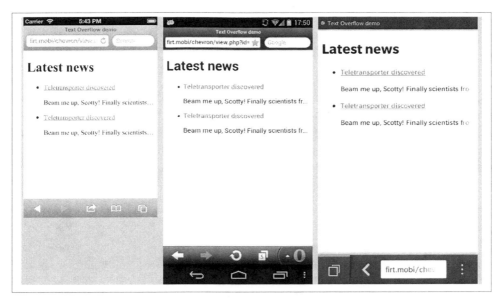

*Figure 11-4. With text-overflow we can create nice effects for small screens (in this example, Safari on iOS, Opera Mobile for Android, and the BlackBerry 10 browser).*

Here is a sample that produces the result shown in Figure 11-4:

```
<!DOCTYPE html>
<html>
<head>
<meta charset="utf-8" />
<title>Text Overflow demo</title>
<meta name="viewport" content="width=device-width">

<style type="text/css">

ul p {
    text-overflow: ellipsis;
    text-overflow: -blackberry-fade; /* For BB10 only */
    overflow: hidden;
    white-space: nowrap;
}

</style>
</head>
<body>

<h1>Latest news</h1>
```

```
<ul id="news">
    <li>
        <a href="#">Teletransporter discovered</a>
        <p>Beam me up, Scotty! Finally scientists from London have
           discovered teletransportation</p>
    </li>
    <li>
        <a href="#">Teletransporter discovered</a>
        <p>Beam me up, Scotty! Finally scientists from London have
           discovered teletransportation</p>
    </li>
</ul>

</body>
</html>
```

### Text adjustment for small screens

Safari on iOS has created a CSS extension style especially for controlling the size of text, prepared for the zooming action: `-webkit-text-size-adjust`. Other WebKit-based browsers with other rendering engines have adopted the same property, such as Firefox (`-moz-text-size-adjust`) and Internet Explorer from version 9 (`-ms-text-size-adjust`).

This style accepts values of `auto` (the default), `none`, or a percentage (such as `200%`). By default, mobile browsers override a website's font sizes to allow the text to be read without any problems when the user zooms in on a paragraph. We can override this behavior with this style, turning it off (`none`) or defining a percentage zoom level to be applied to the default font size defined for the desktop website.

If we want to enhance a desktop website for mobile browsing, we should leave this style set to `auto`. However, if we want to override the default behavior or autosizing, we can use:

```
body {
    -webkit-text-size-adjust: none;
    -ms-text-size-adjust: none;
    -moz-text-size-adjust: none;
}
```

If a paragraph is prepared to be read in a desktop browser with a large viewport width, we can change this behavior using the `-webkit-text-size-adjust` attribute to enhance the mobile reading experience without changing the desktop appearance. Figure 11-5 shows the same text paragraph with this attribute set to `none` and to `400%`.

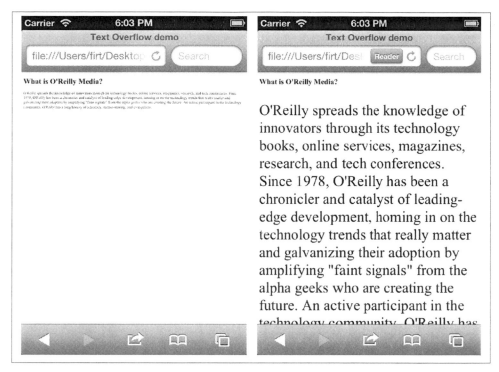

*Figure 11-5. The same text paragraph with text adjustment off and with 400% as the value, in a website without any viewport definition—this feature is useful only in non-mobile web designs.*

### Text stroke and fill

The stroke and fill properties are a handy, nonstandard way of creating fancy effects in titles (with big fonts) without the use of images. At the time of this writing, only WebKit-based browsers support these attributes—that means Safari on iOS, the Android browser, Chrome, and the BlackBerry browser, using the `-webkit-` prefix.

For example:

```
<h1 style="-webkit-text-stroke: blue; -webkit-text-fill-color: yellow">
    Great Title!
</h1>
```

### Multicolumn layout

More suitable for tablets or landscape phones, multicolumn layout (*http://www.w3.org/ TR/css3-multicol*) is a new ability in CSS3 discussed in a separate standard. The feature is fairly self-explanatory: it allows us to define text and other content to be laid out in columns dynamically arranged based on two possible constraints, a fixed column width or a fixed column count. Based on available length, the content will flow automatically between columns, following a newspaper or magazine layout.

Fortunately, all the tablet browsers support this, but at the time of this writing it is prefixed for WebKit-based browsers and Firefox. Internet Explorer 10 (for example, for the Microsoft Surface) and Opera support it without any prefix.

To create a multicolumn layout, we need to define `column-count` or `column-width`. If we define the count, the width will be calculated automatically, and vice versa. We can also optionally define a `column-gap` value that applies to the space between columns and a `column-rule` value (a border-type attribute that draws a line in the middle of the gap).

For example, if we want to apply a three-column layout to an article, as seen in Figure 11-6, we can use:

```
article {
    -webkit-column-count: 3;
    -moz-column-count: 3;
    column-count: 3;

    -webkit-column-rule: 1px dotted gray;
    -moz-column-rule: 1px dotted gray;
    column-rule: 1px dotted gray;
}
```

# Common Patterns

Even the most unique mobile web designs typically rely on a core set of common style patterns.

## Display Properties

The standard `display` values (`none`, `block`, `inline`) are supported on almost all platforms, but in a limited way on older platforms, such as BlackBerry 4.x or 5.x.

There are also table display properties that I do not recommend using in mobile websites: `inline-table`, `table-column`, `table-cell`, and others. If we need a table, we can use the `table` element in HTML, and if we need a table-like layout, well, we should think twice about it.

 Even when we're designing for some new smartphones—like the Samsung Galaxy SIII, which has a screen width of 720 pixels—we should avoid using tables and column layouts with more than two columns. The screen is still small, and we need to remember that it is a mobile device and think about the contexts in which it will be used.

The style `display: none` is used a lot in JavaScript and Ajax development and works without problems on modern mobile browsers.

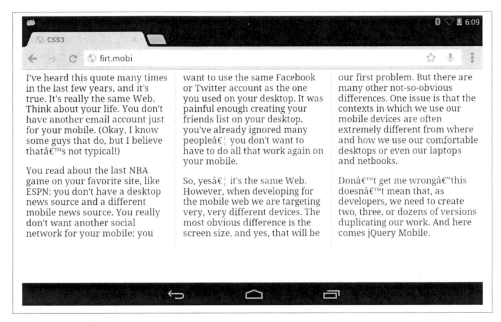

*Figure 11-6. Multicolumn (magazine-like) layouts are mainly useful on tablets, because of the wider screen.*

### Absolute and floating positions

The standard position (`position: static`) is the most widely compatible and is recommended for mobile websites. This means that each element will be rendered in its normal position in the document.

Floating elements do work very well on most mobile devices. However, even on devices with average-sized screens it's best not to have more than two floating elements in the same row. This can be approached using `float: left` and `float: right`.

Relative positioning (`position: relative`) is trickier in mobile browsers. It defines movement (using `top`, `bottom`, `right`, `left`) from the original position as a static element.

The `clear` attribute (`clear: both`, for example) can be used after a floating element to ensure that no floating elements are allowed on the right, the left, or both sides of the element to which this attribute is applied.

### Fixed position

To fix elements on the screen, in classic web development we use `position: fixed`, mixed with the properties `top`, `bottom`, `left`, and `right`. Until 2011, almost no mobile browser had support for fixed position, and it was downgraded to `position: absolute` instead. The main difference is that with absolute positioning the element scrolls with the page, so it's not an ideal solution if we want to have a fixed header or footer in our website.

Fixed position has been supported in Safari from iOS 5.0, in the Android browser since version 2.3, and in the BlackBerry browser since 7.0. The big problem that we still have is that `position: fixed` was prepared for a classic web environment and not for the more complex mobile scenario, where we have two different viewports (initial and current) and zoom abilities.

In compatible browsers, if we use `position: fixed` with a nonscalable viewport (`user-scalable=no`) and the viewport width set to `device-width`, it works great. However, when we allow zooming or if we are browsing a desktop-optimized website, the behavior can be really annoying, as you can see in Figure 11-7. Basically, the fixed elements are fixed to the current viewport and not the device/window viewport. Therefore, when the user zooms the page using the pinch gesture, the fixed elements are zoomed in too, but they remain fixed to the edges of the current viewport (which may or may not be visible on the screen after the zoom action).

If you have a desktop-optimized website with `position: fixed`, it's a good idea to remove that position value for mobile devices to avoid the problem that we can see in Figure 11-7. To do that we can use the following media queries:

```
@media only screen and (max-device-width: 400px) {
    .fixedElement {
      position: absolute; // We can fall back to absolute, hide
                          // elements, or find another solution
    }
}
```

 There is a JavaScript solution for creating a fixed element in noncompatible browsers, called iScroll (*http://www.mobilexweb.com/iscroll*). The main problem with using this kind of JavaScript solution is that it impacts the performance of our websites and consumes battery power.

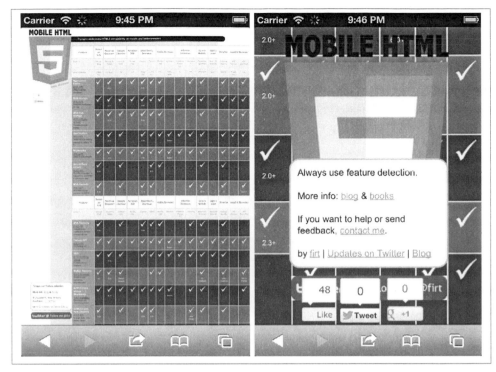

*Figure 11-7. position: fixed when mixed with zoom-enabled viewports will lead to really strange behaviors when zooming in, as we can see in this example.*

### Modern layout techniques

Modern browsers support some CSS extensions for laying out elements on the screen. One technique is CSS Flexible Box Layout (*http://www.w3.org/TR/css3-flexbox*) (also known as Flexbox).

 One of the biggest problems with Flexbox is that over the last few years the specification has changed from the original draft. Some browsers may still support the old spec, not the current and final specification, so you should use Flexbox with care.

When elements are defined as `display: flexbox` (for block elements) or `display: inline-flexbox` (for inline elements), all the children will float and fill the available space. Several CSS styles can be defined to customize the flexible layout, such as `flex-order`, `flex-pack`, `flex-wrap`, and `flex-direction`.

Opera Mobile is the only mobile browser at the time of this writing to support this feature without a prefix. Chrome and the BlackBerry 10 browser support it with the `-webkit-` prefix, while Firefox, Safari on iOS, and Internet Explorer 10 support their own prefixes, but with an old specification (depending on the version).

Microsoft has created a new layout mechanism that has been proposed as a standard, known as *CSS Grid Layout (http://www.w3.org/TR/css3-grid-layout)*. At the time of this writing, only Internet Explorer 10 supports it; it involves the ability to design apps or content in a grid.

## Rounded Corners

Designers seem to love rounded corners (shown in Figure 11-8), and for years this was the nightmare of every web developer who needed to lay out a box with this feature. Table-based layouts for rounded corners are inappropriate for the mobile web, so we can only rely on CSS solutions. If a device doesn't render the style, forget about rounded corners for that device. Any polyfill will just harm performance and isn't worth using on older devices.

> The property for rounded corners is `border-radius`, and it was prefixed on older platforms, such as Safari for iOS before 4.0. If you have a considerable amount of users from those platforms, you can think about adding the prefixed versions too, such as `-webkit-border-radius` and `-moz-border-radius`.

The `border-radius` attribute can be defined as one value (like 5px or 10%), two values (top-bottom and left-right), or four values giving the radius of each corner separately. These are samples of different styles:

```
.rounded {
    border-radius: 10px;
}
.rounded2 {
    border-radius: 10px 20px;
}
.rounded3 {
    border-radius: 3em 2em 3em 2em;
}
```

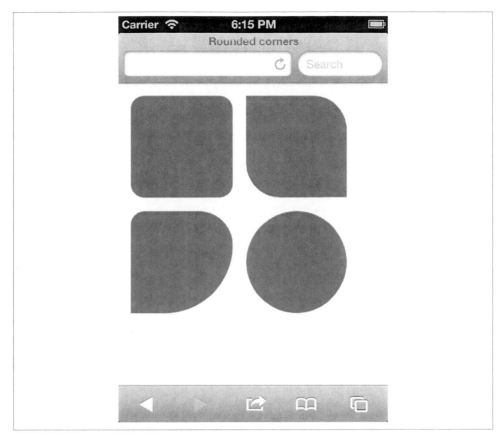

*Figure 11-8. The rounded corners feature allows us to round any defined border or background color on compatible devices.*

## Border Image

The `border-image` CSS attribute is an excellent solution to the problem of creating a dynamically sized rectangle with custom borders. Its implementation is very similar to CSS sprites, and usage is simple. This technique is useful for buttons, titles, content zones, and every area where we want a custom border design without using tables.

The `border-image` attribute is part of the CSS3 standard, but at the time of this writing most mobile browsers still use prefixes (`-webkit-`, `-o-`, and `-moz-`). The exceptions are the BlackBerry browser from version 10 and Firefox from version 15; these no longer require a prefix for `border-image`. The most common syntax is:

```
border-image: url top right bottom left x_repeat y_repeat;
```

The *url* is the image location (or inline image), and the four edge values (*top*, *right*, *bottom*, *left*) are distance values measured from the image's sides. The center box defined by the space not used by these four values will be used for the center pattern. For example, if we define 5 as the top, the box to which we are applying this style will have as the top border the top 5px of the border image.

 The `border-image` property doesn't define the box's width and height or the border size; it is only used to define the contents of the border. If we need to change the dimensions of the box, we need to add `width` and `height` properties. We must also define the `border` property of the element, setting it to the desired size. The border image will be resized to the border size.

The *x_repeat* and *y_repeat* values are optional and can be defined as one of the following constants:

repeat
> The portion of the image extracted using the *top* and *bottom* for *y_repeat* and using the *left* and *right* for *x_repeat* is repeated until it fills the available width/ height of the box.

round
> The image is repeated until it fills the available width/height of the box, but without any partial tile at the end; it is stretched so that it fits in the available space a whole number of times. This value has no effect in many mobile browsers.

stretch
> The image is stretched to fill the entire width or height of the box without repetition.

The border image is cut into nine pieces, as we can see in the Figure 11-9. Four are used as corners and the others are used as background images for the sides and center.

 If you are applying a border image to a button, it will not have any "pressed" effect. To create such an effect, you must change the `active` and/or `focus` pseudoclass, specifying another border image. Problems can occur when you try to change the way buttons are rendered dynamically, though, so for custom designs it is better to use links, or remove the default button rendering on WebKit-based browsers with `-webkit-appearance: none`.

The simplest way to define the border image is with the four values equal, using:

```
border-image: url distance;
```

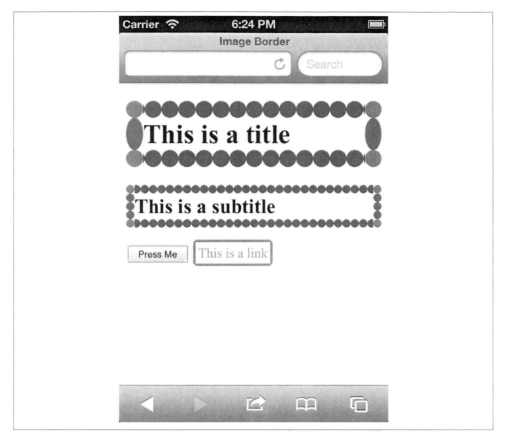

*Figure 11-9. The image is cut into nine pieces and each one is used as either a corner or a part of the background.*

This sample will produce the result shown in Figure 11-9:

```
<!DOCTYPE html>
<head>
<meta charset="UTF-8">
<title>Image Border</title>
<meta name="viewport" content="width=device-width">

<style>
/* We should use input[type=button] too, but for testing purposes
we will not use CSS3 */
input.bordered {
    border-radius: 10px;
    -webkit-border-image: url(border1.png) 6;
    -o-border-image: url(border1.png) 6;
    border-image: url(border1.png) 6;
}
```

```
a.bordered {
    -webkit-border-image: url(border1.png) 6;
    -o-border-image: url(border1.png) 6;
    border-image: url(border1.png) 6;
    color: white;
    text-decoration: none;
    padding: 3px;
}

h1 {
    border: 20px;
    -webkit-border-image: url(border2.png) 50 50 50 50 repeat stretch;
    -o-border-image: url(border2.png) 50 50 50 50 repeat stretch;
    border-image: url(border2.png) 50 50 50 50 repeat stretch;
}

/* The h2 will use the same image border but half size */
h2 {
    border: 10px;
    -webkit-border-image: url(border2.png) 50 50 50 50 round round;
    -o-border-image: url(border2.png) 50 50 50 50 round round;
    border-image: url(border2.png) 50 50 50 50 round round;
}
</style>
</head>

<body>
  <h1>This is a title</h1>
  <h2>This is a subtitle</h2>
  <input type="button" class="bordered" value="Press Me" />
  <!-- Safari applies border image to inline elements too -->
  <a href="http://mobilexweb.com" class="bordered">This is a link</a>
</body>
</html>
```

Another example is the implementation of the classic back button in iPhone user interfaces, using only left, right, and center zones (splitting the image into three parts):

```
<!DOCTYPE html>
<head>
<meta charset="UTF-8">
<title>Image Border</title>
<style>
#back {
    -webkit-border-image: url(border1.png) 0 5 0 15;
    -o-border-image: url(border1.png) 0 5 0 15;
    border-image: url(border1.png) 0 5 0 15;
}

</style>
</head>
```

```
<body>
  <a href="/" id="back">Home Page</a>
</body>
</html>
```

## Pseudoclasses

The pseudoclasses `link`, `active`, `focus`, and `visited` are compatible with all HTML browsers and standards. The question is, when do the pseudoclasses become active? Some situations are well known: for example, `link` is used for not-visited hyperlinks and `visited` is used if the links are in the previous browsing history.

 In Chapter 8, we discussed the validation pseudoclasses for form elements, such as `required` and `invalid`.

What about the `focus` and `active` pseudoclasses, though? The behavior can vary in browsers with focus-based, cursor-based, and touch-based navigation. Some browsers, such as Safari on iOS, support the `active` pseudoclass on every element, while others support it only on anchor elements.

The well-known `hover` pseudoclass is not available in the WAP CSS standard, but it is compatible with most nontouch devices, assuming a similar behavior to `focus`. In touch devices, there isn't a `mouseover` event; the screen doesn't detect the finger or touch position until the user taps it (or clicks it).

 There are a few specific exceptions, such as the Android-based Sony Xperia Sola and the Microsoft Surface tablet with Windows 8 Pro, both of which support hover states. In the case of the Surface tablet, hover events are triggered when using the stylus and not a finger.

Some mobile UIs for touch devices implement a two-tap pattern: if we tap once over an element, it will be like a hover effect, and if we tap again, it will be a click. This can be done with JavaScript and event handling.

## Backgrounds

Changing the background color was the first new feature in XHTML MP that every WML developer used. It was heaven after the old black and white WML. Every mobile browser today understands the `background` property and its specific definitions, like `background-image` and `background-repeat`. However, we need to remember that on mobile devices, the context of the user can be very different from on a desktop. It is not recommended to use a complex background, and it's best to use strongly contrasting foreground and background colors.

 Some cloud-based browsers, such as Opera Mini and the Nokia Xpress browser, will ignore your background image if it's too large for their performance standards. Therefore, it's always a good idea to define a color as a backup for your image.

In compatible browsers, it will be very helpful to use data URI patterns for backgrounds to reduce network requests. One feature that can be buggy on mobile devices is the use of background-attachment: fixed. This allows the background image to be fixed even after scrolling.

CSS3 added the ability to specify multiple background images (separated by commas) and the background-size, background-origin, and background-clip properties.

## Scrollable Areas

A common design pattern in desktop websites is to use a div (or other element) with a fixed size, and content larger than that size. Using the overflow property, we can define a value of scroll, auto, visible (the default), or hidden to indicate what to do with the content that is outside the bounds of the element. If we use a value of scroll, the div will have its own scroll bar on supporting devices. A similar technique involves the usage of the iframe.

For many years in the mobile web environment, scrolling in areas smaller than the whole viewport was discouraged, as it was an impossible mission for users on nontouch devices, and even on touch devices often there was no way to scroll inside them, or to do so the user needed a usually unknown gesture such as a double-finger scroll. This was a problem in Safari on iOS, up to version 4.3.

Since 2011, modern mobile browsers (including Safari on iOS since version 5) have added better support for scrolling small areas, removing the double-finger scroll gesture and adding some extensions to the overflow CSS property to match mobile-specific scrolling behaviors. The Android browser supports overflow from version 2.2.

 For browsers that are not compatible with overflow: scroll or over flow: auto, some JavaScript frameworks have appeared offering a JavaScript-based solution. One example is Scrollability (*https://github.com/joehewitt/scrollability*).

The overflow extensions available in some browsers will generate a scroll with a nice native momentum style (deceleration and bouncing effects). For WebKit-based browsers, compatibility started with Safari on iOS 5, and others followed. In these browsers, we can use `overflow: scroll` and the new `-webkit-overflow-scrolling: touch` extension. In the case of the BlackBerry 10 browser, to get a native scrolling feature we must use `-webkit-overflow: -blackberry-touch`.

 Version 2.x of the Android browser has several issues with `overflow: scroll` elements.

Windows 8 Store apps created with HTML5 support a `-ms-overflow-style` property accepting the values `auto`, `none` (meaning no scroll bars will be visible, even though we can scroll), `scrollbar` (to show scroll bars all the time), and `-ms-autohiding-scrollbar` (to use overlay scroll bars that don't use up space and autohide after the interaction ends). We must use `overflow: scroll` at the sametime as `-ms-overflow-style`.

 When using `overflow: scroll` or `auto` we always need to define fixed dimensions, as in width or height. By default, if we leave automatic dimensions we won't have scrolling behavior and the box will just get the content size.

To have a touch or modern scroll bar area, we can then define:

```
.scrollable {
    /* Always define a fixed width or height */
    overflow: scroll;
    -webkit-overflow-scrolling: touch;
    -webkit-overflow-scrolling: -blackberry-touch;
}
```

## Content

The `content` attribute allows us to use the `after` and `before` pseudoclasses to define an image, some text, or an attribute value to be inserted after or before the selector.

Some browsers allow us to apply the `content` property to any selector, but this is not usually recommended because it will lead us to insert text and content in the CSS instead of the HTML document.

The following sample will add two stars after the link's text and a bullet image before:

```
a:after {
    content: " ** "
}
a:before {
    content: url('bullet.gif');
}
```

## Opacity

Alpha transparency of elements inside a mobile web page will not work on many low-end and mid-range devices, so we should use it with care and be aware that it may not have a visible effect. The `opacity` CSS property allows the usage of a float number from 0 (totally transparent) to 1 (totally opaque). It applies to the element and all of its children.

In CSS3 we can also use the `rgba()` color function to make just the background or foreground colors semi-transparent, instead of the whole box and its contents—the first three parameters to this function represent the color and the fourth is the transparency value, again between 0 and 1. As it may be not compatible with non-CSS3 browsers, though, we should use a fallback mechanism, as in:

```
#myelement {
    color: blue;
    color: rgba(0, 0, 255, 0.5); // Blue with 0.5 opacity
                                 // on compatible browsers
}
```

## Cursor Management

CSS allows any web designer to define which mouse cursor should be used in any situation (generally, the body or a `:hover` selector). In the mobile world this is useful only for devices supporting cursor-based navigation, though, because they have the only browsers that show some kind of cursor over the screen.

The most useful cursors for mobile sites are `default`, `pointer`, and `progress`. The other cursors available (`resize` and `move`) can be very difficult to use in any mobile situation. We should use the `pointer` cursor for defining nonlink clickable zones (using a `:hover` selector), which may be handled by a JavaScript event function.

The `progress` cursor is often applied to the body dynamically with JavaScript to indicate to the user that a current operation is working. In browsers supporting focus and touch navigation, we should generate this pattern using a modal pop-up window with a floating loading image.

---

### Modal Pop-up Windows

A modal pop-up is a floating `div` that displays important information to the user, while disabling and/or fading out the background content.

In the mobile world these are recommended only for smartphones and should be used with extreme care. If we are displaying only simple text, it is better to use the standard `window.alert` JavaScript function, as it will render properly on all devices.

---

# Selection Management

Most smartphone and tablet browsers allow the user to select text and copy it to the clipboard, as seen in Figure 11-10. While this may be a desired feature in most situations, it can lead to some usability problems when we are managing touch events ourselves, or inside apps that will not provide useful content to copy.

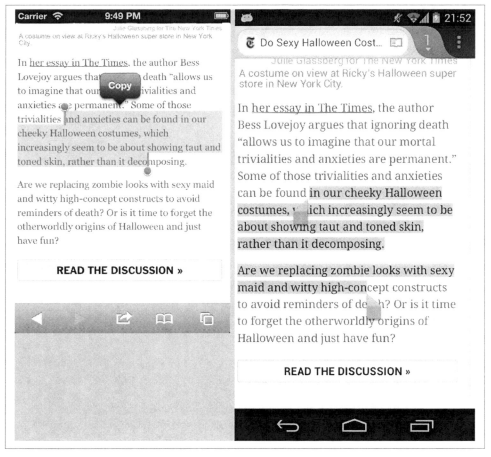

*Figure 11-10. Some mobile browsers allow users to select text using some gesture, such as a double tap or two-finger tap over a paragraph, unless we deactivate the behavior using CSS extensions.*

To remove the selectable behavior on some elements, we can use the not-yet-standard user-select property. This property was proposed in the CSS3 User Interface draft, but never made it to the full standard.

`user-select` accepts the following values: `none` (no content can be selected), `text` (the default; only text can be selected), `toggle` (the element's contents can be selected), `element` (only one child element at a time can be selected, such as a p element), `elements` (one or more elements can be selected), and `all` (only the contents as a whole can be selected).

At the time of this writing, this feature is being implemented with prefixes and not really following the standard possible values.

In WebKit-based browsers, such as Safari on iOS, the Android browser, and Chrome for Android, we can use `-webkit-user-select`, which allows `auto`, `none`, and `text`.

Firefox accepts the `-moz-user-select` variation, supporting the values `none`, `text`, `all`, `element`, and `-moz-none`. The difference between `none` and `-moz-none` is that the latter accepts that a child element can override the parent's `none` if it has a `-moz-user-select: text` attribute.

Internet Explorer 10 uses the `-ms-user-select` prefix and accepts `none`, `text`, `all`, `element`, and `auto`.

 Opera with Presto engine and IE9 don't support `user-select` extensions, but they do support an HTML extension attribute that we can use for the same purpose: `unselectable="on"`.

To simplify, if we want to disable selection for compatible browsers we can use:

```
article {
    -webkit-user-select: none;
    -moz-user-select: none;
    -ms-user-select: none;
}
```

 The CSS3 User Interface draft included a lot of other styles, such as `user-focus` and `toggle-group`, whose implementations are still quite strange on mobile browsers at the time of this writing.

### Selection styles

If we want the user to be able to select content but want to customize the background color or style of the whole selection, we can use some nonstandard pseudoelements that are compatible with some browsers, such as `::selection`, which becomes `::-moz-selection` in Firefox. For example:

```
article {
    -webkit-user-select: text;
```

```
        -moz-user-select: text;
        -ms-user-select: text;
}
article::selection {
    background-color: green;
    color: white;
}
article::-moz-selection {
    background-color: green;
    color: white;
}
```

In Figure 11-11, we can see the selection style being applied in some browsers.

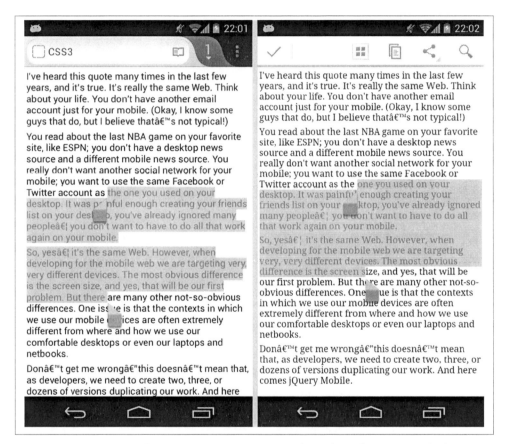

*Figure 11-11. In some browsers we can customize how the selection pseudoelement is rendered, such as modifying the background color.*

## Touch Callout

When you use the long press or touch-and-hold gesture over a clickable area such as an a element, a default callout appears, as we can see in Figure 11-12. In some situations, such as for a JavaScript-based hyperlink, a native web app, or a full-screen web app, disabling the callout may be a good idea. This is also a feature that we may want to disable if we are detecting that gesture in our own code.

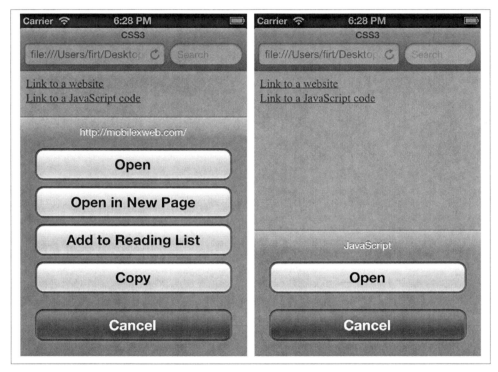

*Figure 11-12. The callout is the pop-up window that appears when we touch and hold a clickable element, such as a hyperlink (even a JavaScript-based link).*

Safari on iOS has added an extension, -webkit-touch-callout: none, that will disable that default pop-up window, as in:

```
a {
    -webkit-touch-callout: none;
}
```

To remove callouts only for JavaScript-based hyperlinks, we can use a CSS3 "starts with" attribute selector:

```
a[href^=javascript] {
    -webkit-touch-callout: none;
}
```

Other WebKit browsers, such as Google Chrome, currently ignore this attribute, and there are no alternatives for other browsers at the time of this writing.

## Highlight Color

When a mobile user taps on a clickable element, such as a link, the default highlight color is shown as a layer of color over the element with a default alpha style. We can override the color or remove the highlight effect using the extension `-webkit-tap-highlight-color`.

If we want to define our own color, we should always make it transparent, with the `rgba()` function. If we provide an opaque color, such as `yellow` or `#CCC`, the clickable element will be totally obscured by that color.

With the `rgba()` function we can override the default alpha value and apply a 0 value (fully transparent) to remove the effect completely, or a 1 value (fully opaque) to obscure the element completely:

```
a.noeffect {
    -webkit-tap-highlight-color: rgba(0, 0, 0, 0);
}
```

This property works on most WebKit-based mobile browsers, such as Safari on iOS, the Android browser, and Chrome.

 Remember that you can use some pseudoclasses, such as `active`, to change an element's properties when the user taps on that element.

## Appearance Override

WebKit-based browsers and Firefox allow us to override the default appearance of an element with the `-webkit-appearance` and `-moz-appearance` properties. For example, we can remove the default platform-specific styling of a button or a text input using the none attribute, as follows:

```
button {
    -webkit-appearance: none;
    -moz-appearance: none;
}
```

If we use one of the available values, we can change the appearance of the element so it resembles a native control in the operating system. A partial list of possible values includes: `button`, `button-bevel`, `checkbox`, `default-button`, `listbox`, `listitem`, `media-fullscreen-button`, `media-mute-button`, `media-play-button`, `radio`, `searchfield`,

searchfield-cancel-button, slider-horizontal, slider-vertical, square-button, textarea, and textfield.

 WebKit-based browsers support the -webkit-text-security extension that defines the character to display in password fields for each character the user enters. Possible values are circle, disc, none, and square.

# CSS Sprites

Using CSS sprites is a great modern web design technique for reducing the number of image server requests on a web page. There are a lot of online resources and books available on this technique. For now, suffice it to say that if you have many images in your site (preferred logos, icons, background images, flags, and so on), you can reduce all of those to one big image with all the originals inside and use a CSS mask to determine which portion of it to show in each container.

This technique has a great impact on web performance, but for mobile applications we should think twice before using it and analyze the possible problems. First, we need full background-position CSS property compatibility (the mobile standards include this, so it's not really an issue). The second consideration is that we will not be using img tags. In their place, we will use any block element (div) or any block-converted element using display: block, such as a span or a tag. This means that we cannot provide alternative text for the images, and the browser won't know how much space to allocate for each image until it renders the CSS file.

Finally, in some browsers this technique can have an impact on rendering performance, because the big image will be duplicated in memory for each usage. We need to balance the performance gained through the reduction of requests with the performance lost in the rendering engine in some browsers.

## Samples and Compatibility

Let's create a sample using two techniques: using an original block element (div) and using an original inline element (a) converted to a block element.

The original document without CSS sprites is the following country list:

```
<!DOCTYPE html>
<html>
<head>
<meta charset="utf-8" />
<title>CSS Sprites Demo</title>
<style type="text/css">
```

```
    ul {
        list-style: circle;
    }

    ul li {
        padding: 0px;
        margin-bottom: 5px;
    }

    ul li img {
        margin: 0px 10px 0px 0px;
        vertical-align: middle;
        border: 1px solid gray;
    }

</style>
</head>

<body>
<h1>The Best Seller</h1>
<h2>Select your nearest country</h2>
<ul>
  <li><img src='ar.png' width='30' height='19' alt='AR'>
    <a href='ar'>Argentina</a></li>
  <li><img src='br.png' width='30' height='19' alt='BR'>
    <a href='br'>Brazil</a></li>
  <li><img src='es.png' width='30' height='19' alt='ES'>
    <a href='es'>Spain</a></li>
  <li><img src='fi.png' width='30' height='19' alt='FI'>
    <a href='fi'>Finland</a></li>
  <li><img src='jp.png' width='30' height='19' alt='JP'>
    <a href='jp'>Japan</a></li>
  <li><img src='us.png' width='30' height='19' alt='US'>
    <a href='us'>United States</a></li>
</ul>
</body>
</html>
```

The previous sample uses six images that can be converted into a single one (saving five requests and the HTTP and PNG headers) with the following code:

```
<!DOCTYPE html>
<html>
<head>
<meta charset="utf-8">
<title>CSS Sprites Demo</title>
<style type="text/css">

    ul {
        list-style: circle;
    }

    ul li {
```

```
            padding: 0px;
            margin-bottom: 5px;
        }

        ul li div {
            /* We define the large image as a background for all divs
               that represent an image*/
            background:url(sprite.png);
            width: 30px;
            height: 19px;
            float: left;
            border: 1px solid gray;
            margin-right: 10px;
        }

</style>
</head>

<body>
<h1>The Best Seller</h1>
<h2>Select your nearest country</h2>
<ul>
  <li><div style="background-position: 0px 0px;"></div>
      <a href='ar'>Argentina</a></li>
  <li><div style="background-position: 0px -29px;"></div>
      <a href='br'>Brazil</a></li>
  <li><div style="background-position: 0px -58px;"></div>
      <a href='fi'>Finland</a></li>
  <li><div style="background-position: 0px -87px;"></div>
      <a href='jp'>Japan</a></li>
  <li><div style="background-position: 0px -116px;"></div>
      <a href='es'>Spain</a></li>
  <li><div style="background-position: 0px -145px;"></div>
      <a href='us'>United States</a></li>
</ul>
</body>
</html>
```

This produces the result shown in Figure 11-13.

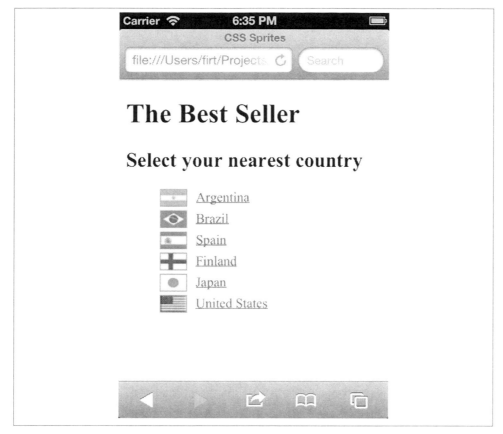

*Figure 11-13. In compatible browsers, using CSS sprites produces the same result using a single image as using six separate images for the flags.*

 There are plenty of online CSS sprites generators where you can upload all your images and receive in seconds one big image and the CSS code to replace each of the original img tags. Examples include Spritegen (*http://spritegen.website-performance.org*) and CSS Sprites (*http://cssprites.com*).

Now let's look at applying the same technique to a nonoriginal block element, such as the a tag. The only problem will be the flag border: as we use the same a tag for the image and the text, we cannot define a border. The code looks like this:

```
<!DOCTYPE html>
<html>
<head>
<meta charset="utf-8" />
```

```
<title>CSS Sprites demo</title>
<style type="text/css">

    ul {
        list-style: circle;
    }

    ul li {
        padding: 0px;
        margin-bottom: 5px;
    }

    ul li a {
        /* We define the large image as a background for all divs
           that represent an image */
        background:url(sprite.png);
        /* We need to create block elements */
        display: block;
        /* We need the background to not be repeated */
        background-repeat: no-repeat;
        height: 19px;
        padding-left: 40px;
    }

</style>
</head>

<body>
<h1>The Best Seller</h1>
<h2>Select your nearest country</h2>
<ul>
  <li>
    <a href='ar' style='background-position: 0px 0px;'>Argentina</a>
  </li>
  <li>
    <a href='br' style='background-position: 0px -29px;'>Brazil</a>
  </li>
  <li>
    <a href='es' style='background-position: 0px -116px;'>Spain</a>
  </li>
  <li>
    <a href='fi' style='background-position: 0px -58px;'>Finland</a>
  </li>
  <li>
    <a href='jp' style='background-position: 0px -87px;'>Japan</a>
  </li>
  <li>
    <a href='us' style='background-position: 0px -145px;'>
       United States
    </a>
  </li>
</ul>
```

```
    </body>
</html>
```

 Using CSS sprites is not recommended for big files or photo images. If you are using PNG images, the best way to approach it is to group icons with a consistent color palette.

## CSS Sprites Alternatives

The idea of minimizing the number of requests to the server is very interesting, even if you reject the usage of CSS sprites. That is why we need to think about alternatives to this technique for some specific situations.

 Image maps are the first technique that comes to mind as a CSS sprites alternative. However, they are not recommended for nontouch navigation, because image maps in nontouch devices can have a negative impact on usability.

### Inline images

As we discussed in the last chapter, inline images are a great technique for compatible browsers. When designing for browsers that understand them, we can copy the first sample (the original document without CSS sprites) and replace the URL of each image with the `data:` representation.

### Join images

If the images are near one another horizontally or vertically, as in our sample, we can consider joining all the images into one. The concept is similar to CSS sprites, but we set up the image as a single-use background, adjusting the margins and padding so that the elements are properly aligned with the different parts of the image. This technique can have poor results on old devices with limited support for margins and padding.

 If we use the original code but define a good cache policy on the server, subsequent pages of the site will load faster than if we used CSS sprites, because no rendering work will be required.

# CSS3 Modules

Besides the standard CSS specification, there are different modules that a browser may or may not support. In this section we will cover the most useful modules that we can use today in mobile browsers.

# Gradients

The CSS3 Image Values (*http://www.w3.org/TR/css3-images*) specification adds a way to define gradients as image functions inside any style that needs an image as a value. Instead of using the `url()` function to provide the URL of the image, we can use the available gradient functions, such as `linear-gradient()`, `radial-gradient()`, `repeating-linear-gradient()`, and `repeating-radial-gradient()`. This technique enables us to create really nice backgrounds for titles, containers, and cells with minimal code.

The specs have changed over time, and compatibility is mixed between old spec, and new spec prefixed and unprefixed. Safari on iOS 3.0 was one of the first browsers to support this feature and we can use it today on most modern mobile browsers, including Safari from iOS 3, the Android browser from 2.1, Chrome, Firefox, the BlackBerry browser from 7.0, Opera from 11.1, and Internet Explorer from version 10.

 For browsers that do not support CSS gradients, such as Internet Explorer 9 for Windows Phone or BlackBerry 5, using a plain color instead of a background image will result in better performance.

Internet Explorer from version 10, Opera from 12.1, and Firefox from 16 don't need prefixes anymore, so we can use the standard code. For all the others we must use the `-webkit-`, `-moz-`, and `-o-` prefixes.

 Repeating gradients have appeared late in mobile browsers—Safari supports them from iOS 5.0, the Android browser from 4.0, and the BlackBerry browser from BB10.

While gradients are beyond the scope of this book, there are some websites that will allow you to design and preview your gradients with a visual tool and get the cross-platform code pretty easily. Some tools allow you to upload a bitmap file with a gradient inside and export it to CSS gradients. Useful online tools include:

- Ultimate CSS Gradient Generator (*http://www.colorzilla.com/gradient-editor*) (Figure 11-14)
- Generate It Gradient (*http://www.generateit.net/gradient*)
- CSS3 Gradient Generator (*http://css3gen.com/gradient-generator*)

**Ultimate CSS Gradient Generator**

A powerful Photoshop-like CSS gradient editor from ColorZilla.

For Firefox    For Chrome    Gradient Generator

Presets

Preview

Orientation: vertical ↓    Size 370 x 50    ☐ IE

Name: Custom                          save

CSS                                    switch to scss

```
background: #f0b7a1;
background: -moz-linear-gradient(top, #f0b7a1 0%,
  #8c3310 50%, #752201 68%, #bf6e4e 100%);
background: -webkit-gradient(linear, left top, left
  bottom, color-stop(0%,#f0b7a1), color-
  stop(50%,#8c3310), color-stop(68%,#752201),
  color-stop(100%,#bf6e4e));
background: -webkit-linear-gradient(top, #f0b7a1
  0%,#8c3310 50%,#752201 68%,#bf6e4e 100%);
background: -o-linear-gradient(top, #f0b7a1
  0%,#8c3310 50%,#752201 68%,#bf6e4e 100%);
background: -ms-linear-gradient(top, #f0b7a1
  0%,#8c3310 50%,#752201 68%,#bf6e4e 100%);
background: linear-gradient(to bottom, #f0b7a1
  0%,#8c3310 50%,#752201 68%,#bf6e4e 100%);
filter: progid:DXImageTransform.Microsoft.gradient(
  startColorstr='#f0b7a1',
  endColorstr='#bf6e4e',GradientType=0 );    copy
```

Stops

Opacity [ ]    Location: [ ] %    delete

Color: ▮    Location: 68 %    delete

Color format: hex ↓   ☐ Comments  ☐ IE9 Support (?)

import from image   import from css

Adjustments

hue/saturation...   reverse

Permalink

Link to, save or share the current gradient using its unique link.

Sponsor

*Figure 11-14. With the Ultimate CSS Gradient Generator, we can design our gradient in a visual drag-and-drop editor and get the CSS standard code ready to paste.*

 Older versions of WebKit-based browsers support only an old specification for gradients, using the `-webkit-gradient()` function and defining `linear` or `radial` as the first parameter. The final spec has different functions for each type.

Just to give you a quick sample, the following code will show you a linear gradient with a fallback plain color for list items:

```
li {
  background: #f0f9ff;
  background: -moz-linear-gradient(top,  #f0f9ff 0%, #cbebff 47%,
      #a1dbff 100%);
  background: -webkit-gradient(linear, left top, left bottom,
      color-stop(0%,#f0f9ff), color-stop(47%,#cbebff),
      color-stop(100%,#a1dbff));
  background: -webkit-linear-gradient(top, #f0f9ff 0%, #cbebff 47%,
      #a1dbff 100%);
  background: -o-linear-gradient(top, #f0f9ff 0%, #cbebff 47%,
      #a1dbff 100%);
  background: linear-gradient(bottom, #f0f9ff 0%, #cbebff 47%,
      #a1dbff 100%);
}
```

In Figure 11-15, we can see different gradients in action, including linear and radial.

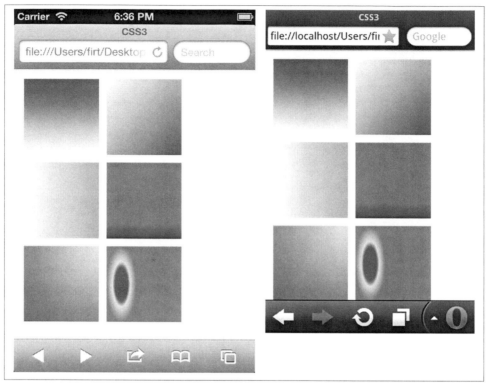

*Figure 11-15. With just CSS you can create different gradient effects for most smartphones and tablets without using images.*

 As of version 6.0, Mobile Internet Explorer supports filters and transitions, using CSS extensions with the filter style. You can create alpha, chroma, shadow, glow, mask, and other effects. For more information, see *www.mobilexweb.com/go/iefilter*.

# Reflection

Reflection or mirror effects are available as an extension for WebKit browsers, but there is no W3C standard behind them. They can be used on any content, including images. Remember, though, that we are designing for mobile screens and we don't want to waste too much space.

 The reflection image doesn't change the layout or the size of the element's original content box. It is only part of the container's overflow.

To create a reflection effect in WebKit-based browsers such as Safari on iOS, use the `-webkit-box-reflect` attribute with the following syntax:

```
-webkit-box-reflect: direction offset [mask-box-image];
```

The *direction* can be `above`, `below`, `left`, or `right`; the *offset* is the distance (in px or %) from the original element at which the reflection should appear; and the optional *mask-box-image* is generally a gradient function that will work as a mask for the reflection image. If no mask image is defined, a normal mirror will be used.

 CSS reflection works in Safari on iOS, the Android browser, Chrome, and BlackBerry from 7.0.

The type of reflection effect typically seen in Web 2.0 websites has the following attribute values, as we can see in Figure 11-16:

```
-webkit-box-reflect: below 3px -webkit-linear-gradient(top, transparent 0%,
                     rgba(255, 255, 255, 0.5) 50%, white 100%);
```

*Figure 11-16. CSS reflection is a nonstandard effect that will not affect the element's original dimensions.*

## Masks

Like reflections, masks are a WebKit-only extension that gives us access to a graphic design feature that has been missing for years in web development: masked images. We can use a masked image to apply any regular or irregular crop to the original image, or, if using an alpha mask (or even a gradient function), to create a really nice visual effect over any image, like a fuzzy border. The mask properties are analogous to the background properties. For applying a mask, we have a shortcut property, `-webkit-mask`, and specific properties for the position.

The syntax of the shortcut version with all the optional parameters is:

```
-webkit-mask: attachment, clip, origin, image, repeat, composite,
    box-image;
```

Of course, we also have access to all the properties separately, as in `-webkit-mask-attachment`, `-webkit-mask-clip`, and so on. There are a lot of possibilities, but typically an image (alpha or not, PNG or SVG) or a gradient function is used as the image value. For example:

```
<img src="london.png" style="-webkit-mask-image:
    -webkit-linear-gradient(top, rgba(0,0,0,1) 0%,
    rgba(0,0,0,0) 100%); ">

<img src="london.png" style="-webkit-mask-image:
    url(old_picture_mask.png)">
```

# Transforms

At the time of this writing, CSS transforms (*http://www.w3.org/TR/css3-2d-transforms*) is a draft standard but is quite safe to use to apply functions to any element to generate visual effects without using images, `canvas`, or SVG. The transformation options work in many browsers and include a main shortcut `transform` property, a couple of CSS functions, and some extension attributes. As with many extensions, some browsers are still using prefixed versions at the time of this writing.

The usage is very simple: we use the CSS property `transform`, applying as a value any of the CSS functions listed in Table 11-1.

*Table 11-1. CSS transform functions available in CSS3*

| Function | Description |
|---|---|
| `matrix(m11, m12, m21, m22, tX, tY)` | Specifies a matrix transformation of six values with two translation elements. |
| `matrix3d(m00, m01, m02, m03, m10, m11, m12, m13, m20, m21, m22, m23, m30, m31, m31, m33)` | Specifies a 3D matrix transformation of 4×4. |
| `perspective(depth)` | Maps a viewing cube onto a pyramid whose base is far away from the viewer. This property is not part of the standard and is available only in WebKit-based browsers. |
| `rotate(angle)` | Defines a 2D rotation around the origin of the element. |
| `rotate3d(x, y, z, angle)` | Defines a 3D rotation with [x,y,z] as the direction vector of the rotation. |
| `rotateX(angle)` | Specifies a clockwise rotation around the x-axis. |
| `rotateY(angle)` | Specifies a clockwise rotation around the y-axis. |
| `rotateZ(angle)` | Specifies a clockwise rotation around the z-axis. |
| `scale(scaleX, [scaleY])` | Performs a 2D scale operation. |
| `scale3d(scaleX, scaleY, scaleZ)` | Performs a 3D scale operation. |
| `scaleX(value)` | Scales along the x-axis. |
| `scaleY(value)` | Scales along the y-axis. |
| `scaleZ(value)` | Scales along the z-axis. |

| Function | Description |
| --- | --- |
| skewX(*angle*) | Performs a skew transformation around the *x*-axis. |
| skewY(*angle*) | Performs a skew transformation around the *y*-axis. |
| translate(*deltaX*[, *deltaY*]) | Specifies a 2D translation vector. |
| translate3d(*deltaX, deltaY, deltaZ*) | Specifies a 3D translation vector. |
| translateX(*value*) | Performs a translation around the *x*-axis. |
| translateY(*value*) | Performs a translation around the *y*-axis. |
| translateZ(*value*) | Performs a translation around the *z*-axis. |

 Rotation transforms, such as rotate and skew, need new kinds of units for defining values. CSS defines deg as degrees (180deg), rad as radians (1rad), and turn as turns (0.5turn).

We can change the origin point of the transformation with the `transform-origin` property. The default value is the middle of the element (a value of 50% 50%); this is particularly useful for rotations.

Internet Explorer since version 10, Firefox since 16, and Opera since 12.1 have removed the need of prefixes for the `transform` property. All the other browsers at the time of this writing still need it, such as `-webkit-transform` for Safari on iOS.

 3D transformations, such as `scale3d` or `matrix3d`, are not available in all browsers.

We can apply more than one transform at a time by declaring more than one function, space-separated. Don't declare more than one `transform` property, though, as the last one will override any previous ones. For example, to rotate an element 45 degrees while making it 10% bigger, we can use:

```
#element {
    -webkit-transform: rotate(45deg) scale(1.10);
    -moz-transform: rotate(45deg) scale(1.10);
    -o-transform: rotate(45deg) scale(1.10);
    -ms-transform: rotate(45deg) scale(1.10);
    transform: rotate(45deg) scale(1.10);
}
```

Remember that transformations don't affect other elements on the screen; therefore, if we translate or scale an element, other elements in the DOM will not be affected and will not be moved (unlike when we increase the margins).

### Perspective

Setting a 3D perspective can be done using the `perspective()` transformation function in WebKit-based browsers only, or the special CSS property `perspective` and its prefixed versions, which take a value in pixels defining the distance from the viewer's perspective. If we use the latter option the perspective will be applied to the children of the element, but if we use the transformation function it will be applied only to the element itself.

### Transform style

The transformation can act differently with regard to its nested (child) elements. We can control this behavior with the `transform-style` attribute, which has two possible values: `flat` and `preserve-3d`. If `flat` is used, the nested elements are flattened as if they were an image and the perspective is applied to that image. With `preserve-3d`, every nested element will have its own 3D perspective, as seen in Figure 11-17.

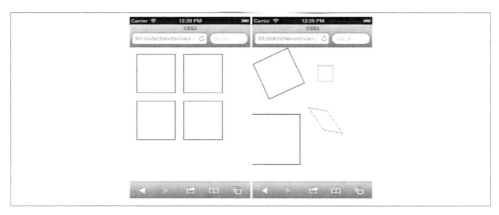

*Figure 11-17. Sample of transformations applied to a couple of elements.*

### Backface visibility

Backface? What? An element in HTML has a backface? It can in CSS 3D transformations defining the `backface-visibility` CSS property. It is not what you might think (two faces in the same element), but the effect can easily be implemented.

The `backface-visibility` property can be defined as `hidden` or `visible`. If `hidden`, when we define a rotation of the *y*-axis of more than 180 degrees the element will disappear, and we can make another element showing a backface appear in its place.

 All transformations can also be applied using JavaScript, by changing CSS styles or by using the `CSSMatrix` JavaScript class (prefixed on some browsers) and defining a couple of objects. The most simple and quick way is to define the transformation as a string and apply it to `element.style.transform` or its prefixed versions, such as `element.style.webkitTransform`.

### The CardFlip pattern

This is one of the most "wow" visual features that Safari on iOS has brought to us. The CardFlip pattern allows us to show an element in a rectangular area and, when some event occurs, perform a transformation that flips the element as if it were a poker card and shows another element of the same size and in the same position as the backface.

Apple provides a full sample (*http://www.mobilexweb.com/go/cardflip*) that can be used as the base template for designing this kind of animation.

A simplified version (without all the prefixes) of the CardFlip sample looks like this:

```
<!DOCTYPE html>
<html>
<head>
<meta charset="utf-8">
<title>Card Flip</title>
<style>
body {
    margin: 0px;
}

#container {
    height: 356px;
    width: 320px;
    background-color: rgba(56,108,179, 0.5);

    /* Disable tap highlighting on WebKit browsers */
    -webkit-tap-highlight-color: rgba(0,0,0,0);

    /* Give some depth to the card */
```

```
        perspective: 600;
}

.card {
    position: absolute;
    height: 300px;
    width: 200px;
    left: 60px;
    top: 28px;

    transform-style: preserve-3d;
    transition-property: -webkit-transform;
    transition-duration: 1.5s;
}

.card.flipped{
    transform: rotateY(180deg);
}

/* Styles the card and hides its "back side" when the card
   is flipped */
.face {
    position: absolute;
    height: 300px;
    width: 200px;
    border-radius: 10px;
    box-shadow: 0px 2px 6px rgba(0, 0, 0, 0.5);
    backface-visibility: hidden;
}

.face > p {
    margin-top: 36px;
    margin-bottom: 0;
    text-align: center;
    font-size: 92px;
}

.front {
    color: rgb(78,150,249);
    background-color: rgb(34,65,108);
}

.back {
    color: rgb(34,65,108);
    background-color: rgba(78,150,249,0.5);
    /* Ensure the "back side" is flipped already */
    transform: rotateY(180deg);
}
</style>
<script>
function flip(event) {
    var element = event.currentTarget;
```

```
        /* Toggle the setting of the className attribute */
        element.className = (element.className == 'card') ?
          'card flipped' : 'card';
    }
    </script>

    </head>
    <body>
        <div id="container">
            <div id="card" class="card" onclick="flip(event)">
                <div id="front" class="front face">
                    <p>♠ ♦<br> ♣ ♥</p>
                </div>
                <div id="back" class="back face">
                    <p>♦ ♠<br> ♥ ♣</p>
                </div>
            </div>
        </div>
    </body>
    </html>
```

Analyzing the code, we see two `div` elements inside a container called `card`. One `div` is the "front" face and the other the "back" face. Both faces are positioned in the exact same position (as absolute elements), and the back side starts with a *y*-axis rotation of 180 degrees. Both faces also define themselves as hidden when backfaced.

When the user clicks the `card` container (with either the front or back face displayed on the screen), via JavaScript we apply (or not) the `flipped` CSS class, which rotates both elements 180 degrees around the *y*-axis. And *voilà!* Only one face will be at the front at any given time; the other will be automatically hidden.

> Remember that for the sake of simplicity, the previous example doesn't include all the necessary prefixed versions. To make it work on all browsers, you should clone every CSS transform style with a `-webkit-`, `-moz-`, and `-o-` prefix.

This process is done with a beautiful, smooth animation, which you can't quite see in Figure 11-18.

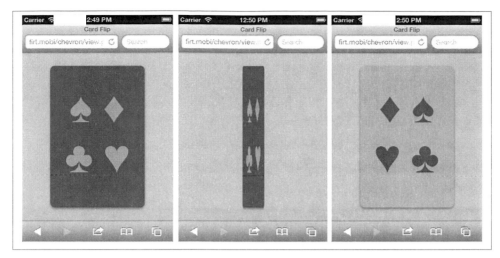

*Figure 11-18. With 3D flipping you can use a beautiful 3D effect to display the backface of an element.*

## Transitions

A *transition* is just an automatic animation that takes place when a CSS property's value changes. The property must be defined by the browser as able to animate. There isn't an official list of properties that animations will work on, but the general policy is that any attribute with numerical or color values should be animated using transitions (we can test different attributes with transition ability using animatable (*http://leaver ou.github.com/animatable*)). There are also a few exceptions, like visibility (a discrete property) and the transform property, which can animate any of the inner functions, such as rotate() or translate(). A version of the CSS transitions spec (*http://www.w3.org/TR/css3-transitions*) is available.

 Remember, these transitions are defined entirely using CSS: we are not using JavaScript or any other technique to create the animations. This may sound a bit strange, but it is a simple and powerful technique. In some browsers, it's hardware accelerated and/or managed by an internal browser timer so it gets the best frame rate possible.

To create a transition, we should:

1. Define the transition properties (duration, delay, where to apply, timing function) in the element(s) we want to animate.

2. Change the values of the attributes of the element(s) to animate using JavaScript, or apply classes to, or remove them from the element.

3. Verify that the animation is working.

Sounds simple, right? Let's do it.

### Animation properties

An animation can be defined using the shortcut property `transition` (and all prefixed versions) with the following syntax:

```
transition: property duration timing_function delay [, ...];
```

We can also use the specific properties listed in Table 11-2.

*Table 11-2. CSS transition properties*

| Property | Description |
|----------|-------------|
| transition-property | Defines which property or properties to animate. We can use a comma-separated list, or the constant value `all`. |
| transition-duration | Defines the duration of the transition. The value can be `0` (no animation) or a positive value in seconds (using `s` as the unit) or milliseconds (using `ms` as the unit). If we want to define different timings for each property, we can use a list of comma-separated values in the same order as the `transition-property` value. |
| transition-delay | Defines the offset delay of the animation, beginning from the time when the property was changed. This can be defined in seconds or milliseconds (using `s` or `ms`), and the default value is `0`. If a negative value is used, the animation starts immediately but with some of the animation already done. |
| transition-timing-function | Defines the function used to calculate intermediate values from the initial to the finishing value of the property. You can use the CSS `cubic-bezier()` function, or any of the following constants: `ease`, `linear`, `ease-in`, `ease-out`, and `ease-in-out` (the most commonly used and default value.) |

Internet Explorer from version 10, Opera from 12.1, and Firefox from 16 have removed the need of a prefixed version for the transition's properties.

 Some modern browsers support staircase-timing functions that separate the animations in repetitive steps. The available functions are `steps()`, `step-start()`, and `step-end()`. These functions are in the standard draft but are not implemented in all browsers.

For example, the following code (with all the prefix versions) produces a fade-in, fade-out animation:

```
<!DOCTYPE html>
<html>
<head>
<meta charset="utf-8" />
<title>Fade Sample</title>
<style>
```

```
#box {
    width: 200px;
    height: 200px;
    background-color: red;
    -webkit-transition: opacity 2s;
    -moz-transition: opacity 2s;
    -o-transition: opacity 2s;
    transition: opacity 2s;
}

.hide {
    opacity: 0;
}

</style>
<script>
function fade() {
    var box = document.getElementById("box");
    box.className = (box.className=="hide") ? "" : "hide";
    box.innerHTML = box.className;
}

</script>

</head>
<body>

<h1>Fading</h1>
<input type="button" onclick="fade()" value="Hide-Show" />
<div id="box">
</div>
</body>
</html>
```

We can do similar transitions for resizing, relocation, color changes, or even 3D transitions using the transform properties that we saw earlier.

### Transition ending

The transition ending can be listened for from JavaScript just like any other DOM event, using addEventListener. You can then initiate another transition or do something else when you are sure that the animation has finished. The event to listen for is called transitionend. The main problem is that in some browsers the event name is prefixed, so we really need to listen to different possible events and apply all of them to the same handler. The possible names are transitionend, webkitTransitionEnd, and otransitionend.

We can listen for this event using the following code:

```
box.addEventListener('webkitTransitionEnd', transitionEnd, false);
box.addEventListener('transitionend', transitionEnd, false);
```

```
    box.addEventListener('otransitionend', transitionEnd, false);

    function transitionEnd(event) {
        alert("Finished transition");
    });
```

## Animations

Transitions are great and are the simplest way to create animations for smartphones and tablets. If you need finer animation control at the keyframe level, you can use the CSS animations module (*http://www.w3.org/TR/css3-animations*). To be completely honest, I thought this was too much to be handled only by CSS—a nonprocedural and nonmarkup language—but it works great.

 There are some visual tools available that will make creating CSS animations easier, such as Sencha Touch Animator (*http://www.sencha.com/products/animator*) and Adobe Edge Animate (*http://html.adobe.com/edge/animate*).

CSS animations are done with the shortcut property `animation` (and prefixed versions), which has the following syntax:

```
animation: name duration timing_function delay iteration_countdirection
```

As you've probably guessed, there are also specific properties for each possible value, listed in Table 11-3.

*Table 11-3. CSS animation properties*

| Property | Description |
|---|---|
| animation-name | Provides the name of the animation to be used by the keyframes. |
| animation-duration | Specifies the duration of the animation, in seconds or milliseconds. |
| animation-timing-function | Defines the function used to calculate intermediate values between the initial and final values of the property. You can use the CSS cubic-bezier() function or any of the following constants: ease, linear, ease-in, ease-out, and ease-in-out (the most commonly used and default value). You can design your own cubic-bezier() variant using Ceaser (*http://matthewlein.com/ceaser/*). |
| animation-delay | Defines the offset delay of the animation, beginning from the time when the property was changed. This can be defined in seconds or milliseconds, and the default value is 0. If a negative value is used, the animation starts immediately but with some of the animation already done. |
| animation-iteration-count | Defines how many times the animation will be repeated. This can be 1 (the default value), any integer value, the special constant infinite, or a float value. |
| animation-direction | Defines whether the animation will play in forward direction (normal) or in alternate mode, playing forward on even iterations and in reverse on odd iterations. |

| Property | Description |
|---|---|
| animation-fillmode | Defines whether the animation changes the element's styles before or after the animation. The default value none means no changes are done when the animation is not active. The forwards value means the last execution keyframe will stay, backwards will apply the initial keyframe before the animation starts, and both applies both behaviors. |
| animation-playstate | Defines if the animation is running or paused. |

After reading this list of properties you are probably asking yourself a few questions. Where is the animation defined? What will be animating? For these, the CSS @keyframes at-rule comes into play.

 If you are moving or scaling an object and you want it to be animated, it is better to use the performance-accelerated transform property rather than the usual CSS properties, such as top, left, or width.

### @keyframes

To define how the animation will work and what it will do, we need to define a special CSS at-rule called @keyframes. This rule is followed by the animation name (the one specified in animation-name).

---

## @keyframes and Prefixes

The big problem with the @keyframes at-rule is that it needs to be prefixed in some browsers—and that means we need to clone the entire keyframe declaration for WebKit-based browsers and for Firefox and Opera.

Opera 12.0 supported only the prefixed version, but the prefix is no longer required from version 12.1, so we can safely ignore it. Similarly, Firefox has removed the need of a prefix from version 16. So, as long as we are not targeting older Firefox editions, we can just define the WebKit prefix for iOS, Android, and other browsers and use the non-prefixed version for Internet Explorer 10 and newer versions of Firefox and Opera. Eventually WebKit browsers will also stop requiring the prefix, but to support 2011 and 2012 browsers we need at least:

```
@keyframes name {
  /* All declarations */
}
@-webkit-keyframes name {
  /* All declarations */
}
```

---

Inside the @keyframes at-rule, we need to specify as many selectors or animation groups as we want keyframes. The selector is defined by a percentage value or the constants from (equivalent to 0%) and to (equivalent to 100%). Inside each selector, we define all the properties and values that we want at that point in the animation. We can also define the timing to use in every animation group using transition-timing-function.

 When the animation finishes, the original values are restored. The elements will not maintain the last keyframe values after the animation stops unless we define animation-fillmode: forwards.

For example, the following sample moves a div in a square path. For reasons of simplicity we are just using the standard code without prefixes, but remember that to support most browsers today we need at least the -webkit- prefixed version:

```
<!DOCTYPE html>
<html>
<head>
<meta charset="utf-8" />
<title>Animation Sample</title>
<style>

#box {
    width: 200px;
    height: 200px;
    background-color: red;
    position: absolute;
    top: 0px;
    left: 0px;
}

.squareAnimation {
    animation-name: squarePath;
    animation-duration: 4s;
    animation-timing-function: linear;
    animation-iteration-count: infinite;
}

@keyframes squarePath {
    /* We can use 0% or "from" as selector */
    from {
        top: 0px;
        left: 0px;
    }

    25% {
        top: 0px;
        left: 100px;
    }
```

```
    50% {
        top: 100px;
        left: 100px;
    }

    75% {
        top: 100px;
        left: 0px;
    }

    /* We can use 100% or "to" as selector */
    100% {
        top: 0px;
        left: 0px;
    }

}

</style>
<script>
    function start() {
        // When we apply the -webkit-animation attributes, the
        // animation starts
        document.getElementById("box").className = "squareAnimation";
    }
</script>

</head>
<body onload="start()">

<h1>Moving over a square path</h1>
<div id="box">
</div>
</body>
</html>
```

 If we define the animation attributes in the element from the beginning, the animation will begin when the page loads. The best solution is to define animations as classes and, when we want to start an animation, apply that class to the element.

So, to start the animation, we apply the class, and if we want to stop it before it reaches the ending value, we should assign an empty value to the transform-name property.

We can define one animation that changes several properties, or use different animations with different names at the same time, each changing a single property.

AliceJS (*http://blackberry.github.com/Alice/*) is an open source Java-Script library that can be used to easily create high-performance CSS3 transitions and animations, including twirl, page-flip, bounce, and dance effects.

### Animation events

As with transitions, we can listen for the events `animationstart`, `animationiteration`, and `animationend`. When fired, they will send an `AnimationEvent` object as a parameter. There is no event to capture each keyframe change.

The event object has the special properties `animationName` and `elapsedTime`, whose value is given in seconds.

Remember that animation events, like transition events, need prefixed versions for some browsers.

## CSS Filter Effects

The CSS filter effects specification is not part of any standard at the time of this writing, but filter effects do work on some browsers, such as Safari on iOS since 6.0, Chrome for Android since version 25, and the BlackBerry 10 browser. They use the `filter` property (`-webkit-filter` is the only prefixed variant available at the time of this writing), which accepts one or more filter functions that can be applied (space separated).

Internet Explorer used to support a nonstandard `filter` property, but it's not compatible with this CSS filter specification. From version 10, Microsoft doesn't recommend the usage of the `filter` property.

Filters come from SVG, and the list of filters already available for usage includes `sepia`, `grayscale`, and `blur`. In compatible browsers, we can even animate or transition within filters.

If you want to try all the possible filters dynamically in a compatible browser, you can point to *mobilexweb.com/go/filters*.

For example, we can define:

```
-webkit-filter: blur(5px) grayscale (.5) opacity(0.66)
    hue-rotate(100deg);
```

## CSS Regions and Exclusions

CSS regions (*http://dev.w3.org/csswg/css3-regions*) and CSS exclusions (*http://www.w3.org/TR/css3-exclusions*) and shapes are two modules proposed by Adobe to cover some design issues with HTML.

With regions, we can define arbitrary regions—not necessarily contiguous—through which the content can flow. Therefore, a long text can flow between different areas on the screen, as you can see in Figure 11-19. With exclusions, we can define "islands" around which the text should flow for richer layouts, as seen in Figure 11-20.

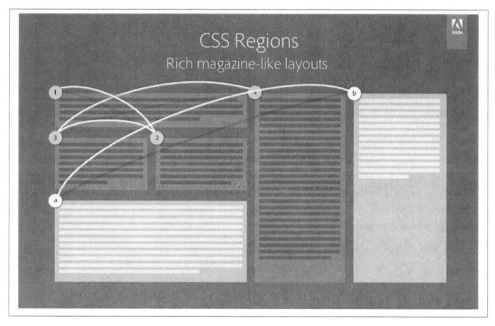

*Figure 11-19. With CSS regions we can define regions through which the content will flow, such as in a printed magazine layout.*

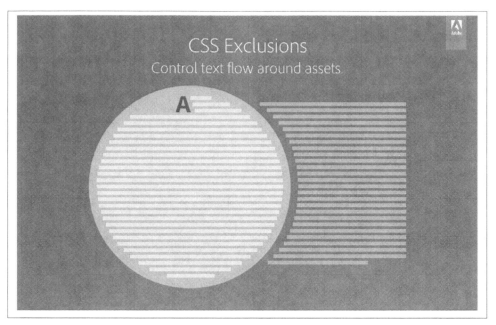

*Figure 11-20. CSS exclusions and shapes allow us to define islands for text to flow around for rich layouts, as we can see in this example from Adobe.*

At the time of this writing, the only browser supporting these specifications is Internet Explorer 10, but we can expect better support in the near future. For updated compatibility information, see Mobile HTML5 (*http://mobilehtml5.org*).

Adobe's commitment to bring us all a richer Web by proposing new standards can be viewed at Adobe's website (*http://html.adobe.com/webstandards*).

## New CSS Values and Units

The CSS3 values and units module (*http://www.w3.org/TR/css3-values*) includes new units and methods that we can use in most CSS declarations.

As we saw earlier in this chapter, we now have angle units, such as deg for degrees, and many other new features.

Safari on iOS 6 became one of the first mobile browsers to support mathematical expressions through the `calc()` function. We can use basic math expressions, such as additions or divisions using different units. For example, we can define something as `width: calc(100% - 24px)`. Internet Explorer, Chrome from version 25, Firefox, and BlackBerry 10 also support the `calc()` function.

Usually, browsers supporting these new values also accept new viewport units that are attached to the viewport, including vw (equal to 1% of the width of the initial containing block), vh (equal to 1% of the height), vim (equal to the smaller of vw and vh), and vmax (equal to the larger of the two).

While these new values and units may be useful, you need to make an analysis of current compatibility before deciding on their usage.

# CHAPTER 12

# JavaScript Mobile

Designing for the Web is about more than content and presentation—users expect websites to be interactive, responding to their choices. Fortunately, although it has some limitations, the JavaScript we use in developing for the mobile web is similar to that used in desktop web development.

We have already talked a bit about the WAP 1.1 standard scripting language, *WMLScript*. Don't worry, we won't go any deeper into this obsolete language.

Thankfully, a couple of years after this standard was released, mobile browsers started to add some support for JavaScript (or ECMAScript, to be totally correct). The standards for mobile scripting are more difficult to define than the standards for CSS. The great benefit is that, excepting some bugs, JavaScript can check at runtime whether some feature, object, or API is available, so we can code for different "standards."

 The standard name for JavaScript is ECMAScript because it is defined by the ECMA (an international, private, nonprofit standards organization). There are three well-known dialects on the market: JavaScript (trademark of Oracle, licensed now to the Mozilla Foundation), ActionScript (trademark of Adobe), and JScript (trademark of Microsoft). At the base, they are the same language, and everyone adds new behavior. In practice, the name JavaScript is so common in the industry today that everyone—including Microsoft—uses it as the language name.

The only mobile-specific standard is called *ECMAScript Mobile Profile* (ESMP). It was defined by the Open Mobile Alliance (OMA), like XHTML MP and WAP CSS. In my 10 years in the mobile web world, I have never heard a developer or a company talking about ESMP. It is a subset of the ECMAScript language and is really just JavaScript with some features left out and some other features added in (imported from WMLScript).

The XHTML MP 1.2 OMA standard has recommended using ESMP, but we will just use standard JavaScript code, as clean as possible, and it will work everywhere.

VBScript is a similar language (created by Microsoft, based on Visual Basic), but it is compatible only with Internet Explorer for desktop. VBScript is not compatible with any version of Internet Explorer for mobile devices.

There are many versions of JavaScript available (at the time of this writing, from 1.0 to 1.8). The most stable version for all browsers (from low-end devices to social phones) is 1.5, and this is the version we should care most about. Newer versions only work in the latest editions of some browsers, and the additions aren't worth the incompatibility. JavaScript developers often aren't aware of different languages' versions, so we will talk about feature compatibility here instead of comparing version numbers.

Some modern browsers support ECMAScript 5, including the strict mode, such as Safari on iOS since 5.0, the Android browser since 3.0, Chrome, and the BlackBerry browser since 7.0.

A number of other scripting languages have appeared in the last years to replace or enhance JavaScript, such as Dart, CoffeeScript, and Type-Script. While no mobile browsers currently support them, you can find compilers that will cross-compile these new languages to standard JavaScript code.

# Coding for Mobile Browsers

When we talk about mobile JavaScript, we are talking about the same code you already know: a `script` tag including some code or a `script` tag with an external source:

```
<script>
// Code goes here
</script>

<script src="mysource.js"></script>
```

ECMAScript Mobile Profile defines two new types for the `script` tag, `application/ecmascript` and `text/ecmascript`, as the preferred types to use for ESMP-compatible code. Beyond that, `text/java script` is the recommendation for XHTML MP documents and is the most compatible type to use for non-MP browsers. My recommendation is to carry on using the well-known `text/javascript`.

## HTML5 Script Extensions

HTML5 includes new attributes to the `script` element that may improve performance on compatible devices. The `script` elements used to block the parallel download of any other resource, and that harms performance. While there are hacks and tricks to load a script asynchronously, HTML5 includes the `async` Boolean attribute that defines that the execution should be done asynchronously without blocking other downloads.

 The `async` and `defer` attributes work in Safari on iOS since 5.0, the Android browser since 3.0, the BlackBerry browser since 7.0, and Internet Explorer since 10, as well as Firefox and Google Chrome. IE9 supports only `defer`.

If we want to defer the execution of the script until the whole document has been parsed, we can use the `defer` Boolean attribute. Both `defer` and `async` work only if we are loading external JavaScript files using `src`.

## Code Execution

You can execute JavaScript code in four different ways:

- From a `script` tag
- From an event handler
- From a link, using the *javascript:* URL protocol
- From a bookmarklet, using the *javascript:* URL protocol

---

### Bookmarklets

A *bookmarklet* is a bookmark in the browser containing some JavaScript code using the *javascript:* URL protocol. When the user activates the bookmark, the JavaScript code is executed over the current document. This allows us to execute a wide range of testing, debugging, and other features over any web page.

There are bookmarklets on the Web that are large applications, encoded in a single line of JavaScript. One of my favorites for desktop usage is Readability (*http://bit.ly/WpPQIe*).

The main problem with bookmarklets in mobile devices is how to add them. In the desktop web, the main way is to drag a link with the JavaScript code to the bookmarks area. This cannot be done in a mobile device, though, so bookmarklets are only useful if you can manage or synchronize them from a desktop (via iTunes for iPhone).

---

There are a lot of bookmarklets for iPhone on the Web, including some that will show the source code of the page inside the mobile browser. These are only really useful for testing or debugging purposes, though, or for "only for geeks" features. Mobile Perf is a bookmarklet created by Steve Souders that will help us with tools to measure and work with performance; you can install it on your browser by following the instructions at Steve Souders' website (*http://stevesouders.com/mobileperf/*).

# Cloud-Based Browsers

We need to pay special attention to cloud-based browsers, like Opera Mini and the Nokia Xpress browser. Remember that these browsers render our websites on their servers and send compressed and compiled content to the clients. Some of these clients aren't really browsers capable of rendering an HTML file or JavaScript code on the device itself. Therefore, all the code that executes before and during the loading process is executed on the server before it sends the rendered result to the browser. Any code executed later, such as because of a click event, will send a request to the server, which will instantiate the web state, execute the code, and send back the changes.

 Some cloud-based browsers execute every line of JavaScript server-side; therefore, we should keep dynamic updates to the minimum, as all of this code will require a server postback.

Some other cloud-based browsers, such as Amazon Silk, execute our JavaScript partially on the server side and partially on the client side, using a nonpublic algorithm that is advertised as making smart decisions to increase the browsing speed.

 For older mobile browsers that do not support JavaScript, or browsers with JavaScript disabled, we can use the noscript tag. Only those browsers will display its content.

### Nokia Mobile Web Library

As we'll see in Chapter 16, when we are working with the Nokia Xpress browser and developing cloud-based Nokia S40 web apps, we have a limited series of functions that we can call that will be executed on the client side, without a server postback. We can make these calls using the Nokia Mobile Web Library (MWL), a JavaScript framework that exposes functions in the mwl global object.

If we call mwl functions directly inside events, these functions will be executed on the client side. Any other calls will be sent to the server. Available functions include show() and hide() for changing an element's display properties, addClass() and remove Class(), and timer() to initiate a time-based operation. For example:

```
<input type="button" onclick="mwl.hide('#content1');
        mwl.show('#content2')" value="Show content 2">
```

For a complete reference of MWL, check out *http://mobilexweb.com/go/mwl*.

# JavaScript Debugging and Profiling

Debugging and profiling JavaScript for mobile browsers and mobile web apps can be a little more complicated than we are used to. Doing the process on the device itself usually is not a good idea, as on-device tools are just not good enough.

In Chapter 18, we are going to look at all the tools available for remote debugging and profiling sessions on many platforms, as well as other hacks for the purpose.

# Battery Consumption

You may be used to working with milliseconds and/or bytes in terms of performance and measures. Do you believe me if I say that now we need to add the unit *joules* to our calculations? Joules is a measure of energy consumption—it reminds us that our JavaScript code will consume battery power. And we know that a low battery is one of the biggest problems for every mobile user.

A team from Stanford University, working in conjunction with Deutsche Telekom R&D Laboratories, has published a study on how much battery power mobile web browsing consumes; it's called "Who Killed My Battery: Analyzing Mobile Browser Energy Consumption" (*http://mobilexweb.com/go/battery*).

While the abstract has lots of useful information, I want to summarize a few key points here:

- Unused, orphan JavaScript code can consume battery power for nothing.
- Not providing a mobile-specific website and viewport means more power consumption, as the browser needs to calculate resizing actions and download big resources.
- Parsing a big JavaScript framework, such as jQuery, may consume around 0.01% of a fully charged battery on some devices.

So, keep your JavaScript code to the minimum—and that includes using frameworks (such as jQuery) only when you really need to, and not just because you're used to it.

# Background Execution

When we see a mobile browser on a smartphone or a tablet, our first thought is that it works in a similar way to a desktop browser. However, browser behavior can be really different, and these differences impact our code's lifetime.

Because of concerns about battery usage and general UI performance, most mobile operating systems, even on tablets, freeze all applications running in the background. Another important difference is that usually closing and minimizing are the same operation. Therefore, from a user's perspective, if she goes to a different app or to the Home screen, the browser (and all the open websites) will be frozen. That means no JavaScript code will be executed in the background. While some exceptions apply, this the expected behavior in most mobile browsers.

A similar situation applies when the phone is in sleep mode, or when the browser is still in the foreground but the user has switched to a different tab or window. Usually, the tabs or windows that are not in the foreground are not being executed and may not be in memory at all.

Safari on iOS, Firefox, the Android browser, and some other browsers freeze all JavaScript code when the user changes tabs/windows, locks the phone, or minimizes the browser. Opera freezes our code when the user locks the phone or minimizes the browser, but it maintains execution if the user switches to a different tab.

On the other hand, Google Chrome for Android keeps our website alive while the browser is still in memory, but if we are using timers the frequency slows down to one second.

 On most platforms, we can only be sure that our JavaScript code will be alive when the browser is in the foreground and our website is in the current tab or window. Typical desktop behavior that uses Ajax calls or similar techniques to update content frequently while in the background will not work in most phone and tablet browsers.

The possible situations that can change a page's visibility status and affect the execution of our code are:

- The browser is in the foreground and our website is in the active window or tab. In this situation, our JavaScript is being executed.
- The browser is in the foreground and our website is not in the active window or tab. However, it is still in memory, usually in a frozen state (no code is being executed). The code will continue its execution from the point at which it was frozen if the user reactivates the window or tab.

- The browser is in the foreground, but our website is not in the active window or tab and is not in memory. This may be because the browser needed memory for other websites, or because the window or tab was opened in a previous browser session. The JavaScript context will be lost in this situation, and when the user reactivates the window or tab our website will be reloaded and will start from scratch.

- The browser is in the foreground, but the device is asleep.

- The browser is in the background and our website is still in memory, usually frozen without any execution possibilities. If the user goes back or opens the browser again, the session will be restored.

- The browser is in the app history (so to the user it appears to still be open), but it has been removed from memory by the operating system, which needed the memory for other purposes. If the user goes back or opens the browser again, it will start from scratch and will reload previous tabs or windows and their contexts.

- The browser is in the background, and it's compatible with background JavaScript execution; in this situation, our code is still being executed.

 At the time of this writing, the only mobile operating system that supports having two apps in the foreground at the same time is Windows 8 for tablets, when using the snap mode (described in Chapter 11). Android devices can have background or service apps, but browsers don't usually fall into this category.

## Status Detection

On most devices, timers (and all JavaScript execution) are paused when the web page is sent to the background. I have an iPod touch, and in Safari I always have my email open in one of the eight possible tabs (or windows). When I want to browse to another website, I change to another tab but leave that one open. That means my email can be frozen for several hours or even days, until I go back to that tab. As developers, this raises an important issue: when our web pages are put into the background, how can we detect when they should "wake up" again?

### The Page Visibility API

The only standard way to capture events indicating when our website is being activated or deactivated is the Page Visibility API (*http://www.w3.org/TR/page-visibility*). With this API we can check the document.hidden property to see whether the document is actually hidden (true) or visible (false). It also exposes the new event visibility change that we can use to detect changes in visibility.

The Page Visibility API also exposes a document.visibilityState property that will give us a value of hidden, visible, prerender, or unloaded.

The Page Visibility API is not available in every browser. At the time of this writing, it is prefixed in some browsers, such as Google Chrome, Firefox (before 18), and Internet Explorer 10. In these browsers, the document.hidden property can be accessed through document.webkitHidden, document.mozHidden, or document.msHidden, and the event name is webkitvisibilitychange, mozvisibilitychange, or msvisibilitychange. Safari on iOS (6.0) doesn't support this API at the time of this writing. Currently, only Opera Mobile since 12.1 and Firefox since 18 support the standard, unprefixed version.

 Don't confuse the Page Visibility API with the pageshow and page hide events available in some browsers on the window object. These events have nothing to do with the visibility of our website; they are equivalent to load and unload but with more control when the page is retrieved from the local cache.

When we detect that our website is not active anymore, we can:

- Store state to be restored on the next load, if the browser or website is deleted from memory.
- Stop timers and animations.
- Pause a game.
- Release big resources that could potentially get our website kicked out of memory.
- Stop server calls.
- Log out the user from the server.
- Close sockets or other server connections.

Remember that when we detect that the website is not on the screen anymore, we should not update the UI, such as showing a dialog. We can send Ajax requests to the server without any problem, though, to inform it that the user is leaving the page for now.

The following code snippet illustrates use of the Page Visibility API:

```
var eventName = "";

if (document.webkitHidden!=undefined) {
    // webkit prefix detected
    eventName = "webkitvisibilitychange";
} else if (document.mozHidden!=undefined) {
    // moz prefix detected
```

```
        eventName = "mozvisibilitychange";
    } else if (document.msHidden!=undefined) {
        // ms prefix detected
        eventName = "msvisibilitychange";
    } else if (document.hidden!=undefined) {
        // standard prefix detected
        eventName = "visibilitychange";
    } else {
        // API not available
    }

    function visibilityChanged() {
        if (document.hidden || document.mozHidden || document.msHidden ||
            document.webkitHidden) {
            // Our website has just hidden
        } else  {
            // Our website is back in the foreground
            // In some situations, the website will load from scratch
        }
    }
    document.addEventListener(eventName, visibilityChanged, false);
```

### Wakeup detection using timers

If the Page Visibility API is not available, such as in Safari on iOS up to version 6.0, we cannot detect when the user is hiding our website. However, we can detect when the user goes back to the website.

Neil Thomas, a software engineer from Google working in the Gmail for Mobile team, has published a very simple and clever solution using a high-frequency timer and a global variable for calculating the time elapsed between calls to that timer. Because the timer will not fire when the application is in the background, if we detect that the delta time from the last execution is greater than a certain threshold value we can assume that the timer firing again indicates that the application has just woken up from hibernation.

 Remember to use a large value for the threshold after deciding that the page has gone to sleep. Otherwise, depending on the tasks being done, the engine behind the browser, and the device hardware, it may take longer for the JavaScript code that's executing to complete than the time defined for the timer.

This is Thomas's public code (with a little variation from me). An explanation can be found at *www.mobilexweb.com/go/timers*:

```
// The time, in ms, that must be "missed" before we
// assume the app has been put to sleep.
var THRESHOLD = 10000;
```

```
var lastTick_;
var detectWakeFromSleep_ = function() {
  var now = new Date().getTime();
  var delta = now - this.lastTick_;
  if (delta > THRESHOLD) {
    // The app probably just woke up after being asleep.
    notifyWakeFromSleep(delta/1000);
  }
  lastTick_ = now;
};
```

In the `notifyWakeFromSleep()` method, you can decide what to do based on the received parameter telling you how many seconds have passed since the last active state. You may want to do different things if the delta time is 10 seconds or 1 day (86,400 seconds). For example, after a big delta you might want to show a warning or a loading animation while new results are fetched using Ajax.

 There is one situation where we won't have the opportunity to wake up. If the device is running out of memory and our page is in the background, it is possible that the browser will delete the page state to release memory, and when the user comes back to it, our page will be loaded by URL as a new session.

Remember that after waking from sleep, the document and the script are in the same state (including their HTML content and JavaScript variables) as they were before going to sleep, unless the operating system or the browser has decided to remove it completely from memory, in which case the website will load from scratch.

## Background Tab Notification Trick

While it can be an annoying behavior from a user's perspective when the page is active, an old HTML mechanism allows us to define a meta tag to reload a window automatically every *n* seconds. Some browsers, such as Safari on iOS, allow us to use this hack to automatically reload inactive tabs and keep them updated:

```
<!-- Updates the page every 1 minute -->
<meta http-equiv="refresh" content="60">
```

 In Chapter 15, we will cover the Web Notifications API, which allows us to send a background notification to the user on compatible devices.

On iPad devices, we can use the `title` element to update the UI and capture the user's attention. This behavior is useful on tablets, as they usually show a tab UI, while on smartphones the titles of any windows that are not in the foreground are hidden from the user's view.

With this technique, the page will reload on the iPad and the inline scripts and the onload event will be executed in the background tab. We can change document.title to send information to the user via the tab's title. No other event or timer will be executed after the onload event until the user goes back to activate the tab.

The problem is how to remove the behavior when the page is in the active tab, so the user doesn't get the reload effect while our website is in the foreground. Every time we set the content attribute dynamically in the meta tag, the browser starts counting again.

To make the trick work on the iPad, we can start a chronometer that will shift the refresh meta tag *n* seconds on every execution. While the page is still active, our chronometer will be executed and the reload action will be shifted every *n* seconds. When the page goes onto a background tab, the chronometer will not be fired and the refresh meta tag will trigger, refreshing the page:

```
<!-- Updates the page every 1 minute -->
<meta http-equiv="refresh" content="60" id="metarefresh">

<script>
// iPad background tab notification trick
var mr = document.getElementById("refresh");
setInterval(function() {
    mr.content=mr.content;  // Shift the reload operation
}, parseInt(mr.content)/2); // Every 30 seconds in our example
</script>
```

## Background Execution Compatibility

Table 12-1 shows how mobile browsers react to background JavaScript code in different scenarios.

*Table 12-1. Background execution behavior in non-cloud-based browsers*

| Browser/platform | When device is locked | When tab/ window is not active | When browser is in background | Supports Page Visibility API |
|---|---|---|---|---|
| Safari on iOS | Paused | Paused | Paused | No up to 6.0 |
| Android browser | Paused | Paused | Paused | Yes from 4.0 |
| Chrome for Android | Executing | Executing | Executing | Yes |
| Nokia Browser for Symbian | Paused | Paused | Paused | No |
| Nokia Browser for MeeGo | Paused | Paused | Paused | No |
| BlackBerry browser for smartphones | Paused | Executing | Paused | No |

| Browser/platform | When device is locked | When tab/ window is not active | When browser is in background | Supports Page Visibility API |
|---|---|---|---|---|
| BlackBerry browser for PlayBook and BB10 | Paused | Executing | Paused | Yes |
| Internet Explorer | Paused | Paused | Paused | Yes from 10 |
| Opera Mobile | Paused | Executing | Paused | Yes |
| Firefox | Paused | Paused | Paused | Yes |

## Push Notifications

Most mobile platforms—including iOS, Android, BlackBerry, and Windows Phone—support push notification services for native installed apps. This kind of service is usually the way to alert the user of some update while the app is in the background or closed.

On iOS the notification can include a badge number, a sound reproduction, and/or a message alert to display; on Android, it includes a message; on BlackBerry it can include an icon change; and on Windows and Windows Phone it can include a message, a badge number, and a live tile update.

Websites can't use push notification services at the time of this writing, but we can definitely use this technique when creating native web apps, such as Apache Cordova/ PhoneGap apps. This behavior is outside the scope of HTML5 and needs to be created in native code, per platform. The technique usually involves the following steps:

1. Get the user's authorization to be notified using native code.

2. Receive a hash authorization string.

3. Send the hash to our own web server and store it mapped to the current user.

4. When we need to send a notification, we create an HTTP/S request to a push notification server with the hash string and the notification details.

5. The notification server sends the notification to the device directly (or the device pulls notifications frequently from the server).

There are some multiplatform solutions that will help us to send notifications to all our users with one simple API, such as Urban Airship (http://urbanairship.com).

# Supported Technologies

We are going to test JavaScript compatibility in the following pages, but you should be aware that making JavaScript work requires more than just support for the language. There are many technologies (or APIs) that are bundled with JavaScript, but they are optional and will not work on all devices.

## The Document Object Model

The DOM is a set of conventions for manipulating, browsing, and editing XML and HTML documents using a set of API conventions that may be implemented in many languages. In fact, although many developers think that the DOM is a JavaScript thing, this is wrong. There are DOM APIs for PHP, .NET, Java, and many other languages.

Even if you've never heard about the DOM, odds are good that you've used it. If you've used the well-known `document.getElementById()` function, for example, you were using the DOM.

Today, the DOM is a W3C specification with several versions available. The most compatible versions for web use are the Level 3 specifications.

With the DOM, we can browse the HTML document structure and make changes and additions dynamically from JavaScript without refreshing the page.

A basic mobile browser can be JavaScript-compatible but without DOM functionality. There are also some browsers that allow us to browse the document tree but not to modify it on the fly, such as older BlackBerry browsers.

Devices shipping from 2010 usually don't have any problem with DOM management.

## The Selectors API

The Selectors API (*http://www.w3.org/TR/selectors-api/*) is an extension to the DOM that allows us to use CSS selectors to retrieve an element result list from the DOM, *à la* jQuery. This mechanism is very popular when using the jQuery JavaScript library, and the API is included natively as part of most modern mobile browsers.

A query is made using `document.querySelector(selector)` for unique results, or `document.querySelectorAll(selector)` for many possible return values. For example:

```
var items = document.querySelectorAll("ul.menu > li");
var option =
    document.querySelector('#form1 input[type="radio"]:checked');
```

## JSON

JavaScript Object Notation (best known as JSON) is a lightweight data interchange format known to be compatible with almost every language in common use. It is sometimes used in JavaScript as a replacement for other transport formats, like XML.

JSON can be used in Ajax requests or to store and load information on the client side. ECMAScript 5 includes a native JSON object that is also included in other older browsers. This object allows us to convert standard objects, arrays, and JavaScript variables to a string JSON format using `JSON.stringify()` and to convert JSON string files to objects again using `JSON.parse()`.

Most modern smartphone and tablet browsers support this object directly, and for older devices we can use a JavaScript polyfill (*https://github.com/douglascrockford/JSON-js*).

## Binary Data

Because of the need for binary data in WebGL—the 3D canvas—modern browsers include a way to manage binary data efficiently, known as *typed arrays*. Even non-WebGL browsers, such as Safari on iOS, support these type extensions. The list of possible types includes `DataView`, `ArrayBuffer`, `Float32Array`, `Int32Array`, and `Uint8Array`. Typed arrays work pretty much the same as normal JavaScript arrays, but their execution is much faster.

We can use these new data types with the Canvas, WebGL, XHR2, Workers, Sockets, and File API, as we will see later in this book.

## Web Workers

Web Workers (*http://www.w3.org/TR/workers*) is a W3C specification that allows JavaScript to create working threads instead of executing all the code in the main UI thread, shared with the browser's rendering engine.

The specification defines two kinds of workers: *workers* and *shared workers*. Creating a worker allows a script to create an isolated thread that can communicate bidirectionally with the opener script and it has its own isolated context. A shared worker can be accessed by different scripts in the same domain that are working in different contexts, such as different tabs, windows, or iframes. Using the idea of ports, the shared worker can communicate with different executing scripts at the same time.

 Shared workers have no real usage in mobile browsers because as we have seen, usually only one window or tab is active and running. Therefore, the need for shared workers is low, although they may sometimes be useful if we are using scripts in iframes.

Mobile browsers vary in terms of worker compatibility, and not every mobile browser supports shared workers.

 We can verify current Web Workers compatibility with mobile browsers at *mobilehtml5.org*; with Modernizr, we can also query on the standard `webworkers` property and the `sharedworkers` and `blobworkers` extension properties.

Workers are not available in the Android browser up to 4.1, Internet Explorer up to 9, and Opera up to 10. Support was incorporated in Safari on iOS from 4.0, Internet Explorer from 10, Opera from 11, and the BlackBerry browser from 7, and workers are available in Google Chrome, the BB10 browser, and Firefox as well.

A worker is always an external JavaScript file that will be executed in an isolated thread, and that means the worker can't access any DOM object, such as `document`, or UI feature, such as `alert`. A worker is especially important for performance purposes to avoid blocking the UI on long calculations and operations, such as a long parsing process. While a worker can't access the DOM, it can send and receive information to/from the main thread though a Messaging API.

To create a worker, we just instantiate it:

```
var worker = new Worker('workercode.js');
```

To enable bidirectional communication, we use the `message` event and the `postMessage()` function:

```
worker.onmessage = function(event) {
    // event.data has the information sent by the worker
}
worker.postMessage(dataToWorker);
```

The message can be a basic data type such as a string or a number, an array, or an object containing other serializable data types. We can't pass native objects, such as `document` or `window`, through the communication channel. Objects being transferred are copied and not shared, so your object will be duplicated on the other side.

 Using an object with JSON syntax, we can create our own communication protocol between the main thread and the worker using different properties to define what we need.

Some browsers support a nonstandard feature that allows us to send and receive shared binary data using a prefixed alternate version of `postMessage()`, such as `webkitPostMessage()` on Google Chrome.

The worker is an external file that has a special `self` object referring to the worker itself. It uses the same Messaging API, including `onmessage` and `postMessage()`, to communicate with the main thread:

```
// workercode.js
self.onmessage = function(event) {
    // event.data has the information sent by the main thread
}
self.postMessage(dataToMainThread);
```

With a hack, some browsers allow the execution of a worker using a data URI or a blob element (binary data of a script) that can be created dynamically from a string file. Therefore, we can avoid the usage of an external file; however, this hack is not safe for mobile browsers today.

 A worker can load external files using the `importScripts()` function and it can be terminated at any time using the `terminate()` method.

# HTML5 APIs

With HTML5, JavaScript supports some new APIs for client scripting and document work. Mobile browsers are already adopting some of these new APIs, even though all the standards are still in discussion. We have already covered some of these APIs, such as Canvas, and in the next chapter we will focus on many others.

## Native Web App APIs

There are other extensions available for native web applications on some devices, and many other JavaScript APIs are supported in installed applications.

These JavaScript APIs can include support for:

- Messaging
- Address book management
- Gallery
- Camera
- Calendar
- Device status information
- Native menus

# Standard JavaScript Behavior

As you move into JavaScript on the mobile web, you'll want to test compatibility and use some old-fashioned features.

Even on JavaScript-compatible devices, a script might not work because of the user's (or company's) profile. For example, older BlackBerry devices have the option to disallow JavaScript from the browser or from the company policies. You should always present a non-JavaScript version of your site's functionality.

## Standard Dialogs

JavaScriptsupports a list of standard dialogs that are undervalued in modern desktop websites, often being replaced by Dynamic HTML or UI libraries. They make great standard dialogs for use in mobile websites, though, as shown in Figure 12-1.

The list of available dialogs is:

- `alert`, for showing a message
- `confirm`, for receiving a Boolean response from the user
- `prompt`, for receiving a string from the user
- `print`, for sending the web page to the printer
- `find`, for invoking the find feature of the browser

The `find` dialog isn't really part of the standard, but it works in almost every non-IE desktop web browser on the market. This dialog receives three optional parameters: the text to find, a case-sensitive Boolean, and a backward Boolean. In general, it should be avoided in mobile browsers. Most of them don't even have a search feature.

The `print` dialog works only in recent versions of Safari on iOS supporting wireless printing, but the `alert`, `confirm`, and `prompt` dialogs are compatible with almost every JavaScript-enabled mobile device. I encourage you to use them when needed. Using a standard dialog will always be quicker, simpler, nicer, and more compatible than using any other solution for the same task.

The `prompt` standard dialog is not compatible with Internet Explorer 9 and 10 for Windows Phone, or with IE10 in Windows 8 Metro mode.

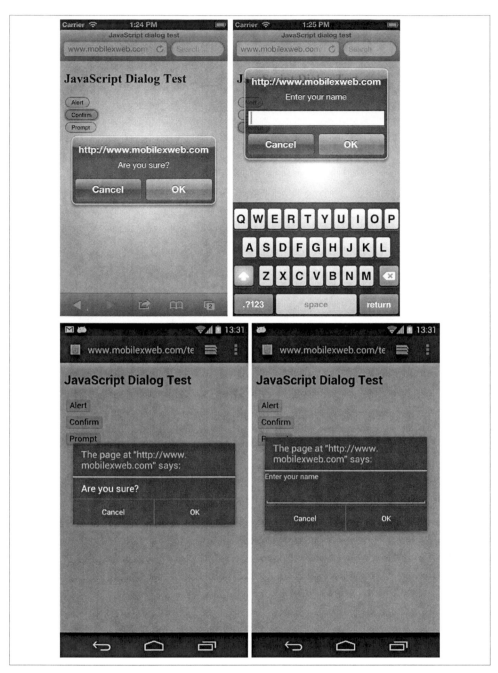

*Figure 12-1. With standard JavaScript dialogs you get rich, multiplatform interfaces for free, using UI controls from the operating system.*

Common problems with the `alert` dialog (and the others) include the usage of the carriage return for multiline text, and how to display text that's too big to fit in the available space. For the first problem, it is common in desktop JavaScript to use the \n (newline) escaped special character. (There are other special escape characters, too, like \t for tabulation.) Let's see what happens with both problems in mobile browsers. Figure 12-2 shows the use of a scrolling area that supports long text.

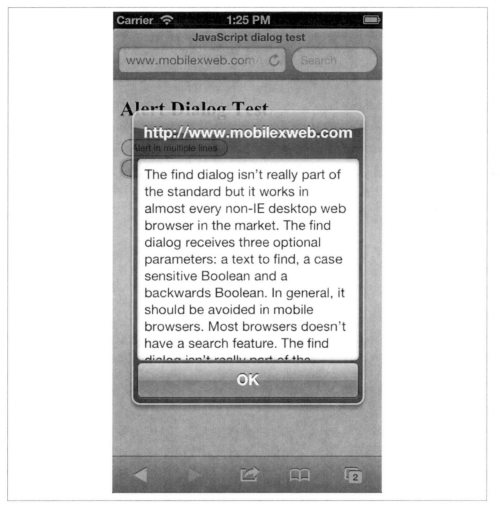

*Figure 12-2. In some browsers, big alerts have scroll bars (or can be scrolled with a finger, on touch devices).*

For usability reasons, if a device has a numeric keyboard, it is best to use a normal text input with numeric capabilities, rather than a selection list. Remember that a numeric keyboard is useful for numeric entries.

# History and URL Management

JavaScript has a few standard mechanisms for browser history management: the `loca tion` and `history` objects. The `location` object has several properties regarding the address, like `href` for the whole URL and `hash` for the anchor part of the URL, if present (the # and everything to the right of it). Changing the `location.href` property will redirect the browser to another page, on compatible devices. It has two useful methods: `reload()`, which refreshes the same page, and `replace(url)`, which sends the user to another page without creating a new history entry.

The `history` object has a few not-very-useful properties and three methods: `back()`, `go(number)`, and `forward()`. The `back()` method is the most commonly used, for emulating a back button:

```
<!-- As a button -->
<input type="button" onclick="history.back()" value="Back" />
<!-- As a link -->
<a href="javascript:history.back()">Back</a>
```

Remember that we are designing for mobile browsers, and sometimes the users will be browsing in full-screen mode without any browser buttons in sight. A link or button for going back will be more useful here than in desktop websites.

## History API extensions

HTML5 has added new abilities to the `history` object that let us replace an existing entry or add a new entry in the history without affecting the page load process. While not a good idea, we can even create nonexistent URLs with this technique (it's not a good idea because if the user bookmarks or reloads the page, the URL will be invalid).

The new methods are `history.pushState(data, title, url)` and `history.replaceS tate(data, title, url)`. *data* is any object we want to store within the current state, and current data can be accessed through `history.state`. In these browsers, once we have pushed a fake URL into the history, we can detect when the user goes back using the `popstate` event of the `window` object.

 `pushState()` does not use the hash (# sign) to change the URL; it will just create a fake complete URL in the history and in the URL bar.

### The hashchange event

HTML5 also adds the `hashchange` event that we can bind to the `window` object: this event is triggered every time the hash part of the URL (after the # sign) is changed. So, we can use `location.href` to add a hash keyword after the current URL and then detect when the user goes forward and backward using `hashchange`.

# Manipulating Windows

One of the most popular (and annoying) features of JavaScript in its early days was the usage of `window.open` to open the classic pop-up windows. For mobile browsers, the usage of this technique is not ideal, for many reasons. Many browsers can't open multiple windows (although Figure 12-3 shows one that can in action), and we cannot define any attributes for the pop-ups; they will just be full-sized, like the main window. Communication between the opener and the pop-up also often does not work well. Finally, closing pop-ups can be problematic on browsers that treat the new window as a normal page and not a pop-up, because `window.close` works only on pop-ups.

*Figure 12-3. The Android browser is one of the few capable of opening pop-ups with a subwindow design; however, this ability was removed in Android 3.x.*

So, if you can, avoid using pop-ups. If you really need one for some reason, open the window after an `onclick` event (avoid opening windows in the `onload` event or inside a timer callback) and remember that some mid-range and low-end devices will not show your window and will just replace current HTML with the pop-up destination.

 The HTML specification from WHATWG (*http://whatwg.org/C*) includes the definition of a `dialog` element that can be used with an API to open modal pop-ups and customized dialogs. While we may see this element implemented in the future, today it is not included in the mobile browser world.

Some browsers will completely ignore a call to `window.close`, while some others, such as Safari on iOS, will close the current window and take the user back to the windows list (on iPhone or iPod devices).

 A better alternative is to use a link with `target="_blank"`. This will have the same result on mobile devices as a `window.open` call, and it will work in every browser. If the browser doesn't support multiple windows, it will just replace the current one.

## Focus and Scroll Management

You can set the focus to a clickable element (such as a form input, link, or button) using the `focus` function of every DOM element. The most helpful usage is for form input controls. The behavior varies in different mobile browsers. On some touch devices, focusing in a text box should automatically open the onscreen keyboard, and in some cursor-based browsers it will position the cursor over the element.

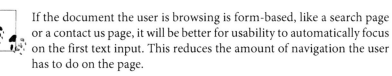 If the document the user is browsing is form-based, like a search page or a contact us page, it will be better for usability to automatically focus on the first text input. This reduces the amount of navigation the user has to do on the page.

On some devices, the global `window` object has a `scrollTo()` function that takes two parameters, `xPosition` and `yPosition`, specifying the position at the top-left corner of the screen to scroll to. On some devices (like the iPhone), using `scrollTo()` emulates the user's scrolling and hides the browser's toolbars, as if the user were scrolling with her fingers. So, for some browsers it is common to use the following code, which automatically hides the toolbars after the `onload` event:

```
window.scrollTo(0, 1);
```

This function can also be used to generate links to the top of the page, on compatible devices:

```
<a href="javascript:window.scrollTo(0, 1);">Go to Top</a>
```

This same behavior can also be applied without JavaScript, using anchors. We have already covered this technique and other similar hacks in Chapter 7.

## Timers

JavaScript offers three kinds of timers: the well-known `setTimeout()` and `setInterval()`, and a new HTML5 timer, `requestAnimationFrame()`. The first one is executed once and the second one is executed every *n* milliseconds until it is cancelled using `clearInterval()`. The latest is not yet supported in every browser, and it's optimized for animations and games.

You can use timers for updating information from the server using Ajax every *n* seconds, for creating an animation, or for controlling the timeout of an operation.

 In mobile browsers, you need to be especially careful about using timers because of the battery consumption. If you need to use many high-frequency timers at the same time, try to manage them using only one timer that will launch different behaviors from the same process.

The first question we need to ask ourselves is, what happens when our web page goes to the background because the user switches focus to another application (in multitasking operating systems) or opens or browses to another tab or window? Another problem is what happens when the phone goes to sleep (because of the user's inactivity while the script is executing). The behavior of timers can be a little tricky in these situations.

Yet another problem is that timers execute on the same thread as the main script. If our script is taking too much processor time (a normal situation with large scripts on low-end and mid-range devices), our timers will be delayed until some spare execution time is found.

If we use a low frequency for the timer (for example, 10 milliseconds), the timer will generally have problems meeting the timetable.

 Remember that the JavaScript execution time depends a lot on the device hardware and the browser's engine. Even if two devices are running the same operating system, like Android, execution times can differ based on the device's processor.

Let's look at a simple example and see what happens normally:

```html
<!DOCTYPE html>
<html>
<head>
<meta charset="UTF-8" />
<title>Using Timers</title>
</head>

<body>

<script type="text/javascript">
var timer = setInterval(timerHit, 200);
var q = 0;
var lastTime = new Date().getTime();

function timerHit() {
    q++;
    var deltaTime = new Date().getTime() - lastTime;
    document.getElementById("content").innerHTML += q + ": " +
        deltaTime + "<br />";
    lastTime = new Date().getTime();

    // Generate some random delay
    var randomNumber = Math.floor(Math.random()*1000)+5000;
    for (var i=0; i<randomNumber; i++) {
        var a = new Array();
    }

    // We will run only 15 experiments
    if (q==15) {
        clearInterval(timer);
    }
}
</script>

<div id="content">
</div>

</body>
</html>
```

The real times are very different on different devices. On low-end and mid-range devices, if they work at all, the result is far from our 200 ms intention—some low-end devices don't even accept timers with a frequency of less than 1 second.

Remember that only a couple of browsers, such as Chrome for Android, maintain execution—including timers—when the device is locked, the tab is in the background, or the browser is minimized. Chrome will reduce the frequency of execution up to 1,000 ms when the page is not in the foreground.

The Gmail for Mobile team discovered some issues with timer behavior on mobile Safari and Android devices, and made the results public in the team blog (*http://www.mobilexweb.com/go/timers*). The conclusions are: for low-frequency timers (1 second or more), there are no performance issues, and you can add as many as you want; for high-frequency timers (for example, 100 ms), though, every new timer created makes the UI more sluggish. The preferred solution is to use only one high-frequency timer.

## Animation timing

Timing control (*http://www.w3.org/TR/animation-timing/*) for script-based animations, also known as animation timing or as the function name `requestAnimation Frame()`, is a W3C draft specification that allows us to use an animation-optimized timer instead of `setTimeout()`.

When using this technique, we don't specify the frequency interval; instead, the browser will determine the best time to update the animation regarding the current scenario. Therefore, the browser specifies the frame rate, and it will pause the animation if it believes the animation should be paused (such as in a background operation).

The standard API is simple: we have a global `window.requestAnimationFrame()` function that receives only the function to execute and returns an ID that we can store, to use with `cancelAnimationFrame()` as we would with `clearTimeout()`. If we want the animation to continue to a next frame we must call `requestAnimationFrame()` in the animation function; therefore, there is no easy way to use this technique with anonymous inline functions.

`requestAnimationFrame()` works similarly to `setTimeout()`, not se tInterval(), as it doesn't execute many times automatically.

To start an animation frame, we can use code like this:

```
var animationId = requestAnimationFrame(animate);

function animate() {
    // animate
    if (!endAnimation) {
        requestAnimationFrame(animate);
    }
}
```

And to stop the animation:

```
cancelAnimationFrame(animationId);
```

At the time of this writing, Internet Explorer 10 is the only browser supporting this API without any prefix. Firefox supports it with a `moz` prefix and Safari from version 6.0, BlackBerry from version 10, the webOS browser for the TouchPad, and Chrome for Android support it using a `webkit` prefix.

On WebKit-based browsers, `requestAnimationFrame()` accepts a second optional argument: a DOM element that is the one that visually bounds the animation.

If we want to encapsulate all the prefixed versions (and we are sure everyone is using the same syntax), we can use the following code:

```
(function() {
  var requestAnimationFrame = window.requestAnimationFrame ||
                              window.mozRequestAnimationFrame ||
                              window.webkitRequestAnimationFrame ||
                              window.msRequestAnimationFrame;
  window.requestAnimationFrame = requestAnimationFrame;
})();
```

Paul Irish (*http://paulirish.com*) has created a nice polyfill so we can use the Animation Timing API on every browser, even falling back to `setInterval()` in noncompatible browsers. It's available at GitHub (*https://gist.github.com/1579671*).

## Changing the Title

In desktop web applications, it is common to change the title dynamically to alert the users of a change in the page, when updates are made in an Ajax application, or simply as an animation (please, don't do this!).

In mobile browsers, this isn't such a good idea, for the following reasons:

- Many browsers don't even display the title.
- If the user is working with many tabs at the same time, dynamically changing the title won't be useful because your web page will be frozen when it is in the background on most browsers.
- Animations in the title can be annoying in a mobile browser.

## Cookie Management

Cookies are a great solution for the problem of statelessness in HTTP. They work in all devices and browsers. This is good. The bad thing is that the lifetime of a cookie can be shorter in the mobile ecosystem than in the desktop world, especially in low-end and mid-range devices because of the lack of memory storage.

It is recommended to maintain cookies' values at below 2 KB for the best compatibility in mobile devices. Be careful when using these server-based techniques in native web apps, where there is no HTTP protocol in the main HTML and script files.

Cookies are normally stored and read by the server, but JavaScript also allows us to read and write them as a client-side storage mechanism.

# Event Handling

One of the most frequently used features of JavaScript is event handling, whether we define it inside the HTML document or by using code. Let's see how mobile browsers work with this way to execute script code.

### Managing events

We can define event handling in scripts using the following methods:

- Using HTML attributes, like `onclick="alert('sample')"`
- Using the JavaScript object property, `element.onclick = function() {}`
- Using the DOM `addEventListener()` method

 Before version 9, Internet Explorer used the `attachEvent` property of the element instead of the DOM `addEventListener()` method.

### Load and unload events

The famous `load` event is available for any HTML element, but it is best used in the body element (the `document` JavaScript object). We'll test compatibility in different types of elements here.

The `unload` event is less famous. In theory it should work for every element, but again the most useful usage is applied to the body element (`document` object) to detect when the user is navigating away from our document.

In modern browsers, the `unload` event does not work as we might want (I remember many battles against the `unload` event when a new pop-up was opened every time I closed one), and it has been replaced by the nonstandard `beforeunload`. The `beforeunload` event is useful for alerting the user about unfinished work so he doesn't lose any changes he's made on the page before going back or browsing to another URL. To do this, it is generally used with a confirm dialog. Unfortunately, `beforeunload` is not so compatible with mobile browsers, so we should store information frequently instead of relying on a confirmation dialog on the beforeunload event.

### Click events

The click event is the most-used event on the Web. In mobile sites, we have to test it to see where it can best be used. We know that there are focus-based, touch-based, and cursor-based browsers. The last ones are the simplest for click events: every time the user moves the cursor arrow and then presses Fire or any other similar key, a click event is generated. In focus-based browsers, it is recommended to use the click event only in clickable elements, such as links or buttons, because the focus may not be active on other elements (such as div, p, or li elements).

For touch devices, the behavior is simple, too: every touch (finger- or stylus-based) is transferred as a click over the screen.

 If the user is using a finger to touch the screen, you need to be aware that the click coordinates can change during the touch (depending on how the user presses the screen), and the precision will not be good. Use big areas as clickable ones. Also, for touch devices we can use touch or pointer events, as we will see in Chapter 15.

**Double tap.** In Chapter 15, we will discuss touch and pointer events, but for now, let's talk about how to emulate a double-click action.

On touch devices, if you want to detect a double-tap gesture, you shouldn't use the nonstandard ondblclick event; in most cases it will not work and it will also fire an onclick. The best solution (also compatible with nontouch devices) is to implement a tap–double tap detection pattern using the following code sample:

```
var doubletapDeltaTime_ = 700;
var doubletap1Function_ = null;
var doubletap2Function_ = null;
var doubletapTimer = null;

function tap(singleTapFunc, doubleTapFunc) {
    if (doubletapTimer==null) {
        // First tap, we wait X ms to the second tap
        doubletapTimer_ = setTimeout(doubletapTimeout_,
            doubletapDeltaTime_);
        doubletap1Function_ = singleTapFunc;
        doubletap2Function_ = doubleTapFunc;
    } else {
        // Second tap
        clearTimeout(doubletapTimer);
        doubletapTimer_ = null;
        doubletap2Function_();
```

```
        }
    }

    function doubletapTimeout() {
        // Wait for second tap timeout
        doubletap1Function_();
        doubleTapTimer_ = null;
    }
```

We can use the previous library like this:

```
<img src="bigbutton.png" onclick="tap(tapOnce, tapTwice)" />
```

supposing tapOnce and tapTwice are two previously declared global functions.

 In general, in a nonclickable element no events will be generated, while in clickable elements events are fired in the order onmouseover, onmousedown, onmouseup, onclick.

Alternatively, we can use it from JavaScript as follows:

```
element.onclick = function() {
    tap(
        function() {
            // This is the code for the first tap
        },
        function() {
            // This is the code for the second tap
        }
    );
}
```

Remember that implementing touch-and-hold (or long press) handling can cause problems in some touch browsers because the browser is already capturing this event for contextual menus. You can apply it only in text blocks with user-select disabled. We may also have problems with the double tap if we have zoom enabled, as the browser may treat it as a zoom in/out action.

### Focusable and form events

Support for the focus, blur, change, and submit (only for forms) events in different mobile browsers is good enough to use them without any worries.

### Over events

The over events include mouseover and mouseout and are typically used for creating a hover effect when the cursor is over an element. Usage of these events in mobile websites is discouraged for must-have features, because they will only work in cursor-based browsers. Touch and focus devices don't have an "over" state; it should be replaced by an active state or a focus one for focus-based browsers.

 Safari on iOS also supports the mousewheel event when the user is scrolling the element using two fingers at the same time.

### Resizing, scrolling, and orientation change events

When the user activates scrolling over the document, some browsers fire the scroll event from the document as a whole. The main problem is that when the scroll has momentum the event is being fired only when the scroll momentum ends, and not continuously, as in desktop browsers. You can find out more about this problem and some workarounds at TJ Vantoll's website (*http://bit.ly/ZCsXyP*).

Some browsers also support the onresize event, which fires when the window size is changed. Users cannot resize mobile browser windows in the way they can resize desktop application windows, but a resize can be generated if the orientation of the device changes from portrait to landscape or vice versa.

Most mobile browsers support the orientationchange window event and the orientation property of the window global object. This property has a value of 0 in portrait mode, 90 in landscape mode, and −90 in inverse landscape mode. Tablets also support the 180 value for inverse portrait mode, which is not possible on phones. We can use this value to make changes in the DOM, or use a body class pattern:

```
if (window.onorientationchange) {
  window.addEventListener("orientationchange", function() {
    var orientation = window.orientation;
    switch(orientation) {
      case 0:     // Portrait
          break;
      case 90:    // Landscape to the left
          break;
      case -90:   // Landscape to the right
          break;
      case 180:   // Up side down portrait
          break;
    }
  }, false);
}
```

If the device doesn't support the orientationchange event, we can query on resize. That is, we can detect the change using the following code:

```
if (window.onorientationchange==undefined) {
  window.addEventListener("resize", function() {
```

```
            if (screen.width>screen.height) {
                // Landscape
            } else {
                // Portrait
        }, false);
    }
```

## Key events

Key events—keypress, keyup, and keydown—allow us to detect keypresses over the whole page (body) or in one element (generally, a text input). On compatible mobile devices, this can be useful for many situations:

- To provide keyboard shortcuts
- To provide navigation or movement in a game or application
- To enable form submission on Enter or another keypress
- To disallow some characters in a text input

If we are going to prevent a key from being used, we should be very careful. Remember that devices can have very different keyboards. Some devices have only virtual keyboards, some numeric, and some QWERTY, and key code management across platforms can be a little tricky.

 If the device has a QWERTY keyboard we can also detect some modifier keys (if they exist), like Ctrl, Alt, or Shift, using the event properties.

A simple test for getting key codes can be created using the following code:

```
<script type="text/javascript">
window.addEventListener("keyup", function(event) {
    // charCode depends on modifiers (such as shift); keyCode does not
    var code = event.keyCode ? event.keyCode : event.charCode;
    alert("code: " + code + " - ASCII value:
        " + String.fromCharCode(code));
}, false);
</script>
```

**Useful keys for some devices.**  In Safari on iOS, while the focus is inside a text input with the keyboard visible onscreen, we can capture every key pressed using only keyCodes. Table 12-2 shows some important codes.

*Table 12-2. Useful keyCodes in Safari*

| Key | keyCode |
| --- | --- |
| Backspace/Del | 127 |
| Enter | 10 |
| Space | 32 |

There are Android and webOS (Palm) devices with physical keyboards, and others without them. The possible special key values for all these devices are shown in Table 12-3.

*Table 12-3. Useful keyCodes in Android and webOS*

| Key | keyCode |
| --- | --- |
| Backspace/Del | 8 |
| Enter | 13 |
| Space | 32 |

> Remember that most touch devices don't have a physical keyboard, and there is no way to open the virtual keyboard whenever we want; it is only opened when some typing-enabled element is in focus, such as a text input or an editable element. Some devices allow the usage of an external keyboard, but the ability to read those keys without an editable element varies per browser.

The Nokia N97 has a full QWERTY keyboard, but the letters don't provide the correct ASCII values unless the user presses the Shift key at the same time. For example, the H and I keys provide the same keyCode (56) but different charCodes. The default Unicode values for the charCodes are the numeric or symbol values of the keys (typically used with the Sym key). If the user is using the onscreen keyboard (only available as a pop-up window when a form has focus), every character typed is delivered (regardless of whether it was entered on the numeric keyboard, by touch recognition, or by predictive text). Table 12-4 shows the common codes.

*Table 12-4. Useful keyCodes and charCodes for Symbian touch devices*

| Key | keyCode | charCode |
| --- | --- | --- |
| Backspace | 8 | 8 |
| Enter | 13 | 13 |
| Space | 32 | 32 |
| Up | 38 | 63497 |
| Down | 40 | 63498 |
| Left | 37 | 63495 |
| Right | 39 | 63496 |
| Fire | N/A | 63557 |

 Even if we can capture keypresses, remember that special keys (Menu, Call, End, Volume) are generally out of our scope as web developers. We cannot detect those keys.

Older Symbian 3rd edition devices (including the Nokia N95, E61, and so on) are non-touch devices with numeric keypads. The few keys we can capture on such devices are shown in Table 12-5.

*Table 12-5. Useful keyCodes and charCodes for Symbian 3rd edition devices*

| Key | keyCode | charCode |
| --- | --- | --- |
| Clear | 8 | 8 |
| Send | N/A | 63586 |
| Cursor and Fire | N/A | N/A |

### Preventing default behavior

For almost every event, we can prevent the default behavior by using the `event.pre ventDefault()` method or capturing the event and returning `false`. This is commonly done with the `submit` event, to cancel the submission when something doesn't validate, or to cancel a link. For example:

```
<a href="news.html" onclick="news();return false">Go to news</a>
```

The preceding code is a standard link to *news.html*, but if JavaScript is supported we can capture the `click` event, call a local function (that can get the news by Ajax), and cancel the normal behavior of the link by returning `false`. This avoids a page load and reduces network traffic.

We can also prevent a key from being used by cancelling the `keyup` event. This feature must be used very, very carefully, and only on tested devices.

# JavaScript Libraries

The life of a JavaScript programmer has changed radically since 2006, with the appearance of Ajax and hundreds of libraries that help us work better with this language. Many of these libraries modify existing behaviors or add completely new behaviors to the language, effectively creating new languages inside (or over) JavaScript.

If the libraries are based on JavaScript, and mobile browsers support JavaScript, why do we care? The answer is that many of these libraries rely on some not-so-clear things in the standard, and while they have been prepared and tested on well-known desktop browsers (Internet Explorer, Firefox, Safari, Chrome, Opera), they have not been tested on all the mobile browsers.

That is the first reason why we need to be careful about using big JavaScript libraries. The second (no less important) reason is the impact on download and execution times, as well as battery consumption. As mentioned earlier, these libraries modify the language and the behavior of standard objects, and even if we don't use any (or very little) of a library's code, the library will need to load itself completely, which takes time. This can lead to performance problems in some browsers, so we are going to test the time that typical libraries take to initialize themselves on mobile browsers.

 Some libraries, in their uncompressed form, are larger than 600 KB. We need to be very careful about performance when using that code, as it will increase network traffic, memory consumption, and execution time. If you can, avoid those big libraries, or use only the code you need.

My first advice is that you should avoid these libraries if you can. If you cannot avoid them, use them only for smartphones, and be aware that some features and plug-ins may not work properly. Look for a way to download only the part of the library that you really need to use; some libraries, such as jQuery Mobile, offer a download builder that creates a customized package for your needs.

When we analyze framework or library usage, we need to understand that the first big problem is just loading and parsing the JavaScript file, even if we are not using it yet. To parse the jQuery core file the browser needs to get and parse around 100 KB of JavaScript code, even if we won't be using it for a while. Downloading and parsing big files can harm your website's performance and use up battery power, so use them with care and only when you really need them.

Just to give you an idea, on some old BlackBerry 4.x devices, the browser needs 8 seconds just to parse the jQuery core file, during which time it shows a "loading" screen and no user interaction with the website is possible.

If you use jQuery just because you don't want to type `document.getE` `lementById()` or `document.querySelector()`, go now and remove all jQuery references in your mobile websites.

## Vanilla JS

Vanilla JS (*http://vanilla-js.com*) is a fast, lightweight, cross-platform framework for building incredible, powerful JavaScript applications. You can create your own modules, including support for animations, regular expressions, closures, array libraries, the DOM, Ajax, and much more. Go now and check out the website: on the site you can compare its performance with jQuery, Prototype, Dojo, and MooTools and see how much faster it is.

Really, go. I'll wait here.

If you've just gotten back from checking out the website, maybe you have already realized that this is an ironic library. Vanilla JS doesn't exist, because it's just plain JavaScript, available by default in every browser! The moral of this story is that you don't need a library for a lot of things, and if you avoid using them your users will be much happier.

## Mobile Libraries

Sometimes libraries are useful, though, and the good news is that many developers have released alternative libraries that are geared for mobile devices and are lighter than the classic ones. There are also full UI frameworks for mobile application development (mostly prepared for iPhone and Android devices) that we will cover later, like jQuery Mobile, iUI, iWebKit, and Sencha Touch. These frameworks will take care of the visualization, events, and interaction of our websites.

There are also other libraries that can replace jQuery and the others on mobile devices. They are very light libraries that provide basic DOM, event, and Ajax support.

### Zepto.js

Zepto.js (*http://zeptojs.com*) is a minimized JavaScript library optimized for performance. Its goal is to provide a 5–10 KB modular library that downloads and executes fast, with a jQuery-like syntax. With its inclusion with the HTML5 Mobile Boilerplate (*http://html5boilerplate.com/mobile/*) template, Zepto.js has become the most popular replacement for jQuery in mobile web development.

As a jQuery-based library it uses the same $ query selector and most of the typical jQuery functions, such as the DOM, Ajax, forms, and event methods.

Zepto includes a Touch module prepared for mobile devices that we can use to detect some basic gestures, such as tap, doubleTap, long Tap, and swipe variations.

## baseJS

baseJS (*http://paularmstrongdesigns.com/projects/basejs*) is a lightweight library (8 KB) compatible with Safari on iOS and other WebKit-based browsers. It has only been fully tested on Safari, from iOS 1.0 to 3.0.

baseJS provides a selector similar to jQuery's, $(*selector*), and some similar methods, like each(), addClass(), hasClass(), removeClass(), toggleClass(), getXY(), fire(), and some Ajax methods.

## jQMobi

jQMobi (*http://www.jqmobi.com*) is a query selector library optimized for mobile devices that takes 5 KB of JavaScript code using a jQuery syntax. Based on Zepto and jQuery, this library focuses on ways to reduce the API to its most useful features and offers a fast version of a similar API. It includes basic DOM and Ajax management through the $ object and chained functions.

## QuoJS

Quo (*http://quojs.tapquo.com*) is a micro JavaScript library (14 KB) optimized for mobile devices that includes DOM, event, and Ajax functionality and a good quantity of touch gesture event handlers, such as pinch out, drag, rotate, hold, swipe, and two-finger tap.

## XUI

XUI (*http://xuijs.com*) is a simple JavaScript framework for building mobile websites that takes up only 4.2 KB compressed. It is available for free and has been fully tested on WebKit-based browsers and Opera Mobile. The developers are working on adding support for IE Mobile and BlackBerry.

XUI is also similar to jQuery, but it is more powerful than baseJS. XUI uses x$ as the main selector object and includes the methods listed in Table 12-6.

*Table 12-6. XUI common methods for a selector query*

| Method | Description |
| --- | --- |
| html(*code*) or html(*location*, *code*) | Defines the inner HTML (or other location, using the second option) of the elements retrieved by the selector query. The *location* is a string and can be one of the following: inner, outer, top, bottom, before, after, or remove. |

| Method | Description |
| --- | --- |
| on(*event*, *function*) | Registers an event listener. The event name can also be used directly as the method name (e.g., click rather than on('click')). The events compatible are: click, load, touchstart, touchmove, touchend, touchcancel, gesturestart, gesturechange, gestureend, and orientationchange. |
| setStyle(*property*, *value*) | Defines a CSS style. |
| getStyle(*property*, *optional_callback*) | Reads the value of a property. If the selector has multiple elements, the callback will be fired. |
| addClass(*class_name*) | Adds a class to the elements. |
| removeClass(*class_name*) | Removes a class from the elements. |
| css(*object*) | Defines CSS styles using a JSON-style object having properties with values. |
| tween(*object*) | Animates one or more CSS properties from one value to another defined in the object. |

So, for example, we can capture an onclick for buttons with a class with the following code:

```
x$('input.button').on('click', function(e){ alert('Ouch!') });
```

or with code like this, chaining the methods *à la* jQuery:

```
x$('input.button').click(function(e){ alert('Ouch!') })
                  .html('Press Me! ').css({color: 'blue'});
```

For Ajax, XUI provides global xhr() and xhrjson() functions to create requests with options.

# UI Frameworks

There are dozens of JavaScript UI libraries for implementing rich controls in desktop websites. The question is: do they work on mobile devices? Usually the answer is no, but even if it's yes it's best to avoid them. They are not usually optimized for touch or focus usage, and the UI will be slow and sluggish.

Many UI libraries have appeared on the market in the past few years to facilitate mobile development. Unfortunately, most of them were designed for specific platforms, but with minor changes or incompatibilities many of them should work on any device.

The browser with the most specific platform is Safari on iOS, followed by the Android browser (and other WebKit-based browsers). Lots of libraries allow us to create rich applications emulating native control behaviors for iOS.

Common iOS-based UI libraries (that also work on Android and may work on other WebKit-based browsers) include:

- iUI (*http://code.google.com/p/iui*)
- jQTouch (*http://jqtouch.com*)

- iWebKit (*http://iwebkit.net*)
- jqUI (*http://www.jqmobi.com*)
- WebApp.Net (*http://webapp-net.com*)
- ciUI (*http://code.google.com/p/ciui-dev*), a C-NET alternative to iUI
- Universal iPhone UI Kit (*http://code.google.com/p/iphone-universal*)

Targeting multiplatform compatibility, we can mention:

- jQuery Mobile (*http://www.jquerymobile.com*), supporting all smartphone and tablet platforms
- Sencha Touch (*http://www.sencha.com/products/touch*), supporting iOS, Android, modern BlackBerry, and Windows Phone 8 platforms
- Lungo (*http://lungo.tapquo.com*), supporting smartphone, tablet, and smart TV platforms

BlackBerry offers the BBUI.js library (*https://github.com/blackberry/bbUI.js*) that gives a native-like UI in web apps for BlackBerry 7, PlayBook, and BB10 automatically. It's optimized for native web apps using the WebWorks packager.

## Sencha Touch

Sencha Touch (*http://www.sencha.com/products/touch*) is a JavaScript-based framework for mobile app development. It has a free commercial license and it is compatible with iOS, Android, BlackBerry 7/10, and Windows Phone 8. It offers a complete multiplatform development environment including the UI, application data management, and binding. The Sencha SDK, from the same company, allows us to make native web apps, compiling the app directly from an IDE.

Sencha Touch includes more than 50 components (see Figure 12-4) and a built-in MVC (Model-View-Controller) system written completely in JavaScript. When using Sencha Touch, our HTML files will consist of just a couple of JavaScript include files and an empty body element. Everything will be instantiated from JavaScript code and rendered by the framework.

A basic "Hello World" application in Sencha Touch will look like this:

```
Ext.application({
    name: 'Sencha Touch Demo',

    launch: function() {
        Ext.create("Ext.tab.Panel", {
            fullscreen: true,
            items: [
                {
                    title: 'Hello World',
```

```
                    iconCls: 'home',
                    html: 'Welcome to Sencha Touch'
                }
            ]
        });
    }
});
```

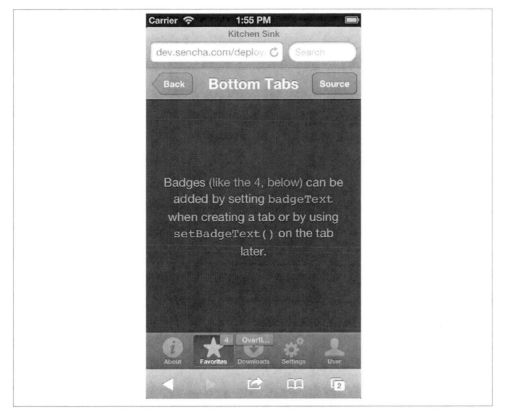

*Figure 12-4. Sencha Touch emulates the native UI in HTML5 browsers using an MVC architecture.*

If you want to learn more about this framework, pick up the book *Sencha Touch 2: Up and Running*, by Adrián Kosmaczewski (O'Reilly).

## jQuery Mobile

jQuery Mobile (*http://jquerymobile.com*) is a cross-platform UI framework optimized for touch smartphones. jQuery Mobile is not a mobile replacement for the jQuery core, like Zepto.js or jQMobi; jQuery Mobile works over jQuery and it manages only the user interface of our web apps.

I've written a whole book about this framework, called *jQuery Mobile: Up and Running* (O'Reilly).

jQuery Mobile is compatible with more than 10 different platforms, including all the modern smartphone and tablet browsers; it's open source and is based on semantic HTML5 markup, so it doesn't require any JavaScript coding.

jQuery Mobile manages a series of rich controls, as well as page navigation and transitions using CSS3 animations. It is compatible with Apache Cordova/PhoneGap apps.

A typical jQuery Mobile document looks like the following code, which we can see rendered in Figure 12-5:

```
<div data-role="page">
  <div data-role="header" data-position="fixed">
    <h1>Hello World</h1>
    <a href="#">Action</a>
  </div>

  <div data-role="content">
    <ul data-role="listview" data-filter="true">
      <li>Option 1
      <li>Option 2
      <li>Option 3
      <li>Option 4
    </ul>
  </div>

  <div data-role="footer" data-position="fixed" data-theme="e">
    <h4>O'Reilly Media</h4>
  </div>
</div>
```

## Enyo

Enyo (*http://enyojs.com*) is a cross-device (desktop, tablet, and phone), cross-platform web app UI framework. The framework originated with the HP Palm team from webOS, but after the open sourcing of that platform (see Chapter 2 for more information) the Enyo effort was converted to a multiplatform solution, including support for iOS, Android, Firefox, Chrome, Windows Phone, BlackBerry, and more.

Enyo is modular and component-based and the basic core is only 25 KB zipped, making it a mobile-optimized framework. It has a range of useful widgets, including image carousels and date pickers, and we can encapsulate our own controls really easily.

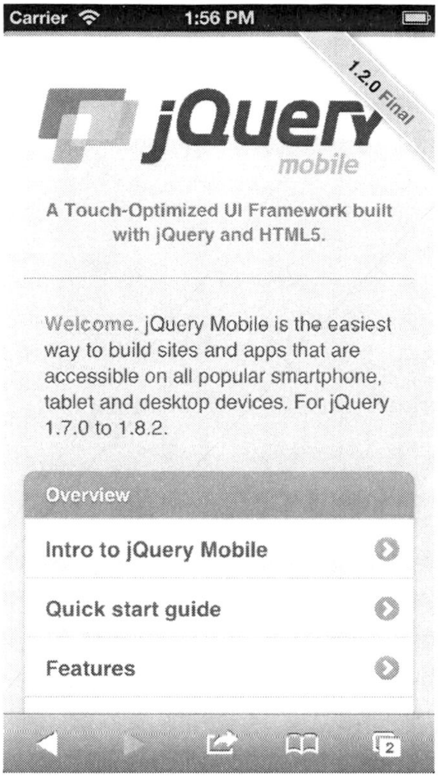

*Figure 12-5. jQuery Mobile offers a touch-optimized UI for almost every platform available on the market, using semantic HTML5 code.*

## Montage

Montage (*http://montagejs.org*) is a complete web app development framework, including a client-side JavaScript library and a server-side Node.js library. One of the big advantages of Montage is the usage of a two-way data binding mechanism using custom HTML5 data, which allows us to simplify the development process and the business logic of our apps. It also includes components and templates, data persistence, and event management.

Montage is an open source project created by Motorola Mobility, now owned by Google. One of the key targets of Montage is Apache Flex (formerly Adobe Flex) developers trying to move into the HTML5 world.

# iUI

iUI was one of the first libraries developed for iPhone-style application development. It was developed by Joe Hewitt (*http://www.joehewitt.com*), author of the popular Firefox plug-in FireBug.

iUI is a very simple-to-use, nonintrusive JavaScript library, including CSS and assets (generally backgrounds) that emulate the native iPhone application controls, animations, and application workflow.

The main features are:

- No JavaScript coding required
- Extends the behavior of standard HTML markup
- Overrides links and forms with Ajax requests
- Updates the page with smooth iPhone transitions with no code

The library uses the master-detail navigation method, copied from the `UITableView` control from Cocoa Touch. `UITableView` is a native iPhone control.

The main structure of an iUI website is just a simple HTML file that includes CSS and JavaScript files and contains a `div` for the top toolbar and one `ul` for each "list page" we want to show:

```html
<!-- Leave this toolbar div with no changes -->
<div class="toolbar">
    <h1 id="pageTitle"></h1>
    <a id="backButton" class="button" href="#"></a>
</div>
<!-- This is the home screen -->
<ul id="home" title="Home Page" selected="true">
    <li><a href="#first">First</a></li>
    <li><a href="#second">Second</a></li>
    <li><a href="#third">Third</a></li>
    <li><a href="ajax.html">Loaded by AJAX</a></li>
    <li><a href="more.html" target="_replace">More...</a></li>
</ul>
<ul id="first" title="Other Screen">
    ... other options ...
</ul>
... other pages
```

iUI uses the child element with `selected="true"` as the home screen when the page loads the first time, and every link with a hash (#) is a link to another screen that loads on the same page and is identified by the ID after the hash, *à la* WML card.

The toolbar is always present and the Back button works automatically, restoring the previous screen's title and using a smooth swipe animation to go back.

---

To reference an external file, we can use a normal link: it will load via Ajax and be inserted below the toolbar. The external file should only have a ul or div element without any other root tag.

We can also implement an in-site pagination design pattern using target="_re place". This will load the href document using Ajax and insert its contents where the li with the replace link is defined. This document should only have lis without any other root element, and it should end with another replace link if there are more elements to paginate.

Other advanced features that iUI supports include:

- Modal dialog pop-ups
- Form designs
- Emulation of native form controls
- Stripped tables
- Right (>) toolbar button

You can find more samples of iUI usage at *www.mobilexweb.com/go/iui*.

# jQTouch

jQTouch is a jQuery plug-in for iPhone web development that produces similar results to iUI, but with more powerful graphics and animations. It is also unobtrusive, but it does require some JavaScript code to initialize the page.

With some visual differences, it also works on the Android and webOS browsers.

The supported features include:

- Native WebKit animations using jQuery methods
- Callback events
- Flexible themes
- Swipe detection
- Extensions: floaty bar, geolocation, offline capability
- Visual controls
- Animations

To use jQTouch we need to first load jQuery 1.3.2 and then the jQTouch script, with two CSS files: the base file (*jqtouch.min.css*) and the visual theme we want to load. For example:

```
<script type="text/javascript" src="http://www.google.com/jsapi">
</script>
<!-- We load jQuery using the Google Ajax API -->
<script type="text/javascript">google.load("jquery", "1.3.2");</script>
<script type="text/javascript" src="jqtouch/jqtouch.min.js"></script>
<style type="text/css" media="screen">
    @import "jqtouch/jqtouch.min.css";
</style>
<style type="text/css" media="screen">
    @import "themes/jqt/theme.min.css";
</style>
```

To initialize the page, we can use:

```
<script type="text/javascript">
$.jQTouch({
    icon: 'iphone-icon.png',
    preloadImages: [
        'themes/jqt/img/chevron_white.png',
        'themes/jqt/img/bg_row_select.gif',
        'themes/jqt/img/back_button_clicked.png',
        'themes/jqt/img/button_clicked.png'
    ]
});
</script>
```

There are dozens of properties we can define at the initialization. You can find a list at *code.google.com/p/jqtouch/w*.

As in iUI, the main markup is done using top-level elements (in this case, divs) with ids and links with hashes for linking in the same document. For example:

```
<div id="home" class="current">
    <div class="toolbar">
        <h1>jQTouch</h1>
        <a class="button slideup" id="infoButton" href="#about">
            About
        </a>
    </div>
    <ul class="rounded">
        <li class="arrow"><a href="#ui">User Interface</a>
            <small class="counter">4</small></li>
        <li class="arrow"><a href="#animations">Animations</a>
            <small class="counter">8</small></li>
        <li class="arrow"><a href="#ajax">Ajax</a>
            <small class="counter">3</small></li>
        <li class="arrow"><a href="#callbacks">Callback Events</a>
            <small class="counter">3</small></li>
        <li class="arrow"><a href="#extensions">Extensions</a>
            <small class="counter">4</small></li>
        <li class="arrow"><a href="#demos">Demos</a>
            <small class="counter">2</small></li>
    </ul>
```

```
    <h2>External Links</h2>
    <ul class="rounded">
        <li class="forward"><a href="http://www.jqtouch.com/"
            target="_blank">Homepage</a></li>
        <li class="forward"><a href="http://www.twitter.com/jqtouch"
            target="_blank">Twitter</a></li>
        <li class="forward"><a
            href="http://code.google.com/p/jqtouch/w/list"
            target="_blank">Google Code</a></li>
    </ul>
</div>
```

# JavaScript Mobile UI Patterns

As we saw in Chapter 5, mobile devices have had to develop alternate paths for handling many common tasks. In this section we'll take a closer look at a few mobile-specific UI patterns.

### Clear text box buttons

In their native UIs, touch devices have added a very nice feature to text boxes: the possibility of clearing all the text by touching a small X at the righthand side of the box (as shown in Figure 12-6). This is especially useful because of the lack of a keyboard on these devices. We can emulate this UI pattern easily by combining an image (or, as we'll see later, a `canvas` tag) and a little JavaScript code.

*Figure 12-6. You can see this pattern implemented in the Yahoo! website for touch devices like the iPhone.*

To implement the clear button, we can use a 20×20-pixel image (great for inline images in compatible devices) with the following CSS style. The image can be shown as a `div` with a background image from the beginning, or only when the user starts typing. It is important to add a right padding to the input box so the X is not overlapped by text:

```css
<style type="text/css">
div.clearx {
    background: transparent url('clearx.png') no-repeat right;
    height: 20px;
    width: 20px;
    margin-top: -26px;
    position: absolute;
    left: 235px;
}
input.clearx {
    padding: 2px 40px 2px 10px;
    width: 200px;
    height: 24px;
}

</style>
```

The HTML should look like this:

```html
<input type="text" id="search" placeholder="Enter your search"
        class="clearx" />
<div class="clearx"
        onclick="document.getElementById('search').value=''"></div>
```

### Autogrowing textareas

This UI pattern was created by the Google Mobile team and is currently used in Gmail. The problem is that if we have a large amount of text in a `textarea`, scrolling inside it is very painful in some browsers (Safari on iOS is one of them). The solution is to grow the `textarea` to fit the contents, so the user can use the normal page scrolling instead of the `textarea`'s.

 All of these JavaScript UI patterns can be created using a nonintrusive, object-oriented approach with a little JavaScript work.

We can capture the `onkeyup` event and grow the `textarea` if necessary. We also need to capture `onchange`, because pasting in iOS doesn't generate an `onkeyup` event.

The complete solution is available at *www.mobilexcode.com/go/autogrowing*. The code, borrowed from the Google Code Blog with a few changes, is:

```
<script>
// Value of the line-height CSS property for the textarea.
```

```
var TEXTAREA_LINE_HEIGHT = 13;

function grow(event) {
    var textarea = event.target;
    var newHeight = textarea.scrollHeight;
    var currentHeight = textarea.clientHeight;
    if (newHeight > currentHeight) {
        textarea.style.height = newHeight + 5 * TEXTAREA_LINE_HEIGHT +
            'px';
    }
}
</script>
<textarea onkeyup="grow(event);" onchange="grow(event);" >
</textarea>
```

 The Google Mobile team is doing a great job with mobile web UI patterns and optimizations, and it releases all the tips to the public in the team blog (*http://googlecode.blogspot.com*).

## Floating bars

Scrolling a large mobile web page just to access a button or a link at the top of the document can be very painful. A floating bar is a great solution for avoiding this problem when `position: fixed` (described in the "Display Properties" on page 404 section in Chapter 11) is not available. A floating bar is just a full toolbar, a drop-down menu, or a mixture of both that always remains at the top (or bottom) of the page when the user scrolls the content.

It is not suitable for focus-based browsers, because there will be usability issues when the user is tabbing between links.

 We need to create a custom floating bar solution only when `position: fixed` is not available. If this feature is available, we should go with it.

For floating bars to work, the browser needs to support the `scroll` event. If the browser supports this event, the toolbar moving can be done automatically, using a smooth animation on some browsers. You can decide whether to have the floating bar appear at the beginning of the navigation or only after scrolling.

The steps to create a floating bar (also known as a *floaty bar*) are:

1. Create a `div` with the content of the floaty bar.
2. Define it as hidden off the screen with negative top values.

3. Define a WebKit transition animation (this will work only on compatible devices).

4. Capture `onscroll`.

5. If the value of `window.scrollY` (the top position of the scroll) is near zero, hide or move the `div` off the screen; if not, move the `div` (changing the `top` value) to the `scrollY` position.

 For Safari on iOS, there is a solution that will have better performance: instead of using a transition animation and changing the `top` value, we can use the `translateY()` function and do a transformation animation. Transformations use hardware implementations for improved performance.

The following code produces a floaty bar with animation for WebKit-based browsers:

```html
<!DOCTYPE html>
<html>
<head>
<meta charset="utf-8">
<title>Mobile Web Test Suite</title>
<style>

    p {
        font-size: xx-large;
    }

    #floaty {
        width: 200px;
        text-align: center;
        border: 2px solid red;
        -webkit-border-radius: 5px;
        background-color: silver;
        right: 0px;
        position: absolute;
        top: -50px;
        -webkit-transition: top 0.2s ease-out;
    }

</style>
<script type="text/javascript">
window.onscroll = function() {
    var floaty = document.getElementById("floaty");
    if (window.scrollY<10) {
        // It is near the top, so we can hide the floaty bar
        floaty.style.top = "-50px";        // out of the screen
    } else {
        floaty.style.top = window.scrollY + "px";
    }
```

```
    }
    </script>

    </head>
    <body>

    <h1>Floaty Bar</h1>
    <div id="floaty">
        This is a floaty bar
    </div>

    <!-- Document goes here -->
    </body>
    </html>
```

### Cascading menus

A cascading menu should be used for large toolbars, typically for touch devices. It can also be used in cursor-based browsers, but remember that in these browsers it may take the user a while to get to the desired zone of the screen using the navigation keys.

As these menus will typically be used on touch devices, we should not use mouseover events to open and close the menu bar, and it is best to use onclick for both the opening and closing actions. We can also hide the menu when the user selects an option, scrolls the page, or moves the focus to another object.

A simple div show/hide interaction with JavaScript will work, or (with care) you can use a JavaScript library for this purpose.

### Autocompletion

An autocomplete (or autosuggest) feature to reduce the user's typing, like the one in Figure 12-7, is a great feature, but it is not as simple to implement in a mobile site as it is in a desktop site. There are two kinds of autocompletes: preloaded and Ajax-based. The preloaded ones involve downloading all the possible values to suggest (not recommended for more than 2,000 values) and storing them in JavaScript variables, and then, if offline storage is available, storing them in the device for future usage.

The first problem is the issue of network latency and bandwidth consumption. If the user is using 2G technologies (GPRS, EDGE), the process of going to the server or preloading all the possible values can be long and costly. The second problem is the UI design, for a few reasons: generating a floating div over other elements can be problematic in many mobile browsers, and browsing between suggestions in nontouch devices can be difficult.

If you are going to use a JavaScript-based autocomplete solution, re-member to deactivate the browser's standard autocomplete feature us-ing autocomplete="off" in the text input.

All that aside, if we can save the users a lot of typing, we will be their heroes.

So, the first conclusion is that this solution is recommended only for touch-enabled smartphones, which we suppose are connected using WiFi or a 3G network. Next, we need to think about the design. The recommendation is not to use a floating div over other content, and instead to use a hidden div that replaces or pushes down the previous content. This div will appear just below the text box, and there must be a close button at the top-right corner.

Another thing to keep in mind for touch devices without QWERTY keyboards is that when the user has the focus in the text box (and our autocomplete feature is working), the virtual keyboard will be on the screen and there will not be much space available. One solution that will ensure that as much space as possible is available for the suggestion list is to scroll the document to the text box position when the user focuses in the text box. This will leave the text input just at the top of the screen, and with the keyboard at the bottom the middle will be open for our suggestion list (as we can see in Figure 12-7).

*Figure 12-7. Google.com autocompletion on an Android device.*

# CHAPTER 13

# Offline Apps, Storage, and Networks

For mobile browsers, HTML5 offers lots of JavaScript APIs that make our web architectures far more powerful than before. In this chapter, we will cover all the offline techniques, storage APIs, and network communication abilities that we have in modern HTML5 browsers.

## Offline Web Apps

HTML5 allows us to create offline-capable web apps using a mechanism known as *application cache*. The concept is very simple. The user first opens the website in normal online mode, and it provides the browser with a package declaration text file called the *manifest file*, which lists all the resources (images, stylesheets, JavaScript, and so on) we want to be stored for offline navigation in the future. The next time the user visits the page, the HTML document is loaded from the cache, as well as all the resources in the manifest.

Our first step is to define what we want. Do we want a full offline application? Do we want some pages or data to be updated from the server every time the application tries to access them? Do we want to have a local data cache and update it whenever online access is available?

The second step is to define the manifest, or the list of files for the browser to download the first time the user accesses our website. This list must include every JavaScript script, stylesheet, image, or other resource that we want to access offline.

Firefox is the only mobile browser that asks the user's permission before storing an application cache (AppCache) package in the local memory. For all the other browsers it's just a transparent action from a user's point of view.

The architecture of our website will be exactly the same as if all the resources had been downloaded from the server. Images, stylesheets, and JavaScript scripts will be loaded, but they will be sourced from the cache instead of the server.

We can use application cache for:

*Performance purposes*
> We can cache our home page and all its resources, resulting in faster load times and reducing the number of requests to the server. Every time the user accesses our URL it will load transparently from the local application cache and not from the network. The Google home page uses this technique on iOS and Android devices.

*Installed apps*
> We can offer the user the option to install our app and add an icon to the Home screen, so it can be launched from there. Installed apps don't require a web server to work. *The Financial Times* web app (*http://app.ft.com*) is a good example of this idea.

*An offline web experience*
> The website will be available even when the user doesn't have an Internet connection—we'll usually rely on other storage APIs for this. The Gmail web app for smartphones is a good example.

## The Manifest File

The package list is delivered through a text file known as a *cache manifest*. This file must have as its first line the literal text CACHE MANIFEST. This line is followed by a list of all the URLs—relative or absolute—of the resources to download to the device. The manifest file must be served as text/cache-manifest and defined as the manifest attribute of the html element:

```
<html manifest="manifest.appcache">
```

The HTML file that is pointing to the manifest, as well as the manifest itself, will be stored locally in the application cache implicitly; we don't need to declare them inside.

 If any file listed in the manifest fails to download while the package is being installed, the entire package is invalidated. That means that if we are defining resources on third-party servers, we will rely on these servers for our apps to be installed.

The initial CACHE MANIFEST line can be followed by a series of relative or absolute URLs that we want to be cached for offline availability. We can comment lines by using a hash (#) at the beginning of the line:

```
CACHE MANIFEST
# This is a comment
ourscript.js
images/logo.gif
images/other_image.jpg
ourstyles.css
```

 While there is no standard definition, the manifest is recommended to use the *.manifest* or *.appcache* extension and must be delivered with the right MIME type: `text/cache-manifest`.

### Reusing the manifest

If more than one HTML page that the user browses points to the same manifest URI, the manifest package will be reused and all the HTML files browsed will be added implicitly to the manifest as "master resources." That is, after a package has been installed, if the user browses to another page that points to the same manifest, all the resources will already be available offline.

## Accessing Online Resources

If our application attempts to access any resource that was not originally defined in the manifest file, the process will fail because the application is sandboxed offline. By default, all the resources are declared in an implicit `CACHE:` section. If we know for sure that we are going to need some information from the Web, we can define it in the manifest file in a special section called `NETWORK:`. (To define a section, we just end the line with a colon.) So, if we want a *countries.json* file to always be delivered from the server, we can change our manifest to:

```
CACHE MANIFEST

# Resources that should be installed on the user's device
CACHE:
ourscript.js
images/logo.gif
images/other_image.jpg
ourstyles.css

# Resources that should always be downloaded from the Web
NETWORK:
countries.json
```

Then, *countries.json* will not be downloaded with the other resources and instead will be accessed online every time the application needs it. If there is no Internet connection, we will not get this file, unless the browser has a cached version (using the typical web cache, not the application cache).

In the network section, we can use wildcards, such as *, or folders; every resource in that folder will be accessible from the Web while we are in an offline operation mode. So, if we want to have an offline application that can access the full Web if the user has a connection, we can just use:

```
NETWORK:
*
```

With this configuration only files listed before the NETWORK: section will be loaded from the offline package; every other resource will be loaded from the Web.

### Fallbacks

Application cache has a mechanism to access external online resources but at the same time provide a fallback to avoid errors if the user is offline: the FALLBACK: group. In this section we provide two URLs, space-separated; the first one can use wildcards while the second one should be a specific URL. For example:

```
FALLBACK:
images/profile.png noconnection.png
```

In this example, when the web app tries to get *images/profile.png*, it will bring it from the server if the user is online and will return *noconnection.png* as a fallback file if the user is offline. The fallback image is stored in the application cache package implicitly.

## Updating the Package

We've said that when the package is installed all the resources—including the main HTML document—will always be loaded from the local storage and not from the Web. Therefore, it's fair to ask: how can we update a resource? What happens if we want to update the theme CSS file, change an image, or add a new page link in the HTML document?

One part of the picture that I omitted earlier is that every time the user opens a cached web app, while the app is always loaded from the local storage, in the background the browser tries to get an updated manifest file from the server.

If there is no Internet connection, nothing happens, and the local version is used. If there is a network connection available, the browser downloads the manifest file from the server and does a byte-by-byte comparison of the new version of the file with the local version from the original web app download. If even one byte has changed, the entire cached manifest is invalidated and every resource is downloaded again, using the new manifest file.

We can force the browser to check for a new manifest file while the application is running, rather than waiting for the next time the app is launched, using `applicationCache.update()`.

Go back to the previous paragraph and read it again. Done? OK, let's take another look at what's happening. If we change the contents of a CSS file but do not change the name of that file, the manifest will be the same, so the downloaded files will not be updated. This is an important point—we need to change the manifest itself for the web app to receive the update.

How should we change the manifest when we make an update to any of the listed resources? The change can involve something as simple as adding a space, changing the resource name (versioning it), or even including a comment line at the start of the manifest file containing a random value or the last-modified date, as in:

```
CACHE MANIFEST
# webapp updated 2013-10-01
```

If we make a single change—for example, the date—the whole manifest will be invalidated and the platform will download all the files again. (Yes, *all* the files—with this API we can't update just one resource.)

 Remember that the resources in the manifest will not be downloaded again until we update the manifest file or invalidate the AppCache.

There's another unpleasant problem that arises when dealing with manifest updates: if there is an update, the platform downloads all the resources in the manifest again, but this download process is done *in the background while the previous files are on the screen*. This means the user will not see the newly downloaded versions of the resources until she reloads the application.

In other words, if we change the manifest, the user must load the page twice to see the new version. As we'll see shortly, we can use events to handle this situation.

## Deleting the Package

How do you remove a package from the application cache? The answer is not so obvious. The only way to do it is to deliver a 404 HTTP code when the browser is downloading the manifest while trying to check for an update. Therefore, if we want to delete a package we need to use Ajax (or some other technique) to communicate to the server that we want the package to be removed on the next reload. The server may physically delete the file, or just store a flag in some sort of server-side storage (such as a session variable) so that on the next manifest request for that user we force a 404 status. After that, we can reload the app or just force an update using applicationCache.update().

 In some browsers, the user can delete the packages from an advanced configuration section, usually called "website data."

## The JavaScript API

There is a global JavaScript object that helps us to know the status of the application cache. The object is applicationCache, and it has a status property that can have one of the values listed in Table 13-1.

*Table 13-1. Status of the applicationCache object*

| Value | Constant | Description |
|-------|----------|-------------|
| 0 | UNCACHED | This is the first load of the page, or no manifest file is available. |
| 1 | IDLE | The cache is idle. |
| 2 | CHECKING | The local manifest file is being checked against the server's manifest file. |
| 3 | DOWNLOADING | The resources are being downloaded. |
| 4 | UPDATEREADY | The cache is ready. |

If the application cache status is 0, our document is loaded from the network; otherwise, it is loaded from the application cache.

We can use constants to ask about the current status. For example:

```
if (window.applicationCache!=undefined) {
    // The API is available
    if (applicationCache.status==applicationCache.UPDATEREADY) {
        // There is an update waiting for reload
    }
}
```

The applicationCache object has the methods update(), which will force an update check, and swapCache(), which will swap from the older cached versions of the resources to the newly downloaded versions (if the object is in the UPDATEREADY state). However, the HTML document and all resources already in memory will not be updated until we do a full page reload (such as with location.reload())

 If your offline application needs to store custom images that are only for one user (for example, pictures of the user's contacts), you can create a manifest file dynamically for each user or, even better, store the images in base64 in offline storage for usage as inline images later.

## Cache events

The `applicationCache` object has events that we can handle to manage every situation. For example, if the user is accessing our website for the first time, we can show a "Downloading app" message while the resources are downloaded so the user will wait, increasing the probability of a complete download.

 We can use the new events `online` and `offline` and the `navigator.on Line` property to detect whether the user has an Internet connection available or not.

The possible events that we can bind to are listed in Table 13-2.

*Table 13-2. Events available for applicationCache*

| Event property | Description |
| --- | --- |
| `checking` | The browser is checking the manifest. |
| `downloading` | The browser has started downloading the resources listed in the manifest. |
| `progress` | A resource has been downloaded (this event is fired for every resource, so we can create a progress bar). The current HTML page and the manifest file count as resources, so this event will be fired $n+2$ times, with $n$ being the number of files in the `CACHE:` and `FALLBACK:` sections. |
| `cached` | The first download process has finished properly. |
| `noupdate` | The cached manifest has been compared with the version on the server, and no update is available. |
| `updateready` | There was an update, and the new resources have been downloaded properly and are waiting for a reload. |
| `error` | There was an error downloading a resource. |
| `obsolete` | When checking for an update it was determined that the manifest is no longer valid, so the web app has been deleted from the storage and will not be available offline the next time the user attempts to use it. |

In a typical situation, we are going to:

- Capture `downloading` so we can show a message to the user and optionally an animated spinner.
- Capture `progress` to make a progress bar.
- Capture `cached` to hide the loading message and tell the user that the app was installed.
- Capture `error` to hide the loading message and tell the user about the situation.
- Capture `updateready` to inform the user that there is an update ready and ask the user if he wants to reload now to access the updated app.

There is no way to polyfill or emulate this API; if a browser does not support application cache it will just ignore the `manifest` attribute and nothing will be downloaded.

We can bind to these events using `addEventListener`. For example:

```
if (window.applicationCache!=undefined) {
   // The API is available

   applicationCache.addEventListener('updateready', function() {

      // There is an update waiting for reload

      if (confirm("There is an update ready. Do you want to load
               it now?")) {

history.reload();
      }

}, false);
}
```

## Compatibility and Limits

Fortunately, application cache compatibility is good in the mobile web, but on some platforms issues do arise that are difficult to debug.

Safari on iOS, the Android browser from 2.1, Google Chrome, Amazon Silk, the Black-Berry browser since 6.0, the Nokia Browser for MeeGo, Opera Mobile, Internet Explorer since 10, and Firefox (Figure 13-1) support application cache. Cloud-based browsers do not support this ability, as they need an Internet connection to parse the website on the cloud.

One of the biggest problems with the specification is the lack of a limit definition. How much space can we allocate for an offline web app? Is there any limit? If so, is it per URL or per domain? Usually, up to 5 MB there are no big issues on any platforms.

Application cache has lots of drawbacks and challenges that developers need to solve. Consequently, a group of well-known companies has created the "Fixing Application Cache" group (*http://www.w3.org/community/fixing-appcache/*) with the aim of defining the future of this API.

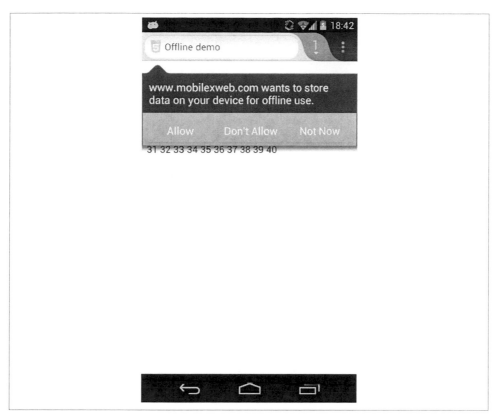

*Figure 13-1. Unlike other mobile browsers, Firefox always asks the user's permission before storing an application cache package.*

Safari on iOS limits have changed with the different versions, as the following list illustrates:

*iOS 3.x*
> 5 MB

*iOS 4.x*
> 5 MB without permission, up to 25 MB with the user's permission. In this version, the permission dialog appears when the download exceeds the 5 MB limit; the browser generates an error event even after the user has granted permission, and only on the next reload will the package be stored.

*iOS 5.x*
> 5 MB without permission, up to 50 MB with the user's permission. From this version, the browser downloads all the files, asks the user for permission if necessary, and, if permission is granted, save the files persistently without any reload needed.

*iOS 6.x*

25 MB without permission, up to 50 MB with the user's permission (as seen in Figure 13-2).

*Figure 13-2. Safari on iOS will ask for permission to store from 25 MB to 50 MB, since version 6.0.*

 AppCache limits are per manifest URI; different HTML pages pointing to the same manifest URI will share resources.

From iOS 5, if you provide files larger than the maximum limit (50 MB on iOS 6), the browser will download every file until the limit is reached and will generate an `error` event after that.

Google Chrome, the Android browser, and Firefox have no predefined limits; the limit is determined by the available space on the device and the amount of time that the user is willing to wait with the page active. In the case of Opera Mobile, the initial limit is 50 MB, and it can be extended with the user's permission.

Be careful: on some platforms (such as Android), when the device goes to sleep or the user minimizes the browser, window, or tab, the download process will be paused. If you want to store large packages, remember that there are no background download processes; the user needs to maintain the HTML page as the active page while the whole package is being downloaded. If not, the download process will be stopped and the whole package will be invalidated. Therefore, be sure to capture application cache events and warn the user to wait until the package is fully installed (signaled by the cached event).

Only Safari on iOS will continue the manifest package download while in sleep mode or when the user changes tabs or windows.

# Client-Side Storage

Working offline is great, but there's a problem: where should a web application store vital statistics and other information when the device is not connected to the Internet? And if the device is not connected to the Internet, how can our applications access helpful databases or information? Client storage solutions come to our assistance, in two flavors: key/value storage and SQL databases (yes, from JavaScript, without server interaction).

Remember that client-side storage mechanisms should be used as temporary and volatile storages, as devices can be restored, lost, stolen, or upgraded. The data should also be stored somewhere else, usually on the cloud (a web server).

Of course, we also have cookies, but they are simpler (only string storage), and we know they are not guaranteed to survive in the browser. However, cookies are the only storage that is shared between the client and the server, through HTTP headers.

## Web Storage

The HTML5 Web Storage API defines two key/value stores through two objects: local Storage and sessionStorage. They are pretty much the same, but the scopes are different: while the local store is used for long-term storage, the session store doesn't persist after the user closes the tab or window.

We should use try/catch blocks when saving items, in case problems occur with the storage or the maximum available space is exceeded.

Both stores are used in the same way:

```
// Save an object or variable in the store
localStorage.setItem("name_in_the_storage", object_to_store);

// Read an object from the store
var object = localStorage.getItem("name_in_the_storage");
```

We can also delete all the objects using clear or delete one key using removeItem. There is also a storage event that we can listen for with window.addEventListener that will be fired when the contents of the local or session stores have changed.

Usually, on mobile devices localStorage is the preferred one as the browser session concept is more ambiguous than on desktops. Remember that from a user's perspective the browser may be opened and minimized, but in practice its session may be closed and out of memory. Therefore, sessionStorage is useful only for caching objects in memory that are volatile.

 If the user is browsing in private or incognito mode, localStorage will not persist values. The only exception is Google Chrome on iOS because of a UIWebView limitation.

Storing information on the device is a synchronous file operation and it takes time, so it will harm performance if you store small items in a loop. Storing a big item once is preferred in terms of performance in some browsers. Just to give an example, it takes Google Chrome four times longer to store 100 elements of 10 KB each than 1 element of 1,000 KB. Version 2.x of the Android browser can take up to 4 seconds to store 1 MB in web storage.

We can only store string values in the local and session stores. However, as we've seen before, we can convert all of the following to string form:

- Any basic JavaScript value, including numbers and Booleans
- Any noncyclic objects or arrays, converting them to JSON
- Images, converting them to data URI format
- JavaScript code to execute using eval()
- CSS styles to be applied in a style element
- HTML parsed code to be injected in the DOM

## Limits

The HTML5 standard has only an arbitrary recommendation of 5 MB per origin (domains and subdomains) that browsers should implement. However, and this is something I've heard from a browser developer firsthand, "All the browsers are just looking at what the others are doing"—and the de facto standard is to maintain a limit of 5 MB per domain to localStorage.

Only Opera Mobile with Presto engine asks for permission to exceed the limit per domain (as shown in Figure 13-3). For other browsers, the user will never receive a confirmation or alert dialog regarding the Web Storage API.

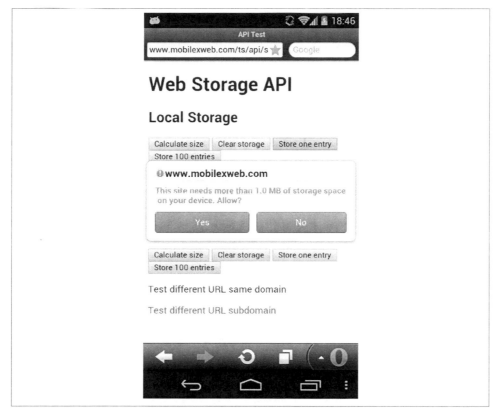

*Figure 13-3. Opera Mobile asks for permission to store more than 1 MB in a sequence of powers of 2 (4 MB, 8 MB, 16 MB, 32 MB, etc.).*

WebKit-based browsers, such as Safari on iOS, Google Chrome, and the BlackBerry browser, support 5 MB per origin (domain or subdomain), per storage (local or session). However, the strings in WebKit are stored in UTF-16 encoding, so each character takes up 2 bytes; this gives us a total of 2.5 MB of UTF-8 text. The Android browser has no limits for session storage, but the WebKit limits apply to local storage.

 The team working on *The Financial Times'* HTML5 web app has released code to compress and decompress strings to take full advantage of the UTF-16 5 MB storage. Using the simple algorithms (*http://mobi lexweb.com/go/ftcompress*), we can store up to 4 MB instead of the 2.5 MB initial limit on WebKit-based browsers.

Table 13-1 shows current limits on the Web Storage API.

*Table 13-3. Web Storage API limits per platform*

| Browser/platform | Initial local storage limit | Session storage limit | Limit can be exceeded |
|---|---|---|---|
| Safari on iOS | 2.5 MB UTF-16 | 2.5 MB UTF-16 | No |
| Android browser | 2.5 MB UTF-16 | No limit | No |
| Chrome for Android | 2.5 MB UTF-16 | 2.5 MB UTF-16 | No |
| Nokia Browser for Symbian | 2.5 MB UTF-16 | 2.5 MB UTF-16 | No |
| Nokia Browser for MeeGo | 2.5 MB UTF-16 | No limit | No |
| BlackBerry browser for smartphones | 2.5 MB UTF-16 | No limit | No |
| BlackBerry browser for PlayBook and BB10 | 12 MB | 12 MB | No |
| Internet Explorer | 5 MB | 5 MB | No |
| Opera Mobile | 1 MB | Shared with local | Yes, with user's permission (Figure 13-3) |
| Firefox | 2 MB | No limits | No |

 Local storage is implemented in the Apache Cordova/PhoneGap library; it replaces the default web view support on some platforms, offering a native storage mechanism.

## The Web SQL Database API

The idea of having a relational database available in JavaScript sounds powerful. The WHATWG team has defined an SQL-based asynchronous API called Web SQL Database that is implemented using the open source SQLite engine. When this API came to the W3C discussion table (*http://www.w3.org/TR/webdatabase*), it was abandoned because it doesn't have any other implementation than SQLite, so it can't be a standard. Therefore, more W3C-friendly vendors, such as Mozilla and Microsoft, have decided to not implement this API and instead to go for the standard alternative, IndexedDB.

While IndexedDB is getting more support as the database standard, there are still big opportunities for Web SQL Database in mobile environments, as Safari on iOS up to version 6.0 does not support IndexedDB. The Web SQL API is implemented in Safari, Chrome, the Android browser, the BlackBerry browser, and Opera Mobile; it's not available in Firefox or Internet Explorer.

Even though IE does not support this API, Apache Cordova/PhoneGap supports it in Windows Phone native web app projects, emulating the feature using an SQL Server engine.

The main method that defines the availability of the SQL database is the `window.open Database()` method, which creates a new database if the *internalName* doesn't exist, or opens it if it does. This method has the following signature:

```
var db = window.openDatabase(internalName, version, displayName,
    sizeExpectable, [callback]);
```

If we use a `try/catch`, we can capture errors during the operation.

 Any script in the same domain can open and edit the same database if it opens it with same *internalName* parameter. The *displayName* is used in some browsers' user interfaces to present a friendlier version of the database name to the user. There is no way to access cross-domain databases.

To execute nonrecordset sentences (`CREATE TABLE`, `INSERT`) we can use a transaction using the `transact()` method, which receives a function as a parameter. As a transaction, if one sentence fails, the others will not execute:

```
db.transact(function(t)) {
    t.executeSql('CREATE TABLE countries (id INTEGER NOT NULL PRIMARY
    KEY AUTOINCREMENT, name TEXT NOT NULL)', [], function() {},
    errorHandler);
});
```

The parameter after the query string is an array of parameters to be replaced in the query (using ? inside), the next parameter is the data handler function (not used in a nonrecordset query), and the last parameter is a function handler for errors in the query.

 There is no way in this API to provide an already created database; all the databases and tables must be created from code and we can't choose where to store them.

To create a typical `SELECT` statement with recordset looping, we can use the following template:

```
db.transact(function(t)) {
    t.executeSql('SELECT * FROM countries', [], countriesHandler,
    errorHandler);
});

function countriesHandler(transaction, data) {
    var record;
    var id;
    var name;
    for (var i=0; i<data.rows.length; i++) {
        // We get the current record
        record = data.rows[i];
        id = record['id'];
        name = record['name'];
        // Do something with record information
    }
}

function errorHandler(transaction, error) {
    alert('Error getting results');
}
```

> The Google Gears project, which predates HTML5, tried to provide similar behaviors, including offline and SQL database support. Gears was compatible with Android 1.x and some BlackBerry devices; it was abandoned by Google in the wake of HTML5.

If you allow working offline you should implement a synchronization method, using Ajax to download changes from and upload them to the server.

## Limits

Apple was the pioneer of the implementation of this API on the iPhone, and today it's still the platform that allows us to have the most control over limits. Safari on iOS supports up to 5 MB per database without requiring the user's permission, and we can extend that limit to 10, 25, or 50 MB if the user accepts it. Other compatible browsers have no specific limits, and usually up to 50 MB there are no problems.

As SQLite uses a binary file, we don't have the problem we had with local storage in terms of UTF-16 usage, and we can store not only strings, but also numbers and binary data.

One of the key problems of the SQL Database API is that there is no way to enumerate or delete a database once it's been created. We can always drop all the tables, but if we've reserved some space, the browser should still save it for the database. The user is in charge of accessing the browser's settings and removing the database.

We define how much space we want to reserve using the fourth parameter of the open Database() method. Therefore, if we want to receive permission for a 45 MB database (45*1,024*1,024 bytes), we can try to open (or create) it and the user will be asked for permission, as we can see in Figure 13-4:

```
var db = window.openDatabase("mydata", "1.0", "My data", 45*1024*1024);
```

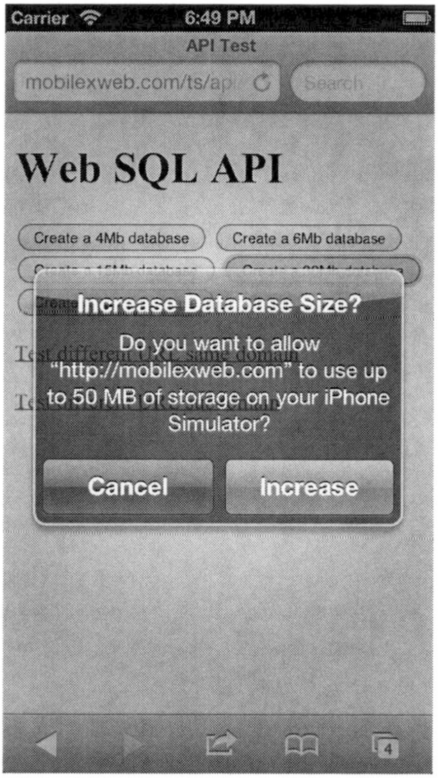

*Figure 13-4. With Safari on iOS we can ask for the user's permission to store large amounts of data (from 5 to 50 MB).*

If we increase the database size automatically, the user may approve the new limit when the current threshold is surpassed, but it's a better idea to pre-reserve all the space we want.

Lawnchair (*http://brian.io/lawnchair/*) is a local client JSON store that uses HTML5 features behind a unique and very simple API. It uses local storage, IndexedDB, Web SQL, the FileSystem API, or other hacks on older platforms.

## The IndexedDB API

The IndexedDB (*http://www.w3.org/TR/IndexedDB*) or IDB API is the W3C standard replacement for the Web SQL Database API. IDB is not yet available in Safari on iOS before version 6.0 or the Android browser prior to version 4.1, but it's implemented in Chrome, Firefox, and Internet Explorer (from version 10), and with time it will probably replace Web SQL on all platforms.

The IDB API allows us to create and query databases, asynchronously or synchronously (useful for web workers). Unfortunately, at first sight the API doesn't look so nice or easy to understand. The interface is a NoSQL (unstructured) database, which can take some getting used to if you're used to working with relational databases.

The basic concepts include a *database repository* having multiple *object stores* (similar to tables) that contain *objects* (similar to records) indexed with a *key* (similar to a primary key). A database, or store, can only be accessed by a same-origin policy, as in the other storage APIs, meaning that we can't access databases cross-domain. IndexedDB provides support for objects to manage indexes, tables, and cursors in a particular transaction. The transaction is the only place where we can execute commands. With IDB there is no way to execute SQL commands.

Using Modernizr we can query about storage API support using the properties `localstorage`, `sessionstorage`, `websqldatabase`, `index eddb`, and `applicationcache`.

While covering the full functionality of IDB is outside the scope of this book, we'll take a quick look at the basics so you can see how to create a database, create an object store, and work with data.

The main functionality happens in the global `indexedDB` object. Some versions of Firefox, the BlackBerry 10 browser, and Chrome up to version 18 use prefixed versions, so to be compatible with previous versions we should check for the prefix first or reassign the global object, as in:

```
window.indexedDB = window.indexedDB || window.webkitIndexedDB || window.mozIndexedDB;
```

Opening a database is done using `indexedDB.open()` and we need to bind events using `on<x>` syntax or `addEventListener`, as in:

```
var dbRequest = indexedDB.open("myDatabase");
var database;
dbRequest.onsuccess = function(event) {
    // The database object appears as event.result
    database = event.result;
}
dbRequest.onerror = function(event) {
    // Manage error
}
```

A big difference between Web SQL and IDB is that when we call the open() method in IDB the database object is not returned. It is available as the result property of the success event parameter.

To create the object stores and schemas we need to implement the upgradeneeded event, which will also be fired when upgrading database versions:

```
dbRequest.onupgradeneeded = function(event) {
    var db = event.target.result;
    // Let's create the object store for books
    var objectStore = db.createObjectStore("books", { keyPath:
      "isbn" });
}
```

To execute commands on an object store we need to use transactions, which receive as parameters a single store name, an array of store names, or an empty array (for all stores) to query on, and the operation type (by default, read-only), as in:

```
var transaction = database.transaction("books", 'readwrite');
transaction.objectStore("books")
            .add({ isbn: "1234567890", name: "Programming the Mobile
                   Web"})
```

To get one element by key from the database, we can use a chained syntax, as in:

```
database.transaction("books")
        .objectStore("books")
        .get("1234567890")
        .onsuccess = function(event) {
            var object = event.target.result;
        });
```

To browse between all objects, we can use a cursor:

```
var allBooks = database.transaction("books").objectStore("books");

allBooks.openCursor().onsuccess = function(event) {
    var cursor = event.target.results;
    if (cursor) {
        var key = cursor.key;
        var currentBook = cursor.value;
        cursor.continue(); // Move to next element and execute
                           // onsuccess again
    } else {
```

```
            // End of object store
        }
    };
```

 Internet Explorer 9 has no support for Web SQL or IndexedDB. Therefore, the only persistent storage is local storage.

# The FileSystem API

The FileSystem API (*http://www.w3.org/TR/file-system-api*), also known as "File API:
Directories and System," is a W3C draft specification—more experimental in terms of
storage compatibility—that allows our domain to have its own full virtual filesystem in
the device memory. We must not confuse this API with the File API (useful to read files
from the user's filesystem), which we will cover in Chapter 15.

With this API we can create and manage folders and files in a virtual filesystem that
may or may not have a corresponding private place in the real device filesystem. Some
browsers may implement it using a database. The API does not allow us to work with
the user's filesystem (private or public); we can only work with the files created by scripts
in our domain.

We can request two kinds of filesystem, PERSISTENT or TEMPORARY, and create our own
structure inside.

To retrieve a persistent filesystem of 4 MB, we can use the following code:

```
window.requestFileSystem(window.PERSISTENT, 4*1024*1024,
function(filesystem) {
    // The filesystem was created/opened

}, function(event) {
    // Handle error
});
```

With this API we can:

- Modify filesystem quotas
- Create and open files
- Append, replace, and delete files
- Create and delete directories
- Copy, rename, and move files and directories
- Read directories' content
- Create filesystem URLs

With this API we also have a new URI, *filesystem:*, that we can use to point from our web app to any file stored in our persistent or temporary storage.

At the time of this writing, only Google Chrome for Android supports this API; check Mobile HTML5 (*http://mobilehtml5.org*) to get updated compatibility information.

 In Chapter 15, we will cover the File API, which can be used in many situations, including with the FileSystem API's files.

## User Intervention

While it may seem that we are in charge of all the storage APIs, the truth is that most modern mobile web browsers allow the user to see and delete a website's data. While the full details are not always given, at least the domain and how much space all the storage APIs are consuming is visible.

In Figure 13-5, we can see Safari's Advanced→Website Data and Google Chrome's Content→"Website settings" screens.

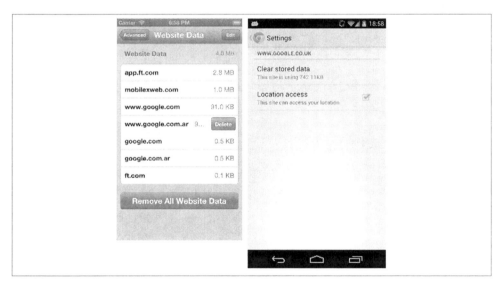

*Figure 13-5. Some mobile browsers allow the user to see and delete website data, including AppCache and storage data.*

## Debugging Storage

Debugging storage (application cache, local storage, databases) can be a little tricky sometimes. We will cover debugging tools in Chapter 18, but for now it's important to know that remote inspection tools, such as the Safari, Chrome, and BlackBerry developer tools, allow us to see all the storage's content and even execute SQL commands on databases, as seen in Figure 13-6.

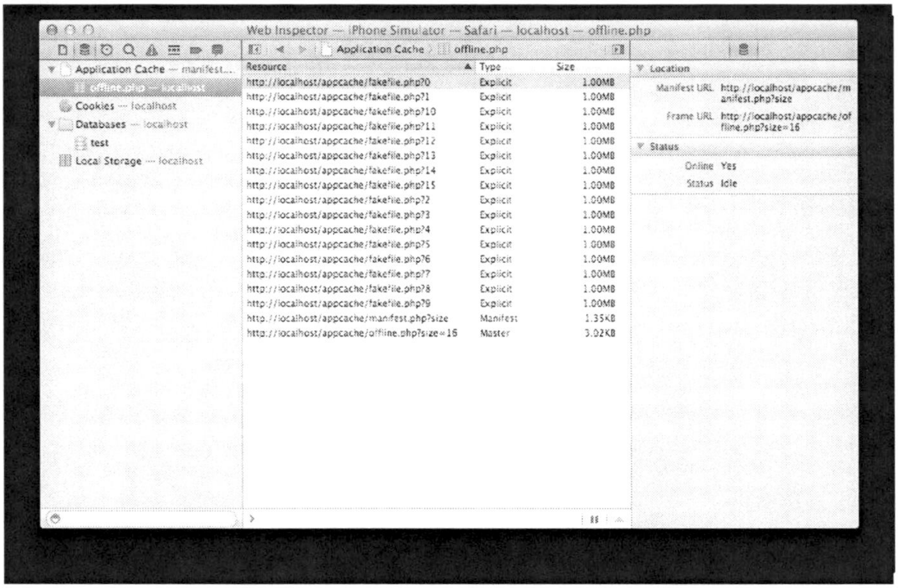

*Figure 13-6. With remote debugging sessions we can check the current storage status for every API covered in this book.*

# Network Communication

Communication between our mobile web apps and a server is usually a must-have feature. Modern mobile browsers have different APIs that will help us with this task, including the well known Ajax and HTML5 APIs.

## Ajax

Ajax, originally an acronym of *Asynchronous JavaScript and XML*, is a technique that involves making asynchronous server requests without refreshing the page, interrupting the user's activity, changing the browser's history, or losing global state variables.

Why did I say "originally an acronym"? Today the term *Ajax* is used in a more general way to define interactive Web 2.0 applications that use asynchronous requests to the server, but may or may not be written in XML. I even hear a lot about Ajax in dynamic websites using the jQuery UI, ExtJS, or other rich control libraries that don't actually make background requests to the server.

The magic behind Ajax is called `XMLHttpRequest`; it is a native JavaScript object available in compatible devices that was based on an ActiveX object created by Microsoft in Internet Explorer 5.0. At the time of this writing, basic Ajax is supported in just about every mobile browser out there. By basic support, I mean `XMLHttpRequest` 1.0 support with the ability to download text (sometimes treated as JSON) and XML.

`XMLHttpRequest` Level 2 (XHR 2, sometimes called Ajax 2) is an extension to the original standard defined by the W3C (*http://www.w3.org/TR/XMLHttpRequest*). With this extension, we can manage a new `load` event instead of managing states in `readystate change`; it also supports the `progress` event as well as the ability to upload and download binary information.

Using XHR 2, a normal Ajax request looks like:

```
var xhr = new XMLHttpRequest();
xhr.open('GET', 'myurl', true);
xhr.onload = function(event) {
    // xhr.responseText includes the server's response as Text
}
xhr.send();
```

XHR 2 also added the `responseType` attribute, allowing us to read the result in different formats. We can set this to `arraybuffer`, `blob`, `document`, or `json`.

Using a Modernizr extension we can detect `XMLHttpRequest` Level 2 and CORS support using the `xhr2` and `cors` properties. We can also verify current compatibility at *www.mobilehtml5.org*.

## Cross-domain requests

While not part of XHR directly, CORS (Cross Origin Resource Sharing) is a way to make Ajax compatible with cross-domain servers. By default, XHR allows calls only to the server on which the resource making the requests resides. With the CORS specification (*http://www.w3.org/TR/cors/*), a cross-domain server can define a couple of headers in the response to allow our or any website to make requests to it using Ajax calls.

If your mobile website gets content using Ajax, you should implement Google's proposal for search engine optimization (SEO). You can find more information about this at *code.google.com/web/ajaxcrawling*.

For example, to allow a script to accept requests from any website, we should deliver the following HTTP header:

```
Access-Control-Allow-Origin: *
```

This is particularly useful to use XHR to call third-party APIs, such as Twitter, Flickr, or Google Maps.

### JSONP

JSON with Padding (JSONP) is a hack for accessing a third-party domain's content without the cross-domain problems of Ajax requests to servers on which CORS is not enabled. Many public web services are offering this new way of communicating with third-party servers.

JSONP uses a script tag generated by JavaScript pointing to a URL with a parameter we define, generally for a local callback function to be called when the script (and the data it fetches) is downloaded and executed.

A very similar technique is used for scripting code: you download only a subset of the scripts in the initial download, and then you download the other scripts that you will need later.

JSONP needs one feature to be working on the browser: the ability to insert a script dynamically from JavaScript. If this feature works, the browser should detect the new DOM `script` element and automatically download and execute this new resource. As this script will call your function with the data, you will be able to receive data from a third-party server.

Modern JavaScript libraries such as jQuery support JSONP requests without dealing with the DOM. You can use `$.getJSON` with a parameter to replace an Ajax query with a JSONP query.

Generally, the third-party server offers some URL to use JSONP as a format. For example:

```
http://api.thirdpartyserver.domain/<jsonp_script>?<callback>=
<our_function>
```

The server will respond with something like this:

```
<our_function>( {<json_data>} );
```

We can test if a mobile browser detects the dynamic creation of `script` elements using the following code:

```
function doJSONP() {
    var head = document.getElementsByTagName('head')[0];
    var script = document.createElement('script');
    script.type = 'text/javascript';
    script.src = 'http://mobilexweb.com/tests/jsonp?cb=finished';
    head.appendChild(script);
}
```

### Ajax with offline resources

Ajax can be used when we are in offline mode in two situations:

- When using web views, such as in Apache Cordova/PhoneGap apps. We can load resources from our application bundle (JSON, text, XML, or binary information) using Ajax, even if there is no web server running.
- When using application cache, if the URL we are trying to get is listed in the manifest file.

## Server Sent Events

Server Sent Events (*http://dev.w3.org/html5/eventsource*) (SSE, also known as *EventSource*) is a network specification draft for enabling web apps to use HTTP for uni-directional real-time communication from the server to the browser. Basically, it's like an Ajax request that doesn't close the connection, so the server can send pieces of information to the client whenever it needs to.

This API aims to replace the long-polling Ajax techniques, sometimes known as Comet techniques, which are not standard and may not work properly on mobile devices.

If for some reason the client or the server closes the connection, the browser starts a polling mechanism, opening the connection again.

At the time of this writing, SSE is compatible with Safari on iOS (since 4.1), Google Chrome, Amazon Silk 2.0, the BlackBerry browser for PlayBook 2.0 and BB10, Nokia Browser for MeeGo, Opera Mobile, and Firefox.

To create an SSE request, we must instantiate an `EventSource` object with the script URL and using a messaging API event mechanism, as follows:

```
var request = new EventSource("/mySSEscript");
request.onopen = function() {
    // An HTTP request has been opened. It can be called more than
    // once if the connection drops
}
request.onerror = function() {
```

```
        // Something went wrong or the connection has been dropped (and
        // it will try to reconnect)
    }
    request.onmessage = function(event) {
        // The server has just sent a message through the connection and
        // it's available in the data property
        var data = event.data;
    }

    // If we want to close the connection later, we call request.close()
```

Every time the server sends a message, we will receive a `message` event handler call. The message data can only be a string.

### The server component

Usually this kind of real-time communication mechanism requires a server-side platform prepared for this kind of work (clients connected for long periods of time), so web servers like Apache or IIS may not be well suited to it. Solutions such as Node.js are much more optimized and prepared. However, SSE can be implemented with any server-side HTTP platform—even PHP, as it's mounted over HTTP.

To answer an SSE request, we must use the MIME type `text/event-stream` and follow the SSE protocol. The basic protocol involves answering with `data: <data>` and a line break. We replace *<data>* with the message we want to send to the client, which will be received in the `message` event. After sending a message, instead of closing the connection, the server should keep waiting in an event loop for new messages to send. Therefore, the server and the client are permanently connected, like a server that is taking a long time to respond and periodically flushing small pieces of information.

Besides the `data:` line, we can also define an `id` that will be used by the client when the connection drops to recover the same session.

In PHP, we can do something like:

```php
<?php
header('Cache-Control: no-cache');
header('Content-Type: text/event-stream');
$end = false;

while (!$end) {
    // Wait for some external event here

    echo 'data: Hello from the server';
    echo '\n\n';   // New line
}
```

```
flush();
?>
```

We are using an $end Boolean variable here that we need to set to true when we want to end the connection. In the meantime, we should wait for something to happen. If you just want a heartbeat, you can use the sleep() PHP function to send messages to the client every *x* seconds. In our example, the message event will receive the Hello from the server data string.

# WebSockets

While SSE is great for real-time apps, it has a big problem: the communication can't be done from the client to the server. WebSockets solve this problem, enabling bidirectional, full-duplex, real-time communication between the browser and a web server.

WebSockets involve two specifications: the WebSocket API (*http://www.w3.org/TR/websockets*), which defines the JavaScript API, and the WebSocket network protocol (*http://tools.ietf.org/html/rfc6455*). Because of their bidirectional nature, WebSockets do not use standard HTTP messages, and therefore a special server is required.

 There are some Apache-based projects to add WebSocket protocol supports, such as Apache WebSocket (*https://github.com/disconnect/apache-websocket*); on the Microsoft side, this protocol was added in Internet Information Server (IIS) version 8 in conjunction with ASP.NET 4.5.

One of the biggest problems of this specification today is that there were many protocol versions during the draft stage, before it was finished by the IETF organization under RFC 6455. Consequently, different browsers may implement different versions. Previous versions of the protocol are known as *hixie-75, hixie-76/hybi-00, hybi-07,* and *hybi-10.*

At the time of this writing, the WebSocket API is available in Safari on iOS (since 4.2), Google Chrome for Android, Amazon Silk (from 2.0), the BlackBerry browser (from 6.1, BB10 and PlayBook included), Internet Explorer (since 10), Opera Mobile (since 12.1), webOS on the HP TouchPad, and Firefox.

 We define WebSocket URLs using the *ws://* protocol definition.

From an API perspective, using WebSockets is easy: we just instantiate a WebSocket object and use the message event and the send() function to receive and send information from/to the server. When we create a WebSocket connection we can optionally define the protocol name as the second argument:

```
var socket = new WebSocket("ws://myserver.com");
socket.onopen = function() {
    // The connection was opened
}
socket.onclose = function() {
    // The connection was closed
}
socket.onmessage = function(event) {
    // We have just received a message from the server
    var message = event.data;
}
// We may send messages
socket.send("Hello server!");
// We can close the connection from the client
socket.close();
```

The WebSocket API is not like low-level socket implementations in other languages, such as C or Java. It supports only string messages, although there is a nonstandard extension supporting binary JavaScript data that works in some browsers.

We need to provide a server solution for our WebSockets. There are frameworks available for almost any server-side language and platform, but remember that WebSockets are more suitable for event-driven platforms that can maintain several connections at the same time instead of closing the connection after the response.

## Socket.IO

Socket.IO (*http://socket.io*) is a powerful open source client- and server-side framework, based on Node.js. Created by Guillermo Rauch (*http://www.devthought.com*), it offers socket abilities using different techniques transparently to the client and server developer, through a very simple but unique API. Socket.IO uses WebSockets but will fall back to other mechanisms based on current browser compatibility, including an invisible Flash socket engine, Ajax, multipart Ajax, forever iframes, or JSONP polling techniques.

Pusher (*http://pusher.com*) is a cloud-based service that allows WebSocket servers to scale easily. It offers a free service supporting up to 20 concurrent connections and 100,000 messages per day, and it also offers commercial services based on the project's needs. It offers a client API and a server API, both communicating with the Pusher infrastructure.

# CHAPTER 14

# Geolocation and Maps

One of the great features of mobile devices is that they can go everywhere with us. That is why the *where* is a very important context to be considered by our websites. Knowing the user's location can help us to show useful contextual information. If I live in London, why should I receive a banner promotion from a shop in New York? Likewise, if I am on holiday in Singapore and I search for "pizza," I would like to receive relevant information about where I can get it.

Location-based services (LBS) are one of the key features of modern mobile web applications. From our mobile websites, we can get the user's location using many techniques. Mapping and LBS are very popular right now, so it is easy to find web services and APIs from different providers that we can integrate into our mobile websites.

## Location Techniques

There are different techniques that we can use to determine the geographical location of a device, based on the platform, the browser, the operator, and so on. Most technologies involve server detection, but others depend on client detection, and we may even rely on the user's input.

### Accuracy

Every location technology has some accuracy error. This is usually specified in a distance metric, like meters or kilometers, but in some techniques accuracy is defined according to levels, such as *city accuracy* or *country accuracy*.

### Indoor Location

When we think about geolocation, we tend to think about the outside location—that is, where on the planet the user is located. Recently, there has been some interest in services that will locate a user inside a building (for example, a shopping mall or an office building). The idea is that we can offer better services for the users inside the building if we can pinpoint what floor they are on or what department they are in. These services may be local services on the Internet, or even services provided on an intranet with the user using a Wireless LAN connection.

---

### Augmented Reality, the Promise

Augmented Reality (AR) is a very popular technology today. It involves the usage of the camera preview with additional information on the screen about the objects and places we are seeing. One of the AR solutions is geographical-based, allowing us to see, for example, the camera preview with a tag over every building and point of interest (POI), with more information displayed about those places.

This solution involves an accelerometer, high-accuracy geolocation (such as GPS), a digital compass, and camera support. Unfortunately, web applications cannot access all of these features on a mobile device today, so we cannot create AR web apps yet; however, it will be possible in the near future.

---

## Client Techniques

Devices support a wide variety of approaches to figuring out where they are. Different approaches may yield different results.

### GPS

The Global Positioning System (GPS) is the first technique most people think of when location detection is mentioned. The United States government created GPS as a system for locating devices, using between 24 and 32 satellites orbiting the Earth. Many mobile devices come with a built-in GPS receiver that can read satellite data to determine location information (data must be received from a minimum of four satellites). In mobile devices, the accuracy error is between 2 m and 100 m. The user needs to have a sky view (outside), and it can take between 5 seconds and 5 minutes to calculate the location.

### A-GPS

Assisted GPS (A-GPS) is a software-based system available for mobile phones connected to carrier networks that can help the devices to determine their locations. The assistance can be in the form of helping the device to find a better satellite signal, or providing less-accurate information about the location of the user until the GPS has connected successfully.

In 2006, I started to use a Nokia N95 with GPS support. In my city, it took 5 minutes to get my location using GPS (with an accuracy error of 10 meters). A firmware update later added A-GPS support to the same hardware, allowing the same device in the same city to connect in 10 seconds, with an initial accuracy error of 100 meters.

### Cell information

Using the operator network's cellular towers, the carrier can triangulate the position of a mobile device. The accuracy will depend on how many cell towers are in range (the more densely populated your location is, the more towers will be in range and the more accurate the reading will be). The carrier knows every cell tower's position, so it can make the required calculations to detect the device's location.

Even knowing which cell tower a device is connected to can provide an idea of its location (near the location of the tower). This might be accurate to within a block, or up to some kilometers in rural areas.

---

## Getting the Cell Location Without the Carrier's Assistance

It is possible to detect a mobile device's position using cell (tower) information without the cooperation of the carrier. OpenCellID (*http://www.opencellid.org*) is an open source project aiming to create a complete database of cell IDs worldwide. If we can get the IDs of every cell in range and calculate the distances to those cells, we can triangulate the device's position.

For example, Google Maps can locate even non-GPS-equipped devices anywhere in the world, thanks to some carrier agreements for cell detection.

---

### WiFi Positioning System

If you have a notebook with WiFi, go to Google Maps (*http://maps.google.com*) and click on the blue circle (the locate me feature). If you are in a large city, you will probably be located very accurately. You were just geolocated, and unless you have a 3G netbook, chances are your notebook doesn't have GPS. This technique also works on a WiFi-connected iPod touch and on tablets. But how?

The WiFi Positioning System (WPS) is a very clever technique that detects your location using the list of wireless routers that are available in your area (even if you are not connected to them). This method relies on a pre-existing database of routers and their geographical locations. Skyhook Wireless (*http://skyhookwireless.com*) is the leading provider, offering developer programs for most mobile and desktop platforms. Google has its own database and is also the provider used by Firefox.

The main problem for us is that as yet there are no mobile browsers that give us the hotspot list.

## Server Techniques

On the server, we can get the HTTP request headers. This is our opportunity to locate the user without using any client technology, such as GPS, and in a way that works even for low-end devices.

### IP address

The main server technique for locating a user is reading the client's IP address. However, this is not as straightforward as it may sound. Depending on the user's connection type (2G, 3G, WiFi), the IP address we receive may be the operator's WAP gateway address, a dynamic IP address in the operator's range, or the IP address of the WiFi connection.

To further complicate our work, we need to bear in mind proxied browsers (discussed in Chapter 2). These browsers use a proxy server to connect to the Internet and to our servers. For example, if the user is browsing using Opera Mini, we will receive the requests from the Opera server instead of from the user's device. Likewise, if the user has a BlackBerry device and is using a corporate Internet connection, we will receive the requests from that connection, which could be based thousands of miles from the user's actual location.

What should we do with the IP address? There are public lists of operators' IP addresses, and there are public and commercial solutions for determining the location of an IP address. The accuracy of this method can be country-level to city-level, although in some special situations, like when the user is using a public WiFi network, we can pinpoint the exact location.

### Carrier connection

Some worldwide operators offer developer programs (both open and private) for web portals that allow any request made from a user to your web server to carry additional headers containing information about the user (identity, location, and billing services). The GSM Association, which encompasses almost all the operators around the world, has launched an initiative called *OneAPI* that aims to provide web applications with access to all this carrier information through its APIs.

### Language

A less accurate mechanism is to use the accepted language of the browser. If the user has set up his device correctly, it should send a header indicating the preferred language, from which we can infer what country the user is in (for example, the browser may send us en-CA as the accepted language, meaning English from Canada). This results in at best country-level accuracy.

### Indoor location

When users are connecting via WiFi hotspots in a single building, we can configure our routers to be queried about those users. Every WLAN user has a unique IP address in the network, so we can tell which hotspot a given user is connected to. With that information, we can identify the floor and zone where the user is located.

## Asking the User

If you need to offer web-based location-based services, the last location mechanism available if all the others fail is to *ask the user*. Even if you have identified the approximate location using another algorithm, you may be able to increase the accuracy by asking the user.

 The user may know her location, or not. For example, if the user is visiting a foreign city, she may not know her exact current location.

So, what should we be asking users? We should allow them to select from a closed list, or to type the location into an open text box. We can query our databases for city names, addresses, POIs (such as parks, hotels, or restaurants), or zip codes. We can also query public databases using web APIs like Yahoo! PlaceMaker, FourSquare, and the Google Places API. To pinpoint the location, we can then use a geocoding query to convert the string into a latitude/longitude pair.

We should allow the users to select their current location from amongst the following:

*Home*
> If the users need to log in to the website, we can ask them where they live when they install the application and store this information in our database for future use.

*Favorite places*
> We can make a users' favorite places database.

*History*
> We can allow the users to select places where they have been recently, ordering the list by frequency.

Records of all of these locations may be stored in a database on our server attached to the user's credentials (for login-based solutions), in a cookie on the client, or even in client storage on devices that support this.

# Detecting the Location

We have two options for detecting the user's geographical location: using the W3C Geolocation API, available under the HTML5 APIs, or using third-party APIs, usually available directly from carriers.

## The W3C Geolocation API

The W3C standard way to query the user's position from JavaScript is called the Geolocation API (*http://www.w3.org/TR/geolocation-API*). The Geolocation API doesn't rely on one location technology. Instead, it allows the browser to decide which method it will use.

With this API implemented in a mobile browser, the `navigator` object in JavaScript will have a read-only property called `geolocation` that will allow us to interact with the API.

Location querying is an asynchronous process. It can take some time to get the user's location (like with GPS); that's why the API relies on callback functions to give us the latitude and longitude.

The user will need to give the site permission to obtain the geolocation data using the API, as shown in Figure 14-1.

### Getting the position

The first way to use the Geolocation API is to get the user's location using the `getCurrentPosition()` function of the `geolocation` object. It receives two callbacks: the function that will receive the position, and an error-handling function. The latter is optional.

Optionally, it may also receive an object that configures some additional properties; this third parameter will be discussed shortly.

Let's look at an example:

```
navigator.geolocation.getCurrentPosition(userLocated, locationError);
```

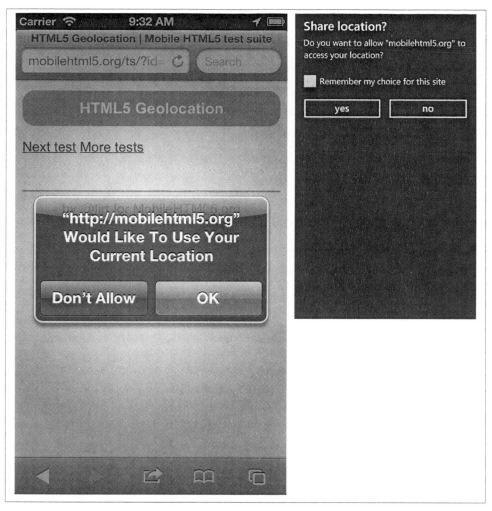

*Figure 14-1. We cannot get the user's location unless permission was granted the first time we tried to get it.*

The first callback will receive one parameter as the `position` object with a `coordi`
`nate` property. The error callback will receive an error code:

```
function userLocated(position) {
    var latitude = position.coords.latitude;
    var longitude = position.coords.longitude;
    var timeOfLocation = position.timestamp;
}

function locationError(error) {
    alert(error.code);
}
```

The coords property has the following attributes, defined in the W3C standard:

- latitude in decimal degrees
- longitude in decimal degrees
- altitude (optional) in meters above the ellipsoid
- accuracy in meters
- altitudeAccuracy (optional) in meters
- heading (optional) in degrees clockwise related to true north
- speed (optional) in meters per second

### Handling error messages

The parameter received in the error handler is an object of class PositionError having a code and a message (useful for logging). The class also has some constant values to be compared with the code property. The constants are shown in Table 14-1.

*Table 14-1. PositionError constants in the W3C Geolocation API*

| Error constant | Description |
| --- | --- |
| PERMISSION_DENIED | The user has denied permission to the API to get the position. |
| POSITION_UNAVAILABLE | The user's position couldn't be determined due to a failure in the location provider. |
| TIMEOUT | The user's position couldn't be determined before the timeout defined in the options. |

To use these constants, we should make a switch for each value:

```
function locationError(error) {
    switch(error.code) {
        case error.PERMISSION_DENIED:
            // error handling
            break;
        case error.POSITION_UNAVAILABLE:
            // error handling
            break;
        case error.TIMEOUT:
            // error handling
            break;
    }
}
```

### Tracking the location

The second way to use the W3C Geolocation API is to track the user's location. With tracking support, we can receive notifications about location changes. For instance, we can make a sports website that tracks the user's steps, makes speed and distance calculations, and stores this information either locally or on our server using Ajax.

For this to work, the user needs to keep the website open in the browser. Also be aware that many browsers stop JavaScript execution when the browser is in the background, as discussed in Chapter 12.

The tracking process involves the `watchPosition()` method of the `navigator.geolo cation` object, which receives two handlers (for location detection and error management) and returns a `watchId`. The handler function will receive the same parameter as the `getCurrentPosition()` function that we saw earlier. To stop the location tracking we can call `clearWatch()`, passing the previously received `watchId`:

```
// Global variable to store the watch ID
var watchId = false;

// This function may be called by an HTML element
function trackingButtonClick() {
    if (watchId==false) {
        // Tracking is off, turn it on
        var watchId = navigator.geolocation.watchPosition(userLocated,
            locationError);
    } else {
        // Tracking is on, turn it off
        navigator.geolocation.clearWatch(watchId);
        watchId = false;
    }
}
```

Using Modernizr, we can check for geolocation support with the `geo location` property; we can also use server-side detection with WURFL, querying whether the `ajax_preferred_geoloc_api` capability has a value of `w3c_api`.

### Defining optional attributes

The third parameter of the `getCurrentPosition()` and `watchPosition()` functions can receive an object with the optional properties outlined in Table 14-2.

*Table 14-2. Optional properties for getCurrentPosition() and watchPosition()*

| Property | Type | Default value |
| --- | --- | --- |
| enableHighAccuracy | Boolean | false |
| timeout | Long (in milliseconds) | Infinity |
| maximumAge | Long (in milliseconds) | 0 |

If the `enableHighAccuracy` property is defined as `true`, the provider should force the best accuracy in determining the user's location (such as GPS if available).

When developing Apache Cordova/PhoneGap applications for Android, you must define enableHighAccuracy as true if you want to test geolocation in the Android emulator.

The maximumAge property is useful when retrieving location data cached on the device. With this property, we can specify how recent we want the cached data to be—if the data is older than the specified maximum age (in milliseconds), the device will have to get a new location. A typical usage might look like this:

```
navigator.geolocation.getCurrentPosition(userLocated, locationError,
    {timeout:10000, maximumAge: 30000, enableHighAccuracy:false});
```

If the maximumAge property is defined as 0 (the default value), the device must always acquire a new location when getCurrentPosition() is called.

 Some older browsers—such as Android 1.x, BlackBerry browser 5.0, and Opera Mobile 9.5—don't support the Geolocation API, but they used to support the Google Gears plug-in, which has a very similar implementation to the W3C standard.

The BlackBerry browser before version 5.0 used the proprietary blackberry.location object, which is faster and less battery-intensive but provides less accuracy and information than Gears or the W3C standard.

## Geolocation API 2.0

The W3C is working on the next generation of the Geolocation API (*http://dev.w3.org/geo/api/spec-source-v2*), including some additions to the current specification (mainly the ability to query about postal addresses).

There are two optional Boolean attributes that we can use when we query about locations: requireCoords and requestAddress. The first forces the system to deliver coordinates, and the second defines whether or not we want to receive a civic address (street, number, city, country).

When we get a location through getCurrentPosition() or watchPosition(), there is an optional address attribute in the argument (in the same place where coords exists). The address object may contain a set of properties including country, region, county, city, street, streetNumber, premises, and postalCode. Every property is optional, so how much information the browser will give us will depend on the current situation.

At the time of this writing, no mobile browser supports these features; however, we can emulate them using a provider API, such as the Google Maps API.

# Carrier Network Location APIs

Some carriers offer custom APIs that developers can use for free, for a monthly fee, or for a geolocation request fee.

## GSMA OneAPI

OneAPI is a cross-operator API organized by the GSM Association. With this API we can access the user's location from our servers, using his phone number. Register as a developer and obtain a token to access the OpenAPI web services (*http://oneapi.aepo na.com*). The API supports SOAP Web Services and REST using HTTP.

One of the services supported by OpenAPI is geolocation. With the Location API, we can get a user's longitude and latitude using the mobile operator's cells' positions. To use the API we need to get a key from the website. Then, if we want to use REST, we can create an HTTP request to a URL like the following:

```
https://developer.aepona.com/TerminalLocationService/Proxy/REST/<key>?
address=tel:<tel>&accuracy=coarse
```

where *<key>* is the key assigned to our developer account and *<tel>* is the international number of the phone we want to geolocate. If the request is successful, we will receive a response like the following:

```
<response timestamp="2010-06-06T12:31:07.014Z" longitude="10.22244"
          latitude="54.601505" altitude="10.0" accuracy="200"/>
```

The list of supported operators is on the website, and the goal is to have all the operators worldwide using the same API.

## Specific carriers' APIs

Table 14-3 shows other carrier geolocation APIs that we may use, using the network services after getting the user's permission.

*Table 14-3. Carrier geolocation API availability*

| Platform | Carriers | URL |
|---|---|---|
| Verizon Network API | Verizon (US) | *developer.verizon.com* |
| BlueVia | Movistar (Latin America, Spain), O2 (UK, Germany), Telenor (Asia, Scandinavia, Eastern Europe) | *bluevia.com* |
| AT&T Location API | AT&T (US) | *developer.att.com/developer* |
| LBS Sprint API | Sprint (US) | *developer.sprint.com* |
| Orange Location API | Orange (France only at the time of this writing) | *api.orange.com* |

LocAid (*http://developer.loc-aid.com*) offers a premium solution that can locate 350 million devices with one API from AT&T, Sprint, T-Mobile, and Verizon. Location Labs (*http://developer.veriplace.com*) offers the ability to locate 250 million devices with a single API too.

# IP Geolocation

There are a lot of free and commercial IP address geolocation services available for use on our servers. When using such a solution, we need to remember that a BlackBerry can browse through a corporate network, so the IP address will be the network IP address and not the user's. The same applies to proxied browsers like Opera Mini.

## Reading the IP address

We can read the IP address from the host using the appropriate mechanism for the server platform. For example, in PHP we read the address using:

```
$IP = $_SERVER['REMOTE_ADDR'];
```

However, we must remember that this IP address may belong to a renderer proxy. For example, when an Opera Mini user accesses our website the IP address will always be the same, because the client contacting our server is actually the Opera Mini server. Fortunately, Opera Mini servers offer us another HTTP header that provides the actual IP address of the requesting mobile device: the X-Forwarded-For header contains a CSV list of the IP addresses of all the proxy servers the request has passed through on its way from the device to the Mini proxy, and the last IP address will be the address of the original requestor (the mobile device).

Once we have the IP address to query, we can use a web service to get the country/city details, or download the Geo-IP open source database (*http://software77.net/geo-ip*).

 We need to keep in mind that IP geocoding is useful only to get the user's country for devices connected to the Internet via 2.5G or 3G, because what we'll receive is the operator's gateway IP address. If the user is using WiFi, depending on the zone, we can usually get more accurate details.

## Google's ClientLocation object

Google provides a set of JavaScript APIs (Maps, Search) that can be used to create feature-rich dynamic websites. Whenever one of these APIs is loaded on a client, the Google Loader attempts to geolocate the user using the device's IP address.

To add support for the APIs, we need to insert this script:

```
<script src="https://www.google.com/jsapi"></script>
```

To use the client location feature, we must then load an API. For example:

```
<script type="text/javascript">
    google.load("search", "1");
</script>
```

Once we've loaded the API, the `google.loader.ClientLocation` object will be populated with properties like the following:

- `latitude`
- `longitude`
- `address.city`
- `address.country`
- `address.country_code`
- `address.region`

 This technique works only on compatible devices and should be used only if we are going to make use of one of the Ajax APIs (Ajax Search, Maps, Ajax Feeds, Earth, Data, Visualization, Friend Connect, or Ajax Language).

# Maps/Navigation App Integration

Some platforms, such as iOS, Windows Phone, and Android, include a native map application outside of the browser that we may want to open in some situations, such as to start a turn-by-turn navigation process. To communicate with this app from our website, we will just use standard URIs, as we will see in Chapter 15.

## Google Maps for Android

To invoke the Google Maps application on Android devices we can just point to *maps.google.com* and optionally send any parameters we want to include, in the basic form *http://maps.google.com/?<attributes>*. Attributes should be URL-formatted, as in *attribute1=value1&attribute2=value2*. Possible attributes include:

*q*

Query parameter; this can be a comma-separated coordinate preceded by a *loc:* prefix (*loc:lat,long*), or any search string, such as *starbucks*

*near*

Applies a location definition for a query, as in *q=starbucks;near=san+mateo+ca ll*

A comma-separated latitude and longitude for the map center

*t*

The type of map (*m*: map, *k*: satellite, *h*: hybrid, *p*: terrain)

*z*

The zoom level, from 1 (the whole world) to 23 (buildings, not available in all areas)

On Android devices, the user will be able to decide if she wants to execute URLs with the Google Maps native API or with the browser.

To force the use of the Maps application, we can also use the *geo:* URI (currently being discussed as a standard; see IETF (*http://bit.ly/Z6uzmz*)). The basic syntax includes:

```
geo:latitude,longitude
geo:latitude,longitude?z=zoom_level
geo:0,0?q=my+street+address
geo:0,0?q=business+near+city
```

Therefore, to make a link to open the Maps application centered on the Eiffel Tower, we can use both options:

```
<a href="http://maps.google.com/?q=eiffel+tower+paris">
    See the Eiffel Tower on a map
</a>

<a href="geo:0,0?q=eiffel+tower+paris">
    See the Eiffel Tower on a map
</a>
```

### Directions and navigation

To initiate a route algorithm and later a possible turn-by-turn navigation, we can use *http://maps.google.com* with the *saddr* (source address) and *daddr* (destination address) parameters, such as:

```
<a href="http://maps.google.com/?saddr=golden+gate&daddr=pier+39">
    Directions
</a>
```

### Street View

Android devices also offer the Street View service on Google Maps. To open a Street View panorama, we can use the nonstandard *google.streetview:* protocol. The parameters are:

*cbll*

The latitude and longitude, comma-separated (mandatory)

*cbp*

A series of optional parameters, such as yaw (center of panorama view in degrees clockwise from north), pitch (center of panorama view in degrees from −90 to 90), and the panorama zoom

*mz*

The map zoom associated with this panorama

If you want to get these parameters, you can just browse to the street view you want to link to and generate a link from your desktop; you will see the parameters there.

To make a link to the White House street view, we can then use:

```
<a href="google.streetview:cbll=38.900214,-77.036509&cbp=12,187.16,,0,2.74">
View the White House</a>
```

## iOS Maps

The Maps application on iOS has changed with time. From iOS 1 to iOS 5.1 the application is Google Maps, and from iOS 6 the application is Apple Maps.

For the Google Maps application we can use the same *http:* protocol as in Android, so linking to *http://maps.google.com* will open the Maps application instead of the website until iOS 6. It accepts the same parameters as in Android.

> While not officially documented, Apple supports the *maps:* protocol in both iOS 5 and iOS 6, accepting at least the *q* parameter for specifying a query.

From iOS 6, *http://maps.google.com* will point to the HTML5 website; to open the native Maps application we need to replace *google* with *apple*. That is, instead of:

```
<a href="http://maps.google.com/?q=eiffel+tower+paris">
    See the Eiffel Tower on a map
</a>
```

we need to use:

```
<a href="http://maps.apple.com/?q=eiffel+tower+paris">
    See the Eiffel Tower on a map
</a>
```

> Full documentation on the Apple Maps URI scheme can be found at *mobilexweb.com/go/applemapsuri*.

The iOS Maps URI scheme adds to the Google scheme some proprietary attributes, such as *cid* for a business ID in the Apple places database.

### Directions and navigation

To initiate a route navigation, we can use the same syntax as in Google Maps from iOS 6. In this case, Apple Maps will calculate the route and offer to the user to start a turn-by-turn navigation (Figure 14-2):

```
<a href="http://maps.apple.com/?saddr=golden+gate&daddr=pier+39">
    Directions
</a>
```

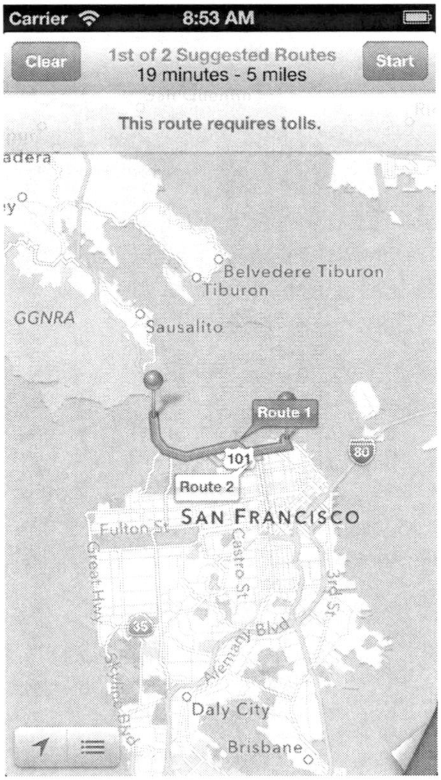

*Figure 14-2. From a mobile website we can open the native Maps application, including the ability to start a route generation and a turn-by-turn navigation operation, using anchor elements and some specific URIs.*

Leaving *saddr* or *daddr* as a blank value, as in:

```
<a href="http://maps.apple.com/?saddr=&daddr=pier+39">
    Directions to Pier 39
</a>
```

causes the user's current location to be automatically filled in as the starting or destination address, respectively.

## Bing Maps

On Windows Phone, we can open the Bing Maps application using the *bingmaps:* protocol, which accepts the following parameters (a partial list):

*cp*
> The center point—a latitude and longitude, separated by a tilde ~ character

*lvl*
> The zoom level (1–20)

*where*
> A search query on places, locations, or landmarks

*q*
> A search query on a local business

*sty*
> The map style (*a*: aerial, *r*: roadmap)

*trfc*
> Whether or not traffic information should be included (*0*: no, *1*: yes)

*rtp*
> The route definition, with the source and destination addresses separated by a tilde ~ character; if either the source or the destination is undefined it will make a route from/to the current location

 Full documentation on the Bing Maps URI scheme can be found at *mobilexweb.com/go/binguri*.

Following the same Eiffel Tower example, to open a map showing this location on Windows Phone, we can use:

```
<a href="bingmaps:?where=eiffel+tower+paris">
    See the Eiffel Tower on a map
</a>
```

# Showing a Map

Once we have located the user (via a client or server solution), we may want to display a map showing the user's position, and/or a list of points of interest or other information superimposed on the map.

To do this, we should use one of the available public maps APIs: Google Maps, Bing Maps from Microsoft, or Nokia Here. We can use all these APIs for iOS and Android devices, as well as other HTML5-compatible devices; Nokia Maps doesn't just work on Nokia browsers.

 As we saw in the previous section, Apple has its own Maps API from iOS version 6.0; however, there is no public API for nonnative iOS apps at the time of this writing, so we can't use it from our websites. We can still link to it using the Apple Maps protocol (*http://maps.apple.com*).

There are actually two Google APIs that are useful for mobile browsers: the Google Maps API v3 and the Google Maps Static API. The first one is the same service that we can find in any website using Google Maps. However, it is currently compatible only with iPhone and Android devices; on other devices, this API will not work properly. The Static API will allow us to show a static map compatible with any mobile browser.

## Google Maps API v3

If we are sure that the device is HTML5-compatible, we should use the Google Maps API v3, as shown in Figure 14-3.

To use the API, we first need to include the script loader:

```
<script type="text/javascript"
        src="http://maps.google.com/maps/api/js?sensor=true">
```

The sensor value must be true if the device has geolocation support via the operating system (this is the case on both iPhone and Android devices). We should check whether the device is compatible either on the server, as discussed in Chapter 10, or using JavaScript.

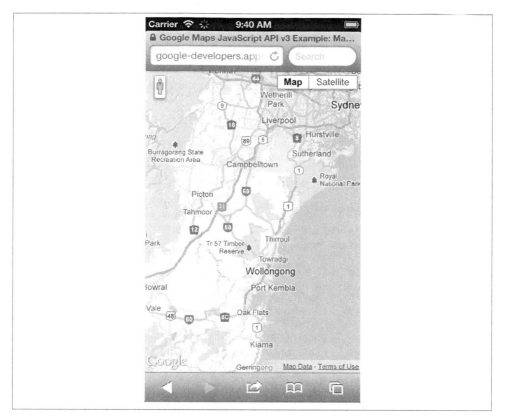

*Figure 14-3. Here we can see the Google Maps API on an iPhone showing the user's current location.*

Then, we need to create a `div` tag in our HTML and define its dimensions as 100%:

```
function showMap() {
    var useragent = navigator.userAgent;
    var divMap = document.getElementById("map");

    if (useragent.indexOf('iPhone') != -1 ||
        useragent.indexOf('Android') != -1 ||
        useragent.indexOf(iPod) != -1 ) {
        divMap.style.width = '100%';
        divMap.style.height = '100%';
        // ...
    } else {
        // Google Maps not compatible with this mobile device
    }
}
```

On feature phones or cloud-based browsers we must use the Google Maps Static API instead.

The other requirement for mobile devices is to define the meta tag to work without user zooming and with an initial scale of 1.0. This is necessary to avoid usability problems with the map zooming. So, in the head we should add:

```
<meta name="viewport" content="initial-scale=1.0, user-scalable=no" />
```

A full sample looks like this:

```
<html>
<head>
<meta name="viewport" content="initial-scale=1.0, user-scalable=no" />
<script type="text/javascript"
        src="http://maps.google.com/maps/api/js?sensor=true"></script>
<script type="text/javascript">
        function init() {
    var useragent = navigator.userAgent;
    var divMap = document.getElementById("map");

    if (useragent.indexOf('iPhone') != -1 ||
            useragent.indexOf('Android') != -1 ||
            useragent.indexOf('iPod') != -1 ) {
        divMap.style.width = '100%';
        divMap.style.height = '100%';
        position = getPosition(); // This needs to be implemented
        var latlng = new google.maps.LatLng(position.latitude,
            position.longitude);
        var options = {
            zoom: 7,
            center: latlng,
            mapTypeId: google.maps.MapTypeId.ROADMAP
        };
        var map =
            new google.maps.Map(document.getElementById("divMap"),
            options);
    } else {
        // Google Maps not compatible with this mobile device
    }
}

</script>
</head>
<body onload="init()">
    <div id="divMap"></div>
</body>
</html>
```

See the full Google Maps API documentation (*http://code.google.com/apis/maps/docu mentation/v3*).

# Google Maps Static API

If we need compatibility with all mobile devices—even the ones without JavaScript support—we can use the free Google Maps Static API, which allows us to show a map as a static image without any automatic interaction.

 Up to 25,000 static map requests per application per day are free. If you need more, you need to purchase additional quota through the API website.

This API is very simple and doesn't require any JavaScript or server code. We will use it inside an HTML `image` tag, in the source URL. The URL will look like this:

```
http://maps.google.com/maps/api/staticmap?parameters
```

To use this API we need to get the location from the server or the client and generate the image URL dynamically, using JavaScript on compatible devices. We need to remember that we may not want to show the user's location, but rather a map of some other place.

 With the Google Maps Static API we can show a map on any mobile phone on the market, even those without JavaScript or Ajax support.

The common parameters include:

sensor
Must be `true` for a mobile device.

center
May be a position using *latitude, longitude*, or a city name.

zoom
The level of zoom required, from 0 (world view) to 21 (building view).

size
The size in pixels of the image required (e.g., 220×300). We should get the device's screen size from the server or from JavaScript.

format
Accepts `GIF`, `JPEG`, or `PNG`. The default is `PNG`, which is suitable for mobile devices.

mobile
Marking this parameter as `true` creates different rendering images optimized for viewing on mobile devices. Google suggests using `false` in the case of iPhone or Android devices.

The API is more complex, and it can even show marks and routes over the map. See the full documentation (*https://developers.google.com/maps/documentation/staticmaps/*).

For example, if we are using PHP and we just have the latitude and longitude (acquired by any method), we should use:

```php
<?php
// $latitude and $longitude already acquired
$url = "http://maps.google.com/maps/api/staticmap?center=$latitude,
$longitude&zoom=14&size=220x300&sensor=true";
?>
<img src="<?php echo $url ?>" width="220" height="300" />
```

## Nokia Here

Here (formerly Nokia Maps) offers a series of free services for mapping on websites (*http://developer.here.net*), including:

*The Mobile HTML5 Framework*
A rich mobile app development framework, including complete functionality for Maps, Positioning, Places, Direction, and Traffic. This API is fully compatible with iOS, Android, MeeGo, Windows Phone, and BlackBerry (see Figure 14-4).

*The JavaScript API*
A classic JavaScript API that is not necessarily optimized for mobile websites.

*REST APIs*
Web Services allowing us to access pre-rendered static map images (similar to the Google Static Maps API), a places database, routing and traffic information, and more.

To work with all the APIs, we need to become a Nokia developer (register for free (*http://developer.here.net*)) and then register an API key to use the mapping services (*http://api.developer.nokia.com*). Usage of the mapping APIs is subject to quotas based on the service we are using; enterprise solutions are available.

To use the Mobile HTML5 API (*http://developer.here.net/mobile_html5*), once we have the API key registered we just need to add some file references, create a map container (usually a div element), and call the API.

jHere (*http://jhere.net*) is a lightweight JavaScript framework that works over Zepto.js or jQuery to simplify the work with Here services, including interactive maps, KML support, and info bubbles.

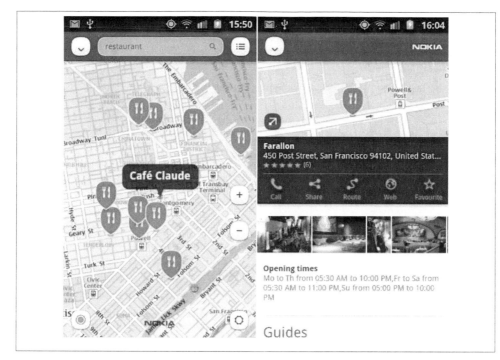

*Figure 14-4. Here for mobile HTML5, while created by Nokia, works on different plat-forms—in this case, an Android browser.*

To add the files:

```
<link rel="stylesheet"
      href="http://api.maps.nokia.com/mobile/latest/lib/mh5.css"/>
<link rel="stylesheet"
      href="http://api.maps.nokia.com/mobile/latest/lib/colors.css"/>
<script src="http://api.maps.nokia.com/mobile/latest/lib/mh5.js">
</script>
```

When we already have a `div` element with specific dimensions defined, we can then create a map reference:

```
nokia.mh5.assetsPath = "http://api.maps.nokia.com/mobile/0.2.0/lib/";
    nokia.mh5.app.embed({
        domNode: "#mymap",
        // API credentials
        appId: OUR_APPID,
        appCode: OUR_APPCODE
    });
```

# CHAPTER 15

# Device Interaction

Mobile browsers have the useful facility of being able to interact with the device—both the operating system and the hardware. Communication can be driven by URIs used in links or JavaScript APIs. Some specific platforms support both an API and a URI scheme for the same feature; in that case the API usually is the preferred way as it's more flexible and less error-prone.

Apache Cordova/PhoneGap and some native web platforms add support for more APIs than the ones available in the standard web view on every platform, as we will see later.

## Mobile-Specific URIs

There are some URI schemes that many mobile browsers understand that enable us to communicate with some phone features. We can use these URIs in typical a elements, and in some browsers we can use JavaScript to force the URI using `location.href`.

Usually we are talking about using a protocol name, a colon, and parameters, such as *tel:2222*:

```
<a href="protocol:parameters"></a>

<script>
   location.href = "protocol:parameters";
</script>
```

 The Wireless Telephony Application Interface (WTAI), part of the WAP 1.x standard, was created in the last millennium; the WTAI libraries were preinstalled on many phones and can be accessed by other applications, such as the browser. To use these libraries (if available), we used to use the syntax *wtai://<library name>/<function name>[(;parameter)*]*. Today, only feature phones still support this library.

We need to be careful about using URI schemes that aren't compatible with a device, however, as the user will not understand the error messages. Figure 15-1 shows an example.

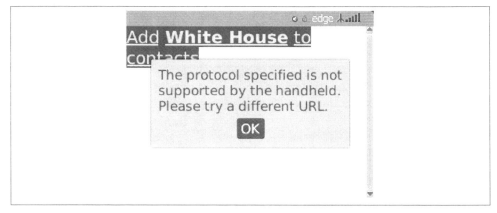

*Figure 15-1. Triggering URI schemes that are not compatible with the user's device can lead to strange error messages.*

## Making a Call

Remember, most mobile devices are also phones! So, why not create link-to-call actions? If you're creating a business guide, or even providing support for your own website, most people will prefer to call a person instead of filling in a form on the device.

Fortunately, there are some URLs that will help us. The first standard (defined by the Internet Assigned Numbers Authority, or IANA) is to use the *tel:<phone number>* scheme. It's a good idea to provide the phone number in the international format—a plus sign (+), the country code, the local area code, and the local number—as we do not really know where our visitors will be located. For example:

```
<a href="tel:+1800229933">Call us free!</a>
```

If they are in the same country, or even in the same local area, the international format will still work.

Some devices also allow sending DMTF tones after the call has been answered by the destination. This is useful for accessing tone-controlled services, help desk systems, or voicemail; you can say to the link, "call this phone number and, when the call is answered, press 2, wait 2 seconds, and then press 913#." You do this using the *postd* parameter after the number: the syntax is *;postd=<numbers>*. You can use numbers, \*, and # (using the URL-encoded %23 value), as well as *p* for a one-second pause and *w* for a wait-for-tone pause. For example:

```
<a href="tel:+1800229933;postd=4">Call us free!</a>
```

This function doesn't work on all mobile devices, but on devices that don't understand it, the primary telephone number should at least be called. The compatibility list for this feature is complex, and I don't recommend relying on it.

If the user activates a call link, she will receive a confirmation alert asking whether to place the call, showing the full number so she can decide. This is to avoid fraudsters tricking the user into calling another country or a premium number. As shown in Figure 15-2, some nonphone devices offer a contextual menu allowing the user to copy or save the phone number instead (the same functionality can be achieved on phone devices after a long-press gesture over a link).

Figure 15-2. Some nonphone devices, such as the iPad or the iPod touch, provide the user with a context menu option to copy or save the phone number instead of placing the call.

Not as well supported today as *tel:*, the other way to originate a call is using the WTAI standard, via the *wp* public library and the *mc* (make call) function:

```
<a href="wtai://wp/mc;+1800229933">Call us free!</a>
```

This link can include tones to be sent to the destination as if the user had pressed them on the keypad, specified using the *wp* library's *sd* (send DTMF tones) function.

 The BlackBerry browser automatically detects phone numbers and email addresses and converts them to links. If you don't want this feature, you should use the meta tag `<meta http-equiv="x-rim-auto-match" content="none">`. Safari also has its own meta tag for the same action: `<meta name="format-detection" content="telephone=no">`.

iDEN networks (like Nextel) use radio packets to make internal calls inside the network. If you are working with customers of such a network—for example, for an intranet—you can allow users to launch internal calls to other members of the team (or external calls) using the Direct Connect URL scheme (*dc:<number>*). This is compatible with BlackBerry iDEN devices:

```
<a href="dc:5040*0077">Ping John</a>
```

 Some models present users with a submenu when they click a *tel:* link so they can choose whether to place a voice-only or a video call (available in 3G systems). Some Japanese phones also allow you to specify that a link should initiate a video call, using the protocol *tel-av:<phone number>*.

## Sending Email

Some modern devices with browsers also have mail applications that can react to the classic web *mailto:* protocol. The syntax is *mailto:<email_destination>[?parameters]*. The detected parameters can change from device to device but generally include *cc*, *bcc*, *subject*, and *body*. The parameters are defined in a URL format (*key=value&key=value*), and the values must be URI-encoded.

Here are some samples:

```
<a href="mailto:info@mobilexweb.com">Mail us</a>
<a href="mailto:info@mobilexweb.com?subject=Contact%20from%20mobile">
    Mail us
</a>
<a href="mailto:info@mobilexweb.com?subject=Contact&
        body=This%20is%20the%20body">
    Mail us
</a>
```

Be aware that the *mailto:* mechanism doesn't guarantee that the message will be sent. It generally just opens the mail application, and the user has to confirm the sending after making optional changes. If you need to actually send the mail, use a server mechanism.

Generally, if we want to insert a newline in the body of the email, we can use the Carriage Return plus Line Feed characters (%0D%0A). This does not work with the Mail application in iOS at the time of this writing; however, it does allow us to insert HTML tags inside the body, so we can use <br> for Safari on iOS (as well as creating complex HTML messages):

```
<a href="mailto:info@mobilexweb.com?subject=Contact&
        body=This%20is%20the%20body%0D%0AThis%20is%20a%20new%20line">
  Mail us
</a>

<a href="mailto:info@mobilexweb.com?subject=Contact&
        body=This%20is%20the%20body<br/>This%20is%20a%20new%20line">
  Mail us from iPhone
</a>
```

The Mail application in iOS supports HTML in the message body, so we can read an HTML content file using XMLHttpRequest or just the innerHTML part of the current page, encode it as a URL, and send it inside the *mailto:* protocol. This enables us to send rich postcards from our websites.

## Sending an SMS

We all like the Short Message Service; that's why mobile browsers generally offer the ability to invoke the new SMS window from a link. To do this, we have two possible URI schemes, *sms://* and *smsto://*. Unfortunately, there is no standard way to know for sure which one is compatible with a user's browser.

WURFL supports a capability to query about which SMS URI scheme is supported on the current device. The capability is xhtml_send_sms_string and the possible values are none, sms:, or smsto:.

The syntax is *sms[to]://[<destination number>][?parameters]*. As you can see, the destination number is optional, so you can open the SMS composer from the device without any parameters defined. The *parameters* usually define the body, but this property is not compatible with all phones for security reasons (to avoid a website sending premium SMS texts, for example). As with an email, an SMS is not automatically sent when the user presses the link. The link only opens the SMS composer window; the user must finish the process manually.

On iOS, from version 5.0, the *sms://* protocol also works on the iPad and iPod touch; the user is redirected to iMessages instead of the SMS application, which is not available.

The destination number should be an international number or, if it is a short number code, we should guarantee that the user is in the right country and is connected with one of the compatible carriers of that short code.

 The BlackBerry platform supports direct messaging between two Black-Berry devices using BBM (BlackBerry Messenger). To create a direct message, you can use the *pin:<number>* URL scheme.

Here are some samples:

```
<a href="sms://">Send an SMS</a>

<a href="sms://?body=Visit%20us%20at%20http://mobilexweb.com">
    Invite a friend by SMS
<a>

<a href="sms://+3490322111">Contact us by SMS</a>

<a href="sms://+3490322111?body=Interested%20in%20Product%20AA2">
    More info for product AA2
</a>
```

---

## Working with MMS

The Multimedia Messaging Service (MMS) is the standard way to send messages with multimedia content (images, video, or any attached content). It depends on the SMS standards and a content file (the multimedia message) that the sender uploads to the carrier and the recipient downloads from the carrier. Symbian devices allow us to define the URI schemes *mms://<url>* to download an MMS file from the specified URL and *mmsto://<destination number>* to open the Multimedia Message Composer.

---

## Other Communication Apps

There are some native applications that can be opened from a link, mostly on iOS. One example is the *FaceTime* video-chat application for the iPhone, iPad, and iPod touch.

---

From iOS 4.1 we can use the *facetime://* URI to open the FaceTime application and call somebody. For example:

```
<a href="facetime://5555555555">Call us free using FaceTime!</a>
```

*Skype* is another application with its own URI scheme, that currently works on iOS and Android. Providing the Skype username with a *?call* parameter will immediately initiate a call when the user clicks the link; without it, clicking the link will bring up the identified user's profile instead. For example:

```
<a href="skype:skype_user">Our Skype profile</a>
<a href="skype:skype_user?call">Call us using Skype!</a>
```

 Skype is one of the only applications with good documentation (*https:// developer.skype.com/skype-uri*) on how to use its URI scheme on different mobile operating systems.

Google Voice on Android will use the standard *tel:* and *sms:* protocols if the user selects it as the application for those protocols. WhatsApp on Android uses a similar mechanism for messaging; it has no specific URI.

## Adding a Contact to the Phonebook

It might be useful to invite users to add your company's contact information (only the phone number, or full details) to their phonebooks for future communication. A WTAI function is available for this purpose for older and WML-compatible devices, and there's also a tricky way of doing it for some modern (and smarter?) devices.

The WTAI library is *wp*, as for making phone calls, and the function is *ap* (add to phonebook). The parameters are the number and optionally a name to be assigned to it, separated by a semicolon. For example:

```
<a href="wtai://wp/ap;+12024561111;White%20House">
    Add <strong>White House</strong> to contacts
</a>
```

For modern browsers (those that don't support WTAI—basically, every modern smartphone or tablet) the trick is to create a *vCard* file (vCard is a standard file format for electronic business cards). If you link to this file, most browsers will send the file to the device's Phonebook application, and the user will be invited to add the contact to the database. Later we will also see some APIs that will help us with this matter.

A simple vCard 2.1 file (the most compatible version for mobile devices) will look like this:

```
BEGIN:VCARD
VERSION:2.1
```

```
N:Maximiliano;Firtman
ORG:O'Reilly Media
TITLE:Author
TEL;CELL;VOICE:+133MFIRTMAN
TEL;WORK;VOICE:+541150320077
END:VCARD
```

For the device to detect this text file as a valid vCard, we must deliver it with the MIME type `text/x-vcard`. The file, if static, is generally a *.vcf* file.

Unfortunately, many modern (again, smarter?) mobile browsers, like Safari on iOS, don't understand vCards if you provide them as links in a document. However, they do understand them if the user receives them by email! The solution, therefore, is to retrieve the user's email address and, from the server, send the vCard as an attachment.

Another excellent feature to provide to compatible devices is to automatically add to the user's calendar details about a meeting or appointment scheduled online, or a reminder about an event for which the user has bought tickets. If you're selling tickets to a concert or a theater show, this is a great way to ensure that the user won't forget it.

There isn't a WTAI way to do this—in fact, in 1998 mobile devices generally didn't have calendar programs. For compatible devices we can use the *iCalendar* format, based on an older vCalendar standard similar to vCard. iCalendar files should be served with the MIME type `text/calendar`.

 Safari on iOS has the ability to show PDF, RTF, Microsoft Office, and Apple iWork files just by linking to them, without the need of any app. Other platforms usually require an app capable of viewing those kinds of files.

# Integrating with Other Applications

Some devices allow us to integrate our websites with other native installed applications. This is dramatically nonstandard, though, and it depends very much on the device and the applications that the user has installed.

### iOS URL schemes

Safari supports some standard URL schemes that will open other native applications. For example, we can open the Maps application simply by using a classic URL pointing to *maps.apple.com*, as we saw in Chapter 14. For YouTube, we can also make *http://* links to *youtube.com* and they will be redirected to the YouTube app (both the default app available up to iOS 5.1 and Google's app from the App Store, available on demand from version 6.0).

From iOS 6 we can take advantage of *Smart App Banners* to communicate with a native app. In this case we are not in control of how the banners are shown, and the operating system decides where to show an installation invitation or an open invitation. We covered Smart App Banners and how to set them up in Chapter 7.

Up to iOS 5.1, we could use *maps://* or *http://maps.google.com* to open the native Maps application. Starting with iOS 6, Google Maps is no longer available as a native app and has been replaced by Apple Maps. We can communicate with this version using *maps://* or *http://maps.apple.com*.

An updated list of URL schemes for iOS is maintained by Akosma (*http://wiki.akosma.com/IPhone_URL_Schemes*), and a list of applications, URL schemes, and optional parameters for Safari can be found at Handle Open URL (*http://www.handleopenurl.com*).

For example, according to these sites we can open the Facebook iOS native application (if installed) showing the user's list of friends using the URL *fb://friends*, and if the user has installed Twitter, we can post a message directly using *twitter://post?message=<msg>*. Here's a sample:

```
<a href="twitter://post?message=I%20have%20just%20visit%20a%20site"> Tweet this post
</a>
```

When passing parameters by URL, remember to properly encode spaces and other characters (for example, using *%20* for spaces).

## Detecting Whether an Application Is Installed on iOS

When the user clicks a link in mobile Safari that is designed to open another application, what happens if that application is not installed on the user's device? In this case, the browser shows an alert to the user and continues displaying the same page. We can take advantage of this behavior to improve the user experience. We can create a timer in JavaScript that starts when the user clicks the link; if the timer is executed quickly, it means that the application could not be opened because it is not installed.

We can't avoid the Safari message, but we can show the user an error message indicating that the application seems not to be installed, while providing a link to the App Store so the user can buy or download it. If we redirect the user to another website or to the App Store itself, the error message will be on the screen for just a couple of milliseconds and it will be replaced automatically by the next call.

Also remember that from iOS 6 we have the ability to show Smart App Banners, as we covered in Chapter 7.

Using these techniques, there are free and commercial services that provide URL shorteners to use in social networks that will try to open the native app, or the store if the app is not installed. mURL (*http://www.murl.cc*) is one of these services.

**X-Callback-URL.** When you open a native app from a link, your website is minimized or closed as in iOS only one app can be opened as the foreground app. Therefore, after doing something with the app, the user needs to come back to the website manually.

 Android and Windows Phone have a Back button that will take the user back to your website from a native app after opening it via a URI mechanism.

To solve that problem, Greg Pierce has developed a specification that some apps are adhering to, called X-Callback-URL (*http://x-callback-url.com*). The basic idea is that we can add some specific parameters to the URL that the app will use as a callback mechanism to return to our website when the operation carried out in the native app is finished. While this mechanism was created for app-to-app communication, it can also be used by websites. The only drawback is that when the user goes back it may open the callback in a new window/tab, leaving the caller in the background.

 On iOS at the time of this writing there is no way to replace the *http://* protocol, and Safari will always open these links. Therefore, Chrome for iOS has registered the *googlechrome://* and *googlechromes://* (for secure connections) protocols, which will force opening a website in Chrome if it's installed.

### Android intents

Android also has the ability to communicate with other applications, via *intents* (abstract descriptions of actions to be performed). A native Android application can register an intent as an explicit call (not available from web applications), from a URL, or from a MIME type.

For example, we can open the default PDF viewer on the user's device by delivering a PDF file with the MIME type `application/pdf`. To open an application without sending a file, we can use the URI schemes defined by the intent. For example, linking to a YouTube video will fire the YouTube internal application (if the user has defined it as the default player).

When the intention call is implicit (using a URL instead of a unique package name), there may be more than one installed application that can respond to that URL. In this case, the user will receive a pop-up asking her to select the application to use. The user can also select a default application for future usages.

 In Android, an intent can be registered as part of an HTTP URL or be activated from a MIME type. For example, if we link to *http:// www.google.com/m/products/scan* in the Android browser, it will try to open a barcode scanner application.

Among the internal URLs that Android supports are those for Google Maps placemarks using *geo:<latitude>,<longitude>*, Google Maps searches using *geo:0,0?q=<search>*, and Google Street Views using *google.streetview:cbll=<latitude>,<longitude> &cbp=1*, as we covered in Chapter 14. More information is available at Android's developer site (*http://developer.android.com/guide/appendix/g-app-intents.html*).

 In Android, when a URI scheme is not registered as an intent, that means the application is not installed. The user will be taken to a new page showing an error message, like when you link to a website that doesn't exist.

Unfortunately, at the time of this writing there are no websites that list all the possible URI schemes to use on Android. Usually well-known applications, such as Facebook or Twitter, use the same URI scheme as on iOS when available.

### Symbian local applications

Symbian devices also allow us to open applications using the nonstandard *localapp:* scheme. For example, to open the Calendar, Contacts, or Messages app, we can use *localapp:calendar*, *localapp:contacts*, or *localapp:messaging*, respectively.

### Windows apps

Windows 8 and Windows Phone from version 8.0 support URI association from native apps. Windows 8 includes some built-in app URIs that are not documented at the time of this writing, such as *maps*, *ms-excel*, *ms-word*, and *wallet*, as well as URI schemes to access the Settings app.

For Windows Phone 8, Microsoft offers a list of URIs (*http://www.mobilexweb.com/go/ wp8uri*) for accessing specific sections of the Settings app and the Windows Phone Store.

# JavaScript APIs

Most device interaction can be achieved through JavaScript APIs. Some of these APIs are specs from the W3C, some are just spec drafts from other sources, and others are proprietary APIs for one specific vendor.

 Data, network, geolocation, drawing, and multimedia APIs are covered in different chapters in this book.

# Touch

Most tablets and smartphones today are touch devices, and some of them also have some kind of a mouse pointer. For example, the Microsoft Surface allows you to use an external mouse or the touch keyboard.

Touches are different than mouse clicks in two main areas:

*Click area*
A touch area is larger than a click area (several pixels as opposed to just one). Even if the user touches quickly, the pressure center may change, and as a mouse event it can be detected as a mouse move.

*Multiplicity*
Modern devices are multitouch, meaning that we may detect more than one touch at the same time. Standard mouse events don't support multiplicity.

While every device still emulates mouse events when touches are used, there are some specific touch events that we can use too. With touch we can also detect gestures manually, or with APIs available in some browsers.

In terms of implementations, today we can find two: Apple's touch and gesture events, and Microsoft's pointer and gesture events.

Before we start talking about the APIs, it's important to understand that some browsers, and some operating systems, have their own touch gestures, and we should avoid trying to detect them at the same time. The following is a list of some gestures to avoid:

- On Safari for iPad, the OS detects four-finger gestures for going home, switching between apps, and accessing the previously opened app list. Therefore, we should avoid four-finger gesture detection.

- Chrome for mobile devices and tablets supports gestures to move between windows or tabs. On phone-factor devices it's a one-finger swipe (or flick) gesture starting from the edge of the window (left or right). Therefore, if we want to use swipe gestures, we should avoid detecting such gestures if they start in the leftmost or rightmost 50 CSS pixels of our page. A visual indicator for the user to know that she should start the gesture inside that area will help.

- MeeGo supports gestures from the borders of the screen to move between open apps, and in some other situations. Therefore, in MeeGo browsers (the Nokia browser, Opera, or Firefox) we should avoid detecting gestures over the edges. The same thing goes for BlackBerry PlayBook and BlackBerry 10 devices.

- Internet Explorer 10 in Windows 8-style mode (also know as Metro mode) supports swipe events (starting anywhere on the screen) to move backward and forward in history.

### Apple Touch Events API

As the first multitouch browser, Safari on iOS invented the touch API as a proprietary extension with the following nonstandard events:

- `touchstart`
- `touchmove`
- `touchend`
- `touchcancel`

After a while, other browsers—including the Android browser, Chrome, the BlackBerry browser, Opera, and Firefox—cloned Apple's implementation.

 While some devices support multitouch gestures, the browser may not support them—for example, the Samsung Galaxy Note I exposes the Touch Events API but its browser supports only single-touch gestures.

When we capture these events, we will receive them both for single touches and multitouches. Every time the user presses a finger on the screen, `touchstart` will be executed; if he moves one or more fingers, `touchmove` will be the event to capture; and when the user removes his finger(s), `touchend` will be fired. What about `touchcancel`? A touch cancel event is executed if any external event with more priority than our website (such as an alert window, an incoming call, or a push notification) cancels the operation. Unfortunately, the `touchcancel` event has several bugs in terms of how it's implemented in different browsers.

 If you are creating a game, a drawing application, or some other solution capturing touches, it is very important to remember the `touchcancel` event and to pause or stop the touch behavior when this event fires.

The four events receive the same event object (TouchEvent) as a parameter. It contains a touches collection representing each touch associated with the current event and a changedTouches collection representing the touches that have changed since the last call. Each collection element is a Touch object having primarily coordinate properties, such as pageX and pageY properties.

 We can bind touch events using either addEventListener or the on<*event_name*> DOM property for either the whole document or any particular element on the page.

A typical scenario, then, will be:

```
<div
  ontouchstart="touchStart(event);"
  ontouchmove="touchMove(event);"
  ontouchend="touchEnd(event);"
  ontouchcancel="touchCancel(event);">
</div>
```

 A touch sequence begins with the first finger and ends with the last finger. The touch events will be delivered to the same object that received the ontouchstart event, no matter where the current touches are located.

We may want to cancel in all events the default behavior of Safari for the gesture the user is doing. This can be done with the preventDefault() method of the TouchEvent object:

```
event.preventDefault();
```

The TouchEvent object supports the array collections shown in Table 15-1.

*Table 15-1. TouchEvent collections*

| TouchEvent attribute | Description |
| --- | --- |
| touches | All the touches actually on the screen |
| targetTouches | Only the touches inside the target element of the event |
| changedTouches | Only the touches that have changed since the last event call (useful in ontouchmove and ontouchend or to filter only new or removed touches) |

When the user lifts a finger from the screen, that touch will be available in changedTouches but not in the other collections. In Android 2.x, however, the removed touch is also available in the touches collection—you should test your code on every browser, as you may find differences.

Every Touch object has the properties outlined in Table 15-2.

*Table 15-2. Properties of the Touch object*

| Touch attribute | Description |
|---|---|
| clientX, clientY | Touch coordinates relative to the viewport |
| screenX, screenY | Touch coordinates relative to the screen |
| pageX, pageY | Touch coordinates relative to the whole page, including the scroll position |
| identifier | A number for identifying the touch between event calls |
| target | The HTML element where the event was originated |

The following sample will show a blue 20px circle below each finger touching the screen:

```
<!DOCTYPE html>
<html>
<head>
<meta charset="UTF-8" />
<title>iPhone Multitouch</title>
<meta name="viewport" content="width=device-width; initial-scale=1.0;
      maximum-scale=1.0; user-scalable=0;">
<style>
    .point {
        width: 20px;
        height: 20px;
        position: absolute;
        -webkit-border-radius: 10px;
        background-color: blue;
    }

</style>
<script>
function touch(event) {
    event.preventDefault();
    for (var i=0; i<event.touches.length; i++) {
        var top = event.touches[i].pageY-10;
        var left = event.touches[i].pageX-10;
        var html = "<div class='point' style='left: " + left +
                    "px ; top: " + top + "px'></div>";

        document.getElementById("container").innerHTML += html;
    }
}

function clean() {
    document.getElementById("container").innerHTML = "";
}

</script>
</head>
```

```
<body>

<div ontouchstart="touch(event)" ontouchend="clean()" id="container"
    style="background-color:red; width: 300px; height: 300px">

</div>

</body>
</html>
```

**Disabling scrolling.** We can use touch events to disable scrolling on our website, which can be useful for immersive apps or games where we don't want the content to be scrolled. Even when there is no overflow content, Safari on iOS allows a momentum scroll where you can even see the background behind the web page.

To disable scrolling, we can just use the following snippet of code:

```
document.addEventListener("touchmove", function(event) {
    event.preventDefault();
}, false);
```

**BlackBerry touch behavior.** The BlackBerry browser since version 7 (including the PlayBook) supports a meta tag to define how the browser should react to touch and cursor events raised by the touchpad or a mouse connected to the PlayBook.

The `touch-event-mode` meta tag defines how the browser handles touch events, and if it should detect browser gestures (such as click, scroll, or zoom) or pass all the raw touch information to the website. The possible values are `native` (no browser reaction to touches, even basic behavior), `pure-with-mouse-conversion` (only basic touches are mapped to `click` events), and `processed` (default value, the browser will manage all touch gestures).

For example, if we are creating a game and we don't want the browser to handle touch interactions, we can use:

```
<meta name="touch-event-mode" content="native">
```

A similar meta tag is available through `cursor-event-mode`, accepting the values `native` (the browser will not handle double-click to zoom or click and hold for a menu) or `processed` (default value).

## W3C Touch Event API

After different vendors started to support the Apple Touch Events API (*http://www.w3.org/TR/touch-events*), the W3C started a working group to standardize it. The BlackBerry browser was the first browser to follow the W3C spec.

The W3C Touch Event API is a superset of the Apple API, adding the `touchenter` and `touchleave` events for dragging purposes. If we are listening for those events on a specific DOM element, `touchenter` will be fired if the user has started a touch outside our element but then drags her finger inside it, and `touchleave` will be fired when a touch that originates in our element leaves it.

 While the W3C has reached a recommendation spec, its implementation for the future is still unclear as Apple has filed a patent claim that may conflict with these events. The discussion is still up in the air, and the last W3C recommendation (*http://www.w3.org/2012/te-pag/pagreport.html*) indicates that Apple's patents don't affect this specification. However, Microsoft has decided to use a different implementation, as we'll see shortly. Apple has also decided to not participate in the W3C Touch Events group.

## Compatibility

The number of simultaneous touches that we can detect may vary per browser and per device. Table 15-3 shows current compatibility with touch and multitouch events as well as support for the mentioned APIs.

*Table 15-3. Browser compatibility with Touch Events APIs and multitouch support*

| Browser/platform | API support | Max simultaneous touches |
| --- | --- | --- |
| Safari on iOS | Apple Touch Events | 5 on iPhone and iPod touch 11 on iPad |
| Android browser | Apple Touch Events | 1–10, depending on device |
| Chrome for Android | Apple Touch Events | 1–10, depending on device |
| IE9 for Windows Phone | No support | N/A |
| IE10 for Windows Phone | Only MS pointer events | 2–4 |
| Symbian browser | Apple Touch Events from version 8.2 (no touch `cancel` support) | Depends on the device |
| Nokia Browser for Series 40 | No support | N/A |
| Firefox | W3C Touch Events since 18 | Depends on the device |
| BlackBerry browser for smartphones | W3C Touch Events since 7.x | 4 |
| BlackBerry browser for PlayBook and BB10 | W3C Touch Events | 10 |
| UC browser | Apple Touch Events | Depends on the device |
| Opera Mobile | Apple Touch Events | Depends on the device |
| Opera Mini | No support | N/A |
| Amazon Silk | Apple Touch Events | 8 |

## Microsoft pointer events

Microsoft arrived late to HTML5, and to touch events in particular. However, that delay allowed Microsoft to be one of the first to realize that Apple has patented the touch events, and that's why (from Internet Explorer 10) it is using its own variation of these events, known as *pointer events*, for touch and stylus detection.

While at the time of this writing the only implementation is the Microsoft prefixed one, Microsoft has proposed it to the W3C as a patent-free standard for touch events; the group has been accepted and is in discussion at W3C's website (*http://www.w3.org/2012/pointerevents*).

The main differences in pointer events are that it is input-type-agnostic, supporting touch, mouse, and stylus touches in one API, and that it supports hover (over and out), pressure, and tilt values for compatible pointer types.

The events available in the Pointer Events specification are listed in Table 15-4. Remember that Internet Explorer 10 on Windows 8 and Windows Phone since version 8 supports these events with the MS prefix; therefore, `pointerdown` becomes `MSpointerdown`.

*Table 15-4. Available pointer events*

| Event | Description |
| --- | --- |
| pointerdown | The pointer enters the active state. |
| pointerup | The pointer leaves the active state. |
| pointercancel | A hardware or operating system operation has canceled the user's pointer action, or a browser gesture has been detected after pointerdown, such as a pinch-to-zoom operation. This can also be triggered if the hardware believes that the touch was accidental or if the user is changing the device's orientation while the pointer is active. |
| pointermove | The pointer has changed coordinates, pressure, or tilt (if supported). |
| pointerover | A pointer has been detected in the area but the pointer is not active yet. For noncompatible input types, pointerover should be fired immediately before pointerdown. |
| pointerout | After a pointerover, the pointer has left the area. |
| gotpointercapture | The element has captured a pointer. |
| lostpointercapture | The element has lost a pointer capture. |

 We can capture pointer events using `addEventListener` or through the DOM interface, which creates one attribute per event following the on<*event*> syntax (such as `onpointerdown` for the standard spec and `onmspointerdown` for IE's implementation).

**Pointer detection.** The Pointer Events specification adds two properties to `window.nav igator`: `pointerEnabled`, a Boolean value to detect API support, and `maxTouch Points`, an integer value for detecting the maximum number of simultaneous touches supported by the device. IE10 supports this prefixed, so the properties are naviga tor.msPointerEnabled and navigator.msMaxTouchPoints.

**Touch action style.** The Pointer Events specification adds a CSS style to define the default touch action in a specific area: the touch-action style, which accepts the values none, auto, and inherit. By defining touch-action: none we can disable the default zooming and scrolling behavior in an area without any JavaScript hack.

In Internet Explorer 10 this property is prefixed (-ms-touch-action) and it also accepts more values, such as pan-x, pan-y, pinch-zoom, manipulation, and double-tap-zoom. Therefore, to disable scrolling and zooming in an element in IE10, the code looks like:

```
#element {
    -ms-touch-action: none;
}
```

> IE10 for Windows Store apps supports several CSS extensions to manipulate zooming and scrolling behavior, such as -ms-content-zoom, -ms-scroll-limit, and -ms-scroll-rails.

**Working with the touches and clicks.** All pointer events, such as MSPointerDown, receive the same PointerEvent object as the event argument. Pointer events differ from touch events in how we receive each touch or point: instead of receiving an array of touches (as in touch events), in pointer events we just receive the current pointer. If the user is pressing with more than one finger simultaneously, we receive one call to the handler per touch, and through the pointerId property we can detect if the pointer is the same as or different than the one in the previous calls.

The PointerEvent object inherits from MouseEvent, including well-known properties such as clientX and clientY for coordinates, and it adds the properties listed in Table 15-5.

*Table 15-5. Most useful PointerEvent properties*

| Property | Description |
|---|---|
| currentPoint | Gets a PointerObject object with basic info for the pointer. |
| hwTimestamp | The time at which the pointer was detected by the hardware. |
| intermediate Points | A collection of PointerObject objects representing the pointer history. |
| isPrimary | Returns whether this pointer is the primary one for the current interaction. In a multitouch operation, the first touch is declared as the primary contact. |
| pointerId | A unique identifier for the current touch or click. It can be used to detect if subsequent events are triggered from the same pointer. |

| Property | Description |
|---|---|
| pointerType | The type of the pointer. Possible values are the constant values of the same PointerEvent object: POINTER_TYPE_TOUCH, POINTER_TYPE_PEN, and POINTER_TYPE_MOUSE. In IE10, the constants are prefixed, as in MSPOINTER_TYPE_TOUCH. |
| pressure | The pressure of the current pointer, from 0 to 255. Available only on selected devices and input types. |
| tiltX | The angle between the Y-Z plane, in the range of −90 to +90. If the angle is greater than 0, that means the tilt is to the right. Available only on selected devices and input types. |
| tiltY | The angle between the Y-Z and transducer-X planes, in the range of −90 to +90. If the angle is greater than 0, that means the tilt is toward the user. Available only on selected devices and input types. |
| timeStamp | The time at which the pointer event was fired. |

 While event names, constants, and CSS styles are prefixed in Internet Explorer, pointer properties, such as pointerId, are not prefixed.

**Simulating touch on desktops.** Google Chrome for desktops supports touch event simulation through the developer tools, as we will see in Chapter 18. With the option in active mode, mouse events will also trigger single touch events on desktops.

Touché (*https://github.com/davidcalhoun/touche*) is an open source JavaScript library that we can use while developing that will map mouse events to Apple touch events. Phantom Limb (*https://github.com/brian-c/phantom-limb*) offers the same functionality with the addition of simulating a second touch using accessory keys on the keyboard.

# Gestures

A *gesture* is a way of combining finger movements over the screen to fire an action, instead of using a simple touch or click. A complete touch (or mouse) move-capturing feature is required in order for gestures to be registered. While we can use low-level touch events and some algorithms to detect them, some browsers support native APIs that will help us with this work.

If the users need to use a gesture in your web application, it is important to train them in what to do by showing a help message, a sample animation, or some other kind of hint.

## Swipe gesture

The swipe (also known as *flick*) gesture is a touch-based browser technique typically used for going forward and backward. For example, it is used in many photo galleries to change the currently displayed image, and in presentations to move from slide to slide. The gesture is simply a finger moving across the *x*-axis from left to right or right to left (a horizontal swipe), or along the *y*-axis from top to bottom or bottom to top (a vertical swipe). It is a one-finger gesture, so it is compatible with almost any touch device.

There is no standard event that captures the swipe action, so we need to emulate it using standard events.

The steps will be:

1. Capture `mousedown` (or `touchstart` for compatible browsers) and start a gesture recording.
2. Capture `mousemove` (or `touchmove` for compatible browsers) and continue the gesture recording if the move is on the *x*-axis (or *y*-axis), within a certain threshold. Cancel the gesture if the move is on the other axis.
3. Capture `mouseup` (or `touchend` for compatible browsers) and, if the gesture was active and the difference between the original and final coordinates is greater than a predefined constant, define a swipe to one direction.

The last item can be replaced with an on-the-fly verification of the gesture inside the `mousemove` event.

 If you are interested in gesture diagrams, Luke Wroblewski has a complete guide (*http://www.lukew.com/ff/entry.asp?1073*).

### Frameworks

Reinventing the wheel is not always a good idea—sometimes it is, but creating algorithms for gesture detection using raw touch movements isn't one of those times! Many application or UI frameworks, such as jQuery Mobile, Dojo Mobile, and Sencha Touch, support some gesture detection in an easier way. There are also some frameworks specifically designed for gesture interactions, such as Hammer.js.

Hammer.js (*http://eightmedia.github.com/hammer.js*) is an open source JavaScript library for multitouch gestures that is available in a compressed format (2 KB). It can detect tap, double-tap, swipe, tap-and-hold, transform, and drag gestures.

Swiper (*http://www.idangero.us/sliders/swiper/*) is a lightweight and multiplatform solution to create swipe effects and transitions using touch or pointer events and CSS transitions, by default.

Other frameworks with gesture support include Jo (*http://joapp.com*), jGestures for jQuery (*http://jgestures.codeplex.com*), Zepto.js (*http://zeptojs.com*), and Lungo (*http://lungo.tapquo.com*).

## Apple Gesture API

One of the coolest features of the iPhone when it was presented as a new phone was the zoom and rotate gesture. Using a pinching gesture with two fingers, the user can zoom in and zoom out on content (generally a picture), and using two fingers moving in a circle, he can rotate that picture.

 For nonmultitouch devices, we should provide zoom features using normal floating buttons or with a slider.

Fortunately, from iOS 2.0, Safari allows us to detect these gestures without using low-level math in the touch events. This specification is known as Apple Gesture API. While lots of vendors have cloned the Apple touch events, at the time of this writing only the Nokia Browser for MeeGo has implemented this Gesture API.

A gesture, from this API's point of view, is a two-finger movement intended to zoom or rotate the document or a specific element on the screen.

 The Gesture API works only with zoom and rotate; it doesn't allow us to detect swipe, touch-and-hold, or any other kinds of gestures.

There are three events available, listed in Table 15-6.

*Table 15-6. Events available in the Apple Gesture API*

| Event | Description |
| --- | --- |
| gesturestart | Fired when the user starts a gesture using two fingers |
| gesturechange | Fired when the user is moving her fingers (rotating or pinching) |
| gestureend | Fired when the user lifts one or both fingers |

The same events are used for rotate and zoom gestures. All three events receive a GestureEvent parameter. This parameter has typical event properties, and the additional properties scale and rotation.

The scale property defines the distance between the two fingers as a floating-point multiplier of the initial distance when the gesture started. If this value is greater than 1.0 it is a pinch open (zoom in), and if it is lower than 1.0 it is a pinch close (zoom out).

The Gesture API for iOS works not only in Safari but in every web view, such as an Apache Cordova/PhoneGap app or any web view–based browsers, such as Chrome for iOS.

The rotation value gives the delta rotation from the initial point, in degrees. If the user is rotating clockwise we will get a positive degree value, and we'll get a negative value for a counter-clockwise rotation.

I know what you're thinking right now: "Great! Rotation and zoom. But we're working in HTML, so what we can do with that?" CSS3 comes to our help with one attribute, transform, and two functions available for manipulating its value: rotate() and scale(). Remember that at the time of this writing, transform is a prefixed attribute in Safari on iOS.

The rotate() function receives a parameter in degrees, and we need to define the deg unit after the number (for example, rotate(90deg)). We can define it from a script using element.style.webkitTransform.

Let's look at a simple sample:

```
<!DOCTYPE html>
<html>
<head>
<meta charset="UTF-8" />
<title>Gesture Management</title>
<meta name="viewport" content="width=device-width; initial-scale=1.0;
    maximum-scale=1.0; user-scalable=0;">

<script type="text/javascript">
function gesture(event) {
    // We round values with two decimals
    event.target.innerHTML = "Rotation: "
        + Math.round(event.rotation*100)/100
        + " Scale: " + Math.round(event.scale*100)/100;
    // We apply the transform functions to the element
    event.target.style.webkitTransform =
        "rotate(" + event.rotation%360 + "deg)"
        + " scale(" + event.scale + ")";
}

</script>

</head>

<body>

<div ongesturechange="gesture(event)" style="background-color:silver;
    width: 300px; height: 300px">
```

```
</div>

</body>
</html>
```

Users can rotate and scale the div (with all its contents) using two fingers on compatible devices. What's the only problem? The transform style is always applied to the original element. So, if we apply a scale of 2.0 to the element and later apply a second scale of 0.5, the new scale value will be 0.5 and not 1.0, as we might expect.

For typical zoom-rotate relative behavior, we should change our function to the following:

```
<script type="text/javascript">
var rotation = 0;
var scale = 1;

function gesture(event) {
    event.target.innerHTML = "Rotation: " +
        Math.round((event.rotation+rotation)*100)/100
        + " Scale: " + Math.round((event.scale*scale)*100)/100;
    event.target.style.webkitTransform =
        "rotate(" +
(event.rotation+rotation)%360 + "deg)"
        + " scale(" + event.scale*scale + ")";
}

function gestureend(event) {
    rotation = event.rotation+rotation;
    scale    = event.scale*scale;
}

</script>

</head>

<body>

<div ongesturechange="gesture(event)" ongestureend="gestureend(event)"
    style="background-color:silver; width: 100%; height: 300px">

</div>
```

 If you have a viewport definition allowing zooming actions, remember to prevent the default behavior when the gesture starts so you can manage the gesture, and not the browser.

## Microsoft Gesture API

Along with its alternative to the Touch Events APIs, Microsoft has also developed a Gesture API. This API was not included by the W3C in the Pointer Events specification.

The Microsoft API supports detection of pinch, swipe, hold, pan, tap, and long press (tap-and-hold) gestures without reading raw pointer events. To start a gesture recognition mechanism, we must configure an `MSGesture` object when a touch starts (`mspointerdown`) and we want to detect gestures on it.

The Gesture API allows the detection of inertia, which is a way to continue receiving events after the user releases his fingers, following the speed of the original gesture. That is, if the user makes a fast swipe, we can receive inertia events based on the speed of the gesture that allow us to create visual effects that decelerate.

> When working with gesture events, it's a good idea to disable zooming, scrolling, and text selection from the elements using `-ms-touch-action: none` and `-ms-user-select: none`.

**Starting a gesture detection.** To start a gesture detection we need to add an element to the gesture engine. We do this using the `MSGesture()` constructor function, passing the `target` element to it. For example:

```
var myGesture = new MSGesture();
var myElement = document.getElementById("gesturearea");
myGesture.target = myElement;
```

To detect a gesture in that element, we need to capture `mstouchdown` and pass the touch identification to our gesture using the `addPointer()` method, as in:

```
myElement.addEventListener("mspointerdown", function(event) {
    myGesture.addPointer(event.pointerId);
}, false);
```

When we have the gesture implemented, we can start listening for gesture events in the element. Possible events are listed in Table 15-7.

*Table 15-7. Events available in the Microsoft Gesture API*

| Event | Description | States |
|-------|-------------|--------|
| msgesturehold | Fired when the user touches down, holds the touch/pointer for a moment, and then releases without moving. | When the user has been holding the pointer down long enough for it to be interpreted as a touch and hold, `event.MSGESTURE_FLAG_BEGIN` is true; when the user has released the contact without moving the pointer `event.MSGESTURE_FLAG_END` is true; and when the user has released the contact after moving it, so the gesture was canceled, `event.MSGESTURE_FLAG_CANCEL` is true. |

| Event | Description | States |
|---|---|---|
| msgesturestart | Fired when a touch has started on the element that may be a gesture. | This event indicates the start of a new contact/gesture. |
| msgesturechange | Fired after a dynamic gesture change, including pinch, rotate, swipe, and pan/drag. | This event fires every time the user moves one touch, and after the user has removed all the touches but there are still inertia events going on. |
| msgestureend | Fired after all associated touches/pointers have been removed from the screen and any inertia movement has finished. | This event fires when the user has removed all the touches for this gesture and any inertia processing has stopped. |
| msgesturetap | Fired after a single, quick interaction with the screen has been made. | This event fires if the touch/pointer is removed quickly, at the same point as where it started. |
| msinertiastart | Fired after the user has removed all touches but, because of the gesture speed, there is still an inertia that will continue "moving" the pointer. | This event fires when the user has removed all touches and there was enough speed in the gesture for inertia. |

We can detect if a gesture is in its inertia phase using the argument's detail property, which we compare to event.MSGESTURE_FLAG_INER TIA. If we don't want to consider inertia for our effects, we can just read this property.

**Gesture change values.** When detecting a dynamic gesture we usually use the msgestur echange event, which receives an argument with different properties that can be easily matched to CSS transformations, such as event.translationX and event.translati onY for translation from the original point; event.rotation for rotation; event.scale for scaling; and event.offsetX and event.offsetY for the center point of the gesture (and the possible transformations).

When detecting swipe (flick) gestures, the msgesturechange event has useful properties such as velocityX and velocityY for the velocity on both axes, and velocityAngu lar for the angular velocity in radians.

Microsoft supports an mscontentzoom event that will be fired after the user has zoomed the target element.

To apply a CSS transformation to the element in which we are detecting gestures, we can use the following snippet, based on a Microsoft official documentation example:

```
myElement.addEventListener("MSGestureChange", function(e) {
    // Get the latest CSS transform on the element
```

```
    var m = new MSCSSMatrix(e.target.style.transform);
    e.target.style.transform = m
// Move the transform origin under the gesture's center
    .translate(e.offsetX, e.offsetY)
    .rotate(e.rotation * 180 / Math.PI) // Apply rotation
    .scale(e.scale)                     // Apply scale
    .translate(e.translationX, e.translationY) // Apply translation
    .translate(-e.offsetX, -e.offsetY); // Move transform origin back
}, false);
```

# Sensors

Touch is not the only input that we can read from an HTML5 mobile app. Most devices after the iPhone included a couple of sensors that we can also use to provide input data for our apps or games, including the accelerometer, magnetometer (digital compass), and gyroscope. Some devices also include pressure and lighting sensors.

While trying to understand how these sensors work is out of the scope of this book, it's important to know what each sensor is useful for:

*Accelerometer*
Measures linear motion (current acceleration) on the device on three axes ($x$, $y$, $z$), including gravity. That means that we can detect how the user is holding the device in three dimensions, as well as any gesture that the user may be doing with the device, such as shaking.

*Gyroscope*
Measures rate of rotation around one axis, based on angular momentum. Gravity does not affect the gyro, and it is usually used in conjunction with the accelerometer to provide trusted information about the device's rotation and orientation.

*Magnetometer*
Measures the device heading in relation to true north, in degrees. This is the necessary sensor to detect yaw, which is orthogonal to gravity.

*Pressure sensor*
Measures barometric information.

While you may think that using the accelerometer will consume battery power, it's important to know that this sensor is always on; it's the one behind the screen rotation mechanism.

## DeviceOrientation Event

The DeviceOrientation Event W3C (*http://www.w3.org/TR/orientation-event*) specification is a draft that is implemented on most tablet and smartphone platforms today. Safari on iOS 4.2 was the first mobile browser to support it, but today it can be found in the Android browser (since 3.0), the BlackBerry browser, and many others, as we can see at Mobile HTML5 (*http://www.mobilehtml5.org*).

This specification adds three events that we can attach to the `window` object: `deviceorientation` for orientation change detection (compatible when a gyro is available), `devicemotion` for accelerometer data detection, and `compassneedscalibration` for when the device detects that the compass needs a calibration to increase data accuracy.

When using `deviceorientation`, every time the user moves the device we will receive an event call that includes the properties `alpha` (0–360), `beta` (–90–90), and `gamma` (–180–180) for the rotation of the device frame around its *z*-, *x*-, and *y*-axes, respectively. These values are typically defined as an offset from an arbitrary direction, usually the direction in which the device was held when the orientation was first obtained. Therefore, `deviceorientation` is more useful for relative movements from the original position.

When `compassneedscalibration` is fired we need to inform the user that she needs to make a figure-eight motion in the air to improve accuracy.

The `devicemotion` event shows gravity and user acceleration on devices with both an accelerometer and a gyroscope. iPhone 3GS, iPad first generation, and older iPod touch devices didn't include a gyroscope; therefore, this API can only measure gravity acceleration on those devices.

The event gives us the `rotationRate` (`alpha`, `beta`, and `gamma` values if a gyro is available), `acceleration` (for the user's acceleration if a gyro is available), and `accelerationIncludingGravity` (for user and gravity acceleration). Acceleration properties include x, y, and z for the acceleration in each axis, measured in m/s$^2$.

We should always query about ranges of values for the accelerometer and orientation and not exact values. Different ways of measuring can be found between different implementations in different browsers, such as one device giving positive values when facing back while others give negative values for the same orientation. Testing and user calibration are important to provide a multiplatform solution today.

There is no better way to understand accelerometer and gyro values than trying this out yourself on a real device. You can point your mobile browser now to *http://t.ad.ag* and look for the JavaScript API→Device Motion tests.

**Moving a ball.** One of the classic examples of accelerometer usage is allowing the user to move the device to give acceleration to a virtual table with a little ball on it. To create this particular example using this API, we can use the following working sample:

```html
<!DOCTYPE html>
<html>
<head>
<meta charset="UTF-8">
<title>Move the Ball</title>
<meta name="viewport" content="width=device-width,user-scalable=no">
<style>
#no {
    display: none;
}
#ball {
    width: 20px;
    height: 20px;
    border-radius: 10px;
    background-color: red;
    position:absolute;
    top: 0px;
    left: 0px;
}
</style>
</head>

<body>

<div id="content">
    <h1>Move the Ball</h1>
    <div id="yes">
    <div id="ball"></div>
    </div>
    <div id="no">
        Your browser does not support the Device Orientation
        and Motion API.
    </div>
</div>

<script>
// Position variables
var x = 0;
var y = 0;

// Speed - Velocity
var vx = 0;
var vy = 0;

// Acceleration
var ax = 0;
var ay = 0;
```

```
    var delay = 10;
    var vMultiplier = 0.01;

    if (window.DeviceMotionEvent==undefined) {
        // API not available
        document.getElementById("no").style.display="block";
        document.getElementById("yes").style.display="none";
    } else {
        window.addEventListener("devicemotion", function(event) {
            ax = event.accelerationIncludingGravity.x;
            ay = event.accelerationIncludingGravity.y;
        }

        setInterval(function() {
            // We calculate new velocity, based on current acceleration
            vy = vy + -(ay);
            vx = vx + ax;

            // We calculate new position, based on current velocity
            y = parseInt(y + vy * vMultiplier);
            x = parseInt(x + vx * vMultiplier);

            // Detect screen boundaries
            if (x<0) { x = 0; vx = 0; }
            if (y<0) { y = 0; vy = 0; }

            if (x>document.documentElement.clientWidth-20) {
                x = document.documentElement.clientWidth-20; vx = 0;
            }
            if (y>document.documentElement.clientHeight-20) {
                y = document.documentElement.clientHeight-20; vy = 0;
            }

            // "Move" the ball to its new position
            var ball = document.getElementById("ball");
            ball.style.top = y + "px";
            ball.style.left = x + "px";
        }, delay);
    }

</script>

</body>
</html>
```

Unless we are creating a native web app, there is no way to force orientation lock in HTML5. Therefore, it's possible that when the user is moving and tilting the device, the orientation will change, and that will lead to some UI problems. We should try to detect these changes and pause/stop the reading until the user goes back to the desired orientation.

Using the accelerometer at the same time as detecting touch events, we can emulate pressure detection, as we can detect how much movement the device had while the user was touching it.

### Compass information

According to the specification, to get the compass heading we just need to handle `deviceorientation` and use the formula `360 - event.alpha`. However, life isn't always that simple, and WebKit-based browsers may differ in their implementation. For example, Apple says that the `deviceorientation` event will show relative information from an arbitrary position and not an absolute position on Earth; therefore, `event.alpha` is not absolute, but a relative measure from the first reading.

On Safari on iOS from 5.0, we can use `event.webkitCompassHeading` to have the heading measured in degrees relative to magnetic north, with `0` being north, `180` south, `90` east, and `270` west. `event.webkitCompassAccuracy` will give us the accuracy measured in degrees; if this property is set to `–1` it's because the compass is not calibrated and the information should not be used.

When the user is changing the device's orientation (e.g., landscape to portrait) the heading may differ, so we can use the `window.orientation` value to act and normalize the `webkitCompassHeading` information.

If you want to see a working example of the compass API with CSS transformations, you can check out the open source solution created by James Pearce at his GitHub page (*https://github.com/jamesgpearce/compios5*).

### Apache Cordova API

Apache Cordova/PhoneGap includes a proprietary accelerometer and compass API to read raw data when creating this kind of app. Two objects are exposed to access the sensors: `navigator.accelerometer` and `navigator.compass`. The API is similar to the Geolocation API, defining methods such as `getCurrentAcceleration`, `watchAcceleration`, `clearAcceleration`, `getCurrentHeading`, `watchHeading`, and `clearHeading`.

Compass handlers will receive an `event.magneticHeading` attribute and accelerometer handlers will receive `event.x`, `event.y`, and `event.z` values for acceleration on every axis.

## Network Information

The Network Information API (*http://www.w3.org/TR/netinfo-api*) allows us to determine some information about the current connection. At the time of this writing, two different implementations of the API are available: an old spec version first implemented by the Android browser and Apache Cordova/PhoneGap apps; and the new W3C spec, including bandwidth information first implemented by the Blackberry 10 browser and Firefox for mobile devices.

## Old specification

The old spec API (*http://bit.ly/10St3bL*) exposes a `navigator.connection.type` attribute that will match one of the following strings: `unknown`, `ethernet`, `wifi`, `2g`, `3g`, `4g`, or `none`.

While the old W3C spec said that the `type` attribute should be a string, the Android browser and Apache Cordova implementations expose its value as an integer, mapped to the `navigator.connection` constants.

This API will give you the connection type of the first node; that doesn't mean that it is working properly or even that it is the ultimate type of connection. For example, it's common to have WiFi on some buses and trains today, and the WiFi access point may be using a 3G connection.

Besides this API, browsers also expose two events—`online` and `offline`—that we can use to detect changes in connection status, as well as the `window.onLine` Boolean property.

When we are offline, we are sure there is no Internet connection, no WiFi, and no cellular connection. If the API is exposing that we are online, that just means that there is a connection available; it doesn't mean it's working.

## New specification

Knowing which type of connection the user has may not be enough—he may be on WiFi under a 2G-connection hotspot or have a nonworking 4G connection. That's why the W3C working group for this API has developed a new draft of it (implemented only in Firefox for Android and the Blackberry 10 browser at the time of this writing).

This new spec is still based on the same `navigator.connection` object, but instead of exposing a `type` attribute it exposes `bandwidth` and `metered` attributes and a `change` event.

The `bandwidth` can be 0 (offline), `infinite` (unknown), or any estimation in MB/s (megabytes per second); `metered` is a Boolean attribute indicating that the current connection may be limited by the Internet provider and that we should be careful about bandwidth usage.

Besides the `online` and `offline` events, this new spec also delivers a new `change` event over `navigator.connection` that will trigger a call every time the connection changes.

Currently Firefox supports this feature through a `moz` prefixed version and Chrome (for desktops only at the time of this writing) with a `webkit` prefixed version.

If this API is available, we can decide what kind of experience we are going to deliver, including SD or HD video and different image qualities, as in:

```
var connection = navigator.connection || navigator.mozConnection ||
                 navigator.webkitConnection;

if (connection.bandwidth!=undefined) {
    if (connection.bandwidth <=1) {
        // Less than 1 MB/s => Low quality
    } else if (connection.bandwidth > 1) {
        // More than 1 MB/s => High quality
    } else {
        // Offline or unknown
    }
} else {
    // API not available or older spec
}
```

## File Management

The File API (*http://www.w3.org/TR/FileAPI/*) is a W3C specification that is available in some modern mobile browsers, including Google Chrome, the BlackBerry browser, Internet Explorer since version 10, and Safari on iOS since version 6. With this API we can read files from the device's filesystem at the user's request.

On some platforms the same API also allows us to navigate through a filesystem and write files, as in Apache Cordova/PhoneGap apps.

> The Directories and System API (also known as the FileSystem API) should not be confused with the File API, as the first one's intent is to create a virtual filesystem for isolated app storage, while the latter works with the user's public filesystem. We can also use the File API on our isolated filesystem.

When working with browser-based apps on mobile devices, this API can be triggered after the user has selected one or more files from a file upload form input control (`<input type="file">`) using the `change` event. In desktop browsers, this API can also be used with the Drag and Drop API (which is useless on mobile devices as there is no way to drag a file from the filesystem to the browser).

> Remember from previous chapters that the file upload control can also be used for taking pictures or recording audio and video using the `accept` and `capture` attributes.

The following example will loop through all the files selected in the form control. Even if we are not using the multiple attribute and it's a single selection, we always receive an array of files. Every file object has a name, a size, and a type (the MIME type of the file):

```
<input type="file" id="selectFiles">
<script>
document.getElementById("selectFiles").addEventListener
    ("change", function(event) {
    for (var i=0; i<event.files.length; i++) {
        var fileObject = event.files[i];
        var fileURL = URL.createObjectURL(fileObject);
        // We are ready to read the file
    }
}, false);
</script>
```

Using the FileReader constructor function, we can read files in three different formats: as text, in data URI string format, and as binary data, using the methods readAs Text(), readAsDataURL(), and readAsBinary(), with every method receiving the file URL as an argument. The file URL (following the *file://* protocol) can be obtained using the URL.createObjectURL() method that is available on the DOM.

File reading is an asynchronous process and we should handle the load and error events of the FileReader, receiving in the first event the file data in the requested format:

```
for (var i=0; i<event.files.length; i++) {
    var fileObject = event.files[i];
    var fileURL = URL.createObjectURL(fileObject);
    var fr = new FileReader();
    fr.addEventListener("load", function(e) {
        var data = e.target.result;
        // We can now save, send, or show the contents of the file
        // in data. We can also revoke the URL to free resources
        // and for security purposes.
        URL.revokeObjectURL(fileURL);
    }, false);
    fr.readAsDataURL(fileURL);
}
```

### Full FileSystem API

Apache Cordova/PhoneGap apps support the full API, including FileWriter to write files, DirectoryReader for folder browsing, and FileTransfer to upload the files to an HTTP server without XMLHttpRequest. For full documentation and working examples, visit Phonegap (*http://docs.phonegap.com*).

Every native app—including native web apps, such as Cordova/PhoneGap apps—usually has two folders available for app storage: a persistent and a temporary storage folder. The persistent folder will keep files for different sessions, and on some platforms that folder is backed up automatically on the computer or in the cloud (such as in iCloud). To use these filesystems, we need to request one using the FileSystem API, as in:

```
window.requestFileSystem(LocalFileSystem.PERSISTENT, 0,
    function(fs) {
        // Filesystem ready to use; we can use DirectoryReader to browse
        // it or FileReader/FileWriter to read and/or write files in it
    },
    function(e) {
        // Failed
});
```

# Full Screen

If we want to get a full-screen experience (no browser UI), we can use the following techniques:

- Package the app as a native web app (see Chapter 16)
- In iOS, create a Home screen web app (see Chapter 16)
- On compatible devices, suggest to the user to force full-screen mode using a browser feature based on current viewport size (at the time of this writing, available only in Safari on iOS 6 in landscape mode and Internet Explorer 10 on Windows 8)
- Use the Full Screen API

The Full Screen API (*http://www.w3.org/TR/fullscreen*) is a way to request the browser to convert one element into a full-screen one, without the browser UI. At the time of this writing, the only browser supporting the API without any bugs is Amazon Silk for the Kindle Fire 2.0. It's possible that other browsers will implement it in the future.

To make a full-screen experience, we need to call the requestFullScreen() method of the DOM element we want to force to this mode. Any sibling elements or elements outside of it will not be on the screen while it is in full-screen mode. On WebKit- and Gecko-based browsers, this API is prefixed, so the method is called webkitRequest FullScreen() or mozRequestFullScreen() instead. It's important to understand that usually the full-screen request can be made only after a user interaction, as a click/tap on the element, and not on load events or timers. For example:

```
function goFullScreen() {
    var element = document.getElementById("fullscreenElement");
    if (element.requestFullScreen) {
        element.requestFullScreen();
    } else if (element.mozRequestFullScreen) {
        element.mozRequestFullScreen();
    } else if (element.webkitRequestFullScreen) {
        element.webkitRequestFullScreen();
    }
}
```

The user usually has a way to get back to the normal web UI through the browser's user interface (in Amazon Silk, there is a UI button), and we can also disable full-screen mode from code by calling `exitFullscreen()` on the `document` object. The previous version of the specification (available on current browsers) defines the exit operation as `cancelFullScreen()` and all the prefixed versions.

 In compatible browsers we can use the new pseudoclass `:fullscreen` to define styles that will apply only in full-screen mode. In other browsers, the pseudoclass must be prefixed, as in `:-webkit-full-screen` or `:-moz-fullscreen`.

The specification (old and new) also adds the Boolean `fullscreenEnabled` attribute and the `fullscreenElement` attribute for getting the current DOM element that is taking up the screen.

## Web Notifications

The Web Notifications API (*http://www.w3.org/TR/notifications*) allows a website to add a notification alert into the operating system notification center. This API is not well supported in mobile devices, primarily because only a few platforms allow a background browser operation that can take advantage of notifications to the user.

At the time of this writing, only the BlackBerry browser for PlayBook and BB10 and Firefox support this API, with the `webkit` and `moz` prefixes, respectively. In Figure 15-3 we can see how Firefox delivers a notification on an Android device.

*Figure 15-3. Firefox for Android supports the Web Notifications API—after getting the user's approval, we can add messages to the notification bar and receive events from the notification (if the user clicks on it).*

The API is based on a global `window.notifications` object that today is prefixed as `window.webkitNotifications` and `window.mozNotifications`. The main problem with this specification is that there are currently two different APIs on the market (the old and new versions).

 The old specification of this API was implemented by Chrome for desktops, but at the time of this writing Chrome for Android doesn't support the new API. For compatibility updates, check Mobile HTML5 (*http://www.mobilehtml5.org*).

We need permission from the user for our website to send notifications. To get that permission, we need to call the method `requestPermission()` from the `notifications` object; this method will receive a callback as an argument. The old specification supports a `checkPermission()` function that returns a 0 value if the permission was granted. The current specification has a `permission` property with the string values `default`, `denied`, or `granted`.

Once we have permission, we can generate a notification using the `createNotification()` method in the old spec or the `Notification()` constructor function in the new spec, which receives a title and an object with options.

In both specs we can handle events for the notification, including `display`, `click`, `error`, and `close`.

 To further complicate our work, for old spec implementations, Mozilla receives the `icon_url` as the last argument and WebKit-based browsers as the first argument.

In the old spec, to create a notification we can use the following snippet:

```
var notificationManager = navigator.mozNotification ||
    navigator.webkitNotification || navigator.notification;

if (notificationManager!=undefined) {
    var notification;
    if (navigator.mozNotification) {
        notification =
            notificationManager.createNotification("icon_url",
            "title", "message");
    } else {
        notification = notificationManager.createNotification("title",
                        "message", "icon_url");
    }
    notification.show();
    notification.onclick = function() {
```

```
        alert('You clicked the notification');
    }
}
```

In the new spec, the same code will look like this:

```
var Notification = window.Notification || window.mozNotification ||
                        window.webkitNotification;

if (Notification!=undefined) {
    var options = {
        iconUrl: "icon_url",
        body: "message",
        onclick: function() {
            alert('You clicked the notification');
        }
    }
    var notification = new Notification("title", options);
}
```

 In the new spec, in the notification's options we have the ability to define a tag. The tag is a string value that will be used to group different notifications from the same source. For example, if we are alerting the user for each mail she receives, we can group all of them into one notification that is updated as more information is received.

# Camera

The ability to access the camera—whether to take a picture, read a QR code, or make a video call—is one of the most interesting features of a mobile web app. Standards around camera access vary, and today there are several different APIs for it:

- HTML Media Capture (covered in Chapter 8), through `<input type="file">`
- The Media Capture and Streams API
- Apache Cordova/PhoneGap's Camera API
- Apache Cordova/PhoneGap's Capture API

### getUserMedia

The Media Capture and Streams spec (*http://www.w3.org/TR/mediacapture-streams/*), defines different mechanisms to capture and stream media from the device. The camera part is also known as the `getUserMedia` API and is the most compatible part of the spec today on mobile browsers.

The API supports `MediaStream` objects representing streams of media data, usually audio or video, having an input and an output. To use the camera as an input, we generate a stream object from a `getUserMedia()` call that uses the camera as the input source for the media stream. The stream's output can be a `file` object or, most probable in a mobile app, a `video` element on the DOM.

> In the future, with the WebRTC (Web Real Time Communication) API, we will be able to use video streams to make video calls or enable two-way video streaming through a web browser.

At the time of this writing, `getUserMedia` is compatible only with Opera Mobile from version 12 and the BlackBerry browser for BB10.

> Streaming camera input is the base for augmented reality apps, as we can point to or show elements over or around the camera preview. On mobile web platforms, it's still not possible to create nice augmented reality web experiences.

To get a stream from the device's camera to a `video` element with the ID `player` we need to use the following code, which we can see in action on a BlackBerry 10 browser in Figure 15-4:

```
window.onload = function(){
    window.URL = window.URL || window.webkitURL;

    navigator.getUserMedia = navigator.getUserMedia ||
                        navigator.webkitGetUserMedia || navigator.mozGetUserMedia;
    var video = document.getElementById("player");

    if (navigator.getUserMedia) {
        // we request a media stream with video and audio
        navigator.getUserMedia({audio:true, video:true},
            function(stream){
            // we create a URL for the input camera stream
            // for the video
            video.src=window.URL.createObjectURL(stream);
            video.play();
        });
    }
}
```

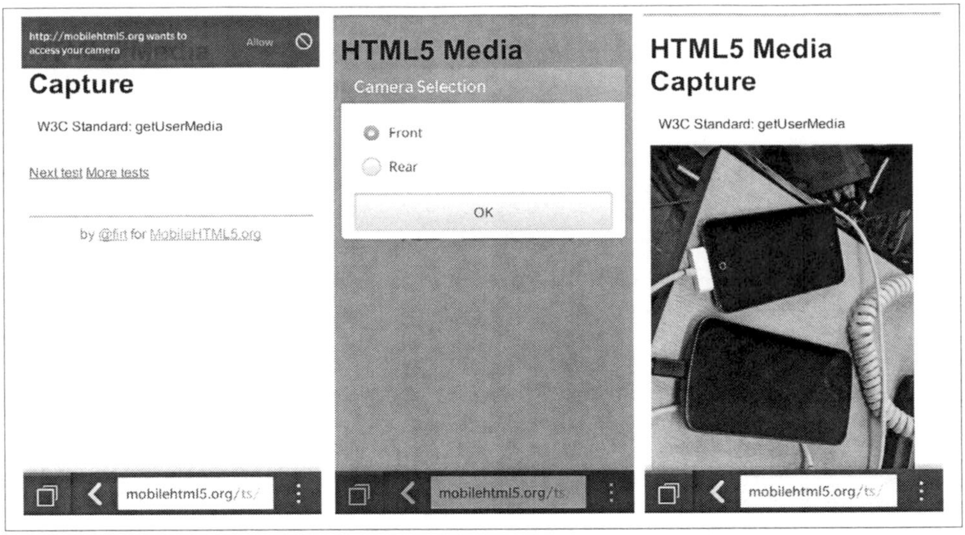

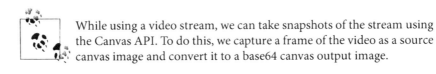

*Figure 15-4. In the BlackBerry 10 browser, when we try to open a camera session the user must give permission and select which camera to use before the stream is sent to a video element.*

> While using a video stream, we can take snapshots of the stream using the Canvas API. To do this, we capture a frame of the video as a source canvas image and convert it to a base64 canvas output image.

## Apache Cordova APIs

When using Apache Cordova/PhoneGap, we have two APIs for managing the camera. The simpler API is through `navigator.camera`, such as in:

```
navigator.camera.getPicture(
    function(imageData) {
        // Success callback
        var imageURL = "data:image/jpeg;base64," + imageData;
    }, function(message) {
        // Fail callback
    },
    {  // Options
        quality: 50,
        destinationType: Camera.DestinationType.DATA_URL
    }
);
```

We can request the resulting image as a data URI string or as a file URL.

The Capture API is a more complex spec that allows us to record videos, images, or audio from the source. Unfortunately, we will receive the final file and not the stream to show on the screen.

To know more about Cordova APIs, check out *http://docs.phonegap.com*.

## Battery

The Battery Status API (*http://www.w3.org/TR/battery-status/*) allows us to read and keep updated on the current battery status, through a `navigator.battery` object. At the time of this writing, only Firefox for Mobile and the Blackberry 10 browser supports it, through a prefixed `navigator.mozBattery` object and a `navigator.webkitBattery` object.

With this API we can detect if the device is being charged or not through the Boolean `charging` attribute; `chargingTime` is the time remaining in seconds until the battery is fully charged, `dischargingTime` is the time available until a system suspension, and `level` is a float number between 0 (discharged) and 1 (totally charged).

The API also exposes some events through the object, including `chargingchange`, `chargingtimechange`, `dischargingtimechange`, and `levelchange`. The following example shows an alert when the battery is low and not being charged:

```
var battery = navigator.battery || navigator.mozBattery;
battery.levelchange = function() {
    if (battery.level<0.2) {
      alert('Battery at low level');
   }
}
```

## Vibration

The Vibration API (*http://www.w3.org/TR/vibration/*) provides a way to vibrate the phone or tablet, if that feature is available, through the `navigator` global object and a new `vibrate()` function. We can start a vibration, sending one value as the duration expressed in milliseconds, or an array of values. When sending an array of values, the first value will be a vibration duration, the second value will be a pause's duration, and so on. For example:

```
// Vibrate the device 2 seconds
navigator.vibrate(2000);

// Vibrate the device 1s, 0.5s pause, vibrate again 2s
navigator.vibrate([1000, 500, 2000]);
```

To stop any vibration, we need to use `navigator.vibrate(0)`. At the time of this writing, Firefox for Mobile are and the Blackberry 10 Browser are the only platforms supporting this API, through a prefixed `navigator.mozVibrate()` and navigator.webkitVibrate function with the same syntax.

## Other APIs

There are numerous other APIs that you may want to investigate.

### W3C

Other APIs with possibilities in the near future for mobile web applications are:

- Pointer Lock (*http://www.w3.org/TR/pointerlock/*)
- Ambient Light Events (*http://www.w3.org/TR/ambient-light/*)
- Proximity Events (*http://www.w3.org/TR/proximity/*)
- Web Intents (*http://www.w3.org/TR/web-intents/*)
- Pick Contact Intent (*http://www.w3.org/TR/contacts-api/*)
- Messaging (*http://www.w3.org/TR/messaging-api/*)
- Calendar (*http://www.w3.org/TR/calendar-api/*)

The W3C maintains a website following updates on all mobile APIs: the Device API Working Group site (*http://www.w3.org/2009/dap/*).

### Apache Cordova

Apache Cordova/PhoneGap apps support other nonstandard APIs, such as:

- Accelerometer
- Contacts
- Globalization

### Mozilla

In its WebAPI initiative (*https://wiki.mozilla.org/WebAPI*), Mozilla has a list of APIs that are implemented in Android and/or Firefox OS and are open to other platforms, including some of the APIs we've covered in this chapter, plus:

- WebTelephony
- Payment (for in-app purchases in web apps)
- WebSMS
- Idle
- Power Management

- TCP Socket
- WiFi Information
- Web Bluetooth
- Alarm
- WebFM

### For the future

The future of HTML5 and the mobile web includes several APIs that may give more power to HTML5 apps, including:

- WebNFC for Near Field Communication, such as reading RFID tags
- WebRTC for Real Time Communication, including bidirectional audio and video calls
- Web Intents for web app communication
- The Social API for abstract sharing to social networks
- The Session and Identification API for login and authorization purposes

 Bowser is an Ericsson Labs browser experiment available for iOS and Android: it's the first mobile browser supporting the full WebRTC draft standard, so you can make video calls between two browsers. More information and demos are available at Ericsson Labs (*https://labs.erics son.com/apps/bowser*).

CHAPTER 16

# Native and Installed Web Apps

Mobile web solutions can run like native installed applications on any platform. This technique is present today in every vendor's roadmap, and many devices are already compatible with some kind of solution for this.

The mobile community hasn't settled on a single name for this kind of application yet; some platforms call them "web apps" and others "offline applications," "JavaScript applications," "hybrid applications," "native web applications," "HTML5 apps," or simply "widgets."

All that said, to simplify our discussion of this kind of application in this chapter, from here on out I will refer to them as *web apps* when they are not packaged and *native web apps* when they are (the power of the author).

 In Chapter 3, we discussed the "native versus web" battle and what it means for us.

We'll define a mobile web app as an application entirely developed using web technologies (HTML, CSS, JavaScript) that is installed on the device's Home screen or in the applications menu and that the user can use when offline as well as online. The usage of web technologies is invisible to the user, and the application can work just like any other software installed on the device.

One of the main features of a web app versus hybrid or native web apps is the hosted-based nature: web apps must be hosted on a web server, while native web apps or hybrids are packaged, signed, and distributed through an app store.

# Web App Pros and Cons

Web apps are the future for most mobile applications, for a number of reasons:

1. The mobile world is fragmented and will be more fragmented in the future. Chapter 1 covered all the platforms that are available today and likely to be available in the near future. If you want wide coverage you need to create an application that will run on iPhone, Android, Windows Phone, Symbian, BlackBerry 7/10, and Nokia Java ME platforms—and you still won't be covering them all.

2. The web environment demands speed to market: we cannot wait months before releasing our mobile application clients. Web apps can be developed quickly.

3. Every vendor roadmap has a native web platform or similar technology implemented or slated to be implemented in the near future.

4. The majority of a web app's code can be shared between all operating systems.

5. A web app can be a great addition to a mobile website, sharing the same code as the "mobile client" version but offering different possibilities, such as integration with the device.

6. Web apps can be on the users' screens all the time, without requiring them to open the browser and type a URL.

7. Web apps are built using well-known technologies (HTML, JavaScript, CSS) for which a lot of human and technical resources are available.

8. We can use any web API for web app development, without waiting for a mobile SDK to appear.

9. Porting is less painful with web apps than with native applications.

10. It is easy to port mobile web apps from and to desktop widgets (Adobe AIR and others).

11. We can distribute web apps freely or sell them in vendors' stores.

12. Web apps can be self-updated (although on some platforms, such as iOS, store rules don't allow this behavior).

13. With web apps, we can access platform services through new JavaScript APIs not available in mobile web browsers.

However, not everything is golden, and we will face some problems when using this technology:

1. Porting is still required between platforms.

2. Debugging is painful, although this is getting better with time.

3. Web apps are not native applications, so the performance will always be worse than with a native app.

4. Web apps are not suitable for all kinds of applications and games.

5. Web apps are not simple websites, but complete applications using JavaScript; best practices and good programming techniques are mandatory.

6. On most platforms, we cannot create background applications.

7. Nonnative web apps can't access all hardware and operating system services.

8. Have I said yet that there are too many platforms? Certainly more than we want!

# Architecture of a Web App

We can define the architecture of a mobile web app as described in Figure 16-1.

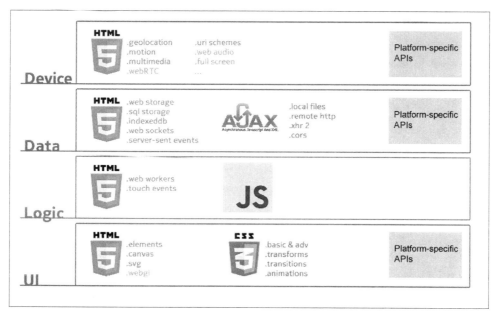

*Figure 16-1. Architecture of mobile web app development.*

# Meta Configuration

Every platform has some kind of metadata configuration file where we generally define the name of the application, the icon to be used for the applications menu, the main HTML or JavaScript file to load when the widget is launched, and other metainformation.

There are widget/web app platforms using all of the following for meta configuration:

- `meta` tags
- XML files
- JSON files
- Property list (*.plist*) files

## Platform Access

Platform access refers to the ability to connect to platform services, using the APIs covered in the previous two chapters.

## Data Storage

Web apps are not simple mobile websites; they are applications. And like all applications, they need to store information—databases, configurations, login data, statistics, or whatever else—in some sort of persistent store. As we saw in Chapter 13, HTML5 storage APIs will help us with this.

## Network Access

To access the Internet we can use standard Ajax requests, like any JavaScript code, or any other similar solution, such as JSONP requests. Most web app platforms accept cross-platform Ajax requests (to any web server, regardless of the origin of the widget code).

 Network communication was also discussed in Chapter 13.

## Logic

The entire model, the controller, and the UI logic will be JavaScript code, and using best practices and high-performance object-oriented code will be mandatory. If you want to learn about JavaScript internals, hacks, and how you can write better code, I strongly suggest that you read the excellent book *JavaScript: The Good Parts* by Douglas Crockford (*http://crockford.com*) (O'Reilly), a JavaScript architect at Yahoo!

The first fear about this is, if the source code is plain JavaScript, can't other people look at and even steal our code? The answer is yes, but it shouldn't be a problem. Every Ajax website today (Gmail, Facebook, Hotmail) is JavaScript code that anyone can look at. Also, nothing stops us from using typical obfuscating techniques for our JavaScript code when we package it up—examining this code will be the same as unpacking a Java ME JAR file or an iPhone native application and trying to decompile the classes. Web apps are no less secure than native applications.

## User Interface

The user interface will be defined using all the technologies we've already talked about in this book: HTML, CSS, images, `canvas`, SVG, and even Flash on supported devices.

Some mobile web app platforms offer us a UI library that we can use to create native-like controls from JavaScript, and some platforms also allow us to define native menus to be used, just like in any other installed application.

## Packaging

Every platform offers some kind of package system where we will include all the static assets for our web apps: HTML, JavaScript, CSS, images, text files, configuration files, and any other required resources. Most packages are just ZIP files with a different extension and MIME type. Some platforms can embed a mobile web application inside a native application, and some others will use the HTML5 Application Cache API (the manifest file) to define a virtual package.

## Distribution

Finally, when we have our package ready to distribute, we can deliver it to users. Options include over-the-air (OTA) delivery (with the appropriate MIME type applied), providing a URL from which the user can access the application for downloading, or distributing it in stores.

# Standards

The standards in this area are still a work in progress, but we can identify some official and de facto standards in the mobile widget world.

## Packaging and Configuration Standards

First, for packaging and for the configuration file, the W3C has the Widget Packaging and Configuration standard, defined by W3C (*http://www.w3.org/TR/widgets*) (not only for mobile widgets). The W3C standard defines a ZIP file as the package format, with a configuration file and an optional icon included in the root folder of the package.

The configuration file must be named *config.xml*. Here's a sample file:

```
<?xml version="1.0" encoding="UTF-8"?>
<widget xmlns="http://www.w3.org/ns/widgets"
        id="http://mobilexweb.com/widget">
```

```
    <name short="Example 2.0">
        The example Widget!
    </name>
    <description>
        A sample widget to demonstrate some of the possibilities.
    </description>
    <icon src="icons/example.png"/>
    <content src="myWidget.html"/>
</widget>
```

The other de facto standard is the Apple Dashboard Widget, used for Mac OS X widget development. It also uses a ZIP file, and a property list file (*info.plist*) is used for configuration.

The property list format stores serialized objects in a file with a *.plist* extension. The contents are in XML format, but without the typical XML tag usage.

In a property file, objects are stored along with their properties. Each property can be a string, a number, a Boolean, an array, a key/value dictionary, or some other type, depending on the system. For each property, we define the name as one key tag and the value as another tag, depending on the type. For example:

```
<?xml version="1.0" encoding="UTF-8"?>
<plist version="1.0">
    <dict>
        <key>Numeric Property</key>
        <integer>2010</integer>

        <key>String Property</key>
        <string>Value</string>

        <key>Boolean Property</key>
        <true/>
    </dict>
</plist>
```

# Official Platforms

Web apps come in a lot of varieties, as different vendors and organizations have come up with different implementations and technologies over time.

## iOS Web Apps

To create JavaScript-based applications for iOS, we have two possible solutions:

- Create a web app (also known as a full-screen web app).
- Create a native web or hybrid solution (for example, a PhoneGap or similar native web project).

A hybrid is a mix between a web and a native application, having the best of both worlds available at the same time.

## iOS web app pros and cons

The advantages of a web app are:

- We don't need a Mac-based computer.
- We can host, manage, and change the web app whenever we want.
- We can create any kind of application, including those that Apple doesn't accept as native applications (for example, adult content or private corporate applications for small- and medium-sized companies).
- The application will have an icon in the Home screen.
- The application will be full-screen, and the user will never know it is a web application once it's installed.
- The application can also work offline using application cache.
- We can use all the HTML5 features and APIs we've already seen in this book.

If you create a web app, you can submit it to Apple's web app gallery (*http://www.apple.com/webapps*) for free promotion.

However, there are also some cons:

- We cannot distribute or sell a web app through the App Store (the official Apple store).
- We will not have access to the APIs not exposed in the browser.
- It is not easy to determine whether a web app is already installed on the system.
- Many users still don't know how to install web apps.

With iOS 4.0, Apple created iAd, an advertising program for iOS native applications. The ads are created using HTML5 and some JavaScript extensions. If we want to create these kinds of ads we can use iAd JS (*http://developer.apple.com/iad*), a JavaScript library.

### Full-screen meta tag

In iOS 2.1 and later, some new meta tags for full-screen mode are available for web apps. First, we must use the `viewport` meta tag and the `apple-touch-icon` link to provide a 1:1-scale interface and an icon for the Home screen, as covered in Chapter 7:

```
<meta name="viewport" content="width=device-width; initial-scale=1.0;
    maximum-scale=1.0; user-scalable=0;">
<link rel="apple-touch-icon" href="/Icon.png">
```

To hide the entire Safari interface when the application is opened from the Home screen, we use the `apple-mobile-web-app-capable` meta tag with a unique possible value of `yes`:

```
<meta name="apple-mobile-web-app-capable" content="yes">
```

This tag will make no difference if the HTML page is opened in the browser. In Safari on iOS, we can query the `window.navigator.standalone` JavaScript object to see if we are working in standalone mode (`true`) or in browser mode (`false`). The standalone and browser versions of the Sun web app (*http://pattern.dk/sun*) are shown in Figure 16-2.

 The latest version of the Nokia Browser for Symbian supports `apple-mobile-web-app-capable` as well as the `mobile-web-app-capable` meta tag for fullscreen standalone mode. First edition of the Blackberry 10 Browser exposes `navigator.standalone` so it may support this mode in later versions.

### Changing status bar appearance

We cannot hide the 20-pixel-high top status bar (40 pixels high in iPhone 4 and other high-DPI devices), but we can change its appearance to be compatible with our design. We do this with the `apple-mobile-web-app-status-bar-style` meta tag. This tag allows values of `black`, `default`, or `black-translucent`, and it only works if we have already defined standalone mode.

When we specify the values `black` or `default`, our website will have available the full height of the screen, minus the 20px of the status bar. If we use the `black-translucent` value we will have the entire screen available, and the toolbar will be overlaid on the top 20 pixels of our website.

*Figure 16-2. Sun is a simple weather app that detects if the user has accessed it using the browser or the Home screen icon—this is the same HTML file, but the version on the right (the version opened from the Home screen) looks like any other native app.*

### Defining startup images

From iOS 3.0, Safari also supports a *startup image* to be used as the initial image before the HTML and JavaScript loads:

```
<link rel="apple-touch-startup-image" href="startup.png">
```

There are different image sizes per device type:

- 320×460 pixels for low-resolution iPhone or iPod touch
- 640×920 pixels for high-resolution 3.5" iPhone or iPod touch
- 640×1096 pixels for high-resolution 4" iPhone or iPod touch
- 768×1004 pixels for low-resolution iPad or iPad mini in portrait mode
- 1024×748 pixels for low-resolution iPad or iPad mini in landscape mode

- 1536×2008 pixels for high-resolution iPad in portrait mode
- 2048×1496 pixels for high-resolution iPad in landscape mode

 iPad devices have Home screen apps compatible specifically with landscape and portrait modes; that is why we can provide both versions of the launch startup image. iPhones' and iPods' Home screens work only in portrait mode. If we want to invite the user to change the orientation to landscape, we can provide a 90-degree-rotated image.

The application launcher also uses this image for the zoom-in animation when the user clicks on the icon. If you don't supply a startup image, it will use a screenshot from the last time the app was used, or a white screen.

 HTML5 Boilerplate includes a JavaScript-based solution that will insert the right startup image for the current device, called MBP.startupImage.

If the file size is not correct for the current device, the operating system will just ignore the image. Therefore, we need a way to provide all the possible alternatives. While this solution is undocumented, media queries work on the link element for the apple-touch-startup-image file. Therefore, we can use this approach to query about the device's screen height, pixel ratio, and/or orientation.

 In iOS 6.0 there is a bug that creates a letterboxed app on iPhone 5 and iPod touch 5th generation (4" screen) devices, with black bars at the top and bottom, unless we define a viewport different than 320 or device-width, such as in:

```
<meta name="viewport" content="width=320.1">
```

Fortunately, we can use JavaScript to force that value when we know we are on this kind of device, as in:

```
if (window.screen.height==568) { // iPhone-iPod 4"
    document.querySelector("meta[name=viewport]").
      content="width=320.1";
}
```

All the possible values at the time of this writing are:

```
<link rel="apple-touch-startup-image" href="startup-iPhone-3.5-1x.png"
    media="only screen and (device-height: 480px) and
    (-webkit-device-pixel-ratio: 1)">
<link rel="apple-touch-startup-image" href="startup-iPhone-3.5-2x.png"
    media="only screen and (device-height: 480px) and
        (-webkit-device-pixel-ratio: 2)">
<link rel="apple-touch-startup-image" href="startup-iPhone-4-2x.png"
    media="only screen and (device-height: 568px) and
    (-webkit-device-pixel-ratio: 2)">
<link rel="apple-touch-startup-image"
    href="startup-iPad-1x-portrait.png"
    media="only screen and
        (device-height: 768px) and (-webkit-device-pixel-ratio: 1) and
        (orientation: portrait)">
<link rel="apple-touch-startup-image"
    href="startup-iPad-1x-landscape.png"
    media="only screen and
        (device-height: 768px) and
        (-webkit-device- device-pixel-ratio: 1) and
        (orientation: landscape)">
<link rel="apple-touch-startup-image"
    href="startup-iPad-2x-portrait.png"
    media="only screen and
        (device-height: 768px) and (-webkit-device-pixel-ratio: 2) and
        (orientation: portrait)">
<link rel="apple-touch-startup-image"
    href="startup-iPad-2x-landscape.png"
    media="only screen and
        (device-height: 768px) and (-webkit-device-pixel-ratio: 2) and
        (orientation: landscape)">
```

Unfortunately, at present there is no way to force an orientation, as the user can change it. We can use media queries and/or JavaScript to show a message to the user when she is in an orientation that we don't want to support, however.

### How it looks

In the applications menu, a web app looks and acts like any other native app, with the only restriction being that we can't push a badge number update as we can for true native apps.

A web app runs in a different process than Safari (internally called *Web.app*), while still sharing the same rendering engine. If we activate the task list (by double-clicking on the Home screen button), we will see that our web app appears as a completely different process than Safari, as shown in Figure 16-3.

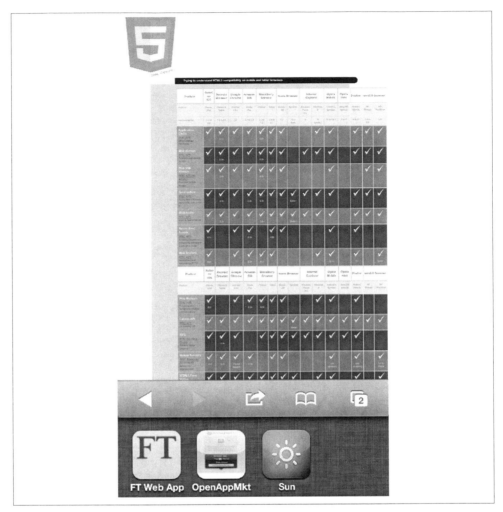

*Figure 16-3. In the task list on iOS, every web app appears with its own icon, separate from Safari; in this case, the three icons are full-screen iOS web apps.*

The icon is defined by the `apple-touch-icon` link and the name of the app is defined by the `title` tag or the `apple-mobile-web-app-title` meta tag, as we saw in Chapter 7.

### APIs

All the same HTML5 APIs are available to us when our website is installed as a web app. Up to iOS 5.1, the same HTML in the browser and as a full-screen web app is considered of the same origin, which means that it shares all the storage data (such as local storage or Web SQL storage).

Starting in iOS 6, web apps are isolated, which means that they have their own storage and the same HTML will access different data when in browser or web app mode. Also, some limits, such as the 50 MB limit for application cache, are lifted when working in full-screen mode.

## Links

The iOS web app mechanism expects to serve a single HTML file that will use JavaScript techniques to deliver a rich experience. Because there is no Safari UI in an installed web app, there is no back button or URL bar for the user to use to navigate our app. Therefore, it is our responsibility to provide a full working user interface for all the possible options.

As the web app mechanism is optimized for a single URL, if we make a link to another site (an external link or even a relative URL), that destination will always be opened in Safari, minimizing our app in the operating system.

Using `XMLHttpRequest` is the preferred way, but if for any reason we want to open a different URL in our current web app context, we can use `location.href` instead, as in:

```html
<a href="javascript:location.href='next.html'">Load other file</a>
```

Mobile HTML5 Boilerplate provides a simple way to override the default anchor element behavior:

```javascript
// Safari in standalone mode
if(("standalone" in window.navigator) && window.navigator.standalone){

    // If you want to prevent remote links in standalone web apps
    // from opening in Safari, change 'remotes' to 'true'
    var noddy, remotes = false;

    document.addEventListener('click', function(event) {

        noddy = event.target;

        // Bubble up until we hit link or top HTML element.
        // Warning: BODY element is not compulsory, so better
        // to stop on HTML.
        while(noddy.nodeName !== "A" && noddy.nodeName !== "HTML") {
            noddy = noddy.parentNode;
        }

        if('href' in noddy && noddy.href.indexOf('http') !== -1 &&
            (noddy.href.indexOf(document.location.host) !== -1 ||
            remotes))
        {
            event.preventDefault();
            document.location.href = noddy.href;
        }
```

```
    },false);
}
```

## Distribution

As a web app is just a normal web document with some meta tags, the user will not "install" it as such; the "installation" just involves adding the website to the Home screen. However, it is still useful to provide a setup assistant or an installation invitation. The user may not understand the full implementation, so talking about installation is still a good idea in terms of communication.

 Remember that some of your users may not be native English speakers. If you are going to give instructions to the user for web app installation, try to provide different language versions, as is done for the device menus.

First, we need to decide if we are going to accept usage of the web app from both the browser and the Home screen, or only as a standalone application. If the last option is our objective, we should provide a single HTML file that detects where the user is accessing it from and either presents the installation link or the app itself (as shown in Figure 16-4), depending on whether it's accessed from the browser or the Home screen.

In the web app HTML file, we first check whether the user is accessing it from the browser or not. If so, we provide instructions for installing the application. For example:

1. Press the + button.
2. Use the "Add to Home Screen" option.
3. The application will be installed on your Home screen for future usage.

The web app HTML should include:

- All the meta tags we've provided
- An offline manifest file (if we want the app to work offline)
- A short title, for use as the application name on the Home screen

We can use any UI library, such as Sencha Touch or jQuery Mobile, to provide an app-like interface.

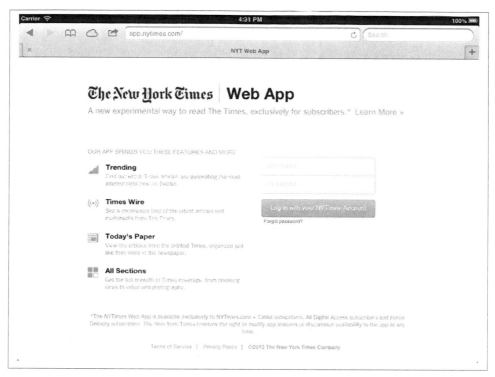

*Figure 16-4. The* New York Times *web app (http://app.nytimes.com) shows a sign-in screen when opened from Safari and not from an installed icon on the Home screen.*

 Remember that when in standalone mode, the user will not have access to the Back, Forward, or Reload buttons, or to the address bar. Therefore, you should provide all of these navigation items in your design.

## Cubiq Add to Home Screen

Add to Home Screen (*http://cubiq.org/add-to-home-screen*) is an open source JavaScript library that creates an invitation bubble for iOS. Its includes device detection to offer the right UI for iPad or iPhone/iPod devices, more than 20 localization languages, and other customization features.

 Mobile Bookmark Bubble (*http://users.softpress.com/topher/iOSBub ble*) is another free library for the "Add to Home Screen" invitation process.

Its basic usage includes code similar to this:

```
<link rel="stylesheet" href="add2home.css">
<script src="add2home.js"></script>
```

The code will show the bubble (as seen in Figure 16-5) only on compatible devices. The framework uses a technique to avoid showing the bubble again in the same session if the user adds the page to the Home screen. Using the advanced setup we can even show the invitation only for returning visitors, to avoid annoying casual visitors who have just landed on our website and are not likely to add it to the Home screen as they don't even know if they like it yet.

*Figure 16-5. Invitation bubbles are a must-have feature when working with mobile web apps.*

 Open App Market (*http://openappmkt.com*) is an open web-based store for HTML5 iOS web apps. Accessing it from Safari on iOS allows us to install the store and then use it to browse through the entire catalog; we can install free web apps and pay for premium web apps.

## Symbian Standalone Web Apps

Following Apple syntax, the Symbian browser from version 8.3.1 (mid-2012) supports chromeless full-screen apps installed from the browser. It supports the same `apple-mobile-web-app-capable` attribute (as well as without `apple-` prefix) and `navigator.standalone` property:

```
<meta name="mobile-web-app-capable" content="yes">
```

If the user adds the page to the Symbian Home screen, the browser will take the current title and it will create an icon (using the techniques described in Chapter 7) that will open the current HTML page in full-screen mode.

# Windows 8 Store Apps

Windows 8 supports native store apps developed using HTML5, besides the .NET/XAML development engine. With HTML5 we can create Windows 8 Store apps (previously known as Metro apps) that can be distributed in the Windows Store for desktops, notebooks, and tablets, such as the Microsoft Surface.

 As of version 8.0, the official HTML5 engine is not available on Windows Phone; on the Phone version we have to use a web view, such as Apache Cordova/PhoneGap, to compile a native web app with HTML5.

Windows 8 apps feel like full native apps in the user interface and they can use all the same native behavior as .NET apps, as we can see in Figure 16-6 (the Wikipedia HTML5 app, available in the Windows Store).

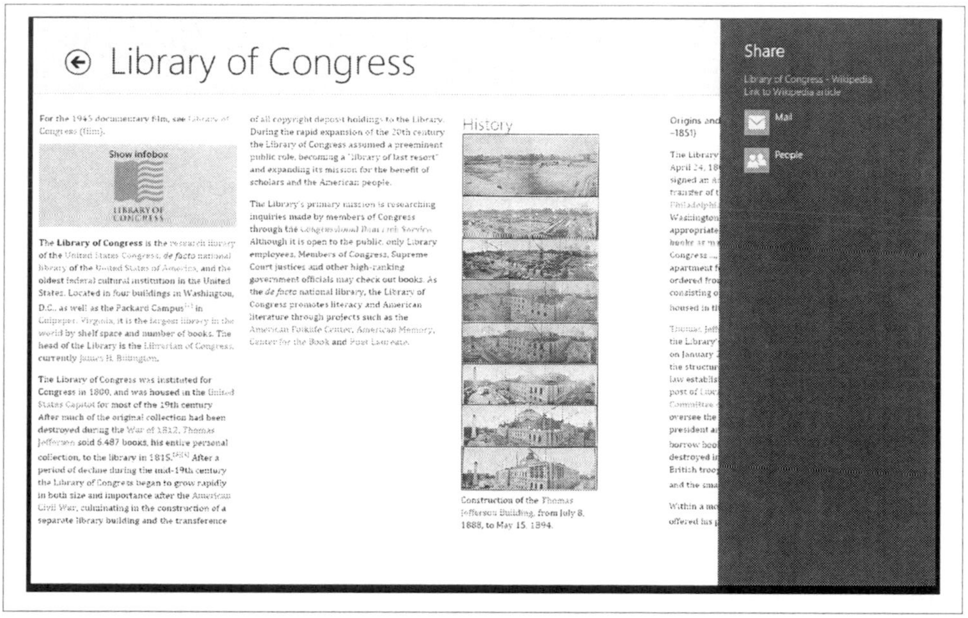

*Figure 16-6. The Wikipedia HTML5 app for Windows 8 looks like a native app, including native charm integration such as the Share mechanism.*

To develop Windows 8 apps we need:

- A Windows 8 Pro device to develop on
- A free developer license that will enable our Windows 8 Pro device to execute apps that have not yet been approved by the Store

- Visual Studio 2012 or Visual Studio Express 2012 for Windows 8 (free edition)
- Blend for Microsoft Visual Studio 2012
- The Windows 8 SDK

You can download all the tools from Microsoft (*http://go.microsoft.com/fwlink/?Link Id=238221*).

 The simplest way to get a developer license is using Visual Studio (even the free Express edition); it will ask if you would like to get one, or you can access the request process from the Store→Acquire Developer License menu option.

To create an HTML5 Windows 8 project, we just use Visual Studio 2012 for Windows 8 and select New Project→JavaScript→Blank App. We can also select one of the many templates already available, as seen in Figure 16-7.

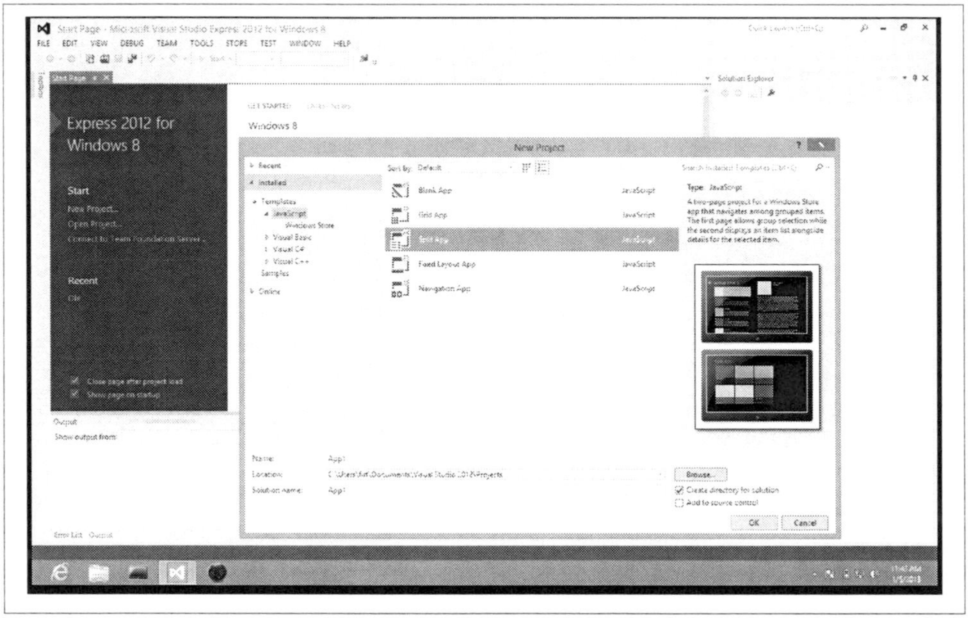

*Figure 16-7. With Visual Studio for Windows 8 we can create HTML5 apps for Windows tablets and desktop devices.*

While all the code is HTML, CSS, and JavaScript, Windows 8 apps have extensions both in JavaScript and CSS that will make our code look like and behave like a native app.

### Windows Runtime

JavaScript apps can access the same Windows Runtime as .NET Store apps, through the global `Windows` object that acts as a namespace. In this object we can find objects and utilities for the core runtime, data and content storage, device management, file management, globalization, graphics, media, networking, printing, presentation, security, and the UI.

There are enough objects, properties, methods, and events available to fill a whole book. Just to give a quick sample, to access the current display's properties, we can use:

```
var displayProperties = Windows.Graphics.Display.DisplayProperties;
```

### WinJS

The Windows Library for JavaScript (WinJS) is a package of JavaScript and CSS files that we can import in our HTML using `script` and `link` tags, to provide native features to our app. In the first edition of the platform, all these files are under the folder *//Microsoft.WinJS.1.0/*.

For UI purposes, we will usually add one of the two main CSS theme files—dark or light—using:

```
<link href="//Microsoft.WinJS.1.0/css/ui-dark.css" rel="stylesheet">
```

or:

```
<link href="//Microsoft.WinJS.1.0/css/ui-light.css" rel="stylesheet">
```

It's important to use one of these stylesheets, because they provide native style to standard HTML controls, automatic support for different languages, and a high-contrast mode.

In terms of JavaScript libraries, usually we will need at least the base library and the UI library:

```
<script src="//Microsoft.WinJS.1.0/js/base.js"></script>
<script src="//Microsoft.WinJS.1.0/js/ui.js"></script>
```

The base framework will add the `WinJS` global object, where we can find application utilities, namespaces for other objects, and object constructors. One of the main objects is `WinJS.Application`; this points to the application itself and exposes several useful events, properties, and functions. Our app can handle different states through this object, such as suspension and reactivation.

The basic code for handling launch events is:

```
WinJS.Binding.optimizeBindingReferences = true;

var app = WinJS.Application;
var activation = Windows.ApplicationModel.Activation;
```

```
app.onactivated = function (args) {
    if (args.detail.kind === activation.ActivationKind.launch) {
        if (args.detail.previousExecutionState !==
            activation.ApplicationExecutionState.terminated) {
            // TODO: This application has been newly launched.
            // Initialize your application here.
        } else {
            // TODO: This application has been reactivated from
            // suspension. Restore application state here.
        }
        args.setPromise(WinJS.UI.processAll());
    }
};
```

Remember, even if we see native objects in JavaScript, we are still working with HTML, CSS, and JavaScript; therefore, we are still using addEventListener or DOM functions for content manipulation.

The setPromise() method informs the application that a task is in progress and should not be considered complete until the "promise" completes. We can use this to show a splash screen while initializing objects, for example. The WinJS.UI.processAll() function will parse our HTML and search for native object declarations to initialize them.

### JavaScript UI controls

While we can create our UI with plain HTML, CSS, SVG, or the Canvas API, we can also use native controls from the operating system—this marks the first big difference between a normal website in Internet Explorer 10 and a native Windows 8 HTML5 app.

These native controls have no markup associated with them, and they will be defined as a div element using the data-win-control attribute. Because these controls are not associated with a DOM element, their attributes are defined in a JSON format inside a data-win-options HTML attribute. For example, to create a Time Picker, we can use:

```
<div id="myTimePicker" data-win-control="WinJS.UI.TimePicker"
    data-win-options="{current: '1:30 pm'}">
</div>
```

To get the control object from JavaScript, we can use any DOM selection mechanism and the winControl attribute of the DOM element. For example:

```
var timePicker = document.getElementById("myTimePicker").winControl;
```

Before accessing native controls from JavaScript we need to wait for the application to be initialized, and that process is different from listening for DOMContentLoaded or load events. Instead, we have to wait for the processAll asynchronous process to finish, as shown here:

---

```
WinJS.UI.processAll().then(function() {
    // Now we can access all native controls here
});
```

The native controls available in WinJS 1.0 are listed in Table 16-1.

*Table 16-1. Windows 8 native controls available from HTML5 using `data-win-control="WinJS.UI.<control>"`*

| Control name | Allows us to... |
| --- | --- |
| AppBar | Display commands in the app's context menu (on right-click with mouse or gesture on touch devices). |
| AppBarCommand | Define a command for the AppBar. |
| DatePicker | Select a date. |
| FlipView | Display a collection of items one at a time, such as photos for an album. |
| Flyout | Display an interactive or noninteractive message in a pop-up that can be dismissed by clicking or tapping outside of it. |
| HtmlControl | Display an HTML page dynamically. |
| Menu | Define a menu layout for displaying commands. |
| PageControl | Define a modular unit of HTML, CSS, and JavaScript that can be navigated to. |
| Rating | Define a rating control. |
| SemanticZoom | Define how the user can zoom between two different views supplied by two child controls (zoomed-out and zoomed-in views). |
| SettingsFlyout | Define in-context access to the application's settings. |
| TimePicker | Select a time. |
| ToggleSwitch | Turn an item off or on (Boolean control). |
| Tooltip | Display rich content to show more information about an object. |
| ViewBox | Scale a single child element to fill the available space without resizing it. |

 Every control has a set of attributes, events, and styles that we can use. The official documentation shows all the possibilities at Microsoft (*http://bit.ly/13YnEAT*).

### Application UI state

A Windows 8 app can work in different states:

- Full-screen portrait (on tablets)
- Full-screen landscape
- Filled (sharing the available space with another app; our app is taking ~2/3 of the screen)

- Snapped (sharing the available space with another app; our app is taking ~1/3 of the screen)

To provide a different UI layout or design in each state, we can use media queries and the `-ms-view-state` extension (available only in Windows 8 Store apps):

```
@media screen and (-ms-view-state: fullscreen-landscape) {
}

@media screen and (-ms-view-state: filled) {
}

@media screen and (-ms-view-state: snapped) {
}

@media screen and (-ms-view-state: fullscreen-portrait) {
}
```

### Navigation

While not mandatory, if we want to have different views and a navigation controller between them we can use the native `PageControl` object mechanism. We can start a project using the Navigation App template or code it on our own.

 Remember we are not creating a website, but an app; therefore, there is no browser UI in our app. We need to provide all the navigation ourselves.

When using this navigation mechanism, we will have a navigation controller and different HTML pages (which can have their own CSS and JavaScript code) for each view. Usually, it's a good idea to use a *pages* folder and one subfolder per view with all the resources inside:

```
<div id="contenthost"
    data-win-control="Application.PageControlNavigator"
    data-win-options="{home: '/pages/home/home.html'}">
</div>
```

 When using `PageControlNavigator`, we have both the main HTML file (*default.html*) and the current page's HTML (such as *home.html*). It's similar to using an iframe, where two HTML files are on the stage at once.

To navigate to a different HTML page we can use the JavaScript `navigate()` method, passing the relative URI:

```
WinJS.Navigation.navigate(URI);
```

We can pass optional state data as a second argument, and we can use a chained `done()` function that will act as an event handler:

```
WinJS.Navigation.navigate("/pages/details/details.html", {id: 444})
              .done(function() { // OK }, function(e) { // Error });
```

 Because some `WinJS` objects are used frequently, it's common to have global aliases defined, such as `app` for `WinJS.Application` and `nav` for `WinJS.Navigation`.

To provide an automatic back button (as shown in Figure 16-6) that will transition to the previous page in the navigation controller, we can use the following snippet:

```
<button class="win-backbutton" aria-label="Back" disabled></button>
```

### Advanced topics

We don't have enough room in this book to cover the entire Windows 8 HTML5 platform. However, you're welcome to continue exploring on your own. Here are some of the things we can use this platform for:

- Creating and managing tiles and secondary tiles
- Toast notifications
- Badges
- Local, push, and periodic notifications
- Saving and restoring state
- Data binding
- Integrating with the Search charm
- Integrating with the Share charm
- Integrating with the Settings charm
- Communicating with other native apps and the operating system
- Uploading and downloading information in the background

## Mozilla Open Web Apps

Open Web Apps (*https://developer.mozilla.org/Apps*) (OWA) is a Mozilla project that allows us to create HTML5 apps that will be executed in a web runtime with a different security model than the browser. While Mozilla's intent is to create a multiplatform open environment, at the time of this writing only Firefox for desktops and Android and Firefox OS support this standard.

Firefox has included a web app engine since version 17 for Android and from the first version of Firefox OS. These apps gain an icon in the Home screen menu and they act like a full-screen app without any browser UI. Firefox calls these apps *open web apps*.

In terms of security, Firefox apps can run in different sandboxes, depending on the type of application/content. The different types are defined as follows:

*Web content*
    Normal website in the browser (not an app).

*Installed web app*
    App with a manifest, downloaded and installed through an unauthenticated website or a store that has no quality assurance (no review on quality and security).

*Privileged web app*
    Authenticated application approved by an app store, equivalent in functionality and security to native apps on other mobile platforms.

*Certified web app*
    Reserved for apps approved by carriers or OEMs that can access core APIs, such as apps for replacing the default dialer, changing the system settings, or power management. This category is not intended for third-party apps.

Every API has a different compatibility based on the sandbox where it is being executed.

An open web app uses standard APIs—such as the Application Cache, Web Storage, IDB, and Canvas APIs—unless the feature is not yet available as a standard, in which case Mozilla uses a custom API.

An open web app must be hosted on our own server or repository using a domain on the Internet, even if it's intended for offline usage.

### App origin

The platform is optimized so there is only one app per origin (combination of protocol, domain, and port). If we want to host more than one app, we must use subdomains (such as *app1.mydomain.com* and *app2.mydomain.com*) to host the manifest and the resource files. This doesn't mean that we can't use resources from other domains, just that the app must be installed from only one trusted domain.

### App manifest

The manifest is a file served with the MIME type `application/x-web-app-manifest` `+json` that provides the installation metadata. It is a text file in JSON format, usually with the *.webapp* extension. Here's a basic snippet:

```
{
  "name": "My App",
  "description": "The description goes here",
```

```
"launch_path": "/",  // Relative URL to the main HTML page of our app
"icons": {
  "128": "/img/icon-128.png"  // >=128 is mandatory
},
"developer": {
  "name": "Max Firtman",
  "url": "http://www.mobilexweb.com"
},
"default_locale": "en",
"permissions": {
  "contacts": {
    "description": "Required to read your contact list",
    "access": "read"
  }
}
}
```

> There is an online manifest validator at App Manifest (*http://appmani fest.org*).

The manifest should include all the API requirements for the user to approve its usage (such as geolocation). The possible properties available for the manifest are listed in Table 16-2.

*Table 16-2. Mozilla open web app manifest properties*

| Property | Description |
| --- | --- |
| name | The visible name of your app (<= 128 chars). |
| description | A description of your app (<= 1,024 chars). |
| launch_path | An optional launch URL (in the same domain) to be used as the initial HTML page for the app. If not provided, the current URL will be used. |
| icons | A map of icon sizes and their URIs. Icons must be square. For Firefox OS, 30×30 and 60×60 are recommended; for Firefox for Android and desktop, 48×48, 64×64, 128×128, and 256×256 are recommended. |
| csp | An optional content security policy for the app. |
| type | The app's type (web, priviliged, or certified). |
| developer | Optional information about the developer, including the properties name and url. |
| locales | A map of locale-specific overrides to the data contained in the manifest. Useful to provide names and descriptions in different languages. |
| default_locale | The default language of the manifest. |
| installs_al lowed_from | An array of trusted origins that you allow the installation from (for example, the Mozilla Marketplace). |
| version | The version number (as a string) for the app. |

| Property | Description |
|---|---|
| orientation | A comma-separated list of orientations the app supports. Available options include: portrait, landscape, portrait-primary, landscape-primary, portrait-secondary, landscape-secondary. |
| permissions | The set of permissions that the app needs. You must list every API you intend to use that requires the user's permission. Permissions have a description so the user knows why you need it and an optional access property defining read, readwrite, readcreate, or createonly. The list of possible permissions is available from Mozilla (*https://developer.mozilla.org/docs/Apps/Manifest*). |
| fullscreen | A Boolean attribute that defines whether the app should be opened in full-screen mode. |
| appcache_path | An optional URL to the application cache manifest file for offline app storage. |
| activities | Specific to Firefox OS, defines a list of "web activities" that the app listens to. With activities, we can handle certain MIME types or specific activities that other apps will delegate to us. |

The full documentation for the web app manifest is available at the Mozilla Developer Network (*https://developer.mozilla.org/docs/Apps/Manifest*).

 Because of an Android limitation, Firefox apps don't have an icon in the applications menu; the icon only appears on the Home screen and in the app launcher inside Firefox.

### Distribution

We can install a Firefox open web app from any website, or we can distribute it through the Mozilla Marketplace (*https://marketplace.firefox.com/developers*). Mozilla doesn't host the apps for us, so even if we want to distribute an app through the store we need to host the files on our own web server or web repository.

To install a web app from our own website, we can use the Apps API available in Firefox from version 17 through the navigator.mozApps object. The basic template to launch an installation process (as seen in Figure 16-8) is:

```
var manifestUrl = "http://mydomain.com/manifest"; // Change this URL
var request = window.navigator.mozApps.install(manifestUrl);
request.onsuccess = function () {
   alert('Installation successful!')
}
request.onerror = function () {
   alert('Installation failed, error: ' + this.error.name);
}
```

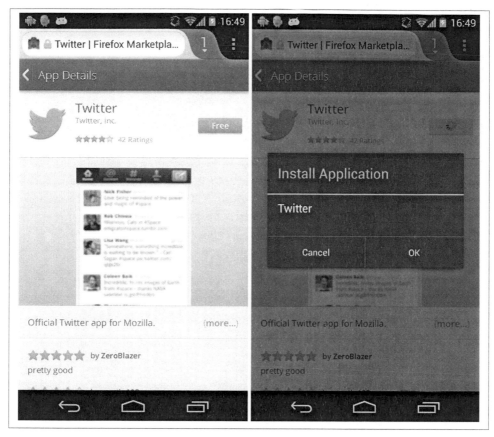

*Figure 16-8. An open web app being installed from the Marketplace website using the Apps API.*

The Apps API offers methods we can use to tell if the app is already installed (`mozApps.getSelf`), get all the apps installed from the current origin (`mozApps.getIn stalled`), and get all the apps installed from any origin (`mozApps.mgmt.getAll`). The latter is known as the apps management API.

### Checking if the app is already installed

As an app is always attached to a domain (or subdomain), on any web page hosted on the same domain we can check if the associated app is installed or not:

```
var request = navigator.mozApps.getSelf();
request.onsuccess = function() {
  if (request.result) {
    // we're installed
  } else {
    // not installed
```

```
        }
    };
```

## Chrome Apps

Google Chrome has its own HTML5 apps engine that is available on Windows, Mac OS, Chrome OS, and Linux at the time of this writing. These apps are also known as *packaged apps*, and all the documentation can be found at the Chrome developer site (*http://developer.chrome.com/apps*).

A version of the Chrome HTML5 apps engine for Android has been announced but not yet launched at the time of this writing. While the desktop and notebook platform includes several APIs and a package mechanism, it seems the Android version will be slightly different, at least in how we will need to package the apps.

To keep updated on Chrome apps, please visit the blog (*http://www.mobilexweb.com*) that goes along with this book.

## Samsung Web Apps

Samsung has released an SDK and a JavaScript API to create multidevice web apps for Samsung devices, including smartphones and smart TVs. The SDK, documentation, and emulators (*http://developer.samsung.com/SamsungWebAPI*) are available.

## BlackBerry WebWorks Apps

BlackBerry launched a new widget engine in 2009 as a first-class citizen of the operating system, starting from Device Software 5.0. The platform was named WebWorks, and it has evolved to support all the BlackBerry platforms, with some kind of portability between them: BlackBerry 5 to 7, BlackBerry PlayBook, and BlackBerry 10.

WebWorks is an open source framework that provides a JavaScript layer over the standard web view available on every BlackBerry platform; therefore, with WebWorks we compile the app as a native app from HTML5 code. Version 5 of the platform is not recommended, as it's too basic and the performance is not good enough to provide even simple list-based apps.

Today, WebWorks is starting to migrate most of its APIs to HTML5 and/or to match the Apache Cordova/PhoneGap framework. Basically all the modern HTML5 APIs can be used in WebWorks, as mentioned in the compatibility tables (*http://mobilehtml5.org*).

### Configuration file

The WebWorks configuration file is an XML document following the W3C configuration file is an XML document following the W3C Widget Package specification, with lots of additions from RIM. The possible properties vary according to the platform we are targeting (5.x to 7.x, PlayBook, or BB10). A basic BB10 file will look like this:

```xml
<?xml version="1.0" encoding="utf-8"?>
<widget xmlns="http://www.w3.org/ns/widgets"
        xmlns:rim="http://www.blackberry.com/ns/widgets"
        version="2.0.0.0" id="myApplication">

   <author href="http://www.mobilexweb.com.com/"
           rim:copyright="Copyright 2013 Firt">@firt</author>

   <name>Programming the Mobile Web app</name>

   <description>
     A sample application for the book
   </description>

   <rim:permissions>
     <rim:permit>access_shared</rim:permit>
     <rim:permit>access_location_services</rim:permit>
     <rim:permit>use_camera</rim:permit>
   </rim:permissions>

   <!-- Icon for BB10 -->
   <icon src="icons/icon-150.png"/>

   <!-- Landscape and portrait screens for BB10 -->
   <rim:splash src="splash-1280x768.png"/>
   <rim:splash src="splash-768x1280.png"/>

   <!-- Main HTML file -->
   <content src="index.html" rim:allowInvokeParams="true"/>

   <!-- Features and permissions -->
   <feature id="blackberry.ui.dialog"/>

   <feature id="blackberry.app.orientation">
     <param name="mode" value="portrait" />
   </feature>

   <feature id="blackberry.app">
     <param name="backgroundColor" value="0xFFFF0000" />
   </feature>

   <access uri="http://www.mobilexweb.com" subdomains="true">
     <feature id="blackberry.app" required="true" version="1.0.0"/>
     <feature id="blackberry.invoke" required="true" version="1.0.0"/>
   </access>

   <license href="http://www.mobilexweb.com/"/>
</widget>
```

The configuration file must be in the root folder of your project, under the name *con fig.xml*. The possible items we can define are listed in Table 16-3, along with their current compatibility per platform.

*Table 16-3. WebWorks configuration file options*

| Element | Description | Platform availability |
|---|---|---|
| access | Specifies that the application can access resources on the Web (the `fea ture` element is used as a child element) | All |
| author | Author information | All |
| content | Initial HTML page to load | All |
| rim:background | A page to be used as a background service | Only 5.x to 7.x |
| description | Description of the app | All |
| feature | Specifies a feature or functionality that the application can use | All |
| icon | Icon(s) for the Home screen; PlayBook accepts only one icon, while the other platforms accept multiple icon sizes | All |
| license | End user and license information | 5.x–7.x and BB10 |
| name | The visible name of the application | All |
| rim:cache | Cache preferences | Only 5.x to 7.x |
| rim:category | Folder location for the application | Only PlayBook |
| rim:connection | Connection timeout | Only 5.x to 7.x |
| rim:invoke-target | Registers your app as the handler for an invocation event | Only BB10 |
| rim:loadingscreen | Properties for the loading screen | 5.x–7.x and PlayBook |
| rim:navigation | Defines cursor navigation behavior | Only 5.x to 7.x |
| rim:orientation | Defines the screen orientation | 5.x–7.x and PlayBook |
| rim:permissions | Container for list of `rim:permit` elements specifying app permissions | PlayBook and BB10 |
| rim:splash | Image to display as the splash screen | Only BB10 |

 The configuration file must have an `access` tag for each Internet domain that we are going to contact using Ajax or some other resource request and a `feature` tag for each API that we are going to use.

## WebWorks APIs

The WebWorks platform supports the features listed in Table 16-4, if they have previously been defined in the permissions area of the configuration file (in the `feature` tag). These APIs are additions to the standard HTML5 APIs that the platforms may support based on operating system version. The full API list (*https://developer.blackberry.com/ html5/apis*) and details on compatibility per platform are available.

These APIs are available on some platforms, including a JS reference to the WebWorks extension APIs. Check the documentation to see where the file is located on every version.

*Table 16-4. Most useful JavaScript BlackBerry WebWorks extension APIs*

| Feature | Object | Allows us to... |
| --- | --- | --- |
| Advertising | blackberry.advertising | Show banners on our app (BlackBerry 6.x and 7.x only) |
| Application | blackberry.app | Access functions and properties for the application, like the background and foreground and Home screen support |
| BBM | blackberry.bbm | Access the BlackBerry Messenger (BBM) system to share content and connect to the social network |
| Event | blackberry.event | Access operating system event handling |
| File I/O | blackberry.io | Access files and directories |
| Identity | blackberry.identity | Access user identification information (IMEI, PIN, phone number) |
| Invoke | blackberry.invoke | Interact with other installed applications |
| Messaging | blackberry.message | Send email |
| Payments | blackberry.payment | Access the In App Purchase API for charging content/services through the store |
| Phone | blackberry.phone | Access the Phone application and call logs |
| PIM | blackberry.pim | Manage the Calendar, Contacts, Tasks, and Memos |
| Push | blackberry.push | Manage the listener for information pushed from the server |
| System | blackberry.system | Get and set system information and event listeners |
| User Interface | blackberry.ui | Manage new JavaScript dialogs and native menus |
| Utility | blackberry.utils | Access useful utility functions like blob converters or URL parsers |

For example, to add an item to the native menu on BlackBerry 7.x smartphones, we should use:

```
var item = new blackberry.ui.menu.MenuItem(false, 1, "Refresh",
    menuHandler);
blackberry.ui.menu.addMenuItem(item);
```

Starting with BB10, WebWorks is migrating its APIs and mechanisms to match the Apache Cordova/PhoneGap project; therefore, for example, we have a `webworksready` event matching the `deviceready` Cordova event.

On BlackBerry 10 devices we can also use platform-specific user interface libraries to implement features such as toast messages, swipe detection, and cover support (the ability to run code while the app is in the background and to update the cover image and text).

### bbUI.js

BlackBerry has released an open source UI framework, similar to jQuery Mobile, to provide a native BlackBerry UI style to WebWorks apps. This framework, called *bbUI.js*, will use different UI concepts if your app is running on BlackBerry 6.x–7.x, PlayBook, or the new BB10, providing the expected UI on each platform.

The project (*https://github.com/blackberry/bbUI.js*) is based on semantic HTML5 code using `data-bb-*` attributes to define roles and behavior. While some controls are only available for BB10, most of the widgets are multiplatform. To make it work, we need to initialize the framework and then push our first screen; every screen is based on an external HTML file.

In Figure 16-9, we can see a sample of what a bbUI.js WebWorks application may look like on BB10.

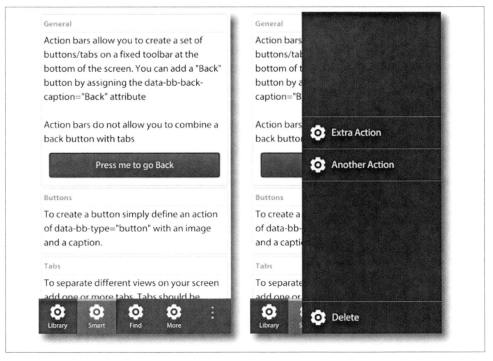

*Figure 16-9. A BlackBerry 10 WebWorks application using bbUI.js.*

The basic template for a WebWorks application is as follows:

```
<!DOCTYPE html>
<html>
<head>
    <link rel="stylesheet" type="text/css" href="bbui-0.9.4.css">
    </link>
    <script type="text/javascript" src="bbui-0.9.4.js">
    </script>
    <script type="text/javascript" src="js/webworks-1.0.2.9.js">
    </script>
    <script type="text/javascript">
        document.addEventListener('webworksready', function(e) {
            bb.init();
            // Open our first screen
            bb.pushScreen('homeScreen.htm', 'homeScreen');
        }, false);
    </script>
</head>
<body>
</body>
</html>
```

Screens are basically HTML files defining elements with data-bb-type="screen", other options, and HTML or bbUI.js controls as children:

```
<!DOCTYPE html>
<div data-bb-type="screen" data-bb-effect="fade">
    <div data-bb-type="title" data-bb-caption="First Demo"
        data-bb-back-caption="Back"></div>

        <div data-bb-type="image-list" data-bb-images="none"
            data-bb-style="arrowlist">
            <div data-bb-type="item" data-bb-title="A"></div>
            <div data-bb-type="item" data-bb-title="B"></div>
            <div data-bb-type="item" data-bb-title="C"></div>
            <div data-bb-type="item" data-bb-title="D"></div>
            <div data-bb-type="item" data-bb-title="E"></div>
            <div data-bb-type="item" data-bb-title="F"></div>
        </div>

        <h3>You can also use plain HTML here</h3>

    <div data-bb-type="action-bar" data-bb-back-caption="Back"></div>
</div>
```

### Packaging and signing

Every platform has its own SDK, including packaging and signing tools that can be downloaded for free from BlackBerry's developer website (*http://developer.blackberry.com/html5*). The available options are:

- WebWorks for BlackBerry 7 or earlier

- WebWorks for BlackBerry PlayBook
- WebWorks for BlackBerry 10

While a few years ago BlackBerry used to offer an Eclipse IDE, today all the SDKs just include command-line tools to package and sign WebWorks applications.

To package a BB10 app, the steps are:

1. Create a folder for your app.
2. Add the *config.xml* configuration file.
3. Add at least one HTML file and optional resources (CSS, JavaScript, images).
4. Find the *webworks-<version>.js* file in your SDK folder, copy it into your package, and add the `script` element to reference it.
5. Create a ZIP archive of your folder with all the contents.
6. Open a terminal session (Command Prompt on Windows).
7. Move to the BlackBerry SDK folder.
8. Compile the application using bbwp *<zip_path>* -o *<app_path>*.

For the other platforms, the steps are quite similar. The resulting application can be executed only on developer platforms.

 Using a command-line tool we can enable the Web Inspector, allowing us to remotely inspect and debug our WebWorks apps.

When we have the *.bar* file (for BB10 and PlayBook), we still need to sign the package before submitting it to the store. The first step is to get a signing key, available for free from BlackBerry's website (*https://www.blackberry.com/SignedKeys*).

To compile and sign the app, we can use the following command line:

```
bbwp <zip_path> -g <KeyStorePassword> -o <app_path>
```

 Don't forget the PIN associated with the key, as it's used to validate your key against RIM's server on every signing process. If you forget the PIN, you will need to get a new key.

## Ripple

While RIM is not offering any IDE at the time of this writing, there is an official tool called *Ripple* (a Google Chrome plug-in) that you can use to help with packaging and signing and for a basic test of the WebWorks APIs, without the need to use a real device or an emulator.

To download Ripple, you have to download the extension from BlackBerry's developer site (*http://developer.blackberry.com/html5/download*), then open Google Chrome on your desktop, go to Tools→Extensions, and finally drag the Ripple file you have just downloaded from the website onto the Chrome UI.

When you have it installed you will see a cyan icon on Google Chrome that will start the Ripple simulation environment, as seen in Figure 16-10. With the extension enabled, you just need to open the HTML file you want to test. To package and sign, you can use the Build panel before setting all the SDK paths manually (Figure 16-11).

*Figure 16-10. Ripple is a mobile web app simulator that works as a Google Chrome plug-in on your desktop.*

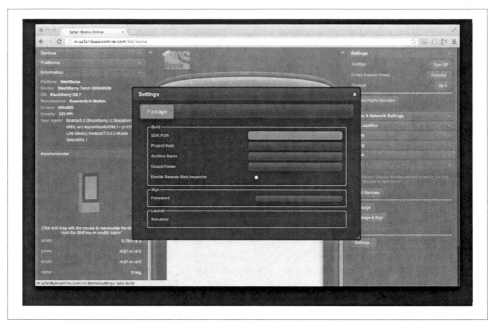

*Figure 16-11. Ripple allows you to define SDK and emulator paths, so it will help you in packaging and testing your WebWorks apps.*

### Distribution

You can distribute a WebWorks app just as you would any other native application, on every platform (in fact, they are the same *.cod* files for 5.x–7.x and *.bar* files for PlayBook and BB10).

To publish applications in App World, you'll need to create an account (*http:// appworld.blackberry.com/isvportal*). Registration is free of charge for developers.

## Nokia S40 Web Apps

Nokia has created a web app platform for its Series 40 social phone devices. If you remember from the first few chapters, Series 40 devices include feature phones, touch and keypad-based phones, and some cheap full-touch phones that are selling well in emerging markets.

These devices include the Xpress browser—a cloud-based browser from Nokia—and the web app engine works on it. Therefore, our apps will live in the cloud and will be delivered compressed to the user. Figure 16-12 shows examples of web apps running on S40 devices.

*Figure 16-12. With S40 web apps, we can create apps for social phones using web technologies and distribute them in emerging markets.*

An S40 web app is a ZIP-based package with the *.wgt* extension; for metadata it uses the W3C Widget Interface specification on a *config.xml* file in the root folder of the package. The rest of the package can consist of HTML, CSS, JavaScript, and images files.

The WGT package is always sent to Nokia's cloud servers, where it is compiled into some custom code that is rendered by the Xpress browser engine on the client. While we are testing, we can just open a URL in the simulator or inside a real S40 browser. We can also compile it into its final Java ME form: the WGT package becomes a Java ME application (containing both JAD and JAR files) that on the device itself acts as a shell for an icon and the app's private URL. When the user opens this app from the applications menu, the Xpress browser is launched and the web app is executed in full-screen mode (no browser UI).

Remember, the Xpress browser is a limited engine and our JavaScript will be executed server-side (with the exception of Nokia Mobile Web Library calls, as we'll see shortly).

 From version 1.5 of the web app platform, all images inside the wgt package will be cached on the device itself so they are not being downloaded every time the app needs them. Any external image that we link to will be compressed on the server side and delivered per request without any caching storage.

In terms of compatibility, at the time of this writing the platform supports XHTML 1.0, CSS 2.1, and the W3C Geolocation API; it also has basic support of CSS3 transitions for fades or slide effects.

S40 web apps work with the idea of a single HTML file; therefore, if you make a link to another HTML page, it will be opened as a web page with the browser UI. If you want to have different pages in your application, you can just use XMLHttpRequest (Ajax) and inject HTML into the DOM. Remember, all these JavaScript behaviors will be executed in the cloud and the client will just receive a pre-rendered compressed version of the result.

 In S40 web apps we should avoid using the *javascript:* protocol in links and use the onclick handler instead.

### Configuration

The web app configuration is done through a *config.xml* file in the root folder of the WGT package, with the following template:

```
<?xml version="1.0" encoding="UTF-8"?>
<widget xmlns="http://www.w3.org/ns/widgets" height="200"
        id="http://mobilexweb.com/superappid" version="1.0"
        viewmodes="windowed fullscreen" width="200">

    <name short="My webapp">My Super webapp</name>

    <description>
        This is my great super app for Series 40
    </description>

    <author email="myemail@mydomain.com"
            href="http://www.mobilexweb.com">
        Max Firtman
    </author>

    <icon src="icon.png"/>

    <content src="index.html"/>

    <license>
        Copyright forever
    </license>

    <feature name="nokia://s40.nokia.com/SAWRT/2.0" required="true" />

</widget>
```

### Mobile Web Library

The Mobile Web Library (MWL) is a built-in JavaScript framework exposed through the mwl global object. It includes basic DOM management functions (for hiding/showing elements, applying/deactivating CSS classes, and event handling), and the main advantage over classic JavaScript code or other frameworks is that all the processing is done on the client side. Any other JavaScript call will be executed as normal, with a round-trip to the server, as this is a cloud-based platform.

For the calls to be client-side only, they must come from JavaScript code inside HTML event handlers, as in:

```
<a onclick="mwl.show('#details')">Show Details</a>
```

If on the onclick event we call a function and that function calls mwl.show(), it will need a round-trip to the server.

### Gesture and keypad events

While we can use the click event, other mouse events, as well as touch events, are unsupported. However, on touch devices the platform supports a gesture extension called *synthetic events* that works with the unique client-side Mobile Web Library. The same events can be used for managing the keypad events.

All the events can be listened for through mwl.add<*Event-name*>Listener, which receives the target node selector and the code to execute. The last parameter should be a string value, and it will be evaluated as string code (don't use a function handler). If you include only mwl calls in the string execution code, you won't need a server round-trip; any other JavaScript call will go to the server.

Possible events are:

- SwipeLeft
- SwipeRight
- SwipeUp
- SwipeDown
- LongPress
- NavLeft
- NavRight
- NavUp
- NavDown

For example, to bind the long-press (or touch-and-hold) event to a JavaScript handler to show a contextual menu, we can use:

```
mwl.addLongPressListener("#myelement", "mwl.show('#menu')");
```

### Storage API

While HTML5 storage APIs are not available, a simple storage API from the W3C Widget Interface specification (*http://www.w3.org/TR/widgets-apis*) is supported. With a limit of 500 keys per app and 256 bytes in length per key-value, we can persist some basic data in our app using the `widget.preferences` collection, as in:

```
// Store data
widget.preferences['mykey'] = 'myvalue';
// Read data
var data = widget.preferences['mykey'];
```

### Tools

To develop, simulate, package, and test our apps, we can rely on Nokia Web Tools (*http://www.mobilexweb.com/go/nwt*) for Series 40, an Eclipse-based IDE that will do all we need (Figure 16-13). We can download this free tool for Mac, Linux, and Windows.

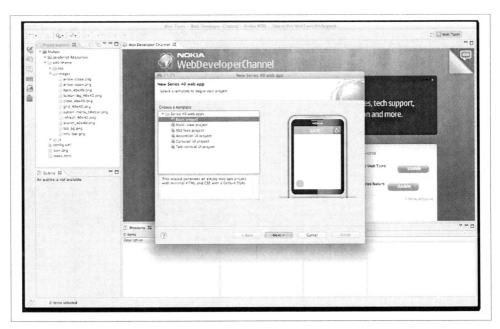

*Figure 16-13. Nokia Web Tools for Series 40 allows us to design, code, simulate, and distribute S40 web apps for Nokia devices.*

Dozens of working demos are available at the Nokia developer website that we can use as the base for our own apps.

This IDE has the ability to communicate via Bluetooth with a real S40 device to test our apps directly on the device (always through the proxy). To make this work we need to install the Nokia Xpress browser on the device (if it isn't installed already), as well as the *Series 40 web app Bluetooth Launcher*, available from the S40 website.

If you don't want to spend a lot of time designing or developing your app, you can use the free online tool Xpress Web App Builder (*http://xpresswebapps.nokia.com*). It will create a Series 40 web app from scratch, based on different templates, such as news, video, pictures, and blog content sharing.

You can learn more about S40 web apps at *mobilexweb.com/go/s40webapps*.

### Distribution

Your web apps can be published to the Nokia Store that every new S40 device includes on the Home screen; to do that you should get a publisher account (*http://publish.nokia.com*). The initial fee at the time of this writing is 1 euro. Users can pay for premium content by credit card or, in some countries, via their operators' billing systems. You will receive 70% of the revenue if the user pays with a credit card and 60% of the revenue if the user pays with operator billing.

The Nokia Store accepts WGT files as a possible app file format.

## Nokia Symbian Web Apps

The oldest mobile web app platform is Web Runtime (WRT) for Symbian devices. While the Series 40 is a live platform from Nokia, the Symbian web app platform is now obsolete, meaning that Nokia is not evolving it anymore. However, we can still create and package web apps for both older and newer Symbian devices, such as the Nokia 500 or the Nokia 808 Pureview, launched in 2012. Every Symbian device on the market (and there are still lots of them in non-US markets) supports WRT apps.

This platform has been available since 2007; for many years Nokia called its applications *widgets*, but it migrated to the *webapps* name in 2011.

WRT is a first-class citizen mobile web app engine. When a WRT widget is installed, it appears like any other Symbian or Java ME installed application, and might look like Figure 16-14. From the user's perspective, there is no difference between widgets and native installed applications. And, of course, the widgets are created entirely using web technologies.

*Figure 16-14. A WRT widget looks like any other installed application; it even has native menu support created using JavaScript.*

Some devices have Home screen support (also known as MiniView), enabling a web app to stay on the device's Home screen all the time, with visual updates possible. This is an excellent solution for applications related to social media, news, or any other information that can benefit from being regularly updated on the user's Home screen.

The platform access JavaScript API does not follow any of the standards we have seen so far, but it has many similarities to Apple's Dashboard Widget API. Modern Symbian devices, from Symbian Anna, also support some HTML5 APIs and CSS3 features in web apps, as listed on Mobile HTML5 (*http://mobilehtml5.org*).

Apache Cordova/PhoneGap has a WRT version that gives us a layer of JavaScript API compatibility with other platforms.

## Package

A WRT web app is a ZIP file with a *.wgz* extension, served as `application/x-nokia-widget`. The configuration file follows the Apple Dashboard standard and not the W3C widget package definition, unlike Series 40 web apps; it is a property list (*info.plist*) file with some mandatory information:

```
<?xml version="1.0" encoding="UTF-8"?>
<!DOCTYPE plist PUBLIC "-//Nokia//DTD PLIST 1.0//EN"
    "http://www.nokia.com/NOKIA_COM_1/DTDs/plist-1.0.dtd">
<plist version="1.0">
<dict>
    <key>Displa
    <stri                        ng>

                        pp_unique_id</string>
```

T                                                see on the screen, the `Identifier` is an
inv                                             ion inside the device, `MainHTML` is the
first                                           ation, and the `Version` is used by the
Appli                                           .g the application again. If we define
AllowN                                          nave any access to the Web (including Ajax
requests                                        .ewEnabled is for compatible devices only.

The icon :                   .u format (the recommended size for the best compatibility is
88×88 pixe         .ust be named *icon.png*, and must be located in the root folder of the
package.

## Features

WRT creates three new global objects in the JavaScript context: `widget`, `device`, and `menu`.

WRT allows us to define multilanguage applications; the version corresponding to the user's defined language will automatically be selected.

In WRT 1.0 we also have a sysinfo object that allows us to access the System Information API, which we can use to access properties relating to the battery, network information, lights, vibration, beep tone, and memory, as well as filesystem information and system language information services. WRT 1.0 doesn't have access to other APIs.

The device object allows us to use the Platform Services API library in WRT 1.1. The standard version of Platform Services is 1.0; if we are using Platform Services 2.0, we can use some new APIs. Table 16-5 lists the available APIs.

*Table 16-5. Nokia Platform Services APIs*

| API | Allows us to... |
| --- | --- |
| AppManager | List applications and launch a specific application or the default handler for a document type. |
| Calendar | Create, access, and manage Calendar entries. |
| Contact | Create, access, and manage Contact entries. In Platform Services 2.0, we can also access Contact Groups. |
| Landmarks | Create, access, and manage Landmark entries that are used by many map applications inside the device. Platform Services 2.0 also allows us to access the Landmarks local database. |
| Location | Retrieve information about the user's location. |
| Logging | Retrieve information about call, messaging, and data logs. |
| Media Management | Retrieve information about media files stored on the device. |
| Messaging | Send and receive messages. |
| Sensors | Access physical sensors on the device (like the accelerometer). |
| System Information | Retrieve system information (similar to WRT 1.0's System Information API). |
| Camera (2.0) | Launch the Camera application and retrieve information on pictures taken (Platform Services 2.0 only). |

If you are targeting devices with WRT 1.x, you can add support for Platform Services 2.0. To do that, download the API and include a *platformservices.js* file in your package and code. You will then be able to access any API using the shortcut nokia.device.load(*interface_name*).

 You can create hybrid applications for Symbian and MeeGo devices using the QtWebKit project. You can find information about porting WRT widgets to QtWebKit at Nokia's developer site (*http://bit.ly/ZqSJHF*).

## JavaScript API

The widget object has the methods and properties listed in Table 16-6.

*Table 16-6. Methods and properties of the native widget object*

| Method/property | Description |
|---|---|
| openURL(*url*) | Opens the specified URL in a browser window, leaving our widget in the background. |
| setPreferenceForKey(*value*, *key*) | Stores a persistent object (the *value*) for a specific *key* that can be read by the same widget anytime. Note that the parameter order is *value*, *key*. |
| preferenceForKey(*key*) | Retrieves a stored preference for a key, or returns undefined if the key doesn't exist. |
| prepareForTransi tion("fade") | Blocks any update on the UI until performTransition() is invoked. This is useful if we are going to change the UI for some controls and we don't want a flick effect. |
| performTransition() | Updates the UI with the changes made since the prepareForTransition() call. |
| setNavigationEnabled (*Boolean*) | Toggles the navigation mode between the default (cursor-based with a pointer on the screen) and focus (tabbed) navigation. |
| setNavigationType(*mode*) | Changes the navigation mode (you can select cursor, tabbed, or none). If none is selected, all the key events can be handled by our code. Available since WRT 7.1. |
| openApplication(*uid*, *param*) | Launches an S60 application, identified by its hexadecimal number. There is a list of common UIDs in the documentation. |
| setDisplayLandscape() | Changes the UI to the landscape orientation. |
| setDisplayPortrait() | Changes the UI to the portrait orientation. |
| onshow | Fired when the application comes to the foreground. |
| onhide | Fired when the application goes to the background. |
| onexit | Fired when the user presses Exit. |
| isrotationsupported | Boolean indicating whether we can change the orientation on this device. |

With the menu object and the MenuItem class, we can create native menus, and we can define the label and handler for the left soft key with menu.setLeftSoftkeyLa bel(*label*, *handler*). The right soft key is by default handled by the platform with an "Exit" label, but after WRT 7.1 we can override it using menu.setRightSoftkeyLa bel(*label*, *handler*). We can also hide and show the soft key labels using showSoft keys() and hideSoftkeys().

The onShow event of the menu object will fire when the user opens the menu.

If we don't define a left soft key, by default it will be an "Options" submenu displaying the native menu we created. A MenuItem can have a label, an id for finding the element, an onSelect event, and optionally child MenuItem objects for submenus. For example:

```
// We define a label and a menu ID
var option1 = new MenuItem("Refresh", 2);
var option2 = new MenuItem("New item", 3);

// We can use the same handler and use the ID to tell
// which one was pressed
option1.onSelect = menuSelected;
option2.onSelect = menuSelected;
```

```
// We append the first option
menu.append(option1);

// We create a third option with a submenu
menu.append(new MenuItem("Submenu", 4));
// We can search for a MenuItem using the ID
menu.getMenuItemById(4).append(option2);

function menuSelected(id) {
    switch (id) {
        // We can query the ID to decide what to do
    }
}
```

> After WRT 1.1, the widget object has a wrt property that we can query
> to get information about the current device and platform, including
> widget.wrt.version, widget.wrt.platform.model, and widg
> et.wrt.platform.romVersion.

### MiniView

The MiniView, or Home screen widget, allows us to display a widget's content (continuously updated) on the device's Home screen, as shown in Figure 16-15. On compatible devices, the widget is installed as normal, but if the MiniViewEnabled property is defined as true in the *info.plist* file the user can opt to add it to the Home screen.

*Figure 16-15. With the MiniView, users can add our mobile web content to their Home screens; using JavaScript, the information displayed in the widget can be updated on a regular basis.*

When a widget is displayed on the Home screen, it shows the same HTML file it would if it were being viewed as a full-screen application. It is up to us to detect the window size change and maybe show and hide a `div` depending on the situation. At the time of this writing, the MiniView size is 312×82 pixels, so we can use a `div` with those proportions when we detect that our widget is being displayed on the Home screen. When the user clicks on the widget in the Home screen it will change to a full-screen display, and when the user exits the widget it will again become small (without actually exiting). The script will be running all the time, so to save the device's battery we should keep our background code to the minimum.

When the user adds a widget to the Home screen, he will receive a confirmation dialog that will allow the web app to make any API call at any time in the future without new confirmation dialogs. So, we can safely use any API (with care, please) in the background.

To update the Home screen UI, we can have a timer defined in JavaScript that queries a server via Ajax, or we can use any other API available on the device (like Location).

We can use the `onshow`, `onhide`, and `onresize` events to detect whether the widget is in full-screen or MiniView mode.

Some devices, like the Nokia N8, allow multipage Home screen support, so the user has more space to add widgets to the Home screen.

### Tools and libraries

We can use any tools we like to create WRT widgets, starting with any text editor and a ZIP packager. However, Nokia has an Eclipse-based tool that will help us in developing, testing, debugging, and packaging Symbian web apps known as Nokia Web Tools 1.2 (*http://www.mobilexweb.com/go/nwt12*) for Symbian.

### Distribution

A WRT web app can be distributed in many ways, including OTA installation from your own server, offline installation from a desktop, and distribution for free or as a premium application in the Nokia Store.

The requirements to publish WRT apps in the Nokia Store are the same as for Series 40 web apps.

# Apache Cordova/PhoneGap Apps

In Chapter 3, we talked about web view–based development and introduced PhoneGap and Apache Cordova (recall that Apache Cordova is the open source engine and PhoneGap is the Adobe implementation). Now it's time to start talking about how to use Cordova for creating native web applications.

 Remember that a Cordova app is a native app from a user's perspective, in terms of installation and usage. It's up to our UI if it "feels" native or webby. If it feels too webby on iOS, Apple may reject it.

Apache Cordova is compatible with the following platforms at the time of this writing:

- iOS
- Android
- Windows Phone
- Windows 8
- BlackBerry
- Bada
- Symbian (deprecated, with a fully working version up to Cordova 1.0)

There are currently also implementations being developed for other platforms, such as MeeGo, Ubuntu for Phones, and Tizen.

The apps that we create are native apps with a full-screen enhanced web view. From a store's perspective it's just a native app compiled for the target platform.

 Apple doesn't allow "packaged websites" as valid apps in the App Store; therefore, if your app looks like a website (with links instead of buttons, for example) it may be rejected even if technically it works properly.

On every platform, Cordova uses the web view that the operating system exposes; that means our code may execute and render differently on every platform, as Cordova is not adding any rendering engine.

## PhoneGap Build

Adobe has launched a service that you can use to compile Apache Cordova apps in the cloud without the need to have every SDK installed on your computer, and even without the need to have a Mac for iOS app compilation.

PhoneGap Build has a free account option that will let you create one private app and infinite public apps; you can also sign up for a premium account that allows you to create up to 25 private apps. To create an account, visit PhoneGap Build's website (*http://build.phonegap.com*); in just a few seconds you will be ready to compile Cordova apps for multiple platforms.

PhoneGap Build is integrated into the Adobe Creative Cloud services, so you can sign up for it as a standalone service or simply use your Creative Cloud membership, if you already have one. You can set up an app from a Git server (including GitHub) where you can push updates, or you can upload a ZIP file with the content of your web app.

The ZIP file should include the main HTML file and every resource—CSS, JavaScript, images, data—that the Cordova app is using. We don't need to provide the CordovaJS file as it varies per platform; the cloud service will inject the right JS file for each compilation, we just need to reference a *cordovajs.js* generic file in our HTML.

To change the default values, including permissions that we request from the operating system, icons, the splash screen, as well as other platform-specific metadata, PhoneGap Build uses a *config.xml* file in the root of the project, following the W3C Widget Packaging specification. You'll find the documentation for this configuration file at PhoneGap Build's documentation page (*http://build.phonegap.com/docs*). PhoneGap Build is a commercial service from Adobe and we should not confuse it with Apache Cordova's openness.

What Cordova does is to enhance all the web views with a common set of APIs that bridge from JavaScript to native code; it also adds several hacks and automatic configuration so the web view will work as expected.

Even though Cordova uses the web view available on each platform, the behavior of some APIs and features may not be the same as in the browser; therefore, testing is crucial for the project's success.

 Apache Cordova/PhoneGap doesn't compile apps; it is just a framework that will help us to compile apps using the official SDK on each individual platform. Don't confuse this with PhoneGap Build, a commercial—with a free option—service from Adobe that will compile Cordova apps in the cloud for us.

## Template Creation

When you download the latest Apache Cordova package from Apache Incubator (*http:// incubator.apache.org/cordova*) or PhoneGap (*http://phonegap.com*), you will receive a ZIP file with one folder per official platform under the *lib* root folder.

> Every compilation has its own "Getting Started Guide" as well as its own permissions and Cordova settings files. You'll find all the guides and documentation at *docs.phonegap.com*.

At the time of this writing, iOS, Android, and BlackBerry have shell commands to create, build, and emulate Cordova projects from the command line. On the other platforms, we need to do this on our own.

In the *<platform>/bin* folder, such as *android/bin*, we will find a *create* shell command (for Linux and Mac) and a *create.bat* command for Windows. To create a file we need to execute this shell command (remember to add *.bat* on Windows), using the following syntax:

```
create path_to_new_project package_name project_name
```

The *path* should be any valid path on the current operating system; the *pack age_name* is a unique identifier using the reverse domain name convention (such as com.oreilly.progmobileweb), and the project name will be the name of the Xcode, Eclipse, or BlackBerry SDK–created project. For example, on Windows we can do:

```
create.bat c:\apps\mybook com.mobilexweb.book MyBook
```

Remember to navigate first to the folder containing the *create* shell command, add it to the default paths, or use a full-path call.

> On BlackBerry, the *package_name* attribute must be omitted.

When the project is created on all three platforms, we will find a *www* or similar folder where all our HTML files and resources should be located, and a *cordova* folder full of tools to use. In that folder we will find the shell commands *debug[.bat]* for building and *emulate[.bat]* for opening the app. For a full list of commands supported, check the documentation.

## Cordova Web View

If we are creating a native app for iOS or Android and we just want to use Cordova in one specific part of it instead of creating a full Cordova app, we can use a feature known as Cordova Web View. On both platforms, we will have a component that inherits the default web view, adding all the Cordova functionality ready to use in our apps.

## CordovaJS

As we said, Cordova adds a layer of APIs that are not available by default on most HTML5 platforms today. This API is now known as *CordovaJS*, and it includes a Java-Script file (different per platform) that acts as a bridge to a native library on each platform.

We will find the right file for the platform after creating a project with the command-line tools or inside the platform folder, usually under the name *cordova.js* or *cordova-<version>.js*.

 At the time of this writing, even though the CordovaJS public interface may be the same for all platforms, the file you need to include varies per platform. Therefore, if we use the iOS version in an Android project, it will compile but the whole JavaScript API will not work.

### DeviceReady event

One of the first things we need to understand about CordovaJS is that most of its functionality relies on a native library that Cordova includes for every platform. Loading that native library can take some milliseconds, and we should wait until it's done before trying to use a Cordova API.

To solve this problem, Cordova adds a new event to the DOM `document` element: `deviceready`. Even some HTML5 APIs should be executed only after `deviceready`, as Cordova is adding a compatibility layer or changing the default web engine behavior. One good example is the Geolocation API on some platforms, such as iOS: if we don't include the CordovaJS file in our project or if we don't wait for `deviceready`, the geolocation will work, but with an "index.html wants to get your location" message. Showing "index.html" in an app doesn't look so good; that's why CordovaJS overrides the default Geolocation API with a native implementation (using the same syntax) that will look more natural to the user.

To detect the event, we use the standard event-handling mechanism:

```
document.addEventListener("deviceready", function() {
    // Cordova is ready
}, false);
```

### Other events

Different events are available on the `document` element after `deviceready` has fired. They may not all work on every platform (check the documentation for details), but the list of most useful events includes:

`backbutton`
> Fired when the Back button is pressed on Windows Phone, BlackBerry, or Android devices.

`menubutton`
> Fired when the Menu button is pressed on Android or BlackBerry devices.

`searchbutton`
> Fired when the Search button is pressed on select Android devices.

`pause`
> Fired when our app is put into the background; we can run only quick processes here before the app is frozen on some platforms.

`resume`
> Fired when the app is brought back to the foreground. On some platforms our app may be reloaded when it comes back from the background.

`batterystatus`
> Fired after the battery status has changed.

`batterylow`
> Fired when the device has reached a low battery threshold.

`batterycritical`
> Fired when the device has reached a critical battery threshold (and may be close to shutdown).

 By default, a Cordova app may be offline in terms of accessing web resources, such as for image loading, accessing analytics scripts, or using XHR to load content. To allow Cordova to use the Internet, we need to add permission. The process varies per platform: we need to edit *res/xml/cordova.xml* on Android, *www/config.xml* on BlackBerry, or *Cordova.plist* on iOS. We can add permission to access the whole Web using the star (*), or whitelist certain domains.

### APIs

Some API usage will require permission in the platform's configuration file; that information will be found in the API documentation available in the *doc* folder of the Cordova package, or at *docs.phonegap.com*.

Cordova also adds a compatibility layer on some platforms for certain HTML5 APIs, such as Geolocation on Symbian, Web SQL on Windows Phone, or a local storage native implementation. Therefore, these APIs will work on those platforms even if the native engine behind doesn't support them.

In addition to the default HTML5 compatibility, CordovaJS adds to most every platform:

- The W3C Network Information API
- The W3C Contacts API, through the `navigator.contacts` object
- The W3C File API
- The Cordova Accelerometer API, through the `navigator.accelerometer` object
- The Cordova Camera API, through the `navigator.camera` object
- The Cordova Capture API
- The Cordova Compass API, through the `navigator.compass` object
- The Cordova Device API, through the `window.device` object
- The Cordova Media API, through the `window.media` object
- The Cordova Notification API, through the `navigator.notification` object

 On iOS from version 6 we can debug Cordova apps (in fact, any web view) using Safari's Remote Web Inspector, including JavaScript debugging and profiling.

**Notification API.** While we have already covered some of these APIs in previous chapters, it is worth taking a quick look at the Notification API at this point.

 The Cordova Notification API has nothing to do with push notification services on mobile devices.

The Notification API allows us to use native dialogs instead of web dialogs, such as alert and confirm. The default dialogs will work, but on some platforms they will not offer the best experience (for example, showing "index.html" as the dialog title). Therefore, CordovaJS adds `navigator.notification.alert()` and `navigator.notification.confirm()` methods that allow us to customize the title, message, and buttons in these dialogs on some platforms.

The following example shows usage of both:

```
navigator.notification.alert("Message",
    function() {
        /* callback */
    }, "Title", "Done button name");

navigator.notification.confirm("Message",
    function(buttonIndex) {
        /* callback */
    }, "Title", "Button1,Button2");
```

Unfortunately, there is no Cordova implementation for the prompt dialog. The Notification API also exposes a `vibrate()` and a `beep()` method.

## Plug-ins

If you can't find what you need using an HTML5 API or a CordovaJS API, don't give up—you may be able to use a Cordova plug-in. A plug-in is a mix of a JavaScript public interface and a native library that can access any native API or feature on every platform. The main problem of plug-ins is that for multiplatform compatibility we need to offer different native code (Objective-C for iOS, Java for Android, Java for BlackBerry 6/7, AIR for PlayBook, .NET for Windows Phone, etc.).

A list of currently available open source plug-ins is located at PhoneGap's GitHub (*https://github.com/phonegap/phonegap-plugins*).

# Distribution

To distribute a native web application, we need to join every publisher's application store program and follow the same instructions as for full native apps.

## iOS App Store

For iOS, you need to join the iOS Developer Program (*http://developer.apple.com/ios/program*). A standard account (personal or business) costs $99 per year. Without an account, your application will only work on the Simulator.

Once your membership has been approved you will have the ability to test your application on real devices, or you can define up to 100 beta testers.

If you apply for a standard account, you will also have the ability to digitally sign your application to be published to the App Store, as a free or premium application. For premium applications, you will receive 70% of the revenue received.

Wikipedia has decided to use Cordova as the platform for its native apps. At the time of this writing, iOS, Android, Windows Phone, Windows 8, and BlackBerry versions are available, and the whole project is open source; therefore, if you want to take a look at Wikipedia Cordova source code you can just point to *https://github.com/wikimedia/Wiki pediaMobile*.

## Android Stores

You can apply for a Google Play Store publisher account (*http://play.google.com/apps/ publish*); the initial fee is $25. You will receive 70% of the revenue from your premium web applications.

You can also distribute your Android applications via the Amazon Appstore. To sign up for a free publisher account, go to Amazon's app developer page (*http://develop er.amazon.com/apps/apps*).

## BlackBerry AppWorld

Publishing to the AppWorld is free of charge, and you can register for a publisher account at the Vendor Portal for BlackBerry World (*https://appworld.blackberry.com/ isvportal*). To sign your BlackBerry apps (required before uploading files to the store) you need to get a free signature from BlackBerry (*http://www.blackberry.com/Signed Keys*). BlackBerry's store supports apps for smartphones, PlayBooks, and the new BB10, and it follows a similar revenue sharing model as the other stores.

## Microsoft Windows Store

For Windows 8, you can get a Store publisher account at the Microsoft Dev Center (*http://msdn.microsoft.com/windows/apps*) (the price may vary based on the developer's country) This enables you to publish free and premium applications for Intel/AMD classic Windows devices and Windows RT (ARM-based) devices such as the Microsoft Surface.

## Microsoft Windows Phone Store

Windows Phone has its own store, previously known as Microsoft Marketplace. To create a publisher account you need to go to *dev.windowsphone.com* and pay the $99 annual fee. This allows you to publish free or premium apps for every Windows Phone manufacturer, including Nokia.

We covered how to sign up to the Nokia Store and distribute Symbian or S40 web apps earlier in this chapter.

# Full-Screen App Patterns

Web app development requires new design patterns to solve the challenges presented. We need to think of our apps as applications, not websites, so some of the techniques we've used for websites will not be useful here.

In the previous chapters we have seen how to technically implement most of the patterns we are going to discuss in this section. We will not talk about pages here, but rather screens or views.

## Multiple Views

The first problem stems from the lack of a browser's toolbar for navigation. Typical web links are bad practice because the user will see a flicker effect, and the back feature needs to be implemented by us.

That is why in a web app, we will generally have only one HTML file and then, using JavaScript, will change the view, using static hidden divs, dynamic content generated by code, Ajax replacements, or other similar solutions.

We will generally use one of the following multiview mechanisms:

- Tab navigation (top or bottom)
- A top toolbar for going back and/or a back key handler, if available
- Key and touch paginating for sequential views (like a slideshow)

## Layout

Even if we are working with only one web app platform, we need to support different screen sizes, orientation modes, and physical screen dimensions. We'll need to decide whether to use a fixed or a liquid design, or a responsive web design approach.

## Input Method

The same problem we encountered when designing mobile websites appears here: the devices on which our web apps are used can have a variety of input methods (touch, keyboards, touchpads, etc.), and we will need to handle all of this by code, supporting all the possible input methods and perhaps changing the layout on touch devices (for larger components).

## One-View Widget

A one-view widget is the simplest (and sometimes the most powerful) kind of web app that we can create. It generally has an information view and, optionally, a second view for configuring the details for the main view. This is suitable for weather, financial, social networking, news, and corporate indicators.

## Dynamic Application Engine

As JavaScript is a dynamic language, we can easily execute code received by a server (using `eval()` or a JSONP request). With this in mind, we can easily create a web app that is only a little engine (like a web browser) that will receive instructions from our server.

All the code (including access to private APIs on some platforms) can be delivered from the server and optionally cached locally in persistent storage. Thus, we can create a self-updating widget mechanism so that no intervention is required from the user to receive the latest version of the application.

There are some security risks and problems, but for most platforms we can easily create a self-update mechanism.

## Reload My Web App

Following on from the previous pattern, while we are developing our apps, adhering to a classic development pattern is not a good idea. That is, we should avoid the process of coding, packaging, signing, and installing every time we want to make a change and see it take effect on a real device or an emulator.

To really accelerate development and testing, we may run our own web server (on the Internet or on the local network) and create a very basic web app that will just load the rest of the files (including scripts, styles, and resources) from our repository. Besides that, we add a simple JavaScript reload feature (`history.reload()`) that we remove when deploying the final version. We then package, sign, and install that application, and every time we want to make a change all we have to do is reload it on the device: all the files will be reloaded from the repository.

When we are done with the testing, we can then move all the files to the package, and create the final web app.

### Live Reload

An extension to the previous tip is to create a live reload mechanism. This pattern involves JavaScript code that we add while in debug mode that will open a session to a server, usually with WebSockets or some other network API. On our development machine we have a resident application (or it can be our own IDE) that detects changes to the filesystem and triggers an update to the web app. Therefore, any time we make a change to a CSS, HTML, JavaScript, or image file, the web app on our testing device will update automatically, without even reloading in some cases.

 Live Reload (*http://livereload.com*) offers apps for Mac and Windows that will automatically refresh a page using WebSockets when it finds changes on the filesystem.

# CHAPTER 17

# Content Delivery

Content delivery is a common need in the mobile web world. Applications, music, video, wallpapers, and any other content can be delivered to compatible devices, but this requires a bit of explanation and expertise.

 We covered video delivery to mobile devices in Chapter 10.

## MIME Types

MIME types, many of which are listed in Appendix A, are a key element for content delivery. Mobile browsers don't care about the file extension; they decide whether or not to accept the content based on the MIME type delivered by the server. Remember that the MIME type travels with the HTTP header response.

### Static Definition

The simplest way to define the right MIME types is to statically define them on your web server. If you are working with a shared hosting service, the control panels often allow you to define document MIME types. If you manage your own server, you can set them up with the following instructions.

#### Apache

In Apache, the simplest way is to open the *mime.types* file located in the *conf* folder of the Apache root. In your favorite text editor, you can add one row per MIME type to be configured.

You will find hundreds of MIME type declarations. The first thing to do is to look for the following line and change the MIME type to the correct one for mobile XHTML documents:

```
text/html                        html htm
```

As you can see, each line contains a MIME type followed by a series of spaces or tabs and a space-separated list of file extensions.

 This technique applies these changes to all the websites on the server. If you want to make changes to only one website or one folder of a website, you should create or edit the *.htaccess* file in the appropriate folder and use the AddType procedure:

```
AddType   text/x-vcard   vcf
```

You can find an Apache configuration file to download and use with all the important mobile web MIME types at *www.mobilexweb.com/go/mime*.

### Internet Information Server

Configuring MIME types in Microsoft IIS can be done via the UI (as opposed to in Apache, where you need to edit a text file).

In IIS from version 7.0:

1. Go to the IIS Manager.
2. Navigate to the level you want to manage.
3. In Features View, double-click on MIME Types.
4. In the Actions pane, click Add.
5. Type the file extension and MIME type and press OK to finish.

 In IIS, you can also manage MIME types from the command line. Check the documentation for more information.

In IIS 7.0, it is also possible to define static MIME type declarations in the *web.config* file in your ASP.NET folder. The syntax is:

```
<configuration>
    <system.webServer>
        <staticContent>
            <mimeMap fileExtension=".mp4" mimeType="video/mp4" />
            <mimeMap fileExtension=".vcf" mimeType="text/x-vcard" />
```

```
        </staticContent>
    </system.webServer>
</configuration>
```

## Dynamic Definition

The other possible way to declare MIME types is to use dynamic header declarations in your server script code.

In PHP, you should define the MIME type before any other output, using the `head er()` function:

```
header('Content-Type: application/xhtml+xml');
```

If you are delivering downloadable content (not markup), like a video, you should also define a filename. If not, when the file is saved it will have a *.php* extension and it will not work.

To define the name of the file we use the `Content-disposition` header, as shown in the following sample:

```
$path = '/videos/video.mp4';
header('Content-Type: video/mp4');
header('Content-disposition: attachment; filename=video.mp4');
// We serve the file from our local filesystem
header("Content-Length: " . filesize($path) );
readfile($path);
```

ASP.NET has a `Response.ContentType` property that we can define:

```
// This is C# code
Response.ContentType = "application/xhtml+xml";
```

The filename should also be defined if it is downloadable content, using `Response.AddHeader`.

In a Java servlet or JSP, you should define the headers using the `setContentType()` method of the `response` object:

```
response.setContentType("application/xhtml+xml");
```

 When you are serving nonmarkup content using a dynamic script, if an error occurs you will not see the error details and the content will be broken (imagine a JPEG with a PHP error as the contents). You should capture any error, send yourself an email or log the error details, and replace the output with generic content.

# File Delivery

To deliver a file, there are three models:

- Direct linking
- Delayed linking
- OMA Download

You can use any of these three methods to deliver the files, either using the physical file (video, audio, game, etc.) directly or via a script (PHP, ASPX, etc.). If you use a script to deliver a file, you can log, secure, and even charge for every download. If the file is available directly through the web server, anyone with the URL can download the file.

 The installation of files using HTTP is also called OTA (over-the-air) provisioning. Some low-end devices don't have a web browser but do have the ability to download files (e.g., ringtones, applications, or images) using HTTP. We can offer files to those devices, but we must send the download URLs by WAP Push using SMS.

## Direct Linking

Direct linking is the simplest way to deliver content. A direct link is just a link to the file (with the right MIME type defined), a link to a script that will deliver the file, or a link to a script that will redirect the user to the file. For example:

```
<a href="game.jad">Download This Game</a>
<a href="download.php?id=22222">Download This Game</a>
```

The *download.php* script can save the download to the database, check permissions, and then deliver the content using the appropriate MIME type, writing the file to the response output or redirecting the browser to the file:

```php
<?php
if ($everything_ok) {
    header('Location: game.jad');
} else {
    header('Location: download_error.php');
}
```

## Delayed Linking

Delayed linking is a technique often used in download sites for desktop browsers. It allows us to show a landing page before the download starts. This landing page will also be the document the user will see after the download has finished or, if the browser supports background downloading, while it is downloading.

Some devices also look for the `type` attribute in a link to decide how to manage the link before downloading the response from the server. For example, we can define a link as a video file using:

```
<a href="video.mp4"
   type="video/mp4">Download This Video</a>
```

The technique involves linking to an HTML document that will show the user some information and will use a `refresh` meta tag to redirect the user to the direct link in $x$ seconds (more than 5 for mobile devices).

So, the download page will redirect to:

```
<a href="download.html">Download This Game</a>
```

And *download.html* will contain code like the following:

```
<!DOCTYPE html>
<head>
<meta charset="UTF-8" />
<meta http-equiv="refresh" content="5;document.pdf" />
<title>Download File</title>
</head>

<body>
<h1>Your document is being downloaded</h1>
<p>If the file is not downloaded in 5 seconds,
    <a href="document.pdf">click here</a>

<h2>Brought to you by "Your favourite ad here"</h2>
<a href="/">More Downloads</a>
</body>
</html>
```

## OMA Download

OMA Download is a standard defined in 2004 by the Open Mobile Alliance to allow us more control over the delivery of media objects. It also has support for Digital Rights Management (DRM) in two versions, OMA DRM 1.0 and OMA DRM 2.0. The specification was used as the basis for the Java ME MIDlet OTA installation method that we will see later in this chapter, so the two are very similar.

Unfortunately, modern platforms—including Safari on iOS and Android browsers—don't support OMA Downloads, and we can use them only on platforms that were on the market before 2008, such as feature phones, older BlackBerry devices, or Symbian devices.

Many browsers support the download of Multimedia Messaging Services (MMS) templates using a format called the *Synchronized Multimedia Integration Language* (SMIL). This is useful if you are offering templates like postcards. You can create messages using Nokia tools (*http://www.mobilexweb.com/go/mms*).

OMA Download adds two phases to the download process: *before download* and *after download.*

The before-download process involves a description file downloaded using HTTP before the real file is downloaded. This description file is an XML file containing meta-information for the operating system and instructions for doing the download. This process gives the user an opportunity to see information about the content (name, compatibility, size) before accepting it.

Using OMA DRM you can protect a file from being sent by MMS, Bluetooth, or any other method after it has been installed on the device. This is to avoid piracy of video, music, Flash Lite, and other multimedia content. Nokia, Sony Ericsson, and Motorola devices are known to have support for this standard.

The after-download process involves an HTTP request posted to your web server from the operating system, confirming the final status of the download. This allows you to confirm that the file has been correctly downloaded and installed.

OMA DRM supports the ability to define the right to play, display, or execute a media object or a file a limited number of times. DRM should be managed with care, and you need to test compatibility with the devices you're targeting before using it.

### Download descriptor

The descriptor is an XML-based file that should be served using the MIME type `application/vnd.oma.dd+xml`.

Here's a simple example of this file:

```
<?xml version="1.0"?>
<media xmlns="http://www.openmobilealliance.org/xmlns/dd">
    <name>The first man on the moon</type>
    <type>video/mp4</type>
    <objectURI>http://mobilexweb.com/video.mp4</objectURI>
    <size>230</size>
    <installNotifyURI>http://mobilexweb.com/download/notify.php?id=3333
    </installNotifyURI>
</media>
```

These are the typical attributes: name, the user-readable name of the content file; type, the MIME type of the file; objectURI, the absolute URL of the file; size, the file size expressed in KB; and installNotifyURI, the URL that will receive the after-download status (this can have GET parameters defined dynamically to log whether or not the download was saved).

Additional properties are also available, like nextURL (the URL of a website to visit after the download has finished), description (a short description of the media file), vendor (the organization providing the file), and iconURI (an optional icon to be shown with the file information).

 There are good resources and tools on the Nokia Developer, Sony Ericsson, and Adobe websites about OMA Digital Rights Management (*http://www.mobilexweb.com/go/drm*).

### Post-download status report

If you define the installNotifyURI in the download descriptor, you will receive a POST request to that URL when the download finishes. This URL will receive as the POST body an integer code with a status message. The important thing is that this request does not come in the normal URL-encoded way, so you can't use the typical $_FORM or Request.Form. To read the status code, you'll need to read the request body in a low-level format. Table 17-1 lists the most common OMA Download status codes to read in our scripts.

*Table 17-1. OMA Download status codes*

| Code | Message | Description |
|------|---------|-------------|
| 900 | Success | The object was downloaded and installed. |
| 901 | Insufficient Memory | The device has no space to download or install the file. |
| 902 | User Cancelled | The user cancelled the download. |
| 903 | Loss of Service | The device lost the network connection while downloading the file. |
| 905 | Attribute Mismatch | The file doesn't match the download descriptor (e.g., the MIME type). The file will be rejected. |
| 906 | Invalid Descriptor | The download descriptor is invalid. |
| 951 | Invalid DDVersion | The download descriptor version is invalid. |
| 952 | Device Aborted | The device aborted the installation process. This can occur for different reasons. |
| 953 | Non-Acceptable Content | The device cannot use the file. |
| 954 | Loader Error | The URL of the file is not working. |

To read the OMA Download response from a PHP script, you can use the following sample code:

```php
<?php
// We get the post body from the input
$post = file_get_contents('php://input');
// We get the first three characters without spaces
$status = substr(trim($post), 0, 3);

if ($status==900) {
    // Download OK, save information to the database
} else {
    // Some error happens, save information to the database
    // to allow the same user to download it again
}

?>
```

If you are delivering premium content that the user has paid for, if the download fails you should deliver the same content without forcing the user to pay again. Even if the download has succeeded, many carriers insist that the content be made available free of charge for 24 hours (or even up to a week). Some new application stores also allow the users to download the premium content again even if they change their mobile devices.

 Remember that you can check for OMA Download compatibility using WURFL with the `oma_support` capability before using this download mechanism.

# Application and Games Delivery

In the beginning, the mobile content delivery world centered around ringtones and wallpapers. To deliver this kind of content, we should rely on what we have seen before: if we deliver the proper MIME type, the file will be saved by the mobile device.

Application delivery can be useful:

- If you are creating a game or application store
- If you are developing a mobile website for a current application
- If you have a richer version of your mobile website available as a widget or application
- If you are providing a shortcut for your website embedded as an application

The application formats that you can deliver from a website are:

- Java ME (formerly J2ME)
- Flash Lite
- Android (if the user allows installation from nonsecure sites)

- Symbian native
- Widgets
- BlackBerry (up to 7.1)

We cannot deliver native iOS, BB10, Windows Phone, or Windows 8 Store applications for end users, as the specific platform store is the unique public way to install and deliver applications for each of these OSs. However, we can provide a link on the screen to the native store application that we want the user to buy or download.

 Always verify, on the server or the client side, that the user is on a compatible device before delivering applications or links to application downloads.

## iOS Applications

If you have your own application that has already been accepted for distribution via the App Store, or if you want to provide users with a link to buy or download an application, game, ebook, music file, movie, or TV show, you can use a special iTunes link that will open iTunes or the App Store automatically, displaying the desired content.

You can create one of these links using the web service iTunes Link Maker (*http://www.apple.com/itunes/linkmaker*). You can select which country's App Store to look for the content in, and then search for the content you want to link to.

 From iOS 6 you can also deliver PassBook (*https://developer.apple.com/passbook*) files, including passes, coupons, and virtual cards.

For example, to provide a link that the user can visit to buy the movie *Terminator Salvation*, we can use the following code provided by the iTunes Link Maker:

```
<a href="http://itunes.apple.com/WebObjects/MZStore.woa/wa/viewMovie?
id=338372479&s=143441&uo=6" target="itunes_store">
<img height="15" width="61" alt="Terminator Salvation" src="http://ax.phobos
.apple.com.edgesuite.net/images/badgeitunes61x15dark.gif" />
</a>
```

 In Chapter 7, we talked about iOS Smart App Banners, a way to connect a website with a related native app in the App Store that will also invite the user to open the app if it's already installed.

### Ad hoc OTA installation

Earlier I said that iOS applications can't be installed from a website, and they have to be downloaded from the App Store. That was not completely true, as there are some exceptions that will allow us to install an app from a website; this is called *ad hoc distribution* or OTA (over-the-air) installation.

We can distribute an app from a website in the following situations:

- We have a Corporate iOS Developer Account that allows us to create internal apps for our company.
- We have a Standard iOS Developer Account (personal or business) and we want to deliver the app to beta testers (up to 100).
- We have a Standard iOS Developer Account (personal or business) and we want to deliver the app to our own devices (up to 100).

In all cases, the app needs to be signed with a specific signature and mobile provisioning file that defines one by one the devices where the app can be installed.

After the compilation process you will have an *.ipa* file (the iPhone Package application) and a *.mobileprovision* file (the counterpart that needs to be installed on the device, which allows installation of nonstore apps).

The mobile provisioning certificate should be delivered from a website as a normal file (no specific MIME type is available, `application/octet-stream` works), but the *.ipa* file needs special attention. If you link to the *.ipa* file directly, it won't work. Instead, you need to create an intermediate download file called the *download manifest*—a similar concept to OMA Download.

The download manifest is an XML file in *plist* (property list) syntax. You can create this file by hand or using Xcode when you do the final archive compilation, with the option "Save for Enterprise Distribution." The manifest file will include the final IPA absolute URL inside.

To link to the download manifest file, you need to use the *itms-services://* protocol and the absolute URL to that file, as in:

```
itms-services://?action=download-manifest&url=<absolute_manifest_url>
```

When the user clicks on a link with this URL, Safari will ask for permission to install the app. If the user accepts, and if he already has the mobile provisioning certificate installed, the app was compiled with it, and the current device is on the list of approved devices for OTA installation, the app will finally be installed on the iOS device, bypassing the App Store.

There are some cloud-based services that will help you install ad hoc apps, such as TestFlight (*http://www.testflightapp.com*), without configuring your own server. Alternatively, HockeyKit (*http://hockey kit.net*) is an open source framework to provide OTA installation for iOS and Android users from your own server.

# Android Applications

Android devices may have different stores for apps, such as the Google Play Store (formerly known as Android Market) and the Amazon Appstore for the Kindle Fire and other devices.

If you make an HTTP-based URI to *play.google.com*, the user will be asked if she wants to open the website or the store app, showing on that content. The best way to link to the details of a native published app is to use the *https://play.google.com/store/apps/ details?id=<package_name>* URL. The *<package_name>* should be replaced with the package name that you defined for your app when creating it. We can also use the *market://details?id=<package_name>* URI mechanism.

On Android 2.x, it was common to use the *market://* protocol to connect to the Android Market, now the Google Play Store. Today, we can use both the *http://play.google.com* and *market://* URIs. The second one will always open the store, while the first one should ask the user what to do.

We can also list all the apps that a publisher has online using *http://play.google.com/ store/search?q=pub:<publisher_name>*. For more options, visit the Android developer site (*http://bit.ly/ZQi7Zj*).

If we have an app published in the Amazon Appstore, we can use the following URI template: *http://www.amazon.com/gp/mas/dl/android?p=<package_name>*. The Appstore app will be opened if it's installed on the device.

## Bypassing the store

Android devices allow app installation from third-party servers if the user has the feature enabled from settings (the menu option varies per version). To deliver an Android application, we just need to serve the *.apk* (Android package) file as `application/ vnd.android.package-archive`.

# Windows Applications

For Windows Phone applications, we can make a link to *http://windowsphone.com/s?appId=<GUID>* that will redirect the user to the specific app in the store. The *<GUID>* is a placeholder for the ID of the application we want to link to.

The ID of your application is a long hexadecimal value; the easiest way to get the full link is to access your account in the Windows Phone Dev Center, go to your app's details, and find the link under the section "Deep Link."

 For other platforms, usually making an *http://* link to the app's details page will trigger the native store application to download that app.

For Windows 8 applications, we can use the *ms-windows-store:* protocol, following the syntax *ms-windows-store:PDP?PFN=<package_name>*. You can find the package name in your project's properties in Visual Studio or by visiting your app's web-based details page and looking at the source code. For example, the ESPN FC app for Windows 8 has a details website at the Windows Store (*http://bit.ly/ZKYU9a*). Digging into the source code, you will find a script with a `packageFamilyName` variable:

```
<script type="text/javascript">

        var autoLaunchStore = false;
        var biEnabled = true;
        var biServer = 'c.microsoft.com';
        var packageFamilyName = 'ESPNCricinfo.ESPNFC_y1atfjxm9t5ma';
        var more='Read more';
        var less='Read less';
        var isDarkText = false;
        var isRtl = false;
        var imageUrl='/webpdp/images/'
        var screenshot='Screen shot {0}';

</script>
```

Therefore, to link to this app, we just use:

```
<a href="windows-store:PDP?PFN=ESPNCricinfo.ESPNFC_y1atfjxm9t5ma">
    Download
</a>
```

While digging into the source code feels like hacking the system, it's one of the suggested mechanisms in the official Microsoft documentation.

For Windows 8 apps, remember that we can add some meta tags so IE10 will invite the user to install or open the native app that is connected to the current website. We covered this ability in Chapter 7.

# Java ME

Java ME was the preferred language for games and applications for years. Its usage is declining today, but it is still the platform behind millions of Series 40 devices, Symbian devices, and BlackBerry smartphones (before BB10). Even Facebook and Angry Birds have versions of their apps in Java ME today, for emerging markets.

A Java ME project is shipped as a *JAR* (Java ARchive) file, which is just a ZIP file containing the application (compiled classes and resources). It must be delivered using the MIME type `application/java-archive`. Many phones accept this file type directly, although the best (and 100% compatible) way of delivering Java ME games or apps is to first deliver a *JAD* (Java Application Descriptor) file. The JAD file is just a text file served with the MIME type `text/vnd.sun.j2me.app-descriptor` that contains metadata about the application, similar to OMA Download's download descriptor files (in fact, OMA Download took this approach from Java).

So, the device first downloads the JAD file and shows the information to the user (name of the application, size, format, etc.). If the user accepts, the JAR file is then downloaded and installed. The Java ME developer usually generates the JAD file, and we receive it in its final state. However, as it is a text file, we can generate it ourselves or change it using a server-side script.

### Serving JAD files

Let's analyze a part of the MIDP 1.0 version of the JAD file sent to the device when a user tries to download Opera Mini 3:

```
MIDlet-Version: 3.1
MIDlet-1: Opera Mini 3, /i.png, Browser
MIDlet-Data-Size: 10240
MIDlet-Description: Opera Mini
MIDlet-Icon: /i.png
MIDlet-Info-URL: http://mini.opera.com/
MIDlet-Install-Notify: http://mini.opera.com/n/13045Bviprdome_en
MIDlet-Jar-Size: 58800
MIDlet-Jar-URL: opera-mini-3.1.13045-basic-en.jar
MIDlet-Name: Opera Mini 3
MIDlet-Vendor: Opera Software ASA
Content-Folder: Applications
MicroEdition-Configuration: CLDC-1.0
MicroEdition-Profile: MIDP-1.0
```

The emphasized parts of the code are the ones that we need to care about when delivering Java ME applications.

 There are a lot of other standard and vendor-specific JAD attributes that can be defined, from virtual keyboard support on touch devices to digital signatures.

MIDlet-Jar-URL defines the relative or absolute URL of the JAR file. We can insert the JAR file directly here, or, if we want to secure and log the download, we can use a URL to a dynamic script using a URL parameter included in the JAD generation.

MIDlet-Install-Notify is the same as the installNotifyURI parameter in OMA Download. It is an optional parameter that defines a URL that will receive by POST the same codes as in OMA Download (from 900 to 906), as seen in Table 17-1.

 There is another optional JAD attribute, MIDlet-Delete-Notify, that defines a URL that will receive by POST a notification when the user deletes the application from the device. Using this attribute is not recommended; it is not reliable, and the user may not want to connect to the Web when deleting an application.

Starting with MIDP 2.0 (the version compatible with almost all Java ME devices on the market today), the standard added new codes that we can receive in the MIDlet-Install-Notify URL. The added status codes are shown in Table 17-2.

*Table 17-2. Additional MIDP 2 status codes*

| Code | Message | Description |
|------|---------|-------------|
| 907 | Invalid JAR | The JAR (executable package) is invalid and could not be installed. |
| 908 | Invalid Configuration or Profile | The device is not compatible with the versions of the libraries used in the package. |
| 909 | Application Authentication Failure | A security problem has occurred. |
| 910 | Application Authorization Failure | A security problem has occurred. |
| 911 | Push Registration Failure | A push notification registered in the JAD file is invalid. |
| 912 | Deletion Notification | The user has deleted the application from the device (used when MIDlet-Delete-Notify was defined). |
| 913 | Required Package Not Supported by the Device | A package or API marked as required by the application is not available on the device. |

### Java ME for BlackBerry

BlackBerry smartphones (not including those using the new BB10 platform) accept the same JAD and JAR files that we've been examining. However, the most compatible way to serve Java ME files on these devices is to use BlackBerry's own format for JAR files: *COD* files.

BlackBerry uses the same JAD files, with two new mandatory attributes: `RIM-COD-URL` and `RIM-COD-Size`. The COD file must be served as `application/vnd.rim.cod`, and it is generated using a free tool from BlackBerry that converts a JAR into a COD file (*https://developer.blackberry.com/java/*).

# CHAPTER 18

# Debugging and Performance

Debugging and performance optimization are the two scariest activities in the mobile web development world, after testing—but don't worry, there are lots of ways to tame them. We discussed tools and techniques for testing in Chapter 4. In this chapter we will focus on more advanced features for debugging and performance.

## Debugging

For years I've complained that web developers were second-class citizens (compared with native developers), in terms of the availability of tools and documentation. Fortunately, in the last year or so vendors have begun to realize that web developers need more tools for debugging and performance measurement, and the tools catalog available today is growing.

## Server-Side Debugging

To debug server-side detection, adaptation, or content delivery scripts, we can use some HTTP tools before turning to the real devices.

### User agent spoofing

User agent spoofing tools allow us to fool the server about the browser that is currently requesting the web page by changing how the client identifies itself to the server. For example, using a desktop browser, we can say it is a mobile browser and the server will fall into the trap. We can use these tools to debug mobile redirects and detection frameworks, as covered in Chapter 9, without the need of real devices or even emulators.

We can then browse to any website and see how the server manages the user agent and which content it serves. (Remember to go back to the default user agent after finishing the debug session, or you may encounter problems in your browser!)

User Agent Switcher (*http://www.mobilexweb.com/go/uaswichter*) is a free plug-in for Firefox (see Figure 18-1).

*Figure 18-1. With User Agent Switcher you can test websites using any mobile user agent and render them with Firefox for desktop.*

 User agent tools don't emulate all the headers of a mobile device, including the accepted MIME types, so you should not rely on this plug-in for testing this kind of detection. You can use other plug-ins to change HTTP headers.

When you've installed this plug-in, you will find a new submenu in the Tools menu of Firefox using the name of the current user agent (it starts with "Default User Agent"). The plug-in changes the user-agent string that Firefox uses for making HTTP requests to the server. It comes with some user agents preinstalled, such as iPhone 3.0, and you can add as many others as you want using the Edit User Agent option.

Keynote MITE (*http://mite.keynote.com*) (Mobile Interactive Testing Environment) is a simulator that can be useful for mobile browser user agent spoofing and HTTP header debugging.

Google Chrome for desktop includes the Chrome Developer Tools, a series of debugging tools for web developers. The latest versions of the desktop browser also include some tools for mobile web debugging, including a user agent cheating mechanism. To use them, go to View→Developer→Developer Tools, access the Settings (the small gear icon at the bottom-right corner), and browse to the Overrides section, as seen in Figure 18-2.

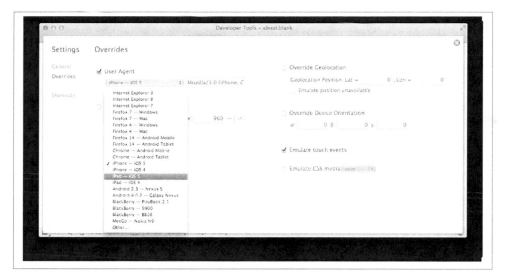

*Figure 18-2. Google Chrome for desktop includes tools for changing the current user agent and matching device metrics with the page's available viewport.*

Opera and Safari for desktop also offer native features to change the user agent without any plug-ins required, using developer tools.

### HTTP sniffing

When using real devices, it will be useful while debugging to store in some log all the request and response headers from the server-side code, so you can see the data the device is sending and receiving. DeviceAnywhere (*http://www.keynotedeviceany where.com*) includes a solution for this purpose for all devices, or you can use any emulator that supports HTTP sniffing, like the Nokia and BlackBerry emulators.

With other emulators and simulators, as well as with some real devices, we can use the typical desktop HTTP sniffing tools, such as Telerik Fiddler (*http://www.fiddler2.com*) or Charles Web Debugging Proxy (*http://www.charlesproxy.com*).

 Some mobile web browsers act differently when connected directly to the Internet than when connected through an HTTP proxy. Therefore, be careful when making conclusions based only on a mobile browser connected through a desktop HTTP proxy.

If you want Android browsers to browse the Web through a proxy (usually connected to a WiFi router and a proxy in the same LAN), you can define this behavior through the desired WiFi connection's "Modify network" contextual menu, activating Advanced Options and selecting Manual Proxy, as seen in Figure 18-3. On iOS devices you need go to Settings→Wi-Fi, edit the hotspot using the blue edit action button, and select Manual HTTP Proxy. On other operating systems, the process is similar.

 If you work with the ASP.NET platform on the server, you can activate the remote tracing mechanism and you will see every header and response from your mobile devices.

### Bandwidth simulators

With bandwidth simulators we can slow down our Internet connection and simulate a real 2G, 3G, or 4G connection to get a better idea of performance and how our website is reacting.

The Charles Web Debugging Proxy (*http://www.charlesproxy.com*) is an HTTP sniffing and proxy tool with a free version available that includes an HTTP throttling mechanism to simulate different bandwidths and latencies (as seen in Figure 18-4). It is available for Windows, Mac, and Linux.

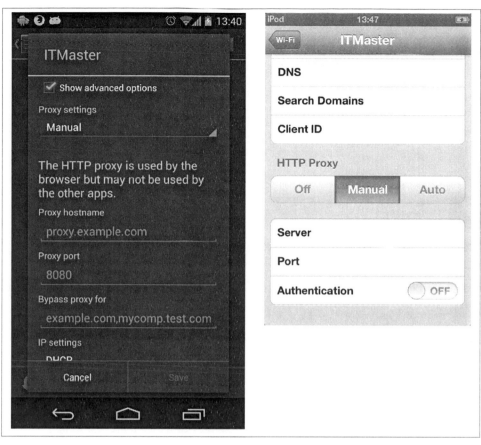

*Figure 18-3. On Android and iOS devices we can define an HTTP proxy for web browsers through the WiFi hotspot advanced settings.*

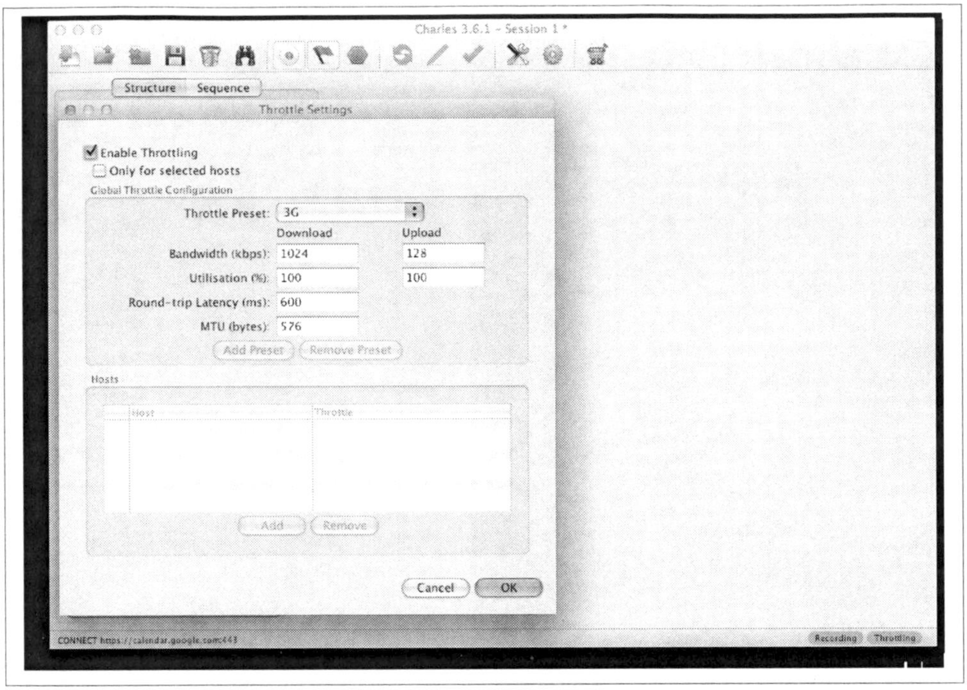

*Figure 18-4. The Charles Web Debugging Proxy allows us to simulate a real bandwidth through the Proxy Throttling feature.*

> On Mac OS, Xcode (from 4.1) includes a System Preferences pane called *Network Link Conditioner* that simulates predefined bandwidth, latency, and packet loss on the whole operating system.

Slowy App (*http://slowyapp.com*) is a Mac-only app that will simulate a real-world connection. It includes several presets, including bandwidth, packet loss rate, and packet latency. Slowy is not a proxy, so when using Mac-based simulators and emulators we don't need to configure any proxy. NetLimiter (*http://www.netlimiter.com*) is a Windows-only app for the same purpose. It includes a free limited version.

Fiddler Connection Simulator (*http://mobilexweb.com/go/fiddlersimulator*) is a Fiddler proxy plug-in adding the ability to simulate different network connections on Windows computers.

## Markup Debugging

There is no automatic way to debug HTML. This is a manual operation on every emulator, device, or remote device you can access. Some browsers include a remote debugger that we can check for markup errors (we'll cover them in a minute), but before doing this it is a good practice to validate the code using one of the online tools available for mobile markup.

### HTML5 validators

If you want to validate your HTML5 code, you can find some beta tools such as W3C's Nu Markup Validation Service (*http://validator.w3.org/nu*) and the Markup Validation Service (*http://validator.w3.org/nu*). However, remember that HTML5 is not finished yet, and there are some extensions outside of the specific standards—therefore, these tools will be useful primarily for getting a big picture of errors and warnings. You should check these one by one to see if they're actually errors or nonstandard features you want to use.

### W3C mobileOK Checker

The W3C offers a mobile markup checker (*http://validator.w3.org/mobile*) that you can use for free. You can upload a file, copy and paste the code, or use a URL if you already have your mobile site on your server.

This markup checker is based on best practices published in the Mobile Web Best Practices standard (*http://www.w3.org/TR/mobile-bp*). It doesn't guarantee that your code will work perfectly on all mobile devices if it passes; it is just intended to help you find possible problems in your code and areas that don't conform to best practices. This tool is intended for XHTML, XHTML MP, and XHTML Basic websites, rather than modern HTML5 websites; however, it will still give us some hints about good practices to follow and potential errors we should investigate.

### ready.mobi

The dotMobi team has created a free validator that includes the W3C mobileOK Checker tests and some others, plus some emulators and detailed error reports with suggestions. The validator is available at mobiReady (*http://www.ready.mobi*). You can use it for a single document by providing a URL or copying and pasting the code, or to report on an entire site, including site-wide testing (registration is required for this last function).

After analyzing your document, ready.mobi will assign you a score on a scale of 1 (very bad) to 5 (excellent). It will also report on the size of your document and resources and the estimated time and download costs for the user.

This report is only suitable today for feature or social phone websites, not for HTML5 web apps.

# Client-Side Debugging

Client-side debugging is one of the most painful activities in mobile web development. Every browser has a different rendering and JavaScript engine, and sometimes code that works on one device doesn't work on another.

Typical desktop JavaScript techniques should be used first to debug logic problems in our code. This includes using the developer tools included with Chrome, Safari, or Internet Explorer, or the classic Firebug (*http://getfirebug.com*) for Firefox. But just because everything works in a desktop browser doesn't mean that it will work in a mobile browser.

The debugging solutions in this area include different kinds of tools:

*Remote debuggers*
> These open a debug session on the device that we can access remotely from a desktop computer, through WiFi or a USB cable. These tools can also be divided into official browser debuggers and injected debuggers, with the latter being a JavaScript file we need to inject in our HTML to provide the debugging session.

*On-device debuggers*
> Here the debug session is seen on the device itself, in a separate window or pop-up.

*Console output viewers*
> These are used only to see console output messages and errors from the browser.

 One problem we will have is that if a JavaScript error is encountered, many devices don't show any notice and the code simply ends its execution.

## iOS Remote Web Inspector

To debug web apps for iOS devices we can use the Remote Web Inspector, available since iOS version 6. The remote session can be connected from Safari 6 for Mac to the iOS simulator or a USB-connected iOS device.

We can open a web remote inspection session to:

- A Safari window/tab on our iOS device or simulator
- A chromeless web app installed on our iOS device or simulator
- A native app using a web view, such as an Apache Cordova/PhoneGap app (this feature is available only for our own native apps; we can't debug an app that was installed from the App Store)

Unfortunately, at the time of this writing there is no way to open the iOS web debugger from a Windows or Linux desktop computer. We must rely on other nonnative solutions if we need to debug from a non-Mac desktop computer.

**Connecting the session.** To use the Web Inspector on iOS 6.0 or newer, we must first enable it from the iOS device or simulator itself, by going to Settings→Safari→Advanced and turning on the Web Inspector feature, as seen on the left in Figure 18-5. The next step is to enable the developer tools in Safari for Mac, via Preferences→Advanced→ "Show Develop menu in menu bar." When we've done all this and the session we want to debug is open on the device or simulator, we can access the Develop menu in Safari for Mac; there we'll see the name of our device as a submenu with all the available web sessions to connect to on it, as seen on the right in Figure 18-5.

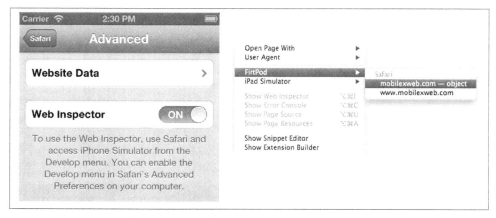

*Figure 18-5. To use the Remote Web Inspector on iOS, we need to first enable it from the device or simulator (left), and then use it from Safari for Mac (right).*

**Working with the session.** When we're connected, Safari for Mac will open a window with our debug session user interface (as we can see in Figure 18-6). In the debug session we will be able to:

- Inspect the HTML, CSS, and JavaScript
- Make changes and see them live, without a refresh
- Touch to inspect (the little hand icon at the top bar)—i.e., we can touch an element on the device to select it on the remote DOM
- Browse storages, such as cookies, local storage, SQL databases, and more

- Record and measure timelines, including network requests, layout and rendering, and JavaScript execution and events
- See warnings and errors
- See web workers (threads)
- See and manage JavaScript breakpoints, including watch expressions
- See the console and execute JavaScript directly on it

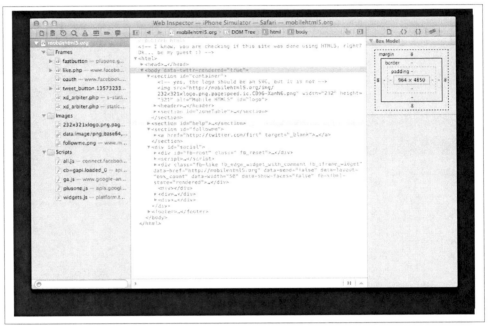

*Figure 18-6. The Remote Web Inspector includes a debug UI similar to Xcode, the IDE for native iOS and Mac applications.*

### Older iOS debugging tools

Previous to iOS 6 (up to mid-2012), the only official debugging solution was a Console view that could be enabled from Safari settings, allowing the developer to see the console and error messages on iOS 3, 4, and 5 devices. This feature was on-device and it was deprecated in iOS 6, as the full Web Inspector replaced it.

In iOS 5, a private API was discovered that opened a Web Inspector session in the iOS simulator only. Using this trick, I created a free tool called iWebInspector (*http:// iwebinspector.com*) that allows developers to open a Web Inspector session and use it easily. This tool is still available if you need to debug iOS 5 web applications, but you should use the official remote inspector for newer devices.

### Chrome for Android debugger

Google Chrome for Android supports remote debugging through a USB connection and the Developer Tools available in Chrome for desktop. To use the debugger, you need to have the Android SDK installed on your computer (see Chapter 4 for details). Then, follow these steps:

1. Enable USB debugging on your Android device (under Settings→Developer options).

2. Connect your mobile device to your desktop using USB. If your host is a Windows-based computer, you will need debug USB drivers from the manufacturer.

3. Open Chrome on your Android device and go to Settings→Advanced→Developer tools. Check the "Enable USB Web debugging" option.

4. Open a terminal or command-line session on your host and execute the following command line from the SDK path's *platform-tools/* subfolder:

   ```
   adb forward tcp:9222 localabstract:chrome_devtools_remote
   ```

5. Open Chrome on your desktop computer and browse to *http://localhost:9222*.

6. Select the mobile tab you want to debug.

When connected you can use the Chrome Developer Tools as usual, to do all of the following:

- Inspect elements
- Access the resources list, including local storage, SQL, and IDB databases
- Access network information
- Add JavaScript breakpoints and debugging tools
- See useful timelines, such as rendering information
- Profile JavaScript code
- See the console and execute JavaScript code on it

Check out more information and tips about the Chrome Developer Tools (*https://devel opers.google.com/chrome-developer-tools*).

### Firefox remote debugging

In Firefox 15 and later, the desktop browser has the ability to connect to a mobile version of the same browser. To use this feature, you need to have Firefox installed on both your desktop and a mobile device. Then, follow these instructions:

1. Open *about:config* in Firefox for desktop and define `devtools.debugger.remote-enabled` as `true`.

2.  Open *about:config* in Firefox for mobile and define `devtools.debugger.force-local` as `false` and `devtools.debugger.remote-enabled` as `true`.

3.  Restart Firefox on the desktop and the mobile device.

4.  Connect your mobile device (using WiFi) to the same network as your desktop computer.

5.  Find your current mobile device's IP address (go to Settings→WiFi and tap on your current WiFi session).

6.  Browse to the desired page on your mobile.

7.  In Firefox for desktop, open the Remote Debugger from the Web Developer menu.

8.  Replace *localhost* in the new window with your mobile IP address.

### BlackBerry remote Web Inspector

The BlackBerry browser for smartphones (7.x), PlayBook, and the newest BB10 platform supports a remote Web Inspector through WiFi. You can enable it through the browser's settings, where you will receive the URL to use on your desktop to open the Web Inspector session.

> When enabling remote sessions using WiFi, as with the BlackBerry browser or Firefox, there is a security risk, as everyone on your own LAN can access the content, cookies, and storages on your mobile browser.

### Opera Dragonfly

From Opera Mobile 9.5, we can debug mobile web applications using the remote debugging tool Dragonfly. To use this tool you will need Opera 9.5 or later (with Presto engine) on your desktop. You can open Dragonfly by going to Tools→Advanced→Developer Tools and checking the Remote Debug option.

When you're done, enter *opera:debug* in the address bar of your Opera Mobile browser and specify your desktop IP address (public or private, if you are connected using WiFi to the same LAN). You will then have access to the same debugging features (DOM, CSS, and JavaScript) that you would if you were debugging a local desktop file.

Complete instructions and tips can be found at *www.mobilexweb.com/go/dragonfly*.

### Android Debug Bridge

While the Android browser doesn't have a remote debugger (at least, as of Android 4.2), we can still read the console errors and even use the same `console` object using the

Android Debug Bridge (*adb*). *adb* is a command-line application available in the *tools* folder of your SDK.

You can find more information on how to use this console at *mobilexweb.com/go/adb*.

## Weinre

Weinre (*http://people.apache.org/~pmuellr/weinre/*) (read it as "winery") is an open source tool now part of Apache Cordova that implements a Remote Web Inspector based on WebKit developer tools. Weinre was created before any platform officially supported a remote inspector, and it is implemented as a server (now a Node.js app; previously a Java servlet) and a debug client (JavaScript code that we need to inject into our HTML).

Because the whole inspection is done directly with the JavaScript code we inject, the inspection session is limited compared to native ones: we can't use breakpoints and there are no profiling abilities.

 As there is no official remote debugger or inspector for the Android browser at the time of this writing, Weinre is the best solution available.

To install it, you can follow the instructions on the website, or you can install Adobe Edge Inspect (covered in Chapter 4), which includes a Weinre server. PhoneGap also provides a free-to-use Weinre server (*http://debug.phonegap.com*). To use it, you need to define a unique ID of your own and inject the following script into your HTML page:

```
<script
src="http://debug.phonegap.com/target/target-script-min.js#<id>">
</script>
```

When you're done, accessing *http://debug.phonegap.com/client/#<id>* from a desktop will open the remote session. (Remember to replace *<id>* with your own unique ID.) The advantages of using this version are that we can debug devices without any other inspection tool, and we can use it through 3G. The main disadvantage is performance, as all the debugging information needs to go through the PhoneGap server on the Web. Installing your own server will improve the performance of the debugging session.

## JSConsole

JSConsole is a free online command-line tool created by Remy Sharp (*http://remy sharp.com*) that can be used directly on the device, by accessing jsconsole.com from the mobile browser, or remotely, for usability purposes. To create a remote session, you need to first open JSConsole (*http://jsconsole.com*) in your desktop browser and then type :listen in the console. You will get a long unique ID that you can use to inject the following script into the HTML page you will load in the mobile browser:

```
<script src="http://jsconsole.com/remote.js?<ID>"></script>
```

Remember to replace *<ID>* with the ID received in your desktop console. When you are connected, you can execute commands from your desktop on the mobile device.

 When injecting debugging session scripts, such as in Weinre or JSConsole, remember to remove those references when you go to the production environment.

### Bookmarklet solutions

Bookmarklets give us access to tools and techniques for testing and debugging that are not typically available on mobile devices. We can use them to access resource lists, inspect source code, and much more. We covered the basics of bookmarklets in Chapter 12. One of the most useful bookmarklet toolkits is Mobile Perf (*http://bit.ly/YI40UG*) by Steve Souders (see Figure 18-7); it gives us easy access to a wide range of tools for debugging and measuring and working with performance.

### Other web-based solutions

There are some scripts that work as a kind of debugger, including DOM and CSS inspectors, and some that work for JavaScript debugging, too. The mobile compatibility for these tools is complicated, though, because of the lack of space on the screen to show all the information. There are also some Ajax-based solutions that will work better, allowing us to view the debug results and panes from a desktop.

 Using alert windows for logging and debugging is annoying and a bit intrusive. Try to use another solution.

The JavaScript Debug Toolkit (JSDT) (*http://code.google.com/p/jsdt*) is an Ajax-based JavaScript debugging tool that works with mobile devices as a standalone desktop application or an Eclipse plug-in.

*Figure 18-7. A bookmarklet (Mobile Perf in this example) injects JavaScript code over any page in a mobile browser, giving us access to functionality including debugging tools.*

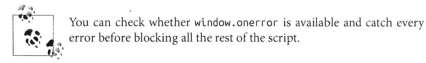

You can check whether `window.onerror` is available and catch every error before blocking all the rest of the script.

Another option is Firebug Lite (*http://getfirebug.com/lite.html*), a plug-in that makes some Firebug tools available in non-Firefox browsers if you add a JavaScript file and a CSS file to your website. It works in many mobile browsers and web app engines, but the navigation is very complicated when the Firebug Lite view is open.

# Performance Optimization

*Most mobile users expect to make sacrifices in terms of content depth and feature-richness in exchange for the convenience of anytime, anyplace mobile Web access. One thing mobile users won't sacrifice, however, is speed.*

—"What Users Want from Mobile"—Equation Research survey, 2011

Performance is the key to mobile web success. People want high-performance websites. We hate to wait on our desktops, and the situation is far worse on mobile devices, with their constrained resources. I could write a whole book about mobile web performance, but for now I will just try to distill some best practices and share some hacks that you can easily apply to enhance your website's performance.

Performance has recently become a hot topic in the desktop web world. In general, mobile web developers should follow the same practices, but there are some new ones to keep in mind as well, and some desktop web best practices that will not work on these devices.

 Web performance optimization is a big topic, and we don't have enough space in this book to cover it completely. If you're just getting started with performance optimization, the first thing you should do is read two excellent books by Steve Souders (*http://stevesouders.com*), *High Performance Websites* and *Even Faster Websites*, both from O'Reilly. You should also follow the Yahoo! and Google performance team blogs at *developer.yahoo.com/performance* and *developers.google.com/speed*.

Mobile browsers aren't the same as desktop web browsers, and not all mobile browsers are created equal. Specifically, the quantity of resources that can be downloaded in parallel and the cache functionality differ. Nevertheless, it is better to approach mobile performance optimization from here than from the ground.

If you want to know more about high-performance mobile websites and mobile browser behavior, check out *mobilexweb.com/go/performance*.

## Measurement

The first thing we need to do is to measure. If we cannot measure, we cannot optimize. However, measuring mobile websites is not easy. Typical desktop measurement and profiling tools don't work for mobile devices, and HTTP sniffers are difficult to implement for mobile browsers on 3G networks.

Steve Souders has created a website listing tool (*http://stevesouders.com/mobileperf/*) that will help us in the process.

### Remote profilers

All the official remote inspectors or debuggers already covered in this chapter, such as the iOS Remote Web Inspector and the Chrome Developer Tools, include precise tools to measure network and rendering performance and profile our JavaScript code in compatible versions of the browsers.

### HTTP proxies

If you are using an emulator or a real device with WiFi capabilities, you can use any HTTP sniffer proxy, configuring the emulator and your device with your desktop IP address and port as the proxy for navigation. There are dozens of tools for doing this, a few of which were mentioned earlier in this chapter. However, bear in mind that browsers may act differently when browsing through a web proxy.

If you have a dedicated server (or even your own development computer with full inbound access to port 80), you can install one of these proxies and a web server and browse your website from any phone on any network to analyze how is it rendering and requesting resources.

PCapPerf (*http://pcapperf.appspot.com*) is a set of open source tools that allow us to capture and analyze traffic generated from a mobile browser through an ad hoc WiFi hotspot created by our desktop computer. When the traffic is captured on the desktop, we can convert the output to the industry HAR standard and display it as a waterfall chart. You can find instructions at the Capture Mobile Traffics wiki (*http://bit.ly/ XUdU7K*).

### Akamai Mobitest

Akamai Mobitest (*http://mobitest.akamai.com*) is a quick and easy way to get waterfall performance charts from mobile browsers, including on iOS and Android devices. On some devices the test is done though a web view and not the browser, though, so the real performance may differ.

You can start a test by just adding a URL, selecting the device, and choosing the optional feature of recording a video, where you can see how your site is being rendered on a timeline (as seen in Figure 18-8).

*Figure 18-8. Akamai Mobitest is a free online service where we can get a waterfall chart of our website being rendered on a mobile browser.*

## Performance APIs

The W3C's Web Performance Group (*http://www.w3.org/2010/webperf/*) is working on different APIs for accurate performance measurement on the browser. The Navigation Timing API (*http://www.w3.org/TR/navigation-timing/*) is already available in some mobile browsers at the time of this writing, including the Android browser from 4.0, Google Chrome, the BlackBerry browser for BB10, Firefox, and Internet Explorer.

The Navigation Timing API allows us to measure times in an accurate way without affecting the measurement. It exposes a series of timestamps for performance hits, such as navigation start, request fetch start, request end, DOM loading, etc.

Therefore, to calculate how much time has passed from the navigation start point, we can use:

```
var now = new Date().getTime();
var page_load_time = now - performance.timing.navigationStart;
alert("User-perceived page loading time: " + page_load_time);
```

# Best Practices

Here are some global best practices you should always have in mind:

- Keep it simple.
- Reduce the HTTP requests to the minimum possible.
- Implement Ajax requests if you can, and if the device supports them.
- Make the cache your friend.

 HTTP request headers are generally larger in mobile websites because of the large `User-Agent`, `Accept`, and other headers. Remember that these headers are sent with each and every request your page makes. That is why it is important to keep the number of requests to the minimum.

## Reducing requests

There are plenty of tips for reducing network requests:

- Use only one CSS and JavaScript external link per page.
- If the script and/or CSS file is only for one document, don't use external code; instead, embed it in the page.
- Use inline images whenever you can.
- Use CSS sprites.
- Reduce the use of images for effects, titles, and text. Try to meet all of these needs using only CSS.
- Use multipart documents when compatible.
- Download only the initially required code and resources and then, after the `on load` event, download all the rest on Ajax devices (lazy loading).

 Every mobile browser supports a cache for resources, and you should definitely use it, with a long-lived expiry for each static resource. Analyze how the cache works (this is outside the scope of this book) and make it your friend, not your enemy!

## Compressing

Compression is a necessity, and there are different techniques you can use for it:

- Minimize your HTML files, removing spaces, comments, and nonuseful tags.
- Minimize your CSS files, removing spaces and comments.
- Minimize your JavaScript files, removing spaces and comments and obfuscating the code.
- Use HTTP 1.1 compression for delivering static and dynamic text-based files (HTML, JavaScript, CSS, XML, JSON).
- Use a cookie-free domain (or alias domain) for static content files.

There are plenty of online and offline tools for minimizing files, such as JSMin (*http://crockford.com/javascript/jsmin*) and YUI! Compressor (*http://developer.yahoo.com/yui/compressor*).

---

### Going Beyond JavaScript Compression

There are plenty of good JavaScript obfuscators and minimizing tools out there, but Google has taken an extra step and created the *Closure Compiler*, a new concept in JavaScript programming. It is not just a minimizing and obfuscating tool, but it is also a compiler: it compiles JavaScript code into better JavaScript code and is very helpful for mobile websites.

You can download the compiler at *code.google.com/closure/compiler* or use the web application compiler at *closure-compiler.appspot.com*.

The code will be rewritten to be lighter and quicker to execute. The resulting code will not be suitable for human reading because it will not use good programming practices, but that is not the goal. We are not going to edit the resulting code; we will always work with the original code (with comments and all the best practices) and recompile it before sending it to the server.

---

### HTTP compression

HTTP 1.1 added compression (using GZIP and *deflate*) as an optional possibility when delivering a file to the client. Using this option is strongly recommended for text-based files on most mobile devices, because it will reduce the traffic between the server and the client by up to 80%. It will add some overhead on the client (to uncompress the content), but it's well worth it. Network traffic will be one of our worst problems if the user is not connected to a WiFi network. Even with 3G connections, the network can have latency problems.

---

If you work with ASP.NET Web Forms, you should be careful about the usage of the ViewState, which generates big hidden input tags in the HTML. Deactivate the ViewState on controls where you won't use it.

You will find plenty of resources on the Web about how to configure HTTP compression for Apache, Internet Information Server, and other products. The most important thing you need to remember is to also compress dynamic scripts delivering markup, like PHP scripts, which by default do not use HTTP compression in Apache.

 As covered in Chapter 9, some mobile browsers already support the SPDY protocol, which improves performance. Implement it when you have users browsing your website on compatible devices.

## Other tips

Here are some other tips to keep in mind:

- Compress images and choose the best format and color palette. You can use the free online tool Smush.it (*http://www.smushit.com*) from Yahoo!.
- Deliver small images for small screens. You can use a dynamic resizing tool, or the free online services covered in Chapter 10.
- Reduce the initial load time as much as possible. You want the web application to be ready as soon as possible.
- Minimize DOM access and simplify your document structure.
- Use HTML5 storage for caching data and resources in base64. You can place a cookie on the client, so the next time the user accesses the website it will know that resources are already stored on the client and don't need to be injected at that time.
- Flush the buffer early, using `flush()` in PHP or `Response.Flush()` in ASP.NET, after `</header>` and after big blocks of visual components.
- Avoid redirects between pages, especially in the home page.
- Use touch events to improve responsiveness, as covered in Chapter 15.
- In very large documents and web apps, using iframes to split the DOM into smaller parts may improve performance.
- Create DOM object pools for reusage instead of creating lots of new elements that will remain in memory when they are off the screen or not useful anymore.
- Create a quick and simple home page.
- Put `script` tags at the bottom to avoid resource download delays and/or use the new HTML5 script attributes covered in Chapter 12, such as `defer`.

- Use a content delivery network or a static server for static content if you have a lot of images or other static content.

- Remove any nonuseful headers from the server responses (like server identification or "powered by").

- Some CSS3 features (mostly on large elements) can impact performance, such as shadows and gradients. Use measurement tools to find problem areas in your project.

---

## Deferred JavaScript Evaluation

The Gmail team, in conjunction with Charles Jolley (*http://blog.sproutcore.com*), has created a very clever and simple way of reducing the initial payload of JavaScript execution. The solution is to deliver the JavaScript code inside a comment block (/* */). This means the JavaScript isn't executing while the page is loading, and it doesn't freeze the UI or block other resources.

When you need to execute that library or code, you just get the script by ID, get its content, remove the comment characters, and just eval() the code. Pretty smart, isn't it? On an iPhone running iOS 2.2, 200 KB of JavaScript code adds 2.6 seconds to the initial page load time, while if it is commented it adds just 240 ms. After all the initial loading is done (or later, whenever you need it), you can parse the code.

---

### JavaScript performance

Again, keep your code simple. Here are some other specific tips for mobile JavaScript coding:

- Don't use `try/catch` expressions for expensive code.
- Avoid using `eval()`, even in situations where you might not think about it being used, like when using a string in `setTimeout()` instead of a function.
- Avoid using `with`.
- Minimize the usage of global variables.
- Avoid the usage of JavaScript frameworks that are not used totally.
- Minimize the number of changes in the DOM, and make the changes in the same operation. Many browsers repaint the whole screen on each change.
- Implement a timeout for Ajax calls.
- Compress (and if you want, compile with Closure Compiler) your code.
- Use CSS transitions/animations instead of JavaScript-based animations.

- In compatible browsers, use the Animation Timing API (also known as `requestA nimationFrame`) instead of `setInterval()`.

 For a while there was a performance tip advocating the use of CSS 3D transforms (for example, `translateZ` or `translate3d`) instead of 2D transforms, as only the former were hardware-accelerated. On modern browsers (from 2012) that is no longer the case, and it can even harm performance on the video card. Modern browsers are smart enough to hardware-accelerate what they can to improve performance.

An excellent book about JavaScript performance tips is Nicholas Zakas's *High Performance JavaScript*, also from O'Reilly.

# CHAPTER 19

# Distribution and Social Web 2.0

So, you've finished your mobile web application and you are ready to go to market (or so you think). However, your work isn't over yet. In this chapter, we are going to analyze some search engine optimization tips, and talk about how to get users to actually visit our mobile websites and encourage them to come back again and again.

We will also explore how to monetize mobile websites using advertising and how to merge our applications with some social features, such as SMS, RSS, and social networks.

## Mobile SEO

Search engine optimization (SEO) refers to a set of best practices that you can follow to help your website be in the best possible place in a search engine's results.

In general, typical desktop SEO techniques apply to mobile websites, too, but some extra care must be taken. As we've already discussed, generating too much code (metadata) and too much text for keyword crawling is not the best solution for the mobile web.

The first thing we need to understand is that mobile search users are not the same as desktop search users. Mobile users are typically searching for something very specific, and we should do our best to facilitate access to those resources.

Mobile search engines (Google, Yahoo!, Bing) localize the search results, so if your service is location-based, you should make sure that your location is properly defined in your text and code. In mobile search engines, the user only types a few characters and the engine tries to suggest the best possible results based on location and previous results, with mobile-specific content given priority.

If your mobile website gets content using Ajax, you should implement Google's proposal for making the content being indexed crawlable. You can find more information about this at *code.google.com/web/ajax-crawling*.

Search engines like Google will try to serve mobile-specific content first, but if someone is looking for the exact name of your application and Google doesn't know that you have a mobile website, the user will be redirected to your desktop site or to a transcoded mobile version of it produced by a Google server.

If you appear in the search engine's databases, you will also be found using the native applications that many search engines are developing, including voice-powered search applications.

## Spiders and Discoverability

The first problem is how to make your mobile website known to the search engines. This can be different depending upon whether you already have a desktop website that has been crawled or not.

If you already have a desktop website, you can give search engines the URL of your mobile site using the alternate link method:

```
<link rel="alternate" media="handheld" href="http://m.yoursite.com" />
```

You can also add your mobile site manually, using these links:

- Bing (*http://bing.com/webmaster*)
- Google (*http://google.com/addurl*)

## Mobile Sitemaps

Google has created an extension to the Sitemap protocol (*http://sitemaps.org*) for mobile web content discoverability, called Mobile Sitemaps. After creating an account in Google Webmaster Central (*http://www.google.com/webmasters*), you can add your mobile site to Google's database. You will need to verify that you are the owner of the site, by inserting a temporal meta tag or HTML file in your site.

Googlebot-Mobile uses the Accept HTTP header to determine whether a site delivers mobile content types. If you want to be sure that the bot can access your site, you can also check that the User-Agent header contains Googlebot-Mobile. Some sites will only allow access to mobile devices, and while Googlebot-Mobile tries to emulate such a device it is not always successful in gaining access unless it is specifically allowed.

Once your site has been validated, you can submit a Sitemap for it. If your mobile site is targeted to only one country using a noncountry top-level domain (like *.com* or *.mobi*), you can also define the geographic target for which your mobile site is prepared.

 Check the Sitemaps documentation (*http://sitemaps.org*) for full tag and option support.

A Mobile Sitemap is an XML file, based on the Sitemap standard, that lists the mobile URLs for your site (XHTML, XHTML MP, WML, cHTML). You can provide URLs for both mobile and nonmobile versions depending on the headers, but you should not list non-mobile-only URLs. A sample Sitemap file looks like this:

```
<?xml version="1.0" encoding="UTF-8" ?>
<urlset xmlns="http://www.sitemaps.org/schemas/sitemap/0.9"
    xmlns:mobile="http://www.google.com/schemas/sitemap-mobile/1.0">
    <url>
        <loc>http://m.yourdomain.com/</loc>
        <mobile:mobile/>
    </url>
</urlset>
```

You should provide one `url` element for each mobile URL and page, including the `mobile:mobile` empty tag. If you have many versions using different URLs (for iPhone, WML, etc.), you should provide them all in the same file.

 To check whether your website is listed in Google Mobile, visit *m.google.com* with a mobile device and use the search operator `site:your_domain`.

The Google Webmaster Team also suggests detecting Googlebot-Mobile in your desktop site and redirecting it to the mobile-specific version of the same page. For example, for information about a product X in your desktop site, you should redirect the bot to the mobile URL displaying information about that product. Otherwise, Google will use a transcoder on the desktop page.

# How Users Find You

Search engines are not the only way for users to discover your mobile website. Obviously, offline marketing is always welcome, but there are also other online features we should implement to facilitate discoverability. These include advertising the new mobile website to your current desktop visitors and implementing newsletters and feed readers.

The first problem to tackle is simplifying the user's first access to the mobile website. Many mobile users still don't know how to go to a URL if it is not on the carrier's home page, and many others will not want to type a long URL on a numeric keypad device.

## SMS Invitation

A good solution is to include in your desktop website a form to collect the user's phone number and then send him a WAP Push or an SMS link. A WAP Push is a special message with a URL inside. This is generally a premium SMS, and some carriers don't allow sending them from a website.

An SMS link is just a normal SMS with a link inside. Almost every modern device with a browser will autodetect a URL inside a text message if it begins with *www* or *http://* and will convert the URL into a link that the user can click after receiving the SMS.

The big question is, how do we send an SMS from a website? The answer is not what you might expect—there isn't a simple or free way to do it. We have to use an SMS provider or gateway that, with a simple web service call, will send the message to users in one country or worldwide. We will have to pay for that SMS, but depending on the business, a new mobile web user will probably be worth the small expense.

 Some SMS gateway providers also allow inbound SMS messages that will be routed to your scripts or will be accessible via an API. This could be an excellent solution to receive queries by SMS to your service.

Some SMS gateway providers include:

- Mogreet (*http://developer.mogreet.com*)
- Lleida (*http://www.lleida.net*)
- Clickatell SMS Gateway (*http://www.clickatell.com*)
- BulkSMS (*http://www.bulksms.com*)
- ClockWork (*http://www.clockworksms.com*)

- Twilio SMS (*http://www.twilio.com/sms*)
- SendHub (*http://www.sendhub.com/developer*)

Alternatively, you can install a 3G or GPRS modem on your server or in any machine and develop a little SMS gateway of your own, with a corporate or personal account. A widget or an application on your device could also work, although this is not the preferred way.

 Most carriers support SMS sending and receiving through an API, but you'll have to sign up with and pay each carrier separately.

You can also use carrier developer networks and the up-and-coming OneAPI to send messages to known networks.

## Email Invitation

If the user accesses her email mailbox from her mobile device, an alternative to SMS is to send the user a free email message containing the mobile URL.

## Mobile Tiny URL

To enable the user to type your URL easily, you can use the free service Mobile Tiny URL (*http://www.mobiletinyurl.com*). It converts any URL into a short form that can be typed with only 13 keypresses on a numeric or QWERTY keypad. By default the generated short URL doesn't work in desktop browsers, but you can add desktop support. These short URLs are useful for publication on desktop websites and in printed advertising.

For example, instead of typing *m.safaribooksonline.com*, a mobile user can type *ad.ag/admtgp* (saving 57 keypresses). As you can see, the generated URL uses only the first letters associated with every key on a numeric keypad, to speed up entry. Even apparently simple URLs like *google.com* will require 37 keypresses on a mobile phone's numeric keypad, and you can save 24 by using the compressed URL (*ad.ag/tgtmjg*). For smartphones and tablets with full QWERTY keyboards, if you have a short domain you can just advertise it; Mobile Tiny URLs are more useful on feature and social phones.

## QR Codes

A QR code is a two-dimensional barcode (also called a *matrix code*) that allows the storage of several bytes in a graphic. These codes have many uses, one of which is to provide a URL that can be read by devices with bar code readers. Many Nokia and

Android devices come with these readers preinstalled, but on other devices, users will need to download one. A sample QR code is shown in Figure 19-1.

*Figure 19-1. Google Maps created the Google Places campaign, sending businesses (like restaurants) stickers like this one that users can scan with their mobile devices to access information, reviews, etc.*

 A QR code can contain 4,296 alphanumeric characters, or 2,953 bytes for binary data. Some devices also support other data inside, like contact information (for example, a vCard file).

QR codes are well known in mobile advertising; many campaigns use these codes in newspapers, on street signs, and even on t-shirts.

To create a QR code, you can use any of these free services:

- Kaywa (*http://qrcode.kaywa.com*)
- Create QR Code (*http://createqrcode.appspot.com*)
- Mobile Tiny URL (*http://www.mobiletinyurl.com*)

If you need to generate a QR code dynamically, there are libraries for almost all server-side platforms that will generate the right image for you.

Google's URL Shortener (*http://goo.gl*) allows us to create a QR code by adding a *.qr* suffix to the short URL; for example, *http://goo.gl/C9pYI.qr*.

## NFC Tags

Modern smartphones and tablets include the Near Field Communication (NFC) technology, allowing the device to "touch" a tag and read some information from it. A tag can be embedded in a product, a sign, a box, or anywhere.

An NFC tag can store a URL, whose length depends on the tag type: a standard Ultralight NFC tag can store up to 41 characters, while other tags can store up to 132 characters.

To create an NFC tag, you can either buy them online from some providers (you provide the URL and the tag type you want and they will create them and send them by postal mail), or you can buy blank tags and write them yourself using an Android device. If you want to learn more about how to create your own tags, check out the article (*http://bit.ly/16uYVTZ*).

Tagstand Writer (*http://writer.tagstand.com*) is an Android app that will let you write URLs on blank NFC tags that you need to buy. The website provides a list of sites where you can buy tags.

## User Fidelizing

Once yyou've gotten a user to your mobile website, how do you encourage him to come back and maintain an interest in your service? If you are not providing a must-use service (such as online banking or email), you may want to implement some of the following techniques to "fidelize" your users:

- Encourage the user to add your site to her bookmarks, or to the Home screen on selected platforms.
- Offer the user an app with richer features.
- Offer the user a shortcut to download for the applications menu or Home screen.
- Offer the user a home widget on supported devices, with automatic updates.
- Create a mobile RSS news feed.
- Provide an SMS alert subscription.

## Web Shortcuts

A *web shortcut* is a native application or web app that has an icon in the applications menu that launches the browser when it is activated. Adding a shortcut is better than adding a bookmark, because it will be installed just like any other application.

## RSS

Some browsers (Opera, Bolt, NetFront, Symbian) detect feed meta tags and offer the user the option to subscribe to the feeds to get updates on the sites that provide them. To offer this service, you should provide an RSS file with a mobile web link inside:

```
<link rel="alternate" type="application/rss+xml" title="Mobile RSS"
    href="http://mobilexweb.com/rss.xml" />
```

If you have an RSS file for your mobile content, there are plenty of online resources that will create a full native app for different platforms based on your RSS content.

 Nokia offers the free Xpress Web App Builder (*http://xpresswe bapps.nokia.com*) for Series 40 that will take your website's content, including RSS, and create a fully capable web app.

## Open Search

If your website provides a search engine, you should supply an Open Search description document that will allow users of compatible devices to add your engine to the list of possible search engines. Not too many mobile browsers support this format at the time of this writing, but a mobile extension is in draft (see Open Search (*http://open search.org*)).

To define an Open Search declaration for discoverability, use the following link tag:

```
<link rel="search" type="application/opensearchdescription+xml"
    href="http://mobilexweb.com/opensearch.xml" />
```

The Open Search descriptor file will look like this:

```
<?xml version="1.0" encoding="UTF-8"?>
<OpenSearchDescription xmlns="http://a9.com/-/spec/opensearch/1.1/">
    <ShortName>Mobile Web Search</ShortName>
    <Description>Search in our mobile web</Description>
    <Url type="text/html"
        template="http://mysite.com/?q={searchTerms}"/>
    <Image height="64" width="64" type="image/png">
        http://example.com/icon.png
    </Image>
    <Language>en-us</Language>
</OpenSearchDescription>
```

## Apple Passbook

Passbook is a native app available in iOS from 6.0 that works as a virtual container for all your passes, tickets, discount coupons, loyalty cards, and gift cards. As a web developer you may want to serve the user with a discount coupon, a ticket to an event, an e-ticket for his next flight, or a loyalty card.

Apple allows websites to deliver these kinds of passes from a website without the need of a native app, as you can see in Figure 19-2.

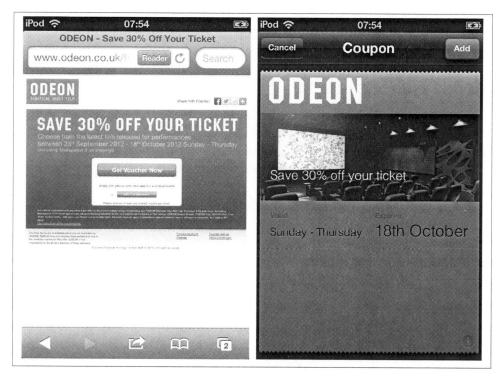

*Figure 19-2. Odeon Cinemas (http://odeon.co.uk) in UK offers discount codes to iOS Passbook directly from their website.*

To deliver the pass via your website you just need to use the MIME type `application/vnd.apple.pkpass` or send the file as an email attachment.

 Apple provides a tool that you can install on your server to package and sign customized passes on the fly that may include current user information.

A Passbook file is a package including just a JSON metadata file and a couple of images. You need to package the file and sign it. Unfortunately, to sign the pass you need a signature from Apple, and that means you need an iOS Developer Program account ($99/year). If you receive the pass already signed, you can just insert it on your own site.

One of the great features of passes is that once they're installed you can provide some web services on your end, and (through Apple's Push Notification Service) the operating system will call your web services to update the information on the passes. Therefore, when you deliver a pass to the user, you can update it from your end without a native app.

More information on Apple's Passbook is available at Apple's Developer website (*http://developer.apple.com/passbook*).

# Mobile Web Statistics

With your website online, you will want to gather some statistics about usage, visitors, and even mobile browsers accessing your site. Typical desktop web statistics systems don't work well with mobile sites, because they don't have mobile user agents in mind when analyzing logs and don't work on non-JavaScript devices or other kinds of services.

However, there are some free and commercial solutions available for mobile web statistics.

## Google Analytics for Mobile

Google Analytics is one of the most used (and most powerful) free web statistics tools for mobile websites, but it is based on JavaScript code that, in the mobile world, only works on high-end devices.

Google Analytics for Mobile Websites (*http://bit.ly/Wgbfob*) works on all web-enabled browsers, with or without JavaScript support. The technology supports script code for PHP, ASP.NET, Perl, and JSP.

 Google Analytics is also available for Android and iPhone native applications, supporting tracking of pages and events.

To use the mobile service, you should apply for a normal Google Analytics (*http://www.google.com/analytics*) account. Create a new Website Profile and, in the Advanced section, select "A site built for a mobile phone," select your server language, and follow the instructions.

## Yahoo! Web Analytics

Yahoo! Web Analytics (*http://web.analytics.yahoo.com*) supports mobile devices, giving the following statistics about your mobile users:

- Mobile device manufacturer
- Mobile device model
- Model device screen size
- Carrier name

You will find these statistics in the Mobile Reports section.

## Mobilytics

Mobilytics (*http://www.mobilytics.net*) provides free and premium metric and visual indicators about your mobile web visitors. It offers scripts for PHP, ASP.NET, JSP, and other server-side platforms. Transcoder detection, mobile device detection, and other capabilities are available in premium plans.

# Monetizing Your Website

You've put a lot of work into building your site. How can you make a return on that investment? One solution could be advertising. Another solution is to charge for content using Premium SMS (through carriers) or Facebook Payments (*http://developers.face book.com/docs/payments*), which is compatible with mobile websites.

## Mobile Advertisements

If you have a free mobile website and you want to monetize it with advertisements, there are a few solutions that you can use. Today, most ad networks offer a mobile version of their services.

 For more information about mobile advertising, visit the Mobile Marketing Association (*http://www.mmaglobal.com*).

### Google AdSense for mobile content

With Google AdSense, you can easily insert mobile-optimized ads for mobile devices. To use it, log in or sign up at Google AdSense (*http://www.google.com/adsense*) and select "AdSense for Mobile Content" on the Account Setup tab.

When you define a mobile campaign for Google AdWords, you can use the Keyword tool to access information about mobile searches in the Google ecosystem.

It is possible to select only advertisements appropriate for the iPhone and other high-end devices, or for all devices (including ads in XHTML, cHTML, and WML format), using server-side code. When you add the server code (for example, PHP) you should start seeing mobile advertisements on your site within 48 hours.

 The Interactive Advertising Bureau (IAB) has released a document with the suggested formats and sizes for mobile ads and banners. It can be found at *www.mobilexweb.com/go/mobileads*.

# Mobile Web Social Features

Your mobile website will not be complete if you don't add some social features to it. In the current social networking era, social integration is a must-have feature to implement.

## Authentication and Sharing APIs

Facebook, Twitter, and Google all offer APIs that can enhance the visibility of your mobile site thanks to the sharing features.

### Facebook Connect

Facebook offers Facebook Connect for Mobile Web (*http://developers.facebook.com/mobile*), an HTML5 library that lets our applications log users in using their Facebook accounts. With this API you can:

- Create a login mechanism easily.
- Get user session data.
- Call methods from the Graph API and prompt for extended permissions (access friends list, send private messages).
- Post on the Facebook timeline.

To use it, you will need to register an app on Facebook, implement the Facebook SDK, log the user in, and use the Graph API.

To get detailed information and samples, visit Facebook developer's site (*https://developers.facebook.com/docs/guides/mobile/web*).

### Twitter for Websites

Twitter for Websites (*http://dev.twitter.com*) allows us to integrate our mobile website with Twitter login. We can also access the user's account, such as for posting new messages or accessing the whole Twitter API.

### Google APIs

Google offers different APIs that are useful for mobile websites, including Google Accounts Authentication and Authorization (*https://developers.google.com/accounts*), useful to log in the user, and the Google+ API (*https://developers.google.com/+/api*) for sharing on that social network.

## Sharing Content

For any content you are serving in your mobile website, you can offer a *Share* service to publish the URL via Twitter, Facebook, and other social networks.

> Remember from Chapter 7 that we have to use some specific meta tags defining the information to share so the sharing mechanism works better. Remember also that some browsers, such as Safari on iOS and Internet Explorer 10 on Windows 8, have a sharing ability built in.

For most social networks, you should use the same URL you would use for the desktop website. On the server, the social network scripts will redirect mobile users to the mobile website.

For Twitter, you can use a link like this:

```
http://twitter.com/home?status=<your message here>
```

Remember that Twitter has a limit of 140 characters, including an optional URL using *http://*, which should be URL-encoded in the status variable. For long URLs, you should use a shortener service API.

For Facebook, you can share a link using:

```
http://m.facebook.com/sharer.php?u=<url to share>&t=<title of content>
```

# MIME Types for Mobile Content

## Markup and Script MIME Types

*Table A-1. Markup and script MIME types*

| Format | Typical extension | MIME type |
| --- | --- | --- |
| WML | *.wml* | `text/vnd.wap.xml` |
| WMLScript | *.wmls* | `text/vnd.wap.wmlscript` |
| HTML 3/4/5 | *.html* | `text/html` |
| cHTML | *.html* | `text/html` |
| XHTML | *.html, .xhtml* | `application/xhtml+xml, text/xml, text/html` |
| XHTML MP | *.html, .xhtml* | `application/vnd.wap.xhtml+xml, application/xhtml +xml, text/xml, text/html` |
| JavaScript | *.js* | `text/javascript, application/ecmascript, application/ javascript` |
| CSS2, CSS3, WAP CSS, and CSS MP | *.css* | `text/css` |
| Multipart document | | `multipart/mixed, application/vnd.wap.multi part.mixed` |

## Image MIME Types

*Table A-2. Image MIME types*

| Format | Typical extension | MIME type |
| --- | --- | --- |
| GIF | *.gif* | `image/gif` |
| JPEG | *.jpeg, .jpg* | `image/jpeg, image/jpg` |
| PNG | *.png* | `image/png` |
| SVG | *.svg* | `image/svg+xml` |

| Format | Typical extension | MIME type |
|---|---|---|
| WEBP | .webp | image/webp |
| Compressed SVG | .svgz | image/svg+xml |
| WBMP | .wbmp | image/vnd.wap.wbmp |
| Nokia Wallpaper | | image/vnd.nok-wallpaper |

# Mobile Content MIME Types

*Table A-3. Mobile content MIME types*

| Format | Typical extension | MIME type |
|---|---|---|
| iOS Passbook | .pkpass | application/vnd.apple.pkpass |
| Java ME Application Descriptor | .jad | text/vnd.sun.j2me.app-descriptor |
| Java ME Archive | .jar | application/java-archive |
| BlackBerry Archive | .cod | application/vnd.rim.cod |
| Android Application | .apk | application/vnd.android.package-archive |
| Symbian Application | .sis | application/vnd.symbian.install |
| Symbian Application | .sisx | x-epoc/x-sisx-app |
| vCalendar | .vcalendar | |
| iCalendar | .icalendar | |
| Nokia Flash Format | .nfl | |
| Adobe Flash Movie | .swf | application/x-shockwave-flash |
| XML | .xml | text/xml |
| JSON | .json | application/json, text/json, text/javascript |
| RSS | .rss, .xml | application/rss+xml |
| Open Search Description | .xml | application/opensearchdescription+xml |
| Mobile Sitemap | .xml | text/xml |
| Multimedia Message | .mms, .smil | application/vnd.wap.mms-message |
| Bookmark | | application/x-wap-prov.browser-bookmarks |
| Sony Ericsson MMS Template | .tpl | application/vnd.sonyericsson.mms-template |
| OMA Download | | application/vnd.oma.dd+xml |

# Audio and Video MIME Types

*Table A-4. Audio and video MIME types*

| Format | Typical extension | MIME type |
| --- | --- | --- |
| 3GPP | *.3gp, .3gpp* | `video/3gpp` |
| 3GPP 2 | *.3gp2, .3gpp2* | `video/3gpp2` |
| QuickTime MOV | *.mov* | `video/quicktime` |
| Windows Media Video | *.wmv* | `video/x-ms-wmv` |
| Windows Media Audio | *.wma* | `audio/x-ms-wma` |
| Real Video | *.rv* | `video/vnd.rn-realvideo` |
| Real Audio | *.ra, .ram* | `audio/x-pn-realaudio` |
| MP3 | *.mp3* | `audio/mp3` |
| Flash Video | *.flv* | `video/x-flv` |
| MPEG-4 | *.mp4* | `video/mp4` |
| Audio WebM | *.webm* | `audio/webm` |
| Video WebM | *.webm* | `video/webm` |

# Webapp MIME Types

*Table A-5. Webapp MIME types*

| Format | Typical extension | MIME type |
| --- | --- | --- |
| Symbian WRT webapp | *.wgz* | `application/x-nokia-widget` |
| Samsung widget | *.wgt* | `application/vnd.samsung.widget` |
| JIL widget | *.wgt* | `application/widget` |
| Opera widgets | *.wgt* | `application/x-opera-widgets` |
| HTML5 Manifest file | *.manifest* | `text/cache-manifest` |
| Server-Sent Event Stream | | `text/event-stream` |

# Index

## Symbols

2D context, 357
3D image formats, 333
3D screens, 53
3GP container, 369
3GP2 container, 369
3GPP (3rd Generation Partnership Project), 351
51 Degrees website, 61, 328
80/20 law, 140

## A

a element, 553
A-GPS (Assisted GPS), 60, 530
AAC codec, 368
absolute positions, 405
Accelerometer API, 583, 594, 649
Accelerometer object (Cordova/PhoneGap)
  clearAcceleration method, 583
  getCurrentAcceleration method, 583
  watchAcceleration method, 583
accelerometers, 60, 60, 579
Accept request header (HTTP), 301, 696
Accept-Charset request header (HTTP), 301
Accept-Language request header (HTTP), 301
accessibility (HTML5), 232
accesskey attribute, 230, 236
accuracy in location technology, 529
active pseudoclass (CSS), 413

Add to Home Screen library, 611
addEventListener() method
  cache events and, 508
  managing events, 477
  transition ending and, 441
Adobe Creative Cloud services, 115
Adobe Device Central, 111
Adobe Dreamweaver, 89, 157
Adobe Edge Animate, 90, 442
Adobe Edge Code, 90
Adobe Edge Inspect, 90, 115–116
Adobe Edge Reflow, 90
Adobe Flash Media Serve, 370
Adobe Flash Player, 123, 365–366
Adobe HTTP Dynamic Streaming, 376
Adobe Intel
  native web apps for, 91
Adobe PhoneGap, 72
  (see also Apache Cordova framework)
  about, 72
  native web apps for, 644–650
advertisements on mobile websites, 705
Advertising API, 627
after pseudoclass (CSS), 415
Ajax
  about, 522–523
  cross-domain requests, 523
  JSONP and, 524
  with offline resources, 525

*We'd like to hear your suggestions for improving our indexes. Send email to index@oreilly.com.*

ajax capability group (WURFL), 316
ajax_supports_javascript capability (WURFL), 318
ajax_support_event_listener capability (WURFL), 318
Akamai service provider
    Internet Observatory website, 61
    Mobitest tool, 687
    streaming services for mobile devices, 377
Alarm API, 595
alert dialog (JavaScript), 467
alert windows, 684
alt attribute, 336
Amazon AppStore, 14, 651
Amazon Silk browser, 76, 311
Amazon.com, 28
Ambient Light Events API, 594
AND operator, 386
Android platform
    about, 13
    apple-touch icon and, 193–195
    application and games delivery, 665
    brands and models in, 13–16
    Debug Bridge tool, 682
    debugging tools, 681
    distributing native web apps, 651
    emulator for, 94–98
    fragmentation and, 16
    Google Maps application, 541
    intents, 562
    online site on screen sizes, 54
    preinstalled browser, 74
    versions, 14
Android SDK Manager, 94
Android Virtual Device (AVD) Manager, 95
animated GIFs, 332, 336
Animated PNG (APNG), 333, 336
animation property (CSS), 442
animation timing API, 475, 693
animation-delay property (CSS), 442
animation-direction property (CSS), 442
animation-duration property (CSS), 442
animation-fillmode property (CSS), 443, 444
animation-iteration-count property (CSS), 442
animation-name property (CSS), 442
animation-playstate property (CSS), 443
animation-timing-function property (CSS), 442
animations
    about, 442–443

keyframes at-rule, 443–445
listening for events, 446
timing control for, 475
transitions and, 439–441
Apache Cordova framework
    about, 72
    APIs for mobile web apps, 594, 649
    managing cameras, 592
    native web apps for, 70, 91, 644–650
    sensor support, 583
    Weinre tool, 683
Apache DeviceMap, 328
Apache platform, MIME types and, 655
apk files, 665
APNG (Animated PNG), 333, 336
APNG-canvas polyfill, 333, 336
app stores, 14
    (see also specific stores)
    Android devices, 14
    Blackberry devices, 25
    distributing native web apps, 650
    Nokia devices, 20
    Samsung devices, 26
AppBar control, 617
AppBarCommand control, 617
Appcelerator Titanium framework, 72, 91
appearance property (CSS3), 421
Apple Corporation
    about, 9
    Adobe versus, 366
    mobile devices, 9–13
Apple Dashboard Widget, 602
Apple Gesture API, 574–576
Apple HTTP Live Streaming (HLS), 376–377
Apple Passbook, 703
Apple Touch Events API, 565–568
Apple TV, 375
apple-mobile-web-app-title meta tag, 191
apple-touch icon, 187–195
application and games delivery
    Android applications, 665
    iOS applications, 663–664
    Java ME and, 667–669
    Windows applications, 666
Application API, 627
application cache
    about, 501
    compatibility and limits, 508–511
    fallback mechanism, 504

manifest file and, 502
uses for, 502
applicationCache object
about, 506–506
addEventListener() method, 508
cached event, 507
checking event, 507
downloading event, 507
error event, 507
events available to, 507
noupdate event, 507
obsolete event, 507
progress event, 507
status property, 506
swapCache() method, 506
update() method, 504, 506, 506
updateready event, 507
AppManager API, 640
Apps API (Mozilla Open Web apps), 622
AppThwack service, 119
Aptana tool, 91
AR (Augmented Reality), 530
arc() method (Canvas API), 358
architecture and design
mobile strategy for, 127–140
navigation tips, 140
user experience, 141–152
ArrayBuffer data type, 464
ASP.NET
MIME types and, 657
reading headers, 308
aspect-ratio attribute, 386
Assisted GPS (A-GPS), 60, 530
async attribute, 453
Asynchronous JavaScript and XML (see Ajax)
AT&T Location API, 539
audio
about, 379
compatibility table for web platforms, 381
containers and codecs, 368–369
inivisible player, 380
MIME types supported, 711
streaming, 376–377
Web Audio API, 380
AudioContext constructor, 380
Augmented Reality (AR), 530
authenticating connections, 706
autocomplete attribute, 267, 499
autofocus attribute, 267, 297

autogrowing textarea, 496
automatic links, removing, 216
autoplay attribute, 374
autosave attribute, 245
AVC (H.264 codec), 368
AVD (Android Virtual Device) Manager, 95
AVI container, 368

**B**

backbutton event (Cordova/PhoneGap), 648
backface-visibility property (CSS), 436
background execution
about, 456–457
background tab notification trick, 460
compatibility table, 461
push notifications, 462
status detection, 457–460
background tab notification trick, 460
background-attachment property (CSS), 414
background-clip property (CSS3), 414
background-image property (CSS), 285, 345, 413
background-origin property (CSS3), 414
background-position property (CSS), 338, 422
background-repeat property (CSS), 413
background-size property (CSS3)
about, 285, 338, 414
percentage values in, 349
Bada emulator, 111
Baidu browser, 86
Baidu Yi operating system, 31
bandwidth simulators, 674
base64 conversion, 334
baseJS library, 486
battery consumption, 455, 593
Battery Status API
about, 593
charging attribute, 593
chargingTime attribute, 593
dischargingTime attribute, 593
level attribute, 593
batterycritical event (Cordova/PhoneGap), 648
batterylow event (Cordova/PhoneGap), 648
batterystatus event (Cordova/PhoneGap), 648
BB10 simulator, 107
BBM API, 627
bbUI.js framework, 488, 628–629
bearer capability group (WURFL), 316
before pseudoclass (CSS), 415

beforeunload event, 477
beginPath() method (Canvas API), 358
bezierCurveTo() method (Canvas API), 358
binary data, 464
Bing Maps application, 545
Bing search engine, 695
bingmaps: protocol, 545
BlackBerry 10 platform, 26, 78
BlackBerry devices
    about, 24
    apple-touch icon and, 192
    preinstalled browser, 78
    Remote Web Inspector, 682
    simulators for, 104–107
    touch behavior, 568
    TunnelTilt game, 363
    viewport declaration and, 214
    WebWorks support, 624–632
BlackBerry Email and MDS Services Simulator
    Package, 105
BlackBerry PlayBook tablet
    about, 25
    simulator for, 107
block elements, 228
BlueVia platform, 539
blur event, 479
bookmarking (mobile browsers), 185
bookmarklets, 453, 684
border-image property (CSS), 409–412
border-radius property (CSS), 287, 408–408
brands (see specific brands)
brand_name capability (WURFL), 317
browsers (mobile devices)
    audio compatibility table for, 381
    background execution, 456–462
    bookmarking support, 185
    browsing types, 43
    canvas compatibility table, 364
    client-side detection, 284–299
    coding with JavaScript for, 452–455
    contenteditable attribute, 250
    direct versus cloud-based, 47
    document margins and, 394
    file upload selectors and, 257, 260–263
    fragmentation and, 50–60
    icon display compatibility table, 186
    image format compatibility table, 336
    JavaScript libraries, 485–487
    key features, 87

legacy, 81
market statistics, 60
MIME types supported, 710
mobile design strategy, 127–140
multipage browsing, 48
navigator object properties compatibility
    table, 298
platform detection, 298–299
preinstalled, 73–82
pseudo-browsers, 69
quantity of simultaneous touches compari-
    son table, 569
reflow layout engines, 46
server-side detection, 300–328
target attribute, 231
testing, 177
useful keys for, 481–483
user-agent string and, 302–303, 307, 309
user-installable, 82–86
vendor prefixes and, 286–290
video compatibility table for, 378
video element and, 372
web engines and, 49
WebGL compatibility, 363
zoom experience, 45
BrowserStack service, 112
Browshot tool, 114
Budiu, Raluca, 145
buttons, 242

C
C# language, 308
cache capability group (WURFL), 316
cache manifest file (see manifest file)
cached event, 507
calc() function, 448
Calendar API, 594, 640
camera access on mobile devices, 590–593
Camera API, 640, 649
Can I Use website, 282
canvas element
    2D context, 357
    about, 357
    advanced features, 359
    as background, 360
    compatibility table, 364
    drawing methods, 358
    exporting drawings, 361
    lines and strokes, 358

as native code, 359
pixel density and, 361
WebGL and, 362
capabilities (WURFL), 316–318
Capture API (Cordova/PhoneGap), 593, 649
Carakan JavaScript engine, 50
CardFlip pattern, 436–438
carrier network location APIs, 539
Cascades UI layer, 26
cascading menus, 499
Chakra JavaScript engine, 50
Champeon, Steven, 132
change event, 479
charCode property, 482
chargingchange event, 593
chargingtimechange event, 593
Charles Web Debugging Proxy, 674
charset encoding, 163
checkboxes, 236, 241
checking event, 507
Chitika website, 61
Chrome (Google)
Android browser and, 74
debugger for Android platform, 681
debugging tool, 673
HTML5 apps engine, 624
HTML5 web apps and, 66
as pseudo-browser, 69
Ripple tool, 104
Chromebook (netbook), 8
cHTML (compact HTML), 158
ciUI library, 487
clear property (CSS), 405
clearRect() method (Canvas API), 358
click event, 478
client-side detection
about, 284
CSS fallbacks, 285
debugging, 678–685
HTML fallbacks, 284
JavaScript fallbacks, 290–292
Modernizr library, 292–297
platform detection, 298–299
polyfills, 297
vendor prefixes, 286–290
client-side location techniques
A-GPS, 530
about, 530
cell information, 531

GPS, 530
WiFi Positioning System, 531
client-side storage
about, 511
debugging, 521
FileSystem API, 520
IndexedDB API, 515, 518–519
user options regarding, 521
Web SQL Database API, 514–517
Web Storage API, 511–514
ClientLocation object, 540
closePath() method (Canvas API), 358
cloud-based browsers, 47, 309–311, 454
Cocoa Touch framework, 12
code development tools
about, 89
Adobe Dreamweaver, 89
Adobe Edge tools, 90
Eclipse, 91
Microsoft Visual Studio, 91
Microsoft WebMatrix, 91
for native web apps, 91
codecs, audio and video, 368–369, 370
column-count property (CSS), 404
column-gap property (CSS), 404
column-rule property (CSS), 404
column-width property (CSS), 404
communication, network (see network communication)
compact HTML (cHTML), 158
Compass APIs, 583, 649
Compass object (Cordova/PhoneGap)
clearHeading method, 583
getCurrentHeading method, 583
watchHeading method, 583
compassneedscalibration event, 580
compressing files, 690
conditional expressions, 385
conditional resource loader (Modernizr), 294
config.xml file (WebWorks), 626, 634
configuration standards, 601
confirm dialog (JavaScript), 467
Connection object, 584, 584
constraints validation API, 274
constructor functions, 291
Contacts APIs, 594, 640, 649
contacts, adding to phonebooks, 559–560
containers, audio and video, 368–369

content (HTML5)
  about, 228
  accessibility, 232
  block elements, 228
  frames, 229
  hyperlinks, 230–232
  lists, 228
  tables, 229
content attribute (meta tag), 461
content delivery
  about, 655
  application and games delivery, 662–669
  file delivery, 658–662
  MIME types, 655–657
content property (CSS), 415
Content-disposition header, 657
Content-Type header (HTTP), 163
contenteditable attribute, 250
context for mobile devices
  defining, 130
  detecting server-side, 307–309
  HTTP headers and, 304
controls attribute, 373, 379
cookie management, 476
coords property, 536
Cordova WebView, 646
CordovaJS API, 647
CORS (Cross Origin Resource Sharing), 523
cors property, 523
createImageData() method (Canvas API), 358
CreateJS toolkit extension, 361, 380
Creative Cloud Services (Adobe), 115
Crockford, Douglas, 600
Cross Origin Resource Sharing (CORS), 523
CSS
  common patterns
    appearance override, 421
    backgrounds, 413
    border image, 409–412
    content, 415
    cursor management, 416
    display properties, 404–408
    highlight color, 421
    opacity, 416
    pseudoclasses, 413
    rounded corners, 408–408
    scrollable areas, 414
    selection management, 417–419
    touch callout, 420

defining extensions, 172–176
Device Adaptation standard, 203
fallback mechanisms, 285, 288
Modernizr properties for, 295
multiple screen densities, 345
noncompatible tags and, 172
resetting files, 393
text formatting considerations, 395–404
vendor prefixes and, 286–290, 291
viewport declaration and, 211
where to insert, 383
CSS 3 conditionals, 286
CSS Animation module, 442–446
css capability group (WURFL), 317
CSS exclusions and shapes module, 447
CSS filter effects specification, 446
CSS Flexible Box Layout, 407
CSS Grid Layout layout mechanism, 408
CSS preprocessors, 288–289
CSS regions module, 447
CSS selectors, 392
CSS Sprites
  about, 422
  alternatives to, 427
  samples and compatibility, 422–425
CSS transforms standard, 433–438
CSS transitions, 439–441
CSS3
  about, 176
  RWD and, 134
  validation pseudoclasses, 273
CSS3 Image Values specification, 428–429
CSS3 media queries
  about, 385–386
  all versus only screen, 388
  CSS conditionals and, 286
  IE 10 snap state, 390–391
  multiple screen densities and, 347
  RWD and, 134
  standard features attributes, 386
  useful queries, 388–389
  viewports and, 212
CSS3 values and units module, 448
CSS4 media queries, 390
CSSPrefixer tool, 290
css_spriting capability (WURFL), 318
cubic-bezier() function, 440
Cunningham, Katie, 233
cursor management (CSS), 416

cursor navigation, 44, 337
cursor-event-mode meta tag, 215, 568

# D

DASH (Dynamic Adaptive Streaming over
    HTTP), 376
data URLs, 334–335, 336
data-blackberry-end-selection-on-touch at-
    tribute, 249
data-win-control attribute, 616
datalist tag, 247
datauri attribute, 335
DataView data type, 464
date input fields, 255, 297
DatePicker control, 617
dc: URI scheme, 556
dd tag, 228
DDR (Device Description Repository), 313–328
Debug Bridge tool (Android), 682
debugging
    about, 671
    client-side detection, 678–685
    client-side storage, 521
    JavaScript on mobile browsers, 455
    markup, 676–677
    server-side detection, 671–676
defer attribute, 453
definition lists, 228
delayed linking model of file delivery, 658
deleting
    margins, 394
    packages, 505
design strategies
    context for mobile device, 130
    for navigation, 140
    progressive enhancement technique, 132–
        134
    Responsive Web Design, 134–138
    RESS, 139–140
    server-side adaptation, 131
    for user experience, 141–152
    when to get out of the browser, 127–129
desktop websites, 36
DetectFree (Movila), 327
detection, feature and device (see feature and
    device detection)
DetectRight engine, 326
Deutsche Telekom R&D Laboratories, 455

development tools
    production environment and, 124–126
    for testing, 91–124
    working with code, 89–91
Device API (Cordova/PhoneGap), 649
Device Central (Adobe), 111
Device Description Repository (DDR), 313–328
device detection (see feature and device detec-
    tion)
device libraries (see specific libraries)
device pixel ratio, 55, 346, 347
device-aspect-ratio attribute, 387
device-height attribute, 387
device-pixel-ratio attribute, 347
Device-Stock-UA header (HTTP), 307
device-width attribute, 387
DeviceAnywhere (Keynote), 120–122
DeviceAtlas product, 324–326
DeviceMap (Apache), 328
devicemotion event, 580
deviceorientation event, 580, 583
DeviceOrientation Event specification
    about, 579
    moving a ball, 581–582
devicePixelRatio property, 346
deviceready event, 647
device_os capability (WURFL), 317
device_os_version capability (WURFL), 317
dialogs, JavaScript, 467–469
Digital Rights Management (DRM), 659
direct browsers, 47
direct linking model of file delivery, 658
directions
    Google Maps for Android, 542
    iOS Maps application, 544
disabled attribute, 268
dischargingtimechange event, 593
discoverability, spiders and, 696–698
display (mobile devices)
    about, 50
    full screen experience, 587
    input methods, 58–58
    physical dimensions, 53–55
    pixel aspect ratio, 57
    pixel density ratio, 55
    resolution, 51–53
display capability group (WURFL), 316
display property (CSS), 404, 422

distribution
    about, 601
    of iOS web apps, 610, 664
    of Mozilla OWA web apps, 622
    of native web apps, 650
    of WebWorks apps, 632
DOCTYPE (Document Type Declaration )
    about, 160
    standards preferences for, 161–164
    WML and, 156
document body (HTML5)
    about, 224
    main structure, 225–226
document object
    getElementById() function, 463
    hidden property, 457
    querySelector() function, 463
    querySelectorAll() function, 463
    visibilityState property, 457
Document Object Model (DOM)
    about, 463
    Web Workers specification and, 465
Dolfin browser, 79
Dolphin browser, 86
DOM (Document Object Model)
    about, 463
    Web Workers specification and, 465
DOM mutation observer, 253
domain considerations, 125
DOMCharacterDataModified event listener, 253
DOMNodeInserted event listener, 253
DOMNodeRemoved event listener, 253
dotMobi TLD, 42
dots per inch (DPI), 53
double exclamation mark, 291
double-tap action, 478
download manifest file, 664
downloading event, 507
DPI (dots per inch), 53
Dragonfly debugging tool, 682
drawImage() method (Canvas API), 358
Dreamweaver (Adobe), 89, 157
DRM (Digital Rights Management), 659
Droid devices, 16, 28
dt tag, 228
Dynamic Adaptive Streaming over HTTP
    (DASH), 376
dynamic definition (MIME types), 657

## E

e-book readers, 72
Eclipse Project, 91
ECMAScript, 451
ECMAScript Mobile Profile (ESMP), 451, 452
Edge Animate (Adobe), 90, 442
Edge Code (Adobe), 90
Edge Inspect (Adobe), 90, 115–116
Edge Reflow (Adobe), 90
80/20 law, 140
Ejecta iOS implementation, 359
email, sending, 556, 699
embedding
    objects, 378
    SVG in XHTML, 354
Emoji (images), 340
emoticons, 342
emptyok attribute, 276
emulators
    comparison chart, 112
    emulators, 92
    remote emulation services, 112
    testing mobile apps with, 92–114
    WML, 157
encoding, charset, 163
Enyo framework, 490
error event, 507
error handling
    Geolocation API, 536
    production environment and, 125
ESMP (ECMAScript Mobile Profile), 451, 452
Event API, 627
event handling
    emulating double click action, 478
    managing events, 477–483
    preventing default behavior, 483
    XMLHttpRequest object and, 523
Event Source, 525–527
events, 477
    (see also specific events)
    animation, 446
    double-tap action, 478
    managing, 477
    pointer, 569–572
    preventing default behavior, 483
    touch, 565–569
exclamation mark, 291
exporting canvas drawings, 361

# F

Facebook Connect for Mobile Web, 706
Facebook site, 70
facetime: URI scheme, 559
fallback mechanisms
    application cache, 504
    CSS, 285, 288
    HTML, 284
    JavaScript, 290–292
    recommendations for, 281
    video element, 374
feature and device detection
    about, 279
    client-side detection, 284–299
    informational websites, 281–284
    possible problems and their solutions, 279–281
    server-side detection, 300–328
feature phones, 4
Fiddler Connection Simulator, 676
fidelizing users, 701–704
fieldset tag, 236
51 Degrees website, 61, 328
File API, 585–587, 649
file compression, 690
file delivery
    content delivery and, 658
    direct linking model, 658, 658
    OMA Download standard, 659–662
File I/O API, 627
file selection fields, 257–263
FileReader object
    readAsBinary() method, 586
    readAsDataURL() method, 586
    readAsText() method, 586
FileSystem API, 520
fill() method (Canvas API), 358
fillRect() method (Canvas API), 358
fillStyle property, 358
fillText() method (Canvas API), 359
filter effects, 446
find dialog (JavaScript), 467
Firebug Lite plug-in, 685
Firefox platforms
    emulator for, 111
    Firebug Lite plug-in, 685
    Firefox OS, 30
    form control attributes, 268
    HTML5 web apps and, 66

    remote debugging, 681
    user agent tricks, 307
    user-installed browsers, 86
fixed position, 406
Flash Player (Adobe), 123, 365–366
flash_lite capability group (WURFL), 317
flash_lite_version capability (WURFL), 318
Flexbox technique, 407
Fling, Brian, 145
flip gesture, 572
FlipView control, 617
Float32Array data type, 464
floating bars, 497–498
floating positions, 405
FLV container, 368
Flyout control, 617
fl_browser capability (WURFL), 318
focus event, 479
focus navigation, 43, 337
focus pseudoclass (CSS), 413
focus() function, 472
@font-face declaration, 397–398
font-family property (CSS), 395
font-size property (CSS), 399
form control attributes
    about, 266
    additional, 270
    autocomplete, 267
    autofocus, 267
    disabled, 268
    Firefox extensions, 268
    input validation attributes, 268
    Modernizr support, 297
    placeholder, 266
    readonly, 268
    Safari extension, 268
    XHTML MP inputmode attribute, 269
form elements
    about, 238
    buttons, 242
    checkboxes, 236, 241
    date input fields, 255
    file selection fields, 257–263
    hidden fields, 243
    non-interactive, 264–265
    radio buttons, 241
    range slider field, 254
    select lists, 238–241
    text input fields, 243–254

form validation
    about, 270
    HTML5, 271–274
    Modernizr support, 297
    WAP CSS, 275–277
formaction attribute, 270
format attribute, 277
formenctype attribute, 270
formmethod attribute, 270
forms (see HTML5 forms)
formtarget attribute, 270
FourSquare website, 533
fragmentation
    about, 50
    Android platform and, 16
    mobile browsers and, 50–60
frames (HTML5), 229
Full Screen API
    about, 587
    cancelFullScreen() method, 588
    exitFullScreen() method, 588
    requestFullScreen() method, 587
full screen apps patterns, 652–654
:fullscreen pseudoclass, 588

# G

games delivery (see application and games de-
    livery)
Gecko rendering engine, 49
General Packet Radio Service (GPRS), 40
geolocation
    about, 60, 529
    Geolocation API, 534–541
    IP addresses and, 309, 540–541
    location techniques, 529–533
Geolocation API
    about, 534
    defining optional attributes, 537
    getting the position, 534
    handling error messages, 536
    tracking locations, 536
Geolocation API 2.0, 538
geolocation object
    clearWatch() method, 537
    getCurrentPosition() method, 534, 537, 538
    watchPosition() method, 537, 537, 538
gesturechange event, 574
gestureend event, 574

GestureEvent object
    rotation property, 574
    scale property, 574
gestures
    about, 572
    Apple Gesture API, 574–576
    frameworks supporting, 573
    Microsoft Gesture API, 577–578
    Nokia S40 web apps, 635
    swipe, 572
gesturestart event, 574
GET request (HTTP), 300
getImageData() method (Canvas API), 358
getUserMedia() method, 590
gif_animated capability (WURFL), 318
Global Positioning System (GPS), 60, 530
Globalization API, 594
Google Accounts Authentication and Authori-
    zation API, 707
Google AdSense, 705
Google Analytics for Mobile Websites, 704
Google Chrome
    Android browser and, 74
    debugger for Android platform, 681
    debugging tools, 673
    HTML5 apps engine, 624
    HTML5 web apps and, 66
    as pseudo-browser, 69
    Ripple tool, 104
Google ClientLocation object, 540
Google Code Blog, 248, 496
Google Glass project, 8
Google Maps API, 546–548
Google Maps application, 541
Google Maps Static API, 546, 549–550
Google Mobile operating system
    about, 13
    UI pattern, 248
Google Nexus devices, 16
Google Places API, 533
Google Play Store, 14, 98, 651
Google search engine, 695
Google Voice on Android, 559
Google+ API, 707
google.streetview: protocol, 542
Googlebot-Mobile, 696
gotpointercapture event, 570
GPRS (General Packet Radio Service), 40
GPS (Global Positioning System), 60, 530

graceful degradation strategy, 132
gradients, defining as image functions, 428–429
GSM Association, 532, 539
gyroscopes, 579

# H

H.263 codec, 368
H.264 codec, 368
Hammer.js library, 573
Handbrake transcoder, 369
Handheld Device Markup Language (HDML),
    40, 153
HAR standard, 687
hashchange event, 471
HDML (Handheld Device Markup Language),
    40, 153
heading structure (HTML5)
    about, 181
    changing navigation method, 215
    hiding URL address bar, 218
    Home Screen icons, 187–199
    integrating native apps, 220–224
    removing automatic links, 216
    sharing meta data, 216–218
    title, 181–182, 191
    viewport declaration, 200
    website icons, 183–186
height attribute
    CSS3 media queries, 387
    img element, 336
    viewports, 205, 211
hidden fields, 243
hiding URL address bar, 218
highlight color, 421
history object
    about, 470–471
    back() method, 470
    forward() method, 470
    go() method, 470
    pushState() method, 470
    reload() method, 506, 653
    replaceState() method, 470
    state property, 470
HLS (HTTP Live Streaming), 376–377
Home Screen icons, 187–199
home screen widget (MiniView), 642
hover attribute (CSS4), 390
HP, Palm devices and, 29
href attribute, 230

.htaccess file extension, 656
HTC devices, 29
HTML
    debugging considerations, 676–677
    DOCTYPE for, 162
    events supported, 477
    fallback mechanisms, 284
    preferred MIME type, 162
HTML Media Capture, 259
HTML5
    APIs for mobile web apps, 595
    boilerplate template for, 227
    compatibility levels, 177–179
    content for, 228–233
    creating templates, 170
    debugging considerations, 676–677
    DOCTYPE for, 162
    document body, 224–226
    fallback mechanisms, 284
    heading structure, 181–224
    history of, 42, 169
    JavaScript APIs, 466
    Modernizr properties for, 295
    new elements in, 172
    offline web apps, 501–511
    preferred MIME type, 162
    script extensions, 453
    storage limits and, 513
    syntax rules, 171
    validating forms, 271–274, 297
HTML5 elements
    canvas, 357–365
    client-side detection and, 284
    for forms, 238–265
    new elements, 172
    picture, 350
    video, 370–376
HTML5 forms
    about, 235
    designing, 235–237
    elements in, 238–265
    form control attributes, 266, 297
    validating, 270–277, 297
HTML5 Test website, 177
HTML5 web apps
    about, 64–66
    e-books and, 72
    Facebook and, 70
HtmlControl control, 617

html_web_4_0 capability (WURFL), 318
html_wi_oma_xhtmlmp_1_0 capability
(WURFL), 318
HTTP (HyperText Transfer Protocol)
    about, 300
    delivering video, 370
    request process, 300–307
    SPDY and, 301
    streaming support, 376–377
    User Agent Profile and, 306
    user-agent string, 302–303
HTTP compression, 690
HTTP Dynamic Streaming (Adobe), 376
HTTP headers
    common, 301
    Opera Mini supported, 310
    reading, 308
    Xpress Browser supported, 311
HTTP Live Streaming (HLS), 376–377
HTTP sniffing, 673, 687
http: protocol, 561
hybrid apps, 69–72
hyperlinks (HTML5), 230–232
HyperText Transfer Protocol (see HTTP)

## I

i-mode XHTML, 230
IAB (Interactive Advertising Bureau), 706
IANA (Internet Assigned Number Authority),
    554
ICANN (Internet Corporation for Assigned
    Names and Numbers), 42
IceCast Server, 377
ICO format, 183
IcoMoon service, 343
icons
    Home Screen, 187–199
    website, 183–186
iDEN networks, 556
Identity API, 627
Idle API, 594
iframe tag, 229, 414
IIS (Internet Information Server), 300, 527, 656
image maps, 337
image-rendering property (CSS), 340
image-set() function, 285, 349
images
    Adobe Flash, 365–366
    CSS Sprites alternatives, 427

formats supported, 331–336
    img element, 336
    joining, 427
    local pictograms, 340–342
    masked, 432
    memory consumption and, 332
    MIME types supported, 710
    multiple screen densities, 342–365
    responsive, 138, 337–340
image_format capability group (WURFL), 316
image_inlining capability (WURFL), 318, 335
IMEI (International Mobile Equipment Identi-
    ty), 304
iMessage service, 558
img element
    multiple screen densities, 344
    SVG and, 355
    usage considerations, 336
importScripts() function, 466
:in-range pseudoclass, 273
IndexedDB API, 515, 518–519
indoor location
    about, 529
    server-side location techniques and, 533
infinite lists, 146
initial-scale attribute, 205
inline images, 334–335, 427
inline SVG, 355
input element
    date input fields and, 255
    file selection fields and, 257
    range slider field and, 254
    text input fields and, 244
input methods for mobile devices, 58–58
input validation attributes, 268
inputformat attribute, 277
inputmode attribute, 269
Int32Array data type, 464
Intel (Adobe)
    native web apps for, 91
Intel computers, 94
intents (Android), 562
Interactive Advertising Bureau (IAB), 706
International Mobile Equipment Identity (IM-
    EI), 304
Internet Assigned Number Authority (IANA),
    554
Internet Corporation for Assigned Names and
    Numbers (ICANN), 42

Internet Explorer
    about, 76
    snap state, 390–391
Internet Explorer Mobile, 214
Internet Information Server (IIS), 300, 527, 656
:invalid pseudoclass, 273
Invoke API, 627
IonMonkey JavaScript engine, 50
iOS AppStore, 650
iOS Developer Program, 650
iOS platform
    about, 10–13
    application and games delivery, 663–664
    creating web apps for, 602–612
    detecting if application is installed, 561
    detection problem for devices, 305
    devices supported per version, 11
    HTML5 web apps and, 65
    Maps application, 543, 560
    reference movies for, 369
    Remote Web Inspector, 678–680
    simulator for, 99–104
    Smart App Banner service, 220–222, 561
    URL schemes, 560–562
IP addresses
    cloud-based browsers and, 310
    geolocation and, 309, 540–541
    ipconfig command for, 114
    reading, 308, 540
    server-side location techniques, 532
iPad device
    about, 9
    iOS detection problem, 305
    iOS Simulator and, 101
    user-agent string and, 304
ipconfig command, 114
iPhone device
    about, 9, 42
    iOS detection problem, 305
    iOS Simulator and, 101
    local pictograms, 341
    Retina display, 55
    streaming support, 377
    user-agent string and, 304
iPhone Safari Viewport Scaling Bug, 210
iPod device
    about, 10
    iOS detection problem, 305
iScroll JavaScript solution, 406

ISO pictograms, 342
is_smarttv capability (WURFL), 317
is_tablet capability (WURFL), 317
is_transcoder capability (WURFL), 318
is_wireless_device capability (WURFL), 317
itms-services: protocol, 664
iTunes Affiliate Program, 221
iTunes Link Maker, 221, 663
iTunes software, 10
iUI library, 487, 492–493
iWebInspector tool, 680
iWebKit library, 487

## J

j2me capability group (WURFL), 317
JAD (Java Application Descriptor) files, 667–668
JägerMonkey JavaScript engine, 50
Japanese mobile web, 82
JAR (Java ARchive) files, 667
Jasmine browser, 79
Java ME (Micro Edition)
    about, 21
    application and games delivery, 667–669
    MIDlet OTA installation method, 659
Java Servlets (JSP), 308, 657
Java Virtual Machine (JVM), 13
JavaScript APIs
    about, 290, 564
    battery status, 593
    camera access, 590–593
    file management, 585–587
    full screen experience, 587
    gestures, 572–578
    HTML5 support, 466
    native web apps and, 466
    network information, 583
    sensors, 579–583
    touch devices, 564–572
    vibrating mobile devices, 593
    web notifications, 588–590
JavaScript Debug Toolkit (JSDT), 684
JavaScript engines, 50
JavaScript language
    about, 50, 451
    applicationCache object, 506–508
    background execution, 456–462
    battery consumption, 455
    changing titles, 476

coding for mobile browsers, 452–455
cookie management, 476
debugging considerations, 455
as dynamic application engine, 653
event handling, 477–483
fallback mechanisms, 290–292
focus and scroll management, 472
history and URL management, 470–471
manipulating windows, 471
mobile UI patterns, 495–500
navigator object, 298–299
performance optimization, 692
profiling considerations, 455
progressive enhancement and, 134
prompt dialog, 254
standard behavior, 467–483
standard dialogs, 467–469
supported technologies, 463–466
timer support, 473–476
UI controls, 487–500, 616
vendor prefixes and, 291
JavaScript libraries, 484–487
JavaScript Object Notation (JSON), 464
javascript: URL protocol, 453
Jehl, Scott, 210, 219
jGestures framework, 573
jHere framework, 550
JIT (Just in Time) compiler, 50
Jo framework, 573
Jobs, Steve, 396
join images, 427
Jolley, Charles, 692
joules (energy consumption), 455
JPS (JPEG Stereoscopic) format, 333
jQMobi library, 486
jQTouch library, 487, 493
jQuery Mobile, 255, 488, 489
jqUI library, 487
JSConsole tool, 683
JSDT (JavaScript Debug Toolkit), 684
JSON (JavaScript Object Notation), 464
JSON object
    parse() function, 464
    stringify() function, 464
JSONP (JSON with Padding), 340, 524
JSP (Java Servlets), 308, 657
Just in Time (JIT) compiler, 50
JVM (Java Virtual Machine), 13

**K**

keyCode property, 481
keydown event, 481
@keyframes at-rule (CSS), 443–446
Keynote DeviceAnywhere, 120–122
Keynote MITE tool, 112, 672
keypress event, 481
keyup event, 481, 483
Khronos Group, 362
KHTML engine, 49
Kindle Fire tablet, 28, 311
Kosmaczewski, Adrián, 489

**L**

label tag, 236
Landmarks API, 640
Lawnchair store, 517
Lawson, Bruce, 287
layout engines
    reflowing pages, 46
    WebKit, 49
layout techniques
    CSS Grid Layout, 408
    Flexbox, 407
    multicolumn layout, 403
LBS (location-based services)
    about, 529
    Geolocation API, 534–541
    location techniques, 529–533
LBS Sprint API, 539
legacy mobile browsers, 81
legend tag, 236
LESS client-side processor, 289
levelchange event, 593
LG Mobile devices
    about, 28
    preinstalled browser, 79
libraries (see specific libraries)
linear-gradient() function, 428
lineTo() method (Canvas API), 358
lineWidth property, 358
link pseudoclass (CSS), 413
list attribute, 248
lists (HTML5)
    about, 228
    navigation lists, 231
    select lists, 238–241
Live Reload, 654

load event, 477
LocAid services, 539
localapp: scheme, 563
localStorage object, 511–514
Location API, 640
location object
    about, 470–471
    hash property, 470
    href property, 470, 471, 553
Location Orange API, 539
location techniques
    about, 529
    accuracy in, 529
    asking the user, 533
    client-side techniques, 530–531
    indoor location, 529
    server-side techniques, 532–533
location-based services (LBS)
    about, 529
    Geolocation API, 534–541
    location techniques, 529–533
Logging API, 640
loop attribute, 374
lostpointercapture event, 570
Lungo framework, 488, 573

# M

m subdomain, 41
Maemo platform
    about, 24
    preinstalled browser, 81
magnetometers, 579
magnometers, 60
mailto: protocol, 556
manifest file
    about, 501, 502, 620
    CACHE: section, 503
    FALLBACK: section, 504
    NETWORK: section, 503
    reusing, 503
maps
    native map applications, 541–545
    showing, 546–551
Maps application (iOS), 543, 560
maps: protocol, 543, 561
Marcotte, Ethan, 134
margins, deleting, 394
market share information, 60
marketing_name capability (WURFL), 317

markup capability group (WURFL), 316
markup debugging, 676–677
markup languages
    delivering markup, 160–164
    historical, 153
marquee element, 174
masked images, 432
Massive Operator Identification Platform, 309
matrix code, 699
matrix() CSS function, 433
matrix3d() CSS function, 433
max attribute, 254, 268, 271
max-height attribute, 211
max-width attribute, 211
max-zoom attribute, 212
maximum-scale attribute, 205
maxlength attribute, 248, 270
max_image_height capability (WURFL), 318
max_image_width capability (WURFL), 318
measuring performance optimization, 686–688
media (see audio; images; video)
Media API (Cordova/PhoneGap), 649
media attribute, 350, 384
Media Capture and Streams API, 590
Media Management API, 640
media queries (see CSS3 media queries)
MeeGo platform
    about, 24
    apple-touch icon and, 191
    emulator for, 111
    preinstalled browser, 78
memory consumption, image size and, 331
Menu control, 617
menu object (Symbian webapps)
    hideSoftkeys() method, 641
    setLeftSoftkeyLabel() method, 641
    setRightSoftkeyLabel() method, 641
    showSoftkeys() method, 641
menubutton event (Cordova/PhoneGap), 648
MenuItem object, 641
menus, cascading, 499
message event, 465
Messaging API, 594, 627, 640
meta data, sharing, 216–218
meter element, 264
MIB (Mobile Internet Browser), 81
Microsoft Gesture API, 577–578
Microsoft Pointer Events specification, 569–572
Microsoft Smooth Streaming, 376

Microsoft Surface tablets, 19
Microsoft Visual Studio, 91
Microsoft WebMatrix, 91
Microsoft Windows Phone Store, 651
Microsoft Windows Store, 651
MIDlet-Delete-Notify attribute, 668
MIDlet-Install-Notify attribute, 668
MIDlet-Jar-URL attribute, 668
MIME types
    about, 160
    audio and video, 711
    content delivery and, 655
    CSS preferences for, 160
    dynamic definition, 657
    image, 710
    markup and script, 709
    mobile content, 710
    standards preferences for, 161–164
    static definition, 655–656
    web apps, 711
min attribute, 254, 268, 271
min-device-pixel-ratio attribute, 347
min-height attribute, 211
min-width attribute, 211
min-zoom attribute, 212
minimum-scale attribute, 205
MiniView (home screen widget), 642
mirror effects (reflection), 431
MITE (Mobile Interactive Testing Environ-
    ment), 112, 672
mixins, 289
MMS (Multimedia Messaging Service), 558, 659
mms capability group (WURFL), 317
mms: URI scheme, 558
.mobi extension, 42
mobile devices, 279
    (see also feature and device detection)
    about, 38
    background execution, 456–462
    battery consumption, 455
    brands, models, and platforms, 9–32
    browsing experience, 43–50
    categories of, 3–9
    client-side detection, 284–299
    coding with JavaScript for, 452–455
    commonly implemented width values, 207
    delivering markup to, 160–164
    device libraries, 313–328
    features of, 1–3

input methods for, 58–58
JavaScript libraries, 485–487
key features, 60
market statistics, 60
MIME types supported, 710
non-phone, 7
quantity of simultaneous touches compari-
    son table, 569
server-side detection, 300–328
technical information, 32
usage statistics on, 37
useful keys for, 481–483
Mobile First concept, 140
Mobile Interactive Testing Environment
    (MITE), 112, 672
Mobile Internet Browser (MIB), 81
Mobile Marketing Association, 705
mobile markup checker, 677
mobile phones, 3
mobile SEO
    about, 695
    how users find you, 698–701
    spiders and discoverability, 696–698
    user fidelizing, 701–704
Mobile Sitemaps, 696
Mobile Tiny URL, 163, 699
mobile web, 89
    (see also development tools)
    advertisements on, 705
    APIs for, 595
    differences in, 38
    gathering statistics for, 704–705
    history of, 39–43
    Japanese, 82
    myths of, 35–38
    native apps and, 37
    navigation design tips, 140
    politics of, 159–160
    social features on, 706–707
    testing considerations, 122
    user experience in, 141–152
Mobile Web Best Practices specification, 677
Mobile Web Best Practices website, 145
Mobile Web Initiative, 177
Mobile Web Library (MWL), 635
MobileHTML5.org website, 282
MobilePerf bookmarklet, 454
mobile_browser capability (WURFL), 317

mobile_browser_version capability (WURFL), 317
Mobilytics website, 705
modal pop-up windows, 416
models (see specific models)
model_name capability (WURFL), 317
Modernizr library
    about, 292–294
    conditional loading, 294
    linking to video files, 370
    local pictograms, 341
    polyfills and, 297
    properties supported, 294–297, 518
monetizing your website, 705
Montage framework, 491
Moore, Andy, 311
Motorola devices, 27
Motorola Mobile Internet Browser (MIB), 81
mousedown event, 573
mousemove event, 573
mouseout event, 479
mouseover event, 479
mouseup event, 573
mousewheel event, 480
MOV container, 368
moveTo() method (Canvas API), 358
Movila DetectFree, 327
Movila Detection, 327
mozactionhit attribute, 268
Mozilla Open Web Apps, 619–623
Mozilla WebAPI initiative, 594
MP3 audio format, 379
MPEG-4 containers, 368
msApplication-Arguments meta tag, 223
msApplication-badge meta tag, 198
msApplication-ID meta tag, 223
msApplication-MinVersion meta tag, 224
msApplication-OptOut meta tag, 224
msApplication-PackageFamilyName meta tag, 223
msApplication-TileColor meta tag, 196
msApplication-TileImage meta tag, 196
mscontentzoom event, 578
MSGesture object, 577
MSGesture() function, 577
msgesturechange event, 578
msgestureend event, 578
msgesturehold event, 577
msgesturestart event, 578

msgesturetap event, 578
msinertiastarted event, 578
multicolumn layout, 403
multiline text control, 248–248
Multimedia Message Composer, 558
Multimedia Messaging Service (MMS), 558, 659
multipage browsing, 48
multiple screen densities
    about, 342
    background images and, 345
    canvas element and, 357–365
    providing image alternatives, 346
    providing single image, 344
    SVG and, 350–357
    vector-based solutions, 343
multitouch navigation, 45
muted attribute, 374
MWL (Mobile Web Library), 635
Myriad browser, 81

## N

\n (newline) escape special character, 469
native apps
    design strategy, 127–140
    HTML5 web apps and, 64
    integrating, 220–224
    mobile web and, 37
    platform-specific solutions, 71
    URI association from, 563
    user experience considerations, 141–152
    web shortcuts and, 702
    Windows 8 support, 613–619
native map applications
    about, 541–545
    showing maps, 546–551
native web apps
    about, 69–72
    code development tools for, 91
    creating, 644–650
    design strategy, 127–140
    distributing, 650
    HTML5, 64–66
    JavaScript APIs, 466
    MIME types supported, 711
    user agent tricks, 307
    user experience considerations, 141–152
navigation (mobile browsers)
    bad example of, 130
    changing default method for, 215

Google Maps for Android, 542
image maps and, 337
iOS Maps application, 544
multiple views and, 652
navigator object, 298–299
types of, 43
usability tips, 140
Windows 8 web apps, 617
navigation link menus, 226
navigation lists, 231
Navigation Timing API, 688
navigator object
about, 298–299
appName property, 298
appVersion property, 298
geolocation property, 534
maxTouchPoints property, 570
onLine property, 507
platform property, 298
plugin property, 298
pointerEnabled property, 570
properties compatibility table, 298
userAgent property, 298
userLanguage property, 298
netbooks, 8
NetFront browser, 79
NetLimiter tool, 676
NetMarketShare website, 61
network communication
about, 522
Ajax, 522–525
Server Sent Events, 525–527
Web Sockets API, 527
Web Sockets protocol, 527
Network Information API
about, 583, 649
new specification, 584
old specification, 584
Network Link Conditioner, 674
network requests, reducing, 689
newline (\n) escape special character, 469
Nexus devices, 16
NFC tags, 701
Nielsen, Jakob, 145, 246
Node.js library, 491, 528
Nokia devices
about, 20
apple-touch icon and, 191
brands, models, and platforms, 20–24

preinstalled browser, 77
reading HTTP headers, 308
remote lab service, 117–119
web app support, 632–643
Xpress Web App Builder, 702
Nokia Here services, 550
Nokia Mobile Web Library, 454
Nokia Mobile Web Templates, 394
Nokia Store, 20, 637
Nokia Web Tools, 91, 636, 643
non-interactive form elements, 264–265
non-phone mobile devices, 7
noscript tag, 454
NOSQL database, 518
not not operator, 291
NOT operator, 386
Notification API (Cordova/PhoneGap), 649, 649
notifications, push, 462, 649
noupdate event, 507
NTT DoCoMo services, 230, 395

## O

Obigo mobile browser, 81
object embedding, 378
object tag, 342
object_download capability group (WURFL), 316
obsolete event, 507
ODP (On Device Portals), 43
offline web apps
about, 501
accessing online resources, 503
compatibility and limits, 508–511
deleting the package, 505
JavaScript and, 506–508
manifest files, 502
updating the package, 504
Ogg container, 369
OMA (Open Mobile Alliance)
ESMA standard, 451
local pictograms, 342
UAProf standard, 306
WAP standard, 39
WML standard, 154
OMA Download standard
about, 659
download descriptor, 660
post-download status report, 661

On Device Portals (ODP), 43
onchange event, 248
onclick event, 472, 479
ondblclick event, 478
one-view widget, 653
OneAPI initiative, 532, 539
onhide event, 643
onkeyup event, 248
onload event, 461, 472
ONLY operator, 386
only screen type, 388
onmousedown event, 479
onmouseover event, 479
onmouseup event, 479
onresize event, 480, 643
onSelect event, 641
onshow event, 641, 643
opacity property (CSS), 416
Open Handset Alliance, 13
Open Mobile Alliance (see OMA)
Open Search description protocol file, 702
Open Web Apps (OWA), 619–623
Open Web Devices, 30
Open webOS, 30
OpenCellID project, 531
OpenDDR project, 328
OpenGL ES 2.0, 362
Openwave browser, 81
Opera Mini browser
    about, 37, 84
    simulator for, 110
    user-agent string, 309
Opera Mobile browser
    about, 84
    Dragonfly debugging tool, 682
    user agent tricks, 307
Opera Mobile Labs, 84
Operator Identification Platform (Massive), 309
OPhone operating system, 31
option element, 247
option groups (select lists), 241
:optional pseudoclass, 273
OR operator, 386
ordered lists, 228
orientation attribute, 212, 387
orientationchange event, 480
OTA (Over-The-Air)
    about, 60, 124
    file delivery and, 658

:out-of-range pseudoclass, 273
output element, 264
Over-The-Air (OTA)
    about, 60, 124
    file delivery and, 658
overflow property (CSS), 414
OWA (Open Web Apps), 619–623

# P

packages
    about, 601
    deleting, 505
    manifest file and, 501
    updating, 504
package_name attribute, 646
packaging standards, 601
Page Visibility API, 457
PageControl control, 617
pagehide event, 458
pageshow event, 458
Palm devices, 29
Passani, Luca, 313
Passbook (Apple), 703
password text input, 246
pattern attribute, 268, 271
patterns
    for tablets, 148
    for touch devices, 145
    JavaScript mobile UI, 495–500
pause event (Cordova/PhoneGap), 648
Payment API, 594, 627
PCapPerf tool set, 687
pdf capability group (WURFL), 317
Pearce, James, 583
Perfecto Mobile, 122–124
performance optimization
    about, 686
    best practices, 689–693
    measuring, 686–688
PERMISION_DENIED error constant, 536
perspective() CSS function, 433, 435
Phantom Limb utility, 572
Phone API, 627
phonebooks, adding contacts to, 559–560
PhoneGap (Adobe), 72
    (see also Apache Cordova framework)
    about, 72
    native web apps for, 644–650
PhoneGap Build service, 72, 645

PHP language
    base64 conversion, 334
    detecting mobile user agents and browsers,
        311
    reading headers, 308
    sleep() function, 527
    WURFL Standalone API and, 319–322
Pick Contact Intent API, 594
pictograms
    about, 340
    ISO, 342
    OMA, 342
picture element, 350
Pierce, Greg, 562
PIM API, 627
pin: URL scheme, 558
pixel aspect ratio, 55, 57
pixel density ratio, 55, 361
pixels per inch (PPI), 53
placeholder attribute, 266, 297
platforms (see web platforms)
playback capability group (WURFL), 317
PlayBook tablet (BlackBerry)
    about, 25
    simulator for, 107
.plist file extension, 602
plug-ins, 650
PNG format, 184, 639
pointer attribute (CSS4), 390
Pointer Events specification
    about, 569
    detecting pointers, 570
    simulating touch on desktops, 572
    touch-action style, 571
    working with touches and clicks, 571
Pointer Lock API, 594
pointercancel event, 570
pointerdown event, 570
PointerEvent object
    about, 571
    currentPoint property, 571
    hwTimestamp property, 571
    intermediatePoints property, 571
    isPrimary property, 571
    pointerId property, 571
    pointerType property, 572
    pressure property, 572
    tiltX property, 572
    tiltY property, 572

    timeStamp property, 572
pointermove event, 570
pointerout event, 570
pointerover event, 570
pointerup event, 570
pointing_method capability (WURFL), 317
polyfills
    about, 281, 297
    APNG-canvas, 333
    local pictograms, 341
    usage suggestions, 280
pop-up windows, 416, 471
popup control, 254
portability, 2, 51
position property (CSS), 405–406
PositionError class, 536
POSITION_UNAVAILABLE error constant,
    536
POST request (HTTP), 300
postMessage() function, 465
Power Management API, 594
PPI (pixels per inch), 53
pre-installed browsers, 73–82
preferred_markup capability (WURFL), 318
-prefix-free framework, 290
prefixes, vendor (see vendor prefixes)
PrefixMyCSS tool, 290
Prefixr tool, 290
preload attribute, 374
preprocessors, CSS, 288–289
pressure sensors, 579
Presto rendering engine, 49
print dialog (JavaScript), 467
production environment
    about, 124
    domain alternatives, 125
    error management, 125
    usage statistics, 126
    web hosting, 125
product_info capability group (WURFL), 316
profiling JavaScript on mobile browsers, 455
progress element, 264, 285
progress event, 507
progressive enhancement technique, 132–134
prompt dialog (JavaScript), 467
proxied browsers, 47, 300, 532
Proximity Events API, 594
pseudo-browsers, 68, 69
pseudoclasses, 413

Push API, 627
push notifications, 462, 649
Pusher service, 528
putImageData() method (Canvas API), 358

## Q

QR Code, 114, 699
Qt framework, 26
quadraticCurveTo() method (Canvas API), 358
QuoJS library, 486
QWERTY keyboard, 58, 481

## R

radial-gradient function, 428
radio buttons, 241
range slider field, 254, 297
Raphaël framework, 356
Rating control, 617
Rauch, Guillermo, 528
RDA (Remote Device Access), 117
:read-only pseudoclass, 273
:read-write pseudoclass, 273
Readability bookmarklet, 453
readonly attribute, 268
ready.mobi validator, 677
readystatechange event listener, 523
Real Time Streaming Protocol (RTSP), 376
Reality display (Xperia), 55
reducing network requests, 689
reference movies for iOS, 369
reflection (mirror effects), 431
reflow layout engines, 46
regressive enhancement technique, 133
reloading web apps, 653
remote debugging, 678, 681
Remote Device Access (RDA), 117
remote emulation services, 112
remote labs
    about, 116
    Keynote DeviceAnywhere, 120–122
    Nokia device access, 117–119
    Perfecto Mobile, 122–124
    Samsung device access, 119
remote profiling, 687
Remote Test Lab (RTL), 119
Remote Web Inspector, 678–680, 682, 683
rendering engines, 49
repeating-linear-gradient() function, 428

repeating-radial-gradient() function, 428
Request desktop site feature, 306
requests (HTTP), 300–307
required attribute, 268, 271, 297
:required pseudoclass, 273
resetting CSS files, 393
resize event, 480
resolution (screen display), 51–53
resolution attribute, 387
resolution_height capability (WURFL), 318
resolution_width capability (WURFL), 318
responseType attribute, 523
responsive images, 138, 337
Responsive Web Design (RWD), 134–138
RESS (Responsive Web Design + Server Side
    Components), 139–140
results attribute, 245
resume event (Cordova/PhoneGap), 648
Retina display (iPhone), 55
rgba() color function, 416, 421
rich text controls, 249–253
RIM-COD-Size attribute, 669
RIM-COD-URL attribute, 669
Ringmark browser testing suite, 178
Ripple tool, 104, 104, 631
Rohrl, Cathy, 155
rotate() CSS function, 433, 575
rotate3d() CSS function, 433
rotateX() CSS function, 433
rotateY() CSS function, 433
rotateZ() CSS function, 433
rounded corners, 408–408
rss capability group (WURFL), 317
RSS files, 702
RTL (Remote Test Lab), 119
RTSP (Real Time Streaming Protocol), 376
RV container, 368
RWD (Responsive Web Design), 134–138

## S

Safari browser
    about, 73
    form control attributes, 268
SailFish OS, 24
Samsung Apps, 14
Samsung devices
    about, 26
    HTML5 web apps and, 66
    preinstalled browsers, 79

remote lab service, 119
web apps support, 624
SASS (Syntactically Awesome Stylesheets), 288
scale() CSS function, 362, 433, 575
scale3d() CSS function, 433
scaleX() CSS function, 433
scaleY() CSS function, 433
scaleZ() CSS function, 433
ScientiaMobile, 313
screen display (mobile devices)
    about, 50
    input methods, 58–58
    physical dimensions, 53–55
    pixel aspect ratio, 57
    pixel density ratio, 55
    resolution, 51–53
screen resolution, 51–53
script attribute (CSS4), 390
script element (HTML5)
    attributes supported, 453
    code execution and, 453
    JSONP and, 524
scroll event, 480, 497
search engine optimization (see SEO)
searchbutton event (Cordova/PhoneGap), 648
security capability group (WURFL), 316
select tag, 238–241
selection management (CSS), 417–419
selectors (CSS), 392
Selectors API, 463
SemanticZoom control, 617
Sencha Touch Animator tool, 442
Sencha Touch framework, 72, 488–489
Sencha.io service, 339–340
sensors
    about, 579
    Apache Cordova API, 583
    compass information, 583
    DeviceOrientation Event specification, 579–
        583
Sensors API, 640
SEO (search engine optimization)
    about, 695
    how users find you, 698–701
    spiders and discoverability, 696–698
    user fidelizing, 701–704
Series 40 (Nokia)
    about, 21
    HTML5 web apps and, 66

preinstalled browser, 77
web app support, 632–637
WML emulators and, 157
Xpress Web App Builder, 702
Server Sent Events (SSE), 525–527
server-side adaptation mechanism, 131
server-side detection
    about, 300
    cloud-based browsers, 309–311
    debugging, 671–676
    detecting the context, 307–309
    device libraries, 313–328
    HTTP, 300–307
    mobile detection, 311
    transcoders, 312
server-side location techniques
    about, 532
    carrier connection, 532
    indoor location, 533
    IP addresses, 532
    language considerations, 532
Session and Identification API, 595
sessionStorage object, 511–514
SettngsFlyout control, 617
Sharp, Remy, 683
Short Message Service (SMS), 41, 557, 698
simulators
    about, 93
    bandwidth, 674
    comparison chart, 112
    testing mobile apps with, 92–114
Sitemap protocol, 696
sizes attribute, 188
skewX() CSS function, 434
skewY() CSS function, 434
SkyFire pseudo-browser, 86
Skyhook Wireless provider, 531
Skype application, 559
sleep() function (PHP), 527
Slowy App tool, 676
Smart App Banner service, 220–222, 561
smart TV platforms, 31
smart zoom, 45
Smart-Fit feature (NetFront), 79
smartphones
    about, 5
    autocomplete feature, 500
    BlackBerry simulators, 105
    JavaScript libraries and, 484

Request desktop site feature, 306
screen resolutions supported, 51
server-side adaptation mechanism, 131
streaming support, 376
SVG support, 351
title compatibility table, 182
video element and, 371
web views and, 67
smarttv capability group (WURFL), 317
SMIL (Synchronized Multimedia Integration
    Language), 659
Smooth Streaming (Microsoft), 376
SMS (Short Message Service), 41, 557, 698
sms capability group (WURFL), 317
sms:// URI scheme, 557
smsto:// URI scheme, 557
snap state (Internet Explorer), 390–391
sniffing, HTTP, 673, 687
Social API, 595
social features on mobile websites
    about, 706
    authentication and sharing APIs, 706
    sharing content, 707
social phones, 5
Socket.IO framework, 528
Sony Mobile
    about, 27
    preinstalled browsers, 81
Souders, Steve, 454, 686, 687
SoundJS API, 380
sound_format capability group (WURFL), 317
SPDY protocol, 301
spiders and discoverability, 696–698
spoofing, user agent, 671
src attribute
    img element, 336, 347
    picture element, 350
    video element, 370
srcset attribute, 350
SSE (Server Sent Events), 525–527
Standard Vector Graphics (see SVG format)
standards, 158
    (see also specific standards)
    current, 158
    delivering markup, 160–164
    DOCTYPE preference, 161–164
    managing multiple, 159
    MIME type preferences, 161–164
    politics of mobile web, 159–160

streaming, 376
    for web apps, 601–602
StatCounter website, 61, 282
static definition (MIME types), 655–656
statistics
    gathering for mobile web, 704–705
    market, 60
    mobile device purchases, 37, 61
status detection
    about, 457
    Page Visibility API, 457
    with timers, 459
step attribute, 268
step-end() function, 440
step-start() function, 440
steps() function, 440
storage capability group (WURFL), 316
storage event, 512
storage, client-side (see client-side storage)
streaming audio and video, 375, 376–377, 591
streaming capability group (WURFL), 316
Street View service (Google Maps), 542
stroke() method (Canvas API), 358
strokeRect() method (Canvas API), 358
strokeStyle property, 358
strokeText() method (Canvas API), 359
submit event, 479
svg element, 355
SVG format
    about, 350
    additional information, 353
    custom fonts versus, 344
    embedding in XHTML, 354
    inline, 355
    multiple screen densities, 343
    Raphaël framework and, 356
    tools for, 352–353
    web platform compatibility table, 336
    website icons and, 184
SVGT devices, 351
svgt_1_1 capability (WURFL), 318
svgt_1_1_plus capability (WURFL), 318
swipe gesture, 572
Swiper utility, 573
Symbian Foundation, 23
Symbian platform
    about, 22–24
    apple-touch icon and, 191
    HTML5 web apps and, 66

local applications, 563
preinstalled browser, 77
web app support, 612, 637–643
Synchronized Multimedia Integration Language (SMIL), 659
Syntactically Awesome Stylesheets (SASS), 288
System API, 627
System Information API, 640

## T

tabindex attribute, 230
tables (HTML5), 229
tablets
　about, 7
　Amazon manufactured, 28
　Blackberry devices, 25
　Nokia devices, 21
　patterns for, 148
　Request desktop site feature, 306
　screen resolutions supported, 51
　SVG support, 351
　video element and, 371
　web views and, 67
Tagstand Writer app, 701
target attribute, 230, 231
target-densitydpi attribute, 205
TCP Socket API, 595
Telefónica (company), 30
Telerik Fiddler tool, 674
terminate() method, 466
Test Center Developer tool, 120
testing mobile apps
　about, 91
　for accessibility, 233
　automating for devices, 122
　emulators and simulators, 92–114
　HTML5 considerations, 177
　importance of, 145
　real device testing, 114–116
　remote labs, 116–124
text boxes, clearing, 495–496
text fill property, 403
text format
　about, 395
　font face, 397–398
　font family, 395
　font size, 399
　multicolumn layout, 403
　text adjustment for small screens, 402

text overflow, 400–400
text shadows, 399
text stroke and fill, 403
text input fields
　about, 243–245
　datalist tag, 247
　multiline text control, 248–248
　passwords as, 246
　popup control, 254
　rich text controls, 249–253
text-overflow property (CSS3), 400–400
text-shadow property (CSS3), 399
text-size-adjust property (CSS), 402
text-stroke property (CSS), 403
textarea
　autogrowing, 496
　multiline text control, 248–248
3rd Generation Partnership Project (3GPP), 351
Thomas, Neil, 459
3D image formats, 333
3D screens, 53
3GP container, 369
3GP2 container, 369
3GPP (3rd Generation Partnership Project), 351
TIMEOUT error constant, 536
TimePicker control, 617
timers
　for animations, 475
　JavaScript support, 473–474
　waking up detection using, 459
Titanium Studio, 91
title (HTML5 heading), 191
titles (web pages)
　about, 181–182
　changing, 476
Tizen platform
　about, 26
　code development tools for, 91
　emulator for, 111
TLD (top-level domain), 42
toDateURL() method, 361
ToggleSwitch control, 617
Tooltip control, 617
top-level domain (TLD), 42
touch devices
　clear text box button, 495–496
　CSS touch callout, 420
　design patterns for, 145
　JavaScript APIs and, 564

label tag and, 236
pointer events, 569–572
touch events, 565–569
user agent tricks, 307
Touch Event API (W3C), 568
touch events, 565
  (see also pointer events)
  about, 565–567
  BlackBerry touch behavior, 568
  disable scrolling and, 568
  W3C, 568
Touch Events API (Apple), 565–568
touch navigation, 45, 337
Touch object
  clientX property, 567
  clientY property, 567
  identifier property, 567
  pageX property, 566, 567
  pageY property, 566, 567
  screenX property, 567
  screenY property, 567
  target property, 567
touch-action style (CSS), 571
touch-event-mode meta tag, 215, 568
touchcancel event, 565
Touché library, 572
touchend event, 565, 573
touchenter event, 568
TouchEvent object
  about, 566
  changedTouches attribute, 566
  event types supported, 565
  targetTouches attribute, 566
  touches attribute, 566
touchleave event, 568
touchmove event, 565, 573
touchstart event, 565, 573
track element, 372
transact() method, 515
transcoders, 225, 312, 369
transcoder_ua_header capability (WURFL), 318
transcoding capability group (WURFL), 317
transform functions (CSS), 433–438
transform property (CSS), 433, 439, 575
transform-origin property (CSS), 434
transform-style property (CSS), 435
transition-delay property (CSS), 440
transition-duration property (CSS), 440
transition-property property (CSS), 440

transition-timing-function property (CSS), 440, 444
transitions
  about, 439–440
  animation properties, 440–441
  considerations ending, 441
translate() CSS function, 434
translate3d() CSS function, 434
translateX() CSS function, 434
translateY() CSS function, 434, 498
translateZ() CSS function, 434
Trident rendering engine, 49
TunnelTilt game, 363
TV platforms, 31
Twitter for Websites, 707
2D context, 357
type attribute
  date input fields and, 255
  file selection fields and, 257
  range slider field and, 254
  text input fields and, 244
  video element, 371
typed arrays, 464

## U

UAProf (User Agent Profile) standard, 306
Ubuntu for phones operating system, 30
UC Browser, 78
UI pattern, 248
Uint8Array data type, 464
UIWebView class, 67
Universal iPhone UI Kit library, 488
unload event, 477
unordered lists, 228
updateready event, 507
updating packages, 504
upgradeneeded event, 519
URI schemes
  about, 553
  adding contacts to phonebooks, 559–560
  integrating with other applications, 560
  making calls, 554
  opening communication apps with, 558
  sending email, 556
  sending SMSs, 557
URL address bar, hiding, 218
URL schemes, 560–562
url() function, 428
User Agent Profile (UAProf) standard, 306

user agent spoofing tools, 671
User Agent Switcher plug-in, 672
user experience
    design considerations, 141
    JavaScript UI libraries, 487–500
    official UI guidelines, 149
    tablet patterns, 148
    touch design patterns, 145
    what not to do, 149–152
User Interface API, 627
User-Agent request header (HTTP), 301–303,
    307, 696
user-agent strings
    about, 302–303
    cloud-based browsers, 309
    user agent tricks, 307
user-installable browsers, 82–86
user-scalable attribute, 205
user-zoom attribute, 212
Utility API, 627
ux_full_desktop capability (WURFL), 317

## V

V8 JavaScript engine, 50
:valid pseudoclass, 273
validating forms
    about, 270
    HTML5, 271–274
    input validation attributes, 268
    Modernizr support, 297
    WAP CSS, 275–277
validating HTML5 code, 677
Vanilla JS framework, 485
VBScript language, 452
vCard file format, 559
VDLs (Virtual Developer Labs), 121
velocityAngular property, 578
velocityX property, 578
velocityY property, 578
vendor prefixes
    CSS and, 286–290, 291
    JavaScript support, 291
    @keyframes at-rule and, 443
    -prefix-free framework, 290
    static tools for, 290
Verizon Network API, 539
versions
    Android platform, 14
    iOS platform, 11

Vibration API, 593
video
    about, 368
    camera access on mobile devices, 590–593
    compatibility table for web platforms, 378
    containers and codecs, 368–369
    delivering, 370
    MIME types supported, 711
    new HTML5 element, 370–376
    object embedding, 378
    streaming, 375, 376–377
video element
    about, 370–373
    advanced declarations, 374
    audio player and, 380
    providing fallbacks, 374
    streaming example, 377, 591
video player API, 375
ViewBox control, 617
viewport declaration
    about, 200
    block elements and, 228
    CSS and, 211
    defining size through meta tags, 203–206
    device width in, 206–207
    landscape behavior, 208–210
    metadata attributes, 205
    for older devices, 214
    pixel availability, 208
    problems using, 200–203
    usage compatibility table, 213
Viewporter mini-framework, 207
viewport_supported capability (WURFL), 318
Virtual Developer Labs (VDLs), 121
visibility property (CSS), 439
visibilitychange event, 457
visited pseudoclass (CSS), 413
Visual Basic language, 308
Visual Studio (Microsoft), 91
VMWare Player, 107
Vorbis audio files, 379

## W

W3C
    animation timing specification, 475
    APIs for mobile web apps, 594
    Contacts API, 649
    Device API Working Group, 594

DeviceOrientation Event specification, 579–583

DOM specification, 463

File API, 649

FileSystem API, 520

Geolocation API, 534–538

IndexedDB API, 515, 518–519

Mobile Accessibility website, 232

mobile markup checker, 677

Mobile Web Initiative, 177

Network Information API, 649

performance APIs, 688

Pointer Events specification, 569–572

Touch Event API, 568

Web Workers specification, 464–466

Widget Interface specification, 636

Widget Packaging and Configuration standard, 601, 624

WAI-ARIA (Accessible Rich Internet Applications), 232, 232

WAP (Wireless Application Protocol)

  history of, 39–43

  HTTP and, 300

  WTAI and, 553

WAP CSS (WCSS)

  about, 172

  extensions for, 172–176

  validating forms, 275–277

WAP Link, 41

WAP Push, 41

wap subdomain, 41

-wap-accesskey attribute, 173

-wap-input-format attribute, 176, 275

-wap-input-required attribute, 176, 275

-wap-marquee attribute, 174

-wap-marquee-dir attribute, 174

-wap-marquee-loop attribute, 174, 174

-wap-marquee-style attribute, 174

wap_push capability group (WURFL), 317

WAV format, 379

WBMP (Wireless Bitmap), 158

WCSS (WAP CSS)

  about, 172

  extensions for, 172–176

  validating forms, 275–277

web apps, 501

  (see also native web apps)

  architecture of, 599–601

  BlackBerry support, 624–632

  creating for iOS, 602–612

  full screen apps patterns, 652–654

  Google Chrome support, 624

  Mozilla OWA support, 619–623

  Nokia support for, 632–643

  offline, 501–511

  pros and cons, 598–599

  reloading, 653

  Samsung support, 624

  server-side adaptation mechanism, 132

  standards for, 601–602

  Symbian support, 612, 637–643

  web shortcuts and, 702

Web Audio API, 380

Web Bluetooth API, 595

Web Clip icon, 187, 189

web engines, 49

web hosting, 125

Web Intents API, 594, 595

Web Notifications API, 588–590

web platforms

  about, 64

  audio compatibility table for, 381

  canvas compatibility table, 364

  client-side detection, 298–299

  e-books, 72

  HTML5 web apps, 64–66

  image format compatibility table, 336

  informational websites for, 284

  native web apps and, 69–72

  navigator object properties compatibility table, 298

  pseudo-browsers, 68

  video compatibility table for, 378

  web views, 67–67

Web Runtime (WRT), 637

web shortcuts, 702

Web Sockets API, 527

Web Sockets protocol, 527

Web SQL Database API, 514–517

Web Storage API, 511–514

web views, 67–67, 307

Web Workers specification, 464–466

WebAPI initiative (Mozilla), 594

.webapp file extension, 620

WebApp.Net library, 487

webapps (see native web apps)

WebFM API, 595

WebGL API, 362

WebKit layout engine, 49
webkitBackingStorePixelRatio property, 361
WebM container, 369
WebMatrix (Microsoft), 91
WebNFC API, 595
webOS platform
    about, 29
    emulator for, 107
    preinstalled browser, 78
WebP format, 332, 336
WebPlatform.org website, 284
WebRTC API, 595
website icons, 183–186
websites
    desktop, 36
    informational, 281–284
WebSMS API, 594
WebTelephony API, 594
WebWorks engine (BlackBerry)
    about, 624
    bbUI.js framework, 628–629
    configuration file, 624–626
    packaging and signing, 629
    Ripple tool, 631
    useful extension APIs, 626
Weinre tool, 116, 683
wgt package, 633
.wgz file extension, 639
WHATWG organization, 169, 269
Widget Interface specification, 636
widget object (Symbian webapps)
    isrotationsupported property, 641
    onexit property, 641
    onhide property, 641
    onshow property, 641
    openApplication() method, 641
    openURL() method, 641
    performTransition() method, 641
    preferenceForKey() method, 641
    prepareForTransition() method, 641
    setDisplayLandscape() method, 641
    setDisplayPortrait() method, 641
    setNavigationEnabled() method, 641
    setNavigationType() method, 641
    setPreferenceForKey() method, 641
Widget Packaging and Configuration standard,
    601, 624
width attribute
    CSS3 media queries, 387

img element, 336
    viewports, 205, 211
WiFi Information API, 595
WiFi Positioning System (WPS), 60, 531
Wikimedia website, 61
Wikipedia website, 129
window object
    cancelAnimationFrame() method, 475
    clearInterval() method, 473
    close() method, 471
    onLine property, 584
    open() method, 471
    openDatabase() method, 515, 517
    orientation property, 480, 583
    requestAnimationFrame() method, 473
    scrollTo() method, 472
    scrollY() method, 498
    setInterval() method, 473
    setTimeout() method, 473
windows
    focus and scroll management, 472
    JavaScript dialogs, 467–469
    manipulating, 471
    pop-up, 416, 471
Windows 8 platform
    about, 18
    native apps support, 613–619
    URI association from native apps, 563
    user agent tricks, 307
Windows Embedded Compact, 19
Windows Mobile platform, 19
Windows Phone platform
    about, 17
    application and games delivery, 666
    Bing Maps application, 545
    emulators for, 107–109
    Nokia devices and, 20
    URI association from native apps, 563
Windows platform
    application and games delivery, 666
    brands and models in, 17
    Start tile, 195–198
Windows Simulator, 109
Windows Store App, 223
WinJS library, 615
Wireless Application Protocol (WAP)
    history of, 39–43
    HTTP and, 300
    WTAI and, 553

Wireless Bitmap (WBMP), 158
Wireless Markup Language (WML), 40, 154
Wireless Telephony Application Interface
    (WTAI), 553, 559
Wireless Universal Resource File (see WURFL)
WML (Wireless Markup Language), 40, 154
WMLScript language, 158
WMV container, 368
wp library
    ap function, 559
    mc function, 555
    sd function, 556
WPS (WiFi Positioning System), 60, 531
wrap attribute, 248
Wroblewski, Luke, 139, 140, 145
WRT (Web Runtime), 637
wta capability group (WURFL), 316
WTAI (Wireless Telephony Application Inter-
    face), 553, 559
WTF Mobile Web website, 149
WURFL (Wireless Universal Resource File)
    about, 313–315
    APIs supported, 319–323
    architecture, 315
    capabilities, 316–318
    emoji property, 341
    linking to video files, 370
    SMS URI schemes and, 557
WURFL Cloud Service, 313, 322
WURFLManager class
    getCapabilitiesNameForGroup() method,
        321
    getDevice() method, 321
    getDeviceForHttpRequest() method, 321
    getDeviceForUserAgent() method, 321
    getListOfGroups() method, 321
WURFL_Device class
    getAllCapabilities() method, 321
    getCapability() method, 321
WYSIHTML5 editor, 253

X

X-Callback-URL specification, 562
X-Forwarded-For header (HTTP), 310, 311, 540
X-Icon Editor, 183
X-Mobile-Gateway header (HTTP), 311
X-Nokia-Device-Type header (HTTP), 311
x-nokia-musicshop-bearer header (HTTP), 308
X-OperaMini-Features header (HTTP), 310

X-OperaMini-Phone header (HTTP), 310
X-OperaMini-Phone-UA header (HTTP), 310
X-WAP-Profile header (HTTP), 306, 311
x-webkit-airplay attribute, 375
xhr2 property, 523
XHTML
    about, 164
    available tags, 165
    creating compatible templates, 167
    DOCTYPE for, 161
    embedding SVG in, 354
    i-mode, 230
    markup additions, 169
    official noncompatible features, 166
    preferred MIME type, 161
XHTML MP (Mobile Profile)
    about, 164
    available tags, 165
    closing elements, 183
    creating compatible templates, 167
    DOCTYPE for, 161
    inputmode attribute, 269
    markup additions, 169
    official noncompatible features, 166
    preferred MIME type, 161
    WAP and, 41
xhtml_file_upload capability (WURFL), 318
xhtml_format_as_css_property capability
    (WURFL), 318
xhtml_make_phone_call_string capability
    (WURFL), 318
xhtml_send_sms_string capability (WURFL),
    318
xhtml_supports_iframe capability (WURFL),
    318
xhtml_support_level capability (WURFL), 318
xhtml_ui capability group (WURFL), 316
XMLHttpRequest object, 523, 523
    (see also Ajax)
Xoom tablet, 16, 28
Xperia series (Sony Mobile), 27, 55
Xpress Nokia Browser, 77, 310
Xpress Web App Builder for Series 40, 702
XUI framework
    about, 486
    addClass() method, 487
    css() method, 487
    getStyle() method, 487
    html() method, 486

on() method, 487
removeClass() method, 487
setStylc() method, 487
tween() method, 487
xhr() function, 487
xhrjson() function, 487

## Y

Yahoo! PlaceMaker API, 533
Yahoo! search engine, 695
Yahoo! Web Analytics, 705

YouTube
    Android intents and, 562
    iOS URL schemes, 560

## Z

Zakas, Nicholas, 693
Zepto.js library, 485, 573
ZIP files, 601
zoom attribute, 212
zoom experience (browsers), 45
Zuckerberg, Mark, 70

## About the Author

**Maximiliano Firtman**, @firt, is a developer focused on mobile and HTML5 development. He is a trainer in mobile technologies and founder of ITMaster Professional Training. He is the author of many books, including *Programming the Mobile Web* (O'Reilly). He has spoken at international conferences such as OSCON, Velocity, Breaking Development, GOTO Europe, Campus Party, QCon, and Adobe en Vivo.

He has been an Adobe Community Professional since 2011, a BlackBerry Elite Developer since 2013, and a Nokia Developer Champion since 2006, and he has developed many mobile-related projects, such as *MobileHTML5.org*, *MobileTinyURL.com*, and *iWebInspector.com*. He maintains a mobile web development blog at *MobileXweb.com*.

He is an expert in native and HTML5 web development, including iOS, Android, PhoneGap, and jQuery technologies.

## Colophon

The animal on the cover of *Programming the Mobile Web, Second Edition* is a jerboa, a small jumping rodent of the family Dipodidae. The 33 species of jerboa are found in deserts of Asia and North Africa. They feed on the leaves and roots of desert plants; many species also eat insects. They extract water from their food so efficiently that they do not need to drink.

Jerboas' powerful hind legs may be four times longer than their front legs and enable them to hop up to three meters. Their tails, which are often tufted, are longer than their bodies and are used for balance. Their ears vary from species to species—they may be small and mouselike or broad and rabbitlike.

Jerboas are well adapted to their harsh desert environments. They are nocturnal and hide in burrows, which they may plug for protection against the elements, during the day. Some jerboas living in hot regions enter a state of torpor (estivation) during the hottest months; jerboas living in cold regions hibernate during the winters.

The cover image is from Riverside Natural History. The cover font is Adobe ITC Garamond. The text font is Adobe Minion Pro; the heading font is Adobe Myriad Condensed; and the code font is Dalton Maag's Ubuntu Mono.

# Have it your way.

# Get even more for your money.

**Join the O'Reilly Community, and register the O'Reilly books you own. It's free, and you'll get:**

- $4.99 ebook upgrade offer
- 40% upgrade offer on O'Reilly print books
- Membership discounts on books and events
- Free lifetime updates to ebooks and videos
- Multiple ebook formats, DRM FREE
- Participation in the O'Reilly community
- Newsletters
- Account management
- 100% Satisfaction Guarantee

**Signing up is easy:**

1. **Go to: oreilly.com/go/register**
2. **Create an O'Reilly login.**
3. **Provide your address.**
4. **Register your books.**

Note: English-language books only

**To order books online:**

oreilly.com/store

**For questions about products or an order:**

orders@oreilly.com

**To sign up to get topic-specific email announcements and/or news about upcoming books, conferences, special offers, and new technologies:**

elists@oreilly.com

**For technical questions about book content:**

booktech@oreilly.com

**To submit new book proposals to our editors:**

proposals@oreilly.com

**O'Reilly books are available in multiple DRM-free ebook formats. For more information:**

oreilly.com/ebooks

Spreading the knowledge of innovators     oreilly.com

CPSIA information can be obtained at www.ICGtesting.com
Printed in the USA
BVOW061123200313

315930BV00003B/3/P